Marriage and Family Today

Second Edition

Keith Melville
City University of New York and The Center for Policy Research

RANDOM HOUSE / NEW YORK

Second Edition

987654321

Library of Congress Cataloging in Publication Data

Melville, Keith.
Marriage and family today.
Includes bibliographies and index.
1. Mate selection--United States. 2. Marriage--United States. 3. Family--United States. I. Title.
HQ728.M36 1980 301.42'0973 79-24898
ISBN 0-394-32346-7

Manufactured in the United States of America

Cover Design: Doug Fornuff
Cover photographs: (*young family*) Mariette Pathy Allen (*extended family*) Bruce Davidson/Magnum
Text Design: Leon Bolognese

Foreword to the Second Edition

In the three years since the first edition of *Marriage and Family Today* was published, the topics dealt with in this book have become even more salient. Precedent-breaking court decisions on mate and child support, custody, and inheritance rights, as well as dramatic headlines have made the American public increasingly alert to the dilemmas and questions grappled with here. The divorce rate is as high as ever, the re-marriage rate is down, and singlehood has indeed become a separate stage in the life cycle; and while the two-child norm seems firmly entrenched, voluntary parenthood and child-free marriage are also receiving attention. The continued exploration of the family is thus a necessity today both for the college student and the concerned citizen.

A second edition is something of a celebration. It attests to the success of one's efforts and to the appreciation of one's work. This is especially the case in this instance since the first edition of *Marriage and Family Today* became the leading family text in the field, read by tens of thousands of students all across the nation. Praised for its readability as well as its comprehensive coverage of research, the first edition made its mark.

This new edition has all these virtues and more. It has been carefully updated, and timely materials have been added in various chapters. Chapter one, for example, includes an assessment of the changes in marriage and family life that have taken place over the past generation. The discussion of changing sex roles has been expanded, with greater emphasis on the problems that are posed for men as well as women. And there is more on cohabitation, sources of sexual information (and misinformation), and the potential for conflict in family relationships. Finally, the book considers the impact of new governmental policies and recent legislation.

The book is current and timely in the facts it presents, and thoughtful in its exploration of their meanings. In thus enlarging upon and enriching the original *Marriage and Family Today,* this revision promises to be an even better book.

Suzanne Keller
Princeton University
January 1980

Foreword to the First Edition

There was a time when the study of marriage and the family would have seemed preposterous. Why study something that everyone already knew through experience? This era and the view it embodied is past. Today, nothing seems more urgent than to explore the structure and meaning of marriage and family life, for both are undergoing changes that no one foresaw. Accordingly, what was once the concern of a few specialists has become the concern of us all.

I have myself long sought a text on marriage and family life that would be both erudite and engrossing. I have also looked for a text that would give students a rounded perspective on important issues without either talking down to them or losing them in remote abstractions. When I began working on this project as consulting editor, these were the goals that I wanted to help the book's author, Keith Melville, to achieve.

Now, looking at the completed book, I believe that the author has been successful in accomplishing what we set out to do. Keith Melville has undertaken a comprehensive review of what is known about the family from a social science perspective. Given the rapidly proliferating studies, this in itself is no mean feat. But he also does something more: He helps the reader to interpret and assess the materials presented and thereby form a broad and substantial understanding of the key issues and problems facing the institution, and the individuals caught up in it.

The sociological imagination is not yet widely developed, even among otherwise intelligent and literate—even expert—individuals. This book helps its readers develop such an imagination by making them aware of the suprapersonal, the collective elements in such seemingly subjective events as love, strife, and the search for happiness. It explores the ostensible as well as the covert motives and reasons for forming—and dissolving—families, the rationale behind passionate attachments, the self-calculus behind "selfless" devotion, and the patterning behind seemingly spontaneous emotions and choices. This alone makes for fascinating and provocative reading.

The book further examines an important social institution—one in which everyone has a stake—in the throes of change. It takes that change seriously without losing sight of the fact that change is never wholesale or irreversible. Accordingly, there are chapters on the changing roles of men and women in marriage, on new domestic arrangements, and some challenging proposals for alternative modes of work and intimacy.

As to its specific virtues, this book is comprehensive in scope and up-to-date in its review of evidence. It deals with such key issues as love, marriage, sex, divorce, and parenting in a serious and balanced way. It poses significant questions but does not impose the answers.

In other words, I consider this book an excellent introduction to an aspect of social life that today is at the forefront of change. It should help students to see the family in social context, while at the same time keep their attention focused on the individual. Above all, the book is a pleasure to read. It makes learning a joy.

Suzanne Keller
September 5, 1976

Preface to the Instructor

It is most gratifying to have written a book that, in its first edition, was received so enthusiastically. Before discussing the changes that have been made in this revision, perhaps it would be useful to reiterate the objectives I had in mind when I began the project. The marriage and family course is a strange hybrid, which differs in some important ways from other courses in the college curriculum. In many colleges, the course serves a dual purpose. On the one hand, the purpose of the course is to introduce scholarly material in order to help students clarify their thinking about marriage and family arrangements. On the other hand—particularly where it is referred to as a "functional" course—its purpose is to help students apply the results of systematic research to their own lives. I have tried to do justice to both objectives, to provide a research-based discussion and to analyze the practical alternatives that today's students face in marriage and family life.

When I began teaching this course, I used several different texts—and each of them seemed inadequate for the type of course I wanted to teach. Some provided a comprehensive digest of thousands of pertinent studies. But in all their cascading detail, they did not really engage the interest of my students because they did not explore the personal applications and implications of the material. Many students come to this course expecting a well-informed technician, but they find instead a theoretician. Their disappointment—I think—is understandable. It seems to me that a good text for an introductory course such as this one should not be an encyclopedia, but rather a judicious choice of material designed to help students think carefully and systematically about important issues as well as personal choices.

Several of the other texts I used focused on more practical matters, but they too seemed flawed in some important respects. Some were simply not well documented; they contained statements for which there is no empirical verification. Worse yet, from time to time their authors seemed to lapse into moral exhortations, whether implied or explicit, of the sort that used to characterize so much of marriage and family studies. At times I felt uncomfortable with these books because their authors offered oversimplified answers to complex questions. This is an area in which honest, well-informed teachers and writers might well speak with a stammer, for the practical implications are staggering. Finally, it seemed to me that most of the texts for the "functional" course focused too narrowly on the interpersonal relationship, and thus encouraged students to think of marriage and family life as something that takes place in a social vacuum.

So what I have tried to do here is to create a text that avoids these shortcomings. For example, I have placed a somewhat heavier emphasis than most "functional" texts do on the ways in which broad social and economic currents influence the marriage relationship, and I included a chapter on kinship and community. Overall, in the choice of topics, writing style, and graphic examples, I have tried to create an appealing invitation to further study.

CHANGES IN THE SECOND EDITION

Rather than change any of the book's main features, what I have done in this revision is to add certain topics, to expand the discussion at a number of points, and of course to update the material, adding new research and perspectives. In the preface to the first edition, I wrote these words: "Because texts are such awkward beasts that it takes a long time to get them moving, their authors often seem to be commenting not on what is happening today or even yesterday, but the day before. My goal in writing this book has been to present important research in order to shed some light on the alternatives we face *today*." Having made that promise, I suppose I have a special obligation to keep the book current, and that is what I have tried to do with this new edition.

Partly in response to suggestions made by instructors who used the first edition, this revision includes new or expanded material on a number of topics. Most of Chapter 1—an assessment of changes that have taken place in marriage and family arrangements over the past generation—is new. Throughout the book, I have tried to do justice to the continuing process of redefining gender roles. In Chapter 8, there is a new discussion of redefined images of masculinity. There are also substantially new sections on several aspects of sexuality, including a discussion of teenage pregnancy and sources of sexual information in Chapter 4, and a new section on the homosexual minority in Chapter 7. In addition, there is new material on such recent developments as the impact of advances in reproductive technology, new legal perspectives on cohabitation, and the effects of double-digit inflation.

Overall, this new edition reflects two of the themes in recent research about marriage and family life. One of those themes—as the readers of any of a variety of reports about child abuse, battered wives, or family violence are well aware—is the recent attention to the dark side of family life, a new willingness on the part of family researchers to ask why family violence is so prevalent. Another theme, discussed in Chapter 1, is that we are now in a better position than we were a few years ago to assess some of the alternatives to traditional marriage and family arrangements that were proposed during the late sixties and early seventies. Recent research allows a better assessment, for example, of the effects of no-fault divorce laws, and we are now in a better position to assess the consequences of the trend toward more participation in the labor force by married women.

NEW MATERIALS FOR THE "FUNCTIONAL" COURSE

There is, I think, a unique challenge for all of us who teach a "functional" marriage and family course, and that is to do justice to the range of instructional objectives that such courses imply. Some years ago, sociologist Nelson Foote (1955) made a comment that still applies: "Those who speak of functional family life courses mean courses in behavioral change, not merely courses that reproduce information. Few courses now given on the family are demonstrably functional in this sense." In the preparation of this new edition, I have given a good deal of thought to the question of what sort of learning tool would help students accomplish such goals as becoming aware of the personal alternatives they face, recognizing and scrutinizing their personal values, and learning how to choose among alternative courses of action.

Over the past few years various social scientists, such as Joseph Bensman and Arthur Vidich, have commented on the "consciousness of choice" that prevails in American society today, particularly among members of the middle class. There is no course where that "consciousness of choice" has a more immediate relevance than it does in this one. But I wonder whether we as educators have given enough thought to how we might help students cope with the multitude of choices they will face. How, exactly, can we do justice to the noncognitive objectives implied in the very title of the course we teach?

As I thought about this, my first inclination was to add material at the end of each of the chapters to accomplish this goal. But as I started to write that material, it became clear that it did not fit a standard text format. Accordingly, I have assembled a student workbook, *Exploring Marriage and Family Today*. Parts of the workbook are familiar, such as self-testing questions that should help students to learn the material. But most of it consists of exercises, projects, and adapted readings designed to help students think about personal implications and applications. You, of course, will be the final judge of whether the workbook, along with the revised text, provides an effective teaching tool for a truly "functional" marriage and family course.

NEW DEVELOPMENTS IN A FLOURISHING FIELD

Perhaps it is appropriate here to make a more general comment about recent trends. Obviously, a great deal has changed in marriage and family studies over the past generation. Once something of an intellectual backwater, the study of marriage and family has moved into the mainstream of academic inquiry. Much of the research in this area is now more objective and less moralistic than family sociology was a few decades ago. New theoretical syntheses such as the two-volume work *Contemporary Theories About the Fam-*

ily (Burr, Hill, Nye, and Reiss, 1979) represent impressive accomplishments. From a different perspective, policy analysts have begun to conduct empirical studies intended not to fill theoretical gaps but rather to provide us with the knowledge to make better collective decisions. And because of recent interest in the history of the family, we now have more accurate perspectives on what happened in the past.

Each of these developments represents an important advance in our understanding of marriage and family arrangements. There is reason for the note of congratulations that the editors of *Daedalus* offered in the preface to a recent issue (Winter, 1978) devoted to the family:

> This issue suggests what happens when a subject becomes a matter of lively curiosity for scholars in a wide variety of disciplines. The subject is made only more important when it also engages the interest of many concerned with the making of public policy. Studies of the family have never been more illuminating than they are at this moment; there has never been a more imaginative use of new documents and data; there has rarely been a more systematic questioning of established opinions. The field is flourishing as it never has before. . . . This is a good time to be studying the family.

And it is a good time to be teaching about marriage and family arrangements, too.

New York City — Keith Melville
January 1980

REFERENCES

Wesley R. Burr, Reuben Hill, F. Ivan Nye, and Ira L. Reiss, eds. *Contemporary theories about the family*. New York: Free Press, 1979.

Nelson Foote. *Identity* and *interpersonal competence*. Chicago: University of Chicago Press, 1955.

Acknowledgments

When I began this project I knew it would be no solitary venture, as most writing is. But I had no idea how many people would lend a hand along the way. As anyone who has written a book knows, that encouragement and assistance is vitally important.

Several years ago, this project was nothing more than a gleam in Roger Emblen's eye, when his infectious enthusiasm was one of the main assets of CRM publishing. It was that enthusiasm that propelled me through a few months of indecision. Thanks also to Rose Somerville, Harold Feldman, and Viktor Gecas, whose comments were so helpful at that San Diego seminar when the project was first taking shape in my mind. Judy Griessman and Ann Levine helped me through the transition to a new publisher, as did my friend and attorney, Joe Mello. Jim and Betty Ramey gave helpful words of encouragement, as they have on many other occasions; they should both be acknowledged as midwives. Many others, including Betty Berry, Peter Stein, Marvin Sussman, Lenore Weitzman, and Robert Francoeur, helped by providing information when I needed it. To Bob Geller, the "media guru" who encouraged my interest in media and the family, I owe a particular debt of gratitude.

Any writer, but most especially a text writer, is indebted to a great many other writers and researchers whose work provides the building blocks out of which a text is constructed. To change the image, a text writer is by definition an intellectual pack rat, taking something from a great many places and in turn leaving something behind. Hopefully, the leavings do justice to the takings.

I am indebted to Jessie Bernard and Arlene Skolnick for demonstrating to me through their writings that it is possible to write with intelligence and insight about marriage and family arrangements for a general audience, and to avoid the triviality that still characterizes much of the worst of contemporary social science.

Ken Gewertz, Sarah English, and Betsy Amster lent a hand in the preparation of several chapters, and Bruce Marcus helped with the appendix on family finance.

In preparing the second edition, I received helpful criticism and suggestions from a great many people, including many of the instructors who used the first edition. I would particularly like to acknowledge the assistance of acquiring editor Philip Metcalf and project editor Anna Marie Muskelly at Random House, as well as reviewers Arline Rubin (Brooklyn College); Gary Lee and Viktor Gecas (both at Washington State University); Alexis Walker (University of Oklahoma); Peter Stein (Wm. Patterson College); Robert Phillips (University of Maryland); Mary Laner (Arizona State University); Marvin Sussman (Wake Forest University); Robert Stout (St. Petersburg Jr. College); Kaye Zuengler (University of Minnesota); and Carl Anderson (Texas Tech

University). Last—and certainly not least—I want to acknowledge the help of a very competent researcher, Brandon Cushing.

To use a few of the superlatives that often sound so perfunctory in other writers' prefaces, but are the only appropriate words here, I owe a special debt to the consulting editor on this project, Suzanne Keller. Evelyn Waugh once remarked that "Two people getting together to write a book is like three people getting together to have a baby." I am delighted to report that this book is the exception to that rule. Suzanne has been a remarkable collaborator—encouraging, intelligent, and critical, all in the right proportions.

Introduction

This book is different from others you will read as part of the college curriculum in one important respect: It explores issues about which you will sooner or later have to make personal decisions.

The most obvious of these decisions is whether or not to marry. Only a few years ago, it was a foregone conclusion for almost all adults in the United States that they would marry, and at a relatively early age. That is no longer so. A wide range of alternatives has opened up for this and almost every other decision you will make in marriage and family life.

Think of the list of choices you will be expected to make. Unlike people who live in cultures where parents choose their children's mates, you will make that choice by yourself. How will you choose between one partner and another? Will you marry at an early age or choose to live on your own for a few years? If you do marry, what meanings will you attach to the marriage contract? What assumptions do you make about sex-role expectations in marriage? Is sexual fidelity important? Do you assume that bearing and bringing up children forms part of that agreement? If you were forced to choose, which would come first, personal growth or family obligations? And if your marriage does not work out, at what point should you seek a divorce, perhaps to look for a new partner?

Many of the issues that you will have to think about did not really come up for most people in the past, because there seemed to be virtually no choice. As the leading character in the musical comedy *Fiddler on the Roof* explains: All life is like the fiddler on the roof, in that we try to maintain our balance while scratching out a little tune. How do we do it? he asks. The question is answered in a word—tradition.

Today, many of those traditions have eroded. Some have disappeared completely. The comfortable, corseting commandments—"Thou shalt not," "Thou wouldn't dare!"—have lost their authority. Because fewer actions are prohibited by custom, religion, or community sentiment, each of us is faced with a bewildering array of choices and lifestyle alternatives. We have more freedom of choice, and although we normally think of freedom as something desirable, it poses problems as well.

Think of the difference between shopping in a small country store and a large supermarket. Because the country store does not have a wide variety of brand names or products, you have fewer decisions to make. Most of the choices are already made for you. Very often you can simply buy the same products that you and your family have been buying for years. But in the supermarket, you are faced with a wide variety of new products and brand names that claim to be superior to the ones you used before. You have to make more decisions. And you have to know more about the products in order to choose wisely.

Since some are better than others, and some are better buys, it can be a bewildering experience to try to make the right choice. You might well feel what futurist Alvin Toffler calls choice overload. You are confronted with more choices than you are willing or able to make intelligently.

In our own lives, as in the marketplace, having more freedom means making more decisions. But where do you get reliable information or useful advice in order to make those decisions? You might turn to the advice columns in newspapers. But there are some serious shortcomings in the information they contain. As one prominent student of marriage and family, Harold T. Christensen, has pointed out, such columns often "treat complex personal problems much too briefly, even flippantly, and with distorted emphases." The individuals who write those columns tend to oversimplify, to sensationalize, and to base their advice on the experience of one or two individuals who may be quite exceptional. "They usually draw upon folklore and common sense more than research findings," says Christensen, "and even when they use the latter it would seem that the temptation to overgeneralize is frequently irresistible" (1964, p. 960).

One of the purposes of this book is to provide information of a more reliable nature than such columns contain. As you learn to read social research, you should learn to distinguish facts and generalizations that are reliable from those that are not. The study of marriage and family life is not limited to any one academic discipline. Rather, it lies at the intersection of a number of disciplines and professions. Although sociology is the most important academic discipline for this book, we will also draw on the work of psychologists, anthropologists, historians, biologists, and economists. You should begin to understand not just their conclusions, but also the research tools they use. And you will be introduced to some of the professions concerned with marriage and family, such as law, family therapy, and marriage counseling.

But any course on marriage and family behavior today must have another goal too. Students in this area, as well as many marriage counselors, have shifted their focus in the past few years. The main concern used to be to ease personal adjustment in marriage. In the 1950s, researchers focused much of their attention on the mate choice, and tried to predict marital satisfaction. Marriage counselors, by and large, played the "fireman" role. They tried to help out when marital tensions mounted. The primary question was: Can this marriage be saved?

Recently, a good deal more attention has been devoted to a very different question: Can the institution of marriage be salvaged? This concern acknowledges that many seemingly personal problems result from a crisis in institutional arrangements. Many of our personal troubles have more to do with problems that are created for us than ones resulting from our own individual failures or shortcomings. In other words, we need to employ a sociological perspective as well as a psychological one in order really to understand marriage and family life.

Our examination of marriage and the family in contemporary society will lead us to the observation that, in many ways, the fact that we live in a society that is impersonal and fragmented defines the problems of contemporary marriage. Many of the functions that marriage performed in the past are now done by outside institutions. But the need for intimacy remains, and today both marriage and family are commonly considered a refuge from the impersonal world outside. Much of the turbulence in marriage today, including a rising divorce rate, might be understood as an attempt to modify marriage and family arrangements so that they will better serve our needs for intimacy.

This is one of the topics that we will explore in the following pages. We will also look more closely at the range of intimate alternatives available today, and try to assess the extent of recent changes. And we will discuss the question: Why do we need to *study* marriage and family? After all, this is a subject about which we all have a good deal of personal knowledge. Most of us have been brought up in families, have lived in and observed family life, and been its beneficiaries and victims. What can we learn from the social sciences that we don't already know? What is the difference between their findings and common sense knowledge?

Before we explore that question, however, let us raise a more topical one: Do the venerable institutions of marriage and family have a future? Or are they, as some observers believe, on their way out, soon to join the Edsel and the Hula Hoop in that pile of discarded ideas which no longer serve our needs? This is the issue discussed in Chapter 1.

REFERENCE

Harold T. Christensen, ed. *Handbook of marriage and the family.* Chicago: Rand McNally, 1964.

Contents

Boxes

I. Research Perspectives on Marriage and Family

II. Point of View

III. What's Happening Today

IV. Introducing the Marriage and Family Professionals

V. Guidelines for Decision-Making

VI. Involvement Exercises

VII. Biological Aspects of Sex and Reproduction

I

Understanding Marriage and Family Today

"Family II" Shirley Gorelick

1 Marriage and Family in a Changing Society

The arrival of a new decade prompts us to reconsider the preceding decades so that we can better understand where we are and where we are going. Even a quick glance back to the 1950s—when the parents of many of today's college students met and married—serves as a vivid reminder of how much has changed in our marriage and family arrangements over a generation, and how rapidly our way of thinking about the institutions that affect us most immediately has been transformed.

In retrospect, the 1950s seem part of another age. As essayist Elizabeth Hardwick writes,

> The 1950s—they seem to have taken place on a sunny afternoon that asked nothing of you except a drifting belief in the moment and its power to satisfy: a handsome young couple, with two or three children, a station wagon, a large dog, a house and a summer house, a great deal of picnicking and camping together. For the middle class, the fifties passed in a dream, a dream in which benevolent wishes for oneself were not thought of as always hostile to the enlarging possibilities of others. The treasured children would do well in school, and the psychiatrist could be summoned for the troubled. The suburbs offered the space and grass that would bless family existence . . . (1978, p. 3)

If this passage disregards those millions of families who were not so fortunate, this too reflects the tenor of the 1950s, for until the publication of Michael Harrington's *The Other America* in 1962 the existence of widespread poverty was not generally recognized and even the professionals who studied family life largely ignored the influence of race, ethnicity, and social class.

During the 1950s, one had the impression that most Americans lived in look-alike families situated in look-alike houses in look-alike neighborhoods. The tired old joke about the inebriated husband who returns home to the suburban development where his family lives, mistakes another house for his own, and does not discover his error until he tries to kiss his neighbor's wife says as much about the alleged similarities among families as it does about the monotony of tract houses in suburbia. This was a decade in which a premium was placed on conformity, and those who did not conform kept a very low profile.

In the decade of the 1950s, there appeared to be little reason for public concern about marriage and family. America at that time was a marriage-oriented society in which the state of matrimony was celebrated in songs and mass-circulation magazines. At about the same time that "Love and Marriage Go Together Like a Horse and Carriage" was a pop hit, domesticity was glorified, "togetherness" was invented by the women's magazines, and the migration to the suburbs was accelerated. Young people got married at an earlier age than ever before, and families were swollen by a large crop of "baby boom" children.

Through the new mass medium of television, millions of people were exposed to a new vision of the modern family in its suburban setting. The images of family life portrayed in such popular television programs as "Ozzie and Harriet" and "Father Knows Best" somehow reflected the mood of the times. To be sure, while the Nelsons had "happy problems" that were resolved by the end of each half-hour segment, the problems of real families of that era were not so easily resolved. But the customs and habits that regulated the relations between men and women and their children seemed satisfactory enough. And a relatively low divorce rate seemed to confirm the impression that the existing institutional arrangements were still sound. The message of much of the writing about marriage and family life was that, with a little bit of personal effort, every family might attain the domestic contentment of the "Ozzie and Harriet" or the "Father Knows Best" model.

Most of the professionals who wrote about these topics conveyed the same impression. Researchers focused much of their attention on the choice of a mate, or ways of predicting marital satisfaction—and thus supported the status quo. An era of general contentment about institutional arrangements is not one in which scholars are likely to ask many searching questions about how things came to be the way they are, or what the alternatives might be.

THE TUMULTUOUS SIXTIES

During the tumultuous decade of the 1960s, much of this changed. If the 1950s had been characterized by a certain bland conformity, and the smug assumption that increasing prosperity would dissolve whatever problems remained, by the early sixties there was a much wider awareness of the "unfinished business" of American society. A 1957 survey of American college youth had concluded that "a dominant characteristic of students in the current generation is that they are gloriously contented both with regard to their present day-to-day activity and their outlook for the future (in Morison, 1958, p. 163). By the early 1960s, many young people were not only aware of poverty, racism, and the problems abroad that attracted the attention of the Peace Corps, but they believed that such problems could be solved by vigorous reform. Several years later, after Kennedy-era idealism had given way to widespread cynicism about the prospects for liberal reform and rebellion against American involvement in Vietnam, a new style of social protest emerged. Political activism gave way to cultural criticism.

By the late 1960s, the new preoccupations were, both literally and figuratively, closer to home. A concern for new lifestyles had become an issue, and the hippie communes to which the media devoted so much attention represented one form of protest against what countercultural spokespeople regarded as the rigidity and isolation of the nuclear household. The word "revolution," which in the mid-sixties was heard most frequently in discussions of political change, was by the late sixties applied in other contexts: everywhere there was talk of a "sexual revolution" that was attributed both to the erosion of parental authority and to the increasing availability of contraceptives, particularly "the Pill." And it was at about the same time that the women's liberation movement became a prominent force. Among radical feminists it became fashionable to attack not only traditional roles, but also the family itself. "The family is what destroys people," said one of the movement's spokeswomen, Roxanne Dunbar. "Women take on the slave role in the family when they have children. It's a trap" (Dunbar, in Danziger and Greenwald, 1971, p. 11).

In sharp contrast to the promarriage climate of the 1950s, by the late 1960s it had become far more common to criticize marriage, as in the lyrics to Carly Simon's song "That's the Way I Always Heard It Should Be." Robert Warshow once commented that "so much of 'official' American culture has been cheaply optimistic that we are likely almost by reflex to take pessimism as a measure of seriousness" (in Moynihan, 1974, p. 132). For a while, this was indeed what happened. Many commentators seemed so concerned about avoiding the unthinking praise of marriage and family arrangements that had been common in the 1950s that they went to the opposite extreme. Hundreds of articles and books appeared with titles such as "The Crisis of the Nuclear Family," "Is Marriage Necessary?" and "Is Monogamy Outdated?" For example, psychotherapist David Cooper began his book *The Death of the Family* (1970, p. 4) with this harsh judgment: The modern family represents the "ultimately perfected form of nonmeeting." Criticism of the family came from another direction as well. Conservatives as well as radicals pointed to the family in their diagnosis of contemporary problems, but for the former the solution was to reestablish family bonds, to reassert those forms of authority necessary for an orderly society, and thus to stem what they regarded as a rising tide of permissiveness.

For years, filmmakers had shied away from any serious treatment of marriage and family life, largely because the topic had been so thoroughly sanitized by television. But, in the early 1970s filmmakers such as John Cassavetes (in *A Woman Under the Influence*) and Ingmar Bergman (in *Scenes from a Marriage*) began again to examine marriage with the same expectant curiosity that used to be reserved for foreign cultures practicing strange customs. To many people the new alternatives, which were attracting so much attention, were indeed strange. Such widely publicized trends as cohabitation, experiments with communal living, the redefinition of traditional sex codes, and a rising divorce rate all illustrated a certain defiance of traditional norms and patterns. And it did often appear that the institution of marriage might be falling apart, literally before our eyes. Advice columnist Ann Landers, who had been dispensing information about how to solve marital problems for years, announced that her own marriage of thirty-five years would not last to the "finish line." She and her husband filed for divorce.

A more graphic illustration of the problems of modern marriage was provided by a documentary series entitled "An American Family," which allowed a nationwide television audience to become acquainted with the William C. Loud family. Despite the handsome presence of Pat Loud in the properly affluent Santa Barbara suburb, it was hardly "Ozzie and Harriet" come to life again. Chosen because they were "typical," Pat and William Loud separated halfway through the series.

Reconsidering "The Death of Marriage and Family"

In retrospect, it is clear that there were at least two developments during the era of the 1960s that convinced many people that the family was falling apart. The first was that increasing attention was paid to the differences between popular beliefs about how people *ought* to act and what actually happens. Within just a few years, both social scientists and the mass media began to devote considerable attention to topics that had previously been considered shameful and private secrets. Public attention was drawn to abortion, child abuse, even incest. For the first time such topics were considered appropriate for daytime "soap operas" as well as prime-time specials.

Another development that caused considerable concern was that intimate arrangements that had long been practiced, but not publicized, began to have vocal advocates. During the fifties, when conformity had been the rule, there had been considerable hostility toward any deviation from majority practices. But in the more permissive climate of the sixties, when there was such an emphasis upon the rights of minorities of all sorts, intimate arrangements that had long been practiced in private—such as homosexual marriages, or couples who lived together without "making it official"—became far more visible than before. As psychologist Arlene Skolnick put it, commenting on the new claims of homosexuals to minority rights,

> What is remarkable here is not the number involved, but the loud proclamation of what was formerly unspeakable and morally dreadful. The open flouting of previous taboos may also be seen in the sudden emergence of unwed pregnancy and motherhood as a viable social role rather than a shameful secret. There is probably no corner of America completely unaffected by the current ferment, even if all that has been provoked is a backlash affirmation of the old morality. (1973, p. 400)

Rather than arguing that such arrangements should be tolerated because some people are unable to conform to the norms, their advocates insisted that the norms (as well as the laws) should be broadened to recognize them as legitimate alternatives.

The discovery of "family pluralism" was an event of considerable importance. It affected the public image of marriage and family life, ushered in a concern for alternatives to prevailing middle-class patterns, and caused social science researchers to pose very different questions from the ones that had been characteristic of family studies in the fifties.

Psychologist Sidney Jourard was one of the people who initiated the discussion of family pluralism when he said that there is a growing realization that we live in "a fantastically pluralistic society" (1970). To a much greater extent than most people have realized, he pointed out, "there exists, in fact, a great diversity of man–woman, parent–child relationships. But only the middle-class design is legitimized." Jourard argued that we have to begin experimenting and exploring the alternatives to our present institutions, and that we need to acknowledge as acceptable alternatives many arrangements that deviate from the middle-class model of what marriage and family are supposed to be (Jourard in Otto, 1970, p. 46).

In fact, a new recognition of alternatives had developed by the early 1970s. One of the reports delivered at the 1970 White House Conference on Children and Youth, for example, was entitled "Changing Families in a Changing Society." It emphasized the importance of recognizing the variety of actual marriages and families. As one of the report's authors, sociologist Marvin Sussman, noted, "This preoccupation with the model nuclear family pattern and efforts to preserve it at all costs prevented sociologists from describing what was becoming obvious to non-sociological observers of the American scene: a pluralism of family forms," each of which has "different problems to solve and issues to face" (1971, p. 42).

As Jourard suggested, considerable attention was devoted to alternatives to traditional marriage and family arrangements during the early 1970s. Some of those alternatives—such as the suggestion that couples draw up a custom-designed marriage contract—were intended to help couples clarify and define roles according to personal preferences and abilities, not traditional assumptions about male and female roles. Other alternatives—such as the O'Neills' proposal for "open marriage" (1972)—were designed to reduce some of the strains of marriage by encouraging spouses to make a greater investment in other relationships. A third set of alternatives—represented by "family clusters," communes, and group marriages—aimed at creating new types of extended families.

By calling attention to such alternatives and discussing their implications, as we will do in the chapters that follow, it is easy to exaggerate their appeal and to commit one of the most common errors of the news media: to emphasize what is novel or unusual and thus to overlook the preferences of the majority. Despite the considerable attention devoted to the new alternatives, the most reliable evidence suggests that very few adults of either sex would want to live in a commune. Few people think that custom-designed marriage contracts are either necessary or desirable. And despite the popularity of *Open Marriage,* polls suggest that sexual fidelity is still very important, both to men and to women (Roper, 1974).

But there is also convincing evidence that certain changes that were first advocated by radical feminists or countercultural spokespersons in the 1960s have gained wide acceptance. Perhaps the most prominent of these changes is a redefinition of sex roles. It is impossible to say for sure whether the changes that have taken place in women's perceptions of their roles can be attributed to the effects of the women's movement. But we do know that, since the mid-1960s, the outlook of American women has converged with that of the movement's leaders. Surveys suggest that attitudes toward sex roles began to change, particularly among college-educated people, in the late 1960s. It became increasingly common for women to challenge the traditional division of labor, which assumes that the husband is the breadwinner and the wife is the homemaker. Then, beginning in 1970, which was about the time at which many Americans first became aware of the women's movement, there is evidence of a significant change in attitudes. Such changes were not confined to any one region, to the college-educated, or to middle-class women. Among married, white southern women, for example, it appears that a substantial minority started to question the traditional division of labor during the early 1970s; and by 1973 a sizable majority of these women endorsed equal rights in the labor market.

Another survey, which focused on changing attitudes among northern working women during the period from 1970 to 1974, showed a more marked shift. By 1974 almost half of these women no longer supported the sex-based division of labor, and large majorities endorsed the idea that husbands should share housework with their wives, and that women should have the same right to jobs, promotions, and pay that men have. By 1974, as the authors of one study point out, more than half of the working women in Detroit expressed attitudes "very much like those espoused by the women's movement" (Brown, 1976; Mason, Czajka, and Arber, 1976).

SEARCHING FOR SELF-FULFILLMENT IN THE "ME DECADE"

Just as a relatively small group of feminists anticipated changes in sex-role attitudes that soon became quite widespread, in the same way by the late sixties adherents to the counterculture, who placed so much emphasis upon immediate enjoyment, self-exploration, and the expansion of consciousness, had anticipated one of the main themes of the decade that followed. The sixties began with a great deal of enthusiasm for the prospects for vigorous reform; but many people became disillusioned with all attempts to bring about social change. The eventual accomplishments of that cornucopia of new programs initiated as part of President Johnson's "Great Society" were meager. By the end of the decade, many people seemed to have given up on the possibilities of effecting political change. One radical student leader who declared a "total moratorium on constructive participation in this society" voiced a sentiment that was widely shared (in Melville, 1972, p. 81). People turned inward. So much of the energy that had been devoted to political change was now redirected to changing oneself, and this preoccupation with self became one of the distinctive themes of the seventies.

If the predominant values of the fifties can be encapsulated by such words as conformity or "togetherness," the label that seems most descriptive of the 1970s is one that writer Tom Wolfe suggested—the "Me Decade." What he and many others have been trying to understand is an apparent shift in the values that people hold, a shift that affects marriage and family life in many ways. What seems to be taking place is a gradual shift away from the traditional ethic that stresses the value of hard work and striving for economic security above all else. Rather than deferring gratification and accepting the necessity of sacrificing for their children, many people in recent years have placed a new emphasis on immediate enjoyment and self-fulfillment.

In 1977, public opinion analyst Daniel Yankelovich completed a survey of parents and children in more than 1000 households. His goal was to determine how, if at all, recent value changes have affected the attitudes and behavior of today's parents. How, in brief, have parents changed, and do such changes shed any light on traditional values that are now being abandoned? The results of this survey showed quite clearly that the 1970s had produced a "New Breed" of parents who are different in important respects from "the Traditionalists," who continue to support the values by which they were raised. As a group, the Traditionalists—who represented 57 percent of the parents in the study—consider religion, hard work, saving, and financial security to be very important. They place a high value on the institution of marriage and having children, and they are prepared to sacrifice for their children. The New Breed parents are different: they appear to have rejected many of the values by which they were raised, such as religion, patriotism, saving, and thrift. And they regard the institution of marriage and their own responsibilities as parents quite differently from the way the Traditionalists do. They consider having children as an option, not an obligation. Perhaps the most revealing difference between the two groups is that the New Breed parents are less willing to make sacrifices for their children. Better educated and more affluent on the average than the Traditionalists, the New Breed parents emphasize self-fulfillment (Yankelovich, 1977).

By the mid-1970s, there was abundant evidence of changing values, as revealed by the new catchwords—words such as "now," "open," "awareness," and most of all, "self." There was considerable interest in almost anything that began with "self-"—whether it was self-actualization, self-enhancement, self-assertion, self-discovery, or self-acceptance. The new best sellers were books with titles such as *I'm OK, You're OK,* and *I Just Met Someone I Like—And It's Me.* There was an event called an "Awareness Extravaganza," a new perfume called "Me!" and a magazine named *Self,* presumably for people who had taken to heart the lesson of Robert Ringer's popular book, *Looking Out for No. 1.*

By the late 1970s, the word "narcissism" began to appear in the commentary about marriage and family life. Narcissism refers to an excessive preoccupation with, or admiration of, oneself. The narcissist is too busy gazing into the mirror to pay any attention to others, so concerned with self that he regards others only in terms of what they can do for him. To some critics, most notably historian Christopher Lasch, many of the fads of the seventies suggested an inexorable drift toward "a culture of narcissism" (1978). Having withdrawn their interest and energy from the outside world, Lasch writes, many people today are preoccupied with the only thing that matters to them, psychic self-improvement. And so they jog, eat health food, get advice on how to get in touch with their feelings and how to relate, and take lessons in ballet or belly dancing. For them, writes Lasch, "Life becomes a never-ending search for health and well-being through exercise, dieting, drugs, spiritual regimens of various kinds, psychic self-help, and psychiatry. For those who have withdrawn interest from the outside world except insofar as it remains a source of gratification and frustration, the state of their own health becomes an all-absorbing concern." Incapable of any enduring relationships, the narcissist seeks instead instant intimacy and companionship without commitment (1977b, p. 140; 1978). To some people, such developments as the increasing popularity of the single

To some critics, notably historian Christopher Lasch, recent fads such as jogging indicate a preoccupation with self-improvement and a never-ending search for health and well-being.

life and a rising divorce rate confirmed Lasch's fears about a new American character type.

Is narcissism on the increase? Does modern society encourage narcissists and reward them with status and power? Does such a shift in values and character types undermine marriage and family, and encourage people not to care about others? Some critics would answer yes to each of these questions. They argue that narcissism is encouraged in today's society, and they point to psychotherapists who perhaps unwittingly encourage people to focus on their own feelings and needs, to the neglect of their spouses, children, and friends. And Lasch is not alone in arguing that narcissistic people may be particularly well-suited to our society's bureaucratic organizations, in which manipulation of others is often required, and where deep personal attachments may be an impediment to success.

Others regard Lasch's diagnosis of "the culture of narcissism" as unduly pessimistic. They point out that a concern for oneself does *not* necessarily keep people from being responsive to others, that only the most aggressive forms of self-assertion are at the expense of other people, and that the quality of relationships—including the marital relationship—may improve as a consequence of recent developments. But no matter what conclusions are reached about their impact, this debate does frame some of the issues that we will be grappling with in the years to come, particularly the question of a proper balance between self-fulfillment and social responsibilities.

Rising Expectations

Much of the concern about the future of marriage and family that has been voiced since the late 1970s stems from this apparent shift in values to preoccupation with the self. For example, Woody Allen's film *Interiors* (1978) explores the dynamics of a family whose members are burdened by their own self-absorption, obsessed with the analysis of their feelings and the pursuit of their personal ambitions. The film illustrates the problems created by the new ideology of self-fulfillment. There is no limit to such expectations, no point at which they are satisfied. As one commentator notes,

> Probably the most widely held and destructive myth is the quest for the *perfect* relationship. The incessant search for "more" is a direct descendant of American optimism and romanticism which

> looks for a marriage which will be loving, full of communication, understanding, mutual respect, joy and fulfillment through children. When all this is found to be as close to the reality of most families as Marcus Welby is to your M.D., a million Americans a year take to the exits, not because they are anti-family, but anti-*their* family. Thus, most divorced persons will try again, and many of those will risk a third time, restlessly looking for that Hollywood made-in-heaven marriage. (Etzioni, 1977)

There is reason for concern about the revolution of rising expectations that seems to have been encouraged by so much emphasis upon self-fulfillment. For it appears that happiness depends less upon what we actually have than upon what we expect to get. From this perspective, it is apparent that—whatever our circumstances—if we believe other people are experiencing what we crave, we are likely to be dissatisfied. Expectations of sexual satisfaction provide a good illustration. Because of a heavy emphasis upon sex in the media and in everyday conversation, many people apparently have the impression that they are missing out on something.

In a recent *Psychology Today* reader survey, 52,000 young adults were asked about their own sexual experience, and also about how many sexual partners they thought the average person their age had experienced. A large majority of the respondents thought that the average person of their age and sex had had more sexual partners and was more sexually satisfied than they were. For example, over half of the men, and about one-third of the women expressed some dissatisfaction with their sex lives. Significantly, they underestimated by far the extent of *other* people's dissatisfaction. And sex therapists report the same thing; people commonly enter therapy complaining about the frequency or intensity of their sex lives, assuming incorrectly that they are missing out on satisfactions that others take for granted (Shaver and Freedman, 1976).

What happened during the seventies was indeed a revolution of rising expectations, and one that affected a very broad spectrum of American society. "Suddenly, new dreams are stirring," writes Lillian Rubin, a marriage counselor and researcher, in a study of working-class families. "*Intimacy, companionship, sharing*—these are now the words working-class women speak to their men, words that turn *both* their worlds upside down" (Rubin, 1976).

THE PERSPECTIVE OF THE 1980s

Having briefly reviewed some of the developments of the past three decades, we return to the present. But where, exactly, are we today? It is much easier to characterize the mood of a decade such as the 1950s or the 1960s that has already been turned over to the historians than it is to get a clear perspective on the recent past and the present. In retrospect, the 1950s seem remarkable because of a general absence of concern about the family. The 1960s seem remarkable because, within just a few years, so many of the social arrangements that had formerly been taken for granted were seen as problematic. And if the early 1970s was a period of widespread experimentation with promising alternatives, the late 1970s was a period when many people started to have second thoughts about those alternatives and their long-term consequences. (See Box 1–1.) Certain of the proposed "solutions," such as communes, had no staying power. The redefinition of sex roles has created a situation of considerable ambiguity about relations between the sexes. (Not the least of the new problems are questions of etiquette. Male gestures, which only a few years ago were obligatory acts of deference to females—such as opening doors, or paying checks—are now sometimes interpreted as acts of intended domination or condescension.) Rapidly increasing numbers of working mothers and single-parent families raise some basic questions about who is taking care of the kids and how well the job is being done.

Some of the recent books that have attracted the greatest attention in dealing with these prob-

What's Happening Today

Box 1–1 / Fourteen New Facts of Marriage and Family Life

You thought you already *knew* the facts of life? They have probably changed since you learned them. These fourteen items might serve as a reminder that marriage and family life are not what they used to be.

1. *The Rise of the Single-Person Household.* The U.S. Census Bureau reports that as of March, 1978, one out of every five households consisted of just one person. This represents a 42 percent increase since 1970, the result of a combination of factors: more young adults are postponing marriage, there is a larger number of elderly widows and widowers who live alone, and there has been a rapid increase in the number of people who are divorced but not remarried.

2. *Contract Marriages with an Option to Renew.* Two members of Maryland's state legislature introduced a bill that would allow three-year contract marriages with an option to renew. As one of the bill's sponsors, Mrs. Hildegard Boswell, said: "I'm sure the church won't like this but with the eighteen-year-old vote coming in, I think the youngsters will look upon this as a totally new approach toward marriage and the family."

3. *Some "Firsts" for Women.* Over the past few years, women have continued to make inroads into positions that have traditionally been reserved for men. Several recent examples: The first female rabbi was ordained in 1972, and even the Episcopal church, which has taken a conservative position on the issue, now has female priests. In 1978 Hanna Holborn Gray became the first woman to head a leading private university when she became president of the University of Chicago. And in Sweden the constitution has been changed, making that country the first to give men and women equal access to the throne. That law, which is expected to go into effect in 1980, could one day make Princess Victoria, the first child of King Gustaf and Queen Silvia, the next ruler, no matter how many brothers she may one day have.

4. *Abortion and Illegitimacy.* Today, only about half of all pregnancies among American women result in legitimate live births. Many people have voiced special concern about the rate of pregnancy among unmarried teenagers. For fifteen- to nineteen-year-olds, the illegitimacy rate increased to 24.2 births per 1000 unmarried women in 1977, which is the highest rate ever observed for this age group.

5. *Househusbands.* Market researchers for household products are beginning to inquire about the preferences of a growing number of househusbands. With more men sharing household duties or assuming them totally, manufacturers and advertisers need to know what men think about foods, cleansers, and child care products.

6. *Living Together.* Recent studies at several American campuses indicate that about 80 percent of college students today would choose to live with an unmarried partner if they were given the opportunity and could find the right partner. And the U.S. Census Bureau reports that the number of unrelated persons living with a member of the opposite sex doubled between 1970 and 1977. Among people under 25, there was an eightfold increase in living together during the same period.

7. *Changing One's Sex, Changing One's Roles.* Item from *The New York Times,* (August 13, 1971):

> Basking Ridge, N.J.—The Bernards Township school board tonight suspended a fifty-two-year-old music teacher who underwent a sex-change operation and wanted to return to class in September as a woman after teaching fourteen years here as a man. . . . A lawyer representing the teacher called the board's move "unfair" since the teacher had not been allowed to teach "in her new role as a woman."

(Box 1–1 continues on page 12)

(Box 1–1 continued from page 11)

8. *Smaller Families.* Between 1970 and 1978, the fertility rate in the United States (the number of births per 1000 women of child-bearing age) dropped from 87.6 to 66.4. Meanwhile, the Gerber Company, which used to advertise that "Babies Are Our Business—Our Only Business" now offers portions of food called "Singles for adults—the whole new way to eat whenever you eat alone."

9. *Brave New World.* Since the birth of the world's first "test tube baby" in Britain in 1978, worldwide attention has been focused on the new facts of life ushered in by advances in reproductive technology. As embryologist Robert Francoeur points out, one of the new options is that "today, a woman whose husband is sterile can conceive a child by artificial insemination with her father-in-law's semen, thus retaining the genetic line of her husband and bearing a child with many of his hereditary traits" (1972, p. 3). Fortunately, we are still far from the situation portrayed in Aldous Huxley's *Brave New World*. But the birth of the "test tube baby" does constitute a step in the direction of separating sex and procreation.

10. *The Abuse of Children and Their Rights.* Judging from recent reports, either child abuse is becoming more common, or recent statistics are more accurate. It appears that the incidence of child abuse is about twice as high as previously estimated. Nearly 4 percent of all children under age seventeen are subject to abuse. Meanwhile, in the nation's courts, there is increasing attention to children's rights, particularly in areas where the state may enforce the child's wish against the parents'.

11. *Salary for Child Care.* For years feminists have complained that housewives don't get the recognition they deserve because they receive no pay for housework. Thus, housewives who may work many more than forty hours a week are, for official purposes, classified as "not in the labor force." The services they perform are not included in the Gross National Product. Professor David Gill has proposed that parents should be paid to raise their own children. Speaking at the First National Symposium on Home-Based Care for Children, Gill argued that the government should recognize that child care is work too, and work that would be more highly regarded if people were paid for it.

12. *Recognizing the Homosexual Minority.* There have been many recent indications that the homosexual minority, which is estimated to include about 20 million Americans, is beginning to gain certain rights that were denied in the past. In December 1978, for example, the United States Court of Appeals for the District of Columbia ruled that the Defense Department could not discharge homosexuals from the military without giving "some reasoned explanation" for the action. Meanwhile, major U.S. firms are acknowledging the buying power of homosexuals and aiming major marketing campaigns at this group. Many companies now advertise in newspapers written mainly for homosexuals, such as *The Advocate* or *After Dark*. Major recording firms now produce records specifically for the gay market. In 1977, most major publishers offered books for and about the homosexual minority.

13. *Something to Think About Before Signing the Marriage Contract.* People who get married in Louisiana now receive a brochure explaining the matrimonial laws and describing some of the changes that couples may make to modify the state's community property law. The state's Civil Code recognizes modifications that a couple can agree to before the marriage—but not afterward.

14. *A "First" for Men.* In May 1978, the Commerce Department announced that from then on, hurricanes would no longer be given only women's names, such as "Hurricane Anna." Richard A. Frank, the director of the National Oceanographic and Atmospheric Administration, said that the agency "decided that in this day and age it was the sensible thing to do to name some hurricanes after men." So the next time a storm causes millions of dollars of damage, we won't necessarily blame "mother nature."

lems—like Selma Fraiberg's *Every Child's Birthright: In Defense of Mothering* (1978)—contain arguments against the tendency to farm mothering out to professionals. Since the percentage of married women in the labor force has substantially increased, both popular magazines and professional journals now probe the consequences, and articles with titles like "Are Working Wives *Really* More Satisfied?" (Wright, 1978) have begun to appear.

Between the passage of "no-fault" divorce procedures in many states and the general erosion of the restraints that used to keep spouses from separating, it is considerably easier now than it was before the 1970s to sever the marital bond; but does this create a situation in which marriages are casually entered into, and just as casually broken apart? Considering the second thoughts that many people are having about the alternatives that were proposed in the seventies, it is somehow fitting that, six years after the publication of *Open Marriage*—a book that portrayed a very appealing alternative for millions of middle-class couples—one of its authors, Nena O'Neill, should write a new book, *The Marriage Premise* (1977), in which she expresses misgivings about some of the newer ideals and alternatives in marriage, including the idea of sexually open marriage.

> We have downgraded the "us" in marriage because we were so dedicated to the search for the "me." In the turmoil of the sixties, many people ignored the sharing aspects of marriage because they were trying so hard to break out of the total-togetherness syndrome. In our haste to correct the obvious inadequacies of the old order in marriage, to revise our roles, and to eradicate the traditions we saw as confining, once again the baby has been thrown out with the bathwater. (O'Neill, 1977, p. 11)

If it is no longer so fashionable to predict the demise of marriage and family as it was a few years ago, we have certainly not returned to the situation that existed in the fifties, when marriage and family seemed to pose so few problems. Indeed, one has the impression today that the topics with which we are concerned have moved to center stage. In many quarters, conversation seems almost obsessively concerned with ourselves, our roles, our relationships. As we move into a situation where there seems to be no widespread allegiance to any one set of norms or expectations, and where rapid change means that yesterday's customs no longer apply, there are new ambiguities in everyday conversation and behavior. (How, for example, should parents refer to the young man with whom their daughter is living? "Friend"? "Lover"? "Boyfriend"? "Partner"? Even the Census Bureau has trouble with this one. Their solution—if it is a solution at all—is to refer to them as "Partners of the Opposite Sex Sharing Living Quarters.")

Today's preoccupation with marriage and family arrangements is not just a private concern. Throughout his presidential campaign in 1976, Jimmy Carter stressed his concern for family life. He often spoke, with apparent sincerity, about his own close family ties. He chose for his vice president a man who was known as "the children's senator." In his inaugural address Carter advocated the strengthening of family ties. And in the first few days of his new administration he sent a memo to the White House staff, reminding them not to overlook their responsibilities at home. ("I want you to spend an adequate amount of time with your husbands, wives, and children," he wrote. "All of you will be more valuable to me and the country with rest and a stable home life.") Partly because of Carter's concern, and partly because of widespread anxiety about the family, there has been considerable discussion about the need for a "family policy." When new legislation is drawn up, the authors are now asked to prepare "family impact statements," which are similar in several respects to environmental impact statements. It appears, in other words, that the family is now regarded—like clean air or unpolluted water—as an essential but threatened resource.

Assessing Recent Changes

That marriage and family attract so much attention today does not necessarily make it any easier to understand what is happening. Most of the articles on this topic that appear in the newspapers seem to support the impression of a general erosion of values and a breakdown in family life. Consider these items that appeared in *The New York Times* in one week:

Item: From an article in the *Times Magazine* entitled "Moving On—Reaping the Rewards of the Women's Movement." The author quotes the words of one young woman who has just had a baby. Unexpectedly, she says, the child is both a "cash drain" and a "time drain." The impression one gets from the article is that the young women interviewed regard their children as regrettable disruptions that distract them from more urgent business. And they seem not to get much satisfaction from their relationships with men either. One woman tried to sum up a general feeling in these words: "When you cut through all of it, men don't like women very much, and women don't like men very much."

Item: The same impression was conveyed by a story in the next day's *Times,* which reported that many people are apparently giving up on sex. Judging from the interviews, it is considered a welcome turn of events. As one woman says, "It's like I no longer drink, I no longer smoke, I no longer take dope."

Item: In an article about the teenage pregnancy "epidemic," we learn that the pregnancy rate among white, teenage girls had increased by about one-third in the previous five years. And in New York City, the Health Department reports that the illegitimacy rate has skyrocketed. Almost one-third of all the children born in the city during the previous year were out-of-wedlock births.

Item: In another article, entitled "Yesterday's Kids Not Having Many," a social scientist is asked to explain why the fertility rate has fallen to a low 1.8 children per woman. His answer: "A lot of people say we're a pleasure-seeking, hedonistic society and all we think about is the here and now, or tomorrow, or next week, or April in Paris."

Item: If such reports seem impressionistic, the *Times* also summarizes a recent bulletin from the Census Bureau that states, among other things, that: (1) an unprecedented number of married women with young children are in the labor force; (2) the percentage of men and women under thirty-five who have chosen not to marry is higher than it has ever been; and (3) for the most recent year for which there were complete statistics, the U.S. divorce rate was once again higher than that of any other industrial nation in the world. The Census Bureau estimates that 40 percent of all marriages involving young women now in their late twenties may end in divorce.

It is news items such as these, from apparently reliable sources, that convince many people that there is a crisis in marriage and family life, and that the attitudes and behavior of millions of Americans have changed—and not just a small minority of militant feminists or the proponents of radically new lifestyles.

What can we conclude from such reports? And is it accurate to say not simply that marriage and family are changing, but that they are in decline? Ultimately, of course, any conclusion that change is good or bad is based upon one's own values or preferences. But before reaching such conclusions it is useful first to consider why such reports may give a mistaken impression. One point worth remembering when reading about marriage and family life is that, on the whole, authors are more likely than their readers to be rebellious individuals, people who reject traditional institutions and propose alternatives for them. Nor can it be denied that writers are aware of the fact that crisis attracts attention and sells newspapers and books. Perhaps the most consistent bias in the media stems from this fact: good news is no news. Therefore, in considering the future of marriage and family, we should consult public opinion polls to find out how what people are actually doing differs from what is written about changing marriage and family practices.

The results of opinion polls give a different perspective on current attitudes. In one nationwide poll conducted in 1974, most of the adult respondents agreed that the institution of marriage was weaker than it had been a decade before. And more than a third of the respondents agreed that "you see so few good or happy marriages that you question it as a way of life." Still, the most impressive conclusion from this survey was that most people believed that marriage was necessary and that traditional forms should be preserved. Only one person in ten agreed that "society could survive just as well without the institution of marriage." Three out of four agreed that traditional family life was important and should be preserved. Four out of five respondents said a happy family life was their most important personal goal (Yankelovich, 1974). A 1978 Gallup survey of American teenagers came to the conclusion that although young people today are apparently willing to endorse certain modifications of existing practices—such as a "trial marriage" period during which couples could test their compatibility—a very large majority (84 percent) expect to get married some day, and only 10 percent intend to stay single.

And—in this area, at least—Americans practice what they preach. The single life is more popular than ever, but there is no convincing evidence yet that many people have decided never to marry. Although the U.S. marriage rate in the late 1970s was lower than it had been at its peak (which was 11.0 per 1000 population in 1972) the 1978 marriage rate of 10.3 was still one of the highest in the world (National Center for Health Statistics, 1978). Demographers still predict that more than nine out of ten Americans born in recent years will marry at least once during their lifetime. Which is to say that the United States is likely to remain one of the most married nations in the world. And most people who terminate their first marriage eagerly seek another. It cannot be concluded that divorce implies a rejection of marriage because four out of five divorced people eventually remarry. Apparently those who remarry think the fault lies in choosing the wrong partner, not in the institution of marriage itself. Or perhaps we should interpret this fact as evidence that there are few alternatives that satisfy the need for intimacy, companionship, and a lifelong partner. Thus, if we examine the results of opinion polls as well as the marriage and remarriage rates, we get a very different perspective on what is happening.

The changes in marriage and family arrangements that we have all observed—and to varying degrees, participated in—over the past decade have been quite drastic for such a short period. Topics that most people only whispered about until a few years ago—such as illegitimacy, or female sexual fantasies—are now widely discussed. The availability of contraceptive information and techniques has substantially changed our thinking about childbearing. New ideas about women's place in the work force are prompting a redefinition of female roles. Biological developments, such as embryo transplants and techniques for artificial insemination, are changing the meaning of parenthood. The recent popularity of the single life means that a new stage may have been added to the life cycle. These changes and many others certainly place new pressures on traditional marriage and family arrangements and require that we substantially modify them.

The Perennial Crisis

It is useful to put the current concern about such changes in perspective by recalling how often in decades past both laymen and "experts" have made anxious pronouncements about the uncertain future of the family. In 1927, for example, John Watson, the founder of behavioral psychology, projected from current trends and concluded that in fifty years marriage would no longer exist. And Watson was by no means the only one in that era who had such sentiments. In 1928 Ernest Groves, who was one of the early and influential advocates of education for marriage and family life, published a book entitled *The Marriage Crisis.* In an article, "Eleven Questions Concerning American Marriages," which appeared at about the same time, sociologist William Ogburn clearly reflected a widespread anxiety. Was marriage a desirable state? What did the rising divorce rate mean?

And, finally—to use Ogburn's quaint phrase—was marriage "diminishing" (1927)? Although Ogburn pointed to the high rate of marriage, his answer to this last question was not completely reassuring. For Ogburn's concern was to understand changes in marriage and family life within the broader context of the transformation of American institutions. Urban life, he wrote, had "greatly reduced" the family's functions, and the family had gradually surrendered its former responsibilities to other institutions. Since the early stages of the Industrial Revolution, the household had not been a place of economic production. Responsibility for education had been transferred to the schools, and responsibility for taking care of the aged and the infirm had been transferred to the state. (A few years later, Ogburn himself encouraged that tendency when he provided expert testimony before the Congressional committee that was responsible for the Social Security Act of 1935.) Such evidence of the gradual "diminishing" of marriage and family led many to agree with Watson that these venerable institutions might no longer exist in another fifty years.

Although we are in a position to see that Watson's prediction was wrong, the process that Ogburn described has continued ever since the 1920s. Today, we might extend his list of functions that the family has surrendered. Many more women are in the labor force than was the case a half century ago, and thus they are no longer so economically dependent upon their husbands. In addition, many of the practical tasks that used to be performed almost exclusively in the home, such as child care and food preparation, are increasingly handled by outside facilities, from day-care centers to nationally franchised fast-food operations. Also, there is considerable evidence that sex, too, is increasingly taking place outside of the context of marriage. One might well become alarmed about what such a long-term tendency could mean, and one might ask how the members of today's family unit are still dependent upon each other. As we have seen, in recent years, as in the 1920s, it has often been asked whether this loss of functions does not mean that the family is about to disappear.

Ogburn answered this question in a report delivered to President Hoover's Committee on Social Trends in 1934. The family has been transformed, he wrote, and certain functions have declined, but the ones that remain—particularly the provision of intimacy and the expression of emotional needs—are crucially important. One of Ogburn's contemporaries, anthropologist Edward Sapir, had already made a similar argument in a popular article entitled "What Is the Family Still Good For?" (1930). His conclusion, like Ogburn's, was that the central function of modern marriage and family arrangements is to provide "intimate companionship." That is a need that no other institution can fulfill as well, and a need that becomes increasingly important in a society where many people spend most of their waking hours in large-scale institutions, interacting in terms of specific roles, and repressing their emotions. Both Ogburn and Sapir agreed that although the form of these institutions would undoubtedly continue to change, the survival of marriage and family is assured because they promise the intimate companionship that is missing elsewhere in modern life (Lasch, 1977a).

There are several things that we might learn from such historical perspectives on the "crisis" in marriage and family arrangements. For one thing, it appears that many commentators in this area assume that any change is a change for the worse. As Mary Jo Bane points out in a book about the future of the family, *Here to Stay,* "In technology, progress is the standard. In social institutions, continuity is the standard, and when change occurs, it is seen as decline rather than advance" (1976, p. 4). It would not be unreasonable to regard many of the changes that we have been discussing as attempts to modify marriage and family arrangements so that they will better serve our needs for intimacy.

In most of the debates about changing marriage and family relationships, there is far less disagreement about what has happened than there is about how we should regard these developments. For example, is the rising divorce rate a symptom of breakdown, or is it a reflection of a widely shared belief that it is better for the spouses and their children to dissolve an unsatisfactory marriage and either to live alone or to remarry? Does today's relatively low birth rate indicate that many adults are more selfish than their parents were? Or should we regard this as a welcome tendency, an indication that because of contraceptive advances today's parents have no more children than they want and think they can care for? Does the recent interest in such facilities as clinics for the treatment of sexual problems and classes in such areas as parenting and couple communication indicate a growing problem, or rising aspirations? Is it a good thing that so many married women are working in the labor force? Since the research suggests that working outside of the home seems to be good for many women, but that the marriages of such wives are somewhat less satisfactory and stable, one's answer to this last question might be regarded as an answer to a more general question as well: Which is more important, marital stability or personal satisfaction?

Empirical studies, such as the ones we will review in the chapters that follow, provide a better understanding of such problems as the effects of labor force participation among married women. But ultimately, whether one concludes that there is indeed a crisis, or that such changes represent welcome modifications of institutional arrangements, any conclusion is largely an expression of one's personal values.

There is something else we can learn by comparing what was written and said about family life fifty years ago with the current debate. As we have seen, Ogburn (1927) called attention to the fact that the family had surrendered many of its former functions—such as education, or the care of the chronically sick or dependent—to outside institutions such as public schools, hospitals, and mental institutions. In the early decades of this century, the state began to perform, at public expense, a task that had formerly belonged to the family—it began to subsidize individuals who were temporarily unemployed or who because of old age or disability were no longer employed. What developed were the vast impersonal bureaucracies designed to deliver personal assistance that are such a common feature of modern life. When Ogburn was writing a half century ago about the changes in family life that such public institutions caused, there was considerable optimism about their effects. It was assumed, for example, that the Social Security system would provide more efficiently for the needs of the elderly, and that publicly subsidized medical plans would allow more people to benefit from advances in medical technology. To a considerable extent, that is what happened.

But what Ogburn had no way of anticipating is something that we can see quite clearly today. In part, the recent emphasis upon the family—which is the only institution in modern life that has not grown to an inhuman scale—derives from a widespread feeling that our major institutions are too large to be either efficient or responsive to our needs. "De-institutionalization" became one of the major themes of the late 1970s. Many people began to argue not only that the size of institutions should be reduced, but also that certain functions should be returned to the family, where they might be performed at lower cost and with more personal attention. For example, over the past few years it has often been suggested that it would be far better for elderly patients if they were allowed to die at home rather than in hospitals.

Disenchantment with the public agencies and institutions that took over the functions once performed by the family has taken other forms, too. Educators such as John Holt—who first tried to convince public school systems of the desirability of certain reforms—have begun to urge parents to keep their children out of school and to teach them at home (*Time*, December 4, 1978, p. 78). It is not very likely that many parents are going to follow Holt's radical advice, but his suggestion does illustrate widely shared feelings of despair about

Part of the appeal of marriage and family life is that they are expected to provide the close personal contact and intimacy that is often missing elsewhere in modern society.

what public schools can accomplish. Since the mid-1960s the most important and influential educational policy studies have shown that schooling does *not* have the independent effect on academic achievement and the eventual attainment of higher income, job status, and social mobility that many people had expected. It is families, and not schools, that appear to have the greatest influence on children's educational careers and their attainment of good jobs and high incomes. Some educational policy-makers therefore concluded that it was unrealistic to expect that greater equality would result from increasing expenditures in public education. The impact of such conclusions was to refocus attention on the family. From this perspective, we can see that recent attention to the family flows not so much from anything that is going wrong in marriage and family life as it does from a general disappointment with what other, large-scale institutions have accomplished (Coleman, 1966; Jencks, 1972; Lasch, 1977a).

The Search for Intimacy

If Ogburn failed to anticipate certain developments that have taken place in the half century since he speculated about the future of the family, in one important respect his analysis is as true today as it was then. It is still true, as Ogburn pointed out in 1927, that the best reason to assume that marriage and family have a future is that they provide—or at least are expected to provide—a refuge from the impersonal world outside. Although there have been enormous changes in American society over the past five decades, there is still no other social arrangement that even comes close to satisfying the need for intimate companionship as marriage often does.

To understand what people expect from marriage and family life, look at the ads for new suburban developments appearing in the real estate pages of most newspapers. Here is one of them: "Through these gates you will find the Impossible Dream!—Full-acre homesites afford the utmost security, privacy, and seclusion from today's hectic tension and turmoil." Evidently marriage and family are expected to satisfy the need for security and acceptance, for warm, human contact—needs that are often frustrated elsewhere. Because of the scale and complexity of the society in which we live, most social relationships are fragmented: we may know someone for many years, but only in one role—as bank teller, grocer, or even work associate—rather than as a complete person. In a bureaucratic society, emotional needs are often ignored and individuality denied. Ours is a nation dominated by symbols of movement and escape—immigration, the frontier, the automobile, and the superhighway. According to U.S. Department of Commerce statistics, about half of the nation's population changes its residence every five years. As a consequence, relationships are frequently severed.

The appeal of a relationship that promises to last "till death do us part" increases in a society where many friendships do not last more than a few years. It is certainly no coincidence that in American society—where individualism has been taken to an extreme, where there has been so much geographical mobility, and where kin ties are less binding—the marriage rate has consistently been one of the highest in the world. The high marriage rate, and an equally high divorce rate, might be regarded as compelling evidence of our collective search for intimate contact, and also as evidence of the difficulties of sustaining this relationship upon which so much depends.

Most human contacts today are defined in functional terms: we expect and get something from most of the people we deal with, and they get something from us. Most relationships presume only a very limited liability. We usually reveal only a part of who we are. Marriage and family life are expected to provide the element that is missing from these other human relationships. In an age of transient relationships, people look to the family for portable roots. As the saying goes, "Home is where the heart is." It is supposed to be a place where we are really in touch with one another.

When people are asked what makes them happy, as the readers of *Psychology Today* were in a survey (Shaver and Freedman, 1976), the responses indicate how common a problem loneliness is, and how often people attribute their happiness not to education, work, or an adequate income, but to those relationships—with friends, lovers, or spouses—that promise some relief from loneliness. Overall, those who filled out the questionnaire—a sample that was on the average younger, better educated, more affluent, and more liberal than most Americans—said that they were quite happy most of the time. But at the same time, about one-third said that they felt "constant worry or anxiety," that they often felt guilty or had trouble concentrating. Strikingly, the most common problem among both singles and married people was loneliness; about 40 percent of the respondents said that they often felt lonely. And, according to the survey, although happiness appears to be easier to achieve for people who are well educated and financially successful, individuals more often attribute happiness to their friends, their social life, their marriage, or being in love than to the satisfactions of work or financial success (Shaver and Freedman, 1976). Education may help to get the job or career people want, and one's work helps to pay the bills and to get recognition, but it appears that most people look to their intimate lives for the deepest satisfactions—and for relief from loneliness.

By keeping in mind how often the need for intimate contact is frustrated in daily life, and how common loneliness is, we can better understand not just the appeal of marriage, but also why so many couples enthusiastically become parents. Partly, of course, most spouses become parents because of the social pressures to do so. But having children also promises many personal satisfactions that are not often available elsewhere. Similarly, one might explain our cultural obsession with sex and physical attractiveness by noting that these are often considered the royal road to intimacy. As anthropologist Ashley Montagu once remarked,

"It is highly probable that sexual activity, indeed the frantic preoccupation with sex that characterizes Western culture, is in many cases not the expression of sexual interest at all, but rather a search for the satisfaction of the need for contact" (1971, p. 167).

Social commentator Alvin Toffler (1974) refers to marriage and family as a "shock absorber" that is expected to help us manage the strains and tensions of everyday life. There is some convincing evidence that it often does exactly that. In 1977, the National Institute of Mental Health (NIMH) sponsored a study (Pearlin and Johnson, 1977) to determine how people cope with the strains of everyday life and who is most vulnerable to stress—as indicated by symptoms of depression. A variety of studies had already shown that people who are married are more likely to enjoy psychological well-being (Gurin, Veroff, and Feld, 1960; Srole *et al.*, 1962; Knupfer, Clark, and Room, 1966; Blumenthal, 1967; Bradburn, 1969; Briscoe and Smith, 1974; Radloff, 1975). In the NIMH study of a representative sample of the Chicago metropolitan population, the investigators wanted to determine why marital status makes such a difference. In more than 2000 interviews, they asked people about life strains, how they coped with them, and what symptoms of disturbance they had experienced.

The results of the NIMH study indicated a clear pattern: the unmarried were far more susceptible to depression than their married counterparts. The investigators found that, on the average, the unmarried experienced greater economic hardship than the married. But even when they compared married couples and unmarried individuals who had experienced roughly equal levels of hardship, they found that the unmarried were less able to cope, more likely to experience depression—and this pattern became more pronounced as the hardships became more severe. The investigators comment that married persons apparently "have the advantage of being able to draw emotional support and concrete help from their partners."

Of course there are other sources of emotional support as well, ones that are equally available to the unmarried, such as close friends, acquaintances in the neighborhood, or people with whom leisure activities are shared. When the investigators compared the social networks of the married and unmarried, they found—as earlier studies had (Gove, 1972)—that single people, especially the formerly married, had greater difficulty in maintaining a durable and emotionally satisfying social life. As a consequence, a larger proportion of the unmarried lead lives of considerable isolation. Studies such as this one suggest that marriage and family life often act quite literally as a "shock absorber." As the authors conclude, "Marriage does not prevent economic and social problems from invading life, but it apparently can help people fend off the psychological assaults that such problems otherwise create" (Pearlin and Johnson, 1977, p. 715).

Other studies provide a different perspective on the importance of the emotional needs that are fulfilled mainly in marriage and family life. When sociologists Norman Bradburn and David Caplovitz (1965) attempted to determine what percentage of Americans feel happy about their lives, they found—as other studies did—that married people report being somewhat happier than singles. But, contrary to the common sense belief that marriage is more important for women, they found that marriage appears to make a greater difference in the happiness of *men*. While almost one-third of the single men reported that they were not very happy, only one out of every six married men felt unhappy. It may be that men, who are under considerable pressure to compete and suppress their emotions at work, depend more heavily on marriage as an emotional outlet.

Surveys such as these help us to understand the continuing appeal of marriage, despite the pronouncements about its erosion and imminent demise. Marriage and family are not so fragile as people have often assumed. But neither are they timeless and unchanging islands of stability in a sea of change. The transition in marriage and family arrangements that we are currently witnessing is not a new phenomenon, nor is it one that is likely to end soon. Here, as elsewhere, change is the only constant; and we will explore in the chapters that follow these changing arrangements.

THREE DIFFICULTIES IN UNDERSTANDING MARRIAGE AND FAMILY BEHAVIOR

One of the basic premises of science is that common sense knowledge is often wrong, and "what everyone knows" may well be false. Early in the seventeenth century, Sir Francis Bacon, one of the first spokesmen for the experimental investigation of nature, pointed out the unreliability of many everyday observations. "These foolish images of worlds which the fancies of men have created," he wrote in *The Advancement of Learning,* "must be scattered to the winds." He referred to the five senses as "a thing infirm and erring," constantly mistaken. And he argued that through carefully controlled observation we might begin to understand the way things *really* are.

Ever since the triumph of the astronomical theories of Copernicus, modern science has lengthened the list of naive beliefs that are wrong. Doesn't the sun pass over the earth? It looks that way. But science has shown that the phenomenon of night and day is produced by the spinning of the earth on its axis, and that the earth and other planets circle around the sun. Isn't the sun where we see it in the sky at this very moment? No, it hasn't been there for something like six minutes. Despite our natural assumption that the sun is exactly where we see it, the truth is that it takes several minutes for the rays to get to us.

In many respects, the social sciences have attempted to repeat the success of the physical sciences in providing knowledge that is more reliable than common sense. Just as the scientific method was applied to problems in astronomy and physics, social scientists have devised research tools that permit systematic and accurate observations of our own behavior.

It may seem obvious that special techniques are required to study such natural phenomena as the rotation of the planets and the properties of light. But it is not at all obvious to most people that special techniques might be necessary to understand our own behavior—and particularly the behaviors this book is about. Most of us, after all, were brought up in families and have spent a good deal of time in and around many different marriages and families, both good and bad. "In no other area," notes Arlene Skolnick (1973, p. 2), "is there such a temptation to use one's own experience as the basis for wide-ranging generalizations." And in no other area are those generalizations so unreliable. Common sense observations about marriage and family are frequently distorted by our hopes and fears, by our ideas about the way things ought to be. Our memories of the way things were in our own families during childhood, and our assumptions about the way they must have been for our grandparents, are frequently clouded. Memory is notoriously selective.

Let us examine three important factors that make it difficult to understand marriage and family behavior with any accuracy: idealization of the past; lack of objectivity; and the belief that our cultural patterns are inevitable or universal.

The Good Old Days That Never Were

One reason why it is difficult to understand marriage and family today is that we commonly idealize the past. An example of this tendency is the popular television series *The Waltons*. Unlike most of the problems that *real*-life families face, such as the ones that struck the William C. Loud family in the documentary series *An American Family,* the Waltons' problems come from outside. Week after week, some wounded person, outcast, or misguided stranger arrives on the mountain and brings in enough of the outside world's tensions to provide drama for an hour. One week it is a humorless missionary student, the next it is a ne'er-do-well writer or a bitter victim of New York's gang wars. No matter how great the bitterness or the tension, the Waltons call upon their reserves of love and understanding and somehow set things right. It is a comforting thought: the problems come from *outside*, not within. And week after week, this family finds the resources to deal with them.

If we had our choice, most of us would probably choose to grow up in a family like the Waltons. Three loving generations in one big house. A rural existence, insulated against the insults of industrial development and urban blight. John Walton, the father, is honest, patient, hardworking, uncompromised. Olivia Walton, the wife and mother, is a woman deeply satisfied with her role. She has dignity and pride. It is all quite satisfying.

From looking at the Waltons, you imagine that things must have been better when times were simpler, that poverty is somehow a noble thing and rural life must offer more satisfactions than life in the city, that large families must work better than small ones, and that—once upon a time—both men and women must have been deeply contented in their roles (Roiphe, 1973).

This is American family life in the 1930s as portrayed in the TV series as well as the 1961 novel on which it was based, Earl Hamner's *Spencer's Mountain*. We are aware that this portrait contains certain exaggerations. In real life, good people aren't *that* good. It is entertainment, after all, not a documentary on family life during the Depression. And yet there is no way of accounting for the popularity of the show if it is regarded only as entertainment. It comes close enough to our ideas about how things must have been in the past to convince us, by comparison, that family life is not nearly so satisfying now.

The Waltons is convincing in the way that appealing fiction often is. Because it describes the individual case in rich detail, it appears to be far closer to reality than most of the accounts presented by sociologists, which offer us not real people but statistical abstractions. Because the sociologist is bound by his vows as a researcher to report only what informants want to reveal about their lives, he seems to know far less than the novelist. The novelist recreates marriage and family life, filling in from imagination whatever is needed to create an appealing story and choosing characters that appeal to us, like Olivia Walton and John-Boy. The sociologist has to forgo concentrating on the attractive individual case so that he can sketch an accurate portrait of how most people live, even if their lives are dull and represent a rather confusing blend of good and bad traits.

The Waltons, a fictional family of the 1930s. As depicted in the popular television series, the family reflects common ideals about what family life is supposed to be like. However, it is a very inaccurate portrait of family life in the past.

Novelists can call upon memory without asking how accurate it is. Sociologists have to be more careful, so as to present a clear picture of reality. When sociologists investigate how marital satisfaction changes over the years, for example, they often have to depend on information gathered at just one point in time. In addition, they must acknowledge that the memories of the person or people interviewed may be clouded by subsequent events.

"I am only trying to clarify the meaning of certain experiences for myself," writes the Mexican poet Octavio Paz, "and I admit that what I say may be worth no more than a personal answer to a personal question" (1961, p. 21). The sociologist claims something more, to be at least somewhat more objective and systematic in collecting data, and to attempt valid generalizations. Thus he cannot depend on experience or memory, least of all when he contradicts the data generated by the research tools. (See Box 1–2.)

This may seem a rather curious way of understanding human behavior. It may seem that social scientists have imposed on themselves an unnecessary set of constraints. Like poets who choose to write in haiku, a form that requires exactly seventeen syllables, the wonder is that, given such exacting rules, anything meaningful can be said at all.

Why, then, are careful research techniques worth the bother? Why can't we settle for our memories of family life in the past, or for those images that novelists create? The answer, quite simply, is that most of them, like *The Waltons,* are inaccurate. One well-informed student of family patterns, William J. Goode, refers to the image created in such misleading portraits as "the classical family of Western nostalgia."

> It is a pretty picture of life down on Grandma's farm. There are lots of happy children, and many kinfolk live together in a large rambling house. . . . Life is difficult, but harmonious because everyone knows his task.
>
> Like most stereotypes, that of the classical family of Western nostalgia leads us astray. When we penetrate the confusing mists of recent history, we find few examples of the "classical" family. Grandma's farm was not economically self-sufficient. Few families stayed together as large aggregations of kinfolk. Most houses were small, not large. We now see more large old houses than small ones; they survived because they were likely to have been better constructed. The one-room cabins rotted away. True enough, divorce was rare, but we have no evidence that families were generally happy. Indeed, we find, as in so many other pictures of the glowing past, that each generation of people writes of a period *still* more remote, *their* grandparents' generation, when things really were much better. (1963, p. 6)

In other words, memory serves us poorly when we try to recall what family life used to be. Perhaps it is comforting to imagine a fictional past when things were better. But such recollections, particularly when they recall family life in the past, are often inaccurate.

What Is and What Ought to Be

It is just as hard to look objectively at what is happening today in marriage and family life as it is to be objective about the past, and one of the social sciences' basic claims is that they can be more objective than most of us usually are. To achieve this degree of objectivity, however, social scientists must overcome some problems that physicists, astronomers, and chemists never have to face. A medical researcher studying bacteria, for example, does not have to be concerned about her own personal feelings or prejudices in the same way that the social scientist does, for she has never been one of the microorganisms she is studying. And presumably no bacteria culture is going to act differently when it knows it is being observed.

In contrast, the social science researcher may have certain prejudices. If they influence what she observes in her experiments or field studies, then the research is contaminated just as surely as the bacteria culture into which a foreign substance strays. And humans do behave differently when they know they are being watched, which creates another problem for the social scientist who would like to observe behavior in a laboratory setting.

If it is difficult to be objective about human behavior in general, it is even more difficult to objectively observe the institutions of marriage

Research Perspectives on Marriage and Family

Box 1–2 / How to Read Social Science Research

Ours is an age of science and statistics, in which one of the most common ploys in persuasion is to preface key claims with such phrases as "Experts agree that . . ." or "Studies indicate that . . ." So toothpaste is sold and arguments won with statements like "Three out of four dentists surveyed recommended Bronzo as the most effective leading dentifrice." Very often, such phrases serve only as a magic wand waved over dubious opinions to make them sound more convincing, more scientific.

How, then, can you judge for yourself the reliability of any observation or generalization? By reading social science research carefully and critically you will learn to detect exaggerated claims. Like well-informed consumers who read labels before making purchases, skeptical readers look for certain clues to determine whether they are being well informed or misinformed. Social science research provides several observational techniques, or methodologies, that allow you to see important facts or relationships more clearly than you could by casual observation or intuition. The language of social science research, however, is difficult. These ten suggestions should help you to read social science research with understanding.

1. *Remember to distinguish between facts and personal opinions.* Like well-coached witnesses in a courtroom, social scientists are trained to stick to facts and avoid personal opinion. You should learn to distinguish between the two. To be sure, there is nothing wrong when a writer argues a case and tries to persuade you to share an opinion. As novelist and essayist Larry McMurtry said in his introduction to *In a Narrow Grave: Essays on Texas* (1971, vi), "I haven't spent thirty years in Texas just to be able to be objective about the place." But you should always know what the writer is trying to do, report some facts or convince you of his own opinion.

2. *The facts don't, as the saying goes, speak for themselves.* Most articles and books consist mainly of inferences or interpretations based on a relatively small number of facts. And research data themselves can often be used to support quite different conclusions. For example, two authors might begin with the same statistics on divorce. If one intended to show how alarmingly high the divorce rate is and the other wanted to argue that many marriages remain intact, they could simply present the same facts from different perspectives. Told that a glass is half full, you are likely to perceive it one way; told that it is half empty, you may see it quite differently.

3. *Pay close attention to the words that researchers use.* In social science research,

and the family. For in this area most behavior is loaded with moral and religious meanings. Having been so carefully instructed on what should take place—the roles that males are supposed to play in marriage, the way parents ought to act with their children, and so on—we make our observations with at least one eye on these rules and expectations. Thus, we may barely be able to perceive what is actually happening: there are so many "shoulds" and "oughts" that it is hard to squeeze in an "is."

That we often perceive what is supposed to happen rather than what is actually happening is shown in research conducted on how young words often have a slightly different meaning from their everyday sense. When you read about studies of marital adjustment, for example, the words don't necessarily mean the same thing that they do in normal usage. Get into the habit of asking whether such terms refer to some specific behavior that the investigator might observe or measure.

4. *Look first at the size and nature of the sample from which a generalization is drawn.* One difference between popular journalism and social science research is that popular accounts are often based upon interesting but unrepresentative anecdotes or individuals. In contrast, social scientists are more frequently concerned with studying a representative sample in order to reach valid generalizations. But even in the writings of social scientists, some generalizations are based largely upon impressions and insights from clinical observations. These can be valuable. You should be aware, however, that such cases may not be representative. Remember to ask whether the population that was studied is representative of the people to whom the conclusions are applied. Scientists, like others, sometimes make the mistake of reaching for the overly ambitious generalization that cannot be supported by evidence from a small or unrepresentative sample.

5. *Learn to distinguish valid generalizations from stereotypes.* Certain generalizations made by sociologists—the statement that blacks have a higher rate of separation and divorce than whites, for example—sound very much like the stereotypes of bigots who insist that black men run out on their families. What is the difference between a valid generalization and a stereotype? The most important difference is that the sociologist begins with careful observation of a representative sample of the population to which the generalization applies. Social science explanations are generally an expression of statistical correlation. This means simply that two factors are associated more frequently than we would expect on a chance basis. Social scientists speak in the language of probability—certain things are more *likely* to happen than others—rather than the more reassuring language of predictability or certainty.

6. *One "fugitive from the law of averages" does not disprove a generalization.* One of the most puzzling things about the language of social research is that you often encounter generalizations to which you can immediately think of an exception. For example, in Chapter 3 you will read that teenage marriages are more likely to end in divorce than marriages between individuals who are a few years older. But you may know several couples who married at an early age and are still happily married twenty-five years later. Is the generalization wrong? No, because generalizations are statistical in nature. Sociologists are concerned not with individual cases, but with the relation between certain factors for the population as a whole. If a connection is discovered, some kind of causal pattern might be assumed even though it cannot be demonstrated in every case. It has been well established, for example, that smoking cigarettes may cause cancer. The most convincing evidence that led the Surgeon General to require

(Box 1–2 continues on page 26)

couples make decisions. Sociologist David Olson (1969) asked a number of couples to fill out a questionnaire, just before the birth of their first child, about which spouse would make such decisions as buying insurance for the newborn, determining the husband's responsibilities in changing diapers, and deciding whether the young mother would return to work within a few months after giving birth. Each spouse filled out the questionnaire individually. Then Olson asked those couples in which the husband and wife gave different answers to participate in a simulated decision-making experiment in a laboratory. He wanted to determine the difference

(Box 1–2 continued from page 25)

the warning that appears on every package of cigarettes was statistical: individuals who smoked cigarettes were much more likely to be victims of lung cancer. The fact that there are many individuals who have been smoking two packs a day for seventy years does not disprove the generalization. There are, to use a phrase from one of Bill Mauldin's cartoons, certain "fugitives from the law of averages." Smokers are, however, much more likely to contract cancer. This is the sort of probability statement that social researchers offer.

7. *Social science research, like bread on a grocer's shelves, does not stay fresh forever.* Rapid social change creates a problem for social researchers. Many studies that were conducted no more than a few years ago are already outdated. They may be useful as social history, to help us understand who we were, but they no longer illuminate who we are. For example, many studies of courtship conducted a few years ago do not describe current behavior and alternatives. You should get into the habit of looking at the date when research studies were conducted. However, an older study may still be valid, and its findings should not be simply dismissed.

8. *Learn to recognize ethnocentric attitudes, in which the standards of one's own group are used to judge another.* Much of what is written about marriage and family behavior still betrays a middle-class bias. It is quite common, as sociologist Hyman Rodman points out, to view any household arrangement or intimate bond that does not correspond to middle-class norms as a problem rather than as a practical solution. He asks,

> Are "illegitimacy," "desertion," and "common law" unions problems of the lower class or are they solutions of the lower class to more basic problems? Do we take the fact that there are few interracial marriages and few full-time career women to indicate that these matters are somehow against human nature and therefore best to avoid? Or do we take these as indicative of cultural obstacles that should be removed? (Rodman, 1965, p. 450.)

9. *Learn how to use statistics and to beware of their misuses.* Statistics are very useful in thinking clearly and precisely about social phenomena. But they are frequently misapplied, as Mark Twain commented when he referred to the man who used statistics "like a drunk uses a lamp-post. Not for light, but for support." You sometimes see articles or books in which the statistics march right across the page, like armies on parade. But don't be too impressed; get into the habit of asking the source of statistics. Figures may be quoted to the third decimal place and still be useless if they come from an unreliable source. Be especially wary of an isolated statistic in an imprecise context.

10. *Remember that social science research cannot provide an answer to moral questions.* Although individuals who wish to act responsibly have to know the likely consequences of their actions, social science research cannot tell you what to do. In many instances, however, it can help you anticipate consequences. Just because a majority shares a certain belief does not prove that this belief is morally right.

between what these young couples said they would do and what they actually did in a laboratory situation closely resembling the real-life situation.

The researcher found no consistent pattern, either among husbands or among wives, of correspondence between the questionnaire responses and their actual behavior in the lab. Significantly, though, he did find that the questionnaire responses were a clear reflection of widely shared ideas about what should take place. The husbands perceived themselves as having more power than they actually did, while the wives perceived themselves as having less. Both husbands and wives seemed to think that most of the decision-making power should rest with the male partner. But the actual decisions were made on a more nearly equal basis. In other words, both spouses agreed in attributing power to the one who is generally assumed to have the right to make important decisions, the husband. Apparently it was not simply a matter of giving the right answers on the questionnaires to present a proper appearance to the investigator; these couples accepted a model of how things ought to be and honestly thought it described their own actual behavior (Olson, 1969).

It is not surprising, of course, that what people say they are going to do differs from what actually happens. But a social scientist can never ignore the problems of gaining reliable knowledge in areas where the "is" and the "ought" are such different things. One sociologist, John Cuber, states the problem in these words:

> In many ways, people in America function in two separate and often contradictory spheres. One consists of a set of prescriptions concerning what behavior ought to occur and why it should follow that outline. The other consists of what people actually do in concrete instances when overt behavior is observed. The two are in direct conflict in almost every aspect of sex, marriage, and family life. (Cuber and Harroff, 1968, p. 36)

Most people share the sort of curiosity that was expressed by one woman interviewed by Cuber and his associate, Peggy Harroff, in a study of the sexual patterns of 437 American adults. "I do at times wonder," this woman said, "what does go on in other people's lives. We all respect each other's privacy to the point where we're really ignorant."

After talking for hours with each of these 437 men and women, Cuber and Harroff comment on the unreality of "the monolithic code" that many of these people apparently believe in and pay lip service to, although it is constantly contradicted by their own behavior. "The monolithic code" is a widely shared sense of what ought to happen sexually within marriage, a code that is assumed to be supported by history and religious tradition. It prescribes that both partners shall be faithful to each other in an active and contented lifelong sexual partnership. "While admittedly living *de facto* lives which are often in sharp contradiction to the monolithic code," write Cuber and Harroff, "they pretend nevertheless that the code is an adequate one to order the relations of men and women" (p. 34).

We know what goes on in our own lives. But we have very little reliable information about the backstage events in other people's lives. What we hear people talk about is their ideas of the way things ought to be, and although we frequently read about certain deviations, we lack reliable information about whether most people's lives correspond to their ideas. Consequently, as Cuber and Harroff write, "a colossal unreality—if not quite a myth—about how men and women in fact live has developed" (1968, p. 41).

Thus, one of the most basic reasons to study marriage and family behavior is to correct pluralistic ignorance, to gain more reliable knowledge of what most people actually do, and not just what the code says is supposed to happen. Investigators of human behavior such as Alfred Kinsey, the pioneer researcher who conducted the first really adequate studies of human sexuality, are often accused of intruding into private areas which, many people believe, should not be studied at all. When those investigations produce evidence like many of the findings in Kinsey's monumental studies, which indicate that behavior does not correspond closely to accepted ideas about what ought to be, many people either deny the validity of the research or despair over declining moral standards.

But the information provided by careful investigations of marriage and family behavior can be useful. Some of it, of course, simply satisfies our curiosity about what does go on in other people's lives. As our curiosity is satisfied, however, we learn more about various marriage and family arrangements not only in other cultures, but even in different parts of our own society. By studying marriage and family life, moreover, we may learn more realistic expectations than the ones we pick up from hearing people talk about the way it is supposed to be. By noticing the point at which our actions commonly diverge from ideals, we may gain some awareness of how institutional arrangements might be redesigned to meet our needs.

It's Only Natural

A third problem in thinking clearly about marriage and family arrangements is that we commonly attribute an inevitability or a universality to the cultural patterns we practice. It seems only natural to many that the family should consist of a husband and wife, along with their children, living in their own household, provided for by the husband's earnings and united emotionally by the wife, who concentrates mainly on home and family. This, for most Americans today, is what constitutes a "family." However, no more than about a third of American families actually correspond to this recipe. We might better refer to such an ideal as the middle-class model of what family life should be. In reality a majority of families, and a very large majority of non-middle-class families, lack at least one of the elements included in this model. For example, families in which a divorce has occurred, households in which the wife holds a full-time job, or that include grandparents or other relatives are deviations from the model and constitute modifications of it.

And yet, although a majority of families do not conform to it, this model of a nuclear family is still widely accepted. Like other cultural models, it is quite resistant to change and seems to be supported by historical tradition and religious authority. For many people, it seems almost inevitable that family life should take the form of the nuclear model.

But when we compare our nuclear family model with the family forms in other cultures, *our* pattern turns out to be something of a curiosity. Our mate selection procedure, our emphasis on love in courtship, our kinship patterns, our assumptions about the distribution of power in marriage, and our pattern of child rearing are almost unique.

More than three centuries ago, one of the founders of modern science, René Descartes, wrote in his *Discourse on Method:*

> It is well to know something of the manners of various people, in order more sanely to judge our own, and that we do not think that everything against our modes is ridiculous and against reason, as those who have seen nothing are accustomed to think.

Since then, anthropologists have had an important effect on our thinking because of the reports they have brought back from other cultures about arrangements that work quite well even though they bear no resemblance to our own. We assume, for example, that children should be raised by their biological parents. But, as anthropologists point out, in *matrilineal* societies—where both the inheritance or descent and the place of residence are determined by the mother's family—it is not the father but the mother's brother who has responsibility for the child. And the biological children of the brother, in turn, are the responsibility of his wife's brother. Many anthropological reports pose a direct assault on the moral beliefs of people who assume that only one right way of acting exists, and that any other way would have disastrous consequences. In our society a great importance is placed on the ideal of marriage to one person at a time and sexual exclusivity and fidelity within marriage. But there are other societies, even ones that practice *monogamy,* where sexual exclusivity is not assumed to be an important element in the marital bond. For example, in Samoan society, as described by anthropologist Margaret Mead, there is no assumption of exclusivity. It is assumed that sex is play, a natural, pleasurable thing in which both hetero- and homosexual expression are allowed, with many variations as acceptable diversions (1928).

In this respect, the social sciences constantly verge on the unrespectable by pointing out the variety of cultural arrangements in different societies, thus puncturing the idea that there is any one right way to take care of basic personal and social needs. Moral codes have always been supported by arguing that people should act in a certain way because it is divinely ordained, because individuals always and everywhere have acted that way, because it is only natural and any alternatives are unthinkable. Many people are upset to discover, in the words of the French philosopher Pascal, that "what is truth on one side of the Pyrenees is error on the other." If we admit that our cultural habits—our customs, beliefs, and institutions—are nothing more than arbitrary choices made at some point in the past, and that they are not inevitable, then we have to allow other groups their choices as well, at least if these do not interfere with our own.

This kind of cultural relativism may seem intolerable to many people, but it is one of the premises of the social sciences. Each society has to be understood in terms of its own values and beliefs. If we were to look at the cultural habits of other people through the distorting lens of our own beliefs, we would inevitably see something different from what is actually there.

But cultural relativism poses a fundamental question: Isn't the basic lesson of the social sciences, then, that "anything goes," because almost every behavior or custom is allowed in some society somewhere? Although such a misunderstanding is common, the answer is no. To see why, it is important to understand the difference between moral judgments and the descriptive accounts provided by the social sciences.

The social sciences are not in the business of making moral judgments, or deciding what ought to be. Their purpose is simply to provide the most accurate observations that can possibly be made, using special techniques. Social scientists have to confine their research to problems that can be tested by observation or experimentation. Since no way exists of empirically testing the truth of any ethical judgment about what ought to be, value judgments of this sort fall outside the realm of the social sciences. Instead, the social sciences have a number of special techniques for observing and describing what is.

Personal values are the criteria we use in choosing among alternative courses of action. In the past few years, a good deal of attention has been given to the study of values clarification, a method of becoming aware of one's own values and learning to act so that the consequences are consistent with these values. Two spokesmen for values clarification, Sidney B. Simon and Howard Kirschenbaum, explain the relevance of personal values in these words:

> Traditionally, educators—parents, the schools, and the churches—have most often taken a common approach toward answering the value questions that young people raise. We call this approach moralizing, which is the direct or indirect transfer of a set of values from one person or group to another. . . . In a world where the future bore a close resemblance to the past, moralizing was a relatively effective means of transmitting or "teaching" values. But consider the young people today. From every side, they are bombarded with different and often contradictory sets of values. Change is so rapid, and new alternatives arise so quickly in every area of life, that no one set of specific beliefs and behaviors could possibly answer all the choice situations of the future. (in Toffler, 1974, p. 259)

If, because there is no longer a consensus about values and because we are confronted with so many new alternatives, moralizing is no longer effective, how can we learn to choose among these alternatives? Simon and Kirschenbaum suggest that we first need to become aware of our own values and personal priorities. We need to learn how to choose among alternatives after examining their probable consequences.

"For example," they say,

> the future will undoubtedly legitimize many different patterns of dating, mating, and marriage. This is already happening. An important part of valuing in this area would be to consider seriously the consequences of each alternative before making a choice, and not just to gravitate toward the alternative that seems most attractive at first glance. (in Toffler, 1974, p. 259)

As sociologist Ira Reiss (1971) suggests, we can illustrate the difference between facts and values by examining how someone might choose to smoke or not to smoke. As most people know, a considerable amount of evidence points to the conclusion that cigarettes cause lung cancer. Of the 50,000 people who die each year from lung cancer, most are cigarette smokers. But do these studies, which link smoking with lung cancer, mean that it is necessarily wrong to smoke? No, says Reiss, because whether an individual chooses to smoke or not is a matter of his or her personal values. Nonsmokers decide that the pleasures of smoking are outweighed by the risk of death from lung cancer. If you decide, on the other hand, that smoking is so enjoyable that its pleasures outweigh the risk to your health, no facts could prove that you are wrong.

Unlike people who lived in the "single answer" cultures of the past, in which more of a consensus existed on moral values and the individual had fewer personal alternatives, everyone in today's society is faced with a long list of choices about marriage and family arrangements. Because of your freedom to choose among those alternatives, you will have to make more decisions. To decide wisely, you will have to be aware of your own personal values and of the likely consequences of each decision.

STUDYING BACKSTAGE BEHAVIOR

Although a systematic study of marriage and family using social science techniques may help to correct our common sense knowledge of these institutions, the techniques themselves have certain limitations. One such limitation stems from the fact that much of the behavior to be investigated is, to use sociologist Erving Goffman's phrase, backstage behavior. It is quite difficult to observe what takes place behind closed doors. Indirect observations, by means of questionnaires or interviews, have obvious shortcomings when they are used to probe into the most private aspects of human behavior. And these shortcomings are only aggravated by the circumstance that women, being more readily available to answer researchers' questions, provide more of the answers than men do. It is quite possible that men would give substantially different answers to many questions, but from the researchers' point of view, they are the silent partners.

Mark Twain once told a story about a policeman who was making his rounds on a particularly dark night. He came upon a drunk who was on his hands and knees under a streetlight looking for something. "What are you looking for?" asked the policeman. "My key," answered the drunk. "Where did you lose it?" inquired the cop, trying to be helpful. The drunk pointed out into the pitch black night. "I lost it out there," he said, "but I can't see out there and I can see here."

It sometimes seems as if social scientists, like the drunk in Mark Twain's story, look only at the areas that are illuminated by their research tools, and thus ignore some of the questions we would most like to have answered. Still, as one writer remarked a few years ago, "practically everything social scientists know about the family has been derived from family members seen alone" (Skolnick, 1973, p. 4). Sociologists know more about courtship and mate selection, and about family disorganization and divorce, than they do about daily family interactions, because normal family behavior is less public. To be sure, many studies are now more objective, are based on more representative samples, and are less moralistic than family sociology was a generation or more ago, but they still do not answer some of the really intriguing questions about marriage and family life. Only recently have researchers—particularly the family therapists described in Chapter 9—begun to do a careful, closeup analysis of family interaction patterns based on direct observation of whole families.

Another problem is that the researcher in marriage and family behavior, like anyone else,

> is shackled by taboos and ancestral superstitions, which he has the more trouble in combating because they are in his mind as well as his environment. We are able to observe only what the social norms permit us to see. (Waller and Komarovsky, in Christensen, 1964, p. 970)

But these shackles are loosening, and this is one reason why the study of marriage and family is considerably more vigorous and exciting now than it was in the 1940s and 1950s. Social norms have changed enough so that new questions can now be asked. It has only been since the late 1960s, when many people began to question the legitimacy of the traditional family unit, that a very active exploration of institutional alternatives began. And it was only after the prevailing social climate about parenthood had started to change that researchers conducted studies indicating that couples without children might be happier than those with them.

Today, there is a very active interest in studying marriage and family behavior, its past, present, and future. Historians, family therapists, and legal experts are examining these institutions with new interest. And there have been some substantial efforts in recent years to construct theoretical propositions that may allow us to build a substantial edifice out of a large pile of conclusions from empirical studies (Hill, Reiss,and Nye, 1979). Some of the studies in this area refute widely shared common sense beliefs. Others provide the facts and observa-

Formal photographs like this one reveal people's beliefs about what a family *should* be. The father sits in the center, with his arms around his wife and daughter, surrounded by three smiling sons dressed in their Sunday best. Even the dog poses for the camera. What we have no way of knowing from this photograph, and what social scientists often have trouble determining, is how the family's "backstage behavior" differs from this proper "public image."

tions that we need in order to think more clearly about alternatives. In the chapters that follow, we will use such studies to examine the institutions of marriage and the family.

Conclusions

This chapter has explored two general questions. First, what changes have taken place in marriage and family arrangements over the past generation, and how have popular ways of thinking about them changed as well? In particular, we noted how common it has been—in recent years as in the more distant past—for people to interpret changing marriage and family practices as evidence of the erosion and demise of these institutions. We have examined some of the changes taking place in these institutions today and noted an increasing awareness of a wide variety of arrangements and preferences. The single standard is beginning to break down, and as a result a widely acknowledged diversity in marriage and family forms with a greater range of personal alternatives is apparent.

Freed from the moral consensus of the past, no longer constrained to live our lives by repeating many of our parents' decisions, we are confronted by many dilemmas as we choose among the alternatives. While social science research cannot tell us what we ought to do, it does offer facts and perspectives that should help us to anticipate the probable consequences of acting in one way rather than another.

The second question raised in this chapter is: Why must we study marriage and family behavior when we already know so much about it from personal experience? The answer is that many difficulties keep us from seeing the realities of marriage and family life with any clarity. Most behavior in this area is charged with emotion and saturated with moral or ethical meanings. We are tempted to argue right and wrong, rather than to observe what is actually happening. We make wide-ranging generalizations based on our own personal experience without considering how different it is from the experience of others. And we assume that many common sense observations about marriage and family life are factual, even when they are only shared opinions. The social science research on marriage and family behavior that provides the material for this book is intended to supply more systematic and reliable knowledge than we can get from other sources.

Finally, there is little reason to believe that the institutions of marriage and family will soon disappear. Most of us—including some of the angriest critics of the family—still marry, and expect that our most basic personal needs will be met in marriage. Although we are currently redefining the institutions of marriage and family, they are by no means obsolete. To one extent or another, almost everyone in American society is involved in this process of redefinition.

REFERENCES

Mary Jo Bane. *Here to stay.* New York: Basic Books, 1976.

Monica D. Blumenthal. Mental health among the divorced. *Archives of General Psychiatry* 16 (1967): 603–608.

Norman M. Bradburn. *The structure of psychological well-being.* Chicago: Aldine, 1969.

——— and David Caplovitz. *Reports on happiness.* Chicago: Aldine, 1965.

William C. Briscoe and James B. Smith. Psychiatric illness—Marital units and divorce. *Journal of Nervous and Mental Disease* 158 (1974): 440–445.

Bertram Brown. How women see their roles: A change in attitudes. *New Dimensions of Mental Health.* Washington, D.C.: U.S. Department of Health, Education and Welfare, Public Health Service, September 1976.

Wesley R. Burr, Reuben Hill, Ira Reiss, and F. Ivan Nye, eds. *Contemporary theories about the family.* New York: The Free Press, 1979.

Harold T. Christensen, ed. *Handbook of marriage and the family.* Chicago: Rand McNally, 1964.

James Coleman. *Equality of educational opportunity.* Washington, D.C.: U.S. Department of Health, Education and Welfare, 1966.

David Cooper. *The death of the family.* New York: Vintage, 1970.

John F. Cuber and Peggy B. Harroff. *Sex and the significant Americans.* Baltimore: Penguin, 1968.

Roxanne Dunbar. Quoted in Carl Danziger and Matthew Greenwald. *Alternatives: A look at unrelated couples and communes.* New York: The Institute of Life Insurance, 1971, p. 11

Amitai Etzioni. The family: Is it obsolete? *Journal of Current Social Issues* 14 (Winter 1977).

Robert Francoeur. *Eve's new rib.* New York: Delta, 1972.

George Gallup. Concept of "trial" marriage has considerable teen-age appeal. *Gallup Youth Survey,* February 1, 1978.

William C. Goode. *World revolution and family patterns.* New York: Free Press, 1963.

Walter R. Gove. The relationship between sex roles, marital status, and mental illness. *Social Forces* 51 (1972): 34–44.

Ernest Groves. *The marriage crisis.* New York: Longmans, Green, 1928.

Gerald Gurin, Joseph Veroff, and Sheila Feld. *Americans view their mental health.* New York: Basic Books, 1960.

Earl Hamner, Jr. *Spencer's mountain.* New York: Dial, 1961.

Elizabeth Hardwick. Domestic manners. *Daedalus,* Winter 1978, pp. 1–11.

Christopher Jencks, et al. *Inequality: A reassessment of the effect of family and schooling in America.* New York: Basic Books, 1972.

Sidney M. Jourard. Re-inventing marriage: The perspective of a psychologist. In Herbert A. Otto, ed. *The family in search of a future.* New York: Appleton Century Crofts, 1970.

Genevieve Knupfer, Walter Clark, and Robin Room. The mental health of the unmarried. *American Journal of Psychiatry* 122 (1966): 841–851.

Christopher Lasch. The siege of the family. *New York Review of Books* November 24, 1977(a) p. 15ff.

———. *Haven in a heartless world.* New York: Basic Books, 1977(b).

———. *The culture of narcissism.* New York: Norton, 1978.

Karen Mason, John Czajka, and Sara Arber. Changes in U.S. women's sex role attitudes 1964–1974. *American Sociological Review,* August 1976.

Larry McMurtry. *In a narrow grave: Essays on Texas.* Austin: Encino Press, 1971.

Margaret Mead. *Coming of age in Samoa.* New York: Morrow, 1928.

Keith Melville. *Communes in the counter culture.* New York: Morrow, 1972.

Ashley Montagu. *Touching: The human significance of skin.* New York: Columbia University Press, 1971.

Elting Morison, ed. *The American style.* New York: Harper & Row, 1958.

Daniel P. Moynihan. *Coping: On the practice of government.* New York: Vintage, 1975.

National Center for Health Statistics. *Births, marriages, divorces and deaths.* Washington, D.C.: U.S. Government Printing Office, 1978.

William Ogburn. Eleven questions concerning American marriages. *Social Forces* 6 (1927): 5–12.

———. The family and its functions. In President's Committee on Social Trends. *Recent social trends in the United States.* New York: McGraw-Hill, 1934.

David H. Olson. The measurement of family power by self-report and behavioral methods. *Journal of Marriage and the Family* 31 (August 1969): 549–557.

Nena O'Neill and George O'Neill. *Open marriage.* New York: Evans, 1972.

Nena O'Neill. *The marriage premise.* New York: Evans, 1977.

Octavio Paz. *The labyrinth of solitude: Life and thought in Mexico.* New York: Grove Press, 1961.

Leonard I. Pearlin and Joyce S. Johnson. Marital status, life-strains, and depression. *American Sociological Review* 42 (October 1977): 704–715.

Lenore Radloff. Sex differences in depression: The effects of occupation and marital status. *Sex Roles* 1 (1975): 249–265.

Ira L. Reiss. *The family system in America.* New York: Holt, Rinehart and Winston, 1971.

Hyman Rodman. The textbook world of family sociology. *Social Problems* 12 (1965): 450–459.

Anne Roiphe. The Waltons: Ma and Pa and John-Boy in mythic America. *The New York Times Magazine,* November 18, 1973, pp. 40ff.

The Roper Organization. *The American women's opinion poll.* New York, 1974.

Lillian Breslow Rubin. *Worlds of pain: Life in the working-class family.* New York: Basic Books, 1976.

Edward Sapir. What is the family still good for? *American Mercury* 19 (1930): 149–151.

Phillip Shaver and Jonathan Freedman. Your pursuit of happiness. *Psychology Today,* August 1976, pp. 26–32, 75.

Arlene Skolnick. *The intimate environment.* Boston: Little, Brown, 1973.

Leo Srole, Thomas S. Langer, Stanley T. Michael, Marvin K. Opler, and Thomas A. C. Rennie. *Mental health in the metropolis: The mid-town Manhattan study.* New York: McGraw-Hill, 1962.

Marvin Sussman. Family systems in the 1970s: Analysis, policies, and programs. *Annals of the American Academy of Political and Social Science* 396 (1971).

Alvin Toffler, ed. *Learning for tomorrow.* New York:

Random House, 1974.

James D. Wright. Are working women really more satisfied? *Journal of Marriage and Family*, May 1978, pp. 302–313.

The Yankelovich Organization, *Public attitudes toward the family*. New York: Institute of Life Insurance, 1974.

Daniel Yankelovich. *The General Mills American Family Report, 1976–77: Raising Children in a Changing Society*. Minneapolis, Minn.: General Mills Consumer Center, 1977.

FOR FURTHER STUDY

There are several books that might be recommended to anyone interested in exploring the ways in which the social climate of the fifties and sixties affected marriage and family life. D. T. Miller and M. Nowack have written a book, *The Fifties: The Way We Really Were* (Garden City, N.Y.: Doubleday, 1977), that helps to correct the prevailing nostalgia for that era. Morris Dickstein's *Gates of Eden: American Culture in the Sixties* (New York: Basic Books, 1977) provides a perceptive and generally well-balanced account of the tumultuous sixties. For a discussion that focuses more specifically on changing values and how images of the family changed during the sixties, see Keith Melville's *Communes in the Counter Culture* (New York: William Morrow, 1972), particularly Chapters 3, 4, and 7.

As noted in this chapter, Christopher Lasch's analyses have been influential over the past few years. Whether or not you agree with his conclusions, his book *The Culture of Narcissism* (New York: W. W. Norton, 1978) provides a useful perspective on changing values and character types in the seventies. Mary Jo Bane's *Here to Stay* (New York: Basic Books, 1976) is a thoughtful and balanced assessment of recent changes. Not only is the family *not* declining, she argues, but there may be more commitment to family today than in the past.

One way to make a forecast about marriage and family life in the 1980s is to look at the attitudes expressed by a nation-wide sample of 17,000 young Americans who graduated from high school in 1979. At the top of their list of priorities is "a good marriage and family life." A very large majority expects to marry; and almost all of them—96 percent— say they would like to have children. See Jerald G. Bachman and Lloyd D. Johnston, "The Freshmen, 1979" (*Psychology Today*, September 1979).

II
Choosing a Partner

"Round Hill, 1977" Alex Katz

2 Mate Selection–The Choice Is Yours

Very few decisions in life are as important as the choice of a mate. At stake are the disposition of property and the heredity of the children, not to mention the happiness of the two mates for several decades of their lives. In the past, this decision was considered too important for young people to make themselves. Parents chose their children's mates with the same care for a good bargain, for practicality and durability, that we would consider appropriate in buying a car.

The choice is no less important now that it is being left to the young people themselves, and it seems to have become particularly difficult because relatively few individuals in modern society share the same social background, interests, and lifestyle expectations. No one is surprised, then, to note that the choice many young people make turns out to be a foolish one. In fact, William Lederer and Don Jackson argue in *The Mirages of Marriage* (1968) that what we learn in American culture about romantic encounters actually prevents us from making a wise choice. "Nature, our culture, and our traditions distract us, prevent us from being intelligent during the mate-selecting process," they write. "Instead, the marriage-bound individual gallops off and gets himself engaged to someone who 'attracts' him" (p. 372).

A lot of time and energy have been spent trying to understand why some people are compatible and others are not. Some of the techniques that used to be popular in assessing compatibility between potential mates now seem very foolish. For example, phrenology—the practice of judging character by the shape of one's skull—was so popular in the nineteenth century that Queen Victoria of England had the royal children's heads examined for this purpose (Murstein, 1974). And yet astrology is used today for the same purpose. When someone asks, "What's your sign?" your answer presumably provides an important clue in figuring out whether the two of you are compatible.

Common sense advice about how to find the right person is unreliable and contradictory. We are told both that "birds of a feather flock together" and that "opposites attract." Is it the similarities between two persons that account for this attraction, or it it the differences? People are not magnets, and no simple formula such as "opposites attract" really explains interpersonal attraction.

Popular beliefs such as "love will overcome all obstacles" express our hopeful fantasies, but they are contradicted by the sober facts. It is commonly said that you will recognize the right person as soon as he or she comes along, but the evidence suggests that permanent relationships are not usually founded on that basis. In one study, more than half the married men and women surveyed said that they had felt no strong physical attraction until at least two months after their first meeting (Burgess and Wallin, 1953).

If it is only in old Hollywood movies that one's ideal mate is revealed by a bolt of romantic lightning, how do we actually go about making this difficult choice? In this chapter, we will look first at some of the social factors that influence the choice of a mate. Although in our society it seems to be mainly a matter of individual preference, the pool of eligibles from which a mate is chosen is limited by a variety of rules. Theoretically, of course, one might be attracted to any member of the opposite sex. However, all but a tiny percentage of those people are ruled out. Some—individuals who are closely related to us by blood—are ruled out by law, and a great many others are excluded because of social pride and prejudice.

After examining the social expectations that limit the pool of eligibles, we will turn to the more individual matter of interpersonal attraction. Why are some people very attractive to us and others not? We often acknowledge—as when we say such things as "What does he see in her?"—being puzzled by those attractions. In this chapter we will explore the importance of appearance as well as romantic love in choosing our mates.

One of the most unique features of our mate selection system is the importance of the apparently irrational factor, romantic love. In contrast to the rational process that sociologists refer to as status matching, love is reputed to be no respecter of social boundaries or common beliefs about a sensible mate choice. Presumably, if you wanted to be entirely rational about the choice of a mate, you might compare various possible mates in terms of intelligence, ambition, stability, family background, genetic makeup, and potential qualities as spouse and lover. And yet very few people go about making this choice in this way. The most common reason why people marry is that they are in love with each other—which tells us something about their attraction, but little about their compatibility.

Is there a conflict between rational and irrational factors in choosing a mate? If the person you are most attracted to is not considered a sensible choice, which inclination should you trust? What are the problems, and perhaps the advantages, in choosing a partner with traits very different from your own? These questions used to be decided by parents who made the choice. In today's society, the choice is yours.

THE MARRIAGE MARKET

Have you ever tried to list the characteristics you want in an enjoyable date or someone you might consider as a spouse? If you are like most people, the list would exclude all but a very few persons. Your list would probably include such considerations as physical attractiveness, the right height, intelligence, good education, certain interests, certain attitudes or beliefs, and characteristics of the person's social background, including religion and family status. For many people, there are certain traits—race, appearance, or education, for example—that automatically rule out most people.

Some items on the list are determined by social custom, which says that you should meet and marry someone who is like you in certain respects and different in others. There are matters of personal preference, too. Dark-complexioned people may be more appealing to you, for example, and you probably enjoy people whose interests are similar to your own.

When you think how long that list of preferences is, you begin to realize why finding a suitable partner is so complicated.

Why is it, after all, that blind dates are considered to be so risky? Clearly, in choosing a partner—even a dating partner—not just anyone will do. Despite the notion that great romantic attractions begin in the most unexpected ways, we prefer to choose partners with our eyes wide open. For both sexes, dating can be a ruthless competition. If things work out, what you stand to gain is a very enjoyable blend of attention and acceptance. But dating involves risks of various sorts, too, ranging from boredom to sexual assault. At its worst, being rejected by a date can be a real blow to one's morale and self-esteem.

Many people avoid blind dates entirely, because the risks are too high. Since the list of expectations we construct is a highly individual set of preferences, dates chosen at random are not often satisfactory. Most people prefer to be "fixed up" by friends who serve as matchmakers. The more these friends know about who you are and who your date is, the more likely they are to succeed in bringing together two people who will enjoy each other's company.

Comparison Shopping

Some of the problems we face in choosing a mate do not arise in simpler societies because there are fewer social differences. But the most important difference between our procedures for mate selection and those followed in more traditional societies is that in the latter the choice is made by the parents. In some cases, a professional matchmaker is called in to serve as investigator and go-between in the same way that we might seek the help of an attorney in a complicated negotiation.

But in all societies, whether it is acknowledged or not, the mate choice takes place within a marriage market. Like other markets, this one involves a commodity—an eligible male or female—to be exchanged at a certain price. The currency in the exchange consists of the socially valued attributes and skills of the two individuals—family background, economic position, education, and personal attributes such as age and beauty. Whatever the qualities are that the society considers valuable, each family or individual seeks as a mate the person who has the most of them.

In societies where marriage is parent arranged, the task of choosing an appropriate mate is largely a matter of matching status characteristics of the prospective bide and groom. As in any other market, the goods are marked with a price, and parents search for a prospective mate for their child only among families of roughly equivalent status because they must pay the price. The exchange is quite explicit in societies where a large dowry—a sum of money or property brought to the marriage by the girl—is sometimes used to marry a daughter into a higher-ranking family. The exchange of money for social rank is considered by both families to be a good bargain.

The bargaining process becomes somewhat more complicated when factors other than social status enter into the negotiations. For centuries a common exchange in our society has been between a powerful, older man from a "good" family and a beautiful, young woman of lower social status. When a woman's beauty enables her to marry above her class, there is likely to be some grumbling among the eligible women in the husband's social circle, but the exchange will generally be regarded as appropriate, if not necessarily wise. Our assumptions about what should happen in an exchange are revealed most clearly when the situation is reversed. What happens when an older woman who has both social position and money marries a much younger man with no discernible advantages other than his physical appeal? Both persons are likely to be laughed at, because the exchange is not considered appropriate.

To us, the practice of parent arranged marriages seems a serious violation of a largely personal matter. It is difficult for us to imagine a situation where most children actually prefer to have their parents make this decision for them, but that is the case in contemporary India. There, marriage establishes an alliance between two kinship groups in which the newly joined couple is merely the most conspicuous link. Thus, marriage is not just an individual affair; the bride and groom marry not only each other, but all their relatives as well.

In societies where marriage establishes this sort of linkage between families, allowing two individuals from very different backgrounds to mate could cause embarrassment, since the two families would not consider themselves equal. Besides, the two individuals might make somewhat different assumptions about the roles and rituals of marriage, thus giving rise to practical misunderstandings. To avoid such difficulties, societies have established the rule of *endogamy*—marriage within one's own group, class, or religion—and parents have taken the responsibility for this important decision.

Both in these societies and our own, there are two primary rules governing marital eligibility. The first is the rule of endogamy, which as we have seen permits marriage only between individuals who are alike in important ways. The other, which is so easy to take for granted that it is likely to go unnoticed, is the rule of *exogamy*. It prohibits marriage within the immediate kinship group. In some societies this taboo applies to all who live within the same clan or village, but in the United States today, it is generally interpreted to exclude first cousins and members of one's immediate family from the pool of eligible mates.

Bargaining for a Mate in India Both parental control of the mate choice and explicit bargaining in reaching that decision are illustrated by the procedure practiced in India today. When David and Vera Mace, two prominent figures in American marriage counseling, went to India in the 1950s to talk with young people about how their mates are selected for them, they asked the question that would be the first to occur to most of us. "Wouldn't you like to be free to choose your own marriage partners?" they inquired. "Oh, no!" answered most of the young women. They actually preferred to have their parents make the decision, because it seemed to them that the American system of mate selection would be humiliating. A young woman would be expected to call attention to herself, perhaps even pretend that she is better than she really is, to attract a boy and get married. In India, the girls don't have to worry because they *know* they'll get married. When girls are old enough, parents find a suitable boy, and everything is arranged. This way girls don't have to go into competition with each other. In India, love comes after marriage, not before (Mace and Mace, 1960).

Although parents still make the mate choice in modern India, they are assisted by ads placed in the matrimonial columns of the Indian newspapers. These ads serve to widen the circle of families from which a mate can be chosen. Thus, when one upper-middle-class family in New Delhi wanted to find a husband for their daughter, they placed this ad in the *Hindustan Times*, a widely respected national newspaper: "Well-placed match desired for accomplished, smart, homely Brahmin girl, 26½ years. B.A. Ed., brother doctor, well-to-do family. Early decent marriage. Caste no bar." Such ads reveal quite clearly the qualities that families look for. The phase "respectable family," which appears in many of them, is a polite way of indicating that family assets—wealth, education, prestige—are desirable. Social status, which in India means one's caste position, is less important than it was. But other factors, such as age, are still important. It is only after such socially defined requirements have been satisfied that the personal qualities of the prospective partner are considered (Weinraub, 1973).

When two Indian families find that their son and daughter seem suitable, certain inquiries are made, often through marriage brokers or professional go-betweens, about the background, character, and personality of the prospective mates to make sure that the ads are accurate. Each family proceeds very carefully, trying to enhance its own status as well as to provide a good match for its son or daughter. The entire procedure shows that marriage represents a contract between two families, not just two individuals. Only at the last stage of the selection process do the prospective bride and groom take any part. In recent years, it appears that because of modernization, more formal education, and increased geographical mobility the attitudes of many college-educated Indians have changed. Although only a very small minority want as much freedom in this matter as most Americans take for granted—namely, ultimate power over the final selection of a mate—an overwhelming majority of college-educated Indians, particularly males, would like to have some voice in choosing their own mates (Rao and Rao, 1976).

Bargaining in the United States The procedure we follow in American culture today seems at first to bear very little resemblance to the Indian system. Since the Colonial period, most marriages here have not been parent arranged. The American pattern has been to eliminate the middleman: When Priscilla said, "Speak for yourself, John" to John Alden when he came to announce another man's affections, she showed how rapidly we were breaking from traditional mate selection procedures (Reiss, 1971). Kinship was not so important in the New World, nor did the choice of a mate affect kin relations so much, so there was far less parental control over the decision. In a culture where social status was more fluid and changeable, the personal attributes of a mate became more important than they had been in Europe. Most of all, traditional mate selection procedures were substantially modified by an idea that became quite popular by the nineteenth century. This was the idea that romantic attraction should precede the mate choice.

Because of our emphasis on romantic attraction and free choice in the selection process, most people today have difficulty accepting that in one important respect our customs are very much like those practiced in India: mate selection still takes place in a marriage market, even though the young person is expected to carry out the bargaining without much help from parents or go-betweens. Think of the types of questions frequently asked in a setting such as a singles bar. Within the first few minutes of conversation you are asked where you go to college, what you plan to do when you graduate, what kind of car you drive. These are the same concerns that Indian parents have when they search for a mate for their son or daughter.

We tend to fall in love with the people who reward us most—by having a pleasing personality or appearance, by sharing their achievements—and are like us in important respects. Modern matchmaking services, though they often use new technologies such as computers and videotapes, perform many of the same services that parents do in traditional societies. The questionnaires that the computerized dating service asks you to fill out, for example, reflect the same assumption that Indian parents make: initially, at least, the important thing is to bring together people who are similar in important respects (see Box 2–1, p. 42).

The crucial question for the design of a matchmaking service is, of course, which characteristics are most significant in predicting compatibility? It would be difficult indeed to program a computer to match the idiosyncrasies described in the ads that appear in the personal column of many American periodicals. In one ad, a man seeking "synergistic closeness" and "bizarre existential adventures when the moon is bright" describes himself as a "ponderer and professional dilettante, successfully marooned in mass communications, who seeks a handsome, bold, and wacky female for anything two loners can work out." But some tastes and preferences can be successfully matched, and that is what computerized dating services promise to do.

As demographer Paul Glick observes, they may provide a much-needed service in a society where young people are left very much on their own:

Involvement Exercises

Box 2–1 / Determining Your Best Match—A Dating Preference Questionnaire

Questionnaires like this are used by modern-day matchmakers, sometimes with the help of computers, to locate compatible dates and potential mates. Notice that the questionnaire asks whether certain social categories are important in a person you would consider an appropriate partner. Then it asks about assets such as education and appearance. Finally, it probes your values and opinions.

Instructions: Answer the questions in all three sections of this questionnaire. Its usefulness, of course, depends upon how truthful you are.

A. *Who are you*? (For each question, circle or fill in the appropriate answer.)

1. My *sex* is Male Female
2. My *age* is _____
   The age preference of my date is _____
   The youngest acceptable age of my date is _____
   The oldest acceptable age of my date is _____
3. My *height* is _____
   The shortest acceptable height of my date is _____
   The tallest acceptable height of my date is _____
4. My *physical build* is Thin Medium Heavy
   My date's physical build should be Thin Medium Heavy
5. My *race* is White Black Oriental
   My date's race should be White Black Oriental
6. My *religion* is Protestant Catholic Jewish Other None
   The religion of my date should be Protestant Catholic Jewish Other No preference
   My religious convictions are Strong Average Mild None
7. My current *educational level* is _____ (current year of study)
   The educational level of my date should be More than mine About the same Less than mine
8. My *marital status* is Single Divorced Widow or Widower
   Would you be willing to date a person who is divorced? Yes No
   Would you be willing to date a person who is widowed? Yes No
9. Do you have any *children* living with you? Yes No
   Would you be willing to date a person who has children living with them? Yes No
10. Members of the opposite sex usually consider my *physical appearance*
    Very attractive or handsome Above average Average Below average Unattractive
    The physical appearance of my date is Unimportant Fairly important Important Very important

B. *Personal Values*. First *circle* the number that best describes the importance of this value for you. Then *check* the number that describes the importance of this value in a date.

	Unimportant	*Slightly Important*	*Important*	*Very Important*
1 Ambition	1	2	3	4
2. Loyalty	1	2	3	4
3. Enthusiasm	1	2	3	4
4. Sophistication	1	2	3	4
5. Popularity	1	2	3	4
6. Daring	1	2	3	4
7. Decisiveness	1	2	3	4
8. Understanding	1	2	3	4
9. Honesty	1	2	3	4
10. Excitement	1	2	3	4
11. Self-Confidence	1	2	3	4
12. Money	1	2	3	4
13. Religion	1	2	3	4
14. Cultural Background	1	2	3	4
15. Consideration of Others	1	2	3	4

C. *Opinions*. Circle the number that best describes how true you believe each statement to be.

	True	*More True Than False*	*Not Sure*	*More False Than True*	*False*
1. God will answer prayers if a person is sincere.	1	2	3	4	5
2. In some instances, stealing can be justified.	1	2	3	4	5
3. All of the prophecies of the Bible are coming true.	1	2	3	4	5
4. Our government should provide more aid to the poor.	1	2	3	4	5
5. Policemen use brutality in too many instances.	1	2	3	4	5

6. How important is it that your date share your views about the questions in this section?
   Unimportant Slightly important Important Very important

Interpreting Your Answers

Can you think of any preferences or criteria that would be important to you in identifying a compatible date but did not appear on this questionnaire? Which person in your class most nearly matches your preferences? Do most of the students in your class share certain values and opinions? If they do, can you conclude that your college represents a preselected pool of individuals with somewhat similar backgrounds and preferences? As you look over your answers, do you find that in most respects you express a preference for characteristics similar to your own? Is there any difference between the preferences you indicated for a date and the ones you would have for a potential mate? What are they?

> One of the first steps in an ideal system for getting the right kinds of people together in marriage . . . would be to acquaint them with a number of the potentially "best" marital partners for persons like them, well ahead of the time when they decide that they should marry. This matching process usually just happens informally through chance meeting at school or at work. Those who are moderately aggressive generally succeed in finding a tolerable-or-better partner and proceed to become married. . . . The point is to help people select an "appropriate" person as a partner to marry during the optimal age for them to marry. (in Bernard, 1973, p. 137)

The newest development in matchmaking services is the use of videotape as a go-between. To use these services you pay about seventy-five dollars for a three-month membership. Then you sit in front of a videotape camera and record a four-minute session, talking about yourself, your interests, and what you find most attractive in the opposite sex. Next, you view the tapes made by some likely date possibilities, and the ones you like best are called and invited to view your tape. Names and phone numbers are exchanged when both parties agree. In short, the videotape service performs almost exactly the same function that matchmakers do in traditional societies: they allow the assessment of potential mates without the embarrassment of a face-to-face rejection.

No matter how you meet potential partners, one thing is common to both a free choice system like ours and a parent arranged system: individuals get as much as their assets will bring. The more committed the relationship, the more likley it will be that the two individuals have a roughly similar social status.

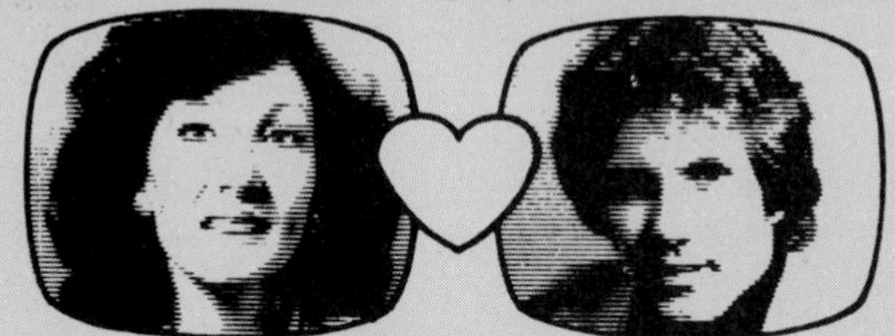

Like the traditional matchmakers—who are not equipped with computers or videotape equipment—today's dating services still bring together those who are looking for partners.

Likes Attract

Since ours is such a heterogeneous society, it would seem likely that individuals who are different in education, family status, or even race would often choose to marry each other. Indeed, people who discuss the hazards of marriage today frequently assume this to be true. For example, the noted anthropologist Margaret Mead once commented:

> Young people are taking extraordinary risks. They are marrying across wide expanses of the world, choosing partners of other classes, other religions, other races. People who are taking those risks . . . feel it is worth it—because they care about intensity, because they care about contrast. (1968, p. 34)

Despite the freedom of choice that our mate selection procedures allow, however, it cannot be assumed that most marriages take place between individuals who are different from each other in important respects. The thesis that love respects no boundaries and dissolves all obstacles is common in folklore and Hollywood movies. Especially in the films of the 1940s and 1950s, we were plentifully supplied with stories of ambitious young women using any means to catch the millionaire or the young doctor on the rise—and of ambitious young men pursuing the boss's daughter. It was an era when actresses like Rita Hayworth and Grace Kelly actually did marry princes. Perhaps this theme was a reflection of the democratic dream of unbounded social mobility. Our hopeful fantasies, like the Cinderella story, reflect the belief that love dissolves social distance and differences.

But after hundreds of sober inquiries into the question of who marries whom, sociologists have come to the conclusion that Cinderella is a fairy tale and nothing more. With remarkable consistency, people who are alike in important ways attract and marry each other. But which ways are the important ones? One way of gauging the importance of various rules of endogamy is to ask parents how they would react if their daughter decided to marry someone of another race or religion. In a 1974 survey, about 70 percent of the mothers said they would find it acceptable if their daughter married someone of another religion; 22 percent said they could accept it but would be unhappy about it; and only 3 percent said it would be unacceptable and would result in a strained relationship. When asked how they would react if their daughter married someone of another race, they responded much more negatively. Only 16 percent said they would accept it; 36 percent said they would accept the decision reluctantly, but

Research indicates that despite the freedom of choice that our mate selection procedures allow, the pattern of *homogamy*—like choosing like—prevails in many more cases than might occur by chance.

would be unhappy about it; 40 percent said they would not be able to accept it (Roper Organization, 1974). In other words, racial distinctions are more important than religious ones in our society, and so racial endogamy—marrying within your own race—is more important than religious endogamy.

While the social pressures to marry someone from a similar religious background are not as strong as they were several decades ago, there are still substantial barriers to racially mixed marriages. Until 1967, seventeen states had laws prohibiting interracial marriage. Those laws were declared unconstitutional in a Supreme Court ruling that year, but the norm that marriage should be racially endogamous has been effectively maintained without legal sanctions. To be sure, interracial dating is fairly common, on campus and elsewhere. According to one survey, almost one in five Americans has dated a member of another race (Porterfield, 1973). And the pattern of greater tolerance toward interracial marriage, as expressed in opinion surveys by both teenagers and adults, is striking. Although disapproval of interracial marriage by adults still outweighs approval—by a margin of 54 to 36 percent—the percentage of adults who say that they approve of interracial marriages almost doubled between 1968 and 1978, from 20 to 36 percent (Gallup, August 1978). Teenagers have fewer reservations about interracial marriage than adults do. In a recent survey, 52 percent of the teenagers polled said that they approved of marriages between whites and blacks. Significantly, a substantially higher percentage of nonwhite teenagers (76 percent) approve of interracial marriages (Gallup, April 1978).

Although public attitudes toward racially mixed marriages are fairly tolerant, actual behavior is something else. It is one thing for people to express a "live and let live" attitude on opinion polls, and quite another for most white people to accept a black person as a neighbor—or a son- or daughter-in-law. Since one of the major reasons why many white parents resisted racially integrated schools was fear that this might lead to interracial unions, it is interesting to look at the actual number of interracial marriages, particularly those between whites and blacks. In the year following the 1967 Supreme Court decision, fewer than one hundred interracial marriages took place in the seventeen states where they had previously been banned (Porterfield, 1973). Although the rate of interracial marriage has increased since then, mixed marriages are still quite rare. More than 99 percent of all the married couples living together at the time of the 1970 Census consisted of husbands and wives of the same race. But a closer look at the results of that census reveals another pattern: the number of racially mixed couples was twice as large in 1970 (330,000) as it had been decade before. Part of this increase may be attributed to the Supreme Court decision, and it is also likely that more people reported their race frankly in 1970 than before (Carter and Glick, 1976, p. 412).

Looking at the proportion of all marriages that are interracial, we can conclude that most people do still conform to the rule of racial endogamy. But we get a different perspective if we ask what percentage of all *minority* marriages are mixed. Among the racial minorities that constitute only a small percentage of the American population—such as the American Indians, Japanese, and Filipinos—well over half of all marriages are racially mixed. Among blacks, who constitute this country's largest racial minority, the rate of racially mixed marriages doubled between 1963 and 1970 to 2.6 percent. In the South, racially mixed marriages are still quite rare; but in the North and West, more than 7 percent of all black marriages in recent years have been interracial. In other words, from the point of view of the white majority, it appears that interracial marriages continue to be a rare phenomenon; but from the point of view of racial minorities, the rate of racial mixing is considerable (Monahan, 1976).

Racial endogamy is perhaps the strongest of all the social expectations that define an appropriate match. A young woman announcing to her parents that she intends to marry would probably not even think to mention that her mate-to-be was similar to her in race; they would all take it for granted. Most likely, however, the parents would ask her about other similarities that they consider important. At some point, they would inquire "How old is he?" and "What does he do?" The question "Have you met his family?" is one way of asking about social status differences. Even if some young people deny the importance of status difference, it still affects the choice of dating partners and mates. When two researchers studied the mate selection process in a campus community they found that steady dating, pinning, and engagement took place mainly within status categories. Men from the high-status fraternities preferred the company of women from high-status sororities. This pattern was more clearly illustrated in the choice of mates than of dates, which is only to say again that the tendency toward homogamy increases with the seriousness of the commitment (Larson and Leslie, 1968).

An obvious explanation of this homogamous tendency is, once again, that in our culture no less than in cultures where parents make the choice of a mate, the matching takes the form of an exchange. The currency in this exchange consists of the social status and the personal attributes of the two individuals involved. Even the language we use in talking about particular matches is saturated with the assumptions of the marketplace. Comments such as "She can do better than that," or "He really got a bad deal in his marriage," reflect the idea that you should shop around before you buy in order to get a good bargain. In the mate selection process, as in the marketplace, if you have a lot to offer, you expect a lot in return. The point is illustrated in hundreds of studies showing that husbands and wives are more alike in a number of ways than can be attributed simply to chance. Family status, age, education, and income, as well as individual personality, determine what one has to offer in the exchange. Individuals who are alike in important respects attract and marry each other because in this way both of them get a good bargain.

The Marriage Gradient—Finding Someone to Look Up To

One partial exception to the rule that likes attract is the tendency in our culture for men to marry women who are slightly their inferiors. This tendency, called the *marriage gradient*, has long been thought to occur on the dimension of social status. Sociologists have argued that since the status of males does not usually depend on the woman they choose to marry, they are not particularly reluctant to marry someone from a somewhat lower social status, provided that she has certain desirable personal characteristics. But because most women do still depend on their mate to determine their future social position, they must make the status of a potential spouse a relatively more important factor in their decision.

If the marriage gradient really does work in this way, it has several interesting implications. One is that men have a wider range of acceptable mates to choose from. Another is that if it is true in general, and not just a few cases, that men marry women who are slightly inferior to them in education, occupation, and family status, then there will be some men who remain unmarried because they can find no one to look up to them—in Jessie Bernard's phrase, the "bottom of the barrel" males. Conversely, the women who remain unmarried would be the "cream of the crop": with very few men superior to them, they have difficulty in finding someone to look up to (Bernard, 1973).

By examining the marital status of different groups in American society, we can see evidence of this pattern. If, for example, we examine the marital status of men between forty-five and fifty-four years of age, we see that those who have a great deal going for them in terms of education, occupation, and income are far more likely to be currently married as compared with those men who have a relatively low socioeconomic status. Because men in this latter category are more likely to have remained single, or to have been widowed or divorced and not remarried, only about three-quarters of them are currently married. With regard to the "cream of the crop" women, we see the same pattern. In 1970, for example, one in every five women who was forty years old, with at least some graduate education and an income of $20,000 or more, had not married, as compared with only one in every twenty women with no college education. One might argue that such relatively advantaged women have a greater range of options, and as a result they more often choose not to marry. But it may also be true that the marriage rates for such women are low because relatively few men are their equals, and fewer still could feel confident in relationships with such women because male dominance is still the norm (Carter and Glick, 1976, p. 405). We will examine some consequences of social status differences for single people in Chapter 5.

The professional literature of sociology does contain evidence that males marry down more frequently than up (Centers, 1949). But at least one study has come to a different conclusion. Comparing the status of the family a woman is born into and the one she marries into, it appears that women today are *not* more likely to marry up than down. Until more conclusive studies are done on social mobility through marriage, this will have to be considered an unanswered question (Glenn, Ross, and Tully, 1974).

Younger Woman, Older Man One dimension on which the marriage gradient certainly does exist today is that of age. At any college it is an obvious rule that younger females date older males. Thus an eighteen-year-old freshman woman thinks nothing of dating a male who is a junior, three years older than she is. But if a twenty-one-year-old woman dates an eighteen-year-old man, the situation is awkward at best. As a consequence of this rule, freshman males and the senior females are left with a relatively small pool of eligibles on campus.

One of the basic determinants of how hard it will be to find suitable partners is the sex ratio in the campus, community, or city in which potential mates live. The sex ratio is defined as the number of males per 100 females in a population. Because of the age gradient, the practical concern is for the ratio of males to females who are slightly younger. Because the population on many college campuses includes more males than females, it creates a favorable market situation for women. But after graduation the situation is reversed, especially in large cities, which typically include a somewhat higher number of young, unmarried females. Where the sex ratio is favorable, finding a suitable partner is a much easier matter.

We can learn something about the matches that are considered most appropriate by looking first at the tendency of American women to marry men who are more nearly their own age than has been the case in the past; we can then look at some implications of the remaining age differences between spouses.

Since the turn of the century in the United States, there has been a substantial reduction in the typical age difference between spouses. In 1900, the difference between the median ages at which men and women got married for the first time was about four years; by 1930, the difference was reduced to three years; and by 1978 the median age of men marrying for the first time (24.2) was about two and one-half years older than the women they marry. Over this period, it has been the age at which men get married that has changed most; the median age at which women get married (21.8) is roughly the same as it was at the turn of the century. One reason for this changing pattern is that since the primary economic responsibility in marriage has been the man's, males have been expected to defer marriage until after they have the economic means to support a wife and family. But gradually this norm has been redefined. Today, it is considered appropriate for men to marry as soon as they complete a college degree.

We can also regard this tendency for spouses to be more nearly the same age from another perspective, by noting that it reflects a preference for a more equal partnership. At the turn of the century, the preference for marriages in which the husband was four or more years older than the wife both reflected and encouraged male dominance. Having had several more years to get established in their careers, and to gain other attributes of status, men who are older than their wives have some important resources that help them meet the cultural expectations of the masculine role, both in courtship and in marriage. Being somewhat older than their wives, they are likely to be more experienced and have more self-assurance. In this respect, marriages between older men and younger women reflect status differences between the sexes. It is revealing to note that for centuries the women who most often violated this pattern have been women with power or wealth of their own. Thus, it is not really surprising that actresses such as Estelle Parsons, Jeanne Moreau, Louise Fletcher, or Kate Jackson are married or living with men who are ten or more years younger than they are. They are exercising a privilege that wealthy and powerful men have long taken for granted. As women gain more power and wealth through their own efforts, we might speculate that such matches will become increasingly common.

The tendency toward partnerships in which men and women are nearly the same age, and have more nearly the same educational experience as well, causes a problem for many young men today. For it appears that, despite their expressed desire for equalitarian relationships, most college students—both male and female—feel more comfortable in relationships where the male is dominant or superior in certain respects. It was this tension between the newer ideal of equality and the older assumption of male dominance that sociologist Mirra Komarovsky examined several years ago in a book entitled *Dilemmas of Masculinity* (1976). When she asked college students of both sexes what their image of the ideal male is, there was general agreement that males should be somewhat superior to their partners in such respects as greater self-assurance and assertiveness. In the author's words, "Despite some changes—such as new expectations of sensitivity and esthetic appreciation which used to be regarded as feminine traits—the traditional ideal of masculinity was still the measure against which the seniors measured themselves" (p. 129).

The problem is that even "liberal" college males who believe in equality between the sexes often act in a way that is inconsistent with their beliefs. As Komarovsky discovered in the course of intensive interviews, many of the "liberal" men chose to be with women who were not their equals because of the difficulties they encountered with females who were as bright as or brighter than they were. As one young man put it:

> Despite my egalitarian proclamations, tugging at my psychic strings is the thought that I am really most comfortable in a situation where my fragile sense of security is not threatened by a woman, where I can maintain a comfortable dominance. Thus my basic insecurity conflicts with my liberated conscience, making me feel like a double-talking hypocrite. (1976, p. 132)

However, finding relationships in which they can be "comfortably dominant" is no easy matter for college males. Many report that women want more support, self-assurance, and responsibility in men than the men are able to provide. In fact, nearly half of the males that Komarovsky interviewed felt anxious about their inability to present a strong, self-assured masculine image. Such anxieties are understandable if we consider the situation of the typical male who is just about to graduate from college. In a culture where manhood is defined largely in terms of economic independence and occupational success, he does not yet have any status or power. And since the women with whom such men generally associate are college students too, and nearly if not actually the same age, the men have few resources with which to establish the male dominance that both they and their female partners desire. In other words, although the gradual narrowing of the age difference be-

Point of View

Box 2–2 / Inequality Between the Sexes Begins at Home

What happens when women marry men who are slightly older, better educated, and draw higher salaries? *Both* sexes, says Judith Stiehm, a professor of political science at the University of Southern California, reach the conclusion that men are superior. She thinks perhaps intelligent and ambitious women should marry relatively inferior men.

> Feminists crisply cite statistics on the availability of "qualified women" and personnel officers solemnly search for them. Nevertheless few American women win fame, power, or distinction. Why? Perhaps because public policies of equality are undercut by personal experiences with inequality.
>
> Marriage is the most intimate, intense, and enduring male–female relationship most people know. If American men and women are only comfortable in marriages based upon an invidious relationship between husband and wife, can they be expected to accept a different, even reversed relationship in public life? If those who are best educated, and with the highest status and highest income—in short, the decision-making men in our society—dominate, outstrip, and are deferred to by their wives, can they be expected to perceive other women as peers?
>
> No one doubts that marriage pairing is highly selective even though there may be disagreement as to the best standards for choice. But social science data suggest that older, more-educated, higher-salaried, higher-status husbands are regularly matched with younger, less-educated, lower-salaried, and lower-status wives.
>
> Men marry for the first time 2.5 years later than women. When they marry for the second time, divorced men pick women an average of 4.5 years their junior while widowers pick women 8.3 years younger than they. Perhaps an age gap would not be significant if women matured earlier than men. However, at age 23 a man is likely to have finished his education, be employed, and to have lived independently. At 20.6 years a women is likely to have less education, little work experience, and

tween partners may well contribute to more equal partnerships, to the extent that both sexes still desire male-dominant relationships, many young men feel the pressure of expectations that are difficult to meet (Komarovsky, 1976).

Such expectations of male dominance help us to explain why, in about 85 percent of all American marriages today, the groom is either the same age or slightly older than the bride. Perhaps the most telling statistic is that in only one marriage out of forty is the wife five or more years older than her husband (Udry, 1974).

The preference for marriage between older men and younger women may also be due to the natural decline in female fertility with increasing age. This decline becomes an important factor in late marriages, or second or subsequent marriages, in which the male is in his thirties or forties at marriage. If he wants to have children, his partner must be close to his own age or younger. There is some evidence of this pattern in census statistics showing that the older the husband is relative to his wife, the higher her fertility. The converse statement is also true: childlessness is more common among couples in which the wife is older (Presser, 1975).

But, especially for younger couples, men prefer younger women for a more obvious reason. Thousands of cosmetic ads promising to restore youthful beauty to anxious middle-aged women—but not to men—reveal that ours is a to be moving directly from her parents' home to her husband's.

It would seem that she is not as mature as her husband. Moreover, she reaches maturity in the context of marriage; there her growth is influenced by her husband's needs and wishes.

In contrast, he is likely to come to adulthood while living as an individual. The two experiences are quite different. For him the emphasis is on self-reliance, for her it is on sharing and sometimes even sacrificing.

Women have the same average education as men although they hold far fewer advanced degrees. The pattern is that the best-educated women marry men with equal or better educations. In contrast, the best-educated men marry women with less or sometimes the same education. Only at the lower levels of education do women outrank their husbands and at this level relative superiority seems to have little social significance.

Indeed, even though women's education closely correlates with income potential, that potential is so low that there is truth to the adage that education is wasted on women.

Virtually all men make more money than their wives. What is interesting is the fact that the best-paid women are married to better, indeed the best-paid men. Further, the best-paid women also are women who make the least as compared to their husbands.

In short, there are mature, educated, high-income, high-occupational-status women in our society. Conventionally they marry older, more-educated, better-paid, higher-status men. Their excellence, then, is always experienced as less excellent. Their significant work is seen as less significant.

Women and men must examine the consequences of pairing based on a mutually agreed-to unequal relationship. What, after all, is the effect on the talents and training of women? What happens to the judgment and emotions of men? Can women achieve high levels of public excellence while maintaining a carefully arranged marital deference? Or should excellent and ambitious women marry relatively inferior men who will nourish and promote their careers? Or should all individuals who wish to pursue a competitive vocation accept singleness as the price of a prized career?

Source: Judith Stiehm. *The New York Times*, July 2, 1975, p. 33.

culture with a double standard of aging. As Inge Powell Bell aptly observes,

> There is a reason why women are coy about their age. For most purposes, society pictures them as "old" ten or fifteen years sooner than men. . . . A man's wrinkles will not define him as sexually undesirable until he reaches his late fifties. For him, sexual value is defined much more in terms of personality, intelligence, and earning power than physical appearance. Women, however, must rest their case largely on their bodies. (in Lopata, 1973, p. 217)

Because of such a double standard, even a couple who are nearly the same age may encounter a problem when they reach their forties. He may appear to be "younger" and more attractive than his wife. The preference for marriage between an older man and a younger woman may be interpreted as a way of anticipating the effects of this double standard.

But the factors that influence the mate choice in one's early twenties are quite different from the typical concerns of middle-aged couples. In fact, if people had so much foresight at the time of choosing, women might marry men who were somewhat younger. Why? One reason is that marital relationships are not likely to be at all equal between two partners if one is several years older than the other and has more education and employment experience (see Box 2–2, p. 50). Another reason is that the present pattern of older men marrying younger women creates a very difficult situation for the divorced or widowed middle-aged woman who is looking for a partner. A man of fifty can choose from women his own age or younger, but a woman the same age has to choose from men who are her own age or older—a much smaller group.

There is a third reason, too, why women might prefer to marry younger men, although it would be one of the last things to occur to a woman in her twenties as she chooses a mate. It is the statistical probability that an older mate will die several years before she does. The life expectancy of American males is now about seven years lower than that of American females. Add to that the two years' difference in age between the average husband and wife, and you realize that many American females are choosing mates who can be expected to die almost a decade before they do.

Who Enforces the Rules in a Free Choice System?

In our culture parents exert less and less direct control over mate selection and courtship. The obvious social pressures that used to be exerted to enforce endogamy have eroded. Many Orthodox Jews, for example, used to express their feelings toward a marriage of one of their own with a non-Jew by *sitting shiva* for the straying person, thus declaring him or her dead. But such things are very rare today.

And yet, the mate choices that most young people make are not dramatically different from what their parents might have made for them. But then who enforces endogamy rules in a free choice system?

One explanation is that individuals from similar backgrounds tend to marry each other because they share the same values, not because they consciously concern themselves with what sociologists refer to as status matching. Without thinking, we tend to associate with people who are like us in more respects than not. Just as we shop in certain stores rather than others because they cater to our tastes, we limit our field of social contacts by associating with certain groups and frequenting certain places. Most of this delimiting takes place without any conscious decision to meet certain types of people.

In choosing where a family will live, parents also choose, in effect, whom their children will associate with. Much of the opposition to busing as a means of desegregating schools undoubtedly stems from parents' desire to control the types of people their children meet, date, and perhaps choose as marital partners.

Despite the belief that love conquers all, including distance, one of the most important determinants of attraction is physical closeness, or propinquity. College students, for example, are more likely to develop friendships with those who attend the same classes and sit nearby, or those in the same dormitory or apartment building. Sociologists who studied mate selection a generation or more ago often remarked on the importance of residential propinquity. One investigator found, for example, that over half the people who got married in Columbus, Ohio, lived within sixteen city blocks of each other at the time of their first date (Clarke, 1952).

It is easy to see how this tendency to date and marry individuals who live nearby helps to explain homogamy patterns. Most people live near others of the same race, social class, religion, and so forth. Thus, again without making a conscious decision to find partners whose traits match ours, we get them nevertheless simply by choosing partners who happen to live nearby.

In the present generation, however, residential proximity has become a less important factor in the mate selection process than it once was. Automobiles allow somewhat more mobility. Mainly, though, this change is due to the much higher percentage of young people attending residential colleges, typically at some distance from their parents' homes. As one investigator has shown, the more contact there is between parents and children during courtship, the more homogamous the child's mate choice will be (Coombs, 1962). Parents can influence their children's mate choice at a distant college only by sending them to a school where many of the students are of the same race and family status, or by encouraging them to participate in campus groups that make it more likely for them to meet the right kind of person. One of the important functions of any college today, particularly the smaller, private institutions, is to provide a pool of approved eligibles. Parents who send their child to one of these colleges can be reasonably sure of the type of person with whom the child will associate. At many colleges, at least a third of all graduates eventually marry someone who attended the same institution (Kirkpatrick, 1963, p. 420). But this percentage may decline in the next few years if the average age of first marriage continues to increase. More and more people are deferring marriage until after they graduate from college.

Upper-class parents have more influence on the mate choice of their children than parents of any other social class—and they have more reason for it. An upper-class person's choice of a mate is not just his or her own affair, but a matter of great concern to many other people as well. In this way, marriage in the upper class resembles marriage in traditional cultures. Questions involving inheritance, maintaining the family business, and even carrying on the family name can be very delicate. As sociologist Ruth Cavan explains it, this class

> tends to form an isolated social world, protecting its isolation by a system of exclusive social contacts. Nurses, tutors, governesses, and maids stand as a bulwark, both physically and in the training they give. . . . The children attend private day or boarding schools, which only admit children of the upper social classes. Clubs, large and small, to which membership may be gained only upon election, also support the social isolation. . . . Long before children are mature enough to think logically of their future the son knows what school and college he is destined to attend, what occupation the family has planned for him; the girl knows the kind of training she will receive and the type of young men she will meet at her debut, one of whom will become her husband. (1969, pp. 90, 96)

If the choice of a mate is not quite so limited for children from other social backgrounds, we have seen that there are still many pressures, direct and indirect, that serve to encourage marriage between the socially similar.

INTERPERSONAL ATTRACTION

In this chapter so far, we have examined the social expectations that limit the pool of eligibles. But we know from personal experience that these expectations are not the only important factors in choosing a mate. In fact, we do not often pay much attention to them. From the viewpoint of a matchmaker or a computerized dating service, they have the advantage of being the easiest factors to test and balance. But far more interesting to the rest of us are the intangibles of interpersonal attraction, the unique personal traits and preferences that make some few people so much more attractive to us than all others.

As one young women said about the dates selected for her by a computer using a questionnaire like that shown in Box 2–1 (p. 42). "You know, that test failed to get us together in the really important matters. . . . A couple of the boys I went out with were really personable people, but there was just that one quality that was lacking. There wasn't that spark. . . ." (Fullerton, 1972, p. 302).

What is "that one quality" which only a few people possess for us, the one that sets these few apart from all the rest in a pool of otherwise eligible people? A large part of it at least begins with the personal asset that provides inexhaustible subject matter for advice columns and everyday conversation and supports several major industries offering products to help us gain and keep it—physical attractiveness.

Mirror, Mirror

Some of the most enduring counsel on the art of interpersonal attraction was written about 2000 years ago by the Latin poet, Ovid.

In our culture beauty is more than skin deep.

> Faults of the face or physique call for attempts at disguise. If you are short, sit down, lest, standing, you seem to be sitting. . . . If you're inclined to be pale, wear stripes of scarlet or crimson. If you're inclined to be dark, white is an absolute must. . . . Have you a bust too flat? Bandages ought to fix that. If your fingers are fat, or your nails brittle and ugly, watch what you do when you talk; don't wave your hands in the air.

These are Ovid's instructions to the woman who must do her own advertising. If they sound slightly mocking, they are also quite practical, for to a considerable extent, we all judge by appearances.

The American beauty industry, a more than billion-dollar-a-year business, is based on the premise that what nature did badly can be improved by means of cosmetics—or surgery. If you have the money to pay for their services, cosmetic surgeons can give you a nose job, hair transplant, face lift, or some other tuck for a body part that is not up to standard. Millions of women endure the pain of electrolysis to have facial hair removed, wear tight girdles, or live for weeks on celery and yogurt to look fashionably thin. Speaking across the distance of 2000 years, Ovid's advice seems quite contemporary. In fact, his message is substantially the same as that of hundreds of beauty magazines appearing on newsstands today. The message is that attractiveness is supremely important because it will win you love and respect.

How important is physical attractiveness in our daily encounters with others? Social psychologists say it counts for more than most of us would be willing to admit. Beauty is, in effect, more than skin deep, because we attribute more desirable characteristics to people who are especially attractive. The Greek poet Sappho stated the belief that to be beautiful is to be good and that the individual who is good will soon be beautiful. Her remark offers a very convenient, if arbitrary, way of judging between good and bad—but no matter how arbitrary this standard is, it is still very much with us. In folklore and films, heroes and heroines are generally portrayed as handsome and beautiful, while evil people are ugly or deformed. Perhaps we should regard this imagery simply as a useful convention. Like the custom in old cowboy films to put the good guys on white horses, this one helps us to identify the characters.

But it is more than just an artistic convention. The stereotype that good is beautiful carries over into everyday life. From infancy, others' perceptions of us are influenced by our appearance. When cute children misbehave, adults see them as less naughty than their less attractive peers who act the same way (Dion, 1972). Teachers commonly assume that attractive children are more intelligent, popular, and likely to go to college, even when their report cards are identical to those of their less attractive classmates (Clifford and Walster, 1973). Nursery school children who have been judged by adults to be less attractive are not as well liked by their classmates and are assumed to misbehave more often (Dion and Berscheid, 1972).

The same assumption shapes adults' perceptions of other adults. Here is a summary of social psychologists' research on the subject in Partrica Middlebrook's words:

> Physically attractive people, both men and women, are generally seen as possessing more socially desirable personality traits, and they are expected to lead happier and more successful lives than unattractive people. Further, the expectations of male and female subjects about the characteristics of attractive people did not differ. No matter whether a man was judging an attractive man or an attractive women, he saw the attractive person as possessing socially desirable personality traits. Women reacted the same way to attractiveness—irrespective of whether they were rating other women or men. Thus, even in same-sex friendships people may tend to prefer attractive people because they believe attractive people are pleasant and intelligent people who will be rewarding to know. (Middlebrook, 1974, p. 422)

Because our self-images are a result of others' responses to us, the assumption that what is beautiful is good becomes a self-fulfilling prophecy.

Physical Attractiveness in Dating When college students are asked what they look for in a date, both males and females mention intelligence, friendliness, and sincerity before they acknowledge the importance of physical attractiveness (Vreeland, 1972). And yet, when confronted with a real-life situation, attractiveness may well be the most important factor, at least in the initial stage of interaction.

To check on the importance of looks in a situation where two people meet for the first time, several social psychologists planned a college dance. Students who came to the dance were under the impression that a computer had selected their dates on the basis of similar interests. Actually, they were assigned on a random basis, though the researchers had taken measures of each student's social skills, intelligence, and personality, as well as physical appearance. Halfway through the evening, at the intermission, the students were asked how they liked their dates. This enabled the investigators to correlate how much each person was liked with his or her other traits. They expected to find that intelligence, personality, and social skills had much to do with being liked, but none of them did. For both the males and females, physical attractiveness seemed to be the sole determinant of whether these college students were liked by their dates (Walster, Aronson, Abrahams, and Rottman, 1966).

In the computer dance setting, and probably in many initial encounters, physical attractiveness is the main determinant of whether there will be any more encounters. One thing that undoubtedly happened in the computer dance, as in other initial encounters, was that students assumed that if their dates were attractive—which could immediately be discerned—they would also be more likable, sensitive, and intelligent. Of course the setting in which this experiment took place allowed for little more than a superficial acquaintance. If the couples had met by themselves and had had the opportunity to talk for several hours, perhaps looks would not have been so important. But investigators who have inquired about the importance of attractiveness over a series of encounters have come to the conclusion that even after each of the partners learns more about the other's personality, the importance of attractiveness does not diminish (Mathes, 1975).

Attractiveness, like social status, can be viewed as an element in the exchange process. There is considerable evidence that people choose mates whose attractiveness is roughly equivalent to their own (Stroebe, Insko, Thompson, and Layton, 1971).

As we noted before, ours is still a society in which the status of the couple usually derives from the occupational position of the male. Thus, when women consider potential mates they do not make physical attractiveness such an important criterion as men do. For women, intelligence and ambition come first in a potential mate because they are good predictors of adult status. Thus it is not very surprising that when two researchers asked, "To what extent is it important that your date be good looking or attractive?" 21 percent of the males but only 6 percent of the females responded that it was very important (Coombs and Kenkel, 1966).

Such responses provide clear evidence of culturally patterned images of masculinity and femininity. Boys are asked what they are going to become; girls are told that they are pretty. Men's magazines concentrate on career-related information, interests, and activities. Women's magazines, with few exceptions, are filled with beauty tips. Despite the changes that have occurred in our culturally defined images of male and female, the lesson still holds: what matters for a male is primarily what he does, for a female, how she looks. This distinction is reflected in the fees paid to fashion models. Because female attractiveness is relatively more important, female models demand and get considerably more for their services than do male models. Modeling is one of the very few occupational areas in which women are paid more than men for identical work.

Recall the words of the Indian girl stated earlier in the chapter: in her system, she said, girls don't have to worry at all. They know they'll get married. Therefore, they don't have to go into competition with each other. In contrast, the high value of physical attractiveness in our culture is, in part, the result of a system in which each person is on his or her own to seek and find a mate. Since physical attraction is, as we have seen, a very important element in dating, it is understandable that we should be so anxious to look good. Ours is indeed a competitive mate selection system. Many of the anxieties of adolescence and young adulthood reflect the fact that, for better or worse, the choice is ours.

LOVE . . . AND MARRIAGE

We have still not discussed what is perhaps the most important and distinctive aspect of our mate selection system. When, in a nationwide survey, people were asked their opinion about the primary reason for marrying today, a large majority of men (77 percent) and women (83 percent) gave the expected answer: love (Roper Organization, 1974).

But what is this thing called love? Of all the words in our language, none has been a source of such perennial interest. Love is an inexhaustible topic on which almost every writer has made some pronouncement. *Bartlett's Familiar Quotations* has only one entry—that for the word "man"—with more quotations than the word "love," about which the book gives 769 different statements. Love is the most fascinating of diversions, the stuff of the *grands amours* of history as well as garden-variety affairs. In this culture, no lesson is taught more thoroughly or repeated so often: One should fall in love, love makes life worthwhile, conquers evil and indifference—and is fulfilled and certified in marriage. Newsstands are filled with magazines bearing titles like *Screen Romance, Young Love*, and *Heart Throb*. Love is easily the most frequent topic for modern-day minstrels, whose lyrics recount the joys and sorrows of love as if nothing else existed.

Love is also an idea that defies both definition and explanation. For all of the attention that has been lavished on it by poets and song writers, social scientists know far less about love than they do about the sober facts of everyday behavior. If other aspects of mate selection can be formulated as a calculated exchange in which each person tries to get a good bargain, love appears to be different. In every sense of the word—whether it is understood as selfless devotion or throbbing passion—love is understood to be a much stronger bond than the exchange we make when you scratch my back and I scratch yours.

It is easy to become excessively cynical about love and destroy its essence by dissecting it. But sometimes an analysis can have great insight. Thus in this *Marriage and Morals* (1929), philosopher Bertrand Russell wrote with characteristic clarity about our motives in seeking both love and marriage:

Love comics. In them, "true" love is the only thing that matters.

> Love is something far more than desire for sexual intercourse. It is the principal means of escape from the loneliness which afflicts most men and women throughout the greater part of their lives. There is a deep-seated fear, in most people, of the cold world and the possible cruelty of the herd. There is a longing for affection, which is often concealed by roughness, boorishness or a bullying manner in men, and by nagging or scolding in women. Passionate mutual love, while it lasts, puts an end to this feeling. It breaks down the hard walls of the ego, producing a new being composed of two in one. (p. 122)

The feelings Russell described in this fine statement are so fundamental and universal that they are rarely expressed. Yet he is describing only passionate love, which apparently does not always last, while we also frequently say that we love our dogs and our parents, our country and our flag. Probably no other word is so much a chameleon, changing its meaning in each new context. Thus the phrase "I love you" is, in turn, a promise, a threat, a bribe, a request, a declaration of sexual passion. When love exists between a mother and child, we think of tenderness and solicitude; when it exists between starry-eyed lovers, we look for the symptoms of distraction, euphoria, and obsession. We are told that love is divine madness, that it means "never having to say you're sorry," and even (in Jules Feiffer's satire, *Harry the Rat with Women*) that love is "a disease spread by the insecure to corrupt the self-possessed."

Passionate love is nevertheless the kind that we are interested in here, and Russell's statement gives us a start toward a useful definition. Romantic love consists of a passionate emotional attachment between two people. Tenderness and affection are as much a part of it as sexual attraction. Romantic love differs from friendship in several respects: it is more intense, and more likely to include elements of fantasy and obsession. Quite commonly, in fact, people fall in love with someone they would not choose as a friend.

The main point is that love, preferably passionate love, is considered by most people to be an essential prerequisite to marriage. If any other motive for entering into a presumably lifelong alliance predominates, we view the marriage with considerable suspicion. The mate selection processes practiced in some other cultures such as the Navajo, where love is not assumed to be essential, strike us as strange, half-hearted, mechanical. As anthropologists Dorothea Leighton and Clyde Kluckhohn explain,

> Though the Navajos have been introduced to the white concept of romantic love in school, it is still not widely held, and almost no emphasis is placed upon psychological compatibility as a prerequisite for marriage. According to the Navajos, one woman will do as well as another, so long as she is healthy, industrious, and competent. (1948, p. 79)

To us, these seem like appropriate criteria in hiring a household helper, but not a lifelong companion.

Examples like the Navajo do not mean, however, that romantic attraction is unknown in other cultures. Something resembling romantic love seems to be common in many societies. What is most peculiar about our own mate selection customs is the assumption that "love and marriage go together like a horse and carriage." In this image love appears to be the animating force and marriage the essential cargo.

Romantic attraction has been considered disruptive in most societies—certainly no foundation for something as practical as marriage. In societies where the newlyweds live with either the bride's or the groom's family, it could be disastrous for a person to fall in love with someone who would be unacceptable to the other members of the household. As sociologist William Goode points out, a variety of strategies, from child marriage or constant chaperonage to isolation of the young from potential mates, have been adopted to prevent love attachments (1959).

The contrast between the traditional mate selection procedures in which love was considered disruptive and the procedures we follow today is illustrated most vividly by what has happened in Japan since World World II. The traditional procedure was for parents to choose the mate for their child. Often the young person was not even involved in the process until the contract was sealed. Romantic love between an unmarried boy and girl constituted a threat to parental authority and therefore was not tolerated, whereas extramarital affairs were actually encouraged (for men) since they could have no effect on the system. As David and Vera Mace point out, in Japan

> the tradition has persisted that a man has two kinds of relationships with women: the dutiful but unexciting obligation he owes to his wife at home, and the less inhibited romantic experience he enjoys in his free time and on a recreational basis at the geisha house. (1960, p. 129)

In contrast to our view of romantic love as a prerequisite for an enduring marital relationship, the Japanese assumed that if the parents made a proper choice, a kind of love could grow between partners who enjoyed a mutually satisfactory relationship. If it seems strange at

Ali McGraw and Ryan O'Neal in *Love Story*—Hollywoods's version of romantic love.

first to suppose that love could develop after marriage between spouses who are chosen for each other, think of our own assumption that mutual love will develop between parent and child even though they do not choose each other either (Turner, 1970, p. 315).

Since World War II, the Japanese system of parent arranged marriages has been substantially altered. Many of the changes that long ago took place in Western Europe and America have begun to undermine traditional assumptions in Japan. Three-generation households have become less common, freeing spouses from many family responsibilities and at the same time making them more dependent on each other. Women have been offered new educational and occupational opportunities and have become more nearly men's peers. The criteria of a good wife have changed accordingly. Submissiveness and fertility are no longer as important as they were. Although there is still no word in the Japanese language for marital companionship, an intimate and affectionate partnership has become possible between husband and wife (Blood, 1967).

As sociologist Robert Blood describes that transition, these changes—along with Western movies and TV shows, which broadcast the idea of a romantic courtship pattern—have ushered in a new era.

> Such changes introduce new complexities into the mate-selection process. No longer can carbon-copy conformity be expected of all prospective brides. Greater variability in attitudes, values, experiences, and perhaps even temperament develops among women. The new emphasis upon love and intimacy raises problems of rapport which can hardly be judged by young people themselves short of a trial period of interaction. These changes shift responsibility from the older to the younger generation. (1967, p. 8)

Today, the idea that romance may lead to marriage has been accepted in every industrialized country in the world, although parents still exercise a variety of direct and indirect controls over the mate choice. In the United States, where the emphasis on romantic love is at its strongest, the contradictions between the intensely personal experience of romantic love and the extremely practical business of marriage have become painfully evident. One way of exploring these contradictions and the problems they pose is to start with the beginnings of the idea of love.

Few ideas have had such a strange career as that of love. Rather than evolving over the centuries, love has been substantially redefined at certain points. In ancient Greece, Plato thought love to be a vital element in human society because it inspires virtue. He distinguished two types of love: common and heavenly. Common love, as Plato defined it, was concerned primarily with physical satisfaction. Although it might be heterosexual, the preferred form as expressed in some of the *Dialogues* was homosexual. The more lofty type of love involved spiritual pleasure, the love of the soul.

In the first century A.D., Ovid defined love as an essential element in the pursuit of pleasure—sensual pleasure, not spiritual. Love was not romantic, not an affair of the soul, not even something that might be expected to last very long. At bottom it was "a game of mutual deceit" in which each person tried to win the attention and the physical pleasures provided by the other (Reiss, 1971, p. 76). Unlike Plato, Ovid was interested only in heterosexual love, but they agreed that love applied only to adulterous affairs and had very little to do with marriage.

Courtly Love

By the twelfth century, love was still restricted mainly to adulterous relationships and still a privilege of the upper classes. Commoners were assumed to be incapable of it. But if its circumstances were the same, its substance was different. The sensual game that Ovid had described was forgotten, and the courtly lover of the Middle Ages practiced an elaborate etiquette designed to heighten the longing for the beloved. This etiquette expressed jealousy, obsession, admiration, and affection, thus setting courtly love apart from marriage, a relationship that allowed for little tenderness.

Unlike the Roman concept of love, courtly love in the twelfth century was a tradition defined mainly by women, the noblewomen of the feudal manors and their lady friends. Men invented the chastity belt to discourage these ladies from misusing their leisure while their husbands were away fighting in the Crusades. The situation was complicated by the abundance of young bachelor knights around many feudal households. One of the favorite activities was the discussion of romantic attraction at a time when so many obstacles prevented its consummation.

By the twelfth century, the troubadours who wandered from manor to manor pictured love as sweet longing, not sensual abandon. Then, as now, love was easily the most fascinating of topics. The troubadours, like the songwriters of today, concentrated on romantic longing and ignored marriage. (When was the last time you heard a popular song celebrating the joys of married love?)

It became quite fashionable to argue the merits of love, to discuss its true characteristics. Long debates took place among the noble ladies about the rules of love. Formal decrees were issued defining a code of conduct appropriate in a relationship between a married woman and a knight. Some of these decrees appeared in a book written late in the twelfth century by Andreas Capellanus, chaplain to Countess Marie of Champagne. Andreas informs his readers that "when a lover suddenly catches sight of his beloved, his heart palpitates." Later he describes love as a very unpleasant state indeed, an obsessive state with a variety of unfortunate symptoms: "A man in love is always apprehensive. He whom the thought of love vexes eats and sleeps very little" (p. 184). If there is an element of exaggeration here, these symptoms are still recognizable as the side effects of the conflicting emotions stirred up by romantic attraction.

Several of Andreas Capellanus' observations help us to understand the tensions between romantic love and what has since been connected to romantic love: the institution of marriage.

For example, it is commonly observed that "the easy attainment of love makes it of little value. Difficulty of attainment makes it prized." Thousands of love stories from *Romeo and Juliet* down to the most recent tales in *Screen Romance* magazine suggest that this observation is still true. The formula is: (1) boy *meets* girl, but then because of some uncontrollable event, evil person, or coincidental obstacle, (2) boy *loses* girl. If, as in *Romeo and Juliet*, there is some fatal misunderstanding, the outcome is tragic and sweet. Few themes are more appealing than two young lovers sacrificing themselves to their passion. More usually, though, the obstacle is somehow removed, the young lovers are reunited, and (3) boy *gets* girl. The relationship is consummated in marriage, "and they live happily ever after."

But why was the obstacle necessary in the first place? Is it simply a dramatic device used by storytellers to keep our interest? The planting and removing of obstacles keeps the story going a while longer—and the storyteller in business. All the same, we know that even in real life, love does flourish in situations that would seem to discourage it. Poets explain that love is essentially illogical; we should expect nothing different. Social psychologists who address the same question come to a conclusion that, if less appealing, is still quite intriguing: "There is some evidence," observes Elaine Walster, "that under the right conditions such unpleasant, but arousing, states as fear, rejection, and frustration do enhance romantic passion." (in Murstein, 1971, p. 90)

Both Andreas and contemporary social psychologists agree, then, that romantic attraction may well be heightened if some obstacle intervenes between the lovers (see Box 2–3, p. 63). The young woman who wonders how to enhance her attractiveness has both the experts and her parents encouraging her to play hard-to-get. But notice that this ploy might be a source of trouble in a culture where love is expected to lead to marriage, and marriage is assumed to be a durable vehicle for love. There

Research Perspectives on Marriage and Family

Box 2–3 / The Laboratory Experiment—Love Loves an Obstacle

There is at least one point that Sigmund Freud, "Dear Abby," and the most recent issue of *Heart Throb* magazine all agree upon: love loves an obstacle. Instant approval is less gratifying and less likely to inspire our passion than approval that we have to win. A woman who is hard to get may be more desirable than one who is not.

Although interpersonal attraction is sometimes a sensible thing that can be explained by our inclination to choose as partners people who offer more affection, beauty, or material rewards, passionate love is not so easily explained. We do *not* necessarily feel passionate about the person who provides the most rewards with the greatest consistency.

Both common sense and folklore tell us that an obstacle coming between lovers is an important stimulant to their attraction. The obstacle can take almost any form; the hard-to-get woman is only one. Storytellers have generally preferred more elaborate obstacles, such as social class barriers (the handsome prince falls in love with the beautiful peasant girl) or parental interference (*Romeo and Juliet*). The important thing is the presence of some obstacle that the lovers must remove. This expresses one of our most cherished fantasies, that love carries the day by defeating all opposition.

Social scientists have eagerly explored the logic of love. Freud tried to explain it in terms of libido, the instinctive force that gives rise to sexual urges: "Some obstacle is necessary to swell the tide of libido to its height," he wrote. "At all periods in history, whenever natural barriers in the way of satisfaction have not sufficed, mankind has erected conventional ones in order to enjoy love" (in Middlebrook, 1974, p. 441). Social psychologists explain the appeal of the hard-to-get woman by pointing out that we are most rewarded by people who do *not* initially have a positve opinion of us. When we win the approval of people who were neutral toward us, we feel the gratification of converting a reluctant partner.

Three social psychologists, Elaine Walster, Jane Allyn Piliavin, and G. William Walster, designed an experiment to see whether the hard-to-get woman is really more attractive (1973). Love may seem out of place in the laboratory, but these researchers devised a way to test the hypothesis that a person whose affection is easily won is less likely to inspire passion.

To study such cause-and-effect relationships, social scientists simulate real-life situations in a laboratory setting where careful observations can be made. One of the chief advantages of this technique is that the researcher can control what is going on more easily than she can in the outside world. Usually her method is to change one variable (called the *independent variable*) in order to determine its effect on another (called the *dependent variable*). Other factors are held constant so that they do not influence the experimental results. Laboratory experiments often involve *control groups* as well. The con-

is a tension between desire and fulfillment. For if the longing for the beloved constitutes romantic attraction, fulfillment in marrage must then bring some disappointment because it ends that longing.

In ancient Greece, love was regarded as rather undesirable, an intoxication, a divine punishment. The troubadours turned the story trol group is placed under identical circumstances except that it is not influenced by the independent variable.

In this case, the experimental design made use of a computer dating questionnaire like the one described in Box 2–1. More than seventy male college students were asked to participate in a study that was described as a comparison of computer matching with random matching. Each of the participants was asked to examine information on five potential dates, some of which had supposedly been selected at random while the others had been computer matched. In fact, all five folders contained information on fictitious women.

In the words of the researchers, the experiment proceeded as follows:

> Each folder contained a "background questionnaire" on which the women had presumably described themselves. Three of the folders also contained five "date-selection" forms. We told the subjects that three of the five women had come in, examined the background information on their matches, and then evaluated the subject and his four rivals on the date-selection forms. On all five forms, each of the women had checked one of twenty scores ranging from "definitely do not want to date" to "definitely want to date." The forms identified each man by number. At this point, we told the subject his number.
>
> We made one of the women who had evaluated her matches appear uniformly hard to get. She indicated that she would date any of the five men, but she was unenthusiastic about them all. We made the second woman uniformly easy to get. She was enthusiastic about dating all five men. We made the third woman easy to get for the subject, but hard to get for anyone else. We labelled this woman "selectively hard to get."
>
> We explained that the other two folders contained no date-selection forms because the other women had not come in to evaluate their matches. Over the course of the experiment, we put each fictitious woman in a new condition. (Walster et al., 1973)

All of the male subjects were asked how well they liked the women described in the folders. They were asked to rate them as potential dates and to indicate the potential assets as well as the liabilities of each woman.

When the results of these questionnaires were tabulated, the researchers found that it was *not* the consistently hard-to-get women who were the preferred dates. They were often regarded by these college men as somewhat undesirable because they appeared to be "snotty" or "picky." On the other hand, the uniformly easy-to-get women were often rejected, too. About them, the men made comments such as "She must be awfully hard up for a date. She really would take anyone." Of the three groups of women, it was the selectively elusive women who were chosen most often as desirable dates. They were also chosen more often than the "control" women, those who did not fill out first-impression questionnaires. As the researchers explain, "the selectively hard-to-get woman possesses all the assets and none of the liabilities of both the elusive and the easy woman" (1973, p. 83). She combined the friendliness and warmth of the available woman with the popularity and selectivity of the distant woman.

It is apparently still true that love loves an obstacle, and that the person whose affection is most easily won does not necessarily inspire our passion. But as this experiment suggests, some women are simply *too* hard to get. It is the woman who is highly selective in her expressions of affection—the one who seems hard for *other* men to get—who is most desirable as a dating partner.

around: love *is* a suffering, they agreed, but a sweet suffering, something to be cultivated. But in a culture like ours, where love and marriage are expected to go together like a horse and carriage, if love is longing or the tension of desire, then marriage, in fulfilling it, also destroys it.

Elaine Walster, who studied the obstacles that

enhance romantic attraction, has arrived at an interesting explanation for what is commonly referred to as love on the rebound. Why are individuals who have just broken off one relationship more prone to enter another? Walster assumed that whenever one's self-esteem is lowered, either because of a severed relationship or for any other reason, a new relationship is actively sought out to regain self-esteem.

She then set up an experiment in order to test her assumption (1965). A group of young women volunteered to take part in an experiment described as an assessment of personality traits. On their way to the room where the experiment was to take place, each encountered a young man—ostensibly by accident—who started a conversation and asked her for a date. Then the women did the official experiment, which consisted of taking several personality tests. After completing them, they were shown the "results": not their actual scores, but a bogus report assigned at random. Some of these "results" were extremely flattering and others were very negative. After they were given a few minutes to look over the "results," the women were asked for honest appraisals of several persons they knew or had just met.

Each of the women whose self-esteem had been lowered by seeing the negative "results" of the personality tests made a positive appraisal of the man who had approached them just before the experiment, while women whose self-esteem had been bolstered by the "results" made a more neutral response. In this setting, and presumably in others where our self-esteem is low, we may have a particularly strong need for the approval of others and may feel a strong attraction to people who promise it. In other words, we may be most susceptible to romantic encounters when we are most insecure.

To return from the social psychologist's lab to the twelfth-century courts of love, we find two more points to explore concerning the contradications between romantic love and marriage. The first is that courtly love was a formula for a highly idealized relationship. The second is that it described an obsession, not a realistic choice. In both respects, romantic love would seem to be a destructive force in a system like ours, where it is expected to provide the basis for marriage.

It is true that individuals who like one another—and this applies to friends as well as lovers—exaggerate their similarities and disguise their differences (Berscheid and Walster, 1969). This behavior helps to explain some of the disenchantment that takes place in the first few months of a marriage, as the young spouses learn through experience that they do not agree with each other in as many respects as they thought they did. But, contrary to the folklore that lovers are blind to each other's faults, researchers who have inquired into the matter conclude that potential mates do not create grossly fictionalized or idealized images of each other.

The second point—that love is an irresistible obsession—is the one that many of the critics of our romantically based mate selection system have been most concerned about. In the twelfth century, love as an obsession did not seem a very strange idea because it was not connected with the practical business of marriage. In fact, Andreas made this point quite clearly: "We pronounce," he wrote, "that love cannot extend its powers over married persons, for lovers must grant everything, mutually and gratuitously, without being constrained by any motive of necessity; while husband and wife are bound by duty" (p. 266). In the past few centuries, however, these two elements, which Andreas and the women in medieval courts considered to be contradictory, have been reconciled—more or less. Love came to be considered absolutely essential, in the *pre*marital period.

Perhaps, as a number of writers have suggested, love was declared appropriate to the premarital period not so much for the individual's sake as for society's. Here, for example, is Sidney Greenfield's explanation of how love serves the needs of modern society:

> What appears to be necessary for the maintenance of American culture is a special mechanism that

> would induce these generally rational, ambitious and calculating individuals—in the sense of striving to maximize their personal achievement—to do what in the logic of their culture is not in their own personal interest. Somehow they must be induced—we might almost say in spite of themselves—to occupy the positions of husband-father and wife-mother. What we are suggesting is that the romantic love complex serves as the reward-motive that induces the individual to occupy the structurally essential positions. . . . A person who falls in love and marries comes to believe that he or she is "doing the right thing" and takes understandable pride in doing so. (1969, p. 346)

It might also be said that love provides a widely accepted justification for a decision that cannot be based mainly on clear, objective criteria. When you make an important decision, as in buying a car, you convince others of the wisdom of your choice (and perhaps even yourself) by reciting the car's merits relative to other makes and models. But such clearly defined criteria do not exist for making a wise mate choice, and so being in love provides a generally accepted explanation that convinces most people.

Notice, however, that now as in the twelfth century, a substantial difference remains between the purpose of love and that of marriage. Ernest van den Haag is only one of the writers who have commented on the differences between the vows of lovers and those exchanged at the altar. He observes,

> If marriage were to end when love does, it would be redundant. Why solemnly ask two people to promise to be with each other for as long as they want to be with each other? . . . Marriage was to cement the family by tying people together "till death do us part" in the face of the fickleness of their emotions. (1962, p. 44)

In our culture, love, marriage, and parenthood are interwoven, made three strands of the same rope even though they are at cross-purposes in several respects. Love is an intense personal experience, while marriage and parenthood are critical to the social fiber. By combining the three, we are encouraged to *want* to do what—from the point of view of society's needs—we *must* do.

The critics of our romantically based mate selection system have been most concerned about its effects on the individual who marries for the wrong reason. In a free choice system like ours, what is to prevent someone from applying the wrong criteria? For people who are influenced by the tradition of romantic love, marriage may be the result of an obsessive passion, when it should be a passionate choice. We speak of "falling in love," which suggests something quite different from a conscious decision. From this perspective, love seems to be "a state to be suffered or undergone," in the words of the French writer, Denis de Rougement. If this conception of love provides the basis for a marriage, it also eliminates the idea of personal responsibility. Again to use a phrase from de Rougement, we might better think of love as "an act to be decided upon," one that involves both passion and choice (1956, p. 303).

What apparently happens in many relationships is that the fragile flower of passionate love gradually gives way to companionate love, a sturdier if less exotic attachment. One researcher, psychologist Zick Rubin (1970), devised several scales by which loving and liking could be measured. In his passionate love scales, for example, he tried to assess such elements as idealization of the partner, the longing to serve and be served by the other, and the exclusivity of the relationship. In contrast, the companionate love scales were designed to assess such elements of liking relationships as respect for the other person, a sense of shared interests, and mutual appreciation. When Rubin and his associates asked married couples to use these scales to determine how the liking and loving elements in their relationships changed over time, they discovered a pattern that we might have expected: couples who had been married longer had lower scores on the passionate love scale. But the critics of our romantically based mate selection system might be relieved to find out that scores on companionate love remained relatively high and did not decline over time as passion did (Rubin, 1970). Perhaps the kind of passionate love that most people in our culture think of as an important prerequisite for marriage is not really incompatible with the bond that is expected to last far longer than passion does.

THE SENSIBLE CHOICE VERSUS THE ROMANTIC ATTACHMENT—IS THERE A CONTRADICTION?

How can one choose a mate intelligently in a culture where parents no longer make the decision, where seemingly few restraints prevent marriages between individuals from different backgrounds, and where the media constantly remind us of the delights of romantic encounters? There seems to be a contradiction among the three factors in mate selection that we have discussed in this chapter. Examining the sober facts of social status, we noticed that whether it was individuals in this culture choosing their own mates or parents in other cultures making that decision for their children, it had the characteristics of a bargaining process. Even though we may not be conscious of it, what sociologists call status matching does take place. The pattern of *homogamy*—like choosing like—prevails in many more cases than might occur by chance. In this respect, the mate selection process seems to be unexpectedly rational.

But then we turned to two factors that are important components in the mate choice, physical attraction and romantic love. Both would seem to be quite irrational. As we have seen, love is reputed to be a violent, irresistible force that strikes where it will, with little respect for class, income, or education. It is somehow pleasing for most people to believe that love is capricious, that their affections could not be predicted by any process so cold-blooded as a computer dating service. Many people are offended by the sociologist's suggestion that a bargaining process seems to characterize even this most intimate of choices.

Which factor, then—the rational process of status matching or the apparently irrational force of love—is more important for most people today? The answer is that both are. The critics of romantic love who worry that it provides a poor basis for marriage are alarmed unduly. We may marry on the basis of romantic attachments, but in most cases romance occurs only when certain conditions have already been met. Social status provides the framework within which love operates. Or, to put it differently, we are most likely to feel the irresistible urges of love for someone who happens to satisfy quite well the cultural expectation of homogamy. As social psychologist Bernard Murstein explains,

> Love, insofar as it involves marriage, hardly appears as a spontaneous bolt of lightning. From my own research and that of others—however cynical it may sound—it seems appropriate to conclude that we generally love or at least marry the best bargain we can get. (1974, p. 396)

Conclusions

In this discussion of mate selection today we have found that we are most attracted to—and thus are more likely to date and marry—individuals who are physically attractive, live nearby, and are similar to us in a number of ways. These similarities are not limited to interests or personal values, but extend as well to the basic dimensions of social status, including family background and education.

We noted that the marriage gradient constitutes a partial exception to the pattern of likes attracting. The marriage gradient is the tendency for people to seek relationships in which the male is slightly superior, or at least gives that impression. While it is questionable whether women "marry up" in social status more frequently than men do today, the marriage gradient definitely does apply with regard to age. We examined several implications of the fact that younger women attract and marry slightly older men.

In general, evidence suggests that homogamy is widely practiced. Most people get in a partner as much as their assets, social and individual, permit.

None of this is very surprising, although it does refute the idea of romantic attractions that strike where they will, with no regard for sensible considerations. Love "across the tracks" is the exception that proves the rule. What takes place in our free choice system is not substantially different from what happens where parents make the mate choice.

One reason why many people object to this kind of explanation is that it is not flattering to realize that one has been chosen as a mate because of social status factors as well as one's personal characteristics. But this recognition need not be a source of discomfort. Inevitably, these more impersonal facts enter into the perception of interpersonal attraction in any setting. And marriage is a practical arrangement in which some impersonal factors may well predict compatibility.

We have compared our mate selection process with that in some other cultures where parents make the choice for their children and the two prospective spouses may even have been strangers to each other before their wedding day. That they may still be perfectly compatible mates is hard for us to understand. We should realize that one of the basic differences between our conception of marriage and that of some other cultures is that, for them, marriage is regarded mainly as a necessary part of the business of living. Where the paramount concern is for each spouse to fill certain practical roles, parents can find a suitable mate for their children by seeking someone who can perform those functions. Today the emphasis has shifted in cultures where spouses are expected to be companions, and not just helpmates. Because it is much more difficult for parents to assess compatibility in such a personal matter as companionship, a free choice system is followed in most cultures where couples expect companionship in marriage. In such societies, courtship becomes a more important occasion for testing compatibility.

REFERENCES

Jessie Bernard. *The future of marriage*. New York: Bantam, 1973.

Ellen Berscheid and Elaine Walster. *Interpersonal attraction*. Reading, Mass.: Addison-Wesley, 1969.

Robert Blood. *Love match and arranged marriage*. New York: Free press, 1967.

Ernest W. Burgess and Paul Wallin. *Engagement and marriage*. Philadelphia: Lippincott, 1953.

Andreas Capellanus. *Art of courtly love*. Translated by John Jay Parry. New York: Ungar, 1959.

Hugh Carter and Paul C. Glick. *Marriage and divorce*. Cambridge, Mass.: Harvard University Press, 1976.

Ruth Cavan. *The American family*. New York: Crowell, 1969.

Richard Centers. Marital selection and occupational strata. *American Journal of Sociology* 54 (1949): 530–535.

Alfred C. Clarke. An examination of the operation of residential propinquity as a factor in male selection. *American Sociological Review* 17 (1952):17–22.

M. Clifford and Elaine Walster. The effect of physical attractiveness on teacher expectation. *Sociology of Education* 46 (1973):248–256.

Robert Coombs. Reinforcement of values in the parental homes as a factor in mate selection. *Marriage and Family Living* 24 (1962):155.

——— and W. F. Kenkel. Sex differences in dating aspirations and satisfaction with computer-selected partners. *Journal of Marriage and the Family* 28 (1966): 62–66.

Denis de Rougement. *Love in the Western world*. New York: Pantheon, 1956.

Karen K. Dion. Physical attractiveness and evaluations of children's transgressions. *Journal of Personality and Social Psychology* 24 (1972): 207–213.

——— and Ellen Berscheid. *Physical attractiveness and social perception of peers in preschool children*. Unpublished mimeo report, 1972.

Gail Putney Fullerton. *Survival in marriage*. New York: Holt, Rinehart and Winston, 1972.

George Gallup. Interfaith/Interracial marriages acceptable to many teens. *Gallup Youth Survey*. Press Release: April 12, 1978.

——— Dramatic changes in white viewpoints on integration and intermarriage. *The Gallup Poll*. Press Release: August 28, 1978.

Norval D. Glenn, Adreain A. Ross, and Judy Corder Tully. Patterns of intergenerational mobility of families through marriage. *American Sociological Review* 39 (1974): 683–699.

William J. Goode. The theoretical importance of love. *American Sociological Review* 24 (1959): 38–47.

Sidney Greenfield. Love and marriage in modern America: A functional analysis. In J. Ross Eshleman, ed. *Perspectives in marriage and the family*. Boston: Allyn and Bacon, 1969.

Clifford Kirkpatrick. *The family*. New York: Ronald Press, 1963.

Mirra Komarovsky. *Dilemmas of masculinity: A study of college youth*. New York: Norton, 1976.

Richard Larson and Gerald Leslie. Prestige influences in serious dating relationships of university students. *Social Forces* 47 (1968): 195–202.

William J. Lederer and Don D. Jackson. *The mirages of marriage*. New York: Norton, 1968.

Dorothea Leighton and Clyde Kluckhohn. *Children of the people*. Cambridge, Mass.: Harvard University Press, 1948.

Helena Z. Lopata, ed. *Marriages and families*. New York: D. Van Nostrand, 1973.

David and Vera Mace. *Marriage East and West*. New York: Dolphin, 1960.

Eugene W. Mathes. The effects of physical attractiveness and anxiety on heterosexual attraction over a series of five encounters. *Journal of Marriage and Family* 37 (1975): 769–773.

Margaret Mead. We must learn to see what's really new. *Life*, August 1968, pp. 30–31, 34.

Patricia Middlebrook. *Social psychology and modern life*. New York: Knopf, 1974.

Thomas P. Monahan. An overview of statistics on interracial marriage in the United States. *Journal of Marriage and Family* 39 (1976): 223–231.

Bernard I. Murstein. *Love, sex, and marriage through the ages*. New York: Springer, 1974.

———, ed. *Theories of attraction and love*. New York: Springer, 1971.

Ovid. *The art of love*. Translated by Rolfe Humphries. Bloomington: Indiana University Press, 1957.

Ernest Porterfield. Mixed marriage. *Psychology Today*, January 1973, pp. 66–72.

Harriet Presser. Age differences between spouses. *The American Behavioral Scientist* 19 (1975): 190–205.

V. Prakasa Rao and Nandini Rao. Arranged marriages: An assessment of the attitudes of college students in India. *Journal of Comparative Family Studies* 7:3 (Autumn, 1976) pp. 433–453.

Ira L. Reiss. *The family system in America*. New York: Holt, Rinehart and Winston, 1971.

Roper Organization. *The Virginia Slims American women's opinion poll*. New York, 1974.

Zick Rubin. Measurement of romantic love. *Journal of Personality and Social Psychology* 16 (1970): 265–273.

Bertrand Russell. *Marriage and morals*. Garden City, N.Y.: Garden City Publishing Co., 1929.

Wolfgang Stroebe, Chester A. Insko, Vaida D. Thompson, and Bruce Layton. Effects of physical attractiveness, attitude similarity, and sex on various aspects of interpersonal attraction. *Journal of Personality and Social Psychology* 18 (1971): 79–91.

Ralph H. Turner. *Family interaction*. New York: Wiley, 1970.

J. Richard Udry. *The social context of marriage*. Philadelphia: Lippincott, 1974.

Ernest van den Haag. Love or marriage. *Harper's*, May 1962, pp. 43–47.

Rebecca Vreeland. Is it true what they say about Harvard boys? *Psychology Today*, January 1972, pp. 65–68.

Elaine Walster. The effects of self-esteem on romantic liking. *Journal of Experimental and Social Psychology* 1 (1965): 184–197.

———, E. Aronson, D. Abrahams, and L. Rottman. Importance of physical attractiveness in dating behavior. *Journal of Personality and Social Psychology* 4 (1966): 508–516.

———, Jane Allyn Piliavin, and G. William Walster. The hard-to-get woman. *Psychology Today*, September 1973, pp. 80–83.

Judith Weinraub. India's traditional arranged marriages take a modern turn. *The New York Times*, June 3, 1973, p. 68.

FOR FURTHER STUDY

On the topic of mate selection, the Maces' *Marriage East and West* (New York: Dolphin, 1960) is an interesting discussion of our pattern as contrasted with patterns in Asia. See particularly Chapter 5, "Romance Is Too Dangerous," and Chapter 6, "Who Picks Your Partner?" Robert Blood's *Love Match and Arranged Marriage* (New York: Free Press, 1967) is another comparative discussion, and a good one. For a well-informed report on American endogamy patterns, see Hugh Carter and Paul C. Glick's *Marriage and Divorce: A Social and Economic Study* (Cambridge, Mass.: Harvard University Press, 1976), Chapter 5, "Intermarriage Among Educational, Ethnic, and Religious Groups."

Most of the contributions to an understanding of

interpersonal attraction have been made by social psychologists, and many are summarized in a volume by two prominent researchers in this area. See Ellen Berscheid and Elaine Walster, *Interpersonal Attraction*, second edition (Reading, Mass.: Addison-Wesley, 1978).

Several books can be recommended on the topic of romantic love. Morton Hunt's *The Natural History of Love* (New York: Funk and Wagnall, 1959) provides a lively historical perspective. From quite a different perspective, French essayist Denis de Rougement traces the fascinating development of romantic love through literature and social history, and concludes with several insightful chapters on the paradoxes of love in marriage. See *Love in the Western World* (New York: Pantheon, 1956). A recent book by Elaine and G. William Walster, *A New Look at Love* (Reading, Mass.: Addison-Wesley, 1978) summarizes much of the research on this, the most elusive of emotions.

"Dance Hall" Rosalind Shaffer

3

Getting to Know You—Dating, Getting Together, Living Together

William Congreve, an eighteenth-century playwright, once defined courtship as "a very witty prologue to a very dull play." Although the word "courtship" has gone out of fashion—perhaps because it suggests something formal and specifically destined to end in marriage—the observation still rings true. For centuries, what leads up to marriage has held far more fascination than what follows. Even though some of the appeal of Hollywood-style romance has worn off, we still have no end of popular fiction, romance magazines, and late-night movies portraying courtship as one of the most exciting episodes in life.

But this portrayal of courtship as drama can be a distraction, too. It diverts attention from the serious business of choosing a mate for a marriage that is intended to last a lifetime. Counselors commonly trace marriage problems back to the initial choice of a partner. "The major errors in the marital process," states writer William Lederer, a man who has spent years studying marriages that do not work, "are made by unmarried people before they commit themselves to be engaged or married. Most brides and grooms stumble into the union as though blindfolded and temporarily deranged" (1973, p. 38).

Compared to the very formal courtship practices of our grandparents' generation, dating or going together would seem to allow a young couple to get to know each other quite well. But critics of the dating system, including psychologists Bruno Bettelheim and Albert Ellis and anthropologist Margaret Mead, point out that it can be a manipulative and exploitative experience. As a rehearsal for adult roles and a school for adult responsibilities, dating may teach all the wrong lessons.

In this chapter we will examine dating and some of the newer courtship patterns practiced in our society. Dating, the standard pattern in the 1950s, is as American as rock and roll. We will analyze it as a game of strategy and skill, and notice what can go wrong when the two players have different goals. But courtship practices change almost as quickly as styles in popular music, and although dating is still common, a more informal practice known only as getting together has grown up alongside it. We will also compare dating and getting together with the newest courtship alternative, cohabitation.

One of the basic ingredients in getting to know anyone is self-disclosure. How much of yourself do you choose to reveal in a given situation? Have you ever met the same person in different settings—a friend's home and a classroom, for example—and realized that your impressions of the person were quite different in the two places? Knowing that it is appropriate to act reserved in some situations and in others to be yourself, you change your behavior from one setting to another. Thus, the rules according to which courtship proceeds, and the settings in which it takes place, have an important influence on what people learn about each other. Dating, getting together, and living together are very different situations. What you might learn about someone on a date is not at all the same as what you would find out if you were living with the person. Throughout this chapter, then, we will explore the self-disclosure process in different courtship settings.

Many divorces occur because, as one writer states, people marry "the wrong partner for the wrong reason at the wrong time" (Macklin, 1974, p. 41). We will see in this chapter that researchers have some idea of what the wrong age to get married is. By looking at the trend toward premarital cohabitation, we can also examine some of the wrong reasons for getting married. And even if no one can tell you with any certainty who the wrong person is, we can examine certain guidelines that might keep people from stumbling into marriage blindfolded.

COURTSHIP IN TWO CULTURES

Few social customs seem so comical and unnecessary as the courting rituals practiced in other times and places. Listen to older people talking about courtship generations ago, using terms like "keeping company," "spooning," "pitching woo" and describing a romance that apparently took place entirely in her parents' parlor, and under their watchful eyes. It is difficult to understand how two people ever got to know each other in those circumstances.

Husband!

Rituals leading up to marriage in other cultures seem even more curious. If you had been born among the Cuna on the islands along the eastern coast of Panama, you would be expected to participate in a drama that is brief and to the point. Marriages are parent-arranged among the Cuna, so the first step is for the fathers of the prospective bride and groom to reach an agreement. The second step is to choose a marriage maker. The marriage maker, aided by his assistants, has the job of picking the prospective groom up bodily and carrying him to the girl's house, calling as they go, "Husband! Husband!" The two mates-to-be are placed together in a single hammock, but the young man immediately jumps out and runs away. Immediately, the marriage maker pursues and recaptures him.

If at that point the prospective groom refuses to return to the hammock, the marriage is called off. Although the male has some freedom of choice, it is assumed that the prospective bride will accept. There may have been a Cuna woman who rebelled, bounced out of the hammock, and voted with her feet, but none of the accounts of the custom records such an event.

If the young man approves of the match, he returns to the hammock only to run away four times more and be recaptured each time. After being thrown in the hammock the fifth time he stays all night, though no intimacies occur. The couple are expected to stay awake throughout the night, for it is considered a bad omen to fall asleep. The next morning, the young man goes with his future father-in-law to collect firewood from the mainland, and this act seals the marriage. After that, the marriage is consummated and the young husband moves in with his wife's family (Biesanz and Biesanz, 1959, p. 25).

From our perspective, this drama seems more like a game of charades than a reasonable way of testing and sealing a lifelong alliance. The Cuna pay no attention to a consideration that is crucial in our system of courtship: assessing compatibility and marital expectations. Whether the two young people are acquainted is less important for the Cuna than the parents' decision that it is an appropriate match. The Cuna society is much simpler and more homogeneous than our own, and so the two young people are likely to have similar expectations of marriage. Courtship in our society is necessarily more complicated because we have the responsibility to choose our own mates and because it is no easy matter in a society with so many diverse marriage and family patterns to find someone with whom one's marital expectations are compatible.

The Dating Ritual

Perhaps the most curious thing about the Cuna ritual is that it seems to allow so little room for improvisation. The young couple follows a script that prescribes every action in their courtship, a script passed down through countless generations. An outside observer investigating our dating system might, however, have the same impression. Sociologist Peter Berger asks us to imagine a young couple sitting in the moonlight. We know that they are destined to choose each other as mates and share "bed, bathroom, and the boredom of a thousand bleary-eyed breakfasts." But first,

> each step in their courtship has been predefined, prefabricated—if you like, "fixed." It is not only that they are supposed to fall in love and enter a monogamous marriage in which she gives up her name and he his solvency, that this love must be manufactured at all cost or the marriage will seem insincere to all concerned, and that the state will watch over the marriage with anxious attention once it is established—all of which are fundamental assumptions concocted centuries before the protagonists were born. Each step in their courtship is laid down in social ritual also, and although there is always some leeway for improvisations, too much adlibbing is likely to risk the success of the whole operation.
>
> In this way, our couple progresses predictably (with what a lawyer would call "due deliberate speed") from movie dates to meeting the family dates, from holding hands to tentative explorations to what they originally planned to save for afterwards, from planning their evening to planning their suburban ranch house—with the scene in the moonlight put in its proper place in the ceremonial sequence. Neither of them have invented this game, or any part of it. They have only decided that it is with each other, rather than with other possible partners, they will play it.
>
> Nor do they have an awful lot of choice as to what happens after the necessary ritual exchange of question and answer. Family, friends, clergy, salesmen of jewelry and life insurance, florists and interior decorators ensure that the remainder of the game will also be played by the established rules. Nor, indeed, do all these guardians of tradition have to exert much pressure on the principal players, since the expectations of their social world have long ago been built into their own projections of the future. They want precisely that which society expects of them. (1963, pp. 85–86)

If this sounds like a description of how courtship *used* to proceed, it is because Berger was writing in 1963 about practices that have changed substantially since then. There are more alternatives now, both before the marriage ceremony and after. There is less emphasis on romance now than in the 1950s, and the stages of courtship are no longer so clearly defined or progress so inevitably toward marriage. But the dating system is still a common one.

One way of examining recent modifications in our courtship system is to look back to the dating patterns of the 1950s, when the parents of many of today's college students met and married, and compare them with current alternatives. As Margaret Mead has noted, dating came as a significant change from the older courtship practices. The date is planned by the young people themselves, and they are not chaperoned. Sexual intimacies are expected rather than forbidden, though there is a complex code specifying how far the young woman is allowed to go at each stage in the relationship. And there is no obligation to continue the relationship beyond the time of the date itself (in Bell, 1969, p. 247).

Stages, Commitments, Concessions

A key feature of the courtship system of the 1950s was that it consisted of a series of well-defined stages. The essence of courtship, as sociologist Willard Waller stated it, is

> to induce young persons into marriage by a series of progressive commitments. In the solitary peasant community, on the frontier, among the English middle classes a few decades back, and in many small communities in present-day America, every step in the courtship process has a customary meaning and constitutes a powerful pressure toward taking the next step. (Waller, 1938, p. 132)

When one investigator (LeMasters, 1957) studied the American courtship system in the 1950s, he found a predictable sequence of six stages: group dating, random dating, steady dating, pinning, engagement, and marriage. Each stage was marked by certain symbols, such as the practice of wearing a boyfriend's high school ring to signify going steady, or his fraternity pin to indicate being engaged to be engaged. Each stage implied a certain level of commitment to the relationship, and an understanding about whether it was an exclusive one. At each successive stage it became more difficult to back out of the relationship. Breach of promise suits, although they had become a thing of the past by the 1950s, illustrate the traditional assumption that at the more advanced stages of courtship there is a definite commitment to marriage. Several generations ago, the presumption was that if her suitor broke the engagement, a young woman's reputation was damaged and her future prospects for marriage impaired.

In the 1950s it was generally agreed that certain sexual intimacies were appropriate at each stage of the relationship. More commitment meant that greater intimacy was allowed. This is what the system looked like to one young man:

> I often had the uncomfortable feeling that the California coed dispensed passion by some sort of rule book. It had all been decided beforehand: the first date, so many kisses; the second date, lips part, tongue enters; fifth date, three buttons; next time, one zipper. . . . (Greene, 1964, p. 131)

If the norms varied somewhat from region to region and from one age group to another, the rule book nevertheless existed. There was a specific sexual code for each stage in the courtship sequence.

Dating was a departure from the traditional courtship system in another important respect: having fun became part of the serious business of choosing a partner. Some students of American courting practices have insisted that a distinction be maintained between dating (regarded as a form of recreation) and courtship itself (which leads to marriage). Listen to one investigator's concern about the "thrill-seeking" encouraged by dating, in a passage written when dating was a new and unfamiliar practice:

> Whether we approve or not, courtship practices today allow for a great deal of pure thrill-seeking. Dancing, petting, necking, the automobile, the amusement park, and a whole range of institutions and practices permit or facilitate thrill-seeking behaviors. . . . The sexes associate with each other in a peculiar relationship known as "dating." Dating is not true courtship, since it is not supposed to eventuate in marriage; it is a sort of dalliance relationship. (Waller, 1938, p. 139)

But even if it became a form of window shopping with no obligation to buy, dating performs several important functions. It serves as a rehearsal for adult roles. It is an informal school that teaches behavior appropriate to one's sex. Dating relationships provide an apprenticeship in intimacy, as well as an occasion to decide which traits are important in a partner. Dating can also provide an occasion for what sociologists refer to as status achievement. An individual can raise his or her prestige among peers by dating and being seen with persons who are considered to be highly desirable.

DATING: THE RULES OF THE GAME

Some of the most important lessons we learn are taught not in classrooms but in social encounters that may be defined as games. Though there is an element of make-believe about them, games serve a serious function, too: they take a real-life problem and remove it from its normal context. Seen in this light, they may be considered information models that help a player learn to process certain facts before deciding to chase or escape, capture or rescue (Melville, 1974).

To say that dating can be regarded as a game is not to say it isn't serious, only that it normally proceeds according to certain rules. Just as a football game would make no sense if the players had not first agreed upon the rules, neither would dating. Even though the participants in the dating game rarely talk about them, these unacknowledged rules specify what is required and permitted as two individuals move toward some arbitrarily defined goal. The fact that the male's goal in dating is often different from the female's only complicates the matter and adds another dimension—deception.

Our examination of dating as a game will show that the rules according to which it is played create an absorbing entertainment as well as a series of dilemmas. But we will find that, as an informal school for teaching adult roles and responsibilities, dating may teach many of the wrong lessons.

His Goals and Hers

One of the interesting things about the dating game as it has been played for at least a generation is that the male and the female are often pursuing different goals. This reflects the fact that males and females have been taught fundamentally different lessons about sexual expression and the desirability of marriage.

"For centuries," writes sociologist Jessie Bernard, "men have been told—by other men—that marriage is: no bed of roses, a necessary evil, a noose, a desperate thing, a field of battle, a curse. . . ." Oscar Wilde once remarked that marriage is a wonderful thing: every woman should be married, but no man. A statement attributed to the American critic H. L. Mencken makes the point even more clearly: since it is in a man's interest to avoid marriage as long as possible and a woman's to marry as favorably as possible, the two sexes are pursuing incompatible goals (in Bernard, 1973, p. 16).

The same theme is reflected in the common stereotypes about unmarried men and women. According to one observer,

> There is, in fact, no altogether acceptable term in common use by which to speak of unmarried women without conveying an overtone of disrespect.
>
> For men, the definition is more ambiguous. Although the older bachelor is generally depicted in a mildly unfavorable light, often humorously, the married man is also pictured as having been trapped—caught in a moment of weakness by the ever-scheming female. By contrast the young man who is both attractive and able to remain single is something of a symbol of strength. (Turner, 1970, p. 50)

This theme—that women want to trap men into marriage while men just as earnestly avoid tying the knot—was a familiar one to the readers of one of the most popular comic strips of the 1950s, *L'il Abner*. The marriage of the befuddled hillbilly, L'il Abner, and his fetching girlfriend, Daisy Mae, was interpreted by some people as cartoonist Al Capp's ultimate satire on the aspiration of every American female: to get married. But it was also a satirical slap at L'il Abner, who feebly protested, "This cain't be happenin'!! N-Not after all th' y'ars ah has successfully d-dodged it!!" What happened in

The reluctant groom/the bride as victor.

Dogpatch was only an exaggeration of a theme familiar to followers of the adventures of L'il Abner and Daisy Mae: the male enters marriage reluctantly, is tricked or bamboozled, or because in love does something he did not really intend. She is the victor. When researchers ask married couples how they made the decision, both male and female recollections correspond very closely to this stereotype. Summarizing a series of interviews on this topic with working-class couples, the author of one recent report concludes that women typically stress the romantic motivations, while men express an "I-don't-know-how-she-caught-me-attitude" (Rubin, 1976, p. 52).

Most males in this culture have been encouraged to express themselves sexually to prove their masculinity. Meanwhile, most females have been pushed toward marriage and motherhood to prove their femininity; self-respect and the respect of others, they are taught, depend on discretion in sexual matters. Therefore, men and women bring different expectations to the dating game. Young women are often more serious about their dating partners. They tend to assess dates as potential mates because their future status and life-chances will be determined, in most marriages, by the husband (Coombs and Kenkel, 1966). Young men, on the other hand, are more likely to view dating as recreation. Thus the two partners on a date may have quite different goals, and neither is likely to declare them. It may be more permissible to admit a desire for a long-term partnership than to acknowledge that one's main object is a temporary sexual encounter, but in fact it is quite unusual to discuss one's real intentions with a date.

From this perspective, we might regard courtship as a game in which he teaches her how to be sexual, and she teaches him how to be romantic. In this sense, the script for male–female relationships can very accurately be referred to as "courtship" because it repeats several characteristics of the courtly love complex of the twelfth century. The first move was for the man to express his longing. The woman was not supposed to grant the amorous award he craved, but she did encourage the pursuit. The man who learned those refined manners referred to as *courtois* behavior, who expressed certain ritualized forms of affection for his lady, and performed certain personal services for her was the one who earned her favor.

Today, of course, the script has changed in one important respect. The emphasis of courtly love, which in theory had little to do with sexual consummation, was on restraint, whereas today's premarital sexual codes specify how much involvement is appropriate at each level of commitment. But then, as now, the script required that males learn the language of love and emotional commitment.

The scene, then, is set for deception. He may indicate a desire for a long-term partnership (which he may not really want) in order to improve his chances for sexual involvement. She may promise sexual adventures (which she may not really want) in order to improve her chances for a developing relationship. In the dating game, as it has traditionally been played, the young woman learns quickly—in the words of the *Je Reviens* perfume ad—"to say 'no' so that he thinks you mean 'not now.' "

Notice what such deception does to the courtship process. Since her goal is to win personal commitment and his is sexual conquest, courtship becomes an escalating game of offense versus defense. As the offensive player, he is expected to make the first move, not just in planning the date but also in taking the sexual initiative. The young woman is in a difficult position. She does not want to lose her reputation, yet at the same time she must make enough concessions to indicate that she likes her date and wants to be asked out again. To complicate the situation, there is no chaperone, and she is left on her own with the responsibility of drawing the line on sexual intimacy. Parents frequently add to the problem by encouraging their daughters to be popular, to date frequently, but not to be "cheap," not to let boys go "too far." This is the dilemma that anthropologist Jules Henry had in mind when he observed that American girls in the dating system live on a "razor edge of sexual competition" (in Skolnick, 1973, p. 187).

The situation gets even more complex when the deception backfires. Picture a young couple negotiating their sexual involvement in the front seat of a car. The male is expected to be the aggressor, pushing toward more intimacy. The female is expected to make some pretense of resisting his advances in order to give the impression that she does not grant sexual favors too freely. As one observer comments,

> A common belief among many young men is that a girl often says "no" when she really means "yes," that she must make some pretense of resisting the intimacy as a face-saving device. Some of the differences in male reactions result from the inconsistencies of the "no"—some girls say "no" and mean it, while others really mean "go ahead." (Bell, 1966, p. 114)

The trouble begins when she *really* means no, but he thinks she means go ahead.

In this game of personal commitment and sexual conquest, the two sexes often display different badges of their achievement. Just as young men enthusiastically discuss and often exaggerate their sexual encounters but say little about their more serious relationships, young women seldom announce their sexual accomplishments but proudly display an engagement ring, fraternity pin, or any other symbol of commitment. And when the process ends in marriage, *her* picture appears in the newspaper, not his. This suggests that "the girl is being congratulated for having won a commitment in a contest with a reluctant partner" (Udry, 1974, p. 192). Many men want to get married, of course, but usually they still feel obliged to play the game.

Exploitation

As in other games, there are losers as well as winners in dating, and ways of taking unfair advantage of one's opponent. The potential for exploitation in the dating game was illustrated by the problems encountered by young women in an urban nursing school, where sociologists James Skipper and Gilbert Nass talked to more than a hundred student nurses and about seventy-five of the young men they dated (1966). These young men, college and medical students, defined dating as recreation and thus were in a position to control the situation because they were less concerned about a continuing relationship.

In any relationship, the individual who is less involved and more willing to end it is in an advantageous position. This is what Willard Waller (1938) referred to as the principle of least interest. When the attachments of two persons are unequal, the one who cares less is in a position of power and may be willing to exploit it. Two common examples are the man who sexually exploits a woman who loves him, or the woman who exploits a man's affection for economic gain.

"It is hard to get them to think about marriage," said one of the nursing students in the 1966 study by Skipper and Nass. It was a common complaint about the men. "They are happy just fooling around with you." Despite the fact that these young women were enrolled in a nursing program, most of them were primarily concerned with attaining the roles of wife, mother, and homemaker.

Skipper and Nass found that many of the nurses they interviewed shared the same problem. Whether or not they do anything to deserve it, nurses have a reputation for promiscuity. They were girls to have fun with, but not to take home to mother. There was a real conflict between the courtship expectations of the student nurses and their dates' anticipation that the women would live up to their reputation.

"The student nurse is placed in a precarious position," write Skipper and Nass.

> If she is not cooperative and does not meet the college boys' expectations of sexual permissiveness, she is likely to be dropped immediately and have no further dates. If she is cooperative, she easily builds a reputation and becomes fair game for her current dating partner, and later his friends and fraternity brothers. [We] suspect that more girls than not choose to solve the dilemma by being more permissive than they normally would, just in order to keep dating. As one young lady commented, "Whether you like it or not, you have to go along with them, at least some of the time. Otherwise, you get left out." (1966, p. 414)

The possibility of exploitation was greatest when the student nurses dated men they met in the medical center. Most of these medical students were occupational transients, men who were only spending a few years in that setting before moving on to establish a practice elsewhere. Not many of them wanted to get serious, or to take on a relationship involving much time or commitment. Because of the demands of their work, they wanted to make the most of their limited free time. In short, they wanted recreation, not courtship; fun, not commitment. To get what they wanted, they sometimes went out of their way to convince their partners that they felt more emotional commitment than they actually did.

Because they were perceived by the student nurses as highly desirable partners, and most of all because they had no strong commitment to a continuing relationship, these men were in a position to control the dating relationship. In any situation where one person feels more attachment than the other, the possibility of exploitation is present.

Other Problems with Dating

So far we have noted that dating, as a game of strategy, encourages deception and exploitation. To say that these elements exist is not to deny real affection or emotional attachment between dating partners, but rather to focus on those aspects of our courtship system that most frequently cause problems. Critics of the dating game have pointed to other problems as well. At least in its traditional form, dating is based on the double standard, and it encourages superficial and insincere relationships. In general, it may not prepare a young couple very well for the realities of married life. Each of these criticisms deserves closer attention.

Much of what we have just observed about the dating system indicates that the double standard is its basic code. Not only are the male's goals different from the female's, but he has more sexual freedom. The question then arises: Does the dating system with its double standard teach the right lessons to a young woman who will be expected to communicate openly with her husband after marriage and to enjoy sex as an equal partner? "The girl who has long practiced coyness and fended off approaches," says one writer, "has been badly trained for the role of equal and joyous wifely sexuality" (Hunt, 1959, p. 359). Psychologist Albert Ellis, one of the most outspoken critics of the system, states the case against dating even more strongly. The traditional dating system, he says, "is almost uniquely designed to sabotage a monogamous marriage. . . . American males develop strong antagonisms toward sex-denying women." What happens to women in this system, says Ellis, is even worse. "They are sexually tortured and maimed in at least as many ways. . . . Women frequently turn out to be orgasmically frigid, both before and after marriage" (1954, p. 57). As we shall see in the next chapter, however, sexual norms have been substantially redefined since Ellis wrote these lines. Because of modifications of the courtship system over the past decade, the "sexual maiming" that he refers to may be much less common now than it was in the 1950s.

Another criticism of dating is that it encourages superficial relationships. Sociologist C. T. Husbands compared dating practices in Europe with those in this country and noticed very different patterns. Especially in the early stages of dating, Husbands observed, the American teenager generally plays the field, while his European counterpart tends to go out with only one partner at a time. Dating in this country, Husbands concluded, is quite superficial (1970). But this conclusion may not be as true now as it was when Husbands reached it. One study, a comparison of dating patterns over a ten-year period at an eastern university, suggests that playing the field may be less popular now. Sociologists Robert Bell and Jay Chaskes (1970) found that although coeds in 1968 went out about as often as coeds had ten years earlier, the tendency was toward more intense relationships with a smaller number of dating partners.

It has also been pointed out that the rules of dating encourage a certain amount of insincerity. What therapists George Bach and Ronald Deutsch write about courting in general applies most accurately to dating:

> Dictionaries define courting as seeking affection, trying to win applause or favor, holding out inducements. So when one courts, one puts on one's best face, inflates strengths, conceals weaknesses, and generally seeks to manipulate the other person. The courter neither presents his own self, nor explores the reality of his partner. The object is to create smoothness without conflict, to capture by pleasing. Whatever might cause roughness or dissonance in the relationship is hidden behind illusions. It is avoided by as much giving-in as one can bear, and by the emotional tip-toeing required by "etiquette." (1970, p. 42)

As a preparation for a lifelong partnership, this style of courtship has obvious drawbacks. If both partners hide behind carefully manicured roles during courtship, neither can accurately anticipate what the other will be like in the day-to-day reality of married life. Dating is a highly contrived social situation, whereas much of married life consists of what sociologists call task-oriented activities—housekeeping, budgeting, child rearing. A courtship consisting largely of dates, therefore, is likely to be a rather deceptive preparation for what lies ahead.

The New Pattern: Getting Together Is Different from Dating

The word "date" now seems almost as old-fashioned as "courtship." It is not a very accurate word to describe an activity often simply called getting together. Dating was originally devised by young people, and in the past few years they seem to have revised it substantially. Many of the criticisms aimed at traditional dating do not apply to getting together.

For example, it used to be improper for a

young woman to call a male friend and arrange a get-together, but this is a common occurrence today. Whereas a date used to consist of a special occasion planned by the male, with an invitation made days in advance, getting together is a more casual matter. It is common for young people to congregate at parties or movies, perhaps to pair off during the evening. Much of the falseness of the older dating style—showing the girl a good time, making a good impression—is gone. As we shall see in the next chapter, the double standard has declined somewhat and premarital sex norms have changed, with the consequence that less bargaining is required now than a decade ago. In many respects, getting together is less like a game than dating. The tendency toward more honesty and less gamesmanship is illustrated best by an increasingly popular practice on campus—cohabitation.

COHABITATION

Back in 1966, Margaret Mead was concerned that the average age of first marriage was quite young. Writing in *Redbook,* she commented on the problems created by early marriage as a means of legitimizing sexual activity for young people. This created at least two difficulties, she said. First, many young couples were trapped into a premature commitment. Second, a high percentage of these young marriages were forced by pregnancy. "There is clear evidence of the fragility of marriage ties," she wrote, "especially among very young couples who become parents before they know each other as man and wife. . . . It is as if having a child sets the seal of permanence on a marriage that is in truth far from permanent" (1966, p. 49).

Mead wondered how marriage might be redesigned both "to give young couples a better chance to know each other, and to give children a better chance to grow up in an enduring family." She was particularly concerned about sexual bargaining between dating partners.

> I should like to see us put more emphasis upon the importance of human relationships and less upon sex as a physical need. I would hope that we could encourage a greater willingness to spend time searching for a congenial partner and to enjoy cultivating a deeply personal relationship. Sex would then take its part within a more complex intimacy and would cease to be sought after for itself alone. (1966, p. 49)

She proposed a simple but radical change in the courtship sequence, a marriage in two stages. The first stage would be an "individual" marriage. It would involve "a serious commitment, entered into in public, validated and protected by law, and for some by religion, in which each partner would have a deep and continuing concern for the happiness and well-being of the other." But it would not, as she conceived of it, involve the economic obligations of a normal marriage. The couple would not have children and the husband would not be responsible for the support of his wife.

Margaret Mead argued that this arrangement would encourage two people to get to know each other, to develop an intimacy that neither a prolonged courtship nor a furtive love affair would allow. And if the couple learned from this relationship that they could not live together compatibly, their postponement of children and the woman's economic independence would allow them to separate without "the burden of misunderstood intentions, bitter recriminations, and self-destructive guilt" (1966, p. 50).

Couples who had tested their compatibility in the first stage and wished to have children could move to the second stage, the "parental" marriage. This would require a separate license and different ceremonies from the first. It would also imply very different responsibilities. The parental marriage would presume lifelong commitment and would have as one of its main purposes the founding of a family. Before a couple could move to this stage, they would have to prove their ability to support a child.

The response to this proposal for marriage in two stages was mixed. Many people, of course, were indignantly opposed to any tampering with the institution of marriage, but others welcomed Mead's idea as a solution to a serious problem. What made this mixed reception interesting was that the idea of a nonprocreative trial marriage was not new: in the 1920s, both Judge Ben Lindsay and Bertrand Russell had made a similar proposal—and both had been denounced for it. But by 1966, when the *Redbook* article appeared, it was clearly an idea whose time had come.

Two years later, in April 1968, a widely publicized story about a Barnard College coed dramatized that cohabitation was a new fact of life on many college campuses. Newspaper headlines referred to sophomore Linda LeClair as Barnard's "Kiss-and-Tell Girl." She had been living off-campus for two years, in violation of college regulations. When the college's judicial council raised charges against her, she responded that the regulation was unjust (McWhirter, 1968). Apparently a substantial number of students at colleges across the country agreed with her, for in the years since then cohabitation has become a well-established alternative on campus, and elsewhere. In several respects it has ushered in something very much like the two-stage marriage that Margaret Mead anticipated.

It is difficult to get an accurate count of the number of cohabitors for several reasons. First, the term itself is vague. If, for example, two people maintain separate residences but spend most of their time together, are they cohabiting? Perhaps the most useful definitions are those, such as the one proposed by Macklin (1974), which specify a minimum amount of time that two people can spend together in order to qualify as cohabitors, thus distinguishing them from people who sometimes stay together. Macklin counts as cohabitors only those who "share a bedroom for at least four nights per week for at least three consecutive months with someone of the opposite sex." Because various researchers use different definitions, the estimates of the number of cohabitors vary widely. A second problem in assessing the extent of this trend is that the Census Bureau's estimate of the number of unmarried men and women living together

During the 1970s, cohabitation quickly became a widely accepted fact of life on campus and elsewhere.

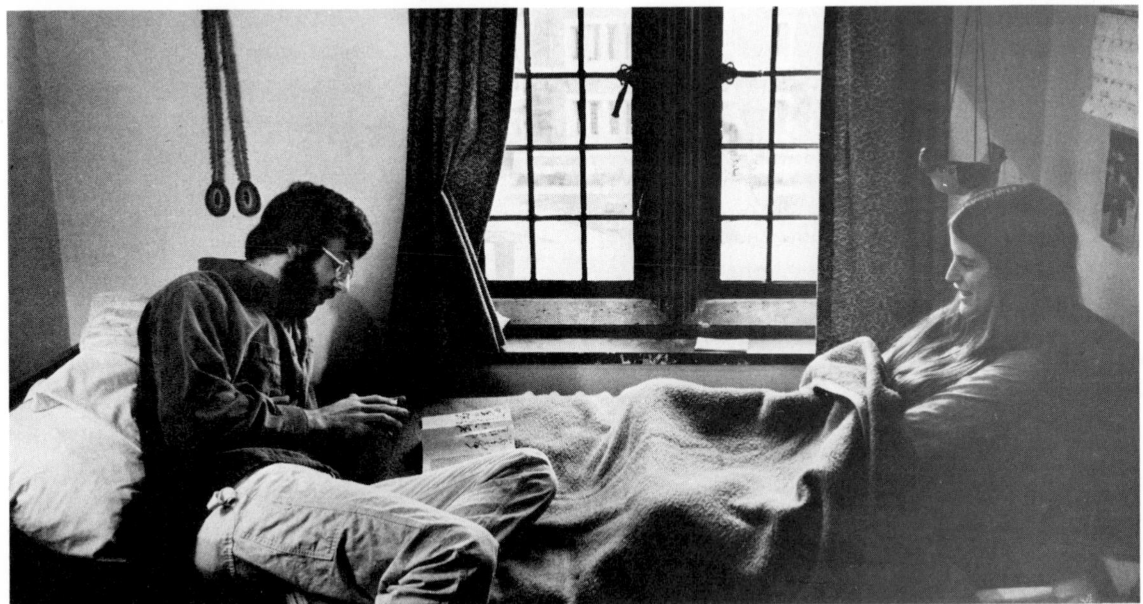

What's Happening Today

Box 3–1 / New Legal Perspectives on Cohabitation

It is often assumed that one of the main advantages of cohabitation is that it allows couples to live together without any of the legal obligations of marriage, and it allows them to break up without bitter legal battles. But recent court decisions about the rights and duties of individuals who formerly lived together have set new precedents. As a result, anyone who contemplates a "living together" relationship should first learn about the newly defined legal obligations that are attached to it.

In December 1978, the California Supreme Court established an important precedent in the widely publicized case of *Marvin* v. *Marvin.* Michelle Marvin, who had lived with actor Lee Marvin for seven years, was suing him for an equal share of the property earned during their relationship. She claimed that while they were living together, they were for all intents and purposes husband and wife, although they had never formalized the relationship. According to her testimony, Mr. Marvin had promised to support her and to give her a share of his earnings if she gave up a career to perform housewife duties. When their relationship ended in 1970, Mr. Marvin continued to support her for a while, and then he stopped. She brought suit, insisting that she had rights to $1 million for her services as a "wife" and $100,000 for the loss of her career. Acknowledging radically changed social practices regarding cohabitation, the court agreed that she did have the right to sue. So long as she was not asking for payment for sexual services, the court reasoned, she had a right to a share of the property accumulated during that relationship. Thus, for the first time, there was legal recognition of an arrangement that, by the mid 1970s, was practiced by at least several million couples in the United States.

The Marvin decision can be regarded as a legal landmark. There had been several earlier cases in which the courts had recognized the rights of individuals to the enforcement of clearly defined agreements between unmar-

in a single household—which, they say, doubled between 1970 and 1977 to 1.3 million—undoubtedly underestimates by far the actual number of cohabitors.

In this context, we will limit our discussion of cohabitation to those who are living together on campus. The best estimates of the total incidence of cohabitation among undergraduates in the United States is that about one-quarter have had some experience of cohabitation (Bower and Christopherson, 1977). Surprisingly, there do not appear to be marked regional differences (Clayton and Voss, 1977). But if only a minority actually cohabit, another statistic is more revealing of current opinion on this issue. Recent reports indicate that a substantial majority of college students support cohabitation. Studies at several campuses suggest that about 80 percent of college students today would choose to live with an unmarried partner, given the opportunity and the right partner (Arafat and Yorburg, 1973; Macklin, 1974; Macklin, 1978).

One Word, Various Meanings

Among parents who courted in the 1950s, one of the most frequent questions about cohabitation is: What does it mean? Their confusion is understandable, for rather than providing a new label for courtship stages that were recognized a generation ago, cohabitation seems to encompass several of them. Parents ask whether it means going *very* steady or a trial marriage. Or ried partners. But in the Marvin case, the courts declared for the first time that the simple act of living together and representing one's relationship as a marriage might in itself imply a contract. In other words, the principle that was affirmed in this case was that agreements—whether written or oral—between couples who decide to divide property or provide support are enforceable. And even where there is no explicit agreement, the courts may infer one where there is an enduring, intimate relationship.

This decision does not mean that cohabitation is, in the eyes of the law, equivalent to marriage. One difference, as the court in the Marvin case stated it, is that California's community property law does not apply to those who are living together; an unmarried person is entitled to those rights only if they are specified in a contract. But the case does suggest some erosion of the legal distinction between marriage and cohabitation. Especially since California has often been in the vanguard of legal and social change, it is widely assumed that the same arguments that were heard in the Marvin case will be considered in other states. As of January 1979, the courts in Georgia had already rejected one case argued along the lines of the Marvin case; but in six other states (Connecticut, Illinois, Michigan, Minnesota, Oregon, and Washington) contractual obligations between those who were living together had been affirmed.

One of the problems created by the Marvin decision is that it recognizes the validity of oral agreements, which are very difficult to enforce because they often boil down to the court having to choose between two different versions of the same story. Because there is not yet any uniform body of law regarding cohabitation, there is a great deal of uncertainty about just exactly what the rights and duties of cohabitating couples really are. One thing is clear, however. Couples who choose to cohabit are not free of all obligations to each other. By choosing *not* to marry, they are also choosing not to avail themselves of certain forms of protection that family law provides. Especially when cohabiting couples share substantial assets, or the responsibility for children, they are well advised to protect their rights by drawing up a contract that defines an equitable distribution of goods and responsibilities should their relationship end.

it is simply a convenient arrangement with no strings attached?

Rather than constituting a socially recognized step toward marriage, as the courtship alternatives in the 1950s did, cohabitation has a variety of meanings. If it is precisely that flexibility which makes cohabitation attractive to college students, the possibility that it may mean different things to the people who are living together also creates new problems.

Very few cohabitors follow Margaret Mead's suggestion that this first-stage marriage begin with a publicly acknowledged commitment. In fact, cohabiting couples often cannot recall any specific decision to live together. Compared to the carefully calibrated stage-by-stage development of relationships in the 1950s, cohabitation typically begins quite casually. "We began studying together," explains one young woman.

> Then I made his dinner before we studied. Then we came back afterward and I made him coffee. At first, I let him out. Then he let himself out. Then he stayed and I made him coffee in the morning. Then he went shopping for groceries and in a week he was here all the time. (McWhirter, 1968, p. 58)

One of the main advantages of cohabitation, say some college students, is that it is so easy—no blood tests, no waiting, no need to "make it official," and no obligation to stay any longer than the affection lasts. (See Box 3–1.) It is a way to avoid "a duty kind of relationship," as one young woman describes it.

> I have seen so many couples who were very happy when they were just living together. Then they decided to get married, and after that things really got to be a drag. I don't know why. Maybe it's because when you are just living together it isn't a duty kind of relationship. You feel free to be yourself and you really try harder to keep the relationship a good experience for both of you. I think if Bill and I were married we would take each other for granted. (Thorman, 1973, p. 251)

Is the experience of living together defined as a form of trial marriage or as a permanent alternative to marriage? As one investigator found when she talked to cohabitors at Cornell, living together is regarded as something quite different from marriage.

> Most of the undergraduate couples did not consider themselves married in any sense of the word. Not only did they not consider themselves married, they rarely considered marriage as a viable alternative to their present cohabitation. When asked, "Did you consider the possibility of getting married instead?" a frequent response was "Heavens no!" Marriage might be seen as a possibility for the future, but the distant future. The future seemed too indefinite to plan that far ahead. They needed more time to grow and develop, and it was financially impractical. (Macklin, 1974, p. 18)

"Most cohabitors still view marriage as a serious, once-in-a-lifetime step," write sociologists Carl Danziger and Matthew Greenwald. "Furthermore, they believe that living together can help them make the right choice before the contract is signed" (1971, p. 17). In other words, cohabitation, like dating, is a form of courtship invented by young people. For most of them it is a new way of assessing compatibility, not a permanent alternative to marriage.

Better than Dating?

One of the most common reasons that college students mention for living together is that they like it better than dating. When thirty cohabiting couples at the University of Texas were interviewed, many mentioned that they objected to the superficiality of dating. One young woman put it this way:

> Before we started living together dating was some kind of game, rather than a real relationship—at least as far as I'm concerned. I was trying to be something I really wasn't. . . . When I look back, it seems like such a waste of time. I never did learn to know the fellows I went out with. And they didn't really get to know me—at least the real me." (Thorman, 1973, p. 251)

Dating encourages a ceremonial image that may be quite different from the "real self." Much of courtship is ceremonial, but

> in close or continuing relationships the ceremonial image is shattered. The transition as the ceremonial curtain is drawn away may be traumatic. But once it is accomplished, there is a relaxation not otherwise possible. Just as there is often a sense of intense relief when a once-guarded secret is out, so elimination of the necessity to maintain the ceremonial image establishes a bond between those involved. (Turner, 1970, p. 86)

Another reason for cohabitation is that it allows sex to be put in its proper perspective. One of the goals Margaret Mead hoped to accomplish with her two-step marriage was to allow sex to "take its place within a more complex intimacy," to eliminate sexual bargaining. In his book *Psychological Factors in Marital Happiness* (1938), psychologist Lewis Terman estimated that only about 20 percent of marital adjustment depends on sexual compatibility. Even if it is impossible to say exactly how much of marital happiness depends on sexual adjustment, Terman's statement raises an interesting question: Does the traditional dating game, with its emphasis on sex as a trade-off for commitment, distract a couple from everything else? How are young people supposed to test the other 80 percent of their future relationship if they are courting in a system that keeps them preoccupied with sex? Courtship rules that are being rewritten by cohabitors to place more emphasis on the relationship itself might have some beneficial consequences. As one male cohabitor said: "Sex assumed its proper place as a part of the relationship, rather than the dominant theme. Together, we were able to find out the more important things about each other in proper perspective" (in Glazer-Malbin, 1975, p. 77).

But in cohabitation, as in dating, the female's intentions may be different from her male partner's, thus creating the same type of conflict we observed before. When two researchers asked students at a large urban university in the Northeast what their reasons were for living together, they discovered some interesting differences between male and female responses (Arafat and Yorburg, 1973). For males, the most frequent reason for choosing to live together was sexual gratification. Females indicated sexual gratification as a primary motive only half as often as males did. Their most common reason for cohabitation was that it might lead toward marriage. This may be the newest expression of an old theme: Daisy Mae is *still* chasing L'il Abner on Sadie Hawkins Day.

Another study sheds light on the same subject. Research conducted in Boulder, Colorado, compared eighteen cohabiting couples with thirty-one couples who were dating steadily but not living together (Davis, Lipetz, and Lyness, 1972). The two groups were matched in several important respects: all couples had come from roughly similar backgrounds; couples in both groups had gone together for about eight months. But the two groups were quite different in their orientation toward marriage. Among the going-together couples, both males and females were equally committed to marriage. The living-together females were almost as committed to marriage as the others, but among their male partners, only three of the eighteen showed any interest in it. The female partners wanted the security of marriage; the males defined living together as an alternative lifestyle.

There was another significant difference between the two groups. As might be expected, the living-together men were more satisfied with their sexual arrangements than were the going-together males. But the living-together males reported less respect for their partners. If this is typical of cohabiting relationships in general, it may provide an important insight into the problems of sustaining a successful cohabitation. The authors concluded that as compared with the couples who were seriously going together, cohabiting couples did not reciprocate the feelings (need, respect, happiness, involvement, or commitment to marriage) basic to a good heterosexual relationship. It seems, then, that parents who wonder what their children's decision to live together means are not the only ones to be confused. Young people who live together often disagree among themselves about what it means, and come to it with quite different expectations.

Cohab: Costs and Benefits

Some of the problems of cohabitors are common to those in any intimate partnership, including marriage. As educational psychologist Eleanor Macklin states it,

> The major emotional problems for Cornell cohabitants was a tendency to become over-involved, and to feel a subsequent loss of identity, lack of opportunity to participate in other activities or to be with friends, and an over-dependency on the relationship. . . . As in marriage, achieving security without giving up the freedom to be oneself, and growing together while leaving enough space so that the individuals may also grow, may well be central to success in the relationship. (1974, p. 30)

Other problems occur because cohabitation is not yet fully accepted. For example, older people generally do not support it. Though living together is at least tolerated in many campus communities, where neither college administrators nor landlords are interested in preventing it, one of the most common problems, as reported in Macklin's studies, is differences between students and parents. "Because of fear of disapproval or unpleasant repercussions, almost 80 percent indicated that they had tried at some point to conceal the relationship from their parents" (p. 51). Females more often than males indicated that their parents did not know they were cohabiting. And almost half of the college students Macklin talked to said their parents had caused problems for the cohabiting relationship.

Parents are often concerned that by living together their children might prematurely narrow their experience with possible partners. There is something to be said for shopping around before making such an important choice. However, the typical cohabitor has already dated about twenty-five persons, and might therefore be regarded as fairly experienced in heterosexual relationships (Schulz and Rodgers, 1975).

Parental objections to cohabitation are hard to understand sometimes. In the 1950s many parents were concerned that their sons or daughters were marrying too young. Immaturity was seen as a cause of marital instability. Observers pointed to the shortcomings of dating that we have just reviewed, and suggested that courtship be redesigned to include more practical tests of compatibility. In many respects, this is what cohabitation provides, a rehearsal that is much more like marriage than dating is. Although average age of first marriage has risen considerably since the 1950s, parents still object to cohabitation, often out of concern for premarital sex standards, which we will examine in the next chapter. Perhaps, however, parental anxiety is inevitable in a society where young people have the freedom to choose their own mates and parents can only stand by, hoping their children will make the right choice.

Cohabiting relationships, like the individual marriages proposed by Margaret Mead, can be terminated more easily than official marriages. They provide a fairly realistic testing ground for compatibility without the expectation that it last "till death do us part." Even engagement is a less reversible step toward marriage than cohabitation is. In a two-year followup study of college couples, one researcher came to the conclusion that cohabiting couples were just as likely to break up as those who were dating (Rubin, 1975). In another study, which compares cohabitors with engaged couples, the authors reach the conclusion that as a group those who live together are less committed to the idea of marriage to their current partner (Lewis and Spanier, 1975). In addition, most cohabitors do not pool their economic resources or make major purchases together (Macklin, 1974). Restrictions of this kind may serve in part to limit the commitment and make it easier to move apart.

When Macklin talked with cohabitors at Cornell, three-quarters of them said they would never marry without first living with their partner (1974). This is one way of gauging the effectiveness of living together as a new means for two people to get to know each other before marriage. Cohabitation is the most drastic modification of the courtship sequence since the invention of dating. Perhaps as cohabitation becomes more acceptable, in campus communities and elsewhere, many couples will put off marriage until they have tested their compatibility by living together a while.

GETTING ACQUAINTED— WHAT YOU NEED TO KNOW

One of the most common stories in the contemporary folklore of marriage is a cautionary tale that we might entitle "The Honeymoon's Over." Picture a young couple, obviously in love, pursuing a whirlwind courtship in which many hours are spent gazing into each other's eyes. The next scene is the wedding, in which the radiant bride is a vision in white, her "illusion veil" in place, her hopes intact. The honeymoon, which takes place at some remote resort, briefly confirms everyone's fondest wishes. But then, not too long after, in that perilous transition between courtship and the demands of everyday married life, the two look at each other and realize, crestfallen, that the honeymoon is over, that after so much make-believe, somehow things are now different.

Even if love is not blind, a culture like ours, which places a heavy emphasis on romance in courtship, sets up a situation in which disillusionment—both with one's partner and with marriage itself—begins to set in at about the time the thank-you notes are sent out. Though the practice of cohabitation seems to indicate a more realistic preparation for marriage, some of the important questions still do not get asked until after the marriage ceremony.

How do so many partners come to form mistaken ideas about each other in courtship today? It may seem unbelievable that a few generâtions ago, when courtship was conducted in her family's parlor or out on the front porch, a couple could make any realistic assessment of their compatibility as mates. But we must remember that in the stable, small-town environment where that courting usually took place, nearly every suitor was already acquainted with the young woman and her family before the courtship began. In our society today, by contrast, people frequently move from place to place, practicing a great variety of lifestyles. Even if two individuals come from similar backgrounds, that is no longer any guarantee of similar marital expectations.

When one researcher compared the courtship behavior of college students in the 1950s with that of their grandparents two generations before, she found a shift toward more exploration of potential trouble spots. In the grandparents' generation, the couples had a longer acquaintance before marriage, but those who married in the 1950s had a more intensive courtship. It is significant that the younger group explored more potential problem areas, such as money management and where they planned to live, during courtship (Koller, 1951).

Too Young

The key question about any courtship is, of course, not how *long* the two people have known each other, but how *well* they know each other. We can see a good illustration of this in the problems of early marriages.

The subject of early marriage received a good deal of attention in the 1950s and early 1960s. When Nat King Cole recorded "Too Young," one of the most popular songs of the period, the number of teenage marriages was at an all-time high. For more than half a century, from 1900 to 1960, the trend had been toward earlier marriages. The median age of first marriage for men during that period declined from twenty-six to twenty-three, for women from twenty-two to twenty. The percentage of females who married before they reached age nineteen increased from 31 percent in 1910 to more than 44 percent by 1960 (Cox, 1968).

The tendency toward early marriage has been reversed in the past decade, but by examining the reasons for instability in early marriages, we can still learn something about what should take place in the courtship period. One of the best-documented facts in research on marriage is the strong relationship between early marriage and poor adjustment. Couples who marry young, and typically have neither a long acquaintance nor a very realistic assessment of each other, are much more divorce-prone than couples who marry later. The divorce rate for young women married before age eighteen has been reported to be almost three times higher than that for young women who marry between twenty-two and twenty-four. Women younger than twenty when they marry are twice as likely to be divorced as those who marry after that age (Carter and Glick, 1970; Glick, 1957). In addition, individuals who marry early are more likely to experience marital discord and to report less marital satisfaction (Clayton, 1975, p. 305).

Although age at first marriage is no sure yardstick of maturity, it appears to be one of the most reliable predictors of successful marriages. Most states recognize the greater risk involved in early marriage by setting a minimum age for marriage with and without parental consent. In general, men who are at least twenty-one and women at least eighteen may marry, but males between eighteen and twenty-one, and females between sixteen and eighteen, must get their

Nowhere are the inducements to "spur of the moment" marriages greater than in Nevada, where easy divorce laws and 24-hour, neon-lit wedding chapels beckon to hopeful couples. No blood tests, no waiting, no fuss, these "come as you are" chapels provide everything—corsages, the bridal outfit, a photographer, even the "Best Man" and the "Maid of Honor" can be hired. Most credit cards are accepted. Buy now, pay later.

parents' consent. In California, legislation passed in 1970 requires teenagers below the age of eighteen to obtain a court order as well as parental consent before they can get married. The court may also require premarital counseling before granting the marriage license. The legislator who sponsored this law argued that of the 87,000 divorces in California in 1968, about 40 percent involved couples in which one or both individuals were under twenty at the time of marriage (Cox, 1968).

But why do early marriages fail so frequently? By examining the reasons for their instability, we may be able to see what needs to be accomplished before any couple decides to marry.

One reason is that many young people marry when there is only a temporary alignment of their values and needs. Teenagers are especially prone to apply criteria that are not very appropriate to the choice of a lifelong mate. The most sought-after qualities in a date are not necessarily the same as those desirable in a husband or wife. This is illustrated in an interview with a married physician who discovered too late the difference between what he wanted in a date and a mate.

> A cutie who can toss the lines with you, get you stared at at the fraternity formal, whose daddy has convinced her that if she's coy enough there'll always be a man to take care of her, can be a hell of a lot of fun while you're living out your adolescence. But *grow up* and her perpetual immaturity, her built-in inability to change from being a girly-girl, her childishness about the real world and the problems in it—why, I've got another child, that's all. She needs more day-to-day wet nursing than my twelve-year-old daughter. (in Cuber and Harroff, 1968, p. 79)

Early marriages, more often than later ones, are prompted by pregnancy. Both the divorce rate and the likelihood of marital dissatisfaction are closely related to premarital pregnancy. The divorce rate for pregnant brides is about double that of marriages begun when pregnancy is not a factor (Christensen and Meissner, 1953). In other words, it is not age at marriage itself but the greater likelihood of pregnancy that causes instability in early marriages. Legislators have begun to acknowledge that in some cases it may be in no one's best interest for a young pregnant woman and her boyfriend to marry. The domestic relations law for the District of Columbia includes this radical provision:

> A marriage license may be issued to an underaged party only if the Court finds that he/she is capable

> of assuming the responsibilities of marriage and that the marriage will serve his/her best interest. Pregnancy alone does not establish that the best interest of the party will be served. (in *Marriage, Divorce and Family Newsletter,* September 1, 1975, p. 4)

That marriages contracted at an early age are more prone to divorce may also be due to the fact that people who are not well suited to marriage at all often marry early. As sociologist Robert Havighurst explains,

> It is more true to say that people with the poorest chance of making a good marriage are more likely to marry early than to say that early marriage causes failure in marriage. There is no evidence that these people would make better marriages if they waited three or four years beyond their present rather early age of marrying. (1962, p. 130)

Another reason for the lack of marital satisfaction and stability among those who marry young is that these people are also more likely to have lower socioeconomic backgrounds. They have less education and fewer means to acquire socially valued rewards and statuses such as prestigious, high-paying careers—and not having these rewards contributes to feelings of dissatisfaction. In many cases, early marriage places one or both spouses in a position where they have to forgo further education in order to earn an adequate income. When they quit school they jeopardize their ability to get high-income jobs later on.

The preceding examples illustrate how hard it is to pinpoint any single explanation in studies that show a correlation between two factors. Although age at marriage and the likelihood of divorce are definitely related, we cannot conclude that any single factor is the explanation. No doubt all are contributing factors. The first two are particularly important in this discussion of the choice of a partner and the timing of a decision to marry. There is more likely to be only a temporary alignment of the partners' values and needs when marriage takes place at an early age. When it is prompted by pregnancy, there is often more concern for social respectability than for mutual compatibility.

How Relationships Grow

As we saw in Chapter 2, such factors as similarity in social status or educational achievement can be useful in explaining interpersonal attraction. They have the serious shortcoming, however, of offering no more than a static view. From experience, we all know that as relationships develop, certain traits become more important than they were when we first encountered the person. For example, though we may be strongly attracted at first by someone's looks, even the best-looking person gets to be a bore if he or she has nothing very interesting to say.

A Stage Theory of Development Social psychologist Bernard Murstein has proposed a theory of marital choice that describes a relationship as developing through three stages: (1) a so-called stimulus stage, in which people are attracted on the basis of physical appearance; (2) a value stage, in which they discover whether or not their attitudes and beliefs are compatible; and (3) a role stage, in which the important thing is how well the two people fit together (1971).

This approach recognizes that different traits are paramount at different stages in the development of a relationship. It also predicts the stage at which certain problems are likely to arise. And it implies that in a brief courtship which skips one of the stages, the two partners may misperceive some important characteristics in each other.

In stage one, the stimulus stage, all that either person knows about the other is what can be immediately perceived about physical appearance, social skills, and intelligence. Initial conversations are an attempt to explore the attributes that are particularly important, such as career aspirations. Almost inevitably, when two people meet for the first time they size each other up and try to arrive at an overall evaluation. We all have a notion of our own attrac-

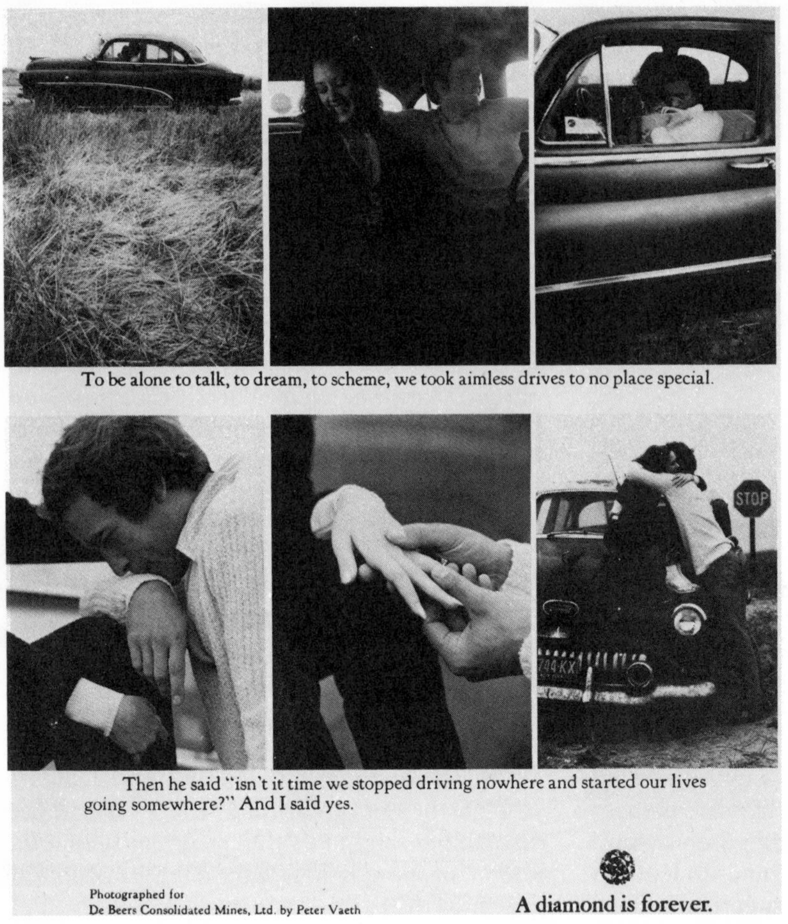

tiveness. People choose partners as well as friends whose total attractiveness—the pluses and minuses of their social status, personality, appearance, and so on—is roughly similar to their own.

This may be why the initial screening process in public meeting places such as singles bars can be so brutal. Anyone can enter the establishment and hence there is no guarantee of generally similar levels of attractiveness. First conversations in such settings are very direct attempts to size the other person up. The chance of rejection, when one person decides the other is not roughly equal, is much higher than it would be in other settings—a private party, for example—where those invited are likely to be fairly similar in the first place.

Once two people have found each other compatible in general attractiveness, Murstein believes, they proceed to the second stage of the relationship, in which the main issue to be explored is compatibility in values and attitudes. As they get to know each other, they reveal their attitudes about religion, life goals, interests, and marriage itself. Couples who get beyond this stage—engaged couples, for example—naturally hold quite similar values (Coombs, 1966).

It is interesting to examine why value differences cause tensions between individuals who are testing their compatibility. "When an individual encounters another who holds similar values, he gains support for the conclusion that his own values are correct," Murstein says.

"Further, many values are intensely personal and are so closely linked to the self-concept that rejection of these values is experienced as rejection of the self" (Murstein, 1971, p. 116).

Intimate relationships strongly affect our self-image. The elation and self-confidence of people in love and the despondency and self-doubts of individuals who have just broken off a relationship illustrate the emotional extremes. Much of the deception in courtship is motivated by the sort of self-doubt that sociologists Richard Sennett and Jonathan Cobb write about so perceptively:

> Whom shall I marry? That question seems obviously to be about my choice, about one of the most important controls I shall establish over my life. The more researchers probe that question, however, the more they find a secret question, more destructive, more insistent, that is asked as well: Am I the kind of person worth loving? This secret question is really about a person's dignity in the eyes of others, but it involves self-doubt of a peculiar kind. (1974, p. 62)

Sennett and Cobb illustrate the point with a quote from a man thinking back to the time of his own courtship, when he was more concerned with maintaining self-esteem than with trying to win the affection of his future wife.

> How did I know what she felt about me? . . . I mean, I felt sort of like I had to prove myself to her for her to love me, that whole Playboy thing. . . . I guess in a way when I was trying to make an impression it was less to impress her than to impress me. (pp. 62–63)

In cultures where parents make the mate choice, anxiety over one's own worthiness is uncommon, but in our society, "the individual is faced with a terrible thought: if he or she is not chosen, then he or she may not be worth choosing" (Sennett and Cobb, 1974, p. 63). The fear of not being worthy of love is one of the most basic anxieties produced by our system of courtship and mate selection.

In the third stage of their developing relationship, the couple tests role compatibility. This information is difficult to gather at an earlier stage, Murstein explains, because "the partner's ability to function in the desired role is not as readily observable as his verbalized expression of views on religion, economics, politics, and how men should treat women" (1971, p. 118). If a courtship is so short that this stage is omitted, the marriage will understandably be precarious. While courting, most people try to project an image of themselves that corresponds to their partners' expectations of them; if there is a discrepancy between the projected image and the person's actual behavior, both partners may overestimate their compatibility.

Some support for this explanation comes from an experiment designed to observe the interaction patterns of young couples (Heiss, 1962). The experimenter carefully recorded the communications and role performances of twenty-four unmarried college-age couples who were casually dating, ten couples who described themselves as seriously dating, and twenty-four who regarded themselves as seriously committed and expecting to marry. He found a substantial difference in the amount of posing between the casual daters and the seriously committed people. The casually dating women played the traditional roles expected of them, apparently for fear of being excluded from the dating market. The people in more serious relationships, however, dropped this traditional façade.

With the decline in posing, each person gains a better knowledge of the other's behavior in different situations. At this stage one finds out how well the other's actual performances fit one's own role expectations. Are the two people compatible in their sexual relationship and their preferences for spending leisure time? Does moodiness or an inability to make decisions together prevent the couple from functioning well as a unit or enjoying each other's company? When one person has a problem, how much comfort or help does the other offer? As each person sees how the other acts in these situations, a comparison is made with one's ex-

Involvement Exercises

Box 3–2 / A Self-Disclosure Checklist—Who Really Knows You?

Getting to know someone depends on what the person reveals about personal likes and dislikes, hopes and fears, strengths and weaknesses. But since much of courtship consists of an attempt to win the other's approval, there is almost inevitably some exaggeration of one's strengths and an attempt to camouflage weaknesses. In part, no doubt, the reason why many couples experience "the honeymoon's over" syndrome is that some important facts about the newlyweds—especially the less appealing characteristics—do not come out until after the marriage ceremony.

What are some of the important things to reveal about yourself and to know about your partner before marriage? The questions in this box, some of which are taken from the self-disclosure questionnaire developed by psychologist Sidney Jourard (1964), might help you to explore the question: Who *really* knows you?

Think of the person you are closest to. First, ask yourself whether you have revealed yourself to that person in each of these subjects. Then ask yourself if you know that person in each of these respects.

If you compare your answers with those of your friend, you will probably find evidence of what social psychologists call the norm of reciprocal self-disclosure. When someone tells you something personal, you are expected to reply with information about yourself that is equally personal (Ehrlich and Graeven, 1971). You may also find that on subjects where self-revelation is difficult, divulging certain personal values or weaknesses would threaten your self-image.

All of these subjects are important in assessing compatibility as mates. One of the most important questions to ask about any courtship pattern is whether it encourages the two people to get to know each other's position on these subjects.

pectations of a future spouse. If they fit, the relationship provides satisfaction and is more likely to progress toward greater commitment.

A Wheel Theory of Development Rather than describing, as Murstein does, the growth of a relationship as progressing through distinct stages, sociologist Ira Reiss (1960) thinks of it as a wheel consisting of four interdependent elements. The elements or spokes of the wheel are rapport, self-revelation, mutual dependency, and personality need fulfillment. At first encounter, a feeling of rapport or ease in being with someone determines that the relationship will continue and leads to the revelation of certain facts about oneself (see Box 3–2 above). Then, as the relationship goes on, the two people begin to feel mutually dependent. This happens, for example, when each person enjoys the other as an audience for one's jokes, or as the two confide in each other. The fourth spoke in the wheel, personality need fulfillment, comes into play when the partners fulfill each other's needs by providing emotional support or encouragement in such areas as career advancement.

Reiss calls his description a wheel theory

Subject

Attitudes and values

1. What are your personal views about religion?
2. Should either or both married partners have the freedom to participate in extramarital relations?

Work or studies

3. What are the strains or pressures in your work that bother you most?
4. What do you consider to be the most serious shortcomings or handicaps that prevent you from working as you would like or prevent you from getting ahead?
5. If you had to choose between moving to a strange city to accept an important promotion or staying in your current job to be among friends or family, which would you probably choose?

Money

6. Should husbands and wives be equal partners in planning the family budget, even if only one is an active wage earner?
7. Do you currently have any personal debts? If so, how much do you owe?

Personality

8. What feelings—worry, anger, depression, jealousy—do you have the most trouble controlling?
9. What is it about your closest friend of the opposite sex that most annoys you?
10. In what situations do you feel most inadequate?

Role expectations

11. How would you describe your expectations about what your future spouse should do without being asked?
12. Should men be expected to share household tasks such as doing the laundry and washing the dishes?
13. Do you want to have children? When? How many?
14. Do you agree that raising children is mainly the mother's responsibility?
15. How do you feel about women in full-time jobs or careers?
16. What responsibilities will you have to your parents after marriage, and which ones do you think your spouse should share?

Body

17. In your judgment, what physical feature—hair, teeth, weight, posture—detracts most from your overall appearance?
18. What is your greatest fear about sexual behavior?

Ambitions and aspirations

19. What is your strongest ambition?
20. What are some important differences between your life today and what you hope it will be ten years from now?

rather than a stage theory because the four spokes can be regarded as elements of a single process. As the relationship develops, the wheel turns in a positive direction: more self-revelation leads to greater dependency and thus to more personality need fulfillment. With each turn of the wheel, the relationship becomes more intense and involves greater commitment. But the wheel can also start turning backwards at any point. Less rapport may make both partners somewhat reluctant to reveal anything more about themselves, and this in turn may lead to a withdrawal of certain habits of interdependency. If the wheel continues to turn backwards, the relationship will eventually come to an end. Reiss explains,

> If love does develop through the culturally directed processes of a primary relationship involving rapport, self-revelation, dependency and need fulfillment, then one would expect that there would be wide differences in the number of needs which were fulfilled in any one relationship, that the very common failure to fully satisfy one's needs might well make one have some doubts and conflicts concerning the value of the relationship; and it also follows that although one has fulfilled some of his needs in one love relation-

> ship, he may fall simultaneously in love with another person who is capable of fulfilling different combinations of needs. (1960, p. 145)

It is not necessary for us to decide which theory, Reiss's or Murstein's, provides the better description of a developing relationship. In their different ways, both of them help us to conceptualize the courtship process and analyze what happens between the initial encounter and a couple's decision to form a long-term partnership.

What Your Partner Knows May Not Hurt You

Few people would deny that courtship is a period of interpersonal assessment, a time for testing compatibility. Some people may think, however, that if it is seen only in this light it looks more like a job interview than one of the happiest, most exciting periods of one's life. It does seem that the warm-hearted aspects of courtship are less accessible to scientific methods of investigation than the coldly calculating aspects. One exception, perhaps, is a study showing that contrary to the pessimistic old saying, love is *not* blind (Burgess and Wallin, 1953). Among the 2000 engaged couples studied, three-quarters of the women and two-thirds of the men said they recognized defects in their partner, things they wished were different: violent tempers, stubbornness, physical imperfections such as dandruff or ears that stuck out too much. But, the investigators report, these flaws were apparently no impediment to love.

Conclusions

A glance back at courtship in the 1950s showed us that dating was more formal than it is now. The courtship system of which it was a part consisted of a series of well-defined stages, each stage implying certain obligations and certain assumptions as to how much sexual intimacy was appropriate.

Even today, males and females often have different goals in the dating game: the male may be seeking only a sexual experience while the female desires a long-term commitment. Much of the gamesmanship in dating revolves around this issue: Which partner will be more successful in reaching one or the other of these incompatible goals? The double sexual standard, insincerity, superficiality, and exploitation are all common elements in the dating game as it has traditionally been played.

Although formal dating is still common, the more casual practice known as getting together has grown up alongside it. Getting together represents a substantial modification of the older pattern. It is less formal than dating and does not consist of well-defined stages. Engagement, the last stage in the traditional premarital sequence, is not so widely recognized today because much of what it used to mean is now taken for granted earlier in the relationship. In many cases, young couples today have intensely personal and sexually intimate relationships without first having moved through a series of preliminary stages.

A most significant change is that the entire process is not oriented to marriage as it was in the 1950s because the alternative of remaining single well into one's twenties has become more attractive to many people today. If the purpose of courtship is "to induce young persons into marriage by a series of progressive commitments" (Waller, 1938, p. 132), then many young couples are not courting at all. They are less concerned with what the relationship may eventually become than they are with the day-to-day satisfactions it offers. In other words, the distinction between courtship and marriage itself is much less clear than it was a generation ago.

The single most important modification in the premarital period since the 1950s, cohabitation, provides a vivid illustration of the greater freedom now allowed before marriage. It is difficult to find any precedent in the 1950s for the many cohabitors who, though they typically have more intimate and extensive knowledge of their mates than did the majority of engaged couples a generation ago, indicate no intention to marry

Guidelines for Decision Making

Box 3–3 / Guidelines in Choosing a Mate

If many marriages end up in divorce courts because people choose the wrong partner for the wrong reason at the wrong time, what are some points to keep in mind when you make this choice? There is, of course, no infallible advice, but these eight guidelines, based on the experience of marriage counselors as well as the research summarized in this chapter, may be worthwhile to keep in mind.

1. *Being in love isn't enough.* There are many reasons to get married. Some of them, such as marrying because all your friends are doing it, or to escape an unhappy family situation, are bad reasons. That two people are in love is the most common reason for getting married, but it is not a sufficient one. Try to examine your *other* reasons for wanting to get married.

2. *Love is different from sexual attraction.* Sex is obviously important in an intimate partnership, but it is only one element in the relationship. If affection, enjoyment, and respect are not part of it, sexual attraction alone, no matter how strong, cannot keep two people together for long.

3. *Are you really compatible?* Differences in such basic areas as life goals, religion, and role expectations can cause real problems later on. Make sure you understand what your partner's assumptions are about the privileges and obligations of marriage.

4. *Try to be honest about fears and inadequacies.* Courtship encourages people to put on their best face, to conceal weaknesses. But everyone has certain fears, problems, and inadequacies. If your partner cannot accept who you really are, it's best to find out before you decide to marry. You might discover some of your partner's fears only when you reveal your own.

5. *Short-term attractions are different from long-term commitments.* Most people have had the experience of finding someone quite attractive in one setting, only to discover that in a different setting the same person was much less appealing. "Shipboard romances" are notoriously unreliable as a preparation for marriage. Ask yourself whether the traits you like in your potential mate are ones that would be equally valuable in other circumstances.

6. *What you see is what you get.* Don't assume that your partner will change after the marriage ceremony, and don't enter a marriage hoping to reform the other person. Even when done with the best of intentions, reforming another person is seldom successful.

7. *Don't make a decision to enter a long-term relationship after only a short-term acquaintance.* Though a long acquaintance is no guarantee of a successful relationship, you are taking a chance if you decide to marry before you really get to know your partner. After summarizing a number of studies on marital breakdown, one writer concludes that if you and your partner have a close acquaintance of nine months or more, you have at least an average probability of marital success (Dominian, 1968).

8. *Don't expect a perfect partner, or total togetherness.* Accepting another person means accepting that person's imperfections, quirks, and moods. And remember that no one person can satisfy all of anyone else's needs. Allow room for friends, interests, and activities that are *not* shared.

their current partner.

In the last section of this chapter we focused on one of the main tasks in the premarital period: getting to know your partner well enough to decide whether you are compatible (See Box 3–3). Early marriages are particularly unstable because they are often based on a temporary alignment of values and needs; not enough time has passed for the couple to test their real compatibility. We examined the process of a developing relationship from the initial encounter to deep involvement. Murstein's stage theory and Reiss's wheel theory both help us to make sense out of the different factors involved in compatibility at various points in the relationship.

Today's alternatives before marriage offer a better chance for partners to get to know each other than did the courtship practices of the 1950s. But, as we noted in the discussion of cohabitation, parental objections are at least as common now as they were then. A frequently voiced concern in the 1950s was that people were marrying too young; their immaturity was presumed to be a major reason for marital instability. Dating was regarded as an impractical prelude to marriage. The average age of first marriage is higher now, and the current courtship alternatives offer a somewhat more realistic preparation for marriage than formal dating did. However, many parents today feel that cohabitation is undesirable because it too closely resembles marriage. One of the most common disputes between the generations focuses on what should be deferred until after the wedding ceremony. Concerns about the morality of premarital sex are at the basis of many of those parental objections. In the next chapter, we will explore recent changes in premarital sex and their effects.

REFERENCES

Ibithaj Arafat and Betty Yorburg. On living together without marriage. *The Journal of Sex Research* 9 (1973): 97–106.

George R. Bach and Ronald M. Deutsch. *Intimacy.* New York: Peter Wyden, 1970.

Daniel Bell, ed. *Toward the year 2000: Work in progress.* Boston: Beacon, 1969.

Robert R. Bell. *Premarital sex in a changing society.* Englewood Cliffs, N.J.: Prentice-Hall, 1966.

——— and Jay Chaskes. Premarital sexual experience among coeds—1958 and 1968. *Journal of Marriage and the Family* 32 (1970): 81–84.

Peter Berger. *Invitation to sociology.* New York: Doubleday, 1963.

Jessie Bernard. *The future of marriage.* New York: Bantam, 1973.

John Biesanz and Mavis Biesanz. *Modern society.* Englewood Cliffs, N.J.: Prentice-Hall, 1959.

Donald W. Bower. University student cohabitation: A regional comparison of selected attitudes and behavior. *Journal of Marriage and the Family* 39:3 (1977): 447–452.

Ernest W. Burgess and Paul Wallin. *Engagement and marriage.* Philadelphia: Lippincott, 1953.

Hugh Carter and Paul C. Glick. *Marriage and divorce: A social and economic study.* Cambridge, Mass.: Harvard University Press, 1970.

Harold T. Christensen and Hanna H. Meissner. Studies in child spacing, III—Premarital pregnancy as a factor in divorce. *American Sociological Review* 18 (1953): 641–644.

Richard R. Clayton. *The family, marriage, and social change.* Lexington, Mass.: D. C. Heath, 1975.

——— and Harwin L. Voss. Shacking Up: Cohabitation in the 1970's. *Journal of Marriage and the Family* 39:2 (1977): 273–283.

Robert Coombs. Value consensus and partner satisfaction among dating couples. *Journal of Marriage and the Family* 28 (1966): 166–173.

——— and W. F. Kenkel. Sex differences in dating aspirations and satisfaction with computer-selected partners. *Journal of Marriage and the Family* 28 (1966): 62–66.

Frank D. Cox. *Youth, marriage, and the seductive society.* Dubuque, Iowa: Wm. C. Brown, 1968.

John F. Cuber and Peggy B. Harroff. *Sex and the significant Americans.* Baltimore: Penguin, 1968.

Carl Danziger and Matthew Greenwald. *Alternatives: A look at unrelated couples and communes.* New York: Institute of Life Insurance, 1971.

Keith Davis, Milton Lipetz, and Judith Lyness. Living together: An alternative to marriage. *Journal of Marriage and the Family* 34 (1972): 305–311.

Jacob Dominian. *Marital breakdown.* Baltimore: Penguin, 1968.

Howard J. Ehrlich and David B. Graeven. Reciprocal self-disclosure in a dyad. *Journal of Experimental Social Psychology* 7 (1971): 389–400.

Albert Ellis. *The American sexual tragedy.* New York: Twayne, 1954.

Nona Glazer-Malbin. *Old family/new family.* New York: Van Nostrand, 1975.

Paul C. Glick. *American families.* New York: Wiley, 1957.

Gael Greene. *Sex and the college girl.* New York: Dial, 1964.

Robert J. Havighurst. *Growing up in River City.* New

York: Wiley, 1962.

Jerold S. Heiss. Degree of intimacy and male–female interaction. *Sociometry* 25 (1962): 197–208.

Morton Hunt. *The natural history of love.* New York: Knopf, 1959.

Christopher T. Husbands. Some social and psychological consequences of the American dating system. *Adolescence* 5 (1970): 451–462.

Sidney Jourard. *The transparent self: Self-disclosure and well-being.* Princeton, N.J.: Van Nostrand, 1964.

Marvin R. Koller. Some changes in courtship behavior in three generations of Ohio women. *American Sociological Review* 16 (1951): 366–370.

William J. Lederer. Videotaping your marriage to save it. *New York* magazine, February 19, 1973, pp. 38–41.

Ersel Earl LeMasters, *Modern courtship and marriage.* New York: Macmillan, 1957.

Robert A. Lewis, Graham Spanier. *Commitment in married and unmarried cohabitation.* Unpublished paper presented at the annual meeting of the American Sociological Association. San Francisco, California, August 1975.

Eleanor D. Macklin. *Unmarried heterosexual cohabitation.* Unpublished mimeo, 1974.

———. Nonmarital heterosexual cohabitation. *Marriage and Family Review* 1:2 (March/April 1978): 1–12.

Marriage, Divorce and Family Newsletter, September 1, 1975, p. 4.

William A. McWhirter. The arrangement at college—Part I, *Life,* May 31, 1968, pp. 56–68.

Margaret Mead. Marriage in two steps. *Redbook,* July 1966.

Keith Melville. Play's the thing. *The Sciences,* January 1974, pp. 12–14.

Bernard Murstein. A theory of marital choice and its applicability to marriage adjustment. In B. Murstein, ed. *Theories of attraction and love.* New York: Springer, 1971.

Ira I. Reiss. Toward a sociology of the heterosexual love relationship. *Marriage and Family Living* 22 (1960): 138–145.

Lillian Rubin. *Worlds of pain.* New York: Basic Books, 1976.

Zick Rubin. *Dating project research report.* Unpublished Manuscript. Harvard University Department of Psychology and Social Relations, April 1975.

David Schulz and Stanley F. Rodgers. *Marriage, the family and personal fulfillment.* Englewood Cliffs, N.J.: Prentice-Hall, 1975.

Richard Sennett and Jonathan Cobb. *The hidden injuries of class.* New York: Random House, 1974.

James K. Skipper and Gilbert Nass. Dating behavior: A framework for analysis and an illustration. *Journal of Marriage and the Family* 28 (1966): 412–420.

Arlene Skolnick. *The intimate environment.* Boston: Little, Brown, 1973.

Lewis Terman. *Psychological factors in marital happiness.* New York: McGraw-Hill, 1938.

George Thorman. Cohabitation: A report on the married-unmarried life style. *The Futurist,* December 1973, pp. 250–253.

Ralph H. Turner. *Family interaction.* New York: Wiley, 1970.

J. Richard Udry. *The social context of marriage.* Philadelphia: Lippincott, 1974.

Willard Waller. *The family: A dynamic interpretation.* New York: Cordon Press, 1938.

FOR FURTHER STUDY

For a perspective on how courtship patterns have changed over the past generation, it is useful to consult E. E. LeMasters' account of the courtship system of the 1950s, *Modern Courtship and Marriage* (New York: Macmillan, 1957). For a contemporary analysis of dating at one midwestern university, see Mark Krain, Drew Cannon, and Jeffrey Bagford, "Rating-Dating or Simply Prestige Homogamy? Data on Dating in the Greek System on a Midwestern Campus," *Journal of Marriage and Family,* vol. 39, no. 4 (November 1977). Results of a major longitudinal study of dating relationships among college students are reported in "Breakups Before Marriage: The End of 103 Affairs," an article by Charles Hill, Zick Rubin, and Letitia Anne Peplau, which appeared in the *Journal of Social Issues,* vol. 32, no. 1 (1976). Three recent perspectives on cohabitation are: Richard R. Clayton and Harwin L. Voss, "Shacking Up: Cohabitation in the 1970s," *Journal of Marriage and Family,* vol. 39 (May 1977); Donald W. Bower and Victor A. Christopherson, "University Student Cohabitation: A Regional Comparison of Selected Attitudes and Behavior," in *Journal of Marriage and Family,* vol. 39 (August 1977); and Eleanor Macklin provides a review of the recent literature on cohabitation in *Marriage and Family Review,* vol. 1, no. 2 (March/April 1978). In an article entitled "Happily Ever After? Following Up Living-Together Couples," Judith Lyness compares dating and living-together couples in *Alternative Lifestyles,* vol. 1, no. 1 (1978).

Anyone interested in further exploring the topic of self-disclosure might first consult a literature review by Paul C. Cozby, which appeared in the *Psychological Bulletin,* vol. 79, no. 2 (February 1973). There are several interesting chapters on patterns of self-disclosure among college students in Mirra Komarovsky's *Dilemmas of Masculinity* (New York: Norton, 1976).

"Alone" Rosalind Shaffer

4

Premarital Sex in the 1970s—Is There a Revolution?

"What if Susan Ford came to you and said, 'Mother, I'm having an affair'?" Morley Safer, a CBS-TV interviewer, asked Betty Ford, the First Lady.

"Well, I wouldn't be surprised," Mrs. Ford responded. "I think she's a perfectly normal human being like all young girls, if she wanted to continue; and I would certainly counsel her and advise her on the subject, and I'd want to know pretty much about the young man that she was planning to have an affair with—whether it was a worthwhile encounter or whether it was going to be one of those. . . . She's pretty young to start having affairs."

"But," Mr. Safer asked, "nevertheless old enough?"

"Oh yes, she's a big girl," Mrs. Ford said.

Commenting further on premarital affairs, she said there seems to be "a complete freedom among the young people now."

(*The New York Times,* August 11, 1975, p. 16)

The former First Lady's comment about her eighteen-year-old daughter was, as Abigail Van Buren later remarked, "the shot heard round the world." Within a few days, Mrs. Ford received nearly 28,000 letters and telegrams, two-thirds of them critical of her remarks.

The reactions she received illustrated the entire spectrum of opinion about this issue. "We deplore the deterioration of morality around the world. Chastity is to be observed before marriage and fidelity after marriage," said Gordon Hinckley of the Mormon Church. A spokesman for Edwin Broderick, Roman Catholic Bishop of Albany, said he was "really shocked" (*The New York Times,* August 11, 1975). Governor Hugh Carey of New York, the widowed father of twelve children, "insisted that he was not old-fashioned but that he believes sex should come with, not before, marriage" (*Daily News,* August 13, 1975, p. 17). In a telegram to the White House, feminist Betty Friedan strongly supported Betty Ford's statement: "As a mother of a wonderful daughter of that age myself, I believe that one can and must trust them to find their own new way. . . . I believe your honesty is what the whole nation is yearning for" (*The New York Times*, August 14, 1975, p. 23).

Should premarital sex be condoned? Under what circumstances? Or should the traditional norm of chastity be reaffirmed? This issue is one of the most difficult dilemmas that young people face today. Its difficulty is compounded by the fact that college students and their parents often take opposite positions on the issue, and not much seems to have changed in the few years since Betty Ford's statement. As of 1977, only about three out of ten adults polled in one nationwide survey agreed that sex before marriage is morally right, while a Gallup Youth Survey taken the following year showed that about six out of ten American teenagers feel that premarital sex is acceptable (Gallup, 1978; Yankelovich, 1977).

At the basis of contemporary confusions about premarital sex is a conflict that has been "created by an uneasy equilibrium between two contradictory values," sex as sin and sex as the ultimate expression of love (Ehrmann, 1963, p. 26). Many people still subscribe to the traditional norm of premarital chastity on moral grounds. But for an increasing number of people, especially college students, the traditional reasons for refraining from premarital sex—religious prohibitions, fear of pregnancy, the desire on the part of women to maintain a good reputation—have eroded. When people are asked how they feel about sex before marriage, a very common answer today is: Why not? To many young people, it seems a very natural expression of affection and love.

It is certainly not true, as Betty Ford concluded, that there is "a complete freedom among the young people now." But what are the new sexual standards? In this chapter we will examine four different sexual standards, each of which has its adherents on any college campus today. We will also discuss these related questions: Is the double standard, which has traditionally allowed the male greater sexual freedom than the female, declining? Why do many parents and children hold such different positions on what the standards should be? What are the problems caused by the emerging sex-with-affection standard?

THE SOCIAL CONTEXT OF CHANGING SEX STANDARDS

Few topics interest us as much as human sexuality, and very few are as difficult to discuss with any objectivity. Attention to premarital sexual behavior is especially significant because it is often seen as a measure of public morality. Like the Mormon spokesman who responded to Betty Ford's comments by deploring "the deterioration of morality around the world," many who defend the traditional norm of chastity use the language of crisis and collapse. Young people who reply by condemning the hypocrisy of their elders only escalate what is already an emotionally charged debate.

In this climate, it is difficult to assess what actually has changed. Are premarital sex behaviors today different from those a generation ago, or do we simply talk more openly about them? Certainly the moral code has changed since the early decades of this century. As historian Henry May described it,

> Chastity was as absolute a good as honesty and (this was tacitly admitted) far more difficult. . . . Paradox lay at the root of the matter: sexual intercourse in marriage was a sacred duty, romantic love the most beautiful thing in life, and sexual lust evil. . . . The millions of people who believed in this code and tried to live by it knew that it was continually broken. Lapses could be forgiven; outright defiance was far more serious. (1959, p. 134)

The most significant change in sexual attitudes and behaviors is this: premarital coitus is now widely regarded, especially by young people, as a legitimate choice. In this sense, there is "outright defiance" of the old code. Norms have changed so much that it is not uncommon for twenty-two-year-old virgins to mask their inexperience and wonder if something is wrong.

However, the abstinence standard has not

been totally abandoned. Despite the widely publicized "sexual revolution," a substantial number of students on most campuses remain virgins. In an atmosphere of sexual candor, we are deluded into thinking that premarital intercourse is more widespread than it actually is. At a large midwestern state university, 78 percent of the women interviewed underestimated the actual number of campus virgins (Jackson and Potkay, 1973). We will examine the evidence on adherence to the chastity standard after looking more closely at several of the factors that have caused the norms to change.

The Decline of Parental Control

Why have premarital sexual norms been redefined? One factor, as we have noted in the preceding chapters, is the decline of parental control. When parents supervised the courtship, complete privacy was rare.

> Taking a stroll after church, going for a buggy ride—in broad daylight—or having some precious moments alone in the parlor or on the porch swing were traditional examples of the privacy allowed couples during the Victorian period. This sanctioned privacy, however, was usually allowed only older youth and young adults who had "serious intentions," and lovemaking was generally limited to "spooning." (Ehrmann, 1964, p. 593)

The rules of courtship changed after 1900, and dating enabled the young couple to plan their own entertainment and get away from parental supervision. Two technological innovations contributed to these changes. The telephone enabled a young suitor to talk to a girl without a formal introduction to her parents. And the automobile became an important accessory on a date because it provided a mobile parlor and far more privacy than the porch swing had in the parents' generation.

Going away to college gave a person still more freedom from parental control. During the 1960s the American college population doubled, from 3.5 to 7 million students. In the 1970s, college enrollment continued to grow—to 9.8 million in 1979. The college environment provided a good deal of freedom, particularly with the decline of such traditions as the all-male or all-female college. During the 1960s, many college administrators began to question whether sexual morality was their concern, whether they should stand in *loco parentis,* in place of the parent. Most concluded that college students ought to be responsible for their own lives.

The only question for college administrators today seems to be whether any limits at all should be placed on students' living patterns. Nothing symbolizes the emancipation of adolescents from adult supervision better than the coed dorms that now exist on more than 70 percent of the residential campuses across the country. It is not uncommon for students to form intimate relationships, sometimes involving cohabitation and lasting for several years, without the knowledge of the parents. Compare this to the situation in the American colonies, when the father in the Puritan family had to give his consent to a potential suitor before the courtship could begin.

Anthropologists have found very few societies that, like our own, provide so many opportunities for intense, unchaperoned interaction of unmarried individuals while still prohibiting premarital intercourse. It is true that

> the great personal "freedom" of males and females in the dating situation was and is, however, in a very real sense a social mirage, because couples were still not supposed to go "too far," and the feeling of guilt was and is still an effective force in human motivation. The development of promiscuous petting was actually only one aspect of a complex set of codes of sexual behavior to deal with this new-found freedom which did not permit, personally or socially, a complete abandonment to lust. (Ehrmann, 1964, p. 593)

But no one would doubt that the decline of parental control intensified the pressure on the traditional norm of premarital abstinence. There is also some recent evidence that the rapid increase in the number of single-parent families may be affecting premarital sex patterns, for it appears that single parents are far more likely to welcome greater sexual freedom, and also that the children of divorced parents typically take more liberal positions on premarital sex than other children do (Gallup, 1978; Yankelovich, 1977, p. 79).

Almost Endless Adolescence

Another factor making the norm more difficult to observe is the lengthening of the period between the end of childhood, as marked by sexual maturity, and the beginning of adulthood, signified by entry into the world of work and accompanied by the privilege of full sexuality. If they practiced premarital abstinence, physically mature adolescents would have to abstain from sex for ten years or more.

To begin with, American boys and girls mature sexually somewhat earlier than they used to. Admittedly the historical record on average age at sexual maturity is incomplete, especially before this century, but it appears that because of nutritional improvements the onset of sexual maturity has been coming earlier in people's lives.

In Great Britain, there is evidence of a drop in the average age at menarche (pronounced ma-NAR-kee), the onset of menstruation, from 17.7 years in the 1830s to 16.5 years in the 1860s, then to 14.5 in the 1920s, and to slightly over age 13 in the 1960s (Tanner, 1966, p. 531). Because nutritional standards have been higher in the United States than elsewhere, American girls have typically begun menstruating somewhat earlier than European girls. From at least the middle of the nineteenth century to about the middle of the twentieth, it appears that the age at menarche declined an average of about four months per decade. But it may no longer be true that each generation reaches sexual maturity at an earlier age than the previous generation did. American researchers have come to the conclusion that the average age at which girls now begin to menstruate—12.8 years—is not substantially different from the age at which their mothers did.

This study also concludes that there is considerable variability in the age at which menstruation first occurs. For some girls, it takes place as early as age nine, for others it doesn't happen until age seventeen or even later. Data such as these suggest that although we can refer to an average age at menarche, there is so much individual variation that there is little reason for concern when girls deviate by several years from that average (*The New York Times,* March 26, 1976, p. 19).

While the onset of puberty in males is not marked by so signal an event as menarche,

Studies of adolescent sexual behavior indicate that more teenagers are sexually experienced today, and that they begin their sexual experience at an earlier age.

there is historical evidence of a dramatic drop in the age of sexual maturity for males, too.

> The eighteenth century records of the Bach Boy's Choir in Leipzig note that on the average the boys stopped singing soprano at about the age of eighteen, while the voices of boys in London choirs now drop out of the soprano range usually in their thirteenth year. (Francoeur, 1972, p. 48)

In other words, over a relatively short period of time there have been significant changes in the age at which children reach sexual maturity. Until about a century ago, sixteen-year-olds were still biological children, both in physical size and sexual development. There was a relatively short period between the time at which physical maturity occurred and the age at which marriage normally took place. But today, teenagers mature sexually at a much earlier age, long before they are intellectually or emotionally mature, and long before they are allowed to marry. Much of the concern about premarital sex might be regarded as a response to this pattern of earlier sexual maturation.

Thus the beginning of adolescence comes earlier, while its ending, postponed by various social pressures and particularly by added years of formal education, comes later. In this "almost endless adolescence," twenty-one-year-old "boys" and "girls" who in most other cultures would long since have had the privileges and responsibilities of adult life thrust upon them live in a campus culture that prolongs their dependence (Berger, 1969, p. 32). Between these two factors, earlier sexual maturity and postponed adulthood, adolescence has become about twice as long as it was a century ago, making premarital chastity that much harder to preserve.

The Erotic Environment

A third factor that has made a substantial impact on sexual norms is the frequent exposure to erotic stimuli experienced by everyone in American society. When the *Report of the Commission on Obscenity and Pornography* was released in 1970, its authors advised against censorship and reported no evidence that pornography leads to delinquency. But they did note that "exposure to erotic stimuli produces sexual arousal in substantial portions of both males and females" (p. 28).

Many of these erotic stimuli appear in the estimated seventy advertisements that the typical consumer pays some attention to every day. Products of all kinds, even detergents and automobile tires, are advertised with the promise of improving the buyer's sex appeal. Sex sells everything from cigarettes ("You make out better at both ends with Big Tip Pall Mall Golds") to women's clothes ("Happy Legs—What she wears on Sunday when she won't be home till Monday") and rental cars ("When an Avis girl winks at you, she means business").

The one setting that advertising does not drench with sex is the marital situation.

> The housewife is generally shown as an unglamorous and frequently unappetizing woman whose peak experiences seem to center on finding a laundry soap or detergent or floor cleaner with magical properties, or hearing about such products from a friendly lady plumber. Wives in advertising are usually not presented as having much interest in their own husbands, and no awareness of other men. . . . There are relatively few advertisements in which a husband and wife are shown together in other than a chaste situation. When married couples are shown in a bedroom, they wear pajamas, do not ordinarily touch each other, and conduct animated conversations at midnight on the relative merits of toothpaste in reducing cavities. (Winick, 1973, p. 164)

In most advertising, sexuality is portrayed as being *outside* the marital relationship—a message that, when repeated so often, may have a special impact on premarital sex norms.

Not just advertising but all the media today carry more explicit and adventurous discussions of sex than they did in the 1950s. Popular magazines frequently include articles on female sexual fantasies, the sexual inadequacies of men, and other such topics that would never have

Biological Aspects of Sex and Reproduction

Box 4–1 / Choosing an Effective Contraceptive

Evolution has produced both a strong drive toward sexual activity and a relatively foolproof means of guaranteeing fertilization; these adaptations have ensured the survival of the human species for millions of years. And although attempts to enjoy coitus without fertilization have been made throughout human history, no method yet devised for circumventing this efficient system has proved to be completely effective.

Probably the most effective means of contraception is surgical sterilization—vasectomy in the male and tubal ligation or vaginal hysterectomy in the female. A vasectomy, in which the seminal ducts are severed and tied off, can be performed in a doctor's office under local anesthetic within a few minutes. Tubal ligation for a woman is a slightly more complex procedure in which the fallopian tubes are cut and tied so that ova cannot be released into the uterus. The operation must be performed in the hospital, requiring about a two-day stay. In both vasectomy and tubal ligation there is a very slight (less than 1 percent) chance that a sperm may somehow manage to reach an ovum despite the elimination of the normal paths.

Next to sterilization, the two most effective means of birth control in use today are the intrauterine device (IUD) and various forms of birth control pills. IUDs are made of soft, flexible plastic, molded into various shapes. It takes only a few minutes for a doctor to insert one of these devices into the uterus. The woman commonly experiences uterine contractions (cramps) for a few hours after the IUD is inserted, and her next few menstrual periods may be irregular, but otherwise the IUD is generally unnoticed by the woman who wears it. Its obvious advantages include the simplicity and the absence of any need to prepare for coitus. However, some women are unable to use the IUD. The device may be expelled spontaneously from the uterus, or symptoms such as bleeding and continued cramps may require the doctor to remove it.

No one yet knows quite how the IUD works, but it seems to interfere with implantation of the developing embryo in the uterine wall. The pregnancy rate for women who use the IUD is 3 to 4 per 100 woman-years. That is, three or four pregnancies will occur each year for every 100 couples who use the IUD as their sole method of birth control. Newer IUDs, such as the Cu-7, are reported to have an even lower pregnancy rate.

Even more effective than the IUD is the birth control pill, or oral contraceptive. The Pill introduces into the body synthetic equivalents of estrogen and progesterone that serve to

been discussed before a mass audience a decade ago. One woman's magazine, *Cosmopolitan,* asks its readers, about half of whom are young, unmarried women, "Is love—sudden, intense, and brief—with an improper stranger bad for you? . . . Spending just one night with a strange man can be delicious or depressing, depending upon what you expect from the experience . . ." (September 1975). This media-created environment in which almost anything goes is a potent force for revising sexual standards.

ADOLESCENT SEXUAL BEHAVIOR

One reason why many people are convinced that a "sexual revolution" has taken place is that for several years the popular media have prevent ovulation. Different brands contain different amounts and proportions of hormones, but the most widely used types have a pregnancy rate of 0 to 0.3 per 100 woman-years.

A major drawback to the Pill is that it has to be taken daily with no omissions for three weeks and then omitted for seven days while the woman menstruates. If the user forgets three or more pills, and sometimes even two or one, the contraceptive effect may be lost for the month, and pregnancy may occur.

The present formulations of the Pill depend highly on estrogen. This hormone has been implicated in a possible side effect of current oral contraceptives—an increased incidence of diseases involving blood clots in the veins. These clots may impair the circulation of the legs and could cause death if they travel to lungs, heart, or brain. The danger of this complication, though, is twenty times less than the risk of similar complications during or following normal pregnancy. Hormones in the Pill are also believed in rare instances to elevate the blood pressure of susceptible women and possibly to alter the metabolism of fats in the body. The new "minipill," which contains no estrogen, has fewer side effects and complications but a slightly higher pregnancy rate.

Until development of the IUD and oral contraceptives, the most common birth control devices were the condom and the diaphragm. The condom, or rubber, is simply a thin, balloonlike rubber sheath that fits over the penis and traps the semen. Its disadvantages include a tendency to develop leaks or tears (particularly if lubricated with petroleum jelly, which dissolves the rubber), a dulling of pleasurable sensations for both partners, and the need to stop foreplay to put on the device after erection is achieved. The average pregnancy rate with condom use is 15 per 100 woman-years.

The diaphragm is a dome-shaped membrane of rubber with a metal ring around the edge, shaped to fit over the cervix and thereby block the passage of sperm. A spermicidal jelly is used to block any leaks around the diaphragm and to help hold it in place. The pregnancy rate with use of a diaphragm is 10 to 12 per 100 woman-years. Improper insertion and forgetfulness probably account for most pregnancies with this method.

Other methods of contraception are rather ineffective but are probably slightly better than nothing. Spermicidal suppositories or aerosol foams may be inserted into the vagina before coitus, or the couple may use the rhythm method, which is based on abstinence during the period when ovulation is most likely to occur. Unfortunately, ovulation can occur at any time during the menstrual cycle (even during menstruation) on some occasions, so that the rhythm method usually proves little better than luck. Withdrawal just before ejaculation (coitus interruptus) is often used to avoid conception but is also very unreliable. Not only does it require good timing and strong willpower, but many active sperm may be released in drops of fluid that ooze from the penis long before ejaculation.

Source: Adapted from *Biology Today*. 2nd edition. New York: CRM/Random House, 1975, pp. 742–743.

been carrying stories about an "epidemic" of teenage pregnancy. While the word "epidemic" does not very accurately describe recent trends, there is cause for concern. Judging from the results of a nationwide survey based upon a sample of 2200 teenagers, it appears that among approximately 10 million girls between the ages of fifteen and nineteen, about 4 million are sexually experienced, and about 1 million have been pregnant at least once as a result. Among the teenagers who had unintended pregnancies, only about one in five had used any contraceptive to try to prevent it. (See Box 4–1.) It is particularly disturbing that so many children are born to girls under fifteen—those who face greater medical risks and are least able to care for a baby (Zelnik and Kantner, 1977).

Some observers have concluded that such trends indicate both a precipitous decline in parental supervision of their children's sexual activity, and also that most sexually active teenagers are apparently unconcerned about preventing the pregnancies that result from sexual activity. But a closer examination of recent trends suggests that neither of these conclusions is entirely justified. In the first place, as we shall see, there have been some significant improvements in the contraceptive practices of unmarried teenage women. Also, contrary to the impression that many recent articles have conveyed, the rate of childbearing among American teenagers has actually fallen in recent years, from a record high of 97.3 births per 1000 women aged fifteen to nineteen in 1957 to 53.5 in 1977.

One reason why births to teenage mothers now attract more attention than they did a decade or more ago is that, because of a rapid decline in the birth rate in older women, children born to teenage mothers now figure more prominently among all births. But while the *rate* of childbirth among teenage mothers has decreased, the *number* of children born to teenagers stayed about the same from 1960 to the mid-1970s because the total number of women in this age bracket increased during that period (Baldwin, 1977). We might conclude from this decline in the teenage birth rate that adolescent pregnancy is actually less of a problem today than it used to be. However, there is still reason for concern about adolescent pregnancy. For while the birth rate among older teenagers has been declining, younger teens, and nonwhite girls particularly, still have relatively high rates of unwanted pregnancy—and a great many of those teenage pregnancies result in unwanted births.

Recent studies provide answers to the following three basic questions about teenage sexual patterns: (1) Is there, as many people assume, more sexual activity among American teenagers today than there was a generation ago? (2) Among those who are sexually active, is the age at first intercourse younger than it used to be? and (3) How frequent is the sexual activity of teenagers?

With regard to the prevalence of sexual activity among teenagers, various studies conducted over the past decade have concluded that there have been at least moderate increases in the sexual activity of this group. In one study, which assessed teenage sexual activity in a white, middle-class community in Michigan, the investigators come to the conclusion that between 1970 and 1973 there was a significant increase in intercourse among fourteen- and fifteen-year-olds, and that by age seventeen roughly one-third of both the boys and girls had experienced intercourse (Vener and Stewart, 1974). From other studies, which have focused on the sexual patterns of other social classes, ethnic groups, and races, we might conclude that black and Hispanic teenagers are more often sexually active and that they begin those activities at an earlier age (Finkel and Finkel, 1975). Those few studies in this area that have used a nationwide sample provide evidence for the common assumption that sexual activity among unmarried teenagers has become more widespread.

In the Kinsey studies (1948, 1953), which report on the behavior of the 1930s and 1940s, it was estimated that about 8 percent of young women had had intercourse by age sixteen. Compare that statistic with the results of a nationwide survey that was conducted in 1971 and then again in 1976 by two researchers at Johns Hopkins University. The latter concluded that the percentage of girls that age who had experienced intercourse has tripled to roughly 25 percent, and that the prevalence of sexual activity among unmarried teenage girls increased by about 30 percent between 1971 and 1976. By the age of nineteen, more than half of all American girls have experienced intercourse. Not only are more teenagers sexually experienced today, they're starting at an earlier age (which may be, in part, a consequence of earlier age at menarche), and they are experiencing sex with a relatively larger number of partners. When considering the meaning of statistics such as these, it is important to remember that "sexually experienced" does not necessarily mean the same thing as "sexually active," for it appears that teenager sexual behavior is typically quite sporadic. In the 1976 survey to which we just referred, the investigators found that about half of all the sexually experienced teenagers had not had intercourse in the month preceding the survey (Kantner and Zelnik, 1977).

Contraception and Unplanned Pregnancies

There are several reasons why so much attention is paid to premarital sex activities. One reason, as we have already noted, is that in America such behavior is regarded by many as an indicator of public morality. But in most societies, it is the fear that premarital sex may lead to pregnancy rather than any moral objection that is the main reason why such activities are restricted. One worldwide study of 158 societies shows that where premarital sex is restricted, as it is in about 30 percent of those societies, the taboo applies mainly to females and is largely a precaution against childbearing out of wedlock (Murdock, 1949, p. 245). One of the primary functions of marriage is the legitimation of parenthood. Almost universally, childbirth among unmarried women is considered a serious form of deviant behavior.

In our society, because contraceptives are now readily available and allow the bait of sexual pleasure to be separated from the hook of reproduction, it is tempting to conclude that unwanted pregnancies would be relatively rare. But when unmarried girls between the ages of fifteen and nineteen were studied in 1971 for the Commission on Population Growth and the American Future (Zelnik and Kantner, 1972), it was found that despite the availability of contraceptives, teenage girls commonly risk pregnancy. The authors of that study characterize them as "very casual contraceptors." Fewer than half had used any protection at last intercourse, and only one in five reported the use of contraceptives on every occasion. A majority had either never used contraception or had sometimes failed to use it (Zelnik and Kantner, 1972). There was little evidence that sexually active teenagers of the late sixties were any better protected against pregnancy than young women had been a generation before, when effective contraceptives were not so readily available.

But during the seventies it appears that the "contraceptive revolution" had a striking impact on sexually active teenagers, for when Zelnik and Kantner repeated their study in 1976 they found that contraceptive practices had improved significantly. There was an increase from 18 to 30 percent in those who always used birth control, and this increase occurred among all age groups and races. And there was a substantial increase in the use of more effective contraceptive methods such as the Pill or the IUD. In 1971, only about one-third of the sexually active teenagers had ever used such measures; by 1976 about two-thirds had. Even teenagers aged seventeen or younger were more likely to have used contraception at last intercourse than were those *over* seventeen in 1971 (Zelnik and Kantner, 1977).

Despite this tendency toward the use of more effective contraceptives, because more young unmarried women are now sexually active, there is a large number of women who risk unwanted pregnancies. Although, as Zelnik and Kantner found, about 40 percent of all teenage women had used contraception the first time they had intercourse, the pattern for the other young women was similar to that of most women in earlier generations who did not typically begin contraception at the same time that they initiated intercourse. Rather, they sought contraceptive methods only after they became sexually active, and thus risked pregnancy in their early sexual encounters. For most people, the risk of pregnancy is highest in their first experience of intercourse. One reason why this is true is that in most cases first intercourse is not expected to happen when it does, and where

What's Happening Today

Box 4–2 / Seven Reasons Why Unmarried Women Get Pregnant

When public health specialist Constance Lindemann visited two clinics in the Los Angeles area a few years ago, she wanted an answer to one important question: Why are there so many pregnancies out of wedlock? Why do young, unmarried women who are having sex so often do nothing to prevent it? After talking with 2500 young women, many of whom had been pregnant, she had some answers. These seven reasons illustrate the conflict between the chastity ideal and the reality for those who have sex before marriage.

1. *I didn't know how to prevent it.* Ignorance about contraception is still a major cause of pregnancy. Because many parents are either ambivalent about or opposed to premarital sex, most girls cannot seek advice or information from them. Lindemann says, "When it comes to what to do, where to go, and which method to use, the family doesn't tell and the girls don't ask." Even parents who have a more permissive attitude often feel that if they offer information on preventing pregnancy it will be taken as a green light on premarital sex.

2. *How can you plan something that's supposed to be spontaneous?* Many young women delay getting birth control until after intercourse has taken place for the first time. This delay is one reason for pregnancy. Another is that while sex is natural, contraception is not. "Sex is better if it's natural," said one young woman, "but birth control is artificial. Getting birth control would shatter romantic ideals. I didn't like the idea of birth control because sex should be spontaneous." Any reliable method requires advance planning, which contradicts the idea that sex should happen on the spur of the moment.

3. *What would he have thought if I'd come prepared the first time?* One legacy of the chastity standard is that young women often feel they should not give the appearance of knowing too much, especially before they have sex for the first time with a new partner. Taking the Pill or having a diaphragm is a sign for some of innocence lost.

there is no planning there is no provision of contraceptives. Such preparations are particularly unlikely when one's first sexual experience is with a partner to whom there is little emotional commitment and when young people do not feel that they can fully accept their own sexuality (Reiss, Bannart, and Foreman, 1975).

Because of the abstinence standard, individuals who engage in premarital sex are often poorly informed about contraceptives and ambivalent about their activities. To choose an effective contraceptive or even to seek counseling on the subject is an admission of sexual activity that is difficult to make, precisely because premarital sex is not yet widely condoned. Pregnancy often occurs because sex "just happens." (See Box 4–2, above).

Thus, the illegitimacy rate among teenage girls, particularly white girls, has been on the rise for more than a decade. Between 1960 and 1974, there was more than a 50 percent increase in the illegitimacy rate of fifteen- to nineteen-year-old girls, from 15.3 per 1000 unmarried women to 23.2 (National Center for Health Statistics, 1976). In certain regions the number of out-of-wedlock births has soared—and about half of those can be attributed to teenage girls. In New York City, for example, the number of

4. *I intended to remain a virgin until marriage.* Even young women who are determined to remain virgins until their wedding day often find it difficult to do so. As Lindemann remarks, "the failure rate of abstinence as a birth control method is considerable."

5. *I didn't care, because we were going to get married.* Males as well as females sometimes fail to use contraceptives because they define the relationship as leading to marriage, and they think pregnancy might cement the relationship. If this really is a motivation for casual contraceptive practices, it doesn't work. In most instances when a child is conceived out of wedlock, the father and the mother do not subsequently marry.

6. *I thought that was his responsibility.* When standards change, it is often true that there is no etiquette, no comfortable way to communicate, even if the message is an important one. As Lindemann comments,

> There is as yet no customary way for the girl who is not prepared with a contraceptive to ask the boy if he has one. Each may arrive at the scene with different expectations and, because of the lack of an etiquette, may not be able to communicate or check out the situation.

7. *It can't happen to me.* Even among those who know about contraceptives, outright denial that pregnancy might result is common. According to one girl, "It just couldn't happen to me. I've read about birth control. I knew the statistics. I could have prepared for it. I knew it was easy to get pregnant, but I thought it couldn't happen to me. It did."

Lindemann concludes that women will have to take on a new self-concept that includes the possibility of premarital sex before they seek out reliable contraceptives. This is difficult in a society still strongly influenced by the chastity standard.

> Girls cannot conceive of sex and pregnancy in a nonmarital context. It is this . . . ambivalence about premarital sex, together with the expressed goal of marriage in which sexual behavior would be approved, that is the source of their birth control behavior. In other words, sex is identified with marriage, not with development, and pregnancy is identified with marriage, not with sex. The result is that even though these girls are sexually active, they have no concern with the consequences of their sexual activities. Or they perceive marriage, not contraception, as the solution to their problem.

Source: Constance Lindemann, *Birth Control and Unmarried Young Women.* New York: Springer, 1974.

such births tripled between 1956 and 1976, from 11,160 to 33,215. There, as elsewhere, the illegitimacy rate of black teenagers is far higher than it is among whites; nationwide, about one in five babies born to white teenagers, as opposed to about three in four babies born to black teenagers, were out of wedlock. But, mainly because of an increase in the sexual activities of white girls, their illegitimacy rate has been increasing more rapidly (*The New York Times,* September 29, 1977, B-3).

This increase in the number of illegitimate births to teenage mothers has caused much of the recent concern about teenage sexual activities, because those mothers and their children commonly face a situation of double jeopardy. Children born to unwed mothers of any age are far more likely than others to be raised in circumstances of economic need and eventually to become dependent upon state support. And becoming a mother is typically a far more difficult thing for a teenager than it is for a somewhat older woman. Because young girls are physically less mature and often do not seek or receive adequate prenatal care, teenagers who bear children face a greater risk both to their own health and to that of their babies. In addition, the teenage mother has to manage not only social disapproval, but also the task of caring for and financially providing for her child—and in order to do so she is typically forced to leave school, to forgo further job training and other opportunities for economic advancement.

Sources of Sexual Information—And Misinformation

If the contraceptive practices of sexually active teenagers have improved, we still have a long way to go before it can be assumed that most young people are both well informed and well equipped to manage their sexual activities. One of the repeated themes in recent studies of adolescents (and college students, too) is their general ignorance about some basic facts of sex and contraception.

For example, when teenage girls who did not use contraception when they last experienced intercourse are asked why they failed to do so, seven out of ten say that they thought they could not become pregnant. And the most common reason why they thought they couldn't get pregnant was that they believed it was the time of the month when they were unlikely to conceive. It appears that only about two-fifths of all unmarried women between fifteen and nineteen realize that the period of greatest risk of conception is about two weeks after the beginning of a woman's period—and knowledge of such basic facts seems not to have improved much in recent years (Zelnik and Kantner, 1977). Most teenage girls know something about contraceptive techniques, but their knowledge is very superficial. Some girls believe that vaseline is an effective contraceptive, or that cola drinks can be shaken and used as douches. Others know about contraceptive methods such as spermicidal foam that can be effective if used correctly, but they don't know how long it is effective, or that such methods have to be used regularly.

Even among teenage girls who do have accurate knowledge of contraceptives, there are problems in obtaining them. This comes as no surprise, since so little information is offered on the subject. Sex education classes do not necessarily offer much advice in this area, and contraceptive advertising on radio and television is banned by the Code Authority of the National Association of Broadcasting, thus blocking another potential channel of contraceptive information. Although there has been a clear trend in recent years toward extending to minors the right to their own medical care, many doctors are still reluctant to deal with sexually active minors, especially without their parents' consent.

Male teenagers are typically no better informed than their female partners. In one study (Finkel and Finkel, 1975), in which male high school students were asked what they know about sex and contraception, the authors concluded that less than half could identify the phase of menstrual cycle when conception is most likely, and only about a third realized that even if a male withdraws before ejaculation his partner may still become pregnant. Significantly, the study concluded that knowledge does *not* appear to increase with age; the oldest group (eighteen- to nineteen-year-olds) did no better on a short quiz on reproduction and contraception than the youngest group (twelve- to fifteen-year-olds).

Learning About Sex

The question we need to pose is: Why do teenagers have so little accurate knowledge about sex and contraception? Consider for a moment the process by which most children learn about sex. In American society since the turn of the century there has been a marked tendency toward more positive attitudes about sex. Rather than warning their children of the perils of "masturbation insanity," as many nineteenth-century parents did, today's parents are more likely to accept the normality of children's sexual impulses. But the early sexual lessons taught by parents are still typically admonitions intended to prevent early intercourse and pregnancy. Children are typically taught what *not* to do, not what to do, or how, or how to prevent its outcome. Just as horror stories about "masturbation insanity" were ineffective in preventing masturbation (but often quite effective in provoking guilt feeling and teaching children to conceal their sexual activities), so parental admonitions to their children that they should refrain from sex until marriage don't very often serve as an effective deterrent to premarital sex. But these admonitions do cause considerable anxiety and convince many young people to conceal what they do. As a consequence, much of what we eventually learn about sex comes from unreliable sources, and much of our early sexual practice has to be covert.

The result of traditional sanctions against premarital sex has not been to curtail premarital sexual activities, but rather to inhibit the flow of information that would allow people to act more knowledgeably. Thus, in a society where the mass media are saturated with sexual themes, and where children become sexually mature ten or more years before they marry, adolescents typically receive little more than admonitions about what they *should not* do from their parents.

It would not be unreasonable to assume that because of the considerable candor with which sexual topics are discussed in the mass media today parents would be more comfortable talking about sex with their children. But the evidence suggests that this is not the case. One report (Yankelovich, 1977), which is based upon a representative nationwide sample of parents who are now raising children under thirteen years of age, includes a list of "Subjects Parents Find Hard to Discuss with Children." At the top of that list are "homosexuality" and "sex"—topics that today's parents still find far more difficult to discuss with their children than other topics, such as their own shortcomings, or problem areas such as money and illegal drugs (p. 98).

Judging from other recent studies, including one that consisted of detailed interviews with 1400 parents in Cleveland whose children range in age from three to eleven (Roberts, et al., 1978), we can conclude that those difficulties effectively prevent any verbal communication about sexuality in many households. Even the discussions with eleven-year-old children who will soon be sexually mature do not include some of the basic information that they need to know in order to understand intercourse or contraception. Only half of the parents had ever mentioned intercourse to their eleven-year-old children, and even fewer parents had ever mentioned contraception. Forty percent of the parents had never mentioned menstruation to their nine- to eleven-year-old girls, who would soon have that experience.

Even if parents do not typically convey much accurate sexual information, they do convey attitudes. Apparently because of the anxieties that parents express in answering the sexual questions of young children, those questions virtually stop by the time the children are about nine or ten. "In word and action," as the researchers conclude, "the Cleveland parents seem to be repeating a pattern set before them by their parents that includes little, if any, verbal communication about sexuality" (Elizabeth Roberts et al., 1978, p. 142).

Why is there such a cloak of silence about sexuality in many households? One reason why many parents are reluctant to talk about sex is their fear that such discussions might be interpreted as an acknowledgment of their children's right to sexual activity, no matter what their age. Another is undoubtedly feelings of embarrassment, which may also help to account for a pattern revealed by the Cleveland study—many parents say they do not often display physical affection with each other in the presence of their children. The information gap between parents and children may also be due to a lack of knowledge about sex on the part of parents, and the absence of a suitable vocabulary for talking about sexual functions.

Considering the silence about sexual matters that seems to be maintained in so many families, it is not surprising that children turn to their peers for information they do not get from their parents. But here, too, there are some serious problems in getting accurate information, partly because it is a situation of the blind leading the blind. Among male adolescents, conversations about sexuality typically consist of tales of sexual prowess, assertions of one's sexuality. Like other tales of physical prowess, such stories of sexual exploits commonly contain an element of exaggeration and reveal far more about adolescent aspirations than they do about actual encounters. And since females have learned from an early age that males are supposed to be the experts in this area, and that females should be careful not to give the impression of too much prior experience, in male–female encounters there is something less than a totally candid exchange of experience and information.

For centuries women have been taught to conform to male expectations in this area and to mask their own experience. Thus, even in marriage, men may not get accurate feedback from their spouses about personal preferences and satisfactions. The modern woman who fakes an orgasm in order to please her husband might, from this perspective, be considered just one more source of sexual misinformation. By responding to his expectations about what she should be feeling, she may also be providing some misleading cues about what really does give her sexual pleasure.

In this area, as in others, it is often assumed that whatever children do not learn from their parents they will learn in school. But precisely because of parental objections, teachers are often reluctant to teach sex education. Today there are only six states (Hawaii, Kentucky, Maryland, Michigan, Missouri, and North Dakota) where sex education is a required part of the public school curriculum. (In one state, Louisiana, the laws expressly forbid such courses.) Only about a third of all junior and senior high schools across the country currently offer sex education courses. Since about half of the sexually active teenagers have their first experience by age thirteen, sex education courses offered at the high school level come too late. Even where those courses are offered to junior high school students, there is some question about how effective classroom instruction is in this area, and how much of it influences actual behavior. In one study that tried to assess the effects of sex education courses (Zelnik and Kantner, 1977), the authors note that there is not much difference in such matters as knowledge about the period of greatest risk of conception between those who take formal courses and those who do not. It may be that sex information provided by adults in classroom settings is discounted, and sometimes dismissed entirely, when it is contrary to the sexual "information" shared in adolescent peer groups.

Considering the obstacles that exist for the teenager who seeks accurate information about sex and contraception, perhaps the most surprising recent development in this area is the improvement in contraceptive practices among sexually active teenagers that we have already noted. Particularly because of the high public cost of supporting out-of-wedlock children and their mothers, we will probably see over the next few years a considerably expanded network of clinics to serve teenagers' needs, offering education, counseling, and medical care. And because of the problems teenagers have in getting reliable sexual information, there will probably be considerable experimentation with new information facilities such as "sexuality hot-lines" for teenagers.

FOUR COMPETING PREMARITAL SEX STANDARDS

The well-known research by Alfred Kinsey and his associates, results of which were first published in 1948, was not the first systematic investigation of human sexual behavior, but it was by far the most comprehensive. Since then, much of the work in sexual behavior has focused on premarital sex. We now can draw on a number of systematic studies of premarital sex standards and behaviors.

It can never be assumed, of course, that what people say they do is what they actually do, especially in so personal and emotionally charged an area as sex. A further caution is that most studies of sexual behavior have been conducted with small samples of college students from middle-class backgrounds; there is little reliable information about the premarital sexual behavior of lower-class adolescents. But especially for the college population, we can sketch a fairly accurate portrait of today's premarital sexual attitudes—and, with some reservations, of behavior as well.

Some of the most valuable studies on attitudes have been conducted by Ira Reiss (1967, 1971), who not only measured premarital sex standards but investigated the social forces—religious commitments, feelings of romantic love, the standards of one's parents and peers, racial and family background—that are significant in shaping those standards. In his surveys he used a questionnaire consisting of two twelve-item scales, one asking his respondents how they felt about male standards, the other how they felt about female standards. First he administered the questionnaire to about 1000 students in Virginia and New York. Then he did what no other researcher in the field had done before: he asked a representative nationwide sample of adults the same questions so that he could compare their attitudes with the students'.

When Reiss tabulated the responses to his questionnaire, he found that males are generally more permissive than females, blacks more permissive than whites, and college students more permissive than adults. He also found substantial regional differences in sexual standards, as have other studies (Packard, 1968, p. 188). In the South, with its large rural population and religious conservatism, there is more support for premarital abstinence and the double standard than there is in other sections of the country.

Just as striking and somewhat less expected than these findings was the evidence for a variety of sexual standards. At every social class level and at every one of the campuses he studied, Reiss found a wide range of attitudes on premarital sex. It is the absence of a consensus on this question—not just between college students and their parents, but also among students of the same age on most campuses—that causes much conflict on this issue.

The range of attitudes that Reiss found can, he believes, be grouped into four different standards. Some support can be found for each of these standards on most campuses today. First is the *abstinence standard,* the position that premarital intercourse is wrong for both men and women, regardless of the circumstances. Second is the *double standard,* which Reiss subdivides into orthodox and transitional. By the orthodox double standard, intercourse is more acceptable for males than for females. By the transitional double standard, the male still has more right to engage in intercourse, but the female may do so when she is in love or engaged. The third standard, *permissiveness with affection,* condones sex for both men and women when there is a stable, affectionate relationship. And fourth, *permissiveness without affection,* or what might be referred to as the recreational sex standard, allows intercourse for both men and women regardless of the amount of affection or stability in the relationship.

Perhaps we can gain some understanding of the current confusion about sex by examining the implications of each of these standards. Exploring the conflicts among these very different standards is more revealing than an estimate of the percentage of students currently subscribing to them.

The Abstinence Standard

Chastity has long been a topic of college humor. At the University of Wisconsin, folklore has it that Abraham Lincoln, who sits in sculpted repose on campus, will stand and salute as soon as a virgin passes. Concerned that the statue had not moved in living memory, someone hung a sign around its neck reading "Out of Order."

Despite the popular assumption of almost universal permissiveness among college students, many people still choose to remain virgins until they marry. The most common reasons for adopting this standard, other than religious, are family training and the desire to wait until after marriage, as well as what has been referred to as the triple threat of infection, detection, and conception.

That people who actively attend religious services are more likely than others to endorse the abstinence standard is not surprising; all three major religious groups in American society—Catholic, Protestant, and Jewish—have opposed premarital sexual relations, if for somewhat different reasons. Researchers studying the sexual experiences of women at a large urban university in 1958 and then again ten years later found that the coeds who attended religious services most often were the least likely to engage in premarital relations and the most likely to feel guilty when they did (Bell and Chaskes, 1970). The writer Vance Packard found additional evidence of a relationship between religious beliefs and support for the abstinence standard when he compared the experiences of women at church-affiliated colleges with those of coeds elsewhere: the percentage of women in state and private colleges who reported that they were not virgins was about four times higher than that of women in church-related colleges (1968, p. 507). It is undoubtedly true that women with more conservative standards in the first place choose to attend church-related colleges, but Vance Packard's study does also suggest that religious beliefs, which have traditionally acted as a very strong restraint on premarital sex for women, are still an important factor.

One of the legacies of a standard prohibiting sex before marriage is strong guilt feelings about premarital relations, and especially one's first experience with intercourse. Because of a general shift toward more liberal sexual standards, fewer students than before now report strong feelings of guilt or remorse after that experience (Christensen and Gregg, 1970), but these feelings are still common. "Sexual liberation notwithstanding, many worries and tensions still surround the first premarital coital experience," comments Morton Hunt, in a discussion of a study conducted by the Playboy Foundation.

> More than a third of our young males and close to two-thirds of our young females experienced regret and worry afterward; and even after many experiences, a fair number continue to worry about pregnancy and VD and to be troubled by emotional and moral conflicts. (1973, p. 75)

It is hardly fair to play on fears of venereal disease or pregnancy in order to frighten people into remaining chaste, but no one can afford to minimize these dangers either. In 1953 Alfred Kinsey took the position that "present methods of simple and rapid cure for both syphilis and gonorrhea make their spread through premarital coitus a relatively unimportant matter" (p. 327). But his optimism proved premature. Thanks in part to penicillin and other drugs, venereal disease had become relatively rare by the 1950s, and Kinsey was not the only one to believe that it no longer posed a serious public health hazard. Since the 1960s, however, venereal disease has become much more common; in some areas it has spread to epidemic proportions. Only 5000 cases of syphilis were reported in the United States in 1958; by 1977, a total of more than 23,000 cases were reported. And, if we can make any reliable generalizations about total incidence from the number of reported cases, it appears that the number of cases of gonorrhea also multiplied rapidly during that same period (*The New York Times,* November 20, 1977, p. 22).

Several explanations, including public ignorance, cutbacks in funds for public health programs, and changing contraceptive practices, have been offered for the dramatic increase in VD (see Box 4–3, opposite). Certainly one of the major factors is the change in sexual standards. The increased acceptance of intercourse before marriage has brought an increase in the number of sexual partners for many people, a condition that enables the disease to spread.

If the reasons for adopting the abstinence standard have not changed much over the years, the percentage of young people who subscribe to it has changed substantially. Most of the writers and researchers who have inquired

Guidelines for Decision Making

Box 4–3 / Recognizing and Treating Venereal Disease

Venereal diseases are spread through sexual contact. Gonorrhea and syphilis are the diseases people generally think of when they refer to VD, but there are others as well. Venereal disease is easily cured by antibiotics and should by now be relatively rare. But, both because of ignorance about its symptoms and consequences and because of social stigma, it has become so common in the United States over the past few years that, among communicable diseases, only the common cold is more prevalent.

Further reasons for the recent increase in VD are: (1) condoms are effective in preventing VD, but newer contraceptive techniques—the Pill, the loop, and the diaphragm—are not; (2) more liberal sexual standards make the communication of VD more likely; and (3) even when individuals recognize its symptoms and seek treatment, they are often unwilling to identify their sexual partners, thus permitting the spread of the disease to go unchecked. Physicians and laboratories are required to report all cases of VD to public health authorities.

Recognizing the Symptoms of Gonorrhea

Gonorrhea (also called the clap, strain, a dose, and other names) is the most common form of VD. It is spread almost exclusively through intimate sexual contact. Genital intercourse is the most frequent method of transmission, though gonorrhea of the rectum and throat as a result of anal and oral sex is not uncommon.

In most cases, men notice the first symptoms within a few days after exposure, although a form of gonorrhea that has no visible signs in males is becoming more common. When symptoms do appear in the male, he first has a white, heavy discharge from the opening of the penis. Then the tip of the penis becomes swollen and urination is accompanied by a burning pain.

If no medication is administered, the infection may seem to disappear. But even when the symptoms are gone, the man can still spread the disease to sexual partners. At the same time, the infection may spread to the prostate gland, the bladder, the kidneys, and the joints, causing a variety of painful and dangerous complications. If left untreated, the man may become sterile.

Most women who contract the disease experience no symptoms at all for the first weeks or even months. In some women, however, there is a noticeable change in the color of vaginal secretions, from the normal whitish color to a green or yellow-green tint. Untreated, gonorrhea may spread up the reproductive tract to enter the abdomen, causing chronic infections that may lead to sterility and other complications.

Recognizing the Symptoms of Syphilis

Syphilis is less common than gonorrhea, but it is more serious. There are no immediate or obvious symptoms. The first sign of infection is a single, painless sore called a chancre (pronounced shank-er) which appears between two to six weeks after exposure. In the male, it usually forms on the penis, but may appear on other parts of the body. In the female, it usually appears on the cervix or on the vaginal walls, and is therefore not noticeable. This sore will disappear, even if the disease goes untreated, but this only indicates that the infection has begun the secondary stage. After the chancre heals, an extremely contagious skin eruption may appear for several weeks, accompanied by fever, headache, sore throat, and muscle pain. These symptoms then vanish, and the disease en-

(Box 4–3 continues on page 116)

(Box 4–3 continued from page 115)

ters its latent phase, in which the microorganisms spread throughout the body. Eventually, the infection may result in heart failure, blindness, insanity, and a host of other symptoms that may lead to death. Even at this late stage, however, antibiotics can cure the disease, though they cannot reverse damage already done.

Syphilis can spread from a mother to her unborn child. The blood tests that are required for a marriage license are designed, in part, to detect the disease.

Examination and Treatment of Venereal Disease

Every sexually active person should be aware of two facts about VD: (1) the only way to be sure that you do not have it is to have periodic examinations by a physician; and (2) if promptly detected and accurately diagnosed, VD can be easily cured by antibiotics. For a medical examination, contact your private physician or the local health department. If you are unable to locate the health department, call National Operation Venus, at this toll-free number: 1-800-523-1885 for information and advice.

The Prevention of Venereal Disease

Aside from abstinence, there are several ways of minimizing the likelihood of getting VD. One is to wash or douche immediately after intercourse. The germs that cause syphilis and gonorrhea are sensitive to soap and water. The use of prophylactics, also called condoms or rubbers, helps to prevent the spread of VD, especially gonorrhea.

Other Sexually Transmitted Diseases

Although gonorrhea and syphilis are the two best-known venereal diseases, there are others that a sexually active person should know about. Some of these are not, strictly speaking, venereal diseases, because they can also be transmitted by means other than intimate sexual contact.

A burning sensation during urination for a male can indicate the presence of *nonspecific urethritis* (NSU). This is not usually dangerous, but should be treated before you resume sexual activities.

Two types of inflammation of the vagina are common. One, called *moniliasis* (yeast) is a fungus that becomes infectious and causes vaginal discharges, itching, and discomfort. The same symptoms may indicate the presence of *trichomoniasis.* In case of either type of inflammation, both male and female sexual partners must be treated simultaneously (even though males may have no symptoms) to prevent reinfection.

Genital herpes is caused by a virus that may be spread through sexual intercourse. The disease causes sores or blisters on the genitals that are similar to cold sores or fever blisters. Though the blisters can be painful, and may reappear after a dormant period of several months, this virus is not as serious as gonorrhea or syphilis. However, it may be related to cancer of the cervix and may be transmitted to a baby at delivery. Thus, a pregnant woman with a history of herpes infection should notify her doctor so that precautions can be taken.

about premarital sexual standards and behavior over the past few decades have regarded abstinence as the norm and considered those who engaged in premarital sex as deviants who were violating an important code. There was good reason for them to take that attitude: traditionally, it has been exceedingly important for young women to preserve their virginity until marriage. In order to encourage women to do so, a great variety of procedures have existed, from chaperoning to restrictions on the freedom that unmarried women could enjoy. But in recent decades, support for the abstinence standard has eroded. Although the precise percentage of young people who indicate support for the abstinence standard varies somewhat from survey to survey, there are at least three conclusions that we can reach from such studies:

1. There is less support for the standard of premarital abstinence than there was in the past, particularly among young people.
2. As we would expect, teenagers more often say that virginity is important to them than their older, unmarried brothers and sisters do; college seniors are more likely than freshmen to say that it is unimportant to them that the person they marry be a virgin.
3. The most important point is that, whatever their age, both teenagers and college students who hold the abstinence standard support a position with which a majority of their peers disagree. Nationwide, only about one-quarter of all college males, for example, indicate that it is important that the woman they marry be a virgin (Gallup, 1978; Sorenson, 1973).

Attitudes toward premarital sex have shifted so much that those who maintain the abstinence standard today often experience considerable peer pressure to abandon what is commonly considered an old-fashioned belief. From the point of view of friends and classmates, a male college senior who adheres to the chastity standard is in a distinct minority. He has the problem of defending a standard that his peers may well regard as a "hang-up." Indeed, when sociologist Mirra Komarovsky (1976) interviewed male college seniors who were still virgins, she found that most of them were troubled by their lack of sexual experience. As a result of this failure to live up to the role expectations set by their peers, some withdrew from dating entirely. In general, Komarovsky concludes, the sexually inexperienced males who subscribed to the abstinence standard felt a lack of self-confidence and had a generally unfavorable self-image. Because young people and their parents so often disagree about premarital sex standards, it is quite common for people to feel caught by the cross-currents of parental expectations that are contrary to the attitudes of peers.

The Double Standard

The second of the four sexual standards distinguished by Reiss, the double standard, expresses an ancient belief in the inequality of men and women. By this standard males are allowed and even encouraged to be sexually active before marriage, while females are obliged to remain virgins until their wedding night. For many centuries our male ancestors have defined themselves as sexual creatures, whether married or not. Women were not supposed to enjoy sex, only to tolerate it—and were permitted to tolerate it only in marriage. Women who were not virgins at marriage were severely punished or killed. It was a tradition of New Testament times that a nonvirgin bride was stoned to death at the doorstep of her father's house (Udry, 1974, p. 105). At the same time, it was assumed then, as it is now, that men would enjoy sex before marriage. In the armed services condoms are routinely left near the sign-out desk for the protection of men and their sexual partners during an evening's entertainment.

Obviously, if all women really were chaste before marriage and faithful afterward, then men would have no one with whom to enjoy their greater freedom. In the past, this problem was solved by prostitutes. As Simone de Beauvoir comments, "A caste of 'shameless women' allows the 'honest woman' to be treated with the most chivalrous respect" (1952, p. 524). But the use of prostitutes is not nearly so common as it was a generation ago. In Kinsey's 1948 study, 22 percent of the college males had patronized a prostitute by age twenty-one; two decades later, only 4 percent of college males of the same age had done so (Packard, 1968, p. 163).

Instead, there was a new definition of the kind of women with whom it was permissible to have sex. Certain types of women—especially those from lower-income groups and ra-

The pure and the impure. There were only two kinds of women: the sexless innocent fit for a husband and children, and the seductress, sexually alive but dangerous.

cial minorities—were defined as bad girls and thus considered to be legitimate objects of sexual exploitation. The virginity standard was kept intact by maintaining the clearest of distinctions between bad girls and good girls. One was to be enjoyed and forgotten; the other was the type you married.

Is the double standard still practiced today? Reiss found that about one-quarter of the students he questioned accepted this standard. With people who follow the double standard, we would expect to find evidence of greater premarital sexual activity among males than females. And indeed, studies conducted until the mid-1960s showed that about 60 percent of college men engaged in intercourse before marriage (which is about the same percentage reported for several previous decades) while only about 20 percent of college women reported being sexually active before marriage (Ehrmann, 1959; Freedman, 1965; Kaats and Davis, 1970; Reiss, 1967). These studies provide clear evidence of the double standard. But, as we shall see when we look at the sex-with-affection standard, research conducted since the late 1960s indicates that college men and women are no longer so different in either their attitudes or their behaviors.

First Intercourse The first experience of intercourse has a different significance for the two sexes, thus providing a vivid illustration of the double standard. First intercourse is, of course, a great divide for both sexes. Individuals who engage in "everything but" consider themselves virgins because they have avoided intercourse. Many societies have made an unbroken hymen the definition of virginity, but in the last analysis any definition is arbitrary. It might make just as much sense to say that any person who has not experienced orgasm with a sexual partner is a virgin.

Many Scandinavians, for example, regard American women as more promiscuous than they are because "the American female defines 'sex' too much in terms of coitus and therefore pets intimately with many boys while remaining virginal" (Reiss, 1967, p. 46). Swedish women are more discriminating about petting than most American women, but are more likely to have intercourse with a partner for whom they feel affection.

In America males and females attach very different meanings to first intercourse. For her, the experience means passing the point of no return to the status of nonvirgin. For him, it is a proof of masculine prowess, a badge to be displayed among his friends. Listen to humorist Art Buchwald's description of his sexual initiation at age fifteen: "It wasn't that good, but I was the first one of my group who got laid so I was sort of a hero. . . . The accomplishment far surpassed the physical pleasure" (Fleming and Fleming, 1975). How many fifteen-year-old girls would eagerly return to their friends under the same circumstances expecting a heroine's welcome?

The way that college students talk about—or conceal—first intercourse illustrates the same point. Men, seeking approval for their sexual exploits from other men, are more likely to talk about the experience. This is especially true when the partners were not emotionally involved. One study of male–female differences in talking about the first sexual experience concluded that much of male sexuality might be characterized as ego sex. When it takes place in casual relationships with little emotional commitment, one of the main rewards for the young man comes from talking about this first sexual experience (Carns, 1973).

The woman's experience is different. If she admits to having sex with a man she does not particularly care for, she may be inviting a bad reputation. Males receive more approval than do females when they talk about their first sexual experience. These differences dissolve, however, when sex takes place between two people who are in love or plan to marry. Sociologist Donald Carns found that for males, the more involved the relationship, the *less* likely it is that friends would approve. For females, the situation is reversed: when there is more involvement, she is much *more* likely to receive approval. When in love or planning to marry, both sexes receive about the same amount of approval from their friends when they discuss first intercourse (1973).

The Transitional Double Standard According to what Ira Reiss calls the orthodox double standard, sex is a man's right but not a woman's, except in marriage. The transitional double standard, on the other hand, allows sexual freedom to women also, but only when they are in love or planning to marry. As with first intercourse, many college students still hold a double standard on sex between partners who are not emotionally involved. But when a woman is in love, sex is considered to be her right as much as it is his. This is a popular standard now among college students, though most adults do not accept it. What the transitional double standard means is that love is the crucial factor in the acceptance of intercourse for women. Women who have been in love at least once are much more likely to accept premarital sex than are women who have never been in love (Reiss, 1967, p. 87).

Though the double standard may have been a male invention, men are not the only ones to have perpetuated it. Researchers asked 400 students at the University of Colorado how they felt about three questions: Is virginity more important for the female? Would students advise their younger sisters more strongly than their brothers not to engage in intercourse before marriage? How did they think family and friends would feel about premarital sex? Their answers show that women, too, hold the double standard. Both male and female students agreed that virginity is more important for the woman. Many students of both sexes also said they would urge sisters more strongly than brothers to refrain from sexual relations before marriage, and responses to the third question followed the same pattern. The researchers concluded: "Not only did these students reject the notion of male–female equalitarianism themselves, but they felt that their close friends, family, and other social groups rejected it as well" (Kaats and Davis, 1970).

Apparently, however, one of the most significant changes taking place today is the rejection of the double standard. Studies conducted at various campuses across the country over the past few years have come to the conclusion that most college students reject the double standard (King, Balswick, and Robinson, 1977; Peplau, Rubin, and Hill, 1977). But as at least one study suggests, actual behavior does not completely correspond to reported attitudes (Ferrell, Tolone, and Walsh, 1977). It appears that although there has been a significant shift over the past few years toward a single premarital sex standard, a significantly larger proportion of males than females reports that they have engaged in full sexual relations. We can interpret this either as evidence of a continuing behavioral double standard that is at odds with the attitudes college students endorse, or as a reflection of the fact that females still feel more reluctant than males do to accurately report their sexual activity.

One reason for the declining popularity of the double standard is that some of the most common arguments for it have come under strong attack. When Reiss interviewed the males who held this position, he heard two common arguments for the double standard. The first is that because the woman can become pregnant and is more likely to be condemned for sexual activities, she has more reason to abstain. That women are more often condemned is true. A woman's sexual activities, as we have seen, are more likely to be disapproved of than are a man's. And women can and do get pregnant, although this is not an entirely convincing argument for refraining from sex. "From a strictly rational approach," comments Reiss, "woman's chance of becoming pregnant may merely mean that she should be more cautious" (1967, p. 173).

The second argument in favor of the double standard is that the female sex drive is much weaker than the male's, and so young women have less need for sexual activity before marriage. But this belief has been vigorously attacked in recent years, and not just in scientific journals. For example, Erica Jong's very popular novel *Fear of Flying* portrays a woman as the aggressor in a no-holds-barred sexual adventure.

The idea that differences in sexual behavior are mainly learned and not biologically determined has been supported by careful research (Ford and Beach, 1951). If sexual behavior is learned, then women need only as much encouragement in their sexuality as men get in order to demonstrate that theirs is not a lesser sex drive. In fact, research by William H. Masters and Virginia E. Johnson demonstrates that, in their orgasmic capability, women far outdo men. The behavior reported in *Human Sexual Response* (1966) is no standard for unmarried women because the females in that research were, with few exceptions, married. All had experienced orgasm during intercourse before the study began. But the fact that 28 percent of the women in that study were capable of multiple orgasms indicates that, though female sexuality is indeed different from male sexuality, there is little reason to believe that women have a weaker drive than men.

The double standard begins when boys and girls are taught very different attitudes toward sexuality: boys are encouraged to be sexual; girls very often are not. The phrase "bad boy" may mean many things, but the phrase "bad girl" generally has only one meaning: that she is a sexual delinquent (Simon and Gagnon, 1969, p. 14). Because of what we are taught,

> sex emerges as something which boys "do to" girls, which girls "let them have" or which boys cheat girls out of. Accounts of boys' early coital experiences with girls show that boys have been unconcerned with and largely unaware of the girls' own behavior. . . . It is sexual conquest. (Udry, 1974, p. 78)

This is a conquest for which young men receive approval from their male friends. Only when sex takes place during affectionate or committed relationships is it likely to have similar meanings for the two partners.

The Permissiveness-with-Affection Standard

The most important change in premarital sex attitudes among college students is the recent acceptance of a new, more liberal, single standard, which Reiss calls the sex-with-affection standard. Males are still permitted more liberty than females, but the difference is not as great as it was.

Behavior seems to have changed along with attitudes. Since the late 1960s, reports from colleges across the country indicate that a substantially higher percentage of young women than before are now having premarital sex. At the same time, there is no apparent increase in premarital sexual activity among college males. Thus, attitudes and behavior seem to be converging toward a single pattern.

Sexual relations are no longer reserved mainly for the engagement period. Coitus is now more likely to happen for the first time earlier in the relationship, when the couple is dating. This does not mean that "anything goes," but rather that a standard allowing sex for both males and females in affectionate re-

Today young, unmarried couples are allowed far more freedom from parental supervision than their parents or grandparents experienced.

lationships is now far more widely accepted.

In recent years, women's attitudes have moved more than men's toward an acceptance of premarital sex. In the past, men consistently endorsed more permissive standards for themselves than women did, and there are still some differences. However, they are not as wide as they were. In 1958 and 1968, sociologists Harold Christensen and Christina Gregg (1970) studied attitudes toward premarital sex at two colleges—one in the Midwest, the other in the Rocky Mountain region. They found that there was a substantial shift for both sexes during the decade toward greater acceptance of premarital sex. By 1968, 38 percent of the males in the predominantly Mormon college in the Rocky Mountain region approved of sex before marriage under some circumstances, and 55 percent of the midwestern males approved. During that decade, the attitudes of women had changed more than those of men. The same thing happened at other colleges. At one of them, the number of women who viewed premarital sex as immoral dropped from 70 percent in 1965 to 20 percent in 1975 (King, Balswick, and Robinson, 1977).

Of course, the values that people endorse do not necessarily describe their own behavior. Several writers have concluded that, although attitudes changed in the late 1960s, premarital sexual behavior did not (Simon and Gagnon, 1970). But the consensus among recent studies at several colleges across the country is that sexual activity among unmarried college women *has* substantially increased. Older studies found that about 20 percent of college females had intercourse; more recent ones suggest that the percentage reporting premarital sex has tripled to about 60 percent (Ferrell, Tolone, and Walsh, 1977; King, Balswick, and Robinson, 1977).

Research Ambiguities Considering the difficulties involved in getting accurate reports on sexual activities, it is not surprising that the percentages in various studies differ. In reporting what they actually do, people are undeniably influenced by what they think they *should do*. It may be that, because of cultural pressures, women understate their activities and men exaggerate theirs. To make matters worse, it is notoriously difficult to make valid generalizations about sex on campus because of regional and cultural variations.

What would happen if people were asked about their premarital sex experiences some years later, after they were married? Two studies that did this found much higher percentages of married women reporting premarital sex experience than the same age group had admitted *before* they were married. When 100,000 readers of *Redbook* magazine were asked, 80 percent of the women indicated that they had engaged in premarital sex, and almost half said the experience occurred before age eighteen (Levin and Levin, September 1975). And when the Playboy Foundation, using a smaller but more representative sample, asked the same question of married women in 1973, 81 percent of the females under twenty-five said they had experienced intercourse before marriage (in Hunt, 1973). These figures are twice as high as the figures reported by studies of premarital sex on campus in the late 1960s and early 1970s.

Perhaps the difference can be explained by the fact that the *Redbook* and Playboy Foundation studies included many women who had not gone to college. Or it may be that married women looking back on their experiences have less to lose by honest reporting than unmarried coeds do.

Despite the ambiguities surrounding the percentages, one trend in premarital sexual behavior is clearly evident: the difference between male and female behavior is no longer as wide as it was. The Playboy Foundation survey showed that a higher percentage of males than females had experienced sex before marriage in every age category, but among those age twenty-five or younger (when the study was conducted in the early 1970s), male–female differences were not nearly so wide as they were among the older people. The younger the women, the higher the percentage of reported intercourse. Much of this increase in premarital

Figure 4-1 Younger women report far more premarital sexual experience than older women. But the percentage of young men who had sex before marriage is *not* much higher than that for men several decades ago. The decline of the double standard is indicated by the smaller gap among younger people between the premarital sexual activity of men and women.

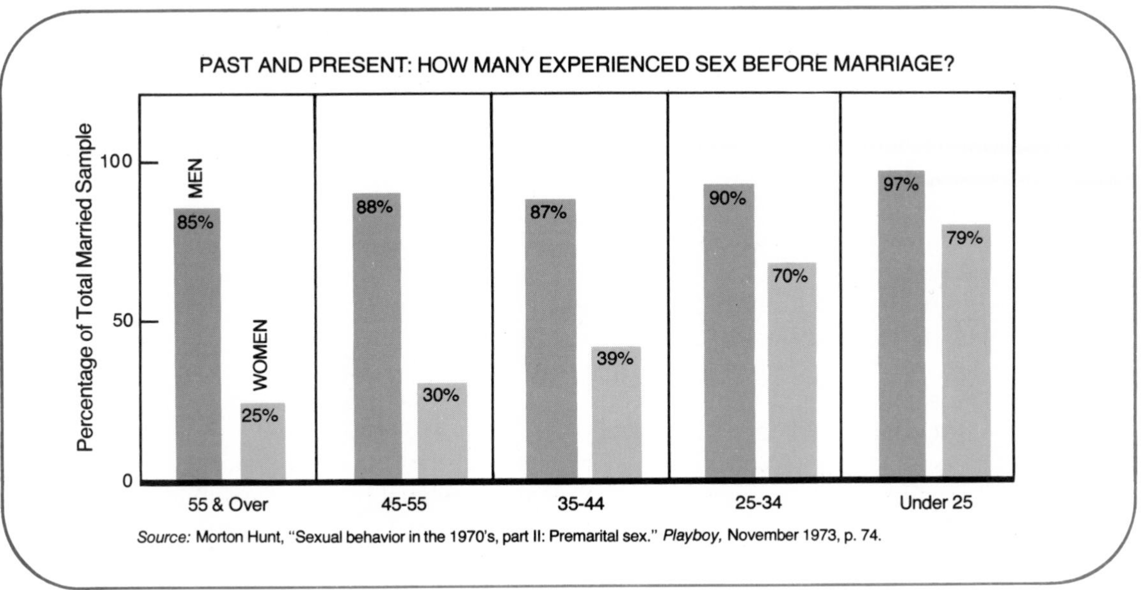

Source: Morton Hunt, "Sexual behavior in the 1970's, part II: Premarital sex." *Playboy*, November 1973, p. 74.

relations for women has taken place within the past ten years, as shown in Figure 4-1.

The Meanings of Premarital Sex Although men and women may be behaving more alike, the meanings they attach to premarital sex still differ in important ways. Writing in 1959, one prominent student of sexual behavior, Winston Ehrmann, expressed the basic male–female difference with respect to sex and love in these words: "Although both sexes are profoundly affected by these matters, females seem more directly and overtly concerned with romanticism and males with eroticism" (1959, p. 264). About ten years later, the Institute for Sex Research conducted a new study on premarital sex patterns (Brody, in Goode, 1971). When the report was released, the institute's director, Paul H. Gebhard, commented that one thing that had *not* changed much was "the enormous difference between how males and females view their initial partner. Females surrender their virginity to males they love whereas males are much less emotionally involved" (in Goode, 1971, p. 104). The study found that 50 to 60 percent of college females reported their first coitus had been with someone they loved and planned to marry. An additional 20 to 25 percent said they loved their partner though marriage was not anticipated.

Among college men, on the other hand, only about 11 to 14 percent said they loved and planned to marry their first sexual partner, and 25 to 30 percent said they felt some emotional attachment but did not love her. Gebhard noted some changes in the direction of greater emotional attachment on the part of males, but concluded that, in general, they still tend to be opportunistic about sex (in Goode, 1971). This difference may give rise to conflict in relationships because the woman will probably assume more emotional involvement than will her male sexual partner.

Sex Before Engagement Apparently, however, she will have less reason for assuming an emotional involvement than she did in former times, for sex is now beginning at an earlier stage in the relationship. In the 1930s, most young women who were not virgins said they had experienced sex only with their fiancés (Terman, 1938). As one writer comments, this might be cynically interpreted as "delivery of the goods upon commitment to purchase" (Hunt, 1959, p. 360). Engagement has changed since the 1930s, but the significance of love and commitment has not. The commitment of engagement is now less important as a justification for sex. Sexual relations more commonly take place at the dating or going-steady stage. In a study of a ten-year trend at one college, researchers concluded that

> the decision to have intercourse is much less dependent on the commitment of engagement and more a question of individual decision regarding the level of the relationship. To put it another way, if in 1958 the coed had premarital coitus, it most often occurred while she was engaged. But, in 1968, girls were more apt to have their first sexual experience while dating or going steady. (Bell and Chaskes, 1970, p. 83)

Permissiveness Without Affection

The last of Reiss' four standards (1967), permissiveness without affection, was epitomized by a *Playboy* cartoon showing a young couple sexually entangled in bed, as he asks her: "Why talk about love at a time like this?" Many people assume that the so-called sexual revolution ushered in an era of unlimited sexuality. A popular image of the college campus is that, in the absence of adult restrictions, sex has been reduced to a form of impersonal recreation in which it is regarded only as a "balling" or "scoring."

Reiss found that sex without affection, which might be referred to as recreational sex, was a standard held only by a small minority. As we might expect, he found more support for this standard among males than females, but even for young men it is definitely a minority position (1971, p. 159). There is little evidence that it has grown substantially in popularity during the past few years. Morton Hunt comments that "while many more single girls are having coitus, they do so with men they love and hope to marry—as did girls a generation or so ago" (1973, p. 74). Other studies have come to the same conclusion. One researcher found that only between 5 and 15 percent of college women find intercourse acceptable on the basis of physical attraction, momentary impulse, or curiosity without any particular affection (Davis, 1971). Other researchers have found that no more than 27 percent of college men and 6 percent of college women in their senior year approve of sexual relations with someone who is only a good friend or a casual date, though slightly larger percentages admitted they had engaged in one-night stands (Luckey and Nass, 1969).

This is hardly a situation of "complete freedom," to recall Betty Ford's words, or one in which "anything goes." For most people who subscribe to the sex-with-affection standard, it is agreed that sex is all right as long as the relationship is mutually rewarding, with a stress on commitment and sensitivity to the partner's needs. According to the Playboy Foundation study (Hunt, 1973), this position is now held by a large majority. Very few of the under-twenty-five singles in that study, which included both college and noncollege populations, had practiced the more unorthodox forms of recreational sex. "Only one male out of six and one female out of twenty have ever experienced such impersonal forms of sexual conduct as partner swapping and sex with more than one partner simultaneously, and most of these have done so only once" (Hunt, 1973, p. 74).

A scene from the movie, *Looking for Mr. Goodbar.* Contrary to the impression of casual or recreational sex so often conveyed by the media, recent studies suggest that relatively few college students subscribe to the permissiveness without affection standard.

What has changed most is the recent emphasis on integrating sex into the relationship, which is expressed well in these words by one young woman:

> For me, the determining factor in premarital intercourse is the quality of the relationship. The relationship is far more important than anything else, no matter what it is! You must have things in common, and it is hard to separate a good relationship and a sexual relationship. (in Hettlinger, 1974, p. 72)

NEW STANDARDS: CONFLICT AND CONFUSION

Young people are generally optimistic about the effects of the new sexual morality, but many older people are not. In 1974, the Roper Organization asked several thousand Americans how they felt about it and whether they believed the new sexual morality would weaken the institution of marriage. The responses, drawn from a representative nationwide sample of the eighteen-and-over population, show how much opposition and uncertainty there is over the new sexual standards. Nearly half the women polled, and only slightly fewer men, viewed sexual freedom before marriage as a change for the worse. Two out of three people believed it would weaken the institution of marriage, and about half thought that as a result, the country's morals would break down. But at the same time, about a third believed that couples would have more honest relationships with each other, which suggests that there may be a

Point of View

Box 4–4 / One Parent's Perspective on the New Sexuality

Betty Ford's casual acceptance of the idea of her teenaged daughter's prospective affair is a perfect example of how we divide what we know into what is true and what is permissible to say out loud. The shock waves she created were like courtesy nods in the direction of an era long past. But even though the President's wife was calm about it, the subject of adolescent sexuality is still a tender, raw spot on the bruised and bent soul of the older parent.

Masters and Johnson, the Pill, legal abortion, breakdown of parental authority, and the woman's movement have reduced the ideal of virginity, male and female, to the size of an appendix, a little organ without much of a future in the evolution of human anatomy. But large social currents aside, it's still a difficult thing when the young daughter who leaves rings around the bathtub, her shoes under the couch, and soup on her algebra homework, turns out to be less of an innocent than you (hiding your copy of *Fear of Flying* under a stack of *National Geographics*) had thought. If a casual inspection of that creature's underwear drawer reveals a container of pills, it's still (in 1975) something of a shock. Any parent who too easily smiles it off is bluffing.

It's always been all right, even desirable, for young males to begin their sexual life early. Most boys found their way to local bad girls or older women. The double standard fostered the myth that boys needed sex for their health and well being while nice girls took up horseback riding. What has changed for boys is the easy access there is now to all kinds of girls. And modern teen-age girls are talking about boys in terms of their value as sex-objects. Locker-room talk has definitely moved into the ladies' lounge.

In some ways, it must have been easier for boys when they could sneak off to the wrong side of the tracks. For females, the changes are massive. Their sexuality need not be kept hidden, used as a lure to keep gentlemen callers calling. They are not afraid of consequences, ruined reputations, or unwanted babies. For girls, the changing morality is filled with promise, but for parents it's still a very confusing problem, arousing conflicting emotions that few of us have dealt with honestly or well.

I have respectable, intelligent friends who know that their daughters at college are living with young men off-campus. They are pleased for their children, delighted that they are loved and loving. But when the young couple come home to visit, they insist that they sleep in separate rooms. The sham is not for the grandparents who live cities away or for younger siblings who have already visited the young couple in their apartment off-campus. The pretense is for the parents themselves whose joy in the new world of sexual mores exists in the abstract but not the particular. Illogical as this seems, it's all very understandable.

A large part of what I've learned as a parent is that we tend to feel opposing emotions at the same time. So, with the emerging sexuality of our children come some dread and some pleasure. After all, we are the generation that knows that one of the signs of good parenting is sexually unrepressed children.

conflict between the traditional morality and honesty in marriage. Many people tolerate the new standards and yet feel quite uncertain about what the effects of more sexual freedom will be. Fully 40 percent admitted to mixed feelings and seemed to be withholding judgment, adopting a wait-and-see attitude toward the new standards.

In this conflict over sexual standards, most of the battles take place between parents and chil-

We toilet trained them casually so as to civilize them with a velvet glove, not a hammer. We told them the truth about the facts of life so that they would be free of the inhibitions and distortions that we had discovered prevented sexual fulfillment. It's ironic but human that, when we get what we wanted, we're not so sure it's what we wanted.

A director of a preparatory school in Maine closed his eyes tightly when I asked him about the sexual activity on his campus. "I'm a Mr. Magoo on the subject," he said. "I prefer to stumble about and bang my head rather than see anything I don't know what to do about." Like most of us who are thirty-five or older, he is caught between the generations. He might even be somewhat jealous of the freedom his students feel but, at the same time, the more repressive voices of his childhood clang in his head, saying "It's not right. It's not right." If he asks himself why it's not right, he may retreat into confusion. "I don't know," he would say. "Do you?" And I don't know either.

Sexuality among teen-agers has created some surprising new problems. The new rules place demands for performance on girls or boys who may be shy or slow, or maturing at a different rate from their peers. Peer pressures and social image have always bedeviled teen-agers, but now the stakes seem higher than ever and "going all the way" is thought to be a sign of that much-desired adulthood. Many think they must act cool and easy about their bodies when the truth is they are still awkward, uncomfortable, and anxious. The new mores do create new problems. But nostalgia for the old ways is no more than nostalgia—they weren't very good either.

Sex is still a taboo subject between the generations. Certain barriers are drawn. Mothers and daughters pretend the other doesn't know anything about it. From the child's point of view, this privacy serves to help the striving for independence. From the parents', the advantages of noncommunication are numerous. Privacy maintains the status quo.

If one of my daughters did tell me that she had begun an affair, I hope I'd be able to ask her if she really wanted to do this, was responding to clues from her own body, not to pressure from her fellow or her friends. I hope I'd be able to tell her the six ways to delay the arrival of my grandchild and I'd hope and expect that she'd already know them. I think then I would tell her to count on the usual mixture of joy and pain that always comes with love. I hope she'd be brave enough, daring enough, to experience all the feelings of anxiety, mixed with pleasure, obsession, and jealousy, tenderness and anger that must accompany any relationship of meaning.

But please, I would ask her, don't forget your work, your mind, your other activities. Don't drown in this relationship. I'd want her to remember that *forever* is mostly for fairy tales. I would tell her that sexual excitements and satisfaction grow with experience and that she should not be disappointed if the beginnings don't meet her expectations. And then I think I might go into my own room, close the door, and weep for the child whose genitals I had once wiped and covered with powder.

Source: Anne Roiphe, excerpted from "Teen-age Affairs," *The New York Times Magazine,* October 5, 1975, pp. 22, 23, 88, 92. Reprinted by permission.

dren. No issue separates the two generations more than this one. (See Box 4–4.) College students are well aware of intergenerational differences, and avoid them by not discussing premarital sex with their parents (LoPiccolo, 1973).

Many parents feel they must defend the traditional ideal of chastity. They expect their children—particularly their daughters—to live by that standard, though they may not have done so themselves. Reiss has observed,

> One of our most prevalent myths is that in the past the typical form of courtship was that of two virgins meeting, falling in love, and doing very little with each other sexually. Then they married, learned about sex together in the marital bed, and remained faithful to each other until death separated them. (1972, p. 167)

Obviously sexual behavior will seem to have changed more than it actually has if you assume that most people conformed to the chastity standard in the past. But many women who married in the 1950s were not virgins at the time; one of the more surprising conclusions of the Kinsey studies was that about 50 percent of the women in that generation had had premarital intercourse (1953, p. 339). In another study, 30 percent of mothers questioned said they had had premarital sex, but only 3 percent were permissive for their daughters and 9 percent for their sons. The fathers took somewhat more liberal positions, but most still did not approve of activities that they themselves had engaged in: 51 percent said they had had premarital sex, but only 9 percent were permissive for their daughters and about 18 percent for their sons (Cannon and Long, 1971).

If many young people now accept premarital sex as a legitimate choice, is it reasonable to predict that in another generation—when the students who are now in college become parents—that there will be a new consensus that accepts the sex-with-affection standard? Not necessarily. How permissive people are seems to be more closely related to family responsibilities and roles than to their age. Reiss observed that childless couples are far less likely to insist upon the abstinence standard than are parents of the same age. When they take on role responsibilities as parents, people become concerned about pregnancy, venereal disease, and the possibility that their children might acquire a bad reputation—and their acceptance of permissive standards declines (Reiss, 1971, p. 169). Probably, therefore, many people who are now college students will take somewhat more traditional attitudes on premarital sex when they become parents.

Even if attitudes have changed more dramatically than sexual behavior in the last twenty years, imagine how the current courtship scene looks to people who met and married in the 1950s. Virginity was a matter of great importance then, even if many women were not virgins at marriage. Many men felt obliged to marry the would-be virgin they had seduced, and women were often pushed into marriage by guilt feelings about sexual involvement. People who courted in the 1950s are not often persuaded that love and affection justify premarital intercourse; from their perspective, a young woman who endorses the sex-with-affection standard is both immoral and foolish. As one observer puts it, she has

> parted too freely with the one thing she had to barter for a husband. Marriage was supposed to be her price and the "good girl" held out for it. . . . The older generation may feel that they can understand why the young are tempted, but not why they apparently feel so little guilt. Behavior that the young regard as guiltless their elders consider shameless. (Fullerton, 1972, pp. 93, 99)

To some extent, then, premarital sex will probably remain an issue between parents and children for a long while. "Over time, the values of parents and the adult community in general may become more liberal and the conflict between generations reduced," writes sociologist Robert Bell. But he sees no reason to believe that the tension between children and their parents on this issue will utterly dissolve:

> In the meantime, and certainly in the near future, it appears that parents and their children will continue to live with somewhat different value systems with regard to premarital sex. Parents will probably continue to hold to traditional values, and assume that *their* child is conforming to those values unless his actions force them to see otherwise. The youth generation will probably continue to develop its own modified value systems and keep those values to itself, and allow parents to believe that they are behaving according to the traditional values. For many parents and their

> children, the conflict about premarital sex will continue to be characterized by parents playing ostrich and burying their heads in the sand, and the youth's efforts to keep the sand from blowing away. (1966, p. 43)

Conclusions

Throughout this book we will see that on many subjects concerning marriage and family there used to be widely shared standards, but now the consensus has broken down. This is certainly true of premarital sex. Rather than taking one standard—premarital chastity—for granted, as most people did in the past, we now must choose among at least four conflicting standards. As Reiss explains, the most important development in the so-called sexual revolution is that premarital sex is now considered a legitimate choice by many young people (1971, p. 140). Sex before marriage, which has always been *practiced* by some people, has now become a respectable *standard,* at least among middle-class college students.

The older standards—abstinence and the double standard—were devised by parents. They made more sense in the male-dominated society of the past, when courtship was more closely supervised. The newer standards reflect a code invented by young people. These standards have evolved in response to new definitions of both sexuality and marriage.

Marriage is no longer the great watershed, with everything but sex allowed on the courtship side, and full sexual relations reserved for the other. We are moving out of an era, as Hunt expresses it, in which "the sexual drives of both partners were supposed to be completely and permanently satisfied within marriage even though there was no testing period beforehand" (1959, p. 342). The old assumption that sex is a man's pleasure and a woman's duty has broken down, and the double standard is gradually being replaced by a more liberal single standard of sex with affection. Sex is less often viewed as a form of currency in premarital bargaining. It has become a more positive element in premarital relationships.

But premarital sex still has a great potential for conflict, not simply between parents and children but between sexual partners as well. "There is a high probability that the man's partner has different values from his own," Udry observes, "and furthermore that he does not know what his partner's standards are" (1974, p. 130). This is a problem that people do not have to cope with in societies where there is more nearly a consensus on sexual norms. On the whole, men still take more permissive positions on premarital sex than women, making it quite possible for a man to make the mistake of assuming that with the decline of the double standard, a woman will probably want full sexual involvement as soon as he does, and under the same circumstances. Though attitudes and behaviors of the two sexes are becoming more similar, men and women still attach substantially different meanings to premarital sex. As we have seen, this difference is most evident in the experience of first intercourse, but even afterward, men and women often make very different assumptions about the importance of affection in sexual relationships, and about the connection between sex and personal commitment.

While a majority of middle-class adults are still debating the morality of premarital sex, many college students seem to have moved a step beyond. It is now commonly assumed that you should be allowed to "do your own thing." One recent study found that 96 percent of the males questioned and 94 percent of the females felt that sexual behavior is a person's own business (Robinson, King, and Balswick, 1972). This is a very different attitude from the moral indignation voiced by many of those who were offended by Betty Ford's permissive attitudes toward her daughter.

In the 1930s, after noticing how much sexual standards had changed in the previous decade, psychologist Lewis Terman predicted that by the 1950s premarital sex would be almost universal, at least among couples intending to marry (1938). Obviously, the chastity standard has proved to be far more durable than Terman thought. Perhaps in another generation it may be considered a curious historical relic, and textbooks will no longer include chapters, like this one, that explore the tensions among competing standards. Although there is far less support for the double standard than there was a decade or more ago, at least among college students, it is likely that the other standards we have examined will continue to have supporters for some time.

So how can we summarize the changes that have taken place with regard to premarital sex? The point of many discussions of the so-called "sexual revolution" seems to be to call our attention to unprecedented change in both attitudes and behavior. As we have seen, there have been some significant changes within the past few decades. Sexual initiation comes earlier than it used to, the double standard has eroded, and the percentage of college students who say that they have had premarital intercourse has increased. But it is inaccurate to conclude from such trends that the sexual scene today is one in which "anything goes." Although the percentage of college students who reject the abstinence standard has increased, it appears that sex is condoned mainly within the context of affectionate relationships. And although the percentage of girls who have experienced intercourse while still in high school has increased, it appears that the frequency of intercourse for such young women is quite low (Zelnik and Kantner, 1977, p. 60).

While acknowledging what has changed, it is also important to be aware of what has *not* changed. For example, the percentage of women who have had only one premarital lover, the man they intend to marry, has remained surprisingly stable. When Kinsey conducted his studies more than a generation ago, he found that just about one-half of the married women had confined their premarital activities to their fiancés; and several recent studies have come to exactly the same conclusion (Hunt, 1973; Tavris and Sadd, 1977, p. 48). And although the double standard has eroded, males and females still play very distinct sexual roles. Males are still the ones who initiate sex most of the time, while females exercise veto power—or indicate a preference for deferring sexual activity (Peplau, Rubin, and Hill, 1977). There is something else that remains the same: despite considerable encouragement from peers and the media to experiment with sex before marriage, early sexual experiences are still often fraught with anxieties about how and where to do it, and how to conceal it from disapproving parents. For while our society has not maintained the elaborate barriers to premarital sex that formerly existed, it does not grant much social approval to such activities either.

REFERENCES

Wendy H. Baldwin. *Adolescent pregnancy and childbearing—Growing concerns for Americans.* Washington, D.C.: Population Bulletin, 1977.

Robert R. Bell. Parent–child conflict in sexual values. *Journal of Social Issues* 22 (1966): 34–44.

——— and Jay Chaskes. Premarital sexual experience among coeds, 1958 and 1968. *Journal of Marriage and the Family* 32 (1970): 81–84.

Bennett Berger. The new stage of American man—Almost endless adolescence. *New York Times Magazine,* November 2, 1969, pp. 32–33, 131–136.

Kenneth L. Cannon and Richard Long. Premarital sexual behavior in the sixties. *Journal of Marriage and the Family* 33 (1971): 36–49.

Donald E. Carns. Talking about sex: Notes on first coitus and the double standard. *Journal of Marriage and the Family* 35 (1973): 677–688.

Harold T. Christensen and Christina F. Gregg. Changing sex norms in America and Scandinavia. *Journal of Marriage and the Family* 32 (1970): 616–627.

Commission on Obscenity and Pornography. *The report of the commission on obscenity and pornography.* Washington, D.C.: Government Printing Office, 1970.

Keith E. Davis. Sex on campus: Is there a revolution? *Medical Aspects of Human Sexuality* 5 (1971): 128–142.

Simone de Beauvoir. *The second sex.* New York: Bantam, 1952.

Winston Ehrmann. *Premarital dating behavior.* New York: Holt, Rinehart and Winston, 1959.

———. The variety and meaning of premarital heterosexual experience for the college student. *Journal of the National Association of Women's Deans and Counselors* 26 (1963): 22–28.

———. Marital and nonmarital sexual behavior. In Harold T. Christensen, ed. *Handbook of marriage and the family*. Chicago: Rand McNally, 1964.

Mary Z. Ferrell, William L. Tolone, and Robert H. Walsh. Maturational and societal changes in the sexual double standard: A panel analysis. *Journal of Marriage and the Family* 39 (1977): 225–271.

Madelon L. Finkel and David J. Finkel. Sexual and contraceptive knowledge, attitudes, and behavior of male adolescents. *Family Planning Perspectives* 7 (1975): 256–260.

Karl Fleming and Ann Taylor Fleming. *The first time*. New York: Simon & Schuster, 1975.

Clellan S. Ford and Frank A. Beach. *Patterns of sexual behavior*. New York: Harper, 1951.

Robert Francoeur. *Eve's new rib*. New York: Delta, 1972.

M. B. Freedman. The sexual behavior of American college women. *Merrill-Palmer Quarterly*. 11 (1965): 33–48.

Gail Putney Fullerton. *Survival in marriage*. New York: Holt, Rinehart and Winston, 1972.

Gallup Youth Survey. *Premarital sex is no sin according to most teens*. October 1978.

William J. Goode, ed. *The contemporary American family*. New York: Quadrangle, 1971.

Richard Hettlinger. *Sex isn't that simple: The new sexuality on campus*. New York: Seabury Press, 1974.

Morton Hunt. *The natural history of love*. New York: Knopf, 1959.

———. Sexual behavior in the 1970s, Part II: Premarital sex. *Playboy*, November 1973, pp. 74–75.

Erwin D. Jackson and Charles A. Potkay. Precollege influences on sexual experiences of coeds. *Journal of Sex Research* 9 (1973): 143–149.

Gilbert R. Kaats and Keith E. Davis. The dynamics of sexual behavior of college students. *Journal of Marriage and the Family* 32 (1970): 390–399.

Karl King, Jack O. Balswick, and Ira E. Robinson. The continuing premarital sexual revolution among college females. *Journal of Marriage and the Family* 39 (1977): 455–459.

Alfred C. Kinsey et al. *Sexual behavior in the human male*. Philadelphia: W. B. Saunders, 1948.

———. *Sexual behavior in the human female*. Philadelphia: W. B. Saunders, 1953.

Mirra Komarovsky. *Dilemmas of masculinity*. New York: W. W. Norton, 1976.

Robert J. Levin and Amy Levin. Sexual pleasure: The surprising preferences of 100,000 women. *Redbook*, September 1975, pp. 51–58.

Joseph LoPiccolo. Mothers and daughters, perceived and real differences in sexual values. *Journal of Sex Research* 9 (1973): 171–177.

Eleanor B. Luckey and Gilbert D. Nass. A comparison of sexual attitudes and behavior in an international sample. *Journal of Marriage and the Family* 31 (1969): 364–379.

William H. Masters and Virginia E. Johnson. *Human sexual response*. Boston: Little, Brown, 1966.

Henry May. *The end of American innocence*. New York: Knopf, 1959.

George P. Murdock. *Social structure*. New York: Macmillan, 1949.

National Center for Health Statistics. *Monthly Vital Statistics Report*, vol. 24, no. 11 (Supplement 2, February 13, 1976), Table 11.

Vance Packard. *The sexual wilderness*. New York: David McKay, 1968.

Letitia Anne Peplau, Zick Rubin, and Charles T. Hill. Sexual intimacy in dating relationships. *Journal of Social Issues* 33 (1977): 88–106.

Ira L. Reiss. *The social context of premarital sexual permissiveness*. New York: Holt, Rinehart and Winston, 1967.

———. *The family system in America*. New York: Holt, Rinehart and Winston, 1971.

———. Premarital sexuality: Past, present, and future. In Ira L. Reiss, ed. *Readings on the family system*. New York: Holt, Rinehart and Winston, 1972.

Ira L. Reiss, Albert Bannart, and Harry Foreman. Premarital contraceptive usage: A study and some theoretical explorations. *Journal of Marriage and Family* 37 (1975): 619–630.

Elizabeth J. Roberts, David K. Kline, and John H. Gagnon. *Family life and sexual learning*. 3 vols. Cambridge, Mass.: Population Education Inc., 1978.

Ira E. Robinson, Karl King, and Jack O. Balswick. The premarital sexual revolution among college females. *The Family Coordinator* 21 (1972): 189–194.

The Roper Organization. *The Virginia Slims American women's opinion poll*. New York: Roper, 1974.

William Simon and John Gagnon. Psychosexual development. *Trans-Action*, March 1969, pp. 9–17.

———. Prospects for change in American sexual patterns. *Medical Aspects of Sexuality* 4 (1970): 100–117.

Robert C. Sorenson. *Adolescent sexuality in contemporary America*. New York: World Publishing, 1973.

J. M. Tanner. The secular trend towards earlier physical maturation. *Tydshrift voor qeneeskunde* XLIV (1966): 527–535.

Carol Tavris and Susan Sadd. *The Redbook report on female sexuality*. New York: Delacorte, 1977.

Lewis Terman. *Psychological factors in marital happiness*. New York: McGraw-Hill, 1938.

J. Richard Udry. *The social context of marriage*. Philadelphia: Lippincott, 1974.

Arthur M. Vener and Cyrus S. Stewart. Adolescent sexual behavior in middle America revisited: 1970–1973. *Journal of Marriage and the Family* 36 (1974): 728–735.

Charles Winick. Sex and advertising. In Robert J. Glessing and William P. White, eds. *Mass media: The invisible environment.* Chicago: Science Research Associates, 1973.

Yankelovich, Skelly, and White, Inc. *Raising children in a changing society: The General Mills American family report.* Minneapolis, Minn.: General Mills, 1977.

Melvin Zelnik and John F. Kantner. Sexuality, contraception and pregnancy among young unwed females in the United States. In Charles F. Westoff and Robert Parke, eds. *Commission on Population Growth and the American Future—Research reports, Volume 1: Demographic and social aspects of population growth.* Washington, D.C.: Government Printing Office, 1972.

———. Sexual and contraceptive experience of young unmarried women in the United States, 1976 and 1971. *Family Planning Perspectives* 9 (1977): 55–71.

FOR FURTHER STUDY

Human Sexuality in Today's World, an anthology edited by John H. Gagnon (Boston: Little, Brown, 1977) includes a number of articles from the popular press about the topics explored here. For a recent and carefully researched account of the various standards mentioned in this chapter, see "Maturational and Societal Changes in the Sexual Double-Standard: A Panel Analysis," by Mary Z. Ferrell, William L. Tolone, and Robert H. Walsh (*Journal of Marriage and the Family,* May 1977). In his book, *Unplanned Pregnancy* (New York: Free Press, 1976), Frank Furstenberg presents a well-documented account of adolescent parenthood in American society.

Two recently completed projects provide some interesting perspectives on how children learn about sexuality. One of them, conducted by the Project on Human Sexual Development, includes an in-depth study of sexual learning among families in Cleveland, Ohio. Reports from this project include *Family Life and Sexual Learning* (1978), and *Human Sexuality: The Learning Contexts* (1980), which explores the significance of the media, peer groups, schools, and other agencies which contribute to sexual learning. Principal contributors to both volumes (which are available from the Project's office at 13 Appian Way, Cambridge, Mass.) are Elizabeth J. Roberts, David Kline, and John Gagnon. For a comprehensive analysis of sex education programs, see *An Analysis of U.S. Sex Education Programs and Evaluation Methods* (1979), a report by Douglass Kirby, Judith Alter, and Peter Scales, published by and available from the Department of HEW's Center for Disease Control in Atlanta. For a recent and comprehensive review of studies in this area, see Catherine Chilman's *Adolescent Sexuality in a Changing American Society* (1979), published by the Center for Population Research, National Institute of Child Health and Development, which is available from the Government Printing Office.

III
The Single Life

"Solitaire, 1974" Audrey Flack

5 Choosing the Single Life—In the Land of the Married

Have you ever played the card game called Old Maid? If you draw the old lady with the spectacles and the cat, you lose. Have you ever heard anyone repeat the superstition that whoever takes the last piece will be an old maid? Or heard someone say, "Three times a bridesmaid, never a bride"? Have you ever been told that unmarried people, no matter what their sex or age, are unreliable, unstable, not really mature?

We live in a society where marriage is the only fully recognized adult status. Nine out of ten people in our culture marry at least once. The decision to marry requires no explanation, but the decision to remain single does. "Beyond a certain age, depending upon where you live and what sex you are," as writer Kathryn Perutz comments,

> society becomes a vast matchmaker. Mothers hanker for grandchildren, or your happiness; gynecologists tell women their periods would be more regular if they settled down; married friends arrange dinners and outings; and, particularly if you're a woman, you begin to be regarded as a freak if you resist too long. (1973, p. 21)

But despite these pressures, one of the most remarkable changes in our traditionally marriage-oriented society is the recent popularity and rapid growth of a singles subculture. The signs of it are visible everywhere: apartment complexes "for singles only," vacation packages and resort facilities designed for the unmarried, bars and discotheques where singles go to meet other singles.

Statistics tell the same story. Recent reports from the U.S. Census Bureau show that there has been a striking increase in the number and proportion of adults living alone. In the period between 1970 and 1978, for example, their numbers increased by more than 50 percent. Though these households are all the same for census purposes, they include a large variety of lifestyles, individuals of different ages, and people who are living alone for very different reasons. The lives of most of the people included in this category do not correspond to the image that usually comes to mind when the word "single" is used—that is, a young, not-yet-married person. In fact, there are also many widowed, divorced, and elderly people in the same category. Of course, certain problems and freedoms are common to them all, but there are also obvious differences between those who choose to remain single and those who, because of death or divorce, have singleness thrust upon them. In this chapter we will be concerned with people who are single because they choose not to marry. Many relatively well-educated, affluent individuals belong to this group.

To marry or not to marry has become a realistic question in many people's lives. No longer is it a foregone conclusion that marriage, undertaken at a relatively early age, is the only way for most adults to live. One alternative is for a man and a woman to live together without a legally contracted marriage. These partnerships have been discussed in Chapter 3. Our subject here, individuals who have never been married and have no exclusive partners of the opposite sex, are in a sense pioneers in unexplored territory.

"Singles": the label itself, as in tennis, suggests something more vigorous, more fun than doubles. These are the people described in the media as "swinging singles," the subject of such popular novels as *Looking for Mr. Goodbar* (Rossner, 1975) and *Sheila Levine Is Dead and Living in New York* (Parent, 1972). Many mass media accounts of the single life reinforce a popular image that singles are people who spend their days lounging by the pools in singles-only apartment complexes, their nights dancing in discotheques. . . .

But this idyllic image of what singles do and how they live is not quite the same as their reality. Living alone in a society where the traditional locus of affection, intimacy, even human wholeness has been marriage poses some difficult problems.

How do singles really live? Why has remaining single become so much more popular? What are the problems and pleasures of the single life? Is it a temporary stage or a permanent status? We will examine some answers to all of these questions in the following pages, after we gain some historical perspective on marriage as a norm.

MARRIAGE AS PRIVILEGE AND OBLIGATION

Benjamin Franklin once referred to single men as "the odd half of a pair of scissors." His observation sums up this culture's traditional attitude toward the unmarried. Those who remain unmarried past a certain age are considered, at best, irresponsible and self-indulgent; at worst, slightly deviant, people no one wanted.

At the root of this assumption that there is "something wrong" with those who do not marry is the extraordinary emphasis that Americans place on marriage. As sociologist Ralph Turner notes, "Marriage is one of the key devices, along with becoming financially self-sufficient, for validating personal adequacy, heterosexual normality, and personal maturity" (1970, p. 50). Adults are defined as those who have "settled down" and chosen a mate.

Think of the popular stereotypes about the unmarried. What images come to mind when you hear the words "spinster" or "old maid"? Do you imagine a thin, dried-up, cranky old lady? She is a fixture of American popular culture, appearing as Miss Watson in *Huckleberry Finn* ("a tolerable slim old maid, with goggles on") and more recently as Aunt Sarah in the Walt Disney movie, *Lady and the Tramp*. Old bachelors receive somewhat kinder treatment, but even they are assumed to be hopelessly eccentric. Henry Higgins in *My Fair Lady* is a representative example: he is charming and lovable, but impossible to live with. Bachelors as well as spinsters have commonly been portrayed as individuals whose fussy preferences lead them to avoid the inevitable complications of day-to-day involvements. Popular images of the unmarried in this culture have been, with very few exceptions, negative.

It was during the 1950s that most of the parents of the present generation of college students married and began to raise their children. You might be better able to understand why those parents are often so eager for their own children to marry and have families if you recall how strong the marriage orientation was then.

There are still, of course, strong pressures toward marriage. Although the number of singles is growing, individuals who do not marry are still a nonconforming minority. The pressure to marry can be blatant, the kind described in *Sheila Levine Is Dead and Living in New York* when the heroine goes to her sister's wedding:

> Sheila, dear, you look wonderful. When are you going to get married? Thank you for coming. . . . You look wonderful. Pretty enough to be a bride yourself. . . . We can't wait to dance at your wedding. (Parent, 1972, p. 135)

Or it can be more subtle, the "nonspecific pressure, a sort of wonderment that at thirty-five I can still be alone," which one single man describes (Stein, 1975, p. 496). The message behind those pressures, however, is the same: young people have a duty to get married. In this culture, marriage has been regarded as an obligation.

So thoroughly are we indoctrinated by the values of a marriage-oriented society that it may be surprising to learn that marriage in Western culture has not always been a universal norm.

In Europe in the Middle Ages, for example, only individuals who had earned economic security could hope to marry, and since land and shops were scarce, gaining economic security was difficult. "Marriage was, in brief, a kind of privilege, a prerogative, a gift bestowed by the community," writes Jessie Bernard. "One had to wait until there was a house or cottage on the commons. A place had to be vacant, land for the luckier ones, or a bakery, a joinery, a loom, or some other productive property" (1973, p. 123). Journeymen and apprentices were not allowed to marry, and the younger sons of the landed aristocracy typically joined the military or the church, which demanded celibacy. Marriage, instead of being a right for almost everyone, as it is in contemporary America, was a privilege granted only to a minority. It has been estimated that as many as two-thirds of the adult women in medieval Europe lived outside of marriage (Noonan, in Bernard, 1973, p. 122).

Medieval society was rich in opportunities for unmarried women. Upper-class women could join convents. Women dominated several craft guilds, most notably the brewers and spinners. This was, in fact, the origin of the word "spinster," which had no negative connotations until the eighteenth century, when the growing textile industry removed spinning and weaving from the home to the factory, turning unmarried women who remained at home from economic assets into liabilities (Lasch, 1973; Watt, 1967). More remarkable even than the economic limitations on marriage was the generally low estimate of it in medieval culture. The church regarded celibacy as holier than marriage. It was not until much later that marriage came to be regarded as a model of the good life.

What demographers refer to as "the European marriage pattern" continues to some extent even today. The pattern is characterized both by late marriage and by no marriage at all for a large percentage of the population. In the early 1960s, for example, the mean age at marriage was about two years older in most European countries than in the United States (Dixon, 1971, p. 218). In France, 28 percent of the women between the ages of twenty-five and thirty-four did not marry. In Ireland, one of the poorest European nations, the comparable figure in the 1960s was a startling 45 percent (Sanders, 1963, p. 83). The high percentage of single women in Ireland indicates that economic factors are still an important influence on the marriage pattern.

The American Pattern: Couples Only

From colonial times, American marriage patterns have differed from the European model.

Economic conditions, far from compelling young people to remain single, encouraged them to marry, for land was limitless and large families were needed to settle the new country. Nor was there any religious tradition of celibacy; the Puritans, in fact, placed an especially high value on marriage and family. In many New England towns, bachelors had to pay extra taxes, on the theory that "sin and iniquity . . . ordinarily are the companions and consequences of the solitary life" (Morgan, 1966, p. 133).

The pressures to marry remained strong even after Puritanism declined. Economic opportunity, social pressure, and the hardships of life on the frontier all contributed to a pattern of early and nearly universal marriage in America. In several respects, this is the reverse of the European marriage pattern. As Jessie Bernard summarizes the American trend through the 1950s,

> Marriage in the twentieth century was no longer dependent on a competence, on property, nor even on maturity. One did not have to wait until one could set up an establishment or manage a large household. Marriage was no longer a class privilege. And the trend in the United States since 1890 has been, until the late 1950s, for marriage at an ever earlier age and for a larger proportion of persons. In fact, the most important characteristic of the American pattern has been the freedom to marry which it encompassed. (1972, pp. 112–113)

The more a culture idealizes marriage, and the higher the percentage of people who actually get married, the greater the pressure on everyone to conform. "It is a rare person," writes sociologist David Riesman, "who does not internalize this [pressure] and become defensive about it" (1964, p. 722).

Since the mid-1960s, the percentage of people who remain unmarried has increased dramatically, but the stereotypes are still alive and well, coexisting somehow with the newer image of swinging singles. In 1975, an ad for the film *Sheila Levine Is Dead and Living in New York* appealed to the fear of becoming an old maid just as directly as the card game used to. The picture showed a woman looking homely, sad, and overburdened. The caption read: "Sheila Levine is every single girl who ever had to attend her younger sister's wedding."

In America, the Talmudic dictum that "whosoever remains unmarried does not deserve to be called a man" has been particularly forceful. During the past decade, however, that assumption has begun to erode.

THE RISE OF THE SINGLES

Recent census reports provide striking evidence of the rise of the singles and allow us to answer several questions: Are Americans now deferring marriage until a later age? How large is the population of young adults who have not married, and how rapidly is it growing? Statistics compiled since 1960 show a sharp reversal of a long-term trend toward ever-younger marriage.

Between 1900 and 1960, the tendency in this country was toward earlier marriages. In 1900, the median age of males at marriage was 25; for females the age was 21. By 1960, the median age of males at marriage was 22.8; for females, 20.3. Since then, the trend has reversed. Young women now postpone marriage longer than did their mothers in the late 1940s and 1950s. Between 1960 and 1977, the median age at first marriage for women increased by a year, from 20.3 to 21.3. The corresponding increase for men during that same period was more than a year, from 22.8 in 1960 to 24.0 in 1977. (Incidentally, there are still substantial regional differences in age at first marriage. In the Northeast, where people typically marry somewhat later than elsewhere, men marry on the average almost two years later than do their counterparts in the South, where early marriages are most prevalent. And women in the Northeast marry about a year and a half later than do women in the South [U.S. Bureau of the Census, March 1977].)

If this tendency toward somewhat later marriage appears to represent no more than a modest change, look at the percentage of people

Figure 5-1 Percentages of young people who have never married: 1960–1978 (by age and sex).

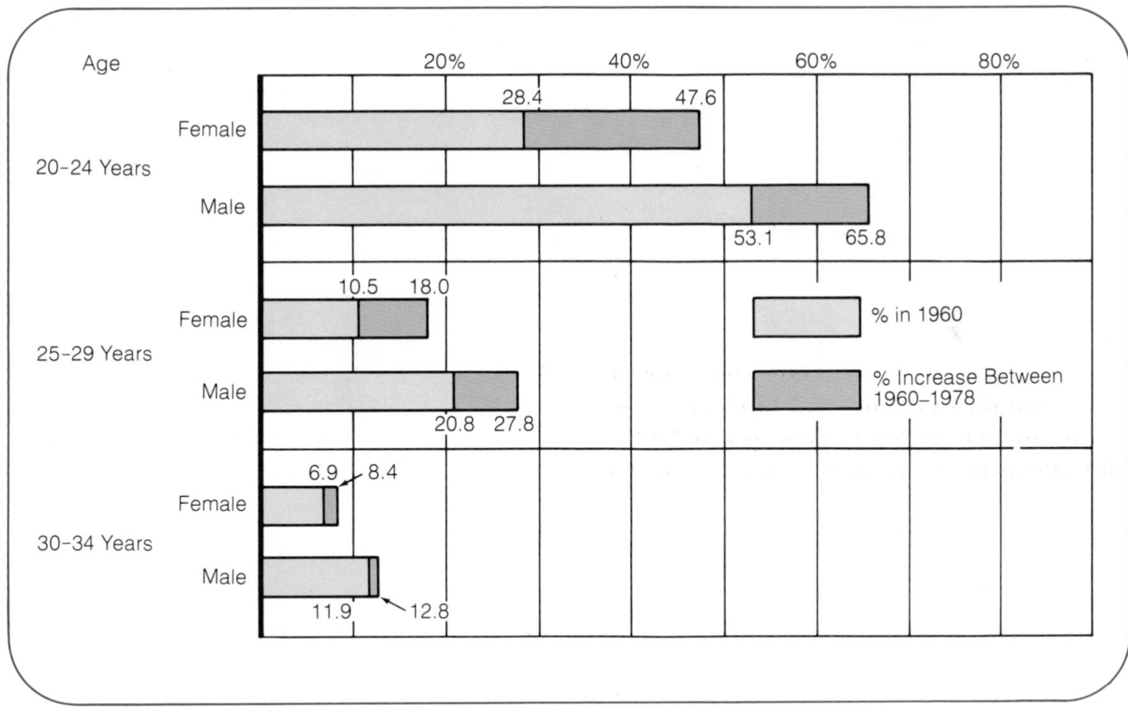

Source for 1960 statistics: U.S. Bureau of the Census: Marital Status & Living Arrangements, March 1977.
Source for 1978 Table 'A' statistics: Bureau of Census: Households & Families By Type, March 1978, Table 4.

who now remain single well into their twenties (see Figure 5-1). Between 1960 and 1978, there was about a 20 percent increase in the percentage of young women between twenty and twenty-four who had not married, and more than a 10 percent increase in the percentage of never-married males in the same age category. In 1978, there were more than 37 million American adults in their twenties who had not married. Since 1970, the size of that group has increased by about 8 million people—which is roughly the size of New York City's population.

The percentage of black adults in their twenties and thirties who do not marry is substantially higher than that of whites. For the age category 25–29, for example, the percentage of black men who have never married, 35.6, is about one-third higher than the percentage of never-married whites; among black women of that same age category, 31.2 percent have never married, which is more than twice the percentage of never-married whites. Among black adults in their thirties, both male and female, the percentage who have not married is about twice as high as the corresponding figures for whites (U.S. Bureau of the Census, March 1976).

The group of more than 40 million young adults who are single has become increasingly visible, especially in the large cities, where they tend to be concentrated. In New York, Washington, Chicago, and Los Angeles the signs of their presence are everywhere. Like other minorities, young singles are not simply growing in numbers. Their public image is changing as well. The "lonely loser" stereotype has partially given way to a new recognition of singleness as a valid lifestyle. Indeed, the recent use of the label "single" reflects changing perceptions. Those who had not married used to be cate-

As the single population grows, so does the number of establishments and services that cater to the unmarried.

gorized with overtly value-laden words like "bachelor" and "spinster." Then during the sixties they were more commonly referred to as a residual category, the "unmarrieds." Like the term "nonwhite," this said more about what they *weren't* than what they *were* and reflected the normative expectation of marriage. Only recently, as the unmarried status has become more widely accepted, has this group been labeled, simply, the "singles."

Changing perceptions of the single status are also evident in the results of recent social surveys. In a 1976 study conducted by the University of Michigan's Survey Research Center, a nation-wide sample of about 2,000 adults was asked this question: "Suppose all you knew about a man/woman was that he/she didn't want to get married. What would you guess he/she was like?" When that question was asked in an identical survey conducted in 1957, four-fifths of the respondents said they thought such a choice was bad: the individual was regarded as sick or immoral; too selfish or too neurotic to marry. Only about one-fifth of the respondents gave neutral answers. The extent to which social norms about marriage have changed in the generation since then is indicated by the very different responses to the same question in 1976, when only one-fourth of the respondents thought the choice of the single life was bad, while two-thirds were neutral and the remaining 14 percent regarded the choice as a positive one. (Veroff, Douvan, and Kulka, 1979.)

Reasons for Choosing the Single Life

It is easier to study what people do than why they do it. The motivations to remain single are complex, and often obscure even to those who make this choice. People who do not marry, as well as people who do, are influenced by cultural pressures even if they are not consciously aware of them. The generation that married in the 1950s, for example, was probably not aware of the strong cultural pressures urging them to marry. A 1950s bride, if asked why she was getting married, would have responded, "Because I love my fiancé," not "I have been seeing idealized images of marriage in magazines and movies as long as I can remember." And yet both factors contributed to the decision.

Since the 1950s, the pendulum has been swinging the other way. Many influences—popular articles and books on the hazards of marriage, feminists' arguments about marriage as a suffocating environment, idealized portraits of the single life—contribute to the current skepticism about marriage.

One of the basic questions to ask about remaining single is: Are most people who are still unmarried in the middle or late twenties single by choice or chance? As two investigators (Carter and Glick, 1970) suggest, a demographic factor which they refer to as the marriage squeeze might have forced many women to remain unmarried against their inclinations. Twenty years after the post-World War II baby boom, which crested from 1947 to 1953, the women born during that period found a scarcity of eligible men because they would typically marry men two or three years older, and there were not enough to go around. For women born during that period, the "marriage squeeze" was a factor that complicated the task of finding an appropriate mate. But the women who entered their twenties in the late 1970s were in a different situation. Because of declining birth rates in the late 1950s, there was a smaller number of females born then compared to the number of males a year or two older. As a consequence, the women who were born during that period have somewhat less reason for concern about finding an appropriate mate because there are more men of the "right" age available.

To discuss such demographic fluctuations is to raise another question about increasing numbers of unmarried adults. Have many people remained unmarried simply because they cannot find an appropriate mate? There is no way to answer the question with any certainty. Few people are as candid as one woman who, when asked by an interviewer for a New York City television special on singles what she was doing in a singles bar, said, "I'm looking for a husband here. I came here to find an eligible man to marry." The number and variety of clubs, bars, apartment complexes, and dating services that provide ways for singles to meet other singles suggest that many do want to get married and are actively seeking partners.

Other evidence suggests, however, that singleness is becoming, for many, an increasingly attractive alternative to marriage, rather than a state to be tolerated. The increasing appeal of the single life is demonstrated by a study of one college where 40 percent of the women in their senior year said they did not know whether they would marry. Moreover, 39 percent thought "traditional marriage is becoming obsolete," and 25 percent agreed that "the traditional family structure of mother, father, and children living under one roof no longer works" (Stein, 1975, p. 3). These answers suggest that for many young people remaining single is a positive choice, not a "failure" to get married.

Why are so many people choosing to remain single today? Perhaps another question should be asked at the same time: Why are many young people wary of entering into traditional marriage? In recent years, two general factors have contributed to the growing appeal of the single life. The first—a shift in values—made the single life increasingly desirable. The second—a growing number of practical alternatives, for example, greater opportunities for women—made it increasingly possible.

It is difficult to chart value changes with any precision, but popular images of marriage and family life are clearly different now from what they were a generation ago. In the 1950s, the nuclear family, complete with children and two cars in the garage of a suburban house, was a widely recognized symbol of the good life. As feminist Caroline Bird argues, it may have been the idealization of marriage in the fifties that contributed to its decline afterward. Since, in her words, "everyone was led to expect a marriage that was a great personal achievement, like the celebrated love affairs of history," some disappointment was almost inevitable (1972, p. 35). Today's young adults, the products of those marriages of the 1950s, may be staying single because they were very much aware of the gap between what was promised and the reality of their parents' marriages. There is some support for this conclusion in the finding that single men report more stressful childhoods than any other group in the population. More than half of the single men in one study viewed their parents' marriages as unhappy (Knupfer, Clark, and Room, 1966, p. 846).

The growing support for zero population growth which has been sparked by the environmental movement, the energy crisis, and fears of a world food shortage may be another reason for the decline in familism. Having a large family is no longer considered desirable by most people.

One factor that quite certainly has contributed to the decline in familism is the women's movement, itself a response to economic changes. As early as 1963, Betty Friedan's *The Feminine Mystique* stated what would become one of the movement's strongest themes: Being a wife and mother, Friedan said, was not a sufficient career for most women. Subsequently, one of the feminists' main targets has been traditional marriage, in which the man is the wage-earner and the woman a housekeeper and mother. Women, many feminists contend, must prove themselves through careers outside the home, just as men do. More extreme feminists see traditional marriage as a legalized form of prostitution, in which the woman exchanges her services as a housekeeper and sexual partner for economic support. As Caroline Bird explains the declining popularity of marriage, "Men no longer had to marry to get sex. Women no longer had to marry to get financial or even social support. . . . The old deal of sex-for-support has long been a dead letter" (1972, pp. 36, 39).

This is an extreme view of marriage as a sordid bargain, a trade of sex for support. But in a more moderate mood, the feminist movement has encouraged many women to remain unmarried and pursue careers. It may also have made some women who stayed home to raise families feel slightly guilty, wondering whether they might have "fulfilled themselves" more completely in other ways.

In addition to the women's movement, there is another more subtle change in values that is contributing to the decline in marriage rates. Since the 1960s, personal growth, freedom, and fulfillment—human liberation, if you like—have been increasingly seen as ends in themselves. Value judgments have become more subjective, less a function of external or absolute standards, whether determined by religious or social norms. The sex-with-affection standard discussed in the preceding chapter is an example of such a shift in values. Young people now tend to judge sexual relationships as good or bad not by whether they are legal but by how the partners feel about each other. Similarly, people are now less likely to require the public validation of a legally constituted marriage before they enter into sexual relationships.

Some widely influential psychologists such as Carl Rogers reflect and in turn contribute to this change in values. Rogers, a well-respected psychotherapist, does not measure his patients' health by their freedom from anxiety or adjustment to society. Instead he uses such standards as openness to experience, *not* measuring oneself by external social standards or the opinion of others, and—perhaps most important—the "willingness to be a process." He argues that *any* external or fixed self-image, any statement like "I am such-and-such a kind of person and I tend to act in such-and-such a way" limits people and keeps them from acting on their feelings from moment to moment. For him, a person is "a fluid process, not a fixed or static entity; a flowing river of change, not a block of solid material" (Rogers, 1961, pp. 115, 122).

The acceptance of change and growth as values is an important reason for the choice of the single life as well as the increasing divorce rate. Excerpts from some of the single people interviewed by sociologist Peter Stein illustrate the point. Here are the words of one young man explaining his divorce: "It's simplistic to think that one person is always going to fill all my needs and that I'm not going to change and she's not going to change." Another explained his reasons for not getting married: "I want freedom of choice, freedom to do what I want instead of being tied to living with just one person and doing the same, mutually satisfying things over and over." Stein came to the conclusion that the most important motivation in the decision to remain single is the belief that marriage is "a restriction and obstacle to human growth" (1975, pp. 10–11).

Several value changes, then, contribute to the decline in marriage. First is the tendency to measure relationships not by fixed, external standards but by subjective and emotional criteria. Second is the tendency to value growth and change over stability and any long-term commitment.

A third change in values encouraging the popularity of the single life is that Americans expect more from marriage and life in general than they used to do. One sign of these rising expectations is the number of self-help books that reach the best-seller list. In the 1970s the crop has included such titles as *How to Be Your Own Best Friend* (1973), *The Joy of Sex* (1972), *The Sensuous Woman* (1970), and *The TM Book* (1975). The outpouring of manuals that teach you how to achieve sexual fulfillment, how to learn to like yourself, how to say no without feeling guilty, even how to have a transcendental experience, suggests that Americans are reaching for personal fulfillment in new and complex ways.

Paradoxically, this quest for fulfillment and personal expression can undermine marriage by leading people to expect too much from it. If people refuse to accept the compromises of a less-than-perfect marriage because of heightened expectations, two things result: a high divorce rate and a high percentage of people who choose not to marry in the first place. Because of their high expectations about marriage, many young people may hesitate before making the commitment. Perhaps, too, the fact that marriage is no longer the economic necessity that it once was allows room for heightened demands that it be emotionally fulfilling. As one young woman said, "Girls really count on marriage as being a deeper experience than they did when they were also counting on it to provide everything else—like shelter, status, and their place in the community" (Roberts, 1971, p. 56).

A number of the singles interviewed by Peter Stein mentioned the desire for a variety of relationships, the freedom to turn to different people to meet different needs. This, too, is an important motivation to remain single. Caroline Bird sums up the argument that men and women can find greater fulfillment outside of marriage than they can in an exclusive relationship with one person:

> Wives can no longer do as good a job of catering, cooking, baking, butchering, nursing, teaching, sewing, child-training or decorating as the specialists their husband's money can buy. Nor can a wife expect to be as good a dancer, hostess, sounding board, business adviser, sexual partner, or showpiece as some women he can find to specialize in one of these feminine roles. So women who are modestly affluent through their own nonbedroom efforts are finding that one man is not necessarily the best partner for chess, sex, camping, party-giving, investing, talking, plumbing, vactioning, gallery-going, and all the other activities which the city offers. *No husband or wife can supply the full satisfaction a single person may derive from a love affair, a sex affair, a job, friends, a psychiatrist, or even, at the end, a top-flight trained nurse.* (1972, p. 39)

Managing Without Marriage The shift of important social functions from the family to outside institutions has been in progress for more than a century. With the rise of factories and

New York, New York

One result of women's economic independence is increased social independence.

the movement of people from farms to cities, the family ceased to be an important productive unit. It is now quite rare for most of a family's food or clothing to be produced in the home. Other functions have been stripped away from the family as well: education is left to the schools; caring for the aged, the sick, and the retarded is left to nursing homes, hospitals, and asylums. Such basic services as cooking, cleaning, and laundry can be bought. By the 1950s it had become a commonplace to say that the only services provided by the nuclear family were the emotional support of its members and the nurturance of small children.

If men no longer need wives to keep their houses, neither do women need husbands to support them as they once did. True, working women still make less than their male counterparts, but the rise of feminism has coincided with growing economic opportunities for women.

As job opportunities for women have become more numerous, women have been offered a wider variety of living accommodations, too. Not long ago, unmarried women were expected to remain in their parents' houses until they married. The only other accommodations for unmarried women were hotels or residences for women only. Although a surprising 43 percent of the single women between twenty-five and twenty-nine were still living with relatives in 1974 (an even more surprising 51 percent of single males of the same age also live with relatives), there are now thousands of studio apartments designed for one person in most urban areas (U.S. Bureau of the Census, 1974).

Singles tend to move to large cities, with the wide range of jobs, services, social contacts, and housing offered there. Cities offer anonymity as well, the freedom to pursue a sexual life outside of marriage without the pressure of traditional standards and gossiping neighbors. In fact, greater acceptance of sex outside of marriage is another reason for the growing popularity of the single life. No one has summed up the traditional argument for marriage as concisely as did St. Paul, who said: "It is better to marry than to burn." When sex outside of marriage was frowned upon, many people married to enjoy sexual fulfillment in a socially respectable way. Now, with more permissive sexual standards, young people need not marry to have sexual relationships. As the manager of one singles-only apartment complex put it. "Sex and love are so free now that you don't need marriage for that part of life. They have everything they want outside of marriage except kids" (Roberts, 1971, p. 56).

The more people choose to remain single, the more convenient a single lifestyle becomes. With so many singles to cater to, new products and facilities are rapidly being designed for this market. And as they advertise their products, businessmen sell the single lifestyle as well. Perhaps the most influential mass media messages in this respect are ones that portray idealized images of masculinity and femininity, images that underscore the allure of the single life. Think, for example, of how masculinity is portrayed in most advertisements. It is relatively rare for men to be shown caring for children, or attending to such ordinary concerns as mortgage payments or dental bills.

Singles as a Newly Discovered Minority

> Like any newly discovered minority singles tend to be viewed by the majority in misleading, monolithic terms. Stereotypes about the unmarried frequently seem as ludicrous as the image of a black population with a universal sense of rhythm and a love for watermelon. (Jacoby, 1974, p. 37)

Neither the old stereotype picturing a lonely, rejected misfit nor the new one which conjures up sexually liberated, fun-loving singles have, in fact, much to do with how most singles live. As one single man complained,

> Five years ago, I was used to hearing sorrowful comments about my "loneliness." Now I get lecherous envy. From reading the press, you'd think every girl is 36–24–36, like the blonde on the cover of *Newsweek*, and every guy lounges by a poolside and waits for the beautiful blondes to admire his rippling muscles. The truth just isn't very glamorous—some single people are happy and some aren't, just like married people. (in Jacoby, 1974, p. 37)

The novel *Sheila Levine Is Dead and Living in New York* humorously describes a single girl's bewilderment upon first encountering the city. After two weeks of job-hunting and apartment-searching, Sheila concludes that "All pathological liars go right from mental institutions into making up classified ads" (Parent, 1972, p. 33). One of the themes of this novel is the discrepancy between the glamorous images of the single life and the life Sheila actually lives.

Like stereotypes about any minority, those about singles imply a certain stigma. Because most adults in this society marry, the minority who do not are viewed with mistrust; they are believed to be immature, incomplete, unstable. The result of this prejudice is discrimination. *Single*, a new magazine, surveyed fifty major corporations to find out whether they discriminated against the unmarried.

> Although 80 percent of the responding companies asserted that marriage was not essential to upward mobility, a majority indicated that only 2 percent of their executives—including junior management personnel—were single. More than 60 percent of the respondents said that single executives tend to make snap judgments, and 25 percent believed singles are generally "less stable" than their married counterparts. (Jacoby, 1974, p. 42)

Are They Really Different? Most employers routinely ask whether job applicants are married or single. You may wonder why they ask, and whether they have any right to. Do employers automatically regard single applicants as questionable? Or do they, as journalist Susan Jacoby suggests, discriminate against *single* men and *married* women? Employers might feel that married men with families to support are less likely to quit than single men who are responsible for no one but themselves. They might also feel that married women work only to earn "pin money" and are likely to leave if they have a child or their husbands are transferred.

There may be a grain of truth in these prejudices. A significantly smaller percentage of single men than married men are employed. Conversely, a higher percentage of single women than married women work, although the gap is closing (U.S. Bureau of the Census, 1960, Table 196; 1970, Table 216). Singles often name freedom, the chance to change and grow in new directions, as the most significant advantage of their way of life. As a thirty-six-year-old lawyer said, when he was planning to leave his practice to move to Europe and begin a writing career, "If I were married, I doubt that I would be able to break away and do this 'crazy' thing. Some of my friends have children who are only a few years away from college. How could I throw over a career in that situation?" (Jacoby, 1974, p. 38). To an employer, such an individual might well pose a greater risk than a man with a wife, two children, and a twenty-year mortgage.

Beneath the prejudices, some fundamental questions remain. Are single people different from those who marry? Is there any truth to the belief that singles are unstable? This image is widely accepted not only by corporate executives but also by bankers, who have found them to be worse credit risks, and insurance companies, who have found that they die younger.

As sociologists Peter Berger and Hansfried Kellner (1964) argue, if we remember that "reality" is socially constructed and maintained, it may be reasonable to conclude that married people are indeed more stable emotionally, more sure of themselves, even more mature. Our self-definitions are to a considerable extent a product of others' responses to us. Those responses emerge from ongoing conversations with certain significant others in which the meaning of day-to-day events, as well as our own actions, is discussed and agreed on. What we experience becomes significant mainly as we talk about its meaning with others. Thus much of the so-called small talk between married partners about daily events has a crucial importance: through ongoing conversation, "world and self take on a firmer, more reliable character for both partners" (1964, p. 5).

This task of carrying on our reality-sustaining conversations in the private sphere becomes even more important in contemporary society where, as Berger and Kellner write, "public institutions confront the individual as an immensely powerful and alien world, incomprehensible in its inner workings, anonymous in its human character." If we are all dependent upon close and continuing relationships in order to carry on these reality-sustaining conversations, then single persons who have no consistent partners may well be less stable. Without such relationships, according to Berger and Kellner, individuals are "powerfully threatened with anomie in the fullest sense of the word" (1964, p. 6). Single persons without consistent partners may be particularly vulnerable to a sense of meaninglessness and confusion, a loss of a secure self-image. This confusion is illustrated in a passage from Judith Rossner's novel about a single woman in New York, *Looking for Mr. Goodbar*:

> Actually, when she thought about it at all, she didn't really feel that she had a life, one life, that is, belonging to a person, Theresa Dunn. There was a Miss Dunn who taught a bunch of children who adored her ("Oh, that Miss Dunn," she'd heard one of her children say once to a parent. "She's one of the kids. A big one.") and there was someone named Terry who whored around in bars when she couldn't sleep at night. But the only

> thing these two people had in common was the body they inhabited. If one died, the other would never miss her—although she herself, Theresa, who thought and felt but had no life, would miss either one. (1975, p. 121)

Individuals who are not regarded as whole persons by someone else may begin to feel fragmented, like a bundle of unrelated roles. One of the most fundamental needs that marriage often satisfies is a consistent partner with whom to carry on the reality-sustaining conversations through which we define ourselves as stable persons.

The social isolation of the unmarried—their lack of close interpersonal ties—may explain why married persons of both sexes are happier than singles (Gurin, Veroff, and Feld, 1960, pp. 231–232). One of the founders of modern sociology, Emile Durkheim, probed into the effects of social isolation on the unmarried in his classic monograph *Suicide* (originally published in 1899), written more than seventy-five years ago. Starting with the observation that married people have lower suicide rates than the unmarried, he discovered that marriage reduces the male suicide rate more than the female suicide rate. To explain this difference he speculated that men, more than women, may need the restraint of marriage; otherwise they "aspire to everything and are satisfied with nothing. This morbid desire for the infinite . . . everywhere accompanies anomie" (1951, p. 271). What Durkheim meant by a "morbid desire for the infinite" was a preference for complete freedom, openness to new experiences, a reluctance to take on any commitment that would limit future choices. As we have seen, these are commonly given reasons for the choice to remain single today, both among males and among females.

And recent suicide statistics in the United States show that singles still commit suicide more often. The suicide rate for single men is now almost twice as high as it is for married men. Among single women, the rate is about one and one-half times greater than it is for married women (Bernard, 1973, p. 18).

Perhaps we can understand this difference better by looking at suicide rates for specific age groups. Among those under the age of twenty-four, the rate is higher for married than for single persons; only in the population aged twenty-five and older does the reverse become true (Dublin, 1963, p. 22). This reversal might be explained as a reflection of social pressures to marry: all people who deviate from the norm, whether by marrying unusually early or by remaining unmarried long past the average age of first marriage, have a higher suicide rate. Thus we might speculate that as the social pressures to marry decline and remaining single becomes more acceptable there will be less of a difference between married and unmarried suicide rates in the United States.

Is Marriage Good for You? If like Durkheim we try to examine the effects of social isolation on the unmarried, we may come close to an answer to a very basic question: Is marriage good for you? The answer, it appears, depends on whether one is a man or a woman. Whereas popular stereotypes portray a frustrated old maid who is not nearly so well adjusted to the single life as the unencumbered bachelor, both suicide statistics and mental health ratings paint a very different picture: women are better able to cope with the single life than men.

We have already noted that the effect of marriage on reducing suicide rates is greater for men than for women. This is particularly true among the elderly whose marriages are terminated by the death of a spouse. Suicide is the third-ranking cause of death among widowed men (Bernard, 1973, p. 21). In one study of suicides in a retirement community on Florida's Gulf Coast, it was found that the death of a spouse hits elderly males harder than females. Social isolation was identified as a prominent cause of suicide, and one that poses more problems for males than females. While widows showed a considerable ability to carry on familiar roles like housekeeping, kin relationships, and community activities, widowers tended to become isolated. Men who maintained contact with social clubs and community activities had a suicide rate that was less than half the rate of men without such contacts. From this study the investigator concluded that "the greater number of associations the individual is involved in, the less the probability of suicide" (Bock, 1972).

An impressive number of studies have come to the same conclusion about younger men. As indicated in the results of a recent survey of more than 2000 adults, "Women get along without men better than men get along without women. . . . Single women of all ages are happier and more satisfied with their lives than single men" (Campbell, 1975, p. 38). A 1962 study conducted in Manhattan indicated that roughly twice as many never-married men have mental health impairments than have unmarried women (Srole and Fischer, 1962, p. 177). In a 1960 survey entitled *Americans View Their Mental Health*, the investigators came to the conclusion that single women experience "less discomfort than do single men: they report greater happiness, are more active in . . . working through the problems they face, and appear in most ways stronger in meeting the challenges of their positions than men" (Gurin et al., 1960, p. 233). And a summary of more than a dozen mental health surveys found that while single persons in general have higher rates of mental illness than do those who marry, among the unmarried—including the never-married, the divorced, and the widowed—men more commonly than women have mental health problems (Gove, 1972).

But when we look at these same studies to see the mental health scorecard for *married* men and women, the opposite pattern emerges: married men are healthier than married women. Although women describe themselves as being happier when married, single women report fewer neurotic symptoms, are less fearful, and have fewer feelings of inadequacy, depression, and passivity.

Contrary to the stereotyped belief that marriage is a triumph for women and a defeat for their reluctant partners, these findings suggest that while marriage is good for men, it poses considerable difficulties for women.

How are the results of these studies to be explained? Are the women who marry and the men who stay single psychologically damaged to begin with, inferior to the women who stay single and the men who marry? Or are there strains and contradictions in the role of single man and married woman that cause psychological distress?

It has in fact often been argued that superior men and inferior women are selected into marriage. As we noted in Chapter 2, the expectation in our culture is that, ideally, the husband should be somewhat superior to his wife in certain ways—an expectation that results in a situation called the marriage gradient (Bernard, 1973). Because of the marriage gradient, as you recall, two groups may be disadvantaged in the marriage market and thus less likely ever to marry: the "bottom of the barrel" males, who can find no one to look up to them, and the "cream of the crop" females, who can find no men who are superior to them.

Some evidence has been found to support this explanation. For example, when single men were compared with single women, the men showed more neurotic symptoms, reported more unhappy childhood experiences, and were more frequently only children who became overly attached to their mothers. By contrast, single women had the happiest childhoods of any group (Knupfer et al., 1966, p. 846). When sociologist Floyd Martinson studied high school girls in the mid-1950s, he found that early marriage had the strongest appeal for *less* mature, *less* well-adjusted girls (1955). Those who did not marry early showed better emotional adjustment, were more self-reliant, and showed fewer antisocial tendencies. "The overall adjustment of the single girls," Martinson concluded, "was decidedly better than that of the married girls" (p. 164). In other words, the Martinson study suggested that, at least among younger females, those who are less mature and less well adjusted than other females are more likely to marry males, who presumably, they think they can look up to.

As Jessie Bernard writes, the women who remain unmarried through middle age do indeed appear to be the "cream of the crop."

> Education, occupation, and income all tell the same story of the relative superiority of unmarried women over unmarried men. At every age level, the average single women surpass the average single men. At the earlier ages, from twenty-five to thirty-four, the single men and women are not very different in education, occupation, or income; the marriageables are still mixed in with the unmarriageables. But as the marriageable men drop out of the single population, those who are left show up worse and worse as compared with their feminine counterparts, so that twenty years later, at ages forty-five to fifty-four, the gap between them is a veritable chasm. The single women are more educated, have higher average incomes, and are in higher occupations. . . . At every age bracket, the more income a woman has, the lower the rate of marriage, a situation just the reverse of that of men. Similarly, the better her job, the lower the rate of marriage. A good job that pays well is a strong competitor to marriage for many women. (1972, pp. 32, 35)

But this "bottom of the barrel, cream of the crop" phenomenon is probably not the only factor causing the relatively poor mental health ratings of single men and married women. The difficulties of these roles should be examined, too. One researcher speculates that having to do housework, having to adjust career expectations to the demands of a husband and "unclear and diffuse" expectations about roles all contribute to the poor mental health of married women (Gove, 1972).

We will look more closely at some of the contradictions of the wife's roles in Chapter 8; here, let us consider some problems that the single man has. One of the chief reasons why women get along better without men than do men without women is that men have more difficulty in establishing and maintaining close relationships. Despite the models of male friendship appearing in books and films—Huck Finn and Jim, the Western hero and his sidekick, Robert Redford and Paul Newman—American men have fewer close friendships than women do. One researcher found, for example, that single women were more likely to turn to their

Close male friendships—such as the one portrayed in *Butch Cassidy and the Sundance Kid*—between actors Robert Redford and Paul Newman—have long been a staple in Hollywood films. Research, however, suggests that in real life men have fewer close friendships than women do.

friends when they were unhappy (Gurin et al., 1960). A study of the unmarried population in San Francisco found that although single men see friends more often than single women (going out at night can be hazardous for women, and they have few places where they can go without male companions), friendships between women were more intimate and stable. Male friendships often involve little more than "hanging out together" (Knupfer et al., 1966). Whereas women are typically taught from early childhood to be friendly, to express feelings, to talk with others about personal problems, men learn different lessons. The "strong, silent type" may indeed be a lone ranger who is not happy with the single life.

Contrary to the popular image of the reluctant groom who somehow, against his better judgment, ends up at the altar, almost twice as many married as never-married men report that they are very happy (Bradburn, 1969).

We began this section by asking whether single people are really different from those who marry, as is commonly believed. As indicated by such measures as mental health statistics and suicide rates, singles do not compare favorably with the married population. But the difference between single and married men is much more striking than that between single and married women. Compared with single men, single women are not only happier, they have better mental health, and more intimate and stable friendships. And at least from middle age on, never-married women appear to be superior to never-married men in a number of respects such as education and income. Contrary to popular beliefs, "the truth is," as one observer writes, "that there are more carefree spinsters and anxious bachelors" (Campbell, 1975, p. 38). Why are men less successful in coping with the single status? The answer lies partly in the same factor that Emile Durkheim examined more than seventy-five years ago: social isolation. Because single men have relatively more difficulty in maintaining close relationships, marriage has a more dramatic effect on their well-being.

These studies suggest that we need to revise the old stereotypes, particularly the idea that single women are frustrated, neurotic old maids. It will be interesting to see whether new studies of the mental health of the unmarried follow the same pattern as the studies conducted between 1954 and 1968, which indicated that singles are not as stable as married people. Other studies of psychological distress paint a more positive portrait of the mental health of singles, particularly women, as compared with the married population (National Center for Health Statistics, 1972; Radloff, 1975). As the single status becomes more acceptable, individuals who remain unmarried may feel fewer strains. Quite possibly the unmarried population now includes somewhat healthier individuals than it did in the past, individuals who chose the single life when they might have married.

LIFESTYLES OF SINGLES

As the single population grows, it creates a huge new market. Young married couples with children have much of their income tied up in mortgage payments, insurance policies, and the various expenses of child rearing. Singles who are free from those responsibilities can spend much more on expensive wardrobes, entertainment, automobiles, and travel. Single women spend over one-third more money on clothes than married women do. Forty percent of singles, but only 15 percent of married people, go to the movies once a week. And almost half of the Porsches sold in the United States are bought by singles (*U. S. News and World Report,* 1974).

Singles have money to spend, and over the past few years hundreds of firms have created new products and services for this expanding market. Apartment complexes, resort communities, therapy groups, computer dating services, tennis clubs—the variety is endless.

The advertising for these products and services helps to create a glamorous, sexy, fun-loving, freewheeling image of the single life. One apartment complex appeals to affluent singles by offering "a millionaire-like atmosphere with pool, jacuzzis, air conditioning, outdoor barbeques, recreation rooms, and billiards, plus a wild and exciting decor!" (Moran, 1975, p. 343). Magazines written for young singles, like *Cosmopolitan*, dwell on the excitement of the single life with articles on topics such as "bedroom etiquette." What is *Cosmo*'s advice to young women who want to "turn that one-night romp into a long-term passion"? "Refrain from doing grubby chores while he's at the apartment (like cleaning the kitty litter)," a typical article advises, and "Never grab the covers away from a sleeping man even if you're freezing!"

At the same time, there is another, very different theme in some of the articles and advertising written for and about singles. One writer notes the frequent references in *Cosmopolitan* to "the lonesome city," "post-dawn emptiness," and "creeping depression" (Key, 1973, p. 142). Much of the advertising aimed at singles plays on a fear of loneliness. An ad for a singles weekend at the Concord Hotel in the Catskills includes a long list of facilities to satisfy your every whim, and then, in its last line, promises something more: "This may be your last 'singles party.' " Thus the same magazines and advertisements that help to create the image of swinging singles convey another message too: the lifestyle of singles is lonely and desperate.

These images say less about the way single people actually live than about the ambivalence toward the single life in a marriage-oriented society. One way of moving beyond these stereotypes is to regard singles as people who seek to meet basic human needs for companionship, satisfying sexual lives, and stable intimate relationships outside the framework of marriage. In New York, the New School for Social Research offers a course for adults entitled "Alone and Female: The Social and Psychological Determinants of Loneliness and Autonomy." The title points to the central problems of the single state: meeting the needs for autonomy and companionship without a long-term commitment to a partner.

Meeting those needs is especially difficult in a society where most adults are married. (See Box 5-1.) Social activities are often organized around couples, not individuals. What do you as a single person do, for example, when married friends ask you to bring a date to a party? One single man, a young professor, complained that at faculty parties "The men would get into shop talk and the women, in some other part of the house, would talk about their families or the school system" (Stein, 1975, p. 49). When he brought a date to such parties, both of them felt out of place. Single women are often perceived as a threat. Friendship with a married couple who reserve their deepest communication for each other can be particularly unsatisfying; such a friendship may only increase the single person's sense of loneliness.

Friends and Strangers

The most genuine sense in which singles are pioneers venturing into unexplored territory is in their search for intimate relationships outside of marriage. As Peter Stein commented after interviewing twenty singles: "The greatest need single people feel is for substitute networks of human relationships that provide the basic satisfactions of intimacy, sharing, and continuity" (1975, p. 496). Where do they turn for these kinds of relationships?

The simplest and most obvious people to turn to are, of course, friends. College graduates often move to cities where their friends from college have settled. They arrive with a social network already partly formed. Work relationships are another source of friends. But city life, which offers some freedom from the interference of prying neighbors, also cuts singles off from the more traditional forms of friendship. Neighbors in city apartment buildings are not likely to become close friends. For example, among the singles in Chicago, "neighborhood and housing-based interactions do not significantly contribute to the formation of friendships

Point of View

Box 5–1 / The Problems and Pleasures of Living Alone

Living alone is an obscure blend of joys and terrors. I have never been able to decide whether I love it or hate it, nor have I ever known whether I actually chose to live alone or simply wound up there by default because I was unable to succeed at the more usual task of living with someone else. I am always astonished when someone admires me for my courage, since I am convinced that living alone requires no more courage than living with another person, that it confers no more automatic freedom than marriage confers automatic bondage. Every way of life—being alone no more or less than any other—requires us to walk a delicate tightrope between abysmal loneliness, active engagement, and chilling disengagement.

Still, there seems to be something in our human nature which forces us to cherish the fantasy that life might be better if we lived it some other way than the way we actually *are* living it. I am taken aback when couples say to me, "If only I could somehow manage to get away from my husband and children and live alone the way you do. . . . " Their image of living alone is similar to their image of what it is like to go off to a South Sea Island; it involves a wholly romantic fallacy, which somewhere inside themselves they recognize to be a fallacy; the moment they are given the option to actually *do* it, they become fully aware of the drawbacks.

The most commonplace problem about living alone is, of course, loneliness. It is also the most difficult to acknowledge. Admitting to loneliness has always seemed a breach of dignity, tact, and pride. If anyone dared to ask me whether I was lonely, I would bristle with indignation, saying that my life was much too adventurous to be burdened with such a pedestrian problem as loneliness. I was not bound by any of the humdrum tedium that afflicted my married friends. I was not trapped by living with someone I didn't love. I didn't have to cook for anyone or clean for anyone or schedule my vacations to fit into someone else's life. (I like to spend three months of the year traveling in Europe or South America, three to six months in New York, three to six months working in solitude at my house in

and dating relationships" (Starr and Carns, 1972, p. 45).

Cities do, however, offer newer and more exotic occasions for intimacy. Women's consciousness-raising groups, for example, provide one means of relating intimately outside a one-to-one relationship. The groups are generally small, consisting of no more than a dozen women. The idea behind them is that women learn that their personal problems are not unique, and thus stem not so much from their own inadequacies as from a sexist society. Although the purpose of many of these groups was initially political, their most important accomplishment has been to strengthen friendship and intimacy among women. In them, women talk to each other about parents, childhood, sexual feelings, relationships with men, fantasies and inadequacies, about anger and joy—about topics, in fact, that have traditionally been reserved for conversations between husbands and wives.

In fact, many of the other social innovations of the past decade, including communes and encounter groups, have had as their main purpose the creation of intimacy outside of marriage. Encounter groups, for example, are short-term experiences among people who begin as strangers. These groups allow a kind of closeness that is frustrated by most social settings in

Maine.) And everyone said, "You really do have the ideal set-up."

What I preferred not to admit, however, was that the ideal set-up—although it could be immensely gratifying—could also be immensely lonely. Freedom, like everything else, has its price.

The fact that one requires a great deal of solitude does not mean that it is always pleasurable. There are certain things one learns painfully to live with in order to preserve other things. I am most intact when I am alone, most myself. Being alone develops strength of character. You learn to rely on yourself, and are forced to face yourself. I can cherish my privacy for days on end, spend hours reading or writing or listening to music, going for long walks or riding my bicycle . . . But then suddenly, without any warning, some shock of desperation will gather itself inside of me and I will think "I just can't bear to face that apartment tonight."

The experience of loneliness is of course not limited to people who live alone, nor is being alone equivalent to being lonely. There are times when I have felt most lonely surrounded by a roomful of people. I have lain awake at night next to someone and experienced the complete disintegration of emotional contact, despite a sexual satisfaction which did not diminish my isolation in the slightest. I have also paced my apartment, battling with the need for precisely that sexual satisfaction, knowing that a foray into the wilderness of impersonal intimacy would bring me no closer to myself or anyone else, that empty sex is much lonelier than no sex at all.

In the vast beehive of New York City, in thousands of studio apartments, thousands of single occupancy hotels, hundreds of little diners where old people congregate merely to acknowledge each others' existence, thousands of singles bars where younger people hope for even a moment's alleviation of an overwhelming isolation, hundreds of little clubs formed for "the pursuit of common interests," loneliness is seen as one of the most serious disfigurations of human life, even though it is the most common.

For myself, I know that I have a very active, independent life, good friends, am successful in my work and travel a lot, that I would never go to a singles bar, never have a computer date or even go skiing in the hope of meeting someone interesting. . . . The life I lead suits my character.

And yet—like most people—sometimes I wonder.

Source: Ingrid Bengis. Being alone. In *Couples*. New York: New York Magazine, 1973.

modern society. Carl Rogers, who was one of the founders of the encounter movement, explains its popularity in this way:

> I believe it is a hunger for something the person does not find in his work environment, in his church, certainly not his school or college, and sadly enough, not even in the modern family. It is a hunger for relationships that are close and real; in which feelings and emotions can be spontaneously expressed without first being carefully censored or bottled up; where deep experiences—disappointments and joys—can be shared; where new ways of behaving can be risked and tried out; where, in a word, people approach the state where all is known and all accepted, and thus further growth becomes possible. This seems to be the overpowering hunger which people hope to satisfy through the experience of an encounter group. (1970, p. 11)

Because of their promise of instant intimacy, such groups have considerable appeal for singles. Resorts that have been hosting singles mixers for years now offer singles encounter weekends. But when a social mixer and a therapeutic encounter are combined, the effects can be devastating. One woman went to a church rap session billed as "a joyous social experience integrating the ideas of Buber, Fromm, Rogers, and Reich." She found that the "nonsexual touching" masked blatant sexual desire. "Pick . . . fondle . . . stare. . . . It was like the old high school dance," she reports. "The cuties got pinched and the wall-flowers were passed over" (Mermey, 1975, p. 11). She found, too, that participants who had confessed their most intimate secrets to the group tended to feel embarrassed later if they ran into someone else from the group. Such unreserved intimacy with strangers may be forced and artificial. And it may only be possible within the anonymity of the city; people who live in small towns might be more hesitant about opening up to others they will be encountering for the rest of their lives. The old cliché that people reveal more intimate secrets to perfect strangers than they would to lifelong acquaintances may explain the appeal of encounter groups.

Not all encounter groups for singles are so exploitative. One observer found that through such organized encounters, people were able to achieve "relationships that enabled them to overcome the role-playing, competitiveness and reserve that had characterized their interactions in the past" (Stein, 1975, p. 498). Such groups can, at their best, provide an occasion for intimate communication like that which has been reserved mainly for couples only.

The most visible facilities for meeting other singles in large cities are the singles bars. Young singles who are new arrivals in the city use them most frequently, before they establish more selective means of making new acquaintances. Singles bars function much as mixers used to: they provide a means of meeting members of the opposite sex. Mixers, though, offered a preselected pool of eligibles; singles bars do not. The appeal of many activities designed mainly for singles in the city—theater clubs, cooking classes, ski trips, tennis lessons—is that they provide a more selective setting for people with common interests. If bars seem to many people to be artificial meeting places where everyone rather desperately "checks out" everyone else, the specific activities provide more comfortable occasions for meeting compatible new friends.

Sex and the Single Person

Much of the fascination with singles bars, as with the single life in general, reflects a curiosity about casual sex. In the film *John and Mary*, for example, two young people meet in a bar, then spend the night together, but can't remember each other's names in the morning. In the media, as well as the minds of many married people, the single life promises a sexual smorgasbord.

Some singles, though probably a tiny minority, do in fact live up to this image. When one journalist visited a singles apartment complex in Houston, she found that the pursuit of sexual encounters was nearly universal. The women generally had marriage in mind, the men casual sex, but there were mixers every night and the game never stopped. One not-so-young man had "scored"—the term is appropriate, for he kept a careful record—with seventy-nine women in the past year. This might be understood as one example, although rather extreme, of the recreational sex ethic. But several psychotherapists who treated some of these same single persons believed that their pursuit of pleasure masked a real unhappiness. Their objective, said one of the therapists, was

> to cut themselves off from their pain. They anesthetize themselves with a lifestyle that consists of ritually getting drunk, getting stoned, getting laid. The very nature of their interaction there is one of *not* dealing with anything real or intense, of not dealing with their own feelings. (Proulx, 1973, p. 66).

Another psychotherapist found these people "cut off, afraid of closeness."

Though their lives exemplify a popular image of how singles are supposed to live, these people are only a small minority of the unmarried population. All singles who seek sexual satisfaction, however, still have to do so in a society where sex outside of marriage is widely condemned. Even the words we use to discuss sexuality—"premarital" and "extramarital"—exclude the person who chooses never to marry.

Changing sexual values are expressed very clearly in a study document, *Sexuality and the Human Community*, which was prepared by the General Assembly of the United Presbyterian Church. The report discusses the dilemma of the unmarried who face the traditional morality of the Judeo-Christian tradition, which condones sex only within marriage.

> We are greatly disturbed by the emphasis we have found on marriage and the family as the exclusive model for ordering all sexual activity. By understanding sexuality primarily in terms of its place in the orders of creation, we emphasize its procreative function still, admitting the relational functions of sexual expression but subordinating them to those concerned with childbearing and nurture. . . . Protestantism has suffered from a single-minded preoccupation with marriage and the family, and by its silence has left the impression that the single estate is a deficient one, requiring more explanation and apology. So, less by intent than by omission, Protestantism has left the unmarried in the shadow of an ethical structure designed to serve another manner of life than theirs. (in Francoeur, 1972, p. 50)

Spokesmen for the Catholic church, too, have begun to argue that sex, which has been viewed primarily in relation to procreation, should be regarded as a means of enhancing relationships and personal growth. One Catholic theologian said recently that sex "must be judged on its own merits, by what it contributes in a particular situation to the growth and mutual creativeness of the two persons involved" (in Francoeur, 1972, p. 73). The shift from a legalistic or moralistic view of sex, where the primary concern is whether the participants are married, to a more humanistic perspective that evaluates sex in terms of its contribution to intimate relationships, is a fundamental one.

What information do we have about the sexual activity of single people, and particularly of single women, who have always felt most acutely the restrictions against sex outside of marriage? More than twenty-five years ago, when Kinsey and his associates collected data for their second volume, *Sexual Behavior in the Human Female* (1953), unmarried women were far from the juiceless old maids portrayed in the stereotype. Although Kinsey's research provides

One of the basic problems of the single life is meeting the need for companionship without a long-term commitment to a partner.

no measure of the quality of the relationships in which their sexual encounters occurred, it does give an indication of their sexual satisfaction. Kinsey found that 96 percent of all married women had experienced orgasm by age forty, but so had 73 percent of never-married women the same age (p. 546)—a smaller difference than many people would have expected. Kinsey's conclusion about the sexual activity of unmarried males was even more remarkable. *Sexual Behavior in the Human Male* provides evidence that single males beyond the age of forty may actually exceed married males in the total amount of sexual activity (1948, p. 266).

In the past generation sexual behavior as well as sexual standards have changed dramatically. In a summary of a study sponsored by the Playboy Foundation, Morton Hunt provides a vivid portrait of change, particularly in the sexual lives of unmarried women. In the Kinsey study, one-fifth of the unmarried women between sixteen and twenty were reported to be having intercourse. Among unmarried women between twenty-one and thirty-five, the figure rose to one-third (1953). Hunt found that two-thirds of the single women in his study between eighteen and twenty-four reported having intercourse. Not only were more women having intercourse, they were having it more often, "a little over once a week," reports Hunt, "or anywhere from three to ten times the typical rates of young women a generation ago" (1974, p. 167). And the percentage who had orgasmic experience increased correspondingly. In Kinsey's sample, only half of the young unmarried women experienced orgasm in coitus. Three-fourths of the women in the 1970s did.

The data from the Playboy Foundation study provide little evidence, however, for promiscuity or swinging among young singles. Hunt reports that the median number of partners in the last year for single men under twenty-five was two. For single males between twenty-five and thirty-four it was four. For single women, the corresponding figures were two and three. Sexual standards for most singles are apparently still closely related to feelings of intimacy and affection. As Hunt concludes, "The new sexual freedom operates largely within the framework of our long-held cultural values of intimacy and love" (1974, p. 154).

REASONS NOT TO MARRY

As we have already noted, in the 1950s, when the marriage rate was at an all-time high and the age of first marriage at an all-time low, it was widely assumed that the "failure" to marry was a reflection of social or psychological problems. For example, a popular marriage and family text listed the following reasons for this "failure":

> (1) hostility toward marriage or to members of the opposite sex; (2) homosexuality; (3) emotional fixation on parents causing an inability to love someone else; (4) poor health or deviant physical characteristics; (5) unattractiveness; (6) unwillingness to assume responsibility; (7) economic factors precluding the financial responsibilities of marriage; (8) geographical, educational, or occupational isolation drastically limiting the pool of eligible mates. (Kuhn, in Becker and Hill, 1955, p. 247)

Social norms are patrolled in many ways, even by the unstated assumptions built into textbooks. Few of the students who read the passage could have missed its meaning: everyone *should* be married. The author apparently never dreamed that one might make a conscious, positive decision *not* to marry. To add insult to injury, he assumed that something was wrong with you if you didn't marry.

The single status has a growing number of defenders who stress its advantages and the corresponding disadvantages of married life. Feminists have placed particular emphasis on what women give up by marrying. In love and preparing for marriage, not many people give much thought to the legal tradition that defines their rights and obligations, and yet, "When you say 'I do,' what you are doing is not, as you thought, vowing your eternal love, but rather subscribing to a whole system of rights, obligations, and responsibilities" (Edmiston, 1972, p. 68). In some ways, our laws perpetuate certain traditional beliefs and assumptions that are contrary to the most cherished personal values of many who marry.

In the United States today, single women have a number of rights that married women do not. In the traditional wedding ceremony, the father of the bride "gives" his daughter to the groom. Giving up her maiden name is the most visible sign that she has surrendered part of her former identity and status to become a wife. This custom accurately reflects the traditional assumption that, in the eyes of the law, husband and wife are one person. And "the doctrine has worked out in reality to mean that . . . the one is the husband" (Kanowitz, 1969, p. 35).

The husband is required to support his wife, a factor that we will examine more closely in the next chapter. In return for the right to support, the married woman gives up several rights that she enjoyed when single. The laws vary somewhat from state to state, but in general, married women lose both the right to make contractual arrangements as an equal to men or unmarried women and some rights to control property. A wife is obliged to perform domestic chores such as cooking and cleaning and to care for her husband and children. A husband may even force his wife to have sexual relations as long as his demands are not unreasonable and her health is not jeopardized. Furthermore, the law states that a wife is obliged to follow her husband if he moves. In effect, then, a married woman cannot take advantage of a new job opportunity as easily as her husband can.

In the past few years a good deal of critical attention has been given to these legal obligations and restrictions defining the marital relationship, making marriage—at least insofar as it is influenced by law—seem both less desirable and less inevitable than it once did. According to Caroline Bird,

> Marriage is no longer the only way to fulfill any basic human need. It is still the most satisfactory as well as the easiest way to do a great many things, such as rearing children; but it is no longer the *only* way to make a success even of that. . . . If love, mutual support, face-to-face daily relationships are essential or desirable—and I am sure that they are—wouldn't we do better to start from scratch and design an institution specifically to evoke and produce those desirables? . . . This is not to say that marriage won't survive. Traditional marriage will satisfy many men and women, but it will never again command the prestige of the "one right way" to live. (1972, p. 117)

THE SINGLE LIFE: A TEMPORARY STAGE OR A LIFELONG STATUS?

Clearly, there is much more social support now than there was a generation ago for people who choose to defer marriage. But a fundamental question remains: Is the single life only a temporary alternative to marriage? Or is it likely to be a permanent, lifelong status for a substantial number of people?

It is too early to predict with any confidence that more people in the next generation will choose never to marry. Although in 1975 the never-married population between the ages of twenty and thirty-four was 50 percent larger than it had been ten years previously, there is no way of knowing how many of these people will eventually get married.

But there are several indications that most young singles regard singlehood as only a temporary status. In 1974, when the Institute of Life Insurance conducted a survey of young Americans between fourteen and twenty-five years old, both males and females were asked what lifestyles they thought were most appealing. Among the young women, only a small minority—17 percent—said they thought the single life was the most desirable alternative. Significantly, a somewhat smaller percentage—about 5 percent—said they expected to be single in fifteen years. Twenty-four percent of the young men chose the bachelor's life as the most appealing alternative, but only 9 percent of this group expected to be unmarried in another fifteen years (Institute of Life Insurance, 1974).

Another more recent study suggests the same conclusion, that most people who intend to remain single for a while after leaving college think of it as a transitional status, not a permanent arrangement. In a 1976 survey conducted by the American Council of Life Insurance, 48 percent of the young people aged fourteen to eighteen said that the opportunity to develop as an individual was their most important life goal. This would appear to substantiate the argument of social commentators who stress the significance of increasing concern for self. But when adults in different age categories are asked what their life goals are, there is a significant pattern to their responses. As people get older, they place less emphasis upon the opportunity to develop as an individual, and more upon a happy family life. In a 1975 survey of adults, for example, 67 percent of those eighteen to twenty-four said that a happy family life was their most important life goal; among those thirty and over, 85 percent indicated that this was their most important goal. Such survey results suggest that it is less accurate to characterize the seventies as the "Me Decade" than it is to describe the teens and early twenties as the "Me Stage." From this perspective, we might explain the popularity of the single life among people in their twenties as a reflection of the emphasis that people of this particular age seem to place upon self-development.

Betty Friedan (1963) comments that the short stories in magazines addressed to young married women provide a sensitive barometer of the needs and aspirations of women. In the 1930s, when the first feminist movement was still a strong influence on educated women, the heroines of stories were often young career girls. By the late 1940s and throughout the 1950s the heroines were housewives (Friedan, 1963, p. 28). If we examine recent issues of magazines such as *Redbook*, we find that the stories still focus on women who are housewives, but most of the heroines have worked in the city and lived the single life before getting married.

Perhaps as the singles phenomenon grows, even parents who met and married in the marriage-oriented climate of the 1950s will more readily accept their children's decision to "live on their own" for a while. In fact, one study of women who became adults in the early 1950s has already found evidence of this pattern. Asked whether they would prefer to have their daughters marry when they did, younger than they did, or older than they did, most of the women who married early—that is, at age eighteen or under—hoped their daughters would delay marriage longer than they did. Most of the women who married late—age twenty-two or after—favored the same timing for their daughters (Elder and Rockwell, 1976). In the judgment of those mothers, marrying at a very young age is quite undesirable, but deferring first marriage until at least one's mid-twenties is not.

The Timing of Our Lives

The timing of our lives today is quite different from that of our grandparents': formal education lasts longer than it used to, the childbearing period is considerably shorter than it was when the average family size was larger, and life expectancy is much longer (See Figure 5-2). In societies where the life span is shorter than ours, there is a correspondingly shorter period of freedom before one accepts adult responsibilities, including marriage and the obligations of child rearing. New life stages such as adolescence develop in response not only to social changes, but to modifications of the life cycle as well. Adolescence was defined as a life stage as the need for child labor decreased and the demand for a better-educated work force increased. The acceptance of the single life may mean that yet another stage is being inserted between childhood and adulthood.

In his analysis of a new stage in the life span which he calls "youth," Kenneth Keniston was speaking mainly of college students. But much of what he says helps to explain the expectations of young single people:

Figure 5-2 Even if singles defer the decision to marry for ten years or so beyond the normal age of first marriage there is still a period long enough to bear several children. The couple can spend more years together in marriage than did the average married couple who married at an earlier age at the turn of the century.

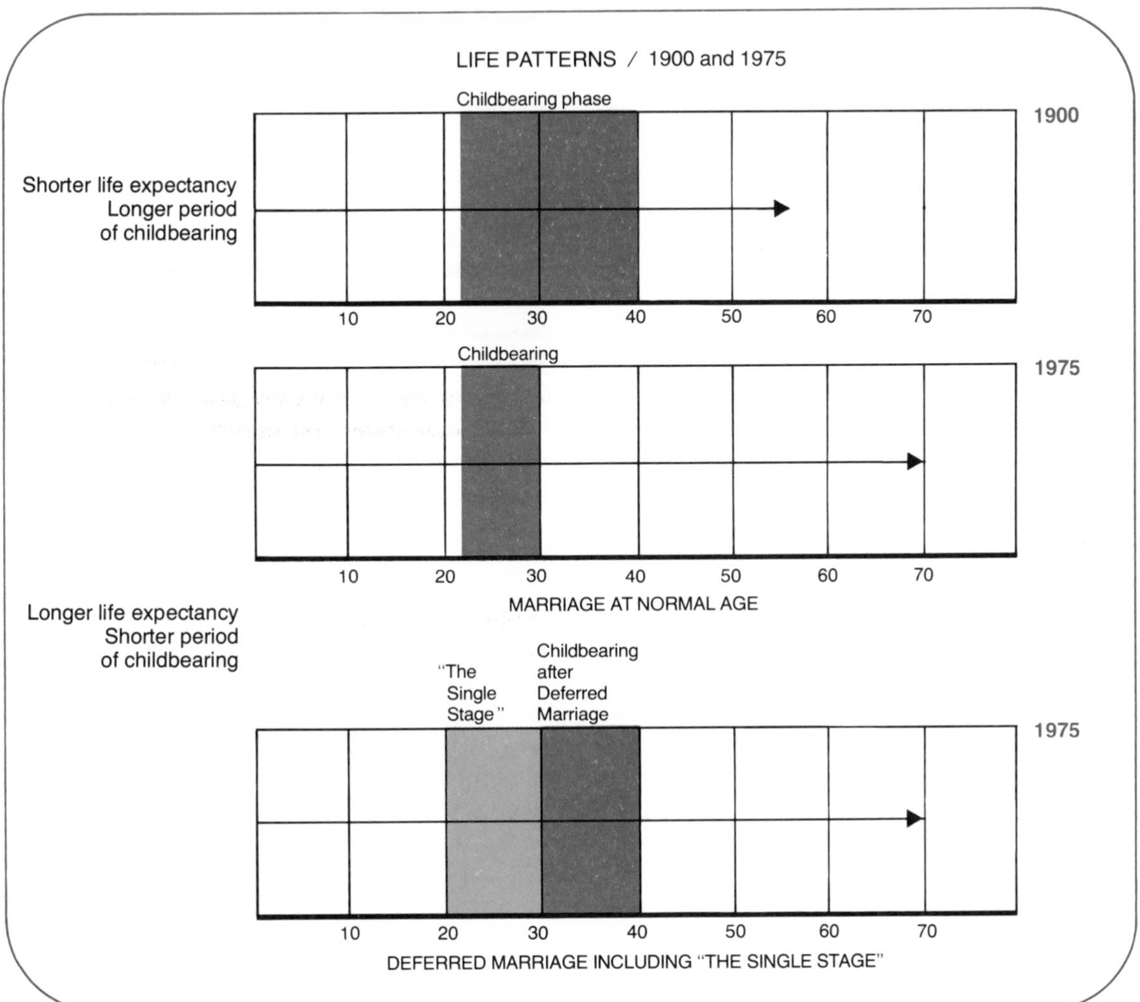

Today, in more developed nations, we are beginning to witness the recognition of still another stage of life. Like childhood and adolescence it was initially granted only to a small minority but it is being rapidly extended to an ever-larger group. I will call this stage "youth" and by that I mean both a further phase of disengagement from society and the period of psychological development that intervenes between adolescence and adulthood. This stage, which continues into the twenties and sometimes into the thirties, provided opportunities for intellectual, emotional, and moral development that were never afforded to any other large group in history. (Keniston, 1971, p. 332)

Since "youth" in contemporary society cannot be defined by chronological age, it is necessary to ask what it does mean. Today, an unmarried graduate student of twenty-eight who is still changing rapidly in terms of his or her self-definition and professional identity might well be "younger" in attitudes than was a fifteen-year-old apprentice a century ago. If we define youth as a stage of being unsure of one's identity or occupation, then it is relevant to ask whether many people will ever become adults in the traditional sense of the word. As psychologist Arlene Skolnick suggests,

> It might be more useful to think of "youth" not so much in developmental terms, but as a particular kind of cultural outlook or psychological perspective. . . . There is no evidence that the generation who are now experiencing "youth" will progress toward adulthood in anything like the old sense. Indeed, it may well be that the psychological themes of youth are not so much a postponement of adulthood as a redefinition of it. (1973, p. 424)

If single persons believe that the commitment to freedom and personal growth is the only commitment they wish to make, youth becomes not a stage that one passes through, but a new way of seeing the world and one's own identity. It may be that the single status, and all that it implies in terms of freedom from long-term commitments, will become a stage to which adults return from time to time throughout their lives. A newly divorced woman in her forties, for example, might experience an identity crisis of the sort we now associate with adolescence. For her, as for the young person who has not yet married, the single life offers a period of freedom to explore the self in a variety of relationships with others.

WHAT IS THE BEST AGE TO MARRY?

If the decision to defer marriage until at least one's mid-twenties is becoming both more popular and more acceptable, what are the consequences of late marriage? In Chapter 3 we examined some of the problems associated with unusually early marriages and saw that they are likely to be unstable. But, surprisingly, so also are marriages in which the partners are substantially older than the average age. Marriages are most likely to be stable ones, as demographer Paul Glick has pointed out, when the man's age is twenty-four and the woman's twenty-two at marriage (in Bernard, 1973, p. 163).

Why are late marriages relatively unstable? If the instability of early marriages can be partially explained by an unrealistic assessment of one's mate, we might suppose that older-than-average persons would choose more wisely. And yet they do not have more stable marriages. Perhaps people who wait until their late twenties are more set in their ways and therefore less able to adapt to a marital partner. Their expectations may be unrealistically high, or they may simply be less conventional to begin with than people who marry "on time." Marital stability may be less important to them. Their somewhat higher divorce rate might be attributed to a greater insistence on personal freedom, which may have been an important motivation in deferring marriage in the first place.

There are advantages as well as disadvantages associated with the decision to defer marriage. To determine the "best age" to marry requires a personal choice among them. In the next few pages we will look at some of the implications of late marriage: the field of eligible mates in their late twenties or early thirties, the economic consequences of late marriage, and childbirth and child rearing for late-married parents.

The Late Mate Pool

If you defer marriage, will most of your potential mates be married already? Remember that according to the marriage gradient, women define as eligible those men who are slightly older than themselves and superior in certain ways, as for example in educational achievement. We might deduce, then, that women who defer marriage to complete their education will have a harder time finding eligible mates, because many of the eligible men who are a few years older will already have married. A well-educated woman, moreover, would have the additional problem of finding someone who is even better educated so that she could look up to him.

It would seem to follow that such late-marrying women would often have no one left to marry but men of lower educational achievement or social backgrounds. But when two researchers examined the mate choices of women who married later than average in the 1950s and early 1960s, that was not what they found. Women who married late were more likely to marry *up* on education. "The mating gradient suggests that a delay in marriage narrows the pool of eligible men who are comparable in background," the authors explain,

> but we find no evidence of this constraint in the marital choice of older brides. These women were more apt to marry up on education and less likely to marry down than other wives. Even among the high school graduates late marriers were far more likely than other women to enter the upper middle class through marriage. (Elder and Rockwell, 1975, p. 30)

Because of their extended work experience, often in white-collar employment, women who deferred marriage were apparently able to meet well-educated men in relatively high-status occupations. They expanded their range of social opportunities and contacts through advanced education and employment.

Although the expectation is that women will marry men who are several years older, college-educated women who marry late expand the field of choice by including younger men. Late-marrying women are much more likely to choose mates their own age or younger than are women who marry early or "on time." This is one way of dealing with the problem of a rapidly narrowing pool of eligible males (Elder and Rockwell, 1975).

Late Marriage and Children

An undoubted advantage of late marriage is that it enables a couple to avoid the economic squeeze often encountered by younger parents. When a couple marries relatively young, the woman typically leaves her job to give birth to their first child. Expenses for the young family rise faster than income because the husband is generally in the early stages of his career, with relatively low earnings. Having had little time or opportunity before marriage and the birth of children to save ahead, the family faces heavy economic pressures. But if they marry late, both individuals have time to accumulate economic resources and get a good start in their careers before taking on the burden of family expenses. On the other hand, a woman who waits much past the normal age of first marriage to bear children takes a greater risk, both to her own health and to the baby's.

A decision to defer marriage is also likely to affect the size of the family. In general, the younger a woman is at marriage, the more children she will bear. People who defer marriage have substantially lower fertility rates (Elder and Rockwell, 1975, p. 21). Thus, one of the consequences of the tendency to defer marriage is a lower fertility rate, since more women in their twenties, the most fertile age, are not yet married. Or we could turn this relation around and say that since women now prefer to have fewer children, they are willing to defer marriage. It is quite unlikely that singles who marry later than average will then decide to have as many children as people who marry "on time."

People who choose to have their first child relatively late will find, of course, that there is a greater age difference between them and their children. Whether an age difference of thirty years or more between parents and children is viewed as a problem depends upon personal values and preferences in child rearing.

To summarize, then, the advantages of marrying "on time" include a larger pool of eligible mates, childbirth with somewhat fewer risks, and a longer span of years in which to give birth to a larger family, if desired. But as more people choose to defer marriage, the pool of eligible mates among those in their late twenties and thirties expands. In any case, individuals who marry late do not appear to encounter substantial problems in finding eligible mates. The recent popularity of the single life is evidence that for many people the advantages of late marriage outweigh its disadvantages.

Conclusions

In this chapter we have examined an increasingly popular alternative to marriage, at least in one's twenties: the single life. Reasons for its popularity include a certain wariness about traditional marriage, less insistence on familism and child rearing than there was a generation ago, and an increasing interest in personal growth and freedom rather than the commitment of marriage. In addition, women are now capable of being self-supporting, and single persons of both sexes can purchase laundry, food preparation, and other services that used to be provided by spouses. As sexual norms for the unmarried become somewhat more liberal, it becomes increasingly possible for people to satisfy most needs outside of marriage.

Pressures favoring marriage, however, are still very strong. It is significant that a recent Gallup Youth Survey found that 84 percent of American teenagers expect to get married some day, while only 10 percent think they will remain single (Gallup, 1978). Although a substantially larger number of young adults in their twenties are unmarried today compared to even a decade ago, there is no evidence yet of what would be an even more significant change: the decline of the assumption that to be an adult means to be married.

In attitudes toward marriage, as in attitudes toward premarital sex, substantial differences exist between people who were brought up in the marriage-oriented culture of the 1950s and their children, many of whom are deferring marriage. Marriage is not considered inevitable by this generation, and the tendency for young people to marry as soon as they leave school because "it's the thing to do" has declined.

Many stereotypes exist about the single life, partly because it is a new alternative. Rather than accepting the popular image of swinging singles, we have discussed the problems of the single life in a culture where most adults marry. In particular, we have looked at some of the ways in which single persons satisfy the need for companionship, a full sex life, and ongoing relationships outside the framework of marriage.

In several respects, the stereotypes exaggerate the differences between married and single people. Loneliness is a common problem for married persons as well as singles, as Peter Stein found when he talked to those who had recently divorced (1975). And although popular belief conjures up either the sexless image of lonely singles or the hyperactive sexuality of "swingers," most singles in fact confine their sexual activities to just a few partners in a year. Frequency of intercourse among young single women is not very different from that of their married counterparts.

We raised the question of whether the single life is a temporary stage or a lifelong status. Some singles do indeed reject marriage emphatically: as one young man said, "There aren't any conditions under which I would consider getting married" (Stein, 1975, p. 496). Undoubtedly, the number of people who choose to remain single into their thirties and beyond will increase. But the attitudes expressed in surveys, as well as active interest in facilities for finding mates, suggest that many are actively looking for long-term partners. Two sociologists who examined the range of social facilities for singles came to the conclusion that

> the appeal of all these establishments is not to provide an adequate alternative to marriage but to provide places where post-college singles can meet, have fun, and contemplate marriage. The successes of such places are the ones who leave to marry, who are able to utilize these facilities to meet the "right one." The short-term reasons for frequenting and participating in the singles scene include the desire for companionship, to escape boredom, to seek security, excitement, to find one's self, to gain social acceptance, and to find affection. The long-range goal of many is marriage—the escape from singleness. (Allon and Fischel, 1973, p. 12)

Young married persons still consistently report that they are happier than single people of the same age. This can be interpreted either as evidence of the normative expectation that adults *should* marry, or as evidence that the married state is still one that offers more contentment for most people.

There are several questions about the single life that we will be in a better position to answer in another decade. Do people who have lived alone as adults for at least a few years form somewhat more equal and independent relationships when they do marry? Among those persons who had as singles the experience of nonexclusive sexual relationships, how many will modify the traditional rule of sexual exclusivity in marriage? We can only speculate about how the new single stage might affect the expectations that people bring to marriage. Perhaps many who experience the single life will insist upon their own definition of marriage. As one young stewardess says,

> I may get married or I just may not. But if I do, it will be on my own terms. I'm no Cosmopolitan girl. I can't stomach the Playboy guy. But I can see nothing wrong with staying single for as long as you please. I mean it's actually a pretty groovy life, isn't it? I mean isn't it?" (*Newsweek,* 1973, p. 58)

REFERENCES

Natalie Allon and Diane Fischel. *The urban courting patterns: Singles' bars.* Paper presented at the annual American Sociological Association Meeting, New York, August 1973.

American Council of Life Insurance. *Youth 1974.* New York: American Council, 1974.

———. *Youth 1976.* New York: American Council, 1976.

Howard Becker and Reuben Hill, eds. *Family, marriage, and parenthood.* Boston: Heath, 1955.

Ingrid Bengis. Being alone. In *Couples.* New York: New York Magazine, 1973.

Peter Berger and Hansfried Kellner. Marriage and the construction of reality. *Diogenes* 46 (1964): 1–12.

Jessie Bernard. *The future of marriage.* New York: Bantam, 1972.

Caroline Bird. Women should stay single. In Harold Hart, ed. *Marriage: For and against.* New York: Hart, 1972.

E. Wilbur Bock. Cited in Suicide over 65. *Human Behavior,* May/June 1972.

Norman Bradburn. *The structure of psychological well-being.* Chicago: Aldine, 1969.

Angus Campbell. The American way of mating. *Psychology Today,* May 1975, pp. 37–43.

Hugh Carter and Paul C. Glick. *Marriage and divorce: A social and economic study.* Cambridge, Mass.: Harvard University Press, 1970.

Ruth B. Dixon. Explaining cross-cultural variations in age at marriage and proportions never marrying. *Population Studies* 25 (1971): 215–233.

L. I. Dublin. *Suicide: A sociological and statistical study.* Translated by John A. Spaulding and George Simpson. New York: Ronald Press, 1963.

Emile Durkheim (1899). *Suicide.* New York: Free Press, 1951.

Susan Edmiston. How to write your own marriage contract. *Ms.* magazine, May 1972, pp. 62–72.

Glen H. Elder, Jr. and Richard C. Rockwell. Marital timing in women's life patterns. *Journal of Family History* 1 (Autumn 1976): 34–53.

Robert Francoeur. *Eve's new rib.* New York: Delta, 1972.

Betty Friedan. *The feminine mystique.* New York: Dell, 1963.

Gallup Youth Survey. *Concept of "trial" marriage has considerable teenage appeal.* Princeton, N.J.: Gallup Organization, February 1, 1978.

Walter R. Gove. The relationship between sex roles, marital status and mental illness. *Social Forces* 51 (1972): 34–44.

G. Gurin, J. Veroff, and S. Feld. *Americans view their mental health.* New York: Basic Books, 1960.

Morton Hunt. *Sexual behavior in the 1970s.* New York: Dell, 1974.

Susan Jacoby. 49 million singles can't all be right. *The New York Times Magazine,* February 17, 1974.

Leo Kanowitz. *Women and the law.* Albuquerque: University of New Mexico Press, 1969.

Kenneth Keniston. Psychosocial development and historical change. *Journal of Interdisciplinary History* 2 (1971): 329–345.

Wilson Bryan Key. *Subliminal seduction.* Englewood Cliffs, N.J.: Prentice-Hall, 1973.

Alfred C. Kinsey, Wardell Pomeroy, Clyde Martin and Paul Gebhard. *Sexual behavior in the human male.* Philadelphia: W. B. Saunders, 1948.

———. *Sexual behavior in the human female.* Philadelphia: W. B. Saunders, 1953.

Genevieve Knupfer, Walter Clark, and Robin Room. The mental health of the unmarried. *American Journal of Psychiatry* 122 (1966): 841–851.

Christopher Lasch. Better than to burn. *The Columbia Forum* 2 (1973): 18–25.

Floyd M. Martinson. Ego deficiency as a factor in marriage. *American Sociological Review* 20 (1955): 161–164.

Joanna Mermey. Instant intimacy: Add cash and stir. *The Village Voice,* August 18, 1975, p. 11.

Rosalyn Moran. Cited in David A. Schulz and Stanley F. Rodgers. *Marriage, the family, and personal fulfillment.* Englewood Cliffs, N.J.: Prentice-Hall, 1975.

Edward S. Morgan. *The Puritan family.* New York: Harper & Row, 1966.

National Center for Health Statistics. *Selected symptoms of psychological distress.* Washington, D.C.: U.S. Department of Health, Education, and Welfare, 1972.

Newsweek. Games singles play. July 16, 1973, pp. 52–58.

Gail Parent. *Sheila Levine is dead and living in New York.* New York: Putnam, 1972.

Kathryn Perutz. *Liberated marriage.* New York: Pyramid, 1973.

Cynthia Proulx. Sex as athletics in the singles complex. *Saturday Review/Society,* May 1973, pp. 61–66.

Lenore Radloff. Sex differences in depression: The effects of occupation and marital status. *Sex Roles* 1 (1975): 249–265.

David Riesman. Two generations. *Daedalus* 193 (1964): 711–735.

Stephen Roberts. The "living alone" phenomenon. *New York Times,* January 31, 1971, p. 56.

Carl Rogers. *On becoming a person.* Boston: Houghton Mifflin, 1961.

———. *On encounter groups.* New York: Harper & Row, 1970.

Judith Rossner. *Looking for Mr. Goodbar.* New York: Simon & Schuster, 1975.

Marion K. Sanders. The case of the vanishing spinster. In William Goode, ed. *The contemporary American family.* Chicago: Quadrangle, 1963.

Arlene Skolnick. *The intimate environment.* Boston: Little, Brown, 1973.

Leo Srole and Anita K. Fischer. *Mental health in the metropolis.* New York: McGraw-Hill, 1962.

Joyce R. Starr and Donald E. Carns. Singles in the city. *Society* 9 (1972): 43–48.

Peter Stein. Singlehood. *The Family Coordinator,* October 1975, pp. 489–503.

Ralph Turner. *Family interaction.* New York: Wiley, 1970.

U.S. Bureau of the Census. Characteristics of the Population. U.S. Summary—1960. Washington, D.C.: Government Printing Office.

———. Characteristics of the Population. U.S. Summary—1970. Washington, D.C.: Government Printing Office.

———. Marital status and living arrangements: March 1977. *Current Population Reports,* Series P-20, No. 306. Washington, D.C.: Government Printing Office, 1977.

U.S. News and World Report. Rise of the singles—40 million free spenders, October 7, 1974, pp. 54–56.

Joseph Veroff, Elizabeth Douvan, and Richard Kulka. Family roles. *ISR Newsletter,* Winter 1979, pp. 4–5.

Ian Watt. *The rise of the novel.* Berkeley: University of California Press, 1967.

FOR FURTHER STUDY

The single life has been examined by a number of journalists. One of the best of these accounts is Susan Jacoby's "49 Million Singles Can't All Be Right," which appeared in *The New York Times Magazine,* February 17, 1974. Various perspectives on the single life, including Caroline Bird's article "Women Should Stay Single," are included in *Marriage: For and Against* (New York: Hart, 1972). In *Is Marriage Necessary?* (New York: Human Sciences Press, 1974) Lawrence Casler writes about developments in modern society that make marriage more dispensable than it used to be. His chapter "The Destructiveness of Marriage" presents a point of view that has seldom been so well documented. Peter Stein's *Single* is a useful book, based largely on interviews with single persons (Englewood Cliffs, N.J.: Prentice-Hall Spectrum, 1976).

For an interesting analysis of the social networks formed by single people, see Mimi Rodin's "Tuesdays and Saturdays: A Preliminary Study of the Domestic Patterns of Young Urban Singles," in *Urban Anthropology,* vol. 2 (1973). There is a detailed demographic analysis of people who marry late, or not at all, in Carter and Glick's *Marriage and Divorce* (Cambridge, Mass.: Harvard University Press, 1976), Chapter 10. The same volume includes a useful discussion of the differences between married and unmarried adults with regard to morbidity, medical care, and mortality. Frances E. Kobrin and Gerry E. Hendershot have also analyzed the mortality statistics on the unmarried in an interesting article entitled "Do Family Ties Reduce Mortality?" *Journal of Marriage and Family,* November 1977. For a recent perspective on the mental health of the unmarried, see the third edition of a classic in this field, Leo Srole's *Mental Health in the Metropolis* (New York: New York University Press, 1978).

IV
Maintaining Intimate Relationships

"Wedding Photo, 1979" Larry Rivers

6 The Marriage Contract—Do You Promise to Love, Honor, and Obey?

The poet W. H. Auden once remarked that "any marriage, happy or unhappy, is infinitely more interesting and significant than any romance, however passionate." It may be true that marriage—in all its variations—is more interesting. But it is also much harder to describe than mate selection and courtship. All that leads up to marriage can be expressed in certain familiar formulas, which provide the plots for so many stories about romantic encounters. Of course, most of these stories end with the words, "and they lived happily ever after." Perhaps this is the storyteller's way of admitting that what follows is so individual a matter that no simple formula can describe it.

Most people have curiously mixed feelings about marriage, one indication of which is the abundance of jokes about it. Almost every stand-up comedian has a repertoire of jokes about wives, mothers-in-law, sex, and other important but potentially troublesome topics. ("Marriage," as one time-worn witticism has it, "is not a word, but a sentence.") Like jokes about any sensitive topic, those about marriage reflect our ambivalence about it and enable us to laugh at our problems.

What marriage means to a forty-eight-year-old construction worker living with his wife in a modest bungalow in the suburbs of Chicago may be very different from what it means to a twenty-seven-year-old nurse in Chattanooga who has been taking care of her disabled husband and their two infant children. And what it means to a semiretired farmer and his wife living in Iowa may again be very different from what it means to a young professional couple living in a luxurious new apartment building in Los Angeles. Obviously, marriage is not one thing but many.

Even among couples with similar backgrounds, marriage takes on a bewildering variety of meanings. When sociologists John Cuber and Peggy Harroff interviewed hundreds of upper-middle-class couples, they came to the conclusion that "aside from the surface requirements," people who live in different types of marriages have "practically nothing in common. Their daily routines, their sentiments, their aspirations, and practically everything about them are foreign to one another" (1968, p. 194).

How can we begin to understand something that has so many facets? The purpose of this chapter is to explore the meaning of marriage. In no society is it entirely an individual matter. Marriage is also an institution, a socially structured means of providing for certain recurrent needs. The bond between spouses celebrated in the public wedding ceremony consists of obligations and duties as well as rights and privileges.

Marriage can be understood as a contractual arrangement. But in American society today there are two significant differences between the marital agreement and other contracts. While most people would never think of signing a contract without reading the fine print, many people who get married are ignorant of the obligations accompanying it. And while a civil contract can be dissolved if the two parties agree to do so, it is not so easy to dissolve a marriage.

To define marriage by describing the implied contract, we must spell out what is required, what is expected, and what is allowed. We will also examine two alternatives, "open marriage" and the practice of drawing up an individually tailored contract. Among all the indications of new personal alternatives in marriage, none is more striking than the apparent popularity of sitting down before marriage to put in writing exactly what both individuals want the contract to mean.

Whether or not you feel that it is necessary to have a custom-designed contract, that exercise might help in understanding what marriage is and what your alternatives are.

DEFINING THE MARRIAGE CONTRACT

"Marriage"—the word conjures up an image of a loving husband and wife with their children. They live in their own house or apartment. Theirs is an economically independent unit; the husband is, if not the sole wage earner, at least the main provider. The wife's responsibilities are different from her husband's. The spouses satisfy each other's sexual needs. And, of course, this is an arrangement that will last till death do them part.

Many people assume that this is a natural arrangement, perhaps even an inevitable and universal one. But as we noticed in Chapter 1, the majority of American families today, not to mention families in other cultures, do not include all the features of the storybook image. The image portrays marriage and family as people believe they *should* be, not as they *are*. It describes a model that is most common among middle-class Americans and disregards the different family structures of other social classes.

Several years ago, psychiatrist John Spiegel and several associates set out to define the normal American family. Their first goal was to describe its structure and function by observing day-to-day behavior. As Spiegel writes, that "apparently simple task" turned out to be unexpectedly difficult:

> Instead of finding a clear-cut definition of the family easy to achieve, we discovered that families exhibited the most astonishing variance in their structure and function. . . . Not only were various and differing functions assigned to the family in different social milieus, but even those functions which were apparently universal, such as the socialization of children, the satisfaction of sexual needs, or the biological and material maintenance of the members of the family, were carried out in such various ways, and with such differing implications, that it proved impossible to obtain meaningful patterns without reference to the surrounding social system. (1971, p. 144)

Because the meanings of the words "marriage" and "family" seem self-evident, we have to be particularly careful about defining them and recognizing how variable actual marriages and families really are. When anthropologist William Stephens (1963) tried to formulate a definition of marriage that would apply both to our own culture and to others, this was the definition he suggested:

> Marriage is a socially legitimate sexual union, begun with a public commitment, and undertaken with some idea of permanence. It is assumed with a more or less explicit marriage contract, which spells out reciprocal rights and obligations between the spouses. (1963, p. 21)

As Stephens suggests, we might use the word "marriage" wherever these four conditions are met: (1) a socially recognized sexual union, (2) begun with a public announcement or ceremony, (3) defined by a certain contract, and (4) undertaken with the intent of permanence (1963). It might be added that marriage provides the social legitimation for bearing children. And in our own society, marriage is limited to unions between two heterosexual partners.

In the traditional wedding ceremony still followed by most couples who get married today, each of the elements in Stephens's definition is expressed symbolically. The traditional ceremony is not a do-it-yourself ritual, but rather a vivid reminder of the power of tradition, the heavy hand of the past. As one writer remarks, almost all the symbolic details of the wedding ceremony are "echoes of the past—everything from the presence of flowers and a veil, to the old shoes and the rice, to the bridesmaid and the processional" (Seligson, 1974, p. 18). The couple is *not* free to attach whatever meanings they please to the marital relationship. The wedding ceremony is more than a public announcement of a new status. It is society's way of reminding the bride and groom that obligations as well as rights are attached to their new status.

In the excitement and the pleasant confusion surrounding a wedding, not many people step back to notice the symbolic meaning of marriage. If they did, they might realize that the traditional commitment is not at all what many young couples today have in mind when they say "I do."

The Wedding Ceremony

The large congregation of family and friends who come together to help celebrate a marriage performs an indispensable function just by being present. Love, romance, sexual attraction—all the things that lead up to marriage—are private matters. But the wedding ceremony is a public act. It asserts that marriage creates new social bonds, as the presence of family members from both sides, whether or not they

Just as the marriage ceremony commonly practiced today symbolizes the nature of the commitment, this fifteenth-century painting by Jan van Eyck portrays the symbols of the Christian marriage. As the couple exchanges vows in the bridal chamber, they are surrounded by reminders of the significance of that act. The dog represents fidelity. Because he is standing on sacred ground, the groom has removed his slippers. The single candle is a reminder of the presence of Christ and the fact that they are partaking of a sacrament.

Guidelines for Decision Making

Box 6–1 / Should a Woman Change Her Name When She Marries?

"Six months ago," writes Diana Altman in a letter to the Center for a Woman's Own Name,

> I was married and decided at that time to continue to use the name that had been mine for twenty-nine years. I did not want to disappear from the telephone book, from the name tag on the mail box, or from charge plates. Exchanging my name for my husband's name would be a symbolic denial of all that I was before marriage. (1974, p. 39)

This letter, like the group to which it was addressed, illustrates one option that more women are deciding to exercise today. A woman's name does not change automatically when she marries. Though a change of name is customary, it is not legally required. In the past few years, more and more women have decided either to keep their own name after marriage or to adopt a hyphenated name combining their maiden name with their husband's name. The common law doctrine is that the husband and wife have a single identity, which is reflected in the custom of one name—the husband's.

The Center for a Woman's Own Name, a nonprofit group based in Illinois, seeks to prevent discrimination against women who want to keep their own names after marriage. One of its activities is to disseminate information about recent court decisions and legislative activities so that women will be aware of their rights. There has been a good deal of controversy about the legal rights of women who choose to keep their own name. In certain cases, women who retain their maiden names have had problems in voting, obtaining a driver's license, running for office, and securing credit. But in general, state courts over the past few years have affirmed the right of women to keep their own names, citing the common law rule that a person may adopt any name he or she wishes provided it is not done for fraudulent purposes.

As Priscilla Ruth MacDougall, an Illinois attorney and a director of the Center for a Woman's Own Name, writes,

> Courts and attorneys general around the country have affirmed and reaffirmed that a woman need not adopt her husband's name. It is legal to retain the name borne at the time of marriage. A woman who elects to do so should experience little difficulty if she is consistent in her usage and insistent upon her right to use her own name. (1976, p. 3)

A married couple can file a joint return to the Internal Revenue Service using two different names. The Social Security Administration asks only that the name on your card be the same one you use at your place of work. Insurance companies now grant policies to married women using their maiden names.

Despite the wider recognition of one's right to do so, some women who chose not to adopt their husband's surname have had to contend with administrative procedures as well as social pressures that reinforce this ancient custom. Married women using their own names have been refused family rates by airlines, for example. And certain banks have refused to give them and their husbands joint accounts.

Many of the women who have decided to keep their own names for both personal and professional reasons consider these to be minor irritations. They agree with these words written by Lucy Stone, who advocated more than a century ago that a woman keep her own name: "My name is the symbol of my identity, and must not be lost" (Center for a Woman's Own Name, 1974, p. 19).

The Center for a Woman's Own Name offers a booklet for women who wish to determine their own names after marriage. Write to 261 Kimberley, Barrington, Ill. 60010, and the cost is $2.50 postage + handling.

ever get together on any other occasion, demonstrates. During courtship, young couples typically have a great deal of freedom to do as they please, to withdraw temporarily from certain obligations and constraints. But, as sociologist Philip Slater points out, marriage is the means by which the couple is tied back into the social structure (1963).

The friends and family members assembled for the wedding are witnesses to the fact that the status of the couple has changed, that they have publicly entered into a commitment of considerable significance, one that cannot be casually dissolved. The vows between husband and wife are thus announced in public, which impresses upon them, as well as on those who attend the ceremony, the significance of the status transition.

Typically, the vows indicate more explicitly than any other part of the ceremony what the marital agreement is. The vows suggested in the Book of Common Prayer, for example, require the spouses to make a commitment that is both permanent and exclusive. He is asked: "Wilt thou love her, comfort her, honor her, cherish her, and keep her; forsaking all others, cleave thee only unto her, so long as ye both shall live?" She is asked to make the same commitment, with just one addition, to "inspire him."

As Stephens suggests in his definition of marriage, one important element of the contract is that it specifies rights, obligations, and role responsibilities. Here is another reminder to the couple contracting a marriage that they are not free to define the relationship on their own terms. This is most explicit in the Jewish wedding, where the reading of the *Ketubah* serves as a reminder of the husband's duties.

Some ceremonies define the man's responsibilities far more carefully than the woman's, but even then the one who is in the spotlight in a traditional wedding is the woman. She is the star of the drama: her picture, not his, appears in the newspaper, and unless she decides to keep her own name (see Box 6–1), it will change but his will not. In these ways the ceremony recognizes that her status changes far more than his in the eyes of the community and the law.

In recent years feminists have complained about the sexism expressed in the traditional ceremony. Notice that the father of the bride gives her away to the husband, an act symbolizing the transfer of ownership. As writer Marcia Seligson points out, this assumption was expressed even more vividly in some marriage ceremonies in the past. In Russia, the father would hit his daughter gently with a new whip, and then hand the whip over to the groom (1974, p. 22).

If the male dominance implied in the act of giving the bride away can be dismissed as merely a curious antique, several other symbols in the traditional wedding fly in the face of modern beliefs and realities. For example, the ring placed on the bride's finger was originally a token of purchase. The rice showering down on the newlyweds as they leave the ceremony signifies fertility, which is far less appropriate today than it was in the past. And the veiled bride, dressed in radiant white, is a symbol of virginal purity, which had great significance in the past, when there was more nearly a consensus that women should remain virgins until they married.

But some elements of the traditional wedding remain basically the same, even if they take a slightly different form today. As Stephens suggests in his definition of marriage, one thing that is always implied is a socially recognized sexual union. In certain cultures in the past, as Seligson notes,

> the wedding night involved public participation as much as the events preceding. Guests would follow the couple into the bedroom, the male attendants undressing the groom and tussling to capture the bride's garter; the parents would make elaborate fertility toasts over the bed; and cowbells, having been surreptitiously affixed to the mattress, would make joyful noise unto the activities that followed. It was not unusual for the "witness" to hang about outside until the first consummation was completed and the husband gave some public sign of satisfaction. (1974, p. 24.)

Today, the same boisterous, ceremonialized sexuality is an important part of what goes on in honeymoon resorts that cater to newlyweds.

The Legal Agreement

If many of the symbolic details of the wedding ceremony reflect ancient assumptions rather than current realities, so do the laws pertaining to marriage and family.

As Norman Sheresky, a New York family lawyer, and writer Marya Mannes comment, "We marry in America with less knowledge of what we are doing than when buying a car." They point out that it is a relatively easy matter to get the state's permission to marry.

> If you are of sufficient age and mental capacity, free of specific diseases, not imprisoned, and not already married, the state will license you to marry anybody of the opposite sex—even if you hate babies, dote on rock music, and believe wholeheartedly in the overthrow of the government while your intended spouse loves large families, likes classical music, and sits on the Republican National Committee. But once married in the state of New York, for example, you are harnessed with several hundred sections of the Domestic Relations Law, the Family Court Act and Rules, and other related statutes and decisions that have the force of law. (1972, p. 33)

Marriage is a contract. It is an agreement undertaken not just between two individuals, but also between them and the silent third party, the state. As sociologist Lenore Weitzman writes, marriage is different from civil contracts, which the contractors are free to define as they please and to dissolve whenever they agree to do so.

> The provisions of the marriage contract are unwritten, its penalties are unspecified, and the terms of the contract are typically unknown to the "contracting" parties. Prospective spouses are neither informed of the terms of the contract, nor are they allowed any options about those terms. In fact, one wonders how many men and women would agree to the marriage contract if they were given the opportunity to read it and consider the rights and obligations to which they are committing themselves. (1975, p. 531)

Recently at least four states, California, Florida, Louisiana, and New York, have considered legislation that would require municipal clerks to distribute information on the legal rights and responsibilities of marriage to those applying for a license. Some women's groups have advocated that anyone wishing to apply should first be tested on the laws, just as people are tested before they can qualify for a driver's license. But these are proposals, not realities. The current situation is that

> no state gives marital applicants the opportunity to read the terms of their marriage contract, nor does any state ask them if they are willing to assume the duties, rights, and obligations it specifies. It is simply assumed that everyone who gets married will want to (and will have to) abide by the state-imposed "unwritten" contract known as legal marriage. (Weitzman, 1975, p. 531)

What is the implied bargain in that unwritten contract? How has the meaning of marriage changed since the law was enacted? "The marriage and family law on the books is archaic," Weitzman observes. "It is the 200-year old vestige of an extinct social structure. The law in action is a patchwork attempt to stretch this old law to deal with modern realities" (1974, p. 1277).

Essentially, as Weitzman summarizes it, there are four provisions in the marriage contract. Significantly, all four are based on the assumption that certain obligations and privileges should be assigned to men and others to women, regardless of individual preferences and capabilities. We will examine each of these four provisions: (1) the husband is the head of the household; (2) the husband is responsible for support; (3) the wife is responsible for domestic services; and (4) the wife is responsible for child care.

The provision that the husband will be the head of the family is observed when a woman gives up her name in marriage. In the eyes of

This is a Jewish marriage contract, or *ketubah,* drawn up for a couple who married in early 19th century Rome. The illuminated border depicting allegorical scenes of the virtues of the wedded life such as "la costanza" (constancy or steadfastness: a woman leaning against a pillar), reflects an Italian influence. The text itself, written in Aramaic, reminds the participants that they are taking part in an unchanging tradition. The *ketubah* specifies both the bridegroom's obligations and what he can expect in return: "Be thou my wife according to the laws of Moses and Israel, and I will work for thee, honor, support, and maintain thee in accordance with the custom of Jewish husbands . . . and I will set aside for thee 200 zuz, in lieu of thy virginity, which belong to thee . . . and thy food, clothing, and necessaries, and live with thee in conjugal relations according to universal custom." In its warning that "This is not to be regarded as an illusory obligation or as a mere form of document" is a reminder of the solemnity of the occasion and the importance of the obligations that the newlyweds are agreeing upon.

the law, she no longer has an independent identity. She has no right to determine her own domicile, or legal place of residence. If a woman refuses to accept her husband's choice of domicile, she is considered to have deserted him. This is true even if moving could jeopardize her own career or job prospects. In some cases women have been forced to give up certain rights or privileges because it was assumed that their husbands' domiciles were their own. For example, a woman who was entitled to free tuition at a state university as a resident of that state might have to pay out-of-state fees if her husband's residence was in another state. Another consequence of the loss of an independent identity is that, until the passage of the Equal Credit Opportunity Act in 1975, it was assumed by creditors that a woman gives up her own credit status upon marriage.

The marriage contract also provides that the man is held responsible for support, regardless of his wife's inclinations or abilities. In the eyes of the law, marriage is no equal partnership, but rather an arrangement in which there is a strict division of labor according to sex. The implied agreement is that in return for support, the wife will maintain the household and care for the children. In most states a woman can never be held responsible for the support of her husband. She is legally obligated to support her children only if her husband is unwilling or unable to do so.

As Weitzman points out, the assumption that a man will provide support is, from the woman's point of view, a mixed blessing (1975, p. 534). Along with the responsibility for support, the laws grant to men the authority to manage family income and property. It is assumed that the wife is dependent on her husband. The extent of the support she may receive depends not on his income but his whim. Normally, the courts become concerned with the level of support only when one spouse is suing for divorce. In most cases, the courts support the right of the husband to determine an appropriate level of support.

The third provision of the implied legal contract is that the wife is obliged to perform domestic services. This does not, of course, mean that a woman who works outside the home is doing anything illegal. It does mean, however, that when marriage and family matters are decided by the courts, the traditional role responsibilities are taken for granted. Because a wife is obliged to perform these services, "the courts have refused to honor contracts in which the husband agreed to pay his wife for housekeeping, entertaining, and other 'wifely tasks,' " (Weitzman, 1974, p. 1189).

Many women have complained that this provision overlooks the fact of female employment and imposes a double burden. That no salary can be paid for housework, some argue, causes women's work to be undervalued. If after years of providing unpaid services the woman divorces, she may, as Weitzman notes, "be cheated out of her fair share of her half of the effort" (1974, p. 1192).

The same criticisms have been made of the fourth provision, that women are responsible for child care. The legal assumption is that this is a "natural and proper" role for women. Critics say that this practice does not take account of the needs of children or the individual traits, capabilities, and preferences of their parents.

In each of these respects, the state steps in when a couple marries and partially defines the nature of their relationship. It has often been asked over the past few years what justification there is for state intervention into what is often assumed to be a private and personal agreement. Jurists refer back to landmark decisions in which the state's "compelling interest" in marriage and family arrangements was first articulated. "Marriage is often referred to as a contract," as one 1888 Supreme Court ruling stated it,

> but it is something more than a contract. The consent of the parties is of course essential to its existence, but when the contract to marry is executed by the marriage, a relation between the parties is created which they cannot change. Other contracts may be modified, restricted, or enlarged, or entirely released upon the consent of the parties. Not so with marriage. The relation once formed, the law steps in and holds the parties to various obligations and liabilities. It is an institution in the maintenance of which in its purity the public is deeply interested, for it is the foundation of the family and of society, without which there would be neither civilization nor progress. (Maynard v. Hill, 125 U.S. 190, in Fleischmann, 1974, p. 38)

Over the past few years there have been increasing pressures for reform in the laws regulating marriage and family, particularly those that are gender specific. Several recent court decisions have responded to those pressures. For example, in 1979 the Supreme Court ruled that state laws specifying that husbands but not wives may be required to pay alimony are unconstitutional, in violation of the equal protection clause of the Fourteenth Amendment. This decision overruled an Alabama law that had been declared constitutional by the courts in that state, and it also overturned similar laws in ten other states. In the words of the majority opinion, written by Justice Brennan, "The old notion that generally it is the man's primary responsibility to provide a home and its essentials can no longer justify a statute that discriminates on the basis of gender" (*The New York Times,* March 6, 1979, p. 1). And although the Court recognized that it is a legitimate state objective to protect the needier spouse in divorce cases, it argued that such objectives could best be met by laws that are "gender neutral."

The 1979 Supreme Court ruling was not the first time that the equal protection clause had been invoked in sex discrimination cases, but it was the clearest statement supporting the principle of "gender neutral" laws that has been made by the Supreme Court. Still, as we have seen, most of the marriage and family laws are gender specific, and it would require many challenges to the constitutionality of such laws for them to be struck down on a case-by-case basis. It is for this reason that the proponents of the Equal Rights Amendment (ERA) feel that its passage is essential in order to end a tradition of sex discrimination in the laws.

The proposed ERA states that "Equality of rights under the law shall not be denied or abridged by the United States or by any state on account of sex. The Congress shall have the power to enforce, by appropriate legislation, the provisions of this article." It was approved overwhelmingly in 1972 by both the House and the Senate. However, before it can be recognized as a constitutional amendment, the ERA must be ratified by three-quarters of the fifty states. As of February 1979, when the amendment was narrowly defeated in both Illinois and North Carolina, it was still three votes short of becoming the 27th Amendment. At the same time, there was action in three states—Indiana, Montana, and South Dakota—to rescind previous approval of the amendment. Although Congress has extended the ratification deadline for the ERA to 1982, there is serious question about whether the amendment's supporters can summon enough support for its approval.

If passed, the ERA would have a substantial impact on marriage and family laws. It would require that spouses be treated equally on the basis of individual capacities, and it would change many of the provisions of the marital contract that we have discussed. Amendments to the Constitution are, by intention, general statements of principle. When they are written, no one can say for sure what their consequences will be. That depends upon how the courts interpret and apply them. However, based on the experience of the seventeen states that have already passed legislation similar to the ERA, we can anticipate some of the probable effects of this amendment, if it is passed.

With regard to marriage and family law, the ERA would probably bring about the following changes: (1) it would prohibit states from imposing greater liability on the husband, solely because of his sex; (2) it would eliminate the presumption that, in most cases, the woman is the proper guardian of the children; and (3) it would prohibit the enforcement of conjugal expectations (such as the performance of domestic services) defined according to sex.

Aside from its impact on marriage and family laws, the ERA would probably bring about other

Supporters of ERA.

Point of View

Box 6–2 / The Equal Rights Amendment—Pro and Con

The Argument Against the ERA

"Women are differ-equal," argues Mrs. Annette Stern, a suburban mother of three—she refers to herself as a "home executive"—and head of Operation Wake-Up, a New York-based group that opposes the Equal Rights Amendment.

> We are physically different and entitled to different treatment under the law. But the ERA would forbid any distinction whatsoever between the sexes, which is not what most women and men want . . . This is a unisex amendment, and we are not a unisex society. (in Klemesrud, 1975, p. 46)

Opponents of the ERA such as Mrs. Stern fear that the amendment would take away more rights than it guarantees, particularly for women who want to be full-time wives and mothers. As they see it, the amendment would cause women to lose pension benefits and widows' insurance; subject women to the draft; open public restrooms to both sexes; legalize homosexual marriages; eliminate the lower insurance rates for which women now qualify; and take away women's rights to alimony and child support payments.

At Stop-ERA rallies around the country, Mrs. Stern and other opponents of the amendment mention examples of the rights that women have lost in states that have already passed such measures. One such story involves a sixty-seven-year-old California woman who was living on alimony. When her husband petitioned the courts to reduce alimony payments, the judge agreed with his request. "The woman was told she had to make provisions for herself," Mrs. Stern says, "but how could she at age sixty-seven? Her husband was able to retire on a pension and Social Security, but she had nothing." In other cases, she says, women's lounges provided at places of work have been taken away after men have demanded equal facilities (in Klemesrud, 1975, p. 46).

One of the most substantial fears about the ERA is that it might nullify many of the labor laws that protect women. While the advocates of ERA say that such "protection" has kept women from seeking better jobs and overtime pay, opponents fear that the measures will be taken away entirely. However, as indicated in a report on the intent of the ERA issued by the Senate Judiciary Committee, certain forms of protection might actually be expanded. "It is expected that those laws that provide a meaningful protection would be expanded to include both men and women, as, for exam-

changes as well. It would, for example, make men and women equally responsible for jury duty. It would prohibit sex-based job discrimination. Women would have the same rights that men currently have to own and manage property and manage an estate. Enlistment requirements for the armed forces would probably be the same for males and females. Certain criminal laws would be changed too. Prostitution, for example, would no longer be defined as a crime committed only by women. Men and women who commit the same crimes would be subject to the same sentences.

Perhaps the most interesting thing about the ERA debate is that in many states a higher percentage of men than women favor it. The fact that this amendment promises equality of the sexes hardly means that most women agree that it represents their best interests. Across the country, citizens' groups with names like WUNDER (Women United to Defend Existing Rights) and Operation Wake-Up have orga-

ple, minimum wage laws . . . or laws requiring rest periods."

Many of the women who oppose the ERA view it as a measure designed and advocated by radical feminists, one which may benefit an élite of professional women but not the ordinary laborer or full-time housewife. Some fear that it will force all women out of the home and into the labor force. As one writer notes, "This is surely the basic reason why fewer women than men favored the [New York State] ERA. They were not saying, 'I am against equal rights.' They were saying 'I am affirming the worth of my life' " (Lear, 1976, p. 30).

The Argument for the ERA

Those who support the ERA accuse its opponents of manufacturing fears and inventing fictitious consequences of the amendment. In states that have passed legislation similar to the ERA, they argue, widows have *not* been deprived of benefits, mothers have *not* been forced to work against their will, and elderly divorcées have *not* been deprived of support payments. Neither will this amendment lead to unisex restrooms; sex-segregated public sleeping quarters and restrooms are protected by constitutionally guaranteed rights to privacy.

Perhaps the most misunderstood issue is the "right to support." The intent of the ERA is not to prevent women from being full-time housewives or to force them to contribute half of the family's financial support. Rather, it more clearly defines the duty of the wage earner, male or female, to support the spouse who performs such work as housekeeping or child rearing, which does not generate income. In a study of court opinions in the fifteen ERA states, attorney Alice Price concludes that "The ERA has not been held to require a fifty-fifty breakdown in terms of financial obligation, but rather a realistic assessment of capacities, including evaluation of nonmonetary contributions to the household" (in Lear, 1976, p. 30).

In any case, as proponents of the amendment argue, at present a woman's "right to support" is uncertain at best. Though the laws require that a husband must provide the "necessaries" of food and shelter for his wife and children, the courts rarely step in to define what those necessaries are, or to force a husband to provide a higher level of support. And despite popular stories about "alimony drones," only a minority of divorced husbands actually pay substantial alimony.

Supporters of the ERA argue that the only way women can be guaranteed their equal rights is to pass a constitutional amendment which would put an end to a long tradition of sexual discrimination. If it is ratified, the ERA would give couples more freedom to define the privileges and responsibilities of marriage according to personal preferences and individual capabilities.

nized to convince voters that they should say "No" to the ERA. Those who oppose the amendment tell us as much as those who favor it about current feelings toward the marriage contract (see Box 6–2).

Individual Marriage Contracts

Over the past few years, there have been arguments of another sort about changes that should be made in the laws regarding marriage and family. As currently defined, the laws not only assign certain responsibilities according to sex, but they also define the nature of the marital commitment. Thus, as Weitzman comments, the laws "allow no individual choice in the degree of commitment and involvement in a relationship. Yet, in our rapidly changing society, not all people want the same degree of intensity in their personal relationships." Furthermore, as she points out, there is a wide variety of individuals—unwed couples, homosexuals, communards, and those who choose to redefine certain obligations and privileges—who are deprived of a legally recognized marriage (1975, p. 547). The recent interest in custom-designed marriage contracts suggests that many people today are taking a closer look at what they mean by the marital commitment and rejecting certain assumptions that have been built into the contract.

Looking at the divorce rate as an index of the number of failures produced by our present system of marriage, some have suggested that the vows be written in the form of a legal contract. "What if we made the tough part of marriage getting in instead of getting out?" ask Sheresky and Mannes. "What if we obliged potential partners to explore together in advance of marriage—and in writing—their motives for marrying, as well as the extent of their intended commitment with regard to children, property sharing, and future alimony, should the marriage fail?" Requiring a couple to look at their motives and potential obligations in this way may seem cold-blooded. It might force them to acknowledge certain incompatibilities that would normally be overlooked in the courtship process, leading them to decide against going through with the marriage. "But that," say Sheresky and Mannes, "is just the point" (1972, p. 33).

It appears that more and more couples have begun to do what Sheresky and Mannes suggest, to write the vow in the form of a legal contract specifying responsibilities and obligations, roles and rights. As we have seen in the last few pages, marriage in any case is a contract. Individuals who custom design a contract are trying to carve out an understanding that suits their personal beliefs and needs better than the unwritten, implied legal contract.

What might be included in such a marriage contract? It should spell out many of the conditions and assumptions according to which marriages are normally structured, even if those assumptions are rarely articulated. The contract would deal with such basic issues as economic expectations, household responsibilities, plans for children, and career intentions (see Box 6–3). One of the potential advantages of designing a marital agreement of this sort is that role responsibilities could be assigned according to personal preferences and abilities, not by the dictates of tradition. As writer Susan Edmiston comments, "Sitting down and writing out a contract may seem a cold and formal way of working out an intimate relationship, but it is often the only way of coping with the ghosts of 2,000 years of tradition lurking in our definitions of marriage" (1972, p. 32).

Certain agreements between partners—a decision for the husband to pay his wife for household services, for example—would violate legal assumptions about the marital relationship. In such cases, the terms of the agreement would be unenforceable if they came up for judgment in court. Why, then, do some couples bother to work out an individually tailored contract that might be declared invalid? As one Hartford, Connecticut, attorney commented when asked whether such contracts were enforceable in his state in 1975,

> I cannot foresee how a court would ever have the occasion to "enforce" most of the provisions which a comprehensive marriage contract should contain. Can you see a husband suing his wife to get her to do the dishes, or a wife trying to obtain relief from her husband's insistence that she take birth control pills? The most important effect of a marriage contract is to help people define how they want to behave. There is no use entering one if you expect to seek a judge's assistance to assure compliance. (in Fleischmann, 1974, p. 5)

In other words, it is the process of defining a contract, not the expectation of its legal enforcement, that is important. The greater part of contract law has to do with the assignment of property, not abstract rights or personal relationships. Courts have traditionally been reluctant to interfere in marital disputes, and the presence of a written contract would not be likely to change that. "Couples should understand," writes Lenore Weitzman,

Involvement Exercises

Box 6–3 / Designing Your Own Marriage Contract

All marriages are based on a long list of assumptions and understandings. A relationship is structured according to these rights, obligations, and role responsibilities, though sometimes they are barely articulated. If in the past it could often be assumed that spouses from similar backgrounds would agree on basic issues and responsibilities, that assumption can no longer be made.

A contract like the one outlined in this box can be used either in lieu of marriage or to define an understanding between two people who intend to marry. Essentially, it is a way to encourage couples to think in specific terms about their compatibility before they commit themselves to a relationship. If, in general, we exaggerate our similarities with people we like and disguise the differences, drawing up a contract is one way to identify potential causes of friction.

Drawing up a contract requires couples to make a conscious decision about household responsibilities, career priorities, and other matters that are often decided by tradition. It requires the exploration, before the commitment is made, of certain potentially troublesome "what if" situations. And it assumes that the relationship will change, and that the contract may require modification later on.

The topics and issues listed here suggest provisions that individuals might want to include in a marriage contract. They are taken from contracts suggested by attorney Karl Fleischmann (1974) and sociologists Lenore Weitzman (1974) and Marvin Sussman (1975).

I. Personal Goals and Expectations

A. What is the relative importance of personal development and job or career satisfactions? Discussions about career objectives should raise questions about the potential stresses that careers place upon personal relationships. Especially when both spouses intend to work, they should agree on the priorities if a career opportunity arises for one partner in another city.

B. Short-term goals and long-term expectations. In general, it is difficult to foresee any situation more than about two years in the future. But it is useful for individuals to discuss the difference between long-term and short-term expectations, and to explore such matters as lifestyle preferences, place of residence, and so on.

II. Financial Matters

A. Will all assets owned by partners when they enter the contract be separately held and managed, or will they be merged and jointly managed? Are both partners clear about what is considered separate property and what is considered common property?

B. Support and living expenses. Couples may agree upon a proportional contribution to total expenses. Or they may decide that each person is responsible for certain types of expenses. A third possibility is that couples may pool their income without determining a specific share for which each is responsible, and then divide equally whatever is left over. It is important to agree on continued support for the partner who, because of pregnancy, child care, loss of employment, or illness, may not contribute to family income. A basic issue is how the partner will be compensated for performing household duties that do not produce income.

C. Managing income. There should be a specific agreement about how income will be apportioned, how much spending money each spouse should have, and who controls the checkbook. A basic issue is deciding on rights in money management, regardless of who the current wage earner is.

(Box 6-3 continues on page 180)

(Box 6-3 continued from page 179)

III. Household Arrangements

A. Domicile. Couples should discuss where they intend to live. If it is possible that a career advancement for one of the partners will require a change in residence, the couple should discuss in advance how that decision should be made, after balancing both personal and job-related considerations.

B. Household management. Some couples share all tasks on an equal basis. Others assign certain tasks to each partner, based on a mutual agreement about personal preferences and abilities. A third option is to agree on a detailed list of household responsibilities, performed according to a specific schedule by each partner. A basic issue is how household tasks may be reallocated as the employment pattern shifts.

IV. Sexual Expectations

A. Individual preferences and expectations. Sexual incompatibility is one of the chief reasons why relationships break up. One issue is expected frequency of sexual activity. Another problem may arise when one individual finds repugnant something that the other expects or requires for sexual gratification. Differences in this area might well be discussed with a sex therapist.

B. Extramarital sex. This is a subject of considerable concern to most people. Some couples agree that if either enters into a serious or prolonged affair, he or she is obliged to disclose that fact to the other.

V. Children

A. One of the basic questions that should be explored in any relationship is the desirability of having children. This involves (1) assigning responsibility for birth control; (2) deciding on family size and spacing of children, if the couple decides to have children; and (3) making a decision about whether adoption is an acceptable alternative.

B. Child care and parenting responsibilities. Some couples divide child care responsibilities by splitting up the tasks. Others agree to take responsibility for specific time periods, stages in the child's life cycle, or for specific children.

VI. Relationships with Others

A. Kinfolk. Both spouses should discuss family obligations. Is it agreed that both will share certain vacations or leisure time with the other's kinfolk? The contract should include some understanding about financial responsibilities to parents and relatives, if the situation arises. A common issue is whether either spouse feels that the couple has a responsibility to take an elderly or infirm parent into their home.

that some of the rights and obligations which they include in their contract may not be subject either to specific performance or money damages. If a breach of contract caused no tangible damage to the other party—as for example where one spouse breaches an agreement to practice a particular religion or to accompany the other to football games or the ballet—monetary damages might be difficult to assess and the award might not comport with the injured party's expectations. . . . Couples writing a contract must realize that some of the provisions in their contract are there to clarify their own thinking and to set forth ideals and aspirations, and they cannot expect that they will all be enforceable. (1974, p. 1271)

Only one state, California, now requires premarital counseling before a couple can be granted a marriage license. And this is required only if one of the applicants is under age eighteen, to encourage the couple to assess their

B. Friends and business associates. One of the basic assumptions in any marriage is how much time will be spent together, in what types of activities. Do both individuals agree about friendships, interests, or activities that may be pursued individually? Do they assume that social invitations extended to one will automatically include the other?

C. Obligations to previous spouse. As divorce and remarriage become more common, this becomes a source of problems. Certain obligations arising from previous marriages—such as those to children or support payments to a former spouse—make demands on one's time and financial resources. These should be discussed.

VII. Duration of Contract, Renegotiation, and Review

A. Duration. Options include a specific term for the contract, such as five or ten years; a contract that lasts until a specific goal is met, such as completing one's education or raising children; or a contract that stays in effect indefinitely.

B. Review and renegotiation. Some contracts call for periodic review. By specifying a review period, an occasion is provided for discussing and resolving any differences that may arise.

C. Unresolved conflicts. Some couples agree beforehand to seek out the help of an objective third party such as a marriage counselor in the event that a difference cannot be resolved.

VIII. Terminating the Contract

A. Grounds and conditions of termination. Some couples try to specify what will constitute breach of contract (neglect or cruelty, for example). There are two options: agree that the partnership can be terminated, uncontested, if either individual wishes to do so, or agree that termination requires the mutual consent of both individuals.

B. Settlement. How will common property, debts, income, and living expenses be divided upon dissolution? The settlement agreement should acknowledge the fact that if one partner has supported the other through school, the one who has supported the other deserves some form of compensation. If a woman passed up career opportunities to take care of the household and children, the contract might specify how she will be compensated for the loss of her earning ability.

C. Children. There should be some agreement beforehand about a custody arrangement in case of dissolution. How are the obligations for child support to be divided?

motives realistically and to anticipate the obligations of marriage. Counseling in such cases involves a process quite similar to that followed by couples who negotiate their own contract. Perhaps the recent popularity of custom-designed contracts indicates a desire to undertake marriage with one's eyes wide open as much as it reflects an interest in discarding some ancient assumptions about the meaning of marriage.

REDEFINING MARRIAGE—NEW PRIORITIES, SATISFACTIONS, AND PROBLEMS

Between the traditional marriage contract and most of the personally tailored contracts that have been drawn up over the past few years there is a dramatic difference, a difference that goes far beyond making the terms of the contract explicit. The real change is in marriage itself. New purposes and redefined functions have transformed the institution of marriage. One of the most significant aspects of that transformation is an increasing emphasis on emotional satisfaction and individual growth in marriage.

The title of a widely used text a generation ago, Ernest Burgess and Harvey Locke's *The Family: From Institution to Companionship* (1953), expresses one aspect of this transformation. We can understand what the new emphasis on companionship means by looking at the results of a 1974 survey in which men and women were asked to list in order of importance the things they considered very important to a good marriage. The responses of both males and females followed a definite pattern. At the top of the list for both sexes was being in love, which was followed by being able to talk together about feelings. Expectations that come closer to the main purposes of the traditional marriage, such things as having children and financial security, emerged eleventh and twelfth, respectively, far below such items as keeping romance alive and liking the same kind of life, activities, and friends (Roper Organization, 1974, p. 45).

One of the most distinctive aspects of modern marriage is its emphasis upon personal compatibility and companionship.

Most people in the United States who look at that list today see nothing remarkable about it. Of course being in love, talking about feelings, and liking the same kinds of activities and friends are important. But if we compare these requirements with the things that most people expected of marriage in the past and in other types of societies, we begin to see what is new in marriage today. In the past, marriage had less to do with companionship and personal growth than it does today. Here, for example, is anthropologist R. H. Lowie's description of the purposes of marriage in one preliterate group, the Kai:

> A Kai does not marry because of desires he can readily gratify outside of wedlock without assuming any responsibilities. He marries because he needs a woman to make pots and to cook his meals, to manufacture nets and weed his plantation, in return for which he provides the household with game and fish, and builds the dwelling. (1920, p. 66)

Notice that nothing is said about the emotional quality of the relationship, or its personal satisfactions. It sounds more like a business partnership than what we conceive of as marriage. The same thing might be said about this brief account of marriage in ancient Greece, from the writings of Demosthenes: "Mistresses we keep for the sake of pleasure, concubines for the daily care of our persons, but wives to bear us legitimate children and to be faithful guardians of our household" (1964, p. 445).

In Finnish society until the nineteenth century, as historian Edward Shorter points out, one had to demonstrate some very practical abilities before qualifying for the business of marriage.

"In order even to be permitted to go out socially," he writes,

> you had to pass a number of community-ordained tests. Boys had to lift heavy stones or sharpen stakes as evidence of their ability to provide for families, and girls had to be able to make a man's underwear and mend the knee of his trousers. "Don't hope for a man before you can shear the sheep's neck, knot the ends of the homespun, and sew a man's shirt," cautioned the villagers. Nowhere does this account say anything about pimples or sex appeal or liking each other, and we may guess that as the Finns chose each other for marriage, they didn't think much about these things. (1975, p. 146)

In other words, the main purposes of marriage were intensely practical. As Jessie Bernard comments, "It was always considered desirable if the partners also found one another congenial, but, in any event, they had to learn to come to terms with each other no matter what happened. The institution was far more important than the individuals themselves" (1973, p. 104).

Not so today. Personal compatibility and companionship are now very important in marriage. This is not to say, of course, that practical skills count for nothing, but rather that they have a different kind of significance. Ever since sociologist William Ogburn's writings in the 1930s, sociologists have stressed the fact that the functions of the family have been transformed. In a classic statement, Ogburn mentioned eight functions of the family: production, status conferral, education, protection, religion, recreation, affection, and procreation. He then pointed out that the modern family has lost many of these functions. The household is no longer a place of economic production; the responsibility for education has been transferred to the schools; the state has taken over many protective functions, such as providing facilities for the aged and the infirm (1934). However, if certain functions have been taken away, the ones that remain—particularly the expression of affection and emotional needs—have become more important. Accordingly, courtship now dwells on personal compatibility, and in marriage we pay much more attention to emotional responsiveness and communication skills.

In the past, companionship between spouses was not nearly so important as it has recently become in American society. In fact, there have been various barriers to companionship in many societies, such as avoidance customs that spouses were expected to heed in public and assumptions that males and females would pursue their leisure separately. As recently as the 1920s, this observation appeared in a report on life in a typical American city: "In general, a high degree of companionship is not regarded as essential for marriage. There appears to be between Middletown husbands and wives of all classes when gathered together in informal leisure-time groups relatively little spontaneous community of interest" (Lynd and Lynd, 1929, p. 118).

Over the past few decades, however, there has been an increasing emphasis upon companionship, shared leisure activities, and mutual friends. As Blood and Wolfe comment, summarizing a 1960 study of marriages in the Detroit area, "When modern Americans think of marriage, they think of companionship more than anything else" (p. 150).

Marriage in the United States today has been transformed because we bring new expectations to an institution designed to serve other, more practical purposes.

"Open Marriage"—Growth Contracts and Individual Fulfillment

From a broader perspective, we can also see that marriage has been affected by the new priority accorded to personal growth and individual fulfillment in every phase of our lives. Wherever we look among the descriptions of family life in the past or in other cultures, we are reminded that the performance of certain obligations to one's family and community took precedence over self-fulfillment. These words appear, for example, in a discussion of marriage in India and Japan: "It is a rigid principle of Eastern life that the stability of the family and the maintenance of the social order always come before the happiness of the individual" (Mace and Mace, 1960, p. 121). Commenting on the American family system in the nineteenth century, sociologist William Goode remarks that "People took it for granted that spouses who no longer loved one another, and who found life together distasteful should at least live together in public amity for the sake of their children and their standing in the community" (1971, p. 480).

Today most people choke on the idea that "at least" a couple should continue to live together, despite their personal dissatisfactions, for the sake of others. We are now influenced by a new set of ideals and assumptions. It is not at all uncommon for personal growth and individual fulfillment to take precedence over traditional obligations.

The puzzled Italian father in the film *Lovers and Other Strangers* takes a traditional perspective on the purposes of marriage. His son tries to explain that the reason he is seeking a divorce is that he and his wife have not been happy together. The father asks: "So what's happiness got to do with marriage?"

For most young people, the pursuit of happiness has a great deal to do with marriage. The popularity of the 1972 book *Open Marriage* tells us something about current values. It also provides a certain perspective on the shape of things to come. As opposed to the older emphasis on personal adjustment in marriage—when a successful marriage was defined by the ease with which each spouse accommodates to the other—"open marriage" is growth oriented.

The authors of *Open Marriage,* anthropologists Nena and George O'Neill, compare two versions of the marriage contract, a "closed marriage" and an "open marriage." Their description of "closed marriage" recalls features of the patriarchal family system of the past, in which distinct limits were placed on individual freedom and personal aspiration. The "closed marriage" contract implies a sense of belonging to one's mate and maintaining a "couple-front." It implies self-denial, rigid role prescriptions, and total exclusivity. At the basis of this family system is the conception of *duty.* One must do certain things regardless of personal inclinations.

Open Marriage is an argument for a new type of marital relationship, one that the O'Neills refer to as a growth contract.

> Open marriage can be defined as a relationship in which the partners are committed to their own and to each other's growth. Supportive caring and increasing security in individual identities make possible the sharing of self-growth with a meaningful other who encourages and anticipates his own and his mate's growth. It is a relationship which is flexible enough to allow for change, which is constantly being renegotiated in the light of changing needs, consensus in decision-making, acceptance and encouragement of individual growth, and openness to new possibilities for growth. Obviously, following this model often involves a departure—sometimes a radical one—from rigid conformity to the established husband–wife roles and is not easy to effect. (1972b, p. 403)

This is indeed a radical redefinition of marriage. It stresses growth, not durability; roles that are negotiated according to personal preferences, not ones defined by tradition. Perhaps most important is the absence of any sense of duty or obligation that would take priority over personal growth. This is a vivid example of how much the meaning of marriage has changed in an era when personal aspirations have a virtually unchallenged priority.

For many people, *Open Marriage* describes an attractive alternative. But it is also very difficult to achieve. Open communication, flexible roles, and individual growth make personal demands that the older styles of marriage did not make. When marriage was defined mainly as a package of role responsibilities, it was an easier matter to determine whether or not it was satisfactory. It was less subjective than the growth-oriented marriage, in which both spouses seek out certain types of individual fulfillment.

Without doubt, many people derive from today's marriages a level of emotional satisfaction that yesterday's marriages only rarely delivered. It is also true that as more demands are placed on the marital bond for the satisfaction of emotional needs, it becomes more fragile. As Philip Slater remarks,

> Spouses are now asked to be lovers, friends, and mutual therapists in a society which is forcing the marriage bond to become the closest, deepest, and most important and most enduring relationship of one's life. Paradoxically, then, it is increasingly likely to fall short of the emotional demands placed upon it and be dissolved. (1968, p. 90)

The popularity of *Open Marriage* and the increasing interest in individually tailored marital agreements both illustrate the fact that many people today refuse to agree to an implied contract established by tradition. The feeling is spreading that no one should have the terms of intimate relationships dictated to them, and that couples should be able to choose the type of commitment they want. We have already begun to see greater public acceptance of different degrees of marital commitment, just as fraternity pins or engagement rings symbolize different degrees of premarital commitment. As Jessie Bernard says,

> . . . We may one day arrive at the idea not of an all-or-nothing marital status, an either-or one, but one of degrees of being married. "How committed are you?" we may ask rather than merely, "What is your marital status?" One may be 100 percent committed to a spouse, permanently and exclusively, or only contingently committed, both the duration and the exclusiveness being contingent on a host of other—specified—factors, such as "How well do I love my partner?" "How dependent am I on the relationship?" "How much more is my work (or whatever) worth to me than my relationship?" and so on. (1972, p. 92)

A society that allows that kind of freedom would also require a good deal of personal decision making on the part of young couples before they say "I do."

Conclusions

Setting out in this chapter to explore the meaning of marriage, we first examined the symbols embodied in the traditional wedding ceremony and noticed that they express all four of the elements in Stephens's definition of marriage. Underneath the variety of its forms, marriage is always (1) a socially recognized sexual union (2) that begins with a public announcement or ceremony, (3) is defined by a more or less explicit contract, and (4) is undertaken with the assumption of permanence. Also, in our society, marriages are heterosexual and provide the social legitimation for bearing children.

The wedding ceremony itself as well as the laws regulating marriage and family indicate that it is more than just a personal commitment between two people. Individuals are not free to give it whatever meanings they please. As defined by law, marriage provides that the husband will be head of the family and responsible for its support, and that the wife will be obliged to perform domestic and child care services. Legislation such as the proposed Equal Rights Amendment would redefine the legal contract by prohibiting conjugal expectations made on the basis of sex. But until or unless such legislation is passed, the law continues to assume sex-based obligations and responsibilities, even if many individuals in today's society do not want to meet them.

Some couples today are writing their own marriage contracts to express their mutual expectations, rights, and obligations. An exploration of the topics normally covered in such contracts provides a better understanding of what is normally implied—if only rarely discussed or negotiated—when two people marry.

In the last few pages of this chapter we compared the implied contract of the traditional marriage with the assumptions and expectations that many couples bring to marriage today. In the past, marriage was a somewhat more practical matter in which each spouse was expected to perform certain role responsibilities, but now the personal relationship has begun to take precedence. More emphasis is placed on companionship, mutual affection, and individual growth.

Throughout this chapter, as in others, we have noted the great range of personal alternatives available to us today. Marriage is no longer considered by many to be a sacrament, an agreement whose terms are preordained and unchangeable. Writing a personal contract is a way of recognizing and choosing among a range of practical alternatives.

In many respects, today's marriages are more demanding and more fragile than were the marriages of the past. They reflect new expectations for companionship and personal growth. Throughout this chapter we have observed the effects of redefined sex roles. In the next two chapters we will direct our attention specifically to sex roles and the question of equality between the sexes.

REFERENCES

Jessie Bernard, *The future of marriage.* New York: Bantam, 1972.

Robert O. Blood, Jr. and Donald M. Wolfe. *Husbands and wives.* New York: Free Press, 1960.

Ernest W. Burgess and Harvey J. Locke. *The family: From institution to companionship.* New York: American, 1953.

Center for a Woman's Own Name. *Booklet for women who wish to determine their own names after marriage.* Barrington, Ill., 1974.

John F. Cuber and Peggy B. Harroff. *Sex and the significant Americans.* Baltimore: Penguin, 1968.

Demosthenes. Against Naera. In A. T. Murray, trans. *Collected works,* vol. 6. Cambridge, Mass.: Harvard University Press, 1964.

Susan Edmiston. How to write your own marriage contract. *Ms.* magazine, Spring 1972.

Karl Fleischmann. Marriage by contract: Defining the terms of relationship. *Family Law Quarterly* 8 (1974): 27–49.

———. Ask a lawyer. *Marriage, Divorce and Family Newsletter,* June 1, 1975.

William J. Goode. Family disorganization. In R. K. Merton and R. Nisbet, eds. *Contemporary social problems.* New York: Harcourt, Brace, 1971.

Judy Klemesrud. As New York vote on equal rights nears, two women disagree about its effects. *The New York Times,* September 18, 1975, p. 46.

Martha Weinman Lear. You'll probably think I'm stupid. *The New York Times Magazine,* April 11, 1976, p. 30 et passim.

R. H. Lowie. *Primitive society.* New York: Boni and Liveright, 1920.

Robert S. Lynd and Helen M. Lynd. *Middletown.* New York: Harcourt, 1929.

Priscilla Ruth MacDougall. Surnames a developing legal and feminist issue for women and men. *Marriage, Divorce and Family Newsletter,* February 1976.

David Mace and Vera Mace. *Marriage East and West.* New York: Dolphin, 1960.

William Ogburn. The family and its functions. In President's Committee on Social Trends. *Recent social trends in the United States.* New York: McGraw-Hill, 1934.

Nena O'Neill and George O'Neill. *Open marriage.* New York: Evans, 1972(a).

———. Open Marriage: A synergistic model. *The Family Coordinator.* October 1972(b), pp. 398–405.

The Roper Organization. *The Virginia Slims American women's opinion poll.* New York: The Roper Organization, 1974.

Marcia Seligson. *The eternal bliss machine: America's way of wedding.* New York: Bantam, 1974.

Norman Sheresky and Marya Mannes. A radical guide to wedlock. *Saturday Review,* July 29, 1972, p. 33.

Edward Shorter. *The making of the modern family.* New York: Basic Books, 1975.

Philip Slater. Social limitations on libidinal withdrawal. *The American Sociological Review* 28 (1963): 339–364.

———. Some social consequences of temporary systems. In W. G. Bennis and P. E. Slater. *The temporary society.* New York: Harper & Row, 1968.

John Spiegel. *Transactions: The interplay between individual, family, and society.* New York: Science House, 1971.

William N. Stephens. *The family in cross-cultural perspective.* New York: Holt, 1963.

Marvin Sussman. *Marriage contracts: Social and legal consequences.* Paper presented at the 1975 International Workshop on Changing Sex Roles in Family and Society, Dubrovnik, Yugoslavia, June 1975.

Lenore Weitzman. Legal regulation of marriage: Tradition and change. *California Law Review,* 62 (1974): 1169–1288.

———. To love, honor, and obey? Traditional legal marriage and alternative family forms. *The Family Coordinator,* October 1975.

FOR FURTHER STUDY

Journalist Marcia Seligson provides a readable account of today's weddings in *The Eternal Bliss Machine* (New York: Bantam, 1974). Jessie Bernard explores the nature of the marital commitment in Chapter 5 of her excellent book *The Future of Marriage* (New York: Bantam, 1973). To better understand how the purposes of marriage have changed, it is still useful to look at William Ogburn's writings from the 1930s. See "The Family and Its Functions," which appeared in *Recent Social Trends in the United States* (New York: McGraw-Hill, 1934).

Anyone interested in further exploring the legal aspects of marriage and family might be advised to begin with the October 1977 issue of *The Family Coordinator,* which includes articles on such topics as sex laws and the likely impact of the ERA. For an interesting analysis of people's attitudes toward the Equal Rights Amendment, see an article by Joan Huber, Cynthia Rexroat, and Glenna Spitze, "A Crucible of Opinion on Women's Status: ERA in Illinois," which appeared in the December 1978 issue of *Social Forces.* Perhaps the best single discussion of the legal aspects of marriage is still Lenore Weitzman's "Legal Regulation of Marriage: Tradition and Change," which appeared in the *California Law Review,* vol 62, no. 4, July 1974. For information on recent court decisions and their implications, see the *Journal of Family Law,* the *Family Law Reporter,* and the *Family Law Quarterly.* For a good discussion of the state equal rights amendments and their impact on domestic relations law, see the article by Paul Kurtz that appeared in the Summer 1977 issue of the *Family Law Quarterly.*

J. Gipson Wells wrote an article entitled "A Critical Look at Personal Marriage Contracts," in *The Family Coordinator,* January 1976, which provides a different perspective from that of this chapter. An article by Cama Clarkson Merritt, "Changing Marital Rights and Duties by Contract: Legal Obstacles in North Carolina," in *Wake Forest Law Review,* vol. 13, no. 85, 1977, provides a detailed analysis of some of the obstacles to individual marriage contracts.

"Stanza i Rainbow" James McGarrell

7 Male and Female—Biological and Sociological Perspectives

No society completely ignores the distinction between male and female in assigning social roles. These roles can be defined as the agreed-upon expectations about how we ought to act in certain situations. One of the main differences between living together and being married, as many couples have discovered, is that marriage is defined by specific sex-role expectations. Here, for example, is a comment from one unhappy ex-husband about what changed as soon as the vows were exchanged. "Before we married," he said, "everything was free and easy and really great. So okay, we marry and right away she begins to take me for granted. Now I'm a husband and should be emptying the garbage. Instead of working it out, like we did before, suddenly I'm supposed to do this, supposed to do that. You'd think she'd know me better, wouldn't you, after all we've been through together?" (O'Neill and O'Neill, 1972, p. 140).

Until recently, it was quite likely that the role expectations among spouses—at least those from similar backgrounds—would match. She would know what he expected of a wife, and he would know what she expected of a husband. Neither would be surprised that the other subscribed to the customary expectations. And both would be upset if every domestic responsibility had to be negotiated, assigned either to the husband or the wife. Social roles are useful because they relieve us of the responsibility of deciding in each new situation what we should do. They also facilitate our interactions with others by telling us what we can expect.

One of the most basic reasons for rapidly changing marriage and family relationships today is that those sex-role expectations are being redefined. It is no longer assumed by many couples that the husband is solely responsible for economic support and that his wife is solely responsible for the children and the housework. In the O'Neills' book *Open Marriage* (1972) it is argued that "tasks, behavior, and attitudes strictly separated along pre-determined lines, according to outdated concepts of 'male' and 'female' are psychologically destructive" (p. 53).

Yet the O'Neills, along with most other responsible commentators on marriage today, admit that totally role-free behavior is impossible to attain, and not even desirable. It is difficult to imagine a marriage in which husband and wife have to "work out," each evening, the question of who will take out the garbage.

Roles are useful in making relationships—especially marital relationships—run more smoothly, but only when the expectations of both partners correspond. Conflict is likely if a man expects the woman he marries to be a full-time homemaker and mother, while she intends to pursue a career and expects him to share the household chores. As we would guess, studies of divorced couples indicate that such relationships are often characterized by contradictory expectations about the roles of husband and wife (Jacobsen, 1952, p. 146). Today, changing ideas about sex-role expectations are putting a considerable strain on many marriages. (See Box 7–1.)

Margaret Mead, like others who have been peering into the future, envisioned a society in which the differences between the sexes would be minimized.

> There would be a growing disregard for sex as a basic mode of differentiation. Boys and girls would be given a similar education and like demands would be made on them for citizenship, economic contribution, and creativity. Adults who functioned as parents would be given special forms of protection. Limitations on the freedom of women would be removed. Boys and girls would be differentiated not by sex-typed personality characteristics, but by temperament. The two-sex exclusive pair would lose its power. Instead, companionship for work, play, and stable living would come to be based upon many different combinations, within and across sex lines, among different-sized clusters of individuals. (1969, p. 872)

This is an interesting vision of a society very different from the one we live in. But before we can disregard sex "as a basic mode of differentiation," we need to answer one fundamental question: How different are the sexes? Do culturally defined sex roles merely elaborate upon innate differences which, because they are biologically determined, are unchangeable? We will attempt to answer these questions in the following few pages.

ANATOMY IS DESTINY . . . OR IS IT?

Sex roles are normally so much a taken-for-granted feature of the social landscape that many people hardly notice them. One way of calling attention to conventional assumptions about masculinity and femininity is to do a role reversal, and to notice how bizarre the result is.

Imagine a society in which all of the traits commonly attributed to men are assigned to women, and vice versa. Feature articles in men's magazines in this upside-down society offer beauty tips for anxious, middle-aged men who have only a few "good years" left. The same magazines offer helpful hints so that the devoted househusband can use his "masculine touch" to transform a house into a home. The good husband is expected to tend to a thousand little details around the house, so that his wife is free to concentrate on more important things, like her career.

Powerful women executives sit around conference tables smoking cigars, and making wisecracks about their gossiping, overly emotional husbands. Female hardhats laugh at men's attempts to get into the construction unions because that, after all, is physically demanding women's work. As everyone knows, men break down under stress, and they are not dependable. Aside from that, the presence of men on the job would cramp the style of the female hardhats. They commonly utter a stream of obscenities to "let off steam," and their favorite on-the-job entertainment is whistling at attractive males who walk past. Even if the men who are the object of that attention are a little embarrassed, no harm is done, because—as all the women know—men are basically vain. . . .

If such a situation seems both improbable and unnatural, it is because we are so accustomed

Research Perspectives on Marriage and Family

Box 7–1 / The Social Survey—Measuring Attitude Changes on Marital Roles and Responsibilities

There are two common problems that we all have in making valid generalizations about the social world around us. First, we pay more attention to the exceptional instance than we do to the less interesting, more commonplace event. Second, we usually assume that our own social surroundings are typical, that the opinions we share with our friends are those that "people in general" hold. In effect, most of us form our own picture of what Americans are thinking and doing by conducting informal "opinion surveys" of our friends and acquaintances. The problem with such everyday generalizations is that we tend to forget how atypical our own surroundings are.

Social surveys provide a more reliable portrait of the attitudes of a large population. They are one of the most commonly used research techniques in the social sciences, and are valuable in assessing changing attitudes toward marital roles and responsibilities.

The first step in designing a social survey is to define the *population* to be studied, and then to select a representative sample of its members. A population may include everyone living in an entire nation. In general, however, it is a considerably more specific group, such as all college seniors, the residents of a certain metropolitan area, or all women under thirty-five. Rarely is the population so small that every one of its members can be questioned. Therefore, the researcher must select a *sample* of that total population which reflects the characteristics of the entire group. With regard to most attitudes, it is important that the sample include people whose age, race, educational achievement, and income level are representative of the entire population. The care with which that sample is chosen is far more important than the total size of the group actually questioned. In the social sciences, researchers draw samples according to specific procedures based upon probability theory. The validity of survey research rests upon the proposition—which is mathematically provable—that one can make accurate inferences about an entire population by sampling only a portion of it.

The validity of survey research also depends upon the care with which the questionnaire or interview schedule is constructed. Questions must be easily understood and unambiguous. And, so far as possible, the interview schedule or questionnaire must be designed so as to minimize the tendency for the respondent to choose the answer that he or she thinks the interviewer wants to hear. Finally, the alternative answers on multiple-choice questions must not distort the respondent's views.

Here is a question about women's status that appeared in a recent survey of the eighteen-and-over population for the entire country, and had also been asked nine years earlier. It provides a perspective on the extent of changing attitudes on women's status:

(Box 7-1 continues on page 192)

(Box 7-1 continued from page 191)

DO YOU FAVOR OR OPPOSE EFFORTS TO STRENGTHEN OR CHANGE WOMEN'S STATUS IN SOCIETY?

1970

	Women say:			Men say:		
	Favor %	*Oppose* %	*Not Sure* %	*Favor* %	*Oppose* %	*Not Sure* %
Total	40	42	18	44	39	17
18 to 29	46	39	15	53	34	13
30 to 39	40	44	16	37	45	18
40 to 49	39	43	18	52	34	14
50 and over	35	45	20	38	41	21
8th grade	36	38	26	40	37	23
High school	38	45	17	43	40	17
College	44	40	16	49	38	13

Source: Louis Harris and Associates: *Virginia Slims American Women's Opinion Poll.* 1970, p. 4.

1979

	Women say:			Men say:		
	Favor %	*Oppose* %	*Not Sure* %	*Favor* %	*Oppose* %	*Not Sure* %
Total	61.2	30.6	8.2	69.7	25.3	5.1

	Both Sexes:		
	Favor %	*Oppose* %	*Not Sure* %
18 to 29	74.3	24.0	1.7
30 to 49	70.8	23.4	5.8
50 to 64	57.4	33.9	8.8
8th grade	39.2	36.3	24.5
High school	59.3	33.6	7.1
College	76.0	20.9	3.1

Source: ABC News/Louis Harris Associates, unpublished data from survey taken February 14, 1979.

Notice that there may be an ambiguity in the wording of the question. Asked about efforts to "strengthen *or change* women's status in society," some respondents may have advocated change which might not be interpreted as strengthening women's position. Assuming, however, that this possible ambiguity does not seriously distort the responses, look at the pattern described in these statistics. In general, men, more so than women, favor efforts to strengthen women's status—and this was true both in 1970 and in 1979. Overall, there was an impressive growth in support for improving women's status during those nine years. A majority of people across the country now take such a position. Support for efforts to strengthen women's status is stronger among the more highly educated.

to the script in our own society that assigns certain traits to males and others to females. It has often been assumed that "it's only natural" for men to be more aggressive and for women to be submissive. It is commonly believed that women are fulfilling their "maternal instincts" by caring for children. Men have gallantly tried to protect the "weaker sex" and have assumed that woman's place is at home. Meanwhile, of course, males take the positions of power and privilege, and enter into marriages where women are the junior partners.

In our society, the differences between men and women have not been simply superficial. For example, when a team of social scientists conducted an in-depth study of one suburban community in the 1950s, they found that "the deepest cleavage in the belief system in Crestwood Heights—more basic and deeper than differences in age, ethnic group, or status—is created by the striking divergence in the belief systems of men and women" (Seeley, Sim, and Loosley, 1956, p. 503). Women, they found, tended to believe that individuals are more important than groups, while men valued the organization over the individual, and tended to support general rules. Women valued people over things, freedom over order, happiness over achievement. Men's priorities were the reverse.

Are these differences innate, biologically determined? Is male dominance inevitable? Does anatomy determine one's destiny? Or should male dominance be regarded as the product of a sexist plot that has been handed down from one generation to another? "One of the oldest gambits," observes sociologist Philip Slater, "has been to maintain that dominance is sex-linked (as indeed it is, in some species). Thus, if a woman assumes any other than a submissive pose she is accused of being 'unfeminine.' This is an ingenious device for maintaining superior status and has been quite successful" (in Bernard, 1973, p. 165).

One way of answering these questions is to look at the cross-cultural evidence to determine if men in *all* cultures are aggressive and authoritarian, in contrast to women who are submissive and nurturing. If the evidence suggests otherwise, it would seem to support the argument that socialization patterns—and not biology—determine masculinity and femininity.

It is for this reason that a book published in 1935 by Margaret Mead, *Sex and Temperament in Three Primitive Societies,* has been so influential and so widely quoted. When she left for New Guinea in 1931, Margaret Mead said that she "shared the general belief in our society that there was a natural sex-temperament which at most could be distorted or diverted from normal expression" (1935, p. xvi). But after living among three neighboring tribes—the Arapesh, the Mundugumor, and the Tchambuli—she changed her mind.

Each culture, she found, makes a different assumption about the connection between sex and temperament. Among members of the first tribe, the Arapesh, it is assumed that there are no temperamental differences between men and women. Both males and females have what we normally think of as feminine traits. Both are gentle and passive, and share the tasks of child rearing. In contrast, both males and females of the second tribe, the Mundugumors, have what we commonly think of as masculine traits; both sexes are aggressive and combative. The members of the third tribe, the Tchambuli, believe that the sexes are different in temperament. But rather than following the role prescription of Western culture, they reverse it. The Tchambuli women, who have shaven, unadorned heads, are described as solid, practical, and powerful. In contrast, it is the Tchambuli men who seem to be the outsiders. They devote their lives to self-adornment, they bicker and pout, and they exhibit the emotional ups and downs more commonly attributed to women in our culture.

How can these temperamental differences be explained? Mead attributes most of them to socialization practices. But an anthropologist who has visited the Tchambuli more recently stresses a different set of factors. The main "cash crop" among the Tchambuli is the plaited mosquito bags, made exclusively by women, which are traded to other tribes. Because women control the main industry, they have a source of wealth that enables them to gain status and power. It may be that women's temperament—as well as men's—is as much a product of economic arrangements as it is of socialization practices (Gewertz, 1976). It should be noted that socialization practices also reflect economic arrangements.

In any case, the implications of Margaret Mead's study of these tribes are highly significant. She concludes that the characteristics that we assign to one sex or the other are "mere variations of human temperament to which members of either or both sexes may, with more or less success in the case of individuals, be educated to approximate" (1949, p. xvi).

But you might look at the cross-cultural evidence and come to quite a different conclusion. If there is no natural connection between sex and temperament, then we may assume that personality traits would be assigned on a random basis to males and females in various cultures. However, when anthropologist William Stephens compared sex roles and work roles of men and women in more than a hundred primitive societies, he came to the conclusion that "there is much less intercultural variation than one might expect" (1963, p. 281). Work around the house—such as cooking, cleaning, and child care—is almost everywhere the responsibility of the wife. Tasks such as hunting, herding, and handicraft with metals or stone are almost always done by men. In other words, if we look at the division of labor by sex in a variety of cultures, for many tasks a virtual consensus exists about what is woman's work and what is man's.

The anthropological evidence suggests that while there is nothing inevitable about the connection between sex and temperament, there are significant cross-cultural consistencies, especially in the division of labor. Some of these can be explained on the basis of physiological differences, but not all of them. The cross-cultural evidence indicates that biological factors are not solely or inevitably responsible for certain temperamental traits in males and females. But, at the same time, it does not rule out the influence of biology in shaping sex roles. Masculinity and femininity represent cultural exaggerations of the biological facts of maleness and femaleness. It is no longer possible to defend the position that either nature or nurture is entirely responsible for the differences between the sexes. Sexual identity results from the interweaving of both biological and sociological factors.

TWO PERSPECTIVES ON SEX, GENDER, AND IDENTITY

How many times have you been asked to "Check one: ———Male; ———Female"? In our society, as in most others, it is assumed that your answer says a lot about who you are. And it is assumed that male/female is an obvious distinction, based upon anatomical features. But the closer we look at this complex thing called gender identity, the more complicated it becomes. One's genetic sex does not necessarily coincide with the fetal and pubertal hormones normally associated with it. Internal and external sexual anatomy do not always match. Not all babies are born clearly boys or girls. In some few cases, the sex to which children are assigned does not match the biological facts. More significantly for most people, there is a great deal of variation among both males and females, as well as between them.

Jessie Bernard comments that "as a corrective to this nonsense on nature's part and to tidy up her [*sic*] carelessness, concepts like masculinity and femininity evolve to show the two collectivities what to be like vis-à-vis one another, regardless of their heredity" (1973, p. 273).

Because the nature-versus-nurture controversy has become a heated debate in the past few years, it is important to understand the relative importance of both biological and sociological factors in determining sexual identity. The most vocal spokeswomen for the nurture position have been the radical feminists. Opposed to them are people like those who talked to sociologist Mirra Komarovsky when she studied blue-collar marriages. Many of these individuals took the position that, after all, men and women are different, and not much can be done about it (1967).

The Biological Perspective

In any culture there is little question about how to determine whether the newborn child is male or female. Though the anatomical differences are obvious in most instances, what may come as a surprise is how similar the body plan is in both sexes. An individual's genetic sex is determined at the moment of conception. All humans have twenty-three pairs of chromosomes. All are alike except one pair. The sex chromosomes in a normal female are xx; in a normal male, xy. The female ovaries produce eggs, all of which carry the x chromosome; and the male testes produce sperm, some of which carry the x chromosome, some the y. If the egg fuses with a sperm carrying the x chromosome, the infant born nine months later will be a genetic female; if it connects with one carrying the y, a genetic male results.

For the first six weeks, the embryo is not sexually differentiated. All embryos have a gonad that will develop into either the sex organs of a male or those of a female. Hormonal differences between the sexes are important at two points of human development: the first is during the prenatal stage about six weeks after conception; the second is at puberty. Normally, if it is a male embryo, the gonad will release one hormone that inhibits the development of the female sex organs, as well as another hormone, testosterone, that will trigger the development of the male sex organs. Without these two hormones, all embryos would develop as females, regardless of the genetic sex. In the words of John Money and Anke Ehrhardt, two prominent researchers in the biological aspects of sex differences, "Nature's rule is that to masculinize, something has to be added" (1974, p. 7). The development of the ovaries in females occurs about six weeks later than that of the testicles in males and requires no extra hormones.

Despite our emphasis on the differences between males and females, there are some significant biological similarities between them. Normal individuals of both sexes produce male as well as female hormones. As sociologist Ann Oakley comments, the body's "ground plan" is similar in either case:

> Far from falling into two discrete groups, male and female have the same body ground plan, and even the anatomical difference is more apparent than real. Neither the phallus nor the womb are organs of one sex only: the female phallus (the clitoris) is the biological equivalent of the male organ, and men possess a vestigial womb, whose existence they may well ignore until it causes enlargement of the prostate gland in old age. (1972, p. 18)

If you look through the window of any hospital nursery, it is difficult to tell which of the babies swaddled in white are girls and which are boys. To tell them apart, you have to read the tags that say "Female Jones" or "Male Smith." At birth, the baby is sexually unfinished. What is yet to be accomplished is the process of learning one's gender identity, which begins as soon as the blue blankets are assigned to the boys and the pink ones to the girls. *Gender identity* is one's subjective sense of being either a boy or a girl, a man or a woman.

It is easy, of course, to distinguish between adult males and females. The hormones become important again at puberty, when females produce larger amounts of estrogen and progesterone and males produce testosterone and the androgens. These trigger off the development of the secondary sex characteristics. Males' voices change, females' breasts develop, and the mischief caused by hormonal changes temporarily ruins the complexion of many young teenagers at the same time that it prepares them for the act of reproducing the species.

But by the time of puberty, gender identity is already fixed—and by processes that are social, not biological. For example, in our culture, from the earliest stages of infancy, females are treated differently than males. According to one study, by the time infants are no more than three weeks old, mothers hold male infants longer than females (Moss, 1967). This cannot be explained entirely by the fact that males observed in this study were more irritable, slept less, and fussed and cried more than the female infants. Even with babies in the same state—awake or asleep, crying or content—the mothers stimulated the males more, with both tactile and visual stimulation. In other words, even at this early age, mothers reinforce different types of behaviors in male and female infants and contribute to gender identity.

If differential treatment of the sexes begins so soon, how can it be said that masculine or feminine behavior, even in a two-year-old, is biologically determined? Most of the differences commonly regarded as "natural" male or female characteristics can be accounted for by the very different social scripts taught to infants from the time that those first tags are attached to the cribs in hospital nurseries.

In one study of four-year-olds in a Project Head Start classroom, the investigator found that even at that young age the children's attitudes were sexually stereotyped. Under close observation it was determined that the teachers, who thought that they were treating boys and girls in identical ways, were actually encouraging somewhat different aspirations and self-images (Chasen, 1977).

The importance of nurture in determining gender identity is illustrated most clearly by those rare cases of "deviant gender." Not all babies are born clearly boys or girls; a few have undeveloped organs of both sexes. Such infants provide a "natural laboratory" for the study of sexual identity. Investigators, like Money and Ehrhardt, have concluded that genetic sex is less important to the formation of gender identity in these children than is the sex of assignment (1974). For example, hermaphrodite children, given the appropriate hormone therapy and corrective surgery, may be raised either as girls or boys. Commenting on such cases, Money and Ehrhardt remark: "To use the Pygmalion allegory, one may begin with the same clay and fashion a god or goddess" (1974, p. 159).

Even the gender identity of "normal" children is malleable. One case has been reported in which a boy, an identical twin, was accidentally castrated when he was seventeen months old. Physicians advised his parents to raise him as a girl. By age seven, with the encouragement of the parents, the child was behaving in conventionally feminine ways and was sure of her identity as a girl. She was quite different from her twin brother. If done at an early age, such reassignments of sex can be successfully accomplished (Money and Ehrhardt, 1974, p. 123).

In other cases, individuals grow to adulthood with a gender identity that is the opposite of their biological sex. During the past few years, a number of successful sex-change operations have been performed. One of the most widely publicized is the case of Jan Morris. As James Morris, he served in the British army, went to Oxford, climbed Mount Everest, married, and fathered five children. But as Morris wrote in a recent autobiography, "I was three or perhaps four years old when I realized I had been born into the wrong body, and should be a girl" (in Gagnon and Henderson, 1975, p. 3). In 1972, after surgery, he finally became Jan Morris.

As yet, we know little about why individuals such as Jan Morris identify themselves as members of the sex opposite to their own anatomy. However, such cases clearly demonstrate that developing a sense of gender identity is not an automatic consequence of being born male or female.

But can we conclude, then, that our cultural conception of masculinity and femininity has nothing to do with the biological differences between men and women? The answer is a qualified no. Recent research suggests that certain biological differences—particularly the presence of male and female sex hormones—predispose individuals to behavior normally regarded as masculine or feminine. Some girls, either because their mothers are given hormone treatments or because of a malfunction in their own adrenal glands, receive androgens, the male sex hormones, while they are still in the womb. Money and Ehrhardt compared twenty-five of these girls to a control group that had not received fetal androgens (1974). The comparison revealed the effect of those hormones on the girls' personalities. The androgenized girls were more likely to be tomboys than were the controls, preferring outdoor play, rougher and more vigorous physical activity, and tending to dominate and become leaders in their play groups. Compared to the control group, they showed little interest in dolls. In contrast to the control girls, all of whom wanted to be wives and mothers when they grew up, one-third of the androgenized girls wanted no children at all, while the rest were as interested in having a career as in marriage (p. 107). It should be noted, however, that the mothers knew what they had been given and its possible effects. This knowledge may have influenced the way in which they raised their daughters.

This study suggests that a high level of physical energy, a desire to compete and dominate, and a relative lack of interest in dolls are all related to the presence of the male hormone in the fetus. Several writers have cited this study as evidence for their conclusion that traditional sex roles—which assign to women the nurturing and mothering roles, and to men the competition for status and power outside the home—are natural and inevitable. In his book *The Inevitability of Patriarchy* (1973), sociologist Stephen Goldberg mentions this study, as well as the cross-cultural evidence for the division of labor according to sex. He concludes that if women are encouraged to seek competitive, high-status jobs as equals to men, they are doomed to failure. Other writers, such as anthropologist Lionel Tiger, reach the same conclusion based on evidence about primate behavior. Male monkeys, for example, play more roughly than females, compete for dominance in social groups, and are uninterested in nurturing small monkeys (1970).

Many common assertions about "inevitable" male/female differences are dubious, and unsupported by empirical investigation. When psychologists Eleanor Maccoby and Carol Jacklin compiled an exhaustive summary of the research on sex differences, they concluded that many widely held beliefs about sex differences are mythical. For example, the consensus among researchers is that girls are *not,* as is commonly thought, more "social" than boys, and that boys are *not* more analytic in their thinking style than girls. Among the sex-related differences that are commonly held, the only one with any substantial social significance that may be due to biological factors is aggressiveness. But Maccoby and Jacklin disagree with Goldberg's position that because aggression is the primary means by which men dominate women and compete with one another, it explains why they occupy the positions of high status and authority. According to Maccoby and Jacklin, "Aggression is certainly not the method most usually employed for leadership among mature human beings." The fact that it is "entirely possible to achieve status by other means," such as negotiation, cooperation, and persuasion—skills that are at least as common among women as men—means that male dominance in a society such as ours is not inevitable (1974, pp. 360, 368).

As we have seen, Money and Ehrhardt's study of androgenized girls fueled the argument that traditional sex-role distinctions may be inevitable. However, the most important point in their study is that both groups—those who received the androgens and the control group of normal girls—were capable of functioning happily within the limits this society defines as normal behavior. Normal individuals of both sexes produce male as well as female hormones—though in different proportions—and individual variations in masculine and feminine characteristics are common.

We might well emphasize this overlapping of male and female social characteristics, rather than the differences. "Although there is a natural biological tendency for males to be rougher and tougher and more active than most females, there is also considerable overlap between the sexes: some women are bigger and stronger and rougher and tougher than some men. . . . If you wanted to hire a door-to-door salesperson, you'd be wiser to hire a determined, aggressive woman than a shy, retiring male" (Skolnick, 1973, p. 157).

A Sociological Perspective—Gender Roles Aren't Natural

Learning gender roles is a longer and more complex process than most people realize. "A gender role is not established at birth," write researchers John Gagnon and William Simon, "but is built up cumulatively through experiences encountered and transacted—through casual and unplanned learning, through explicit instruction and inculcation, and through spontaneously putting two and two together to make sometimes four and sometimes, erroneously, five" (in Gagnon and Henderson, 1975, p. 4).

By the age of three, most children can label themselves as boys or girls, but they cannot accurately label the sex of others. And even after they learn to apply those labels accurately, until about age six children believe that gender can be changed, just like age—that girls can be boys if they want to, and vice versa (Kohlberg, 1966, p. 139). For Freud, it was the differences in physical anatomy that were assumed to be crucial in one's sense of gender. However, research by Lawrence Kohlberg suggests that social differences are clearer and more important to children than are anatomical ones: children identify people in pictures as male or female because one figure is a fireman and another wears a dress (1966).

According to Kohlberg, gender *identity*—being able to say, "I am a boy"—is inseparable from learning gender *role*—behaving in certain "boy" ways and doing certain "boy" things. *Gender role* is what one says and does to indicate to others, and to oneself, one's maleness or femaleness. It is the outward expression of one's gender identity (1966).

Children began to learn gender roles at a very early age. For example, a mother describes how she treated each of her twins—one of whom was a boy, the other a girl:

> I started dressing her in little pink slacks and frilly blouses. . . . She likes for me to wipe her face, and yet my son is quite different. I can't wash his face. . . . She seems to be daintier. Maybe it's because I encourage it. I've never seen a little girl so neat and tidy. She is very proud of herself when she puts on a new dress. . . . The boy once went and took a leak in the garden. He was quite happy with himself. And I just didn't say anything. . . . The girl once took off her panties and threw them over the fence. I gave her a little swat on the rear, and I told her that nice little girls don't do that. (Money and Ehrhardt, 1974, pp. 124–128)

Parents, of course, are not the only people who teach children what it means to be masculine or feminine. Brothers and sisters, and other children, also assist in socialization. Television, movies, advertisements, and books are important agents in the process, too. The importance of the cultural stereotypes children learn is illustrated by one four-year-old girl who insisted that mothers could not be doctors—only nurses—even though her own mother was a doctor (Maccoby and Jacklin, 1974, p. 364).

Learned behavior has an enormous importance in determining all human activity. Compared to other species, we have a longer period of dependency. A correspondingly greater part of who we are is what we are taught to be. As we have seen, this applies to a great extent to human sexual identity. The infant is "sexually unfinished" at birth; and whatever hormonal predispositions do exist, apply to only a few behavior patterns. And even in these areas, the predispositions of males and females overlap. It is the parents, the child's peers, and the communications media that act as a "finishing school." Expectations and instructions about sex roles teach males and females to be different in more respects than biology dictates.

Becoming a Man

Margaret Mead once commented that "The worry that boys will not grow up to be men is much more widespread than that girls will not grow up to be women" (1949, p. 195). She was speaking specifically about the South Sea Islands, but her comment applies to almost all cultures. In most preliterate societies, there are rites of passage for males, but not for females. There are ceremonial dramas, supervised by the men, which ease the difficult transition from boyhood to manhood. But why is so much attention paid to the male adolescent, and not to the female? This difference in emphasis might be interpreted as one manifestation of male dominance. The older men lavish attention upon the younger boys because males are assumed to be more important than females. Or it might be argued that, in any culture, "something extra" is required to make a boy into a man. There is no society where the transition from the status of the child into that of adult is entirely smooth. But it appears in certain respects, at least, that the contradictions between the two roles are greater for boys than for girls. In many societies, first menstruation is considered a natural sign that a girl has come of age. But whereas attaining womanhood is seen in terms of a biological process for girls, becoming a man is a cultural process for boys: the rites of passage are "man"-made ceremonies.

Can we say the same of our own society? Is it harder to learn to be a man than to become a woman? How, exactly, are we taught what is masculine and feminine? It is important to examine this process because male–female differences—as well as the movement toward removing certain of those differences—are at the basis of marriage and family arrangements.

We have already seen that "something extra"—androgens, the male hormones—is required for the fetus to develop into a male. As John Money suggests, the same pattern may be repeated in the socialization of children: something extra is demanded of boys, and their sexual identity may be more fragile (Money and Ehrhardt, 1974, p. 154).

One reason why this may be so is that the transition from infancy to adulthood for males is full of contradictions. All infants are "feminine" in their orientation to the world, as our culture usually defines femininity. Thus, babies are dependent and passive. Small children cry and cling to their mothers. But for males, the transition from boy to man is sharper. Sooner than girls, they are told not to cry. They are pushed to be independent at an earlier age. They are often taught not to be emotionally expressive, which—as we noticed in the discussion of the problems of single men in Chapter 5—may well pose difficulties later on. Many boys are taught that the expression of normal human feelings—such as pain, inadequacy, love, and affection—is "unmanly."

The socialization of boys is further complicated by the natural tendency of children to identify more closely with their mothers. Even as adults, both men and women are more like their mothers than their fathers in characteristics that are not sex-typed (Lynn, 1966, p. 25). Boys, though, are expected to shift their identification from their mothers to their fathers. This process of change is made more complicated because the father's main role—his work role—takes place away from the home. Unlike his sister, the young boy cannot learn what the same-sex adult does by watching and imitating. Boys learn the masculine role by responding to many negative sanctions. They are often told what *not* to do to be a man: "Don't act like a girl!" "Don't be a sissy!" "Men don't cry!" This is a fine recipe "for inducing anxiety—the demand that the child do something which is not clearly defined to him, based upon reasons he cannot possibly appreciate, and enforced with threats, punishment, and anger by those who are close to him" (Hartley, 1959, p. 458).

We can draw two negative implications for marriage from this pattern of sex-role socialization. The first is that boys who are told that it is bad to act like a girl may grow up convinced that everything feminine is bad. In our culture, male hostility toward women is tolerated—even encouraged in certain ways. Think of the films that portray the cowboy who loves his horse more than his girl, or pugnacious Jimmy Cagney smashing a grapefruit in his girl-

Even in an era of greater equality between the sexes, the gender training process still encourages boys and girls to learn somewhat different attitudes and behaviors.

friend's face in *The Public Enemy*. On the other hand, women who are hostile toward men are considered slightly monstrous.

Media images of "masculine" men—whether they are tough guys like John Wayne or smooth manipulators of women like the James Bond/*Playboy* ideal—hardly paint a picture of the good husband. "The on-screen John Wayne doesn't feel comfortable around women. He does like them sometimes—God knows he's not *queer*. But at the right time, and in the right place—which he chooses. And always with his car/horse parked directly outside, in/on which he will ride away to his more important business back in Marlboro country" (Balswick and Peek, 1971, p. 366). As for the ideal male portrayed in *Playboy,* he seems to devote more attention to women than John Wayne does. But this attention is not directed toward an equal. For the *Playboy* male, women are accessories, decorative and useful like the right sports car or stereo receiver. The Playboy regards women as commodities, not persons with whom one might have a multi-dimensional relationship.

It has also been observed that boys—and men—often seem to be more anxious about their sex-role identification than women. Certainly, parents seem more anxious about the gender identity of their sons. It's acceptable if little girls wear jeans, climb trees, and play baseball. But little boys who prefer dolls are less tolerated. It is somehow much worse to be called a sissy than a tomboy. As sociologist Richard Udry says, "parents are not as confident of their boys growing up to become 'masculine men' as previous generations were" (1974, p. 53).

Boys, then, may have trouble learning the male role because it is taught in a negative way—they learn more about what it *isn't* than what it *is*—and because children are so segregated from the workaday world that they have only the vaguest ideas about what male figures do outside the home. School, too, is a feminine world, at least in the early grades. Most elementary school teachers are women, and many reward neatness, obedience, and passivity—qualities that are more likely to be identified in later life with females than males (Maccoby, 1963, p. 244).

Becoming a Woman

Both the pressures exerted on girls to attain femininity and the contradictions that result from moving to another life stage are quite different from those a male faces.

Most of us have seen, in movies or on television, innumerable scenes where the father grips the boy's shoulder and says, "Son, be a man." It is harder to imagine a mother telling her daughter, "Be a woman." If learning to be a man in this culture means facing certain challenges, learning to be a woman very often means accepting certain limitations.

The socialization of girls is smoother and less stressful than that of boys. Clinging, dependent behavior seems to be tolerated longer. In one study of two-year-olds who were left alone in a strange room with their mothers, the girls remained with their mothers longer than the boys did, and they returned to their mothers more often. The researchers sum up the differences: "Dependent behavior, normal to all young children, is permitted for girls and prohibited for boys. Thus, girls are not encouraged to give up old techniques of relating to adults and using others to define their identity, to manipulate the physical world, and to supply their emotional needs" (Bardwick and Douvan, 1971, p. 227).

In general, girls are taught more prohibitions and restrictions. But sexual identity is considered to be less of a problem than it is for boys: it is not something to be accomplished, or something one learns, but rather something that comes naturally.

Gender training, which begins at home in the interactions between parents and children, becomes more explicit as the child is exposed to other sources of information such as teachers, books, and television. Studies of the content of children's textbooks, for example, have pointed out that many of these books still perpetuate sexual stereotypes. Females are portrayed in nurturant roles, while males are more apt to be active, aggressive, seeking recognition for their achievements. And it has been argued that the educational testing process as well as the curricular offerings in school also promote sex-role stereotyping (Saario, Jacklin, and Tittle, 1973).

An analysis of books written for preschool children that won the Caldecott medal between 1938 and 1970—the Caldecott medal is awarded to the best books in the industry—shows that the ratio of titles featuring males to titles featuring females was 8:1. In addition, the award-winning books contained 261 pictures of males and only 23 of females. As a result, at the same time that young children learn the three R's, they also learn another lesson—that girls are not as important as boys because no one bothers to write books about them (Weitzman, Eifler, Hokada, and Ross, 1972). But statistics do not tell the whole story. Girls in children's books do not usually have adventures. They are princesses locked in towers waiting for a prince to come to the rescue, or housewives who wait in the background while the action takes place around them. In a typical scene "Mrs. Woods went to work washing dirty dishes, and Officer Woods set about his plan . . ." (U'Ren, 1971, p. 322).

The same thing might be said of the influence of TV programing and commercials (see Box 7–2). During the 1970s, women began to be portrayed in the media in a wider variety of roles. It is no longer true that women appear in only a few stereotypical roles—such as the featherhead wife portrayed in *I Love Lucy*, or the maternal housewife portrayed in the *Donna Reed Show*. There are new TV images of the "liberated" woman in active, traditionally male roles such as the police officer or detective. But the most common role for the "liberated" woman in TV offerings in recent years is the chic, hard, sexy swinger—an image that has more to do with male fantasies than social realities. Despite a greater diversity of female roles in the media, systematic analyses of the portrayal of women on TV during the seventies show that TV programing still reinforces sex-role stereotypes. For example, while women are portrayed as younger and less mature, white men are older, more mature. A much higher proportion of the males' roles are serious ones. While white men in TV roles are identified more often than women by their occupational roles, women are more often defined by their family roles. And while TV males commit more violent acts, females are the most frequent victims (U.S. Commission on Civil Rights, 1977). In other words, the world depicted in TV programing still differs conspicuously from social reality, and it still reinforces traditional sex stereotypes. TV programing is a particularly important agent in gender training for young children not just because children spend so many hours watching television, but also because they are not yet exposed to many alternative sources of information. Thus it comes as no surprise to find that children who are heavy TV viewers are more likely than others to hold traditional views on sex roles (Frueh and McGhee, 1975).

The influence of such agents of gender training as children's books and TV programing undoubtedly contributes to the very different self-images and aspirations of males and females. Despite impressive growth in the numbers of women entering into the professions and other occupational areas that have been dominated by males (which we will examine more closely in the following chapter), it still appears to be true that a much smaller proportion of teenage girls than boys expect to fill jobs at the top of the occupational status hierarchy—such as executive or managerial positions. In a recent study of 3,200 junior and senior high school students in upstate New York, researchers found no differences in the educational aspirations of males and females, but they did find that adolescent boys have more ambitious occupational aspirations. Apparently the gender training process still influences boys and girls to channel their energies in the direction considered appropriate to their sex. With increasing age, adolescent girls are more likely to aspire to stereotypically feminine occupations. Perhaps this can be explained by the realistic fear held by

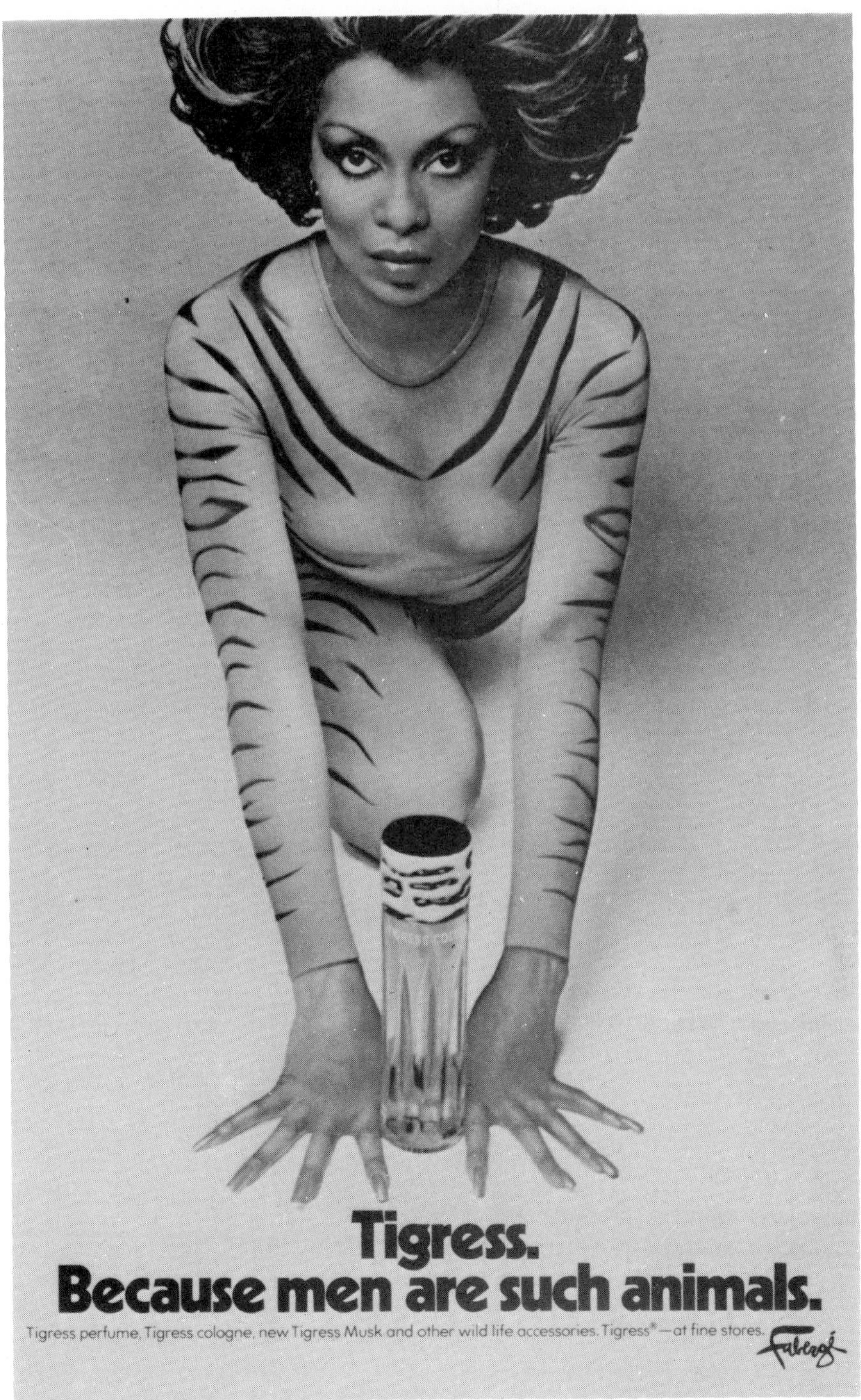

Most of what we associate with masculinity and feminity is a product of social learning, not biological necessity—and such ads as this one are an important part of the gender training process.

What's Happening Today

Box 7–2 / Woman's Image in Advertisements

"We'll return to tonight's exciting adventure after a 60-second insult to women, brought to you by the makers of that washday miracle . . ."

TV commercials may not be subtle, but their messages are repeated so often that they serve as one of the most effective agents of sex-role socialization. The messages about sex roles are particularly effective in giving young children certain images of masculinity and femininity long before they have the sophistication to dismiss their stereotyped content.

Women have become increasingly disturbed by their image as portrayed by advertisements. A few years ago, an angry group of feminists broke up a CBS stockholders' meeting, shouting that, "You use our bodies to sell products! You blackmail us with the fear of being unloved if we do not buy!" If you think about the message—both explicit and implied—in many of those commercial minutes on television, women have something to complain about. There she is, Mrs. American housewife, anxious that her guests not have water-spotted glasses, crushed with despair as the little voice chants, "Ring Around the Collar!" She stalks dirt, dust, and household odors with the fervor of an evangelist, and she anxiously compares her laundry with that of her neighbor, which is, alas, "brighter than bright."

The following are some of the basic lessons about What It Means to Be a Woman as taught in these 60-second sagas:

Lesson 1: Failure to perform the wifely tasks causes your husband's disapproval, while success wins his love. As portrayed in commercials, women are fanatics about cleanliness. They waltz around the living room in chiffon skirts polishing the furniture. They frantically scrub the sink, or wonder whether the toilet bowl smells. But why should a woman care so much about a level of perfection that's almost unattainable? The lesson taught in many commercials is that, if she doesn't attain that perfection, she'll lose the respect and love of her husband, family, and friends. Guests register their disapproval at scuffed floors; neighbors wrinkle their noses at household odors. And, worst of all, husbands withdraw their approval. The Wisk ad, for example, shows a husband and wife—on a carefree vacation—getting off the plane in Hawaii. A Hawaiian woman in a hula skirt comes up to greet them, and to put a *lei* around the husband's neck, only to draw back in horror as the mortified wife hears the words "Ring around the collar!" There they are, on a romantic vacation, and all of a sudden the wife is threatened with the evidence of her inadequacy—and by a beautiful woman, no less. The wife's reaction is to recoil, distraught and guilty. The ads never suggest that perhaps *he* ought to wash his neck more often.

Lesson 2: Woman's place is in the home. Lesson 2 is that woman's place is at home, and particularly in the kitchen ("Nothin' says lovin' like something from the oven. . .") and the laundry room. The millions of American women who work are all but forgotten in commercials. From the point of view of advertisers, the important thing is apparently to convince women to buy more things for the house. Because housewives buy more household products than career women, females are not often shown in occupational roles. Furthermore, in commercials where women are shown deciding which products to buy, relatively inexpensive purchases are involved, such as food, cosmetics, and cleaning products. When the product is a "big ticket" item such as a home appliance, men are brought into the ads.

Lesson 3: Women are envious. One of the most consistent themes in advertisements for household products is that women are competitive and envious. They are shown in an anxious competition with other women, measuring their adequacy as wives and mothers against the performance of neighbors and friends. ("How does she get her wash so *bright* when mine is so dingy?") Women reveal their "washday secret" to other women as if they were revealing the recipe for some priceless love potion. As a matter of fact, women are not often portrayed interacting or working with other women. They are shown operating independently in their homes, or anxiously comparing their skills as homemakers with others. One analysis of the content of ads in seven major publications revealed that men are more than twice as likely to be shown interacting with members of their own sex in a cooperative way (Courtney and Lockeretz, 1971).

Lesson 4: Women are dependent upon men. It is particularly ironic that housewives, who spend many of their waking hours in the kitchen or the laundry room, are instructed by men about how to do their housework. Arthur Godfrey, for example, who probably never entered a laundry room except to tape a commercial, instructs women about the virtues of Axion pre-soak. This undoubtedly reinforces lesson 4: the man's voice is the voice of authority. The theme is expressed most clearly in ads where a big, strong man—such as "the White Knight," or "Mr. Clean," or "the Giant-in-the-Washing Machine"—rushes in to rescue women from their household woes.

Lesson 5: Women are valuable mainly as sex objects or pretty accessories. This is a theme that appears in ads for many products. "Handsome is as handsome does," but for "the fair sex"—as portrayed in commercials—the important thing is what she looks like. The clearest expression of the theme of the woman-as-commodity/the wife-as-possession appears in the Geritol ad where the admiring husband says of his wife, who, though well into middle age, is still healthy and beautiful: "I think I'll keep her!" He might say the same thing of a dependable car or a faithful dog. The wife is admired for her commodity value, her health, her looks, the extent to which she resembles the physical ideal of woman. Imagine how strange this ad would seem if the sexes were reversed: "I think I'll keep him!"

The rumbles of a counterattack against such sexist ads are being heard in the advertising business. One woman, Franchellie Cadwell, who is president of her own agency, sounded many of the themes of that revolt in an ad placed in a trade journal called *Advertising Age:*

> When over 55% of the women in the country are high school graduates, and 25% have attended college, when women have achieved sexual freedom aren't they beyond 'house-i-tosis'? At the very least, women deserve recognition as being in full possession of their faculties. . . . The revolution is ready, and one of women's first targets will be moronic, insulting advertising. No force has demeaned women more than advertising.

Advertisements from *The Insurance Salesman.*

many teenage girls and young women that high occupational expectations will bring disapproval from males (Rosen and Aneshensel, 1978).

The woman's dilemma of having to choose between high occupational aspirations and social approval by many members of the opposite sex is also demonstrated by the relatively low self-esteem of college-age women. A study of women attending six of the nation's most prestigious colleges showed that women have both lower self-esteem and lower occupational aspirations than do men who are performing at the same level (*The New York Times,* December 10, 1978, p. 12). In general, it appears that college-age women—more so than women in any other age group—lack confidence in their ability to do well on new tasks and feel that they have less control over their fate. This lack of confidence may well be related to other events beginning to occur in a young woman's life. It is at this age that women are typically forming enduring relationships with men. "In the dating and mating game, women are traditionally expected to take less initiative than men. Perhaps it is at this period of their lives more than any other that individuals define themselves in terms of their masculinity or femininity, and when greater sex differences may therefore appear" (Maccoby and Jacklin, 1974, p. 359). In other words, for college-age women, in contrast to men of the same age, there is a contradiction between living up to the expectations of one's sex role and achieving at a high level at the same time. The woman who wants to combine marriage with a career may experience great anxiety about actually doing so.

Thus, many young women today feel confused because they are caught in the cross-fire between two contradictory sets of attitudes about how to be feminine. On the one hand, childhood experiences and parental pressures push a young woman toward the traditionally female roles. If she follows this set of instructions, she is supposed to attain the social graces, be careful about her appearance, and find the "right" man so that she can fulfill the expectations of marriage and motherhood. But because of more recent pressures that she fulfill herself by seeking at least part-time work or a career, the woman who fulfills the traditional formula might feel anxious that she is missing something. In this area, as in many others discussed in this text, there is no longer a consensus about basic norms.

THE HOMOSEXUAL MINORITY

According to the most reliable estimates, somewhere between 5 and 10 percent of the American population today is homosexual. But such statements raise as many questions as they answer, because they imply that everyone can be categorized as either homosexual or heterosexual. As Edward Sagarin suggests, the word "homosexual" is a social label; it is important to distinguish between a person's sexual preference and his or her self-identity.

> It might be useful to start from the premise that there is no such thing as a homosexual, for such a concept is . . . an artificially created entity that has no basis in reality. What exists are people with erotic desires for their own sex, or who engage in sexual activities with same-sex others, or both. The desire constitutes feeling, the act constitutes doing, but neither is being. . . . However, people become entrapped in a false consciousness of identifying themselves as *being* homosexuals. They believe that they discover what they are. . . . Learning their identity, they become involved in it, boxed into their own biographies. (1973, p. 4)

Data compiled by Kinsey and his associates (1948) suggest that there are far more people who engage in homosexual activities than there are people who identify themselves as homosexuals. Only half of the total male population they studied could be regarded as exclusively heterosexual, as defined by both sexual acts and feelings since puberty. Thirteen percent of the males had experienced homosexual desires that they had not acted upon, and 37 percent had had at least one homosexual contact in which they reached orgasm. About 18 percent of the men had had as much homosexual as heterosexual experience, and 8 percent had spent at least three years since adolescence in exclusively homosexual relationships. However, only 4 percent of the males had been lifelong exclusive homosexuals. In contrast, there was considerably less homosexuality among the women Kinsey studied. Fifteen percent had experienced homosexual desires but had not acted upon them. Thirteen percent had had some homosexual contacts, but only about 2 percent of the female population was found to be exclusively homosexual. For present purposes, we are interested mainly in that group whose sexual preferences are predominantly or exclusively homosexual, and whose self-identity is homosexual as well.

It appears that homosexuality has existed in all cultures, but the extent to which it has been condoned has varied enormously. One survey of preliterate societies determined that in forty-nine out of seventy-six of them some form of homosexual activity was regarded as normal or acceptable, although it was seldom sanctioned for the majority of the community (Ford and Beach, 1951). In the modern world, as Kinsey (1948) pointed out, there is no society where homosexuality has been more harshly condemned than in American society, where criminal sanctions have applied to homosexual acts, and where homosexuality has been regarded as a form of mental illness.

In 1973, when the American Psychiatric Association approved a resolution declaring that "homosexuality per se cannot be classified as a mental disorder," that decision reflected a widespread tendency in recent years to reconsider the nature of homosexuality. But just as the wording of that statement left some question as to whether homosexuality had been declared "normal" or labeled a symptom of underlying problems, there is a good deal of confusion today as to whether homosexuality should be regarded as an unnatural and perverse act, the result of genetic or hormonal abnormalities, or simply as a minority sexual preference.

A variety of perspectives on the origins of homosexuality have been proposed, and none are conclusive. A point of view that at one time enjoyed considerable support is the idea that homosexuality can be explained by certain biological abnormalities. One early study that seemed to support the position that genes exert a powerful influence over an individual's sexual predisposition was F. J. Kallman's (1952) research with eighty-five male homosexuals who were twins. Kallman found that among the fraternal twins (who were no more similar than brothers normally would be) the brothers of the homosexual subjects were not much more likely to be homosexual than one would expect in a random sample; but among the identical twins, the homosexual subjects all had brothers who were overt homosexuals. But subsequent research has not confirmed Kallman's findings. More recent research suggests that homosexual tendencies cannot be explained on the basis of genetic influences (Rosenthal, 1970).

Another biological theory holds that a hormonal imbalance may contribute to homosexual behavior. From this perspective, it is assumed that homosexual males have lower than average levels of the male sex hormone, testosterone, and that homosexual women have low levels of estrogen. Several studies support this hypothesis. For example, one research team found that the urine of homosexual men contains less testosterone than that of heterosexual men. In addition, the urine of lesbians was found to contain higher levels of testosterone and lower levels of estrogen than the urine of heterosexual women (Loraine, Adamopoulos, Kirkham, Ismail, and Dove, 1971). However, other studies of this sort have found no differences between homosexuals and heterosexuals. In any case, findings such as these have to be interpreted with caution because they are correlational. That is, they do not establish that hormonal imbalance is the cause of homosexual behavior, only that these two factors are somehow associated. Another finding is inconsistent with a simple cause-and-effect explanation: when the glandular balance in males is changed by increasing testosterone levels, no change in sexual preference results. Thus, there is no conclusive evidence that biological factors alone exert any determining influence on sexual orientation.

Learning theory provides another perspective on the origins of homosexuality, emphasizing the importance of conditioning rather than biological factors. This was the perspective that Kinsey adopted as he tried to explain the factors that contribute to homosexual behavior. As Kinsey (1948) pointed out, humans, like other mammals, are capable of responding to a variety of sexual stimuli. Thus, one might account for homosexual preferences by noting that some individuals have their earliest sexual experiences with persons of the same sex. Regular patterns of sexual behavior or exclusive preferences for one sex or the other come only with experience and as a result of social pressures that encourage us to follow one pattern or another. As Kinsey suggested, perhaps the question we should pay more attention to is "why each and every individual is not involved in every type of sexual activity" (Kinsey et al., 1953, p. 447).

Psychoanalysts have a different perspective on homosexuality. Like Kinsey, Freud and the analysts who followed in the tradition he founded emphasize the importance of early learning in accounting for the origins of homosexuality. But while Kinsey emphasized a broad range of factors that may predispose individuals to learn to be attracted to their own sex, psychoanalysts have focused more narrowly on specific factors that may contribute to a homosexual orientation. In one influential study, Bieber and his associates (1962) examined the case records of 106 homosexual patients and 100 heterosexual patients who were undergoing psychoanalysis. His conclusion was that fear of the opposite sex ("heterophobia") could be traced to events in early childhood and laid the basis for the subsequent choice of same-sex partners.

Bieber noted that compared with heterosexual patients, the homosexuals had mothers who exerted on their sons an unhealthy preferential treatment, which combined seductiveness with a smothering and over-controlling attitude. In contrast, the fathers were often found to be detached and hostile. The son often became the most important individual in the mother's life and replaced the husband as the predominant "love object." These conclusions, consistent with psychoanalytic theory, have been attacked by critics who point out that the data were collected by analysts who were looking for precisely the pattern they discovered. Yet similar results were obtained in a more carefully controlled study in which nonpatients filled out anonymous questionnaires asking about their childhoods (Evans, 1969). For people who hold the view that homosexuality is a "condition" resulting from blocked heterosexuality, psychotherapy is regarded as an appropriate form of intervention.

How successful is psychotherapy in changing an individual's sexual orientation when both patient and therapist desire such a change? The answers to this question—like many others about homosexuality—are inconsistent and inconclusive. On the one hand, Kinsey's Institute for Sex Research has had a long-standing offer to evaluate people whose basic sexual orientation has changed as a result of therapy. Researchers there have not found a single case that they consider conclusive evidence of a basic change in sexual orientation. On the other hand, in their recent volume on homosexuality, Masters and Johnson (1979) claim considerable success in treating fifty-four men and thirteen women who wanted to convert to heterosexual patterns; although at this time their five-year followup study has not been completed, it appears that more than half of the homosexuals Masters and Johnson treated who wanted to change their sexual orientation have been quite successful in doing so.

Pride and Prejudice

There are several reasons why the American Psychiatric Association decided that homosexuality should no longer be included on its list of recognized forms of mental disorder. One is that there is no convincing evidence that there is any more pathology among homosexuals than among heterosexuals. In several studies, batteries of psychological tests have been used to determine if there are any differences between randomly chosen groups of homosexuals and heterosexuals in a nonpatient population. The conclusion of these studies is that there are no major differences in psychological adjustment between these two groups (Hooker, 1957; Oberstone and Sukoneck, 1976).

A more basic flaw in the explanations that seek to account for homosexuality in terms of certain biological or psychological abnormalities is that they minimize or overlook entirely the effects of the social climate in which homosexuals live. One of the most significant changes that has taken place in recent years is that it is becoming more common for homosexuals to be regarded as a minority group that has experienced many of the same types of prejudice and discrimination that members of racial and ethnic minorities have experienced. Over the past decade, the homosexual minority has become far more visible than it was formerly, partly because of the activities of such groups as the Mattachine Society and the Gay Activists' Alliance, which have organized events such as "Gay Pride Week." The goal of these groups, and the aim of much of the recent literature that depicts homosexuality sympathetically, is to gain legal rights and to prevent further discrimination on the basis of an individual's sexual preference.

There are some indications of a growing tolerance of homosexuality. When Morton Hunt (1973) replicated the Kinsey study, he found that the percentage of people who expressed tolerance of homosexual behavior—about half of his sample—was about twice as high as it had been a generation earlier. About a quarter of the people in Hunt's sample agreed that "being homosexual is just as natural as being heterosexual." Recent polls show that people who live in large cities tend to be more tolerant of homosexuality. People older than fifty, those who are frequent churchgoers, and residents of the Middle West and the South more often disapprove of homosexuality. A 1977 Gallup poll taken just after a widely publicized campaign in Dade County, Florida to repeal an ordinance banning job discrimination because of sexual preference found that 56 percent of a nationwide sample agreed that homosexuals should have equal rights in terms of job opportunity. However, almost two-thirds of the people in that sample were opposed to allowing homosexuals to be elementary school teachers. Although the gay minority has become far more visible, and in many quarters more socially acceptable than before (by the late 1970s, several TV shows routinely depicted gay characters), continued opposition to gay rights laws suggests how much resistance there is to legislation that might be interpreted as an endorsement of homosexuality.

Stereotypes about homosexuals serve the same purpose as stereotypes about other minorities—such as those about Jews and blacks—to distort their characteristics so as to justify continued discrimination. Recent accounts of homosexual lifestyles allow a somewhat more objective view and challenge the belief that all homosexuals are alike. Some of the older misconceptions are being challenged, such as the idea that many homosexuals have disturbed personalities, or that they are identifiable by mannerism, body type, or the way they dress. The title of the recent volume prepared by Alan Bell and Martin Weinberg (1978) under the auspices of Kinsey's Institute for Sex Research—*Homosexualities: A Study of Diversity Among Men and Women*—underlines its main point, that there are many different homosexual lifestyles. This book, which is based upon interviews with about 1,500 homosexuals, most of them residents of San Francisco, provides evidence that contradicts many of the stereotypes about gays. Like most heterosexuals, the majority of gays in this sample support themselves in stable jobs—and not in stereotypically gay fields such as hairdressing. Contrary to the popular stereotyped notion that male homosexuals are incapable of any enduring relationship, this study concludes that almost all of the respondents had had long-lasting love relationships involving considerable emotional commitment (Bell and Weinberg, 1978).

The Bell and Weinberg study also sheds some light on the substantial differences between male and female homosexuals. Whereas three-quarters of the lesbians they studied lived in stable relationships, only half of the male homosexuals did. Compared with the men, homosexual women are far less sexually active; most had had fewer than ten sexual partners over their lifetime. In contrast, three-fifths of the white homosexual men had had more than 250 sexual partners. (1978, p. 308) Although this may be partly explained by the fact that there is little institutional encouragement for stable partnerships in homosexual culture, this finding does provide support for the common belief that homosexual men are far more promiscuous than heterosexuals.

Overall, perhaps the most revealing thing about the Bell and Weinberg study, like the recent Masters and Johnson volume on homosexuality (1979), is that its authors are far less concerned with understanding the origins of homosexuality than they are with pointing out what homosexuals and heterosexuals have in common—such concerns as making a living, choosing a coherent lifestyle, and achieving sexual compatibility with their mates.

Conclusions

We have been examining one of the fundamental elements in marriage—gender roles. In the past, most societies assigned distinctly different personality traits and tasks to the two sexes. Men and women lived in substantially different worlds, and marriage and family life was based upon rigidly defined male and female roles.

Such rigid sex segregation was reinforced by popular beliefs about the inevitable differences between men and women. In the Chinese religion, Taoism, for example, men are *yang*—creative and aggressive, associated with the sky and the sun—while women are *yin*—dark, hidden, receptive, associated with the earth. In astrology, the air signs, which stand for intellect, and the fire signs, which signify action, are masculine. The earth signs, signifying practicality, and the water signs, which refer to intuition, are feminine. Implicit in these myths, as Simone de Beauvoir comments, is the idea that women are different, mysterious, *other* than men (1952).

As we have noted, these myths have little basis in biology. Although males may be slightly more aggressive as a consequence of biological factors, most of what we associate with masculinity and femininity is a product of social learning, not biological necessity.

Recent evidence suggests that both parents and teachers are moving away from the traditional pattern, which was to teach boys and girls very different patterns of behavior. This change may be a realistic response in a society where extremely sex-stereotyped individuals—both unusually aggressive, competitive, and insensitive men, and passive, unassertive women—are at a disadvantage. In modern society, the biological differences between men and women—men are generally taller and stronger and only women can bear and nurse children—matter less than they did. Women no longer spend most of their adult lives producing and raising children, and physical strength is no longer required in most work. Consequently, ours is a society where it is no longer necessary or even practical to label certain tasks "men's work" and others "women's work."

REFERENCES

Jack O. Balswick and Charles W. Peek. The inexpressive male: A tragedy of American society. *The Family Coordinator* 20 (1971): 363–368.

Judith Bardwick and Elizabeth Douvan. Ambivalence—the socialization of women. In Vivian Gornick and Barbara K. Moran, eds. *Women in sexist society*. New York: Basic Books, 1971.

Alan P. Bell and Martin S. Weinberg. *Homosexualities: A study of diversity among men and women*. New York: Simon and Schuster, 1978.

Jessie Bernard. *The future of marriage*. New York: Bantam, 1973.

Irving Bieber *et al*. *Homosexuality: A psychoanalytic study*. New York: Random House, 1962.

Barbara Chasen. Toward eliminating sex-role stereotyping in early childhood classes. *Child Care Quarterly* 6 (1977): 30–41.

Alice E. Courtney and Sarah Wernick Lockeretz. A woman's place: An analysis of the roles portrayed by women in magazine advertisements. *Journal of Marketing Research* 8 (1971): 92–95.

Simone de Beauvoir. *The second sex*. New York: Bantam, 1952.

Robert B. Evans. Childhood parental relationships of homosexual men. *Journal of Consulting and Clinical Psychology* 33 (1969): 129–135.

Clellan S. Ford and Frank A. Beach. *Patterns of sexual behavior*. New York: Harper, 1951.

Terry Frueh and Paul E. McGhee. Traditional sex role development and amount of time spent watching television. *Developmental Psychology* 11 (1975): 109.

John Gagnon and Bruce Henderson. *Human sexuality*. Boston: Little, Brown, 1975.

Debra Gewertz. Personal communication, 1976.

Stephen Goldberg. *The inevitability of patriarchy*. New York: Morrow, 1973.

Robert E. Hartley. Sex-role pressures and the socialization of the male child. *Psychological Reports* 5 (1959): 456–462.

Evelyn Hooker. The adjustment of the male overt homosexual. *Journal of Projective Techniques* 21 (1957): 18–31.

Morton Hunt. *Sexual behavior in the 1970's*. New York: Dell, 1974.

A. H. Jacobsen. Conflict of attitudes toward the roles of husband and wife in marriage. *American Sociological Review* 17 (1952): 146–150.

Frederick J. Kallman. Comparative twin study in the genetic aspects of male homosexuality. *Journal of Nervous and Mental Disease* 115 (1952): 283–298.

Lawrence Kohlberg. A cognitive-developmental analysis of children's sex role concepts and attitudes. In Eleanor E. Maccoby, ed. *The development of sex differences*. Stanford: Stanford University Press, 1966.

Mirra Komarovsky. *Blue-collar marriage*. New York: Vintage, 1967.

Joseph A. Loraine. Patterns of hormone excretion in male and female homosexuals. *Nature* 234 (1971): 552–555.

David B. Lynn. The process of learning parental and sex-role identification. *Journal of Marriage and the Family* 28 (1966): 466–470.

Eleanor Maccoby. Women's intellect. In S. M. Farber and R. H. L. Wilson, eds. *The potential of women.* New York: McGraw-Hill, 1963.

Eleanor Maccoby and Carol Jacklin. *The psychology of sex differences.* Stanford: Stanford University Press, 1974.

William H. Masters and Virginia E. Johnson. *Homosexuality in Perspective.* Boston: Little Brown, 1979.

Margaret Mead. The life cycle and its variations. In Daniel Bell, ed. *Toward the year 2000: Work in process.* Boston: Beacon Press, 1969.

———. *Male and female.* New York: Morrow, 1949.

———. *Sex and temperament in three primitive societies.* New York: Morrow, 1935.

John Money and Anke A. Ehrhardt. *Man and woman, boy and girl.* New York: Mentor, 1974.

H. A. Moss. Sex, age, and state as determinants of mother-infant interaction. *Merrill-Palmer Quarterly* 13 (1967): 19–36.

Ann Oakley. *Sex, gender, and society.* New York: Harper, 1972.

Andrea K. Oberstone and Harriet Sukoneck. Psychological adjustment and life style of single lesbians and single heterosexual women. *Psychology of Women Quarterly* 1 (Winter 1976): 172–188.

Nena O'Neill and George O'Neill. *Open marriage.* New York: Evans, 1972.

Bernard C. Rosen and Carol S. Aneshensel. Sex differences in the educational-occupational expectation process. *Social Forces* 57 (1978): 164–186.

D. Rosenthal. *Genetic theory and abnormal behavior.* New York: McGraw-Hill, 1970.

Terry N. Saario, Carol Nagy Jacklin, and Carol Kehr Tittle. Sex role stereotyping in the public schools. *Harvard Educational Review* 43 (1973): 386–416.

Edward Sagarin. The good guys, the bad guys, and the gay guys. *Contemporary Sociology* 2 (1973): 3–13.

John R. Seeley, R. A. Sim, and E. W. Loosley. *Crestwood Heights.* New York: Wiley, 1956.

Arlene Skolnick. *The intimate environment.* Boston: Little, Brown, 1973.

William Stephens. *The family in cross-cultural perspective.* New York: Holt, 1963.

Lionel Tiger. Male dominance? Yes, alas. A sexist plot? No. *New York Times Magazine,* October 25, 1970, p. 36 et passim.

J. Richard Udry. *The social context of marriage.* Philadelphia: Lippincott, 1974.

United States Commission on Civil Rights. *Window dressing on the set: Women and minorities in television.* Washington, D.C.: Government Printing Office, 1977.

Marjorie B. U'Ren. The image of women in textbooks. In Vivian Gornick and Barbara K. Moran, eds. *Women in sexist society.* New York: Basic Books, 1971.

Lenore J. Weitzman, Deborah Eifler, Elizabeth Hokada and Catherine Ross. Sex-role socialization in picture books for preschool children. *American Journal of Sociology* 77 (1972): 1125–1150.

FOR FURTHER STUDY

For useful summaries of research on sex roles, see Arlie Russell Hochschild's "A Review of Sex Role Research" (*American Journal of Sociology,* vol. 78, 1973) and particularly Eleanor Emmons Maccoby and Carol Nagy Jacklin's *The Psychology of Sex Differences* (Stanford: Stanford University Press, 1974).

During the past few years, several new books have appeared for the general reader who wants a well-informed overview on maleness and femaleness, masculinity and femininity. *The Longest War: Sex Differences in Perspective* by Carol Tavris and Carole Offir (New York: Harcourt, Brace, Jovanovich, 1977) is a lively and clearly written account. *Sexual Signatures: On Being a Man or a Woman,* by John Money and Patricia Tucker (Boston: Little, Brown, 1975) is another useful discussion, with chapters on such matters as prenatal development, the effect of sex hormones on the brain, and gender identity. *Human Sexuality in Four Perspectives,* an anthology edited by Frank A. Beach (Baltimore: Johns Hopkins, 1976), includes several articles pertinent to the themes of this chapter and contains particularly good coverage on the effects of hormonal changes and other biological factors. See especially the chapters by Milton Diamond ("Human Sexual Development: Biological Foundations for Social Development"), Jerome Kagan ("Psychology of Sex Differences"), and Frederick T. Melges and David Hamburg ("Psychological Effects of Hormonal Changes in Women").

For decades, social scientists have tended to minimize or overlook entirely the relevance of human biology to our social behavior. In recent years, social scientists have begun to consider the implications of the fact that males and females are not at all identical. In an article entitled "A Biosocial Perspective on Parenting," Alice Rossi argues that there is more to sex roles, and to the division of labor in the family, than differences in socialization (see *Daedalus,* vol. 106, Spring 1977). Drawing upon evidence from endocrinology, Rossi argues that with regard to such matters as maternal interest in children during the first few years of life, the influence of biological factors may be far greater than many people have assumed. For obvious reasons, such research on biological differences is particularly susceptible to misinterpretation; critics of research in this area are concerned about the possibility that it will be used as scientific justification for sexism. For two additional perspectives on the issue see Milton Diamond, "Sexual Identity and Sex Roles," *The Humanist,* March/April 1978; and Daniel Goleman, "Special Abilities of the Sexes: Do They Begin in the Brain?" *Psychology Today,* November 1978.

One of the most interesting discussions of gender training to appear in recent years is Erving Goffman's monograph entitled "Gender Advertisements," which filled the entire Fall 1976 issue of *Studies in the Anthropology of Visual Communication.* (A hardbound edition has been published by Harvard University Press, and a paperback edition by Harper & Row, 1978). The monograph includes a portfolio of 500 photographs that portray cultural assumptions about patterns of dominance and subordination, body positions and postures that reveal the relative statuses of males and females.

Domingo

8

His Marriage and Hers—Redefining Sex Roles and Relationships

His—The Male Role in Marriage

Hers—The Female Role in Marriage

Box 8–1: In Response to the Liberated Woman—The Total Woman

The Strains and Rewards of Being a Housewife

Working Wives

The Dual-Career Marriage

Toward Role Equality in Marriage—Is It Possible? Is It Desirable?

Box 8–2: Revising a Sexist Language—of Wopersons, Herstory, and People-power

Have you ever seen *The Newlywed Game?* On that television show, recently married husbands and wives are asked about each other's preferences, or what their spouse would be likely to do in certain situations. Then the answers of the husband and wife are compared. Of course, their responses often don't match at all. The difference between his perceptions and hers is what makes the program entertaining. If the question is "What does your husband like most about you?" and her answer is "My intelligence," his is likely to be "Her backrubs." Like many situations that provoke laughter, this one is common—and a common source of problems—in everyday life.

Sociologists find the same kinds of discrepancies between his version of what is going on in a marriage and hers, even among couples who have been married for years. It is often true that husbands and wives give quite different answers to questions about decision-making, how often they have intercourse, or how often they laugh together. About half of the couples even disagree about seemingly clear-cut matters such as who pays the bills; a quarter do not even agree about who mows the lawn (Bernard, 1973, p. 5).

For years, novelists, philosophers, and psychologists have been demonstrating that our perceptions of the world are fundamentally subjective. What we see depends upon our angle of vision. This subjectivity is certainly true in marriage, where so often there seem to be two completely different realities—the husband's and the wife's. Two very interesting novels about marriage and family life by Evan Connell provide a vivid illustration. The first, *Mrs. Bridge* (1958), describes the reality of her marriage in a series of vignettes. The second, *Mr. Bridge* (1969), describes the reality of his marriage. And though many of the same events and situations occur in both books, they take on very different meanings to the two spouses. The Bridges' marriage is a "good" one by most conventional standards; the two love each other and share most of the important events in their lives. But they don't understand each other. The most important moments in the lives of each pass by without the other noticing them. The same objective events have very different meanings. In this respect, they are like most couples. We will look first at his marriage and then at hers in order to examine the difference between these two realities.

In particular, we will focus on how women's roles—as wife, mother, and worker—have changed, and how those changes affect marriage and family. Consider how quickly women's roles have been redefined over the past generation, and how different the experience of mothers who married in the 1950s was from that of their daughters who grew up in the 1960s and 1970s. In the 1950s, it was widely assumed that women's main roles were the ones they performed at home, and college-educated women were no exception. In a commencement address delivered at Smith College in 1955, Adlai Stevenson told the graduating women that their main role was to "influence us, man and boy," their mission was to "restore valid, meaningful purpose to life at home," and to keep their husbands "truly purposeful." These words reflect the characteristic emphases of that decade on child rearing and domesticity.

But the social and economic trends of the past generation have drastically altered women's roles. Unlike their mothers, young women today grew up in an era when zero population growth became a widely discussed goal, when contraceptives were readily available, when women were encouraged to have fewer children, and to consider the possibility of having none at all. Today, young women no longer assume that motherhood is destiny, the only career they need, and the only one for which they will receive social approval. A majority of women now want to have both a family and a career. A woman who expressed that preference in the 1950s would have been a member of a small, even deviant minority. Today, although there are still groups which adamantly believe that woman's place is in the home, a woman who combines work and family roles can expect to receive considerable social approval, partially because a majority of intact families now have two wage earners. Unlike their mothers, young women who are now in college grew up during a decade when feminist complaints about sexism in the labor force, in the media, and in marriage were commonplace.

As a result of such developments, expectations of marital roles have been substantially redefined. In this chapter, we will examine the male and female roles in marriage and explore the implications of recent demands for equality between the sexes.

HIS—THE MALE ROLE IN MARRIAGE

To be a man in a society still largely dominated by males would seem to be a highly desirable status. It is men, of course, rather than women, who dominate most of the professions, run the corporations, as well as the cultural and educational institutions. The social customs and legal regulations that discriminate against other groups in the society give men—at least white men—a privileged position. When performing the same tasks that women do, men are often paid more, and they are more likely to be promoted.

But there are costs as well as benefits for males. Most health statistics, as well as the criminal records, demonstrate that males are more vulnerable to stress, and they commit more serious crimes. Men have more heart attacks than women; they die younger; they are more likely to develop ulcers, commit suicide, and to become alcoholics. Perhaps these are symptoms of the pressures that males feel as they try to meet masculine role expectations. Both health statistics and criminal records demonstrate that men and women still live in different worlds, and feel different social pressures.

Industrialization contributed to the split between the man's world and the woman's. In many respects, the family is—to use again Alvin Toffler's phrase—the "shock absorber" in a society whose institutions are rapidly changing. The changes that industrialization brought

Studies of the division of household labor show that even when wives take jobs outside the home, they generally continue to perform a disproportionate amount of household work, including cleaning, cooking, and childcare.

about caused marriage and family roles to be substantially redefined. The family used to be a unit of production as well as consumption. Farms, grocery stores, inns and, later, gas stations used to be family enterprises. Wives, children, and frequently grandparents were integral parts of a flexible labor force. But as more and more enterprises took the form of businesses or factories located at some distance from the home, work roles and family roles became more distinct. The husband's role changed from that of head of the family business to the provider of an income earned away from home. At the same time, as we shall see in the next few pages, the woman's role became that of a full-time housewife and mother.

One of the consequences of this shift is that today family members often have only a vague idea of what their father does. Here are the thoughts of Mr. Bridge, as described in Evan Connell's novel, as he ponders over the split in his life between work and family roles:

> He sipped his drink, feeling too tired to eat, and wondered why he could not talk to his family about his work as an attorney. He knew that he did want to confide in his family . . . but after all, they could not possibly care about the testimony of a conductor involved in a traffic accident, or the observation of his secretary, Julia, about the mechanic with the infected tattoo. None of this would make sense at the dinner table. . . . No, he thought, there is almost nothing I can say to them. My life is cut in half. The halves remain side by side in perfect equilibrium, like halves of a melon. I suppose the same is true of most men. (1969, p. 107)

Even though a man might feel split in half between his two roles, both the marriage laws and the vast majority of wives agree that a man's most important role is that of breadwinner and provider (Lopata, 1971, p. 91). How successful a man is in his occupational role has a direct effect on his influence and decision-making power in his family. Several studies have shown that the higher a husband's income, the more decision-making power he will have at home (Blood and Wolfe, 1960, p. 31). Thus family life is influenced in a very direct way by the economy, the labor force, and the demands made on breadwinners by various occupations and professions.

Some of the most important changes in marriage and family life in recent years have resulted from the fact that more women are now in the labor force, thus redefining expectations about who is responsible for family support. The Census Bureau recognized this trend by announcing that, beginning with the 1980 Census, it would replace the term "head of household" with a new one, "householder," and that it would abandon its practice of assuming that the husband is the "head of household" even if his wife works.

Just as responsibilities for economic support have changed, so have images of masculinity. The traditional masculine stereotype—as exemplified by such film heroes as John Wayne—is now widely regarded as a handicap. There is a new image of masculinity evident, among other places, in the films of the past few years. The older image was that of the competitive male, who defined himself and was defined by others in terms of his achievements. The film heroes of the 1930s, 1940s, and 1950s—whether cowboys, gangsters, or cops—were typically loners, men who seemed capable at best of enjoying the companionship of other men. What was not depicted in film was the thoughtful hero, one who was emotionally competent, who liked women and enjoyed their companionship, or who triumphed through collective action. In contrast, the new masculine ideal is portrayed by actors such as Alan Bates in "An Unmarried Woman" or Jon Voight in "Coming Home." As one commentator remarks,

> In these films, the more conventional male is usually portrayed by the heroine's husband and the "new man" is epitomized by her lover. The husband is self-absorbed, aggressive, and emotionally distant from his wife, while the lover is tender, considerate, responsive, and easygoing. (Starr, 1978)

The husband in these films exemplifies the older image of masculinity. By the traditional standards of achievement, competitiveness, and virility he does quite well. But he is portrayed in these films as being seriously handicapped, and he is compared unfavorably with men who are emotionally competent, affectionate, capable of expressing feelings, and responding to the feelings of others.

This new type of screen hero reflects social reality more accurately than the mass media generally do. Although many people seem to have trouble defining what they mean by masculinity today, the traits now commonly associated with the "ideal man" are very different from those of the John Wayne image of masculinity. When, for example, women of various ages were asked in a nationwide survey what qualities they admire in a man, young women answered far more frequently than older ones that they admire and seek out men who can express their feelings (Roper, 1974). And when 28,000 readers of the magazine *Psychology Today*—a group that is younger, more liberal, better educated, and more affluent than the population as a whole—completed a questionnaire about how they define masculinity, the results showed that they, too, value emotional competence in males. At least among members of this group, it appears that both sexes reject the image of the macho male who is strong, tough, aggressive, and has many sexual conquests (Tavris, 1977).

The most striking pattern in the *Psychology Today* survey, and in other recent studies of how young adults define masculinity (Komarovsky, 1976), is that most of the traits that people consider important in the "ideal male" are the same ones that people look for in the "ideal female." At the top of the list for both the "ideal man" and the "ideal woman" are some traditionally female traits (such as personal warmth and the ability to love) and some desirable but sexually neutral ones (such as intelligence and self-confidence), while such traditionally male traits as competitiveness, aggressiveness, or physical strength are considered by both sexes to be much less important than these other traits in the "ideal man." There are, however, some exceptions to this generally egalitarian pattern: substantially more women than men consider occupational success to be essential for the "ideal man"; and men consider the physical attractiveness of members of the opposite sex to be more important than women do. But the overall trend is clear: traditional differences between masculine and feminine ideals are eroding, as are the differences between male and female roles (Tavris, 1977).

To the extent that we can generalize from

surveys such as this one, it appears that masculinity has been substantially redefined—at least by young, college-educated adults—and the new expectations of men have many implications for marriage and family life. Though the man's most important role in family life may still be that of breadwinner, it appears that masculinity is no longer defined mainly by activities performed outside the family unit.

While many people consider this newly defined image of masculinity to be a desirable change, it might also be observed that these new expectations place new and sometimes inconsistent demands on men. As Carol Tavris comments in her summary of the *Psychology Today* survey, women "don't just want a man who is merely sweet, thoughtful, loving, gentle, and faithful; they also rate being successful at work more heavily than men do. . . . The ideal men are strong but gentle, tough on the outside and soft on the inside, able to express emotions but not a slave to them" (1977, p. 39). To the extent that occupational success requires traits that are quite different from the loving and gentle qualities valued at home, this new ideal of masculinity requires that men be successful in very different realms.

Changing definitions of the masculine ideal have an obvious impact on the husband's role. Inconsistent demands, such as the ones we were just considering, might well create new stresses, but there are as yet no data that confirm that this is happening. What we do know—as we discussed in Chapter 5—is that, in comparison with their single counterparts, married men appear to be better able to cope with personal and occupational stresses. As we also noted in Chapter 5, it may be that men who choose to marry have superior mental health and career prospects—in comparison with single men. There is no way, finally, to determine how important this selective factor is. But the statistics on survival rates, suicide, occupational success, and mental health ratings all tell the same story. In sociologist Jessie Bernard's words, "There are few findings more consistent, less equivocal, and more convincing than the sometimes spectacular and always impressive superiority on almost every index of married over never-married men" (1973, p. 17). Despite the perennial complaints of husbands about the burdens of their role, the evidence suggests that marriage is quite beneficial for many men.

But—to recall another point discussed in Chapter 5—if we look at those same studies to compare the statistics for single and married *women,* a different pattern emerges. Compared with single women, married women report more neurotic symptoms, are more fearful, and have more feelings of inadequacy, depression, and passivity (Bernard, 1973, p. 30). To understand this remarkable pattern, we need to look more closely at the female role in marriage.

HERS—THE FEMALE ROLE IN MARRIAGE

Particularly for college-educated women, marriage often comes as a shock. One reason is that it changes a woman's life more than a man's. The transition between the role expectations of the college woman and those of the full-time housewife and mother are particularly abrupt. Think of the changes that take place for the young woman who marries at graduation to become a housewife, and—soon after—a mother. She moves from a world where there is little sexual segregation—where men and women attend the same classes, compete for grades on an equal basis, perhaps even live in the same dorms—into a world where males and females have substantially different experiences. She becomes the person who takes care of others. She moves from the openness of the university—an environment designed to provide a stimulating mixture of people and ideas—into the much more restricted world of homemaking and child rearing.

Considering how different these two environments are, perhaps it is not surprising that women's personalities seem to change when they marry. After marriage women tend to become more submissive and conservative (Bernard, 1973, p. 42).

In fact, whereas one of the main purposes of a college education is to train people to think and act independently, marriage may teach women to be just the opposite. Study after study has shown that wives adjust to their husbands far more than husbands do to their wives. Women make more adjustments in marriage than men do because they have more at stake. The wife's status—how much money she can spend, where and how she lives, and where her children go to school—depends, in most cases, upon her husband's efforts more than her own.

In fact, marriage seems to be more important to women than to men at every stage in the life cycle. Teenage girls and young women look forward to marrying more than young men do. For wives, marital success is crucial to their overall happiness. But for men, this is not necessarily true. It is much more common for men to tell interviewers that their marriages are not very happy, but that they are generally satisfied with their lives (Bernard, 1973, p. 148).

Perhaps because marriage is a more important ingredient in overall satisfaction for women than men, wives are less likely than their husbands to be happy in their marriages. Here, again in Jessie Bernard's words, is what the research indicates:

> There is a very considerable research literature reaching back over a generation which shows that: more wives than husbands report marital frustration and dissatisfaction; more report negative feelings; more wives than husbands consider their marriages unhappy, have considered separation or divorce, have regretted their marriages; and fewer report positive companionship. Only about half as many wives (25 percent) as husbands (45 percent) say that there is nothing about their marriages that is not as nice as they would like. (1972, pp. 26–27)

Not only are married women unhappier than married men, but they also show more of the symptoms of psychological distress. Wives are more likely than their husbands—or single women—to be depressed, anxious, and passive. Studies that have been conducted over the past few decades show that married women are more likely than their husbands "to be bothered by feelings of depression, unhappy most of the time, to dislike their present jobs, to be afraid of death, terrified by windstorms, worried about catching diseases, sometimes thinking of things too bad to talk about, and bothered by pains and ailments in different parts of the body" (Bernard, 1973, p. 32). Recent research suggests that this pattern may have changed since those older studies were conducted. One major mental health survey conducted in the 1970s, a replication of the Midtown Manhattan study first conducted in the 1950s, suggests that the psychiatric impairment rate of women between the ages of forty and sixty is no longer substantially higher than that of men. The authors of this study, Leo Srole and Anita K. Fischer (1978), speculate that changes in women's status have brought about a radically different social climate, and that an important reason for the relative well-being of these women is that they did not submerge their identities in domestic roles. But we should be careful about generalizing from studies, such as this one, that focus on a population that (as its authors acknowledge) is not representative of the nation as a whole. In large cities, relatively few women are full-time housewives. The metropolitan milieu, as Srole and Fischer comment, encourages women to be independent and to use their new-found freedom of self-expression outside the home.

Another recent study of psychological and physical stress has inquired about symptom patterns of a more representative group of American adults, and it concludes that full-time housewives, at least, still experience far more psychological distress than their husbands do. They are, for example, far more likely to have frequent headaches, to feel sometimes that "they just can't go on," to experience considerable anxiety, loneliness, and a sense of worthlessness (Shaver and Freedman, 1976).

Of all the questions being raised about marriage today, one of the most important is why

Point of View

Box 8–1 / In Response to the Liberated Woman—*The Total Woman*

Author Germaine Greer offers one of the most pointed statements of the feminist position in *The Female Eunuch* (1970):

> So what is the beef? Maybe I couldn't make it. Maybe I don't have a pretty smile, good teeth, nice tits, long legs, a cheeky arse, a sexy voice. Maybe I don't know how to handle men and increase my market value, so that the rewards due to the feminine will accrue to me. Then again, maybe I'm sick of the masquerade. I'm sick of pretending eternal youth. I'm sick of belying my own intelligence, my own will, my own sex. . . . I'm sick of pretending that some fatuous male's self-important pronouncements are the objects of my undivided attention. I'm sick of going to films and plays when someone else wants to, and sick of having no opinions of my own about either. I'm sick of being a transvestite. I refuse to be a female impersonator. I am a woman, not a castrate. (p. 53)

However, there is another book on being female today that has sold far more copies than Germaine Greer's feminist manifesto. Rather than instructing women on how to avoid "male tyranny," this book is packed with advice on how to please a man: "It is only when a woman surrenders her life to her husband, reveres and worships him, and is willing to serve him, that she becomes really beautiful to him." The book's title is *The Total Woman* (1975). It was written by Marabel Morgan, the wife of a successful Miami attorney. Along with other popular books written in the same vein, such as Helen Andelin's *Fascinating Womanhood* (1974), it is a how-to book for women more concerned about pleasing their husbands than raising their consciousness. For many of the readers of *The Total Woman*, women's liberation makes far less sense than suggestions on how to put a little romance back into their marriages.

(Box 8–1 continues on page 222)

women who are full-time housewives so commonly experience psychological distress. To explore this question, we need to examine the role expectations of the housewife.

Until roughly the turn of the century, housekeeping was not considered a full-time occupation for women. Previously, women were expected to perform both productive and housekeeping tasks. The pioneer women, for example, as described in Robert Smuts' *Women and Work in America*, "worked side by side with her husband, planting, harvesting, building, fighting grasshoppers and prairie fires" (1972, p. 7). Farm women commonly used to share the responsibilities for livestock and tend the gardens; they sewed their own clothes and often contributed to the family income by selling eggs or cheese, or taking in laundry.

In contrast, middle- and upper-class women had more leisure; their condition was closer to that of modern housewives. It is interesting that the first feminists in England came from relatively privileged circumstances. Their complaints, like the following voiced by the heroine of Charlotte Bronte's *Shirley*, written in 1849, sound quite modern:

> Women should have more to do—better chances of interesting and profitable occupation than they possess now. What do men expect women to do at home? If you ask, they would answer: sew and cook. Men expect women to do this only, contentedly, regularly, uncomplainingly all their lives long, as if they had no germs of faculties for anything else. (p. 315)

(Box 8–1 continued from page 221)

Here are instructions from Marabel Morgan and Helen Andelin about how to be female. They reveal a world that is far apart from Germaine Greer's:

Admire Him—"Women need to be loved; men need to be admired. Your husband needs you to see him as he sees himself. Tell him you love his body. If you choke on that phrase, practice till it comes out naturally" (Morgan, p. 63).

Adapt to Him—God planned for woman to be under her husband's rule. God ordained man to be the head of the family, its president, and his wife to be the executive vice-president. Allowing your husband to be your family president is just good business" (Morgan, p. 82).

Be Feminine—"A feminine woman is dependent upon her husband to guide her, protect her and provide a living for her and her children. She can develop her femininity by living her feminine role as the wife, mother and homemaker. . . . But when a woman steps into the man's world and tries to be a shining light there she sacrifices her own special beauty and grace. And when a woman divides herself between two worlds it is difficult for her to succeed in either" (Andelin).

How to Turn Him On—"Once this week call him at work an hour before quitting time to say 'I wanted you to know that I just crave your body!' Eat by candlelight; you'll light his candle! Thrill him at the front door in your costume. Costumes provide variety without him ever leaving home. You may be a smoldering sex-pot, or an all-American fresh beauty. Be a pixie or a pirate—a cowgirl or a showgirl. Keep him off guard. . . . One gal took the course being held in her Southern Baptist Church. She welcomed her husband home in black mesh stockings, high heels, and an apron. That's all. He took one look and shouted 'Praise the Lord!' " (Morgan, pp. 163, 119).

Sources: Germaine Greer. *The Female Eunuch.* New York: McGraw-Hill, 1970. Marabel Morgan. *The Total Woman.* New York: Pocket Books, 1975. Helen Andelin. Personal communication, 1977.

Even the unusually privileged women of the mid-nineteenth century, though, had more responsibilities than most housewives do today. Mrs. Beeton's *Book of Household Management,* published in England in 1861, contained not only recipes and certain tips on how to make a home more attractive, but also instructions on nursing the sick and making medicines, drawing up legal contracts, and managing a household that included a butler, a footman, a coachman, a groom and stableboy, a valet, a lady's maid, housemaids, a dairy maid, a nursemaid, a laundress, and a wet nurse.

Smaller houses, smaller families, ready-made clothing, electricity, appliances, convenience foods, the support of outside institutions like schools and hospitals—all these innovations have changed woman's role at home. But the most important change has resulted from an economic innovation that we have already discussed: the replacement of family-owned and operated craftshops and businesses by factories and offices at some distance from the household. With this change, the family, once a unit of production, became primarily a unit of consumption. Men became wage earners and spent their working hours away from their families. And many married women, for the first time in history, were removed from the world of productive work.

Of course modern women can—if they choose—make the family's clothes or bake the bread. The number of books about raising organic foods, baking, sewing, and doing pottery suggests that many housewives are still pursuing fulfillment through women's traditional crafts. However, the housewife who makes the family's bread is probably spending more money than she would if she bought it. She is consuming, not producing.

The full-time housewife, then, is a relatively new occupation, and until a few years ago, most discussions glorified it. Here, for example, is a 1940s description of the role:

> A woman who is an effective homemaker must know something about teaching, interior decoration, cooking, dietetics, psychology, social relations, community resources, clothing, household equipment, housing, hygiene, and a host of other things. She is a general practitioner rather than a specialist. . . . The young woman who decides upon homemaking as her career need have no feeling of inferiority. One may say, as some do, "Men have careers because women make homes." One may say that women are released from the necessity for wage earning and are free to devote their time to the extremely important matter of homemaking because men specialize in breadwinning. . . . (Bowman, in Friedan, 1963, p. 130)

Today, however, feminists have turned the statement around: the housewife's job is often regarded as menial drudgery, a waste of woman's time and energy. Much of what has been written and said about it in the past years is summarized in sociologist Philip Slater's terse comment: "The housewife is a nobody" (in Bernard, 1973, p. 48). In the next few pages, we will examine the housewife's role.

The Strains and Rewards of Being a Housewife

An important strain of being a housewife results from a fairly new tendency—she is more isolated from other adults than she used to be. Philip Slater comments on a pattern that is most common today in middle-class and upper-middle-class families:

> The idea of imprisoning each woman alone in a small, self-contained, and architecturally isolated dwelling is a modern invention, dependent upon an advanced technology. In Muslim society, for example, the wife may be a prisoner, but at least she is not in solitary confinement. In our society,

Some people attribute the psychological distress of full-time housewives to the isolation of such women, and the monotony of the work they perform.

> the housewife may move about freely, but since she has nowhere in particular to go and is not a part of anything her prison needs no walls. Her only significant relationships tend to be with her husband who, however, is absent most of the day. Most of her social and emotional needs must be satisfied by her children, who are hardly adequate to the task. (*Washington Post,* March 1, 1970, p. 68)

In the past, women commonly spent many of their daytime hours around other adults who were either members of the household, or neighbors in settings that posed fewer obstacles to sharing day-to-day tasks.

A second strain in the housewife's role—one that we have already mentioned—is that she no longer works part-time in the family-owned and -operated business. The removal of production from the home, as novelist and feminist Elizabeth Janeway notes, creates an anxiety-provoking situation in which housewives no longer have "an objective standard by which to measure their actions":

> Our great-grandmothers may not have been able to support themselves by their earnings, but . . . they could look beyond the family for a judgment on their abilities. Some of them turned out goods that went to the market and had to pass the test of saleability. But even if they didn't, their repute in their own communities supplied a public yardstick. Mrs. Appleton's pickles, Mrs. Matthews' baked goods, the special dyes Mrs. Mayhew used for her yarn, Mrs. Lockhart's quilts—these might win only local fame, but they existed apart from their makers. Such a reward may be no more tangible than ribbons from a country fair, but public judgments of this kind simply reflected and represented the existence of a whole area of housewifely skills. (1971, p. 170)

A woman whose only task is caring for her husband and children has no such objective standard, as her great-grandmother did, to measure her success or failure. Perhaps this is the reason why advertisements for household products so frequently show women in an anxious competition with their peers. ("How does she get her wash so bright when mine is so dingy?") Advertisers know that, in the absence of any objective standard of household cleanliness, most women can be persuaded to try a little harder, and to buy cleaning products that used to be unnecessary.

Also, in America, we tend to value work according to how much one earns for it. Because housewives are not paid, they are dependent upon their husbands' status. Women are commonly asked what their *husbands* do, not what *they* do. It is ironic that the wives of successful,

Marguerite Panet

Marguerite Panet, wife of retired Maj.-Gen. Edouard de Bellefeuille Panet, died yesterday.

Gen. Panet, 93, is well-known for his work with the Canadian Paraplegic Association, for which he served as its Quebec division chairman for several years.

The general is a member of a distinguished Canadian military family which had a soldier in the army of Montcalm. He served in the First World War, rising to the rank of brigadier-general and was made a Companion of the Order of St. Michael and St. George and the Distinguished Service Order.

Funeral service for his wife will be held Tuesday at the Cathedral of Montreal at 1 p.m.

Source: Obituary column, Montreal *Star.*

In a society where identity is determined by one's occupation, the woman who is "just a housewife" finds herself, in Gail Fullerton's words, with a "pseudo-occupation and a second-hand identity."

affluent men are—in several respects—most likely to be in a vulnerable position as full-time housewives. With adequate money, many of the housewives' tasks can be performed by specialists; household appliances take care of many of the others. If the husband makes a good living, whatever economic contributions the wife might make through part-time work are likely to be relatively insignificant. In addition, affluent families can afford houses that are architecturally more isolated from those of neighbors, which may make it more difficult for the wife to contact others throughout the day.

Another strain in the housewife's role results from the fact that men in relatively prestigious careers are expected to move from one place to another as a condition of advancement. Myrna Weissman and Eugene Paykel of the Depression Research Unit at the Yale University School of Medicine studied the relationship between moving and depression in women. Although most of the moves made by women in this study were voluntary and meant career advancements for their husbands, the women often responded with symptoms of stress. Women often feel helpless and victimized because men initiate moves, but *they* bear the responsibilities. During the early and most demanding years of a man's professional life, the details of selling a house, packing up, and locating a new home are often left to the wife. The study found that the depressive feelings of these women were "by-products of faulty adaptation to stresses and changes created by moving." Moving turns out to be one of the most frequent causes of depression in women (in Melville, 1972, p. 20).

Because the housewife's role is not defined as work in the same sense that her husband's job is, women commonly belittle their contribution by making comments such as "I'm just a housewife." Whereas men justify their leisure as a necessary form of recreation that helps them to return to their productive roles, women who have no productive roles often feel guilty about the "frivolous" activities with which they fill their leisure time. As sociologist David Riesman comments, "Our definitions of work mean that the housewife, though producing a social work-product, does not find her work explicitly defined and totaled, either as an hour product, in the national census, or in people's minds" (1961, p. 262).

Many feminists feel, like the French novelist Simone de Beauvoir, that housework is "like the torture of Sisyphus . . . with its endless repetition: the clean becomes soiled, the soiled is made clean, over and over, day after day. The housewife wears herself out marking time" (1952, p. 425). There is nothing new in women doing such work. In even the simplest hunting and gathering societies, the routine tasks are considered to be women's work. And even if those routine tasks include gathering the foods that provide most of the nutrients in a family's diet, the work that is considered to be more important—such as hunting, which is also more exciting and less monotonous—is men's work. What is relatively new, as we have seen, is the idea that housework should be considered a full-time occupation.

A summary of the most common complaints about the housewife's role, then, includes these items: the housewife is often isolated throughout much of the day from other adult companions. From the point of view of this society's values, the housewife's work is not considered productive. Moreover, much of it is monotonous and repetitive. Thus a situation is created whereby women are dependent upon their husbands' status. Each of these factors helps to explain why the transition to the housewife's status is difficult for many women, and why the symptoms of psychological distress are common among housewives.

One of the main reasons why so many middle-class and upper-middle-class women today support the feminist cause is that they spent at least several years in a college community treated as men's equals. During the 1960s, the percentage of American women who attended college more than doubled. Consequently, many of those college-educated women no longer take it for granted—as most of their

"You say you're only a housewife, and I say what do you mean, 'only'?"

mothers did—that they are destined to be homemakers and mothers. Recent complaints about the housewife's role are an important consequence of teaching women to have new and different expectations of themselves.

However, none of the strains in the housewife's role is inevitable. Housewives can—if they choose—move outside the home into friendly relationships with their neighbors and community activities. They can define themselves in ways that are not limited to routine household tasks.

In a study of Chicago-area housewives, sociologist Helena Lopata interviewed 571 women and concluded that the feminist stereotype of housewives as "basically passive, unimaginative, uninterested in events outside their walls, chained to routine tasks, and unable to understand the work their husbands and children perform away from home" was false (1971, p. 362).

Lopata did find a number of "restricted housewives" who had few relationships outside the family, saw their relationships with their husbands in terms of male dominance and resented it, and defined their role as a series of chores. But she also found another pattern—more prevalent in relatively affluent families—that suggests some of the rewards of the housewife's role.

One of those rewards, Lopata discovered, is a feeling of competence. To be an intelligent consumer in a society that offers as many choices as ours takes skill. To decorate a home, to clothe a family, to pick and choose among a variety of stores in any metropolitan area demand both intelligence and creativity. Being a housewife can involve far more than routine tasks, and highly educated women are more likely to turn to books and magazines for help in household management.

Another reward of being a full-time housewife is the freedom to build "a many-faceted life, an opportunity few other vocational roles allow, because they are tied down to single organizational structures and goals" (p. 373). Suburban housewives are more likely to define obligations to the community as an important part of woman's role, and they are also more likely to regard obligations to the self—such as artistic expression—as important (p. 48). The same study suggests that women with young children typically form close relationships with their neighbors; a few years later, when those children enter school, many of these women become involved in a wider range of community activities.

Finally, Lopata's highly educated housewives derive considerable satisfaction from their relationships with their families. They tend to see "husband–wife relations not as a struggle for authority, but as a process of developing interpersonal depth suited to the unique needs of both personalities." Housewives with less education are more likely to define their roles in terms of specific tasks that have to be performed. They often agree with the description of the ideal housewife as "the one who has her house in perfect order, and her children cleaned and fed." More highly educated wives emphasize their contribution to relationships, and describe the ideal housewife as "one who has a happy family" or "one who is satisfied with herself—receives recognition from her husband and children and is looked upon in the community with respect" or even "one with a sense of humor to meet all occasions with understanding and love" (1971, pp. 375, 221, 220).

More than most jobs, the housewife's occupation depends upon what she makes of it. To use a phrase from the classified ads, it requires a "self-starter." The perils of isolation, loss of self-esteem, feeling trapped by routine work, and even psychological distress are real. Interestingly, success in the role seems to require traits not traditionally associated with femininity, such as administrative skill and the willingness to take the initiative. And, as Helena Lopata comments, some women who quit their jobs to become full-time housewives

> miss the time and work controls and systems of the job, and women not accustomed to being self-motivating or initiative in their behavior have to undertake major personality changes in the way they handle themselves, their duties, and their relations with others. Passive stances, or awaiting the initiative of others, may be effective and even desired of secretaries to charismatic and ever-present bosses, but the modern housewife cannot afford such an approach to her roles. This stage demands a good deal of work to be planned, organized, and executed by the same person. (1971, p. 36)

Running a household, disciplining children, taking the first steps to make friends and become active in a community require activity and initiative. Perhaps the housewives who lack those qualities are most likely to experience the difficulties sometimes associated with the role, such as a loss of self-esteem and certain neurotic symptoms.

As we have noted, the symptoms of psychological distress seem to be more common among full-time housewives than among women who work in the labor force, and some of the characteristics of the housewife's role that we have discussed—such as the differences between her work and the work that is highly valued in American society—may help to explain the pattern. But while studies of psychological well-being hardly support the image of the happy homemaker that was so widely accepted in the 1950s, the results of nationwide surveys taken during the 1970s suggest that we should not underestimate the satisfactions of the housewife's role either. So much of what has been written and said about the housewife's role during the past decade has been negative that it may come as something of a surprise to see how positively full-time housewives regard the work they perform.

In one survey, for example, fewer than one in five women expressed any dislike for housework; more than half said without qualification that they liked it. When employed women were asked whether their housework or their outside work was more important to them, a large majority responded that housework is more important. And although, as we have noted, many people have expressed concern about the housewife's isolation from other adults, a large majority of the housewives surveyed said that they did have ample opportunity to spend time with other adults during the day. The evidence from a series of nationwide surveys suggests that the recent image of the discontented housewife performing menial work that no one values is as inaccurate as the myth of the happy homemaker was in the 1950s. Even though full-time housewives suffer more symptoms of psychological and physical distress, survey data do not reveal any significant differences in expressed satisfaction between working women and housewives (Wright, 1978).

But whether or not there are any differences between full-time housewives and working women with regard to feelings of satisfaction with life, women are far less likely today to remain full-time housewives than were their mothers or grandmothers. It is the women who combine the roles of wife and worker that we will examine in the next section.

Working Wives

Until the end of the nineteenth century, one of the most common arguments for keeping women out of the labor force was based on the assumption that the female was a fragile flower, easily crushed. "In the interest of the race," wrote one influential physician, Edward Clarke, in a book published in the 1870s, "woman possesses a set of organs peculiar to herself, whose complexity, delicacy, sympathies and force are among the marvels of creation. If neglected or mismanaged, they retaliate on their possessor. . . . Muscular effort, brain work, and all forms of mental and physical excitement germinate a host of ills" (in Smuts, 1972, p. 114).

But such arguments applied only where men could afford to treat women as delicate flowers. Long before the nineteenth century, women had worked outside the home whenever it was necessary. By the early years of this century, it was common for women to work as teachers, in the sweatshops of the garment industry, in textile factories, and—in increasing numbers—as salespeople and clerical workers. But most of the women who worked before the 1940s were single. "Only among Negroes and among the immigrant populations of New England textile towns were a large minority of wives employed outside of the home. By and large, the married women who did work away from home were those whose husbands were permanently or temporarily unable to support their families" (Smuts, 1972, p. 22). Despite the feminist agitations in the first two decades of this century, the proportion of women who were gainfully employed rose little between 1910 and 1940.

World War II caused a dramatic change in the employment patterns of women. The jobs vacated by men who joined the armed forces were filled by women. "Rosie the Riveter" became a national heroine. As William Chafe remarks in his history of American women, "The woman with an acetylene torch became almost as familiar a figure to magazine readers as the girl with the Palmolive smile" (1972, p. 147). Many of the new recruits to full-time employment during the war were married women. Before the war, only 15 percent of married women worked; by the time it ended, nearly 25 percent of all married women worked. For the first time, there were as many married women over forty in the labor force as young, single women (p. 144).

Despite some feeling that women who had worked during the war should give up their jobs to returning veterans in the mid-1940s, most of

Figure 8–1 Married women (in households where husband is present)—their increasing participation in the labor force (1950–1978)

Sources: U.S. Bureau of the Census. *U.S. Working Women—A Databook.* 1978, p. 19. U.S. Department of Labor. "Marital and Family Characteristics of the Labor Force.

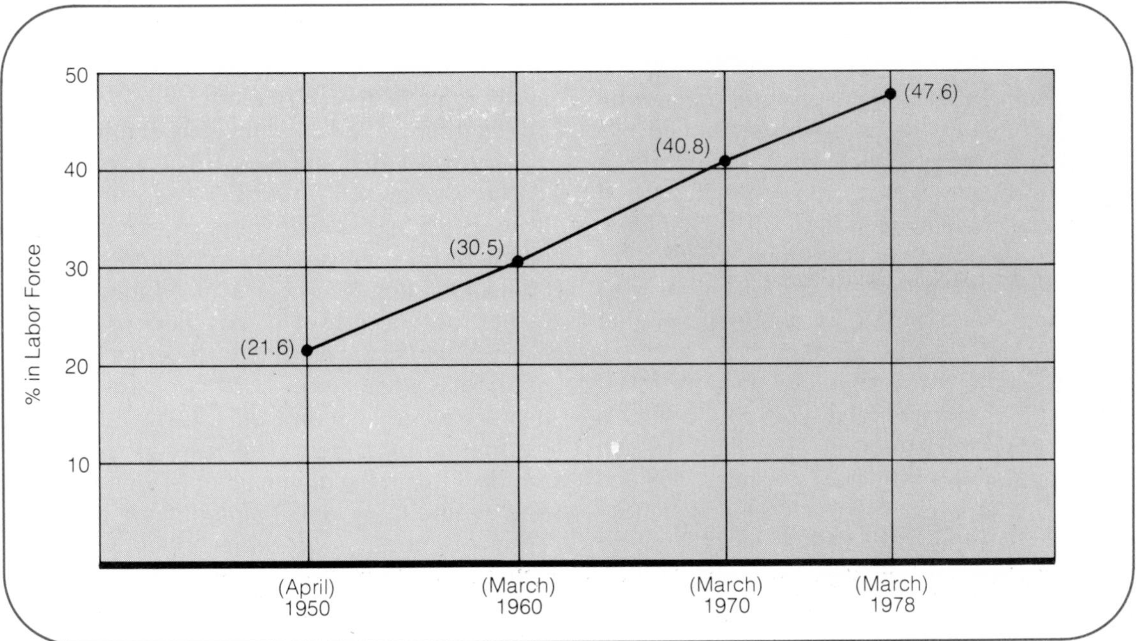

those women continued on the job after the fighting ended. In fact, one southern senator suggested that an act of Congress be passed to force wives and mothers "back into the kitchen" (Chafe, 1972, p. 177). But a variety of factors encouraged women to keep their jobs. During the postwar years there was a shortage of young people entering the labor force because of low birth rates during the Depression. Furthermore, government-sponsored programs were designed to encourage returning vets to go to college, and many of the young men who would have reentered the labor force went instead to college. At the same time, the economy was expanding very rapidly. Most of the demand for new employees occurred in white-collar occupations—such as clerical or secretarial work—that had traditionally been defined as women's work. Rapid inflation and rising aspirations were two other reasons why so many married women stayed in the labor force (Chafe, 1972, p. 190).

In her influential book, *The Feminine Mystique* (1963), Betty Friedan argued that in the 1950s many women took family togetherness quite seriously, and left the offices and factories and returned home. But the statistics tell a different story. (See Figure 8-1.) The percentage of married women living with their husbands and who are gainfully employed has increased steadily from 22 percent in 1948 to about 50 percent in 1979. The majority of wives with school-aged children now work. An even more dramatic change has taken place among women with small children. The percentage of women with children under five who work has tripled since 1948 (Hoffman and Nye, 1974, p. 5).

There are several reasons why we might assume that this trend will continue. Women are catching up with men in educational attainment. This is significant because the more educated a woman is, the more likely she is to be employed. Furthermore, more young women expect to work. And because family size is somewhat smaller than it was, and life expectancy is somewhat longer, young women who expect to work are being quite realistic: a woman who marries relatively early and has a small family can expect to have her last child by her late twenties, and have all her children in school before she is thirty-five. That leaves her more than thirty years to work on at least a part-time basis, and about twenty years after her oldest child leaves home.

Although the percentage of women in the labor force has changed, the types of work most women perform has not. In 1890 most women who worked were domestic servants, unskilled factory workers, teachers, salesclerks, stenographers, or typists. By 1970 more women worked in clerical and sales positions, and far fewer in factories or as domestics. Only two new "women's professions" have been added since the turn of the century: nursing and social work. Both represent traditionally female roles—taking care of the sick and the poor—that have been professionalized. In fact, many of the jobs that women perform today might still be understood as extensions of the traditional female role. Secretaries, for example, are typically expected to handle details that are too trivial to demand the boss's attention. Like wives, they are expected to soothe the boss's ego, and to keep things tidy. It is not just coincidental that men often refer to their secretaries as "office wives."

Despite legislation—such as the Equal Pay Act of 1963—designed to ensure equal pay for any job regardless of who performs it, women still face job discrimination and relatively low wages. But these factors have not deterred a substantial percentage of married women from entering the labor force. Why do married women enter the labor force? And what effect does that work have on their marriages?

Most working wives have a simple and direct answer to the first question. They work "for the money," and not—at least initially—to gain the other satisfactions that work sometimes offers (Nielsen, 1978). The very practical motivations for many working wives are demonstrated by the fact that women are more likely to enter the labor force if their families' income has declined than if it has remained stable or increased (Hoffman and Nye, 1974, pp. 36, 40).

The woman who works to keep her family from the edge of poverty or to pay for the down payment on a house or her children's college education often views her work as an extension of her familial role. Her paycheck is another contribution to the family's well-being. For most married women, jobs—whether part- or full-time—have quite a different meaning than they do for married men. The roles of wife and mother remain the dominant ones for most married women. As one commentator remarks, "Most of today's working wives . . . work mainly in order to earn money they don't absolutely have to have" (Smuts, 1972, p. 148).

However, many wives work for reasons other than the financial rewards. It is easier for a working wife—especially the mother of small children—to say that she works because her family needs the money rather than to admit that she wants to because it is enjoyable. Yet the majority of working wives—whatever their reason for joining the labor force in the first place—do like to work. When asked, "Would you continue to work if your family no longer needed the money?" a majority of women say they would continue in their jobs (Hoffman and Nye, 1974, p. 39).

What, then, are the satisfactions that work offers to married women? One of them is that it makes women feel both useful and important, in a way that being a housewife does not. For example, working mothers are more likely to mention their jobs as a source of such feelings than their roles as wives or mothers (Hoffman and Nye, 1974, p. 46). Working may satisfy the needs for achievement; it also provides the satisfactions of being with other adults. Even poorly paid, low-status jobs can be rewarding.

In the armed forces, as in the civilian labor force, traditional distinctions between "men's work" and "women's work" have begun to break down.

One forty-six-year-old woman who, inspired by a consciousness-raising group, took her first job as a file clerk, describes her satisfactions:

> Well, I know it's not much of a job in the eyes of anyone else. But to me the job is something. . . . What do I get out of the job? For one thing, I get to meet a lot of different people who give me new things to think about. The young girls ask me, "Mrs. Levine, why are you working at your age when you have a husband and children? We're just waiting to get married and get out of this hole." I tell them I'm working because it's better than sitting home and being a vegetable. . . . It makes me feel both that I'm independent and that I'm contributing something to the household. (in Jacoby, 1973, p. 31)

Working affects not only the wife's psychological well-being, but her marriage as well. A wife's decision to take a job often changes the division of labor within marriage as well as decision-making patterns, even though most families with working wives still seem to accept traditional role definitions. In families where the woman works, the wife still spends more of her time on housework and child care than her husband does, even if they both have full-time jobs. But some responsibilities for housework and child care in such families are shifted to the husband (Blood and Wolfe, 1960, p. 62; Hoffman and Nye, 1974, p. 181).

When wives work, the balance of power shifts. Studies of working wives show that they often have more power than full-time housewives. Although working wives tend to make fewer day-to-day decisions about what to have for dinner, or whether to punish a child, they have more power in making major decisions. The wife who brings home a paycheck, for example, has considerably more influence in decisions about how to spend the family income (Hoffman and Nye, 1974, p. 167). But if the husband's occupation is the primary source of family income, he still has the upper hand in most major decisions as money appears to be a crucial ingredient in marital power. Women in low-income families gain far more power by working than do women in more affluent families because their wages have a more dramatic effect on total family income.

Studies conducted in the 1950s and early 1960s indicated that conflict and dissatisfaction in marriages where the wife worked were more frequent than in marriages where the wife was a full-time homemaker and mother. These findings may be attributed to factors other than the wife's work. Families with working wives tend to be older, to have lower-income husbands, and to live in urban areas—and all of these conditions are associated with lower marital satisfaction (Hoffman and Nye, 1974, p. 205).

From the woman's perspective, her employment is most likely to cause dissatisfaction if she feels that she has to work. Sociologists Susan Orden and Norman Bradburn found that women who said that they would *not* continue working if the family didn't need the money were the women most likely to report marital dissatisfaction. But if the wife *chose* to work, both partners reported fewer marital tensions, and the wives indicated an increase in sociability. Marriages where the wife works part-time seem to be the ones where both partners report the greatest satisfactions with their roles. Where both the husband and his wife are highly educated, her employment is most likely to be associated with high marital satisfaction (1969). Few people would disagree with the observation that the increase in the number of working women is one of the most important changes to have taken place in American society over the past generation. However, there is considerable disagreement among the various studies that have attempted to assess the effects of women's labor force participation upon marital satisfaction (see, for example, Ferree, 1976; Burke and Weir, 1976; Bahr and Day, 1978; Wright, 1978). The only overall conclusion that can be reached at this point is that there appear to be no consistent and statistically significant differences in the reported marital satisfaction of working women and full-time housewives.

THE DUAL-CAREER MARRIAGE

It is important to remember that the employment of most wives is still part-time in several senses. It does not continue throughout their adult lives. Most women stop working for a while to have children. Many married women work for only part of the year, or at part-time jobs. For most of these women, the roles of mother and housewife come first, and the husbands' contribution to family income is far greater than theirs. But what happens to a marriage when the wife chooses not just to hold down a job, but to pursue a career? Dual-career marriages, in which both spouses are highly committed to their occupations, are different in several significant ways from the marriages we have been examining. It is in dual-career marriages that traditional male and female roles are most likely to be redefined.

A career might be defined as a succession of jobs, each related to the next. Anyone pursuing a career usually moves in a predictable sequence from positions of lower prestige and responsibility to those that confer more authority, prestige, autonomy, and income. A college teacher, for example, moves up through the academic hierarchy from the position of lecturer to full professor. As in any other career, each new position demands certain skills and knowledge acquired in previous positions. In addition, careers typically require more education and training than most jobs do, they make more time demands, and they require a greater personal commitment.

Compared with men, relatively few women have pursued careers. The few American women who have pursued careers have, in the past, tended to remain single. In 1920, for example, only 12.2 percent of professional women were married. Seventy-five percent of the women who earned PhDs before 1924 never married. Between the 1930s and the 1950s—decades in which more and more women were marrying, and doing so at younger ages—the percentage of women who taught at the college level steadily declined (Chafe, 1972, pp. 94, 100). Even today, female PhDs who are single advance further than those women who are married, and a majority of women who become successful in science, engineering, or the civil service are unmarried (Coser and Rokoff, 1974, p. 501).

In other words, if considerable evidence exists that married men are more successful than single males, the opposite seems to be true for women. A contradiction between marriage and occupational success still seems to exist for a great many women.

Women are trained to feel ambivalent about success long before they enter the job market. The married woman who pursues a career has to face not only conflicts about ambition, but also a more fundamental conflict in roles. One of the reasons why most career areas have been almost exclusively the domain of males is that they require the type of personal commitment that women are encouraged to make only to their husband and children. As two prominent sociologists put it, in most families "allegiances are sex-typed: a man owes to his profession what a woman owes to her family" (Coser and Rokoff, 1974, p. 505). A woman who wants to combine a career with marriage and family responsibilities may feel considerable conflict about where to put her major commitment. There is another reason why married women hesitate about pursuing careers. Unlike men and single women, most married women don't have to pursue a career to support themselves. Careers, after all, are difficult and demanding. For many women, their costs outweigh their benefits.

Yet, despite those strains, growing numbers of women want to combine marriage with a career. In one 1974 survey, more young women said they preferred a life that combined both rather than any other way of life (Roper Organization, 1974). Another survey, of high school students in Los Angeles, indicated that nearly half of the young women wanted to combine marriage and a career. The main reasons given for choosing this alternative were not financial. Most of these young women assumed that their future spouses would be able to support them. Also, no difference existed between the material aspirations of females who anticipated a career and those who did not. This survey suggests that young women who desire to have careers want them because of their intrinsic satisfactions (Turner, 1970, p. 273).

If the number of dual-career marriages today is still quite small, there is good reason to assume that it will increase rapidly in the next few years. Since the early 1970s, the percentage of women in most professional schools has skyrocketed. Many of these women are now entering dual-career marriages that are substantially different from arrangements in which the wife works, but has no long-term commitment to her work.

What is it like to have a dual-career marriage? Two social scientists, Rhona and Robert Rapoport, conducted an intensive study of sixteen English families in which both the husband and the wife were highly committed to successful careers (1971). They found that these marriages were high in both strains and satisfactions. What the Rappoports refer to as "overload" was one of the most common strains. Since both spouses were involved in careers as well as the normal responsibilities for child care and maintaining a household, time was seen as a precious commodity. Consequently, it was particularly difficult for such couples to have any free time together.

Social disapproval causes other strains. In some circles, a mother's career is still frowned upon. In addition, such couples face—in an extreme form—the conflicting demands of career and family. Decisions about whether and when to have children are particularly troublesome, because the birth of a child often causes one of the spouses—generally the wife—to fall behind in attaining career goals. However, if there are considerable strains in dual-career marriages, they yield unusual rewards, too. Where both spouses pursue successful careers, a high family income means that money can relieve many strains. Maids or housekeepers, day-care centers, dinners out, and laundry service help to ease the burden of housework.

But the financial rewards were not the most important ones for the couples the Rappoports studied. For the wives, the major reward was "self-expression." Most of the women indicated that they would experience a sense of loss if they had to give up their careers. And their husbands were interested in, and proud of, their wives' work. Dual-career marriages are high in both role-sharing and companionship. One couple talked about the rewards of their relationship in these words:

> Both of us look upon it as an absolutely fifty-fifty partnership. . . . Everything is done jointly, almost everything as far as possible, as a family. Very few of my friends at home and very few other people here (except the other married couples) have somebody with whom they can turn over ideas about what one might do in one's own job. . . . One of the outstanding features of this situation is that we have a tremendous interest in common. We've never really quarreled over anything serious because we both realize it's a matter of deciding jointly and we're prepared to compromise. (pp. 193–196)

Not unexpectedly, however, one of the most common problems in these marriages concerns role expectations. The Rappoports found that tensions often resulted over differences about whether the wife was being "a good wife and mother when she chose to pursue her career involvements." For the husband there were problems about whether he was "sacrificing his 'manliness' " by taking a greater part in household management. Traditional role expectations, it seems, appear even in marriages where the provider role is shared, and where each spouse has a high commitment to a career. As in more conventional marriages, inclinations toward male dominance are still apparent: "It takes a husband who is either very strong or closely identified with the efforts of his wife to allow her to equal or exceed his own accomplishments without major disruption in the relationship" (p. 285).

Dual-career marriages represent a profound innovation despite the persistence of some traditional ideas about sex roles. As sex roles have traditionally been defined, each of the spouses is dependent upon the other. Each fulfills specific needs for the other—he is the provider and she is the mother and housekeeper. But in dual-career marriages, those assumptions are substantially modified. The wife does not depend on her husband for support. And he does not depend on her for services that he can either buy or perform for himself. If expecting companionship from one's spouse is much more important in most marriages today than previously, it is in the dual-career marriage that it is most important. Because spouses in such marriages are not dependent upon each other in as many practical respects as other couples are, dual-career relationships ought to provide real and substantial emotional satisfaction.

TOWARD ROLE EQUALITY IN MARRIAGE—IS IT POSSIBLE? IS IT DESIRABLE?

The idea of equality has been at the basis of many of the agitations for social change over the past two decades. Its effect on marriage is immeasurable. As political scientist Andrew Hacker remarks

> The major changes in the family in recent years, and the problems of the future, are summed up in one word: women. . . . Today, women are involved in much greater expectations and frustrations. The trouble comes from the fact that the institution we call marriage can't hold two full human beings—it was only designed for one and a half. (1970, p. 34)

Ancient assumptions about women's proper role are being discarded. Sociologist Robert Blood comments, as have others for several decades, that marriage defined by rigid sex roles has begun to give away to companionship marriage. This phenomenon, he says, ushers in "a new phase in American family history":

> One distinguishing characteristic of this family is the dual employment of husband and wife. Employment emancipates women from domination by their husbands and, secondarily, raises their daughters from inferiority to [a more equal status with] their brothers. . . . The classic differences between masculinity and femininity are disappearing as both sexes in the adult generation take on the same roles in the labor market. The roles of men and women are converging for both adults and children. As a result the family will be far less segregated internally, far less stratified into different age generations and different sexes. The old asymmetry of male-dominated, female-serviced family life is being replaced by a new symmetry. (1965, p. 29)

Figure 8-2 Percentage of professional degrees* awarded to women (1967-1979)

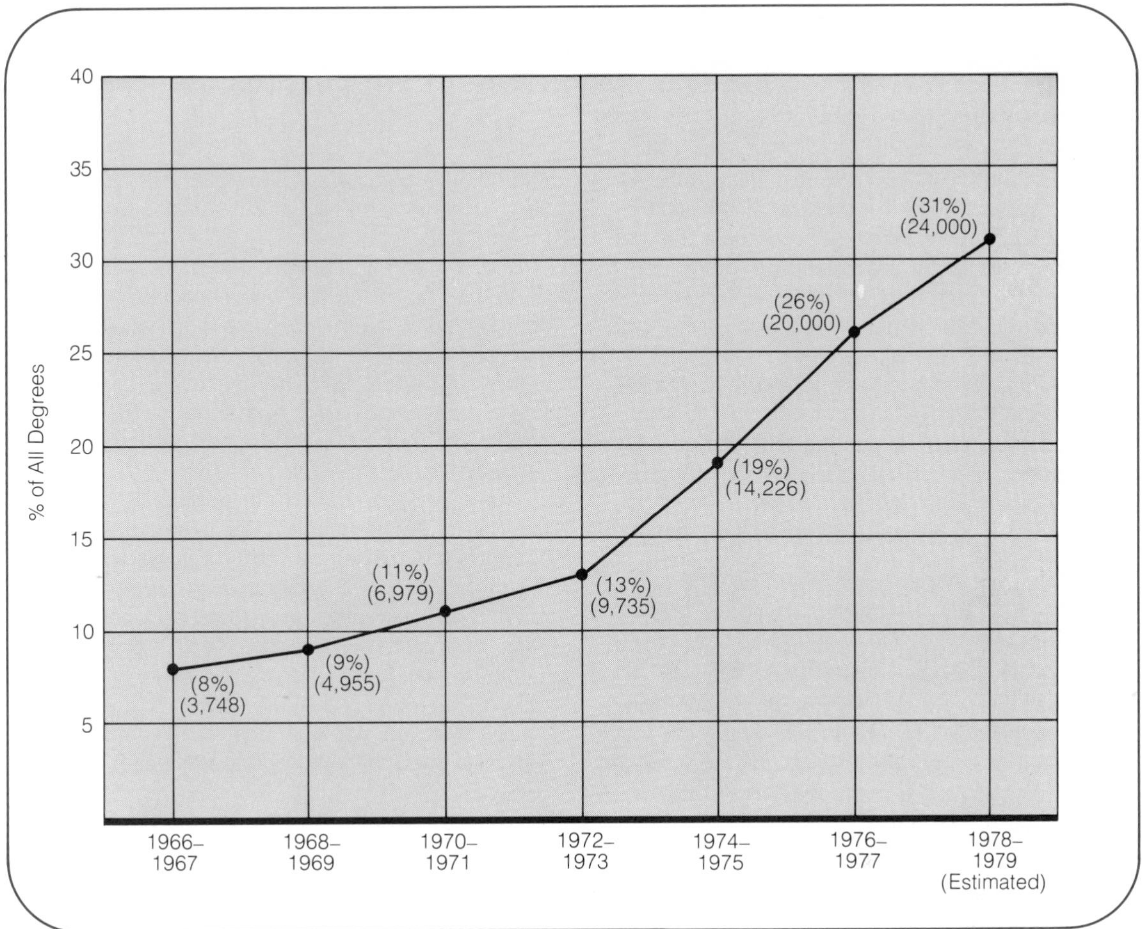

*Includes all academic doctorates, plus first-professional degrees in medicine, law, dentistry, theology, veterinary medicine, and optometry.
Source: Chronicle of Higher Education, November 13, 1978, p. 13.

There are a number of reasons why demands for sexual equality will become even more widespread. A college education is apparently a powerful influence for sexual equality. Highly educated couples have more shared friends; they are more likely to share personality traits than are couples with less education. The results of personality tests indicate that college men score relatively high on measures of femininity and college women score high on masculinity (Osofsky and Osofsky, 1972, p. 416). Women who have completed a college degree are more likely to enter the labor force, even if they marry. As we have seen, working wives have more power than nonworking wives in family decision-making. The college-educated population, in this sense, serves as a social barometer. It tells us what changes we might expect in marriage as an increasing number of women receive a college education and professional training. (See Figure 8–2.)

There are two other reasons why the trend toward sexual equality will probably become more vigorous in the next several years. First, the sectors of the labor force that are growing most rapidly—such as clerical work—are also

What's Happening Today

Box 8–2 / Revising a Sexist Language—of Wo-persons, Herstory, and People-power

Language reflects our mental habits. Because we think in a language, the assumptions that are built into it perpetuate the mental habits of the past. Appropriately, one of the chief targets of feminists who have been trying to attach new meanings to the categories of male and female is that living museum—which has been tended almost exclusively by men—the dictionary.

If you look at any of the dictionaries—such as the Oxford English Dictionary—that carefully trace the origins of the words most commonly used to refer to women, it does indeed look as if this is the last bastion of male supremacists. The word "lady," for example, originally meant "bread-kneader," a term that defined a woman in relation to her lord, or "bread guardian." The word "female" has been altered over the centuries to look like a derivative of "male." When it was originally taken over from the French and incorporated into Middle English as "femelle," the root "fem" meant "woman" and the suffix "-elle" meant "little."

One of the few changes that have caught on is the use of the title *Ms.* Feminists have complained, with some justification, that while *Mrs.* and *Miss* identify women by their marital status, *Mr.* does not. The implied lesson is that marriage defines a woman more than it does a man, and that her identity as well as her status derive from her husband.

These represent only the beginning of a long list of sexist usages. For example, it is common to use the pronouns *he* or *his* when referring to people in general, as in "Everyone must renew *his* automobile license once a year." It is quite awkward to use "his or her" in every sentence where a pronoun is required. But what is the alternative? The first issue of *Ms.* magazine proposed the common gender pronouns "tey, ter, and tem" as a so-

the ones that employ mostly women. Second, women are likely to continue their preference for relatively small families. This decision is significant because childbearing and the first years of child rearing are the most decisive activities that perpetuate traditional feminine roles. To the extent that women defer marriage for at least a few years, then choose after marriage to defer childbearing slightly longer than their parents did, and subsequently decide to have relatively small families, they are also more likely to choose nontraditional roles in marriage.

There is good reason, then, to predict that fewer and fewer people will conform to rigidly defined sex roles. But marital equality is still largely an ideal, not an accomplished fact. Research shows that "Neither decision-making nor the division of labor in the family (even among middle-class spouses) has been found to be equalitarian, nor has the conception of marital roles by married people been reported as companionate or equal in any sense" (Safilios-Rothschild, 1970, p. 539).

Studies of the division of household labor in families where wives work at full-time jobs illustrate the point. It would be reasonable to assume that as wives take on more wage-earning responsibilities their husbands would share more of the household tasks, but this has apparently not happened in most families. Various studies of time-budgets show that husbands contribute about the same amount of time to household tasks whether or not their wives work outside the home (Stafford, Backman, and DiBona, 1977; Walker, 1977). In other words, it appears that the husbands of many working lution. Now, several years later, these still sound like a foreign language. Perhaps the alternative is to use the plural form, as in "Drivers must renew *their* licenses."

Think also of the sexism that is perpetuated by the use of those terms that have female and male versions. For example, the word *nymphomania* is frequently tossed about in casual conversation, with an undeniably negative connotation. Yet *satyriasis,* which is its male counterpart, is almost unknown. Consider also those terms for which the male form—such as widower—suggests an active partner, while the female form—widow—is passive. The message is more subtle than that of the aggressively male Marlboro man, but the meaning is the same.

The meaning is the same, too, when a masculine noun is used in many common expressions, such as *man of letters, Renaissance man,* or *man about town.* To turn these phrases around—for example, *woman of letters, Renaissance woman,* or *woman about town*—would undoubtedly cause more than a few raised eyebrows.

In any revolutionary era when old assumptions are discarded, words are among the first casualties. But think of the words that will have to be retired or rebaptized if we are to have a nonsexist language. First-year college students, for example, would be referred to as *fresh-persons.* You might sign up for a course in *herstory,* rather than *history.*

And what should we do with phrases like "Mother Nature"? To feminists, these are fighting words. By implication, they assign to women the tasks of gardening, cooking, and child rearing, while the important and creative work is reserved for "Father Culture."

There are some signs of progress, however. The Labor Department's Manpower [*sic*] Administration recently announced that 3,500 jobs will be renamed in the new listing of job titles "to achieve some degree of neutrality and sexlessness." So bus boys will henceforth be called dining room attendants. Governesses are now to be referred to as child mentors. And within the three-mile limit, fishermen will be ordered to drop the suffix. If that isn't enough to convince you that we have a long way to go before we achieve a nonsexist language, consider the title of this agency that is so conscientiously trying to change woman's image. . . .

wives do nothing to relieve the double burden that their spouses bear. However, it would not be entirely accurate to attribute this pattern to the insensitivity of males who simply refuse to perform household tasks traditionally defined as women's work. For it appears that many wives are reluctant to turn over the responsibility for household tasks to their husbands. In a national survey conducted in 1973, fewer than one-quarter of the women said that they wanted more help from their husbands in this area, and the responses of working women were not much different from those of full-time housewives (Robinson, 1977, p. 184).

In the division of household labor, even more than in the performance of other roles, it appears that a very traditional pattern is often maintained. The tasks that men perform most often are the traditionally "male" tasks, particularly the "outside" work, such as mowing the lawn, shoveling the snow, home maintenance, and the "outside" cooking performed on the barbecue. Wives do most of the day-to-day cooking and dishwashing, as well as the other "inside" tasks such as housekeeping and childcare (Blood and Wolfe, 1960). Perhaps the main reason why such a traditional division of labor in household tasks persists is that it is in these areas where the sex-role modeling of children is most vivid. The division of household labor provides a clear example of considerable resistance to change, even among couples who express a belief in the equality of the sexes.

More evidence of the difficulty of redefining sex roles comes from other societies. In Sweden, for example, the official policy is that men should work shorter hours and share in the housework to provide more equality of opportunity to women. But despite the encouragement of government policy, there is a great deal of resistance to change. Predictably, Swedish men favor traditional sex roles far more frequently than the women do (Palme, 1972).

What has happened in the Israeli kibbutzim provides an even more vivid illustration of resistance to change. The pioneers who established these collective settlements decided that women would have to join men in the labor force, leaving traditional "housewife" tasks to be performed in communal nurseries and dining rooms. But despite this attempt to eliminate sex-typing in the division of labor, men and women in the kibbutzim today are as different as the two sexes in our own society. Why do these role differences persist even in a society where the distinction between "men's work" and "women's work" has been almost eliminated? One reason is that sex stereotypes have not been altered. Even in the kibbutzim, it is still assumed that the personal traits of men and women are different, although the work they perform is the same (Keller, 1973; Schlesinger, 1977).

As the Israeli experience suggests, sex roles may not change substantially even if boys and girls are taught the same skills in school and men and women are asked to perform the same tasks. By the time children reach school, the personality traits associated with masculinity or femininity may be relatively fixed.

Significantly, although many college men belittle the housewife's role, few show a willingness to redefine their own marital roles to facilitate their future wives' careers. In a recent survey of college males, sociologist Mirra Komarovsky found that 24 percent intended to marry a woman who would be satisfied to remain at home as a housewife and mother. Sixteen percent indicated a willingness to allow their wives to work, but hedged their approval with a set of qualifications that no woman could meet. Forty-eight percent said that their wives could work, but they would be expected to interrupt that work for childbearing and at least the early years of child rearing. Only 7 percent indicated that they would change their own marital roles in substantial ways in order to facilitate their wives' careers (1973, p. 873). To the extent that males feel ambivalent about both the housewife role and their wives' full-time work role, some conflict is bound to result.

As Jessie Bernard points out, men have always wanted contradictory things from their wives. Many want security without being tied down. They want a woman who is both safe and sexy, a mother and a mistress. The same theme is expressed in many American novels, which portray two types of women—the romantic Dark Lady and the good Fair Maiden. The Dark Lady is openly sexual, adventurous, and aggressive. She is the woman with whom the hero would dally for a while. But even though the Dark Lady is more attractive to the heroes portrayed in these novels, she is not the one that they marry. That honor is reserved for the Fair Maiden, who is blonde, passive, and conventionally feminine (Bernard, 1973, p. 248; Fiedler, 1962).

If this sounds like a contradiction expressed in fiction but not in everyday life, here are the words of a Princeton senior describing what he is looking for in a wife:

> I would not want to marry a woman whose only goal is to become a housewife. This type of woman would not have enough bounce and zest in her. . . . I want an independent girl, one who has her own interests and does not always have to depend on me for stimulation and diversion. However, when we both agree to have children, my wife must be the one to raise them. She'll have to forfeit her freedom for the children. I believe that when a woman wants a child, she must accept the full responsibility for child care. The person I'll marry will want the child and will want to care for the child. . . . I believe that women should have equal opportunities in business and the professions, but I insist that a woman who is a mother should devote herself entirely to her children. (Komarovsky, 1973, p. 254)

But how is any woman to take advantage of "equal opportunities in business and the professions" if she is solely responsible for the children? And how is she to remain "an independent girl" with her own interests if she devotes herself for a considerable number of years to child rearing? Very few women can fulfill both sets of expectations at the same time. As Komarovsky comments, "Such ambivalence on the part of college men is bound to exacerbate role conflict in women" (1973, p. 254).

If traditional sex roles stifled both men and women by encouraging them to act in certain prescribed ways, at least they had the virtue of clarity. Both men and women know what was expected of them, and what they could expect of their spouses. Specialized sex roles, like the division of labor on an assembly line, allow routine work to be performed more efficiently. As traditional sex roles break down, we can expect more conflict and confusion in marriage. Increasingly, married couples are working out for themselves a fair distribution of the costs as well as the dividends of marriage and family life. And many women are beginning to discover that their roles will not change substantially until male roles do.

Married couples are also discovering the benefits that may result from a more equally balanced union where greater friendship and companionship between men and women become possible. As the stereotypes of the "strong, silent" male and the emotional but incompetent female break down, both sexes are freed to display the better traits traditionally associated with the opposite sex. Women can feel free to be strong, and men to be gentle. A wider, more interesting world opens up for women, and men are given a chance to be less emotionally dependent upon occupational success and more involved with their children.

The strains and conflicts of living in a period of transition about sex roles are real. But so also are the potential benefits. In Greek myth, man and woman were originally one. As a form of punishment, the Gods split them in two. Consequently, as we are told in Plato's *Symposium,* "each half yearned for the half from which it had been severed." Man and woman needed each other in order to be whole again. According to Plato, when they met they threw their arms around each other and embraced in their longing to grow together again.

The word "androgyny" is a combination of the Greek words for man and woman. Perhaps this word best describes the new ideal that each sex should share the personality traits of the other. "Men must learn to sing, to decorate, to garden, to play, to cry, to open up huge areas of self once blocked off, while women must escape from the isolation of housework, from their low self-esteem, from their denial of self. Androgyny suggests a spirit of reconciliation between the sexes, and a spectrum upon which human beings choose their places without regard to propriety or custom" (Heilbrun, 1974, p. 132).

Conclusions

Just as marriage has changed in the past in response to new social and economic conditions, it is changing today. In this chapter we have looked at the differences between his marriage and hers, and examined some implications of the fact that an increasing percentage of married women are working. Our society is now reversing several of the tendencies that have existed since industrialization caused the place of work to be separated from the household. Now as women again become an important part of the labor force, the man's world and the woman's become less segregated. As the new ideal of androgyny replaces the old reality of rigid sex segregation of personality traits and tasks, the husband's involvement in child care and household management is being stressed at the same time that his wife is encouraged to spend much of her adult life in the labor force. Interchangeable roles have begun to replace sex-segregated roles.

We might describe the range of personal alternatives in this area as a spectrum of choices. At one end of that spectrum is the role-segregated pattern that has been typical of many working-class families. In such families, it is not just the economic and homemaking responsibilities that are assigned according to traditional assumptions about the man's world and the woman's. In role-segregated marriage, there is little sharing of leisure activities either.

A second alternative is the full-time housewife/mother pattern in which the wife accepts all of the responsibilities for homemaking and child rearing, and the husband bears the entire economic responsibility. But, unlike the highly role-segregated marriage, this pattern does not presume separate leisure preferences or separate groups of "his" and "her" friends.

A third alternative is the family in which the woman bears the major responsibility for homemaking and child rearing, but also has a part-time job or career. That work outside the home is often viewed as a source of personal satisfaction as well as additional family income. Among couples choosing this alternative, husbands generally take over a portion of the household tasks. There is considerably more role-sharing than generally exists in either of the first two alternatives.

A fourth alternative is the dual-career pattern, in which both spouses are equally committed to work roles. There is no assumption that childbearing and rearing take precedence over the woman's career development. Among couples who choose this alternative, there are typically few distinctions between the man's world and the woman's. Combining work and marital roles is not nearly so difficult for the couple without children. For those couples who want to have children, however, role conflict is more likely to arise. Especially for dual-career couples, successfully balancing the demands of work and family roles requires a juggler's skill.

REFERENCES

Helen Andelin. *Fascinating womanhood.* New York: Bantam, 1974.

Steven J. Bahr and Randal D. Day. Sex role attitudes, female employment, and marital satisfaction. *Journal of Comparative Family Studies* 9 (1978): 55–65.

Jessie Bernard. *The future of marriage.* New York: Bantam, 1973.

Robert O. Blood. Long-range causes and consequences of the employment of married women. *Journal of Marriage and the Family* 27 (1) (1965): 27–34.

——— and Donald M. Wolfe. *Husbands and wives.* New York: Free Press, 1960.

Charlotte Bronte (1849). *Shirley.* London: Collins Press, 1953.

Ronald J. Burke and Tamara Weir. Relationship of wives' employment status to husband, wife, and pair satisfaction and performance. *Journal of Marriage and Family* 38 (1976): 279–287.

William H. Chafe. *The American woman: Her changing social, economic and political role 1920–1970.* N.Y.: Oxford University Press, 1972.

Evan S. Connell, Jr. *Mrs. Bridge.* Greenwich, Conn.: Fawcett, 1958.

——— . *Mr. Bridge.* New York: Knopf, 1969.

Rose Laub Coser and Gerald Rokoff. Women in the occupational world: Social disruption and conflict. In Rose Laub Coser, ed. *The family: Its structures and functions.* New York: St. Martin's, 1974.

Simone de Beauvoir. *The second sex.* New York: Bantam, 1952.

M. Ferree. Working class jobs: Housework and paid work as sources of satisfaction. *Social Problems* 23 (1976): 431–441.

Leslie Fiedler. *Love and death in the American novel.* New York: Meridian, 1962.

Betty Friedan. *The feminine mystique.* New York: Dell, 1963.

Germaine Greer. *The female eunuch.* New York: McGraw-Hill, 1970.

Andrew Hacker, in The American family—Future uncertain. *Time,* December 28, 1970, pp. 34–40.

Caroline Heilbrun. Recognizing the androgynous human. In Robert T. and Anna K. Francoeur, eds. *The future of sexual relations.* Englewood Cliffs, N.J.: Prentice-Hall, 1974.

Lois Hoffman and F. Ivan Nye. *Working mothers.* San Francisco: Jossey-Bass, 1974.

Susan Jacoby. What do I do for the next twenty years? *The New York Times Magazine,* June 17, 1973, pp. 30 et passim.

Elizabeth Janeway. *Man's world, woman's place.* New York: Morrow, 1971.

Suzanne Keller. The family in the kibbutz: What lessons for us? In Michael Curtis and Mordecai S. Chertoff, eds. *Israel—Social structure and change.* New Brunswick, N.J.: Transaction Books, 1973.

Mirra Komarovsky. Cultural contradictions and sex roles: The masculine case. *American Journal of Sociology* 78 (1973): 813–844.

Helena Z. Lopata. *Occupation: Housewife.* New York: Oxford University Press, 1971.

Keith Melville. On our way to where? *The Sciences,* November 1972, pp. 18–20.

Marabel Morgan. *The total woman.* New York: Pocket Books, 1975.

A. C. Nielsen Co. Press release. Nielsen survey, September 1978.

Susan Orden and Norman M. Bradburn. Working wives and marriage happiness. *American Journal of Sociology* 74 (1969): 392–407.

Joy D. Osofsky and Howard J. Osofsky. Androgyny as a life style. *The Family Coordinator* 21 (1972): 411–418.

Olof Palme. The emancipation of man. *Journal of Social Issues* 28 (1972): 237–246.

Rhona Rappoport and Robert Rappoport. *Dual-career families.* Baltimore: Penguin, 1971.

David Riesman. *The lonely crowd.* New Haven: Yale University Press, 1961.

John P. Robinson. *How Americans use time.* New York: Praeger, 1977.

The Roper Organization. *The Virginia Slims American Women's Opinion Poll.* N.Y.: Roper, 1974.

Constantina Safilios-Rothschild. The study of family power structure. *Journal of Marriage and the Family* 32 (1970): 539.

Yaffa Schlesinger. Sex roles and social change in the kibbutz. *Journal of Marriage and the Family* 39 (1977): 771–779.

Philip Shaver and Jonathan Freedman. Your pursuit of happiness. *Psychology Today* 10 (1976): 26–32.

Robert W. Smuts. *Women and work in America.* New York: Schocken, 1972.

Leo Srole and Anita K. Fischer. *Mental health in the metropolis.* N.Y.: New York University Press, 1978.

Rebecca Stafford, Elaine Backman, and Pamela DiBona. The division of labor among cohabiting and married couples. *Journal of Marriage and the Family* 39 (1977): 43–57.

Paul Starr. Hollywood's new ideal of masculinity. *The New York Times,* July 16, 1978.

Carol Tavris. Masculinity. *Psychology Today,* January 1977, pp. 34–39.

Ralph Turner. *Family interaction.* N.Y.: Wiley, 1970.

Kathryn E. Walker. Household work time: Its implications for family decisions. *Journal of Home Economics,* October 1977, pp. 7–11.

James D. Wright. Are working women really more satisfied? *Journal of Marriage and the Family* 40 (1978): 301–314.

FOR FURTHER STUDY

The topics discussed in this chapter have received a great deal of attention in recent years, and there are many articles and books that might be recommended. Jessie Bernard's comments about "his marriage and hers," which appear in *The Future of Marriage* (New York: Bantam, 1973) are particularly insightful. Two of Evan Connell's novels provide a vivid illustration; see *Mrs. Bridge* (Greenwich, Conn.: Fawcett, 1958) and *Mr. Bridge* (N.Y.: Knopf, 1969).

To get a clearer understanding of just how sex-role attitudes have changed, see an article entitled "Change in U.S. Women's Sex-Role Attitudes, 1964–1974," by Karen Oppenheim Mason, John L. Czajka, and Sara Arber in *American Sociological Review,* vol. 41, August 1976. For a more specific discussion of changing attitudes among female college students, see Ann P. Parelius, "Emerging Sex-Role Attitudes, Expectations and Strains Among College Women," in *Journal of Marriage and the Family,* February 1975.

The following titles are particularly valuable for understanding how women's roles have changed: Sheila M. Rothman's *Women's Proper Place: A History of Changing Ideals and Practices, 1870 to the Present* (New York: Basic Books, 1978); Janet Zollinger Giele's *Women and the Future* (New York: Free Press, 1978), and Suzanne Keller's "The Woman's Role: Constants and Change," in *Women in Therapy,* edited by Violet Franks and Vasanti Burtle (New York: Brunner/Mazel, 1974). William H. Chafe's *Women and Equality* provides a thoughtful assessment of the women's movement (New York: Oxford, 1977). Rosabeth Moss Kanter's *Work and Family in the United States* (New York: Basic Books, 1978) focuses on labor force participation of women and its implications. For a comprehensive discussion of the various roles involved in marriage and family life, see F. Ivan Nye (ed.) *Role Structure and Analysis of the Family* (Beverly Hills, Calif.: Sage, 1976).

For different perspectives on the housewife's role, see Helena Z. Lopata's *Occupation: Housewife* (New York: Oxford, 1971); Philip Slater's essay "Kicking the Domestic Habit," in his book *Footholds* (New York: E. P. Dutton, 1977); and Linda Burzotta Nilson's "The Social Standing of a Housewife," which appeared in the August 1978 issue of *Journal of Marriage and the Family.*

Readers interested in thinking about how changing images of masculinity affect the husband's role might consult a special issue of the *Journal of Social Issues* (vol. 34, no. 1), which was devoted to various aspects of the male experience, and an anthology, *Men and Masculinity,* edited by Joseph Pleck and Jack Sawyer (Englewood Cliffs, N.J.: Prentice-Hall Spectrum, 1974).

One of the few book-length studies of dual-career families is *Dual-Career Families Re-Examined,* by Rhona and Robert Rappoport (New York: Harper & Row, 1976). The same authors have compiled a useful review of the literature on dual-career families, which appeared in the September/October 1978 issue of *Marriage and Family Review.*

"The Cruel Discussion" Private Collection, photograph courtesy of Holly Solomon Gallery

9 Communication and Conflict–Talking Without Speaking, Listening Without Hearing

"The objective of companionship between husbands and wives in addition to sexual compatibility is surely brand new, a luxury item," writes sociologist Jessie Bernard. "That husbands and wives like as well as love one another, enjoy one another's company—this is a very exalted conception of marriage." Looking back to the relations between men and women in times past, Bernard calls attention to the new expectations we bring to marriage. In the past, she remarks, men and women either

> hopped into bed or they turned their backs on one another. The only times there has been good talk between the sexes socially were when a determined effort was made to achieve it, as in the eighteenth century salons. . . . Marital companionship cannot, therefore, be taken for granted. It is not something that just naturally happens. . . . (1964, p. 33)

Though we hear much about having lost the ability to communicate with each other, it is more accurate to say that we have become more concerned about being able to do so. This is particularly true of the relationship between husband and wife. In societies where each of the spouses is assigned well-defined roles and responsibilities, it is not assumed that there is much community of interest between them. For example, sociologist Ezra Vogel reports that many Japanese women are both curious about and puzzled by the companionship of American couples. When one Japanese woman was told about an American couple who had gone on a trip together, she replied, "How nice!" And then after a moment's reflection, she asked, "But what would they talk about for so long?" (1971, p. 113).

Today, there are many books that promise to show us how to communicate. The O'Neills' popular book *Open Marriage* (1972), for example, discusses marital communication at greater length than any other single topic. Another book, *The Intimate Enemy* (Bach and Wyden, 1968), explores the art of marital combat, and *I'm Okay, You're Okay* (Harris, 1967),

Games People Play (Berne, 1978), and *Body Language* (Fast, 1970) examine the communications strategies of friends, lovers, and spouses.

After an extensive four-year research project, the Family Service Association of America reached the conclusion that ineffective communication is the principal cause of marriage failure (Mace, 1975, p. 41). Training courses in couple communication are now being offered throughout the country. Texts on marriage and family life like this one now routinely discuss marital communications, though the topic rarely came up in such courses fifteen or twenty years ago. "It may come as a surprise," the authors of one article remark, "to realize that very few references to communication—its function and importance—can be found in marriage counseling or functional marriage texts before the mid-1960s" (Miller, Corrales, and Wackman, 1975, p. 143).

By now, in fact, so much attention has been devoted to the problems caused by faulty communication that more effective communication is often considered a cure-all, something that will dissolve all differences. One investigator interviewing couples about to marry found many of them preoccupied with communication. They believed their marriages would last "because we can talk to each other, because we can discuss our problems together." It had become for them, according to the investigator, an almost magical belief (Hilsdale, 1962, p. 142).

Unfortunately, however, communication is not a marital panacea. Complete openness about all topics is not necessarily the best policy. But effective communication is important in marriage, although it is difficult to achieve. In this chapter we will examine marital communication patterns by observing, first, how subtle and significant patterns of family communication actually are. In family life, even more than in other interactions, the simplest gestures are loaded with meaning. It is often more difficult to communicate effectively with intimates than with people who are not so close to us—and in this chapter we will try to see why. We will also see how these difficulties may be overcome through such elements of effective communication as self-disclosure, sending consistent messages, learning empathy, and providing useful feedback.

This is also a chapter about marital conflict. No two spouses ever agree completely about basic values, claims to certain privileges or scarce resources, or the precise meaning of role responsibilities. Airing and resolving these differences are a crucial part of any relationship; the absence of bargaining about differences signals the presence of real problems.

THE FAMILY DRAMA

As we noted in Chapter 1, what behavioral scientists know about marriage and family behavior was until recently almost entirely based on indirect observation. Sociologists used interviews or questionnaires to ask people what went on in their families—how decisions were made, what roles family members were expected to play, and so on. Those who have studied behavior in small groups have typically observed a group of strangers unacquainted with each other before the experiment began; thus their behavior bears little resemblance to those small groups called families. Psychotherapists, too, have been interested in family behavior, but had only their patients' reports of it. They could not directly observe family behavior themselves.

It is ironic that, in an area where we all have so much personal experience, it has been so difficult for researchers to carefully observe and conceptualize what actually happens in the intimate environment of marriage and family life.

Over the past two decades, however, some investigators and therapists have taken the unprecedented step of observing what actually takes place among family members. Rather than having to depend upon the reports of family members—which for obvious reasons are both incomplete and somewhat unreliable—these investigators are making direct observations of family dynamics. The first studies of this type concerned the families of schizophrenic children. Therapists began to bring whole families into their office in hopes of understanding why psychiatric disturbances developed in the first place (see Box 9–1).

The seemingly bizarre behavior they saw did indeed help to explain the psychiatric disorders of the person labeled the patient. For example, family members made verbal statements that were immediately contradicted by the tone of voice in which they were conveyed, or by the speaker's body language. Sometimes two family members formed an unstated alliance, teaming up against a third. Or they systematically disqualified each other's statements, telling the therapist that the other person didn't really mean what he or she said (Haley, 1959). Then the therapists discovered many of the same patterns in normal families, and a general study of communication and conflict among intimates, conducted by direct observation, was under way. Investigators pursuing this study have identified three themes that help to understand the subtle and complex network of family interactions:

1. All marriages and families are defined by certain rules, of which family members are not generally aware.
2. Family communications shape and maintain our images of ourselves.
3. Much of family behavior makes sense as a game—a series of transactions in which each player moves toward certain goals.

Rules and Realities

In the beginning, for most of us, there were three or more: father, mother, perhaps sisters or brothers, and ourselves, together forming a social unit creating and sustaining a unique reality. Each family has its own language, myths, and taboos which, because they have served the family, seem right, logical, even inevitable.

Therapists working with a family discern this unique pattern of norms, values, and role expectations, which to the outsider often seems an obvious distortion of reality. One therapist recalls a family in which the wife was the sole breadwinner, handled all the money, gave her husband an allowance, and had him sign over their house to her as sole owner because of his "incompetence." In meetings with the couple, the therapist could find no evidence that the husband actually was incompetent. It appeared to be a mutually agreed-on unreality (Melville, 1973, p. 18).

In *Open Marriage,* the O'Neills recall a story in which a reporter asks three umpires how they distinguish between a ball and a strike. The first umpire says, "There are balls and there are strikes, and I call them as I see them." The second answers, "There are balls and there are strikes, and I call them as they is." And the third responds, "There are balls and there are strikes, *but they ain't nothing until I call them.*" It is the attitude of the third umpire that describes best how families define reality. It is what the family members agree it is (1972, p. 112).

One therapist uses the term "family myth" for what he has described as

> a series of well-integrated beliefs shared by all family members, concerning each other and their mutual position in the family, beliefs that go unchallenged by everyone involved in spite of the reality distortions which they may conspicuously imply . . . the family myth is an image to which all family members contribute and apparently strive to preserve. It refers to the identified roles of its members. (Ferreira, 1963, p. 457)

Perhaps the best image for family life as seen by therapists is a drama or game for which there is a script, or certain rules. Children are recruited into family roles. They have no alternative but to take a part in that drama, and to cope with the meanings that the other family members attach to their behavior.

The bonds that tie the family members together consist of an intricate weaving of shared realities, interdependent roles, and certain family secrets. Thus, even though spouses may by

Introducing the Marriage and Family Professionals

Box 9–1 / The Family Therapist

"In a family, there is no such thing as one person in trouble." This is the motto of the Family Institute, which occupies a handsome townhouse on New York City's Upper East Side. Like affiliated units in Boston, Philadelphia, Chicago, Palo Alto, Cincinnati, and Atlanta, the institute offers family therapy and serves as a training center for therapists. This relatively new therapeutic strategy is rapidly gaining acceptance.

As described by Dr. Nathan Ackerman, founder of the institute and a leading advocate for its approach, family therapy represents not just a new treatment method, but also a new strategy for observing family interaction.

> Originally, psychoanalysis was basically a nonsocial form of treatment. Currently, therapy turns increasingly in the direction of a true social experience. Concern with family life is direct, rather than indirect. Intervention points not to the individual away and apart from the family, but rather to persons within the family and to the family as a living whole. (in Melville, 1973, p. 17)

In other words, family therapists depart from the procedures followed by more traditional psychotherapists in two important ways: (1) they emphasize that individual behavior cannot be understood apart from the network of social relationships that the individual shares with others; and (2) they treat entire family units, interviewing them together at regular intervals. Generally, those participating in family therapy include parents, children, and other *de facto* family members such as housekeepers or close friends who live in the same household.

Since the early 1960s, when substantial numbers of family therapists started to observe and treat whole families, they have become an important source of information about patterns of family communication and conflict. Families ordinarily enter therapy with a specific problem to solve. Often one person, generally a child, is labeled the sick one because of obvious symptoms, such as a history of drug abuse or delinquency. The therapist then attempts to unravel the tangled skein of family tensions in order to understand how family conflicts may lead to a situation in which one member is made the scapegoat or symptom-bearer. The therapist's goal is to help the family achieve a clearer understanding of what the real conflicts are. Typically, parents will complain about the "sick" one's problem without realizing how their own actions, the unstated family rules, or their rigid control over their own feelings may have contributed to it.

The major advantage of family therapy is that the therapist can observe ongoing family relationships. As the family drama unfolds, the therapist watches for certain clues. How does the family arrange itself physically in the therapist's office? Are there contradictions between what is said and what is conveyed through body language? What are the unstated alliances and fears? What expectations do family members have of one another? How do family members try to win the therapist's approval, and each other's?

Essentially, the family therapist serves as an observer whose function is to show family members what is actually happening, and to teach them new ways of communicating with each other. They are encouraged to understand and talk about how they communicate and to acknowledge and discuss their unstated rules.

their own admission be unhappy with each other, they may also be unwilling to give up a shared reality that neither could maintain if they separated. As in the play *Who's Afraid of Virginia Woolf,* the reality of shared illusions may seem incomprehensible to outsiders who catch a glimpse of normally concealed secrets.

From the first days of any partnership, the two people involved are deciding how they are going to behave with each other and what kinds of communications will be allowed and prohibited. The couple may never talk about them directly, but certain issues must be settled in any relationship: dominance and submission, closeness and distance, as well as rules about making rules. Here is an illustration of how rules emerge in the early stages of a relationship:

> Assume that through their interactions up to this time, a newly married man and woman, on their honeymoon, have established an unspoken "rule" that each is to fill the other's needs without being asked. Mary prepares John's favorite meals, compliments him, straightens his clothes; and John buys small gifts for Mary, compliments her cooking, makes all travel arrangements, and so forth. In this interaction, neither has to ask the other to fulfill his role according to their mutual expectations.
>
> Now suppose that on the fifth day of the honeymoon, Mary . . . sees a ring which she would like to own and asks John if he will buy it for her. At this point, one unspoken rule of their relationship has been broken. Mary has asked for a gift. (Lederer and Jackson, 1968, p. 92)

A trivial episode, perhaps, but the rules defining a relationship develop from a tapestry of thousands of such episodes. Depending on how John responds to Mary's request, he will be redefining the rules of the relationship. If he complies without complaining, he establishes the rule that she can make such requests. If he refuses, Mary's response will affect his behavior in the future. She might, for example, accept his refusal, but resentfully; then he would remember her resentment and prepare to deal with it in case of any future refusal. Especially in the early months of a relationship, some of the most heated battles, even when they concern apparently trivial matters, arise over the rules that structure the relationship and the rules for changing those rules.

This helps to explain why skilled therapists can help troubled families. As perceptive outsiders, they can often identify the unspoken rules that structure a relationship. By encouraging families to talk about those rules and how they communicate in general, therapists can often change behavior as well.

The Sources of Self-Esteem

One reason why it is often more difficult to communicate effectively with family members than with strangers is that the people who are closest to us affect our self-concept most powerfully. Though initially established in early childhood, self-concept is shaped throughout our lives by others who respond to us, praise or criticize us, encourage us to think more or less of ourselves. And it is in intimate relationships, where we reveal more of ourselves, that we are most vulnerable to attack, ridicule, and criticism. When, for example, a husband attacks his wife's self-concept, she may reject his evaluation, though that would leave a discrepancy between the concept she holds of herself and the concept her spouse has of her; such discrepancies are serious matters between intimates. One way to resolve the dilemma is for the wife to adjust her own self-concept so that it accords with her husband's. Or she may dismiss her spouse's judgment altogether, thus increasing the distance and mistrust between them. In short, there is no satisfactory way out.

Because spouses (and other family members) play such an important part in either confirming or denying our sense of self-esteem, self-disclosure among family members is a particularly tricky business. As we noted in Chapter 3, self-disclosure refers to the act of revealing personal attitudes, feelings, or experiences to others. It is obvious that the extent of self-disclosure affects relationships in many ways, and determines how intimate a relationship may become. It is also clear that judgments about how much self-disclosure is appropriate in specific situations, and with certain people, are an important element in our communications. From an early age, most of us learn *not* to disclose certain judgments—particularly negative judgments—about other people, just as we learn that it is not necessarily appropriate to act spontaneously in all situations.

Although intimate relationships might be defined as those in which partners feel free to talk about aspects of themselves that they normally keep hidden, it is certainly not to be assumed that there is a consistently high level of self-disclosure in all intimate relationships. In fact, several studies show that the most intimate disclosures happen in isolated interactions (with strangers, for example) where there is a low probability of any future interactions, and thus little risk (Altman and Haythorn, 1965).

Some studies (Shapiro, 1968) show that high self-disclosers have more self-esteem than do people who reveal less of themselves; and people who disclose more about themselves provide an important clue for us in understanding what risks are involved in self-disclosure. Some instances of self-disclosure reveal aspects of ourselves that our partners may not regard as desirable. To the extent that our sense of self-esteem depends upon the evaluations of people who are closest to us, any such revelation constitutes a risk to a person who does not initially have a very high sense of self-esteem. Self-disclosures, such as comments about how our opinions or values differ from those of our partners, may also be interpreted as attempts to alter the relationship in ways that our partners do not consider desirable. From this perspective, we can see why total self-disclosure is so rare, and may not even be desirable. The level of self-disclosure that can be tolerated in a relationship is related not only to the level of self-esteem of each of the partners, but also to the strength of the bond between them. As therapists often suggest, one of the most important interpersonal skills is to learn how to express positive judgments as well as negative ones, thus bolstering the self-esteem of one's partner, and also to express criticism in descriptive rather than judgmental terms.

Things get really complicated, as psychiatrist Lyman Wynne and his associates (1958) point out, when both spouses have little self-esteem to begin with. Calling such cases pseudomutual marriages, Wynne finds that both spouses participate in an illusion that neither can afford to acknowledge. Since neither began with a sense of self-esteem, each believes that the other is deceived or would never have entered the relationship. It is also impossible to admit the deception, since a person with low self-esteem is convinced that he or she could never win another. Thus, because they think they are unlovable, such couples attach a high value to maintaining a sense of relatedness. Fitting together becomes the primary goal. Any personal traits that do not dovetail, any sign of conflict that indicates potential fissures in the relationship, must be covered up. Bound by fear of losing the relationship and being revealed as the unworthy person each spouse secretly believes he or she is, both deny their individuality, repress conflict, and are preoccupied with maintaining a consensus.

The Marriage Game

Therapists have also called attention to the systemic nature of family relationships: in normal as well as disturbed families, almost every action stimulates some sort of reaction. Communications are not necessarily verbal. In fact, a whole series of communications can take place without a word being exchanged, and even without the family members being conscious of their reactions to each other's facial gesture, posture, or tone of voice.

"In the course of time," write William Lederer and Don Jackson,

> as partners experience recurring patterns of behavior in their relationship, certain predictable

> successions of events are established. The wife's left eyelid may quiver almost imperceptibly when the husband has badgered her too much about how boring her parents are. After this sequence has been repeated a few times, they both "know" that if the husband continues nagging, the wife will lose her temper and may walk out. . . . Neither party is consciously aware of their exchange. In this situation, they are an error-activated system; they are behaving exactly like a thermostat on a furnace—when it becomes too cold, on goes the heat; when it becomes too warm, it shuts off. The spouses govern each other's behavior to maintain the expected or usual emotional temperature for their relationship. (1968, p. 177)

Such situations, in which each action calls forth a predictable reaction, can accurately be described as games. There are moves, countermoves, and rules about what can and cannot be done. Though both parties are pursuing goals that at times are incompatible, they agree to interact within the boundaries set by the rules. The point of popular books like Eric Berne's *Games People Play* (1964) is not to persuade us to stop playing games, but rather to be aware of the personal transactions that take place in *all* communications. Such an awareness can lead to more effective communication.

THE ART AND SCIENCE OF COMMUNICATION

Trying to understand the message in some communications is like watching a foreign language film—without subtitles. You know something is happening, but you can't figure out what it is. In the following example, notice that what the spouses actually say to each other conveys very little of their real message:

> A husband and wife, driven to the point of spontaneous combustion by their three small children and a few dozen other eroding pressures, escape for the evening to a party in their neighborhood. They have been looking forward to this evening for a week. The party is great. In about an hour, however, the wife develops a headache. After waiting a short while to make sure that the headache is not going to leave her, she dismays her husband with the entreaty, "You'd better take me home." He resists momentarily. "Every time we start having fun, you seem to get a headache." She doesn't feel like arguing. "You take me home and then you come back to the party." He pauses, rehearses in his mind all the reasons why he should return to the party and says, "Okay, let's go." They are both quiet during the drive home. Arriving home, he escorts her into the living room, asks her if there is anything to do to help her get comfortable, and announces his departure. "Where are you going?" she asks. "I'm going back to the party." He notices the pained expression and a small tear welling up in the corner of her eye. "What's the matter now?" "You're leaving me alone." "But you told me I should go back to the party." "I know, but if you really loved me, you wouldn't want to. . . ." (McCroskey, Larson, and Knapp, 1971, p. 169)

This is a common example of faulty communications, and it is easy to see what has gone wrong. Neither spouse pays much attention to the other's nonverbal messages or to the other's preferences and needs. The wife tacitly assumes the husband would not return to the party without her, but he takes her words literally and criticizes her for contradicting herself. Both avoid the real issue: which is more important, her care or his fun? He may be thinking, "I know what her headache *really* means. It's her way of depriving me of something I enjoy." Then, as if this were not enough, she accuses him of not loving her. Now he knows she will feel rejected if he returns to the party and will probably treat him coolly as a result. Though the episode is not very significant in itself, it has really raised one of the basic issues in any relationship—how much the partners care for each other.

Happily married couples seem to have more effective communications than do those who seek marital counseling to improve an unhappy situation. One study compared the communication patterns of two dozen couples who

"Do you suppose I could ask for 'Dear Abby' without getting half a grapefruit shoved in my face?"

sought counseling with a group of couples who were presumably happy. To no one's surprise, the investigator found that the happily married couples talked more often with each other, felt they understood what the spouse was saying more often, were more sensitive to each other's feelings, and were more aware of nonverbal cues as well as explicit messages (Navran, 1967).

But if effective communication is so important in marriage, why do so many couples fail to achieve it? A communication consists of a sender, a receiver, and a message. The message may be sent by several means, more by gestures than words, more by the emotional tone of the statement than by its content. It involves interpretation, too. The receiver always has to make some judgment about what the message means, for even plain words mean different things in different contexts. As one writer remarks,

> Words are slippery customers. The full meaning of a word does not appear until it is placed in its context, and the context may serve an extremely subtle function—as with puns or *double entendres*. And even then the meaning will depend upon the listener, upon the speaker, upon their

Point of View

Box 9–2 / Communication Problems in the Working-Class Marriage: His Perspective and Hers

Lillian Rubin's book, Worlds of Pain, *is a portrait of working-class families based upon roughly one hundred interviews conducted separately with husbands and wives. In this excerpt, Rubin discusses a characteristic communication problem that she discovered in the course of those interviews, a problem that results from the different socialization practices of males and females. As the author recognizes, this is not a problem that is limited to working-class couples.*

Once marriage is conceived of as more than an economic arrangement—that is, as one in which the emotional needs of the individuals are attended to and met—role segregation and the widely divergent socialization patterns for women and men become clearly dysfunctional. And it is among the working class that such segregation has been most profound, where there has been the least incentive to change.

Such couples talk *at* each other, *past* each other, or *through* each other—rarely *with* or *to* each other. He blames her: "She's too emotional." She blames him: "He's always so rational." The problem lies in the fact that they do not have a language with which to communicate, with which to understand each other. They are products of a process that trains males and females to relate to only side of themselves—she, to the passive, tender, intuitive, verbal, emotional side; he, to the active, tough, logical, nonverbal, unemotional one.

Both honestly believe what the culture has taught them. To be rational is the more desired state; it is good, sane, strong, adult. To be emotional is the less desired state; it is bad, weak, childlike. She says: "I know I'm too emotional and I can't really be trusted to be sensible a lot of the time." He says: "She's like a kid sometimes, so emotional. I'm always having to reason with her, to explain things to her. If it weren't for me, nothing very rational would happen around here." This equation of emotional with nonrational, this inability to comprehend the logic of emotions lies at the root of much of the discontent between the sexes.

Her lifetime training prepares her to handle the affective, expressive side in human affairs; his to handle the nonaffective, instrumental side. A *real* man, he has been taught, is the strong, silent type. For a lifetime, much of his energy has gone into molding himself in that image—and into denying his feelings, refusing to admit that they exist. Without warning or preparation, he finds himself facing a wife who pleads: "Tell me your feelings." He responds with bewilderment. "What is there to tell?" One man says: "Yakketty-yakkers, that's what girls are. Guys talk too. But, you know, there's a difference. Guys talk about things and girls talk about feelings."

When they try to talk, she relies on the only tool she has; she becomes progressively more emotional and expressive. He falls back on the only tools he has: he gets progressively more rational—determinedly reasonable. She cries for him to attend to her feelings, her pain. He tells her that it's silly to feel that way; she's just being emotional. Repeatedly, the experience is the same, the outcome predictable. They play out the same theme over and over again—he, the rational man; she, the hysterical woman.

Is this just a phenomenon of working-class life? Clearly it is not. Still, there are important class differences. The norms of middle-class marriage for much longer have called for companionate relationships—for more sharing, for more exploration of feelings, and for more exchange of them. Thus, middle-class

(Box 9–2 continues on page 252)

(Box 9–2 continued from page 251)

women and men have more practice and experience in trying to overcome the stereotypes. And they have more models around them for how to do so.

This, however, is only part of the explanation of why sons of the professional middle class are brought up in a less rigidly stereotypic mode. Parents do not, after all, raise their children in a vacuum. Professional, middle-class parents, who assume that their children are destined to do work like theirs—work that calls for innovation, initiative, flexibility, creativity, sensitivity to others, and a well-developed set of interpersonal skills—call for an educational system that fosters those qualities. But, by contrast, in most working-class jobs such traits as creativity, initiative, and flexibility are considered by superiors a hindrance. Those who must work at such jobs may need nothing so much as an iron-willed discipline to get them to work every day. No surprise, then, that working-class parents look suspiciously at spontaneity, whether at home or in school. No surprise, either, that early childhood training tends to focus on respect, orderliness, cleanliness—in a word, discipline—especially for the boys who will hold those jobs, and that schools are called upon to reinforce these qualities.

Among working-class couples, the demand for communication, for sharing, is newer. For generations, it was enough that each did their job adequately. Intimacy, companionship, sharing—these were not part of the dream. But dreams change—sometimes before the people who must live them are ready. Intimacy, companionship, and sharing are now the words working-class women speak to their husbands, words that turn *both* their worlds upside down. For both women and men, fears and uncertainties are compounded by the fact that there are no models in their lives for the newly required and desired behaviors.

The men are even worse off. Since the new dream is not *their* dream, they are confused about what is being asked of them. They only know that, without notice, the rules of the game have been changed. What worked for their fathers no longer works for them. They only know that there are a whole new set of expectations—in the kitchen, in the parlor, in the bedroom—that leave them feeling bewildered and threatened.

Source: Excerpted from Lillian B. Rubin *Worlds of Pain*. New York: Basic Books, 1976.

> entire experience of the language, upon their knowledge of one another, and upon the whole situation. (Cherry, 1966, p. 10)

For example, imagine a woman who complains to her husband at dinner that she is "very tired." What those words mean depends upon the way in which they are said. He may assume that the real message is that she is fatigued. However, when the same couple is in bed later on, and she responds to his tentative caresses with the words "I'm very tired," he may interpret them as a rejection and conclude that she no longer finds him attractive.

Considering how different the socialization pattern for males is from that for females, it is hardly surprising that spouses often misinterpret each other's messages.

In her discussion of blue-collar families, sociologist Mirra Komarovsky refers to the male's "trained incapacity to share." She points out that

> the ideal of masculinity into which these men were socialized inhibits expressiveness both directly, with its emphasis on reserve, and indirectly, by identifying personal interchange with the feminine role. Childhood and adolescence,

> spent in an environment in which feelings were not named, discussed, or explained, strengthened these inhibitions. (1967, p. 156)

Trained *not* to express emotions or to acknowledge feelings of hurt or inadequacy, many men neither welcome the opportunity to talk with their wives nor are they able to do so (see Box 9–2).

In the next few pages, we will examine some of the characteristics of effective communication—including empathy, the ability to send consistent messages, and the capacity for responding, or providing feedback.

Empathy and Mutual Understanding

Ever since the work of George Herbert Mead (1934), sociologists have been exploring the importance of taking the role of the other. Mead applied this idea mainly to the stages of childhood socialization, but it also helps us to understand why some adults communicate well and others do not. As Mead noticed, young children are incapable of seeing things from others' viewpoints. Only gradually do they become capable of empathy, of sharing another's thoughts and feelings, sufferings or joys. We adults are of course able to take the role of the other to some extent, but there are obvious differences in our abilities. To note just one consequence of these differences, people who are particularly good at taking the role of the other do better on tests of social interaction (Feffer and Suchotliff, 1966).

Empathy is particularly important in marital communication. One of the stock cartoons about married life shows a man hiding behind

In all communications, but particularly those in marriage and family life, many messages are transmitted through the "language" of facial expression, posture, physical proximity, and body movement.

his newspaper over coffee in the morning while his wife tries without much success to gain his interest. This picture typifies a grievance among wives about the empathy they receive from their husbands, a complaint supported by research, which shows that females do appear to be more empathetic than males (Hoffman, 1977).

There are indications from various studies that due to boredom, indifference, or the mistaken belief that one already knows how the other feels, spouses often overestimate their understanding of each other. Thus, for example, misunderstandings may arise because a husband does not make his feelings or preferences known, and his wife is not even aware that he is not doing so (Shapiro and Swensen, 1969). Real communication is replaced by a guessing game in which husbands and wives make certain assumptions about each other rather than seeking out further information that might lead to real understanding.

Unspoken Messages, Contradictory Cues

Family therapists have discovered that faulty communication is often caused by mixed messages: two verbal messages contradict each other or a nonverbal message contradicts a verbal one. The sender of mixed messages is not aware of what he or she is doing, and the receiver is of course confused.

Here are two examples of mixed messages. A husband responds to a suggestion made by his wife with the words "That's a good idea." At the same time, however, he brushes an invisible speck from his sleeve in a gesture of indifference or dismissal. Which is the real message, the verbal or the nonverbal one? Another example: a family is sitting in a therapist's office, the father next to his daughter. When the therapist asks the father how he feels about his daughter, he replies, "I love her. She means the world to me." But while making this statement his legs are tightly crossed, he does not even glance at his daughter, and he speaks in a flat tone. Thus his actions appear to contradict the verbal message he apparently intended to convey.

We have learned much over the past few years about the importance of unspoken messages or "body language." One researcher found that in the communication of an emotional message, 55 percent of its impact on others is due to the speaker's facial expression, 38 percent to the tone of voice, and only 7 percent to the words themselves (Mehrabian, 1972). Thus, an important communication skill is to gain an awareness of the range of nonverbal cues—for example, facial expression, posture, tone of voice, eye movement, rapidity of speech—and learn how to use them.

Of course, it is possible to pay so much attention to nonverbal cues that the verbal message slips by unnoticed. One weakness of nonverbal communication is that it lacks precision and can therefore be confusing. How, for example, would you distinguish a nonverbal expression of anger from one of determination or one of disgust from one of contempt? As the work of family therapists demonstrates, a very effective technique for changing behavior is to teach family members how to talk about their style of communicating—to put it all in words.

Feedback

Family therapists have emphasized that poor communications are not just the sender's fault. For an individual to communicate effectively, he or she must get some sort of feedback. In fact, the accuracy and frequency of feedback are some of the best indications of real communication.

In the disturbed families of schizophrenic children, therapists find extreme cases in which no one accepts, acknowledges, or confirms what anyone else says. One prominent student of family communication systems, Gregory Bateson (1956), accounts for the extreme confusion of schizophrenic children with his theory of "double-bind" messages. In such messages, the feedback of parents to their children contains such contradictory cues that it sets up a painful dilemma. Bateson illustrates the "double bind" with the following example of contradictory messages:

> A young man who had fairly well recovered from an acute schizophrenic episode was visited in the hospital by his mother. He was glad to see her and impulsively put his arm around her shoulders, whereupon she stiffened. He withdrew his arm, and she asked, "Don't you love me any more?" He then blushed, and she said "Dear, you must not be so easily embarrassed and afraid of your feelings." (Bateson, 1956, p. 266)

The child's dilemma is clear: If he assumes that his mother's apparent warmth is genuine, and responds to her affectionately, she withdraws. But if he perceives her to be emotionally cold and rejecting, and thus does not respond to her with affection, she criticizes him as an unloving son. In other words, no matter what he does, her reaction disconfirms his response. As Bateson explains, the only alternative to such self-defeating strategies would be to recognize the ambiguity of his mother's reactions; but in order to do that, he would have to acknowledge the fact of her coldness and her simulated affection. Terrified by the prospect of emotional abandonment, the schizophrenic child is unable to acknowledge his mother's real feelings. As a result, the illusion of intimacy is sustained, but at a very high cost: to remove himself from the dilemma in which his behavior—no matter what it is—is disconfirmed by his mother, the schizophrenic child resorts to sending messages that are deliberately ambiguous and gradually removes himself from reality by pretending to be someone else (Bateson et al., 1956).

Fortunately, it is only in the most extreme cases that such contradictory communications may lead to schizophrenia; and there is by no means a consensus among psychiatrists that Bateson is correct in regarding schizophrenia as a result of disturbed communications. But here, as elsewhere in the study of human communications, there is much to be learned by asking the same questions about how normal families communicate that have already been investigated in manifestly disturbed families.

One of the most common conversational patterns is what philosopher Abraham Kaplan once called a duologue, two people taking turns at separate conversations, neither listening nor responding to the other. A husband, for example, might be talking about his day at the office, discussing his upcoming business trip, while his wife recounts her day at home, and worries about a child's illness. It is not really a communication because neither is providing feedback to the other; nothing that either says really modifies what the other will say next. Real communication involves not only careful listening, but also inquiries about how the other feels, or whether the listener has understood correctly. Phrases such as "Do you mean that . . . ?" or "You sound discouraged about that . . . " or "Would it help if you . . . ?" indicate that the other person was listening to what was said and recognizing the speaker's thoughts and feelings.

MARITAL CONFLICT AND FAMILY VIOLENCE

We are often encouraged to think of marriage and family life as an emotional oasis, a retreat from the competitiveness and tension of the world outside. This conception of the family is reflected in much of what has been written and said about marriage and family for more than a century. In the nineteenth century, for example, there was a commonly expressed sentiment that husband and wife would find solace and spiritual renewal in each other's companionship. Wives were expected to serve—to recall a common phrase of that era—as "angels of consolation." What was largely ignored was the behavior that contradicted this image, the evidence that the group we look to for the satisfaction of our most intimate needs is also the one most commonly characterized by violence and physical abuse. Such phenomena as wife beating or child abuse did not go completely unnoticed, but when acknowledged, these practices were often regarded as the behavior of a small group of disturbed individuals. For decades, even students of family life ignored the evidence of marital violence; an analysis of the articles that appeared in the *Journal of Marriage and the Family* between 1939 and 1969 shows that there was not even one title in which the word "violence" appeared (O'Brien, 1971).

But since the early 1970s, family violence has attracted a great deal of attention in both the popular press and professional journals, and there has been widespread recognition of how different the ideal of the family-as-haven is from the reality. Partly as a result of the women's movement and its concern for the victims of family violence, in many American cities there are now special shelters for battered women, "hotlines" that abused wives can use to seek help, and police teams specially trained for domestic intervention.

This recent attention to the violent side of family life raises several questions: How common is such violence? If, as the evidence suggests, physical abuse is not a rare or isolated phenomenon, but rather a recurrent pattern in millions of households, then how can we explain why the family is such a crucible of extreme conflict?

It is difficult to gauge the extent of family violence because this is not only "backstage" behavior, but it is also behavior that people feel ashamed of and are thus reluctant to acknowledge. In addition, the records kept by law enforcement agencies in this area are not very helpful. Instances of family violence are considered to be the most underreported crimes. But several recent studies based upon representative samples do allow us to estimate the extent of family violence. Extrapolating from one study, Suzanne Steinmetz (1977) concludes that among 47 million American couples, 3.3 million wives and more than .25 million husbands have experienced severe beatings from their spouses. Another survey suggests that at least 1.7 million of those married individuals have at some point had a gun or knife forced upon them by their spouse (Straus, Gelles, and Steinmetz, 1978). Since these studies included only intact families, where both spouses are currently living together, we can conclude that the statistics greatly underestimate the actual level of marital violence. Although much attention has been drawn to wives who are physically abused by their husbands, it appears that wives commit violent acts against their spouses about as often as their husbands do (Straus, 1974). As we might expect, the two sexes resort to somewhat different modes of violence: husbands more often use direct physical strength as they push, grab, or choke their spouses, whereas wives more often throw things, or use objects such as kitchen knives, which do not require as much physical strength (Steinmetz, 1977).

Studies of violence between parents and their children provide more evidence of how common physical abuse is in family life. In interviews with more than 1,000 families that include children between the ages of three and seventeen, Richard Gelles and his associates (1977) found that 63 percent of the respondents reported at least one violent episode during the previous year. Extrapolating to the 46 million children in this age range who lived with both parents in 1975, the authors estimated that roughly 2 million children had been beaten up by their parents, and at least 1 million had been threatened by a parent wielding a gun or a knife (Gelles, Straus, and Steinmetz, 1977). When considering what such statistics mean, it is important to remember that these studies are based upon self-reports, thus underestimating the incidence of family violence.

In the United States, as in many countries, the most extreme form of violence—homicide—occurs more often between people who are acquainted or related than between strangers. In recent years, more than 25 percent of all the murders in the United States have involved members of the same family, and in about 15 percent of all homicides one spouse kills the other (*Vital Statistics,* 1976).

Clearly, violence among family members is not a rare or isolated phenomenon. Although physical abuse is more common in households

Scene from the movie, *Who's Afraid of Virginia Woolf?*

where the father has recently experienced unemployment (Gil, 1970), it is not limited to any specific social class. And although studies have found a distinct connection between the use of alcohol and family violence (Wertham, 1972) it would be misleading to conclude that most of the violence among family members can be attributed solely to the effects of drinking. The most satisfactory explanations of this phenomenon are those that acknowledge the unique potential for conflict in family dynamics.

We can begin to understand why there is such potential for conflict in intimate relationships by considering how family behavor typically differs from behavior in other areas. One important characteristic of family life is that much of it consists of what sociologist Erving Goffman refers to as "backstage behavior" (1959). In contrast to those situations where we are obliged to perform well-defined roles—as worker or student, churchgoer or salesperson—here there is greater freedom to act naturally, to "be yourself," to set aside the etiquettes we normally observe. This freedom to abandon pretense that intimate relationships allow is also the source of considerable conflict. When people are "at ease" in the backstage area, spontaneity and an easy familiarity are possible, but so also are inconsiderateness, disrespect, and outright personal attacks.

As Goffman points out, there are certain similarities between family life and what takes place in other "backstage areas," for example, faculty lounges to which instructors can retreat and indulge in behavior not considered appropriate to their official role, such as smoking, or exchanging candid comments about the attributes of their students. In many respects, the rules of "backstage behavior" are the contrary of the rules that we follow elsewhere. Public behavior normally requires a certain formality; in our speech and dress we are supposed to convey a proper impression. In public, we normally maintain a certain distance from others (as reflected by the terms of address employed), and we refrain from obvious acts of disrespect (such as mockery or sarcasm). But in the backstage area, we feel free to drop the pretense of an outwardly cheerful manner, to engage in a relaxed slovenliness of both dress and demeanor that may include uncomplimentary nicknames, open grumbling, profanity, and incoherent mumbling. Notice that this backstage behavior typically includes acts—such as belching, humming, and shouting—that are potentially offensive indications of disrespect. And notice, too, the similarities between the way in which we convey affection and the way we express aggression:

> Thus, although lovers stare at each other, so do enemies. Standing very close to a person, calling him or her "baby," remaining silent for long periods, or handling that person's possessions can signal either intimacy or hostility, depending upon the emotional context of the situation. Since lovers are used to giving one version of these signals, it seems relatively easy for them to slip into the other mode. (Skolnick, 1978, p. 229)

Goffman's comments about "impression management" provide another insight that allows us to understand the potential for conflict in family life. He points out that we try to control the impressions that others have of us and attempt to conceal anything that is incompatible with the image of ourselves that we intend to convey. One of the simplest ways of conveying the intended impression, says Goffman, is to make sure that the audience for any one of the roles we play is different from the audiences for all the others (1959). This may be an effective technique in performing public roles, but audience segregation is impossible among family members. In the "backstage" area of family life, we not only reveal very different and sometimes contradictory aspects of ourselves but more vulnerable ones as well. Consequently, in intimate relationships there is the constant possibility that others may use the information and insights they have to attack or discredit us, to tell us that we are not really what we pretend to be. One commonly hears about lovers who betray each other by revealing secrets shared in confidence. This is the paradox of intimate relationships. "You always hurt the one you love," as the song lyric has it, because it is here that you have the most potent weapons for inflicting pain.

To complicate the matter, family life typically consists not only of highly charged emotions but also of mixed emotions. Several decades ago, therapist Theodor Reik commented that one of the main reasons why people seek psychiatric help is that they feel intense guilt about the hatred they bear toward the people they love. We might add that there is a substantial literature in social psychology pointing to the conclusion that ambivalence adds to the intensity of passion. Consider the conflicts that love relationships often pose: as revealed by countless tales of romantic love, the raptures of falling in love are often accompanied by the gradual realization of one's dependence. The more we get from the people we love, the more we have to lose if that affection is withdrawn. Thus love is commonly associated with a jumble of mixed emotions because of our ambivalence about dependence. Such mixed emotions are a potent source of conflict and anger.

In addition to all the preceding explanations, one of the most important reasons for family violence, as sociologist Murray Straus (1978) notes, is that the family is where many people

Over the past few years, increasing attention has been paid to violence among family members.

get their "basic training" in the use of force; they observe parents resorting to physical punishment and other forms of violence. Under certain conditions, social norms condone the use of physical force in family life. For example, parents have the legal right to strike their children in order to discipline them. Part of the problem for parents as well as researchers is to determine the point at which appropriate discipline becomes unreasonable and harmful abuse. (We will return to the question of child abuse in Chapter 12.) When police intervene in domestic disputes, battling spouses often protest that they have a right to hit each other, and researchers have found that even the victims of family violence commonly justify it with such explanations as "I asked for it" or "I deserved it." Many people feel that violence is justified under certain circumstances. These attitudes may have been learned in childhood, since various studies suggest a strong association between exposure to violence as a child and violent behavior as an adult. It appears that in many families the use of physical force is passed down from one generation to another. Children who observe violence or who are its victims are more likely to justify violent acts and to resort to them as adults (Owens and Straus, 1975; Steinmetz, 1977).

The Uses of Conflict

Conflict does not necessarily lead to violence, of course. Indeed, a common goal of marital therapy is to get spouses to admit their differences and to air their grievances. One therapist, George Bach, has argued that fighting is not only inevitable between intimates, but it is also highly desirable—if couples know how to fight properly. As Bach and his associate Peter Wyden write,

> the notion that a stress- and quarrel-free emotional climate in the home will bring about authentic harmony is a preposterous myth, born in ignorance of the psychological realities of human relationships. Fighting is inevitable between mature intimates. Quarreling and making up are hallmarks of true intimacy. However earnestly a mature person tries to live in harmony with a partner he will have to fight for his very notions of harmony itself and come to terms with competing notions—and there are always competing interests. (1968, p. 11)

One element of the encounter group experience that Bach endorses is the venting of aggressive feelings. Many of the therapeutic strategies that have been developed since the 1960s are based on the assumption that dropping inhibitions, letting it all out, punching, biting, and smashing can be helpful expressions of "therapeutic aggression." In his "aggression labs," Bach uses padded foam paddles to assist his patients in letting out their true feelings. An advertisement describes the "Olympic model" paddle as "best for continued heavy use" and goes on to explain that it offers a "safe, satisfying release for anger, hostility, frustration and excess energy. Perfect for assertiveness training!"

Murray Straus questions whether such "aggressive therapy" really accomplishes its aim. Is it true that by giving free expression to aggressive feelings, individuals can vent their anger and hostilities and thus reduce subsequent aggression? After conducting a study of several hundred couples, he came to the conclusion that the evidence fails to support the value of aggression release. "In fact," he concludes, "the weight of the evidence suggests that such an approach may be dangerous because, rather than reducing subsequent aggression, expressing aggression against others probably tends to increase subsequent aggressive acts" (1974, p. 27).

Most students of marital communication patterns agree on the importance of leveling—communicating where one stands, airing grievances, and expressing real feelings about the partnership. Leveling, write Bach and Wyden,

> means that one should be transparent in communicating where one stands and candid in signaling where one wants to go. . . . With a casual acquaintance or a business associate, leveling is rarely worth the trouble. It may even be unwise. With a loved one, the art of aggressive leveling calls for careful cultivation. (1968, p. 50)

This may sound like a relatively easy skill to master, but many couples habitually avoid issues that need resolution. In her study of blue-collar marriages, Komarovsky describes some of the common strategies for avoiding conflict and tells what happens eventually when unresolved differences are allowed to pile up. A greater proportion of husbands than wives, she found, simply withdraw in the face of conflict. Husbands more often withdraw by leaving the house. Wives commonly withdraw psychologically, resorting to a sullen silence. One woman said, "When I get real mad I just won't talk, sometimes I won't talk for days. I won't say a word. My husband and daughter feel it after a while. I have one kind of mad and I holler at them; then the other times I keep quiet. I think that's the worse time" (1967, p. 193).

Not unexpectedly, the failure to air grievances commonly leads up to a blowup. As one man explains, "You don't quite know what you feel, you're just sore and mad so you don't say nothing and it gets worse, and after a while you blow up" (p. 195).

Another generally unsatisfactory strategy for dealing with conflict is displacement. This refers to a tendency to avoid the real issue by arguing about something else. Fights about money, for example, are often really an expression of more basic, harder-to-discuss conflicts, such as marital roles or the partners' affection for each other.

Destructive Fighting

"The list of ways to discourage intimacy is almost inexhaustible," write Bach and Wyden, "and some love-killing fight-styles require no words at all." In *The Intimate Enemy,* they provide a list of tactics used by spouses who lack the skill or desire to resolve conflict (1968, p. 97). By examining three of those tactics we can perhaps understand why some fights resolve conflict and others produce greater anger and differences.

One popular tactic among educated, articulate people is spouse-probing. In this exchange, a female spouse-prober makes it clear to her husband that she knows him better than he does himself:

> *Wife:* I'm telling you, you're just kidding yourself.
> *Husband:* That's ridiculous! I know what I'm doing.
> *Wife:* No, you don't! You're totally unaware. I know you inside out. . . ." (1968, p. 99)

Character analyses of this sort are particularly infuriating because they disqualify what the other person says or does. An exchange that begins like this is likely to lead only to further insistence on the part of the husband that he really does know what he's doing.

Another tactic, this one particularly appealing to people who have some knowledge of the diagnostic categories used by psychiatrists, is character analysis through the use of stereotyping. Between spouses as much as strangers, the use of such stereotypes as alcoholic, sadist, or neurotic is depersonalizing, and likely to lead to an exchange of insults (1968, p. 101). Putting such labels on someone is particularly destructive because it attacks the other's self-concept. In general, the response to such attacks is an angry defense of one's self-worth. Being told who you are in negative terms is much harsher than being informed of something specific you did that displeased your partner. Moreover, such labeling is not likely to lead to the resolution of any specific issue. Not surprisingly, people who are unhappily married attack the self-concept of their mates more than do happily married people (Mathews and Mihanovich, 1963).

A third example of destructive aggression is the "kitchen sink" fight, illustrated by a married couple who meet for a dinner date. The wife arrives twenty minutes late.

> *He:* Why were you late?
> *She:* I tried my best.
> *He:* Yeah? You and who else? Your mother is never on time either.
> *She:* That's got nothing to do with it.
> *He:* The hell it doesn't. You're as sloppy as she is.
> *She:* (getting louder) You don't say! Who's picking whose dirty underwear off the floor every morning?
> *He:* (sarcastic but controlled) I happen to go to work. What have you got to do all day?
> *She:* (shouting) I'm trying to get along on the money you don't make, that's what.
> *He:* (turning away from her) Why should I knock myself out for an ungrateful bitch like you? (Bach and Wyden, 1968, p. 3)

In this destructive volley, the husband and wife have made a whole series of mistakes. Bach and Wyden call it a "kitchen sink" fight because, almost literally, everything gets thrown in. There is no specific grievance or issue, but rather a mess of complaints and accusations. In comparing her with her mother, the husband throws an irrelevant barb from the past. She counterattacks by accusing him of being a bad provider; he questions her usefulness and calls her a bitch. It is a good example of how many things can go wrong in a destructive fight where no specific issues are raised; both overload the other with grievances and nothing is resolved (see Box 9–3).

Coping with Conflict—The Bargaining Process

For some couples, conflict is a way of life. John Cuber and Peggy Harroff call such marriages conflict habituated and describe them as relationships in which "incompatibility is pervasive, conflict is ever-potential, and an atmosphere of tension permeates the togetherness." One of the women interviewed by the researchers looks back over her own marriage and characterizes it as "a running guerrilla fight. . . . It's hard to know what it is we fight about," she says. "You name it, and we'll fight about it. . . . We don't really agree about anything." As the authors suggest, in such cases it is reasonable to assume a deep need on the part of both spouses to maintain the psychological battle. For conflict-habituated people, the differences serve as a cohesive factor that keeps the marriage together (1968, pp. 44–45).

But for most couples, conflict is neither customary nor cohesive. Issues have to be recognized and resolved in order for the conflict to be constructive. Learning how to fight might be compared with learning how to dance. Both involve certain understandings and both are based on the premise that in the long run the two individuals get the greatest satisfaction out of performing together.

Bach and Wyden recommend that husband and wife have the general understanding that when differences develop, both will follow this three-step procedure. First, the "recipient" listens without comment or interruption while the "aggressor" states the complaint, airs feelings related to the complaint, and makes a specific request for change. The procedure stipulates that the recipient will not interrupt, comment, or make any countercomplaints, but will give feedback to satisfy the aggressor that he or she

Guidelines for Decision Making

Box 9–3 / Fifteen Suggestions for Constructive Conflict

1. Be specific when you introduce a gripe.

2. Don't just complain, no matter how specifically; ask for a reasonable change that will relieve the gripe.

3. Ask for and give feedback of the major points, to make sure you are heard, to assure your partner that you understand what he wants.

4. Confine yourself to one issue at a time. Otherwise, without professional guidance, you may skip back and forth, evading the hard ones.

5. Do not be glib or intolerant. Be open to your own feelings, and equally open to your partner's.

6. Always consider compromise. Remember, your partner's view of reality may be just as real as yours, even though you may differ. There are not many totally objective realities.

7. Do not allow counterdemands to enter the picture until the original demands are clearly understood, and there has been a clear-cut response to them.

8. Never assume that you know what your partner is thinking until you have checked out the assumption in plain language; or assume or predict how he will react, what he will accept or reject. Crystal-ball gazing is not for pairing.

9. Don't mind-rape. Don't correct a partner's statement of his own feelings. Do not tell a partner what he should know or feel.

10. Never put labels on a partner. Call him neither a coward, nor a neurotic, nor a child. If you really believed that he was incompetent or suffered from some basic flaw, you probably would not be with him. Do not make sweeping, labeling judgments about his feelings, especially about whether or not they are real or important.

11. Sarcasm is dirty fighting.

12. Forget the past and stay with the here-and-now. What either of you did last year or month or that morning is not as important as what you are doing and feeling now. And the changes you ask cannot possibly be retroactive. Hurts, grievances, and irritations should be brought up at the very earliest moment, or the partner has the right to suspect that they may have been saved carefully as weapons.

13. Do not overload your partner with grievances. To do so makes him feel hopeless and suggests that you have either been hoarding complaints or have not thought through what really troubles you.

14. Meditate. Take time to consult your real thoughts and feelings before speaking. Your surface reactions may mask something deeper and more important. Don't be afraid to close your eyes and think.

15. Remember that there is never a single winner in an honest intimate fight. Both either win more intimacy, or lose it.

Source: George R. Bach and Ronald M. Deutsch, 1974, *Pairing*. Copyright, Wm. C. Brown Co., Publishers. Reprinted by permission of the publisher.

is understood. Only at the second stage does the "recipient" respond to the "aggressor's" complaints, feelings, and demands—and now it is the "aggressor" who must limit himself or herself to providing feedback about whether the message was clear. Then, at the third stage, both offer possible solutions to the problem, being careful to keep their suggestions pertinent to the issue under discussion (1968). Obviously such procedures for constructive conflict also require an appropriate time and place for the quarrel.

Any constructive conflict ends with some bargaining over potential solutions. Sociologist Ralph Turner notes that "bargaining" may seem

> a cruel word to apply to the deliberations of members in the intimate family relationship. But bargaining is simply a general term for any interaction in which the concessions that one member makes to another are expected to be reciprocated in some manner, so that over the long run the sacrifices of each will balance out. (1970, p. 106)

Between intimates, what one party gets for making concessions to the other is generally implied. But, as Turner suggests, in marital bargaining as in international diplomacy, if there is little underlying trust to begin with, or if one party feels that concessions are not being fairly reciprocated, it is not likely that differences will be resolved to the satisfaction of both.

Conclusions

Recent interest in the quality of communication between spouses is another indication of the importance of companionship in marriage today. At the same time, family psychiatry has provided many new insights into the dynamics of family communication. It has been discovered, for example, that all family interaction is structured by rules that, although generally unstated, define the unique reality each family constructs and maintains, and specify the roles to be played by family members. Therapists note that something is *always* being communicated in families, but the message is often subtle, unintended, or misunderstood.

Everyone knows that many communications are not very effective. The question is, why are some messages misunderstood? In this chapter we have examined the problems involved in accurately interpreting messages, in achieving empathy, reading nonverbal cues, and giving appropriate feedback.

We have also discussed marital conflict, family violence, and some techniques for resolving them. Differences are a part of any close relationship. In marriage, spouses can either deny them and withdraw from the tensions they produce or level with each other and try to achieve better accommodation and personal growth.

REFERENCES

I. Altman and W. Haythorn. Interpersonal exchange in isolation. *Sociometry* 28 (1965): 411–426.

George R. Bach and Peter Wyden. *The intimate enemy*. New York: Morrow, 1968.

Gregory Bateson. Toward a theory of schizophrenia. *Behavioral Science* 1 (1956): 251–273.

Jessie Bernard. Developmental tasks of the NCFR—1963–1988. *Journal of Marriage and the Family* 26 (1964): 33–38.

Eric Berne. *Games people play*. New York: Grove Press, 1978.

Colin Cherry. *On human communication: A review, a survey, and a criticism*. Cambridge, Mass.: MIT Press, 1966.

John F. Cuber and Peggy B. Harroff. *Sex and the significant Americans*. Baltimore: Penguin, 1968.

Julius Fast. *Body language*. New York: Evans, 1970.

Melvin Feffer and Leonard Suchotliff. Decentering implications of social interactions. *Journal of Personality and Social Psychology* 4 (1966): 415–422.

Antonio J. Ferreira. Family myth and homeostasis. *Archives of General Psychiatry* 9 (1963): 457–464.

Richard J. Gelles, Murray Straus, and Suzanne Steinmetz. *Violence toward children in the United States*. Paper presented at the September 1977 meeting of the American Association for the Advancement of Science, Denver, Colorado.

David G. Gil. *Violence against children: Physical child abuse in the United States*. Cambridge, Mass.: Harvard University Press, 1970.

Erving Goffman. *The presentation of self in everyday life*. Garden City, N.Y.: Doubleday Anchor, 1959.

Jay Haley. The family of the schizophrenic: A model system. *Journal of Nervous and Mental Disease* 129 (1959): 357–374.

Thomas Harris. *I'm ok, you're ok*. New York: Harper & Row, 1969.

Paul Hilsdale. Marriage as a personal existential commitment. *Marriage and Family Living* 24 (1962): 137–143.

M. L. Hoffman. Sex difference in empathy and related behaviors. *Psychological Bulletin* 84 (July 1977): 712–722.

Mirra Komarovsky. *Blue-collar marriage*. New York: Vintage, 1967.

William J. Lederer and Don D. Jackson. *The mirages of marriage*. New York: Norton, 1968.

James McCroskey, Carl E. Larson, and Mark L. Knapp. *An introduction to interpersonal communication*. Englewood Cliffs, N.J.: Prentice-Hall, 1971.

David R. Mace. The outlook for marriage: New needs and opportunities. *Foundation News*, November/December 1975, pp. 16, 36–42.

Vincent D. Mathews and Clement S. Mihanovich. New orientations on marital maladjustment. *Marriage and Family Living*. August 1963, pp. 300–305.

George Herbert Mead. *Mind, self and society*, part 3. Chicago: University of Chicago Press, 1934.

Albert Mehrabian. *Nonverbal communication*. Chicago: Aldine-Atherton, 1972.

Keith Melville. Changing the family game. *The Sciences*, April 1973, pp. 17–19.

Sherod Miller, Ramon Corrales, and Daniel B. Wackman. Recent progress in understanding and facilitating marital communication. *The Family Coordinator*, April 1975, pp. 143–152.

Leslie Navran. Communication and adjustment in marriage. *Family Process* 6 (1967): 173–184.

J. E. O'Brien. Violence in divorce-prone families. *Journal of Marriage and the Family* 33 (1971): 692–698.

Nena O'Neill and George O'Neill. *Open marriage*. New York: Evans, 1972.

D. M. Owens and Murray A. Straus. The social structure of violence in childhood and approval of violence as an adult. *Aggressive Behavior* 1 (1975): 193–211.

Lillian B. Rubin. *Worlds of pain*. New York: Basic Books, 1976.

Arnold Shapiro. The relationship between self-concept and self-disclosure. *Dissertation Abstracts International* 39 (1968): 1180–1181.

Arnold Shapiro and Clifford Swensen. Patterns of self-disclosure among married couples. *Journal of Counseling Psychology* 16 (1969): 179–180.

Arlene Skolnick. *The intimate environment*. Boston: Little, Brown, 1978.

Suzanne K. Steinmetz. *The cycle of violence: Assertive, aggressive, and abusive family interaction*. New York: Praeger, 1977a.

——— Wife beating, husband beating: A comparison of the use of physical violence between spouses to resolve marital fights. In M. Roy, ed. *Battered women: A psychosociological study of domestic violence*. New York: Van Nostrand Reinhold, 1977b.

Murray A. Straus. Leveling, civility, and violence in the family. *Journal of Marriage and the Family* 36 (1974): 13–28.

———, Richard J. Gelles, and Suzanne K. Steinmetz. Violence in the family: An assessment of knowledge and research needs. In M. Van Stolk, ed. *Child abuse: its treatment and prevention—An interdisciplinary approach*. Toronto: McClelland and Stewart, 1977.

——— *Violence in the American family*. Garden City, N.Y.: Doubleday Anchor, 1978.

Ralph Turner. *Family interaction*. New York: Wiley, 1970.

Vital Statistics Reports: Births, deaths, marriages and divorces. vol. 24, no. 13. Washington, D.C.: National Center for Health Statistics, 1976.

Ezra Vogel. *Japan's new middle class*. Berkeley: University of California Press, 1971.

F. Wertham. Battered children and baffled adults. *Bulletin of the New York Academy of Medicine* 48 (1972): 887–898.

Lyman Wynne, Irving Ryckoff, Juliana Day, and Stanley Hirsch. Pseudo-mutuality in the family relationships of schizophrenics. *Psychiatry* 21 (1958): 205–220.

FOR FURTHER STUDY

Two journals that provide articles on the topics discussed in this chapter are *Family Process* and *The Journal of Communications*. For a discussion of the relationship between social class and different styles of marital communication, see James L. Hawkins, Carol Weisberg, and Dixie L. Ray, "Marital Communication Style and Social Class" (*Journal of Marriage and Family*, vol. 39, 1977, pp. 479–490). Janet Malcolm has written an interesting account of how family therapists work with troubled families, which appeared in *The New Yorker* (May 15, 1978).

For a review of the literature on nonverbal communication, see *Nonverbal Communication: The State of the Art*, by Robert G. Harper, Arthur N. Wiens, and Joseph D. Matarazzo (New York: Wiley, 1978).

Violence in the Family, edited by Suzanne K. Steinmetz and Murray A. Straus (New York: Dodd, Mead, 1974), is a valuable collection of articles on conflict, aggression, and violence among intimates. Among the recent publications in this area are several other useful and informative books, including *Violence in the American Family,* by Murray Straus, Richard J. Gelles, and Suzanne Steinmetz (Garden City, N.Y.: Anchor, 1978). The May/June 1978 issue of *Marriage and Family Review* includes a comprehensive review of the rapidly growing literature in this area, prepared by Suzanne Steinmetz.

For perspectives on the conflicts in intimate relationships, the reader might be interested in a recent anthology entitled *Jealousy*, edited by Gordon Clanton and Lynn G. Smith (Englewood Cliffs, N.J.: Prentice-Hall, 1977).

Several popular books include valuable discussions of marital communications. These include *The Mirages of Marriage*, by William J. Lederer and Don D. Jackson (New York: Norton, 1968), which has a particularly good analysis of marital bargaining; and *The Intimate Enemy*, by George R. Bach and Peter Wyden (N.Y.: Morrow, 1968) on the art of fair fighting.

"Bedroom Ensemble" Claes Oldenburg

10 Marital Sexuality—As Work and Play

Several years ago a new store called Eve's Garden opened in midtown Manhattan, featuring a selection of "pleasure products for women" ranging from books about female sexuality to "love oils." "We grow pleasurable things for women," the store advertised. "Now is the time to declare your sexual independence, or share it."

This is no sex shop, like the ones in the Times Square area several blocks away. Customers—mainly women—entering the store find a friendly, businesslike atmosphere. Owner Dell Williams says, "I wanted to create an environment in which women would feel comfortable about their bodies and their sexuality. The more positive women feel about their bodies, the better they feel about themselves. We want to help women to get around all the negative lessons about sexuality that have been around for so long. . . ."

If stores like Eve's Garden are not yet common in other American cities, many of the attitudes it fosters are rapidly gaining acceptance. The emphasis on sexual pleasure as a woman's right, on the belief that sex is necessary to well-being and neither a moral threat nor a drain on one's energies—these are characteristics of a distinctly modern way of thinking about sex.

Only slightly more than half a century ago, Sigmund Freud, having treated many casualties of the repressive sexual codes of Vienna at the turn of the century, wondered "whether our 'civilized' sex code is worth the sacrifice" (in Epstein, 1975, p. 61). Whether the sexual code of Freud's time was more civilized than that of today is debatable, but it is unquestionably true that the new sexual morality departs radically from the sexual beliefs of the late nineteenth century.

Describing the sexual attitudes of that era, historian Arthur Schlesinger denounces "the sickness of prudery" and the "appalling gentility" that governed the relationships between the sexes. Some art galleries insisted that men and women view classical statues in separate groups, on the assumption that exposure to the human anatomy portrayed in those statues

Today's revealing swimsuit fashions, like candid discussions of sexual pleasure in the mass media, would have seemed scandalous to previous generations.

would be embarrassing in mixed company. In other galleries, statues were discreetly draped if their sculptors had not provided decent attire. In deference to female sensibility, legs were alluded to in ordinary conversation as "limbs"; pregnancy was "a delicate condition" (Schlesinger, 1973, p. 18). The Victorian wife was an "Angel in the House," as the title of a popular poem by Coventry Patmore described her. Even her mode of dress—bell-shaped skirts sweeping the floor—gave the impression that her physical self ended at the waist.

Writers of that era, including even medical authorities, also denied women a sexual existence. The English historian John Acton, for example, dismissed as a "foul aspersion" the suggestion that women were capable of orgasm (in Comfort, 1963, p. 20). Masturbation was regarded as a pernicious vice that led to various mental and physical disorders. Sex in marriage was regarded as a necessary evil, the purpose of which was procreation, not pleasure.

Today, just a few generations later, we have entered an era in which for a substantial part of the population, at least, sexual repression has given way to a more liberal set of beliefs. Contemporary confusions about sex result from this very rapid transition from one set of beliefs to another (see Box 10–1).

Confusion is also created by the contradictory instructions we receive about sex at various stages in our lifetime. In many families, there are still strong taboos against the sexual explorations of children: "If you touch it, you'll go

Point of View

Box 10–1 / Two Views on Sexuality

Ours is an age of divergent and often contradictory views on sexual ethics and practices. Here are excerpts from two statements that take opposing views on such basic matters as masturbation and premarital sex.

Sex

Excerpts from the declaration on sexual ethics issued by the Vatican Congregation for the Doctrine of the Faith (*The New York Times*, January 16, 1976).

> In the present period, the corruption of morals has increased, and one of the most serious indications of this corruption is the unbridled exaltation of sex. Moreover, through the means of social communication and through public entertainment this corruption has reached the point of invading the field of education and infecting the general mentality.
>
> As a result, in the course of a few years, teachings, moral criteria, and modes of living hitherto faithfully preserved have been very much unsettled, even among Christians. There are many people today who, being confronted with so many widespread opinions opposed to the teachings which they received from the church, have come to wonder what they must still hold as true.

Excerpts from Dr. Alex Comfort's book *Sex in Society* (Secaucus, N.J.: The Citadel Press, 1963).

> The fact of having made sex into a "problem" is the major negative achievement of Christendom.
>
> Our real need is for a mentality in which the word "problem" is banished permanently in favor of "enjoyment." The essence of the "problem" is that for many people and for various reasons enjoyment is lacking. So is security—and so too, very often, is love. (p. 54)
>
> The net impact of Christian teaching over nineteen centuries has produced several clear-cut assumptions: that of all moral delinquencies, sexual misdeeds are the most serious; that sexuality in itself is a trap, fraught with ritual and personal danger; that suffering, abstinence, and virginity are desirable as indices of moral value. (p. 67)

(Box 10–1 continues on page 270)

blind." In the teen years, sex is surrounded with guilt: "What if you get pregnant?" But then, at marriage, it is assumed that sex will take its place as a regular and satisfactory part of conjugal life. In one's later years, regardless of individual inclinations or capacities, it is often assumed that sexual interests are abandoned, and that elderly couples who maintain an active sex life are a bit strange.

Other confusions arise from regarding sex sometimes as work, sometimes as play. The premise of hundreds of sex manuals is that "sexual adequacy" is something to be attained through much knowledge and training. If sex is play, therefore, we are instructed to work at it.

These changes in the sexual code and the confusions that stem from them obviously have a profound effect on marriage. But exactly how have the sexual activities of spouses changed? How does sex contribute to or detract from the marital bond? How do sexual beliefs and activities vary from one couple to another, and from one social class to another? We will consider these questions in this chapter.

(Box 10–1 continued from page 269)

Masturbation

(Vatican)

The traditional Catholic doctrine that masturbation constitutes a grave moral disorder is often called into doubt or expressly denied today. . . . Whatever the force of certain arguments of a biological and philosophical nature, which have sometimes been used [to defend masturbation as a normal phenomenon] in fact both the magisterium of the church—in the course of a constant tradition—and the moral sense of the faithful have declared without hesitation that masturbation is an intrinsically and seriously disordered act . . .
The tradition of the church has rightly understood it to be condemned in the New Testament when the latter speaks of "impurity," "unchasteness," and other vices contrary to chastity and continence.

(Comfort)

Fear of the entirely illusory physical effects of masturbation still underlies a proportion of neurosis in young men; this fear is traceable almost entirely to books and pamphlets dating from the mid-nineteenth century, many of which are unfortunately still in print. In all branches of health education, the refutation of fallacies takes longer than the spreading of new knowledge.

There is no evidence that frequent orgasm obtained through masturbation is in any way harmful, provided that there is no adult-fostered guilt or anxiety attached to it. It seems an important aim of sex education to see that the boy's or the girl's first encounter with sex in this form shall be frankly pleasurable, not merely tolerated. (p. 108)

Premarital Sex

Today, there are many who vindicate the right to sexual union before marriage. . . . This is especially the case when the celebration of the marriage is impeded by circumstances or when this intimate relationship seems necessary in order for love to be preserved.

This option is contrary to Christian doctrine, which states that every genital act must be within the framework of marriage. Experience teaches us that love must find its safeguard in the stability of marriage if sexual intercourse is truly to respond to the requirements of its own finality and to those of human dignity. These requirements call for a conjugal contract sanctioned and guaranteed by society.

If, indeed, we want to talk to the young in terms of sensible moral prohibition (and there is no reason why we should not) then the two most important commandments . . . are "Thou shalt not exploit another person's feelings and wantonly expose them to an experience of rejection" and "Thou shalt not under any circumstances risk producing an unwanted child." These are prohibitions which apply quite as much within marriage as outside it. Unlike the injunction of chastity they make sense. (p. 95)

SEX AS WORK AND PLAY

Among the Yoruba of West Africa, the male organ is depicted as an agent of the God of Mischief, an autonomous and unruly force that threatens the social order. This concept is not totally incomprehensible to us, for we commonly regard sex as an imperious drive, a biological necessity, a natural urge that is difficult to restrain.

Obviously, sex is a biological function, one that we share with other species. But human sexuality differs from that of other animals in the same way human culture in general differs from the social interactions of other species—it is mainly *learned* behavior, not instinctive. Sex appears to be one of the most natural of human functions, but it is also channeled by cultural instructions and shaped by the symbolic environment.

From one perspective, the prohibitions and regulations that have surrounded sexual behavior reflect an ancient attitude of venerating the powers of sexuality. From another perspective, the social controls over sexual behavior can be understood as a means of channeling it in socially desirable ways. Prostitution, for example, is disapproved of in many cultures not so much because it implies that sex is an exchangeable commodity available to anyone who can pay the price, but because it contradicts the most basic assumptions about the role of sex in marriage. Prostitution implies not only promiscuity, but also emotional indifference, and thus flies in the face of the assumption that sex will cement an exclusive affectionate bond between spouses.

One way to understand how much of sexual behavior is a social product that has to be learned is to regard erotic situations in theatrical terms, as John Gagnon and William Simon do when they argue that such behavior is "scripted." These social scripts are rules of conduct that "define the situation, name the actors, and plot the behavior" (1973, p. 19).

> Our use of the term "script" with reference to the sexual has two major dimensions. One deals with the external, the interpersonal—the script as the organization of mutually shared conventions that allow two or more actors to participate in a complex act involving mutual dependence. The second deals with the internal, the intrapsychic, the motivational elements that produce arousal or at least a commitment to the activity. (1973, p. 20)

Since the script that channels sexual activities is written by society, people in different historical periods and cultures, as well as individuals from different social classes in the same culture, may follow different sexual scripts. The concept of a sexual script helps us to understand a pattern we noted in chapters 3 and 4, when we discussed courtship and premarital sex in the United States today: males and females are typically taught to attach quite different meanings to sex. Adolescent males learn from their peers to regard sex as recreation, an occasion for proving one's prowess. The common use of phrases such as "scoring" is only one of many indications that male sexuality is largely oriented toward impressing same-sex peers. The sexual script taught to most females, on the other hand, emphasizes the relational aspects of sex, not the recreational or specifically genital ones. Gagnon and Simon note that

> girls appear to be well trained in that area in which boys are poorly trained—that is, a belief in and a capacity for intense, emotionally charged relationships and the language of romantic love. When girls describe having been aroused sexually, they more often report it as a response to romantic rather than erotic words and actions. (1973, p. 74)

By noting the differences between the sexual scripts that males and females typically follow, we can get a better understanding of how the erotic responses of the two sexes differ. Indeed, one might conclude, as several researchers have, that most of what we normally define as pornography—such as erotic pictures or hard-core films—might more accurately be labeled *men's* pornography; whereas the stimuli that often produce intense arousal in women—such as "true romance" and "confessions" magazines—are not normally considered pornographic. The typical porno film overlooks precisely that aspect of eroticism that the "confessions" magazines and romantic novels dwell upon—the seduction, the creation of suspense about the outcome of some male–female encounter. To the extent that women have been taught to respond sexually to romantic overtures, hard-core porno films that focus narrowly on genital contact are not very likely to create arousal (Money and Ehrhardt, 1974).

The differences between male and female sexual scripts are evident even in what would seem to be the most private and nonsocial form of sex—masturbation. Alfred Kinsey (1948) found that masturbation is a nearly universal practice among males from early adolescence; among females it typically begins somewhat later and is not practiced by quite so many. More interesting, however, is the fact that in masturbating, males usually fantasize about imaginary encounters—sexual experiences they would like to have—while females recall actual experiences that were pleasurable. Thus, the masturbatory fantasies of males seem to follow a recreational script, while those of females seem more relational in content.

Sex in Other Societies

If sexual scripts differ from group to group within one culture, they vary even more widely from one culture to another. In some cultures, sexual pleasure is defined as a man's right, but not a woman's. In some—such as the Keraki of New Guinea—homosexual relations before marriage are expected among males; in others, any homosexual contact is strongly taboo (Ford and Beach, 1951, p. 265). According to the script in some societies, sexual pleasure is strongly condemned. In others, such as the Lepchas of India, sex is regarded as both morally and emotionally neutral. Among the Lepchas, writes anthropologist Geoffrey Gorer,

> sexual activity is practically divorced from emotion. It is a pleasant and amusing experience, and as much a necessity as food and drink; and like food and drink it does not matter from whom you receive it, as long as you get it. (in Stephens, 1963, p. 204)

Like most of the Western European cultures, American society is emerging from an era of strong antisexual feelings. The predominant sexual script in the nineteenth century defined procreation as the only legitimate motive for sexual activities between spouses.

Marital sexuality had long been regarded as no better than a shameful necessity by some Christians. In St. Paul's words, "it is better to marry than to burn." In the seventeenth century, the prominent English chaplain Jeremy Taylor stated that marital sexuality was allowed in order to avoid fornication, to bear children, and to show endearment. But, Taylor warned, "He is an ill husband that uses his wife as a man treats a harlot, having no other end but pleasure. The pleasure should always be joined to one or another of these ends," that is, procreation or showing endearment (in Scanzoni and Scanzoni, 1976, p. 297). If pursued mainly for pleasure, sex between spouses was still regarded as sinful.

In Europe and America during the nineteenth century, religious teachings combined with other social currents to create an extremely repressive, antisexual morality. However, since the first few decades of this century, our sexual scripts have been revised very rapidly. For many, the image of sex as sin has been replaced by the image of sex as play.

Sex as Play

The studies of human sexuality published by Alfred Kinsey and his associates in 1948 (*Sexual Behavior in the Human Male*) and 1953 (*Sexual Behavior in the Human Female*) had a profound effect on how people thought about sexuality. For one thing, Kinsey found that fewer than half of the orgasms experienced by American males came in intercourse with their wives. Many of his readers were shocked at the considerable evidence of sexual activities in childhood, premarital sex, homosexual encounters among apparently heterosexual men, and extramarital sex. A majority of most men's sexual experiences, in other words, are socially disapproved and many are illegal (1948, p. 568). These findings struck a blow at the hypocrisy of a sexual ethic that condemned much of what people actually did. (See Box 10–2.)

Since then, a number of states have passed legislation that legalizes all sex acts among consenting adults. In May 1975, for example, California passed a law repealing all prohibitions of private sexual behavior among consenting

Research Perspectives on Marriage and Family

Box 10–2 / The Sex Researchers

Sexuality has posed more difficulties for investigators than almost any other aspect of human behavior. It is an area in which direct observation has generally been ruled out, and one in which responses to interviewers' questions are often incomplete or distorted. Because much of what is written about human sexuality is still distorted by preconceived judgments and tainted by poorly designed research, it is particularly important to be aware of the strengths and weaknesses of the various studies mentioned in this chapter.

Until the Kinsey studies were begun in the late 1930s, no one had conducted a really adequate investigation of the sexual behavior of a cross section of the population. Earlier analyses of sexual behavior, such as the seven-volume work of Havelock Ellis, *Studies in the Psychology of Sex* (1897–1928), had been based upon medical or psychiatric case histories and accounts from individuals who volunteered information about their own experiences. What no one had accomplished, however, was a survey of the sexual practices of a "normal" population, which might illuminate the differences between widely shared norms and actual behavior. This is what Alfred C. Kinsey, a biology professor at Indiana University, accomplished. The Kinsey research, based upon interviews conducted between 1938 and 1951, was an investigation of the various ways in which humans reach orgasm: nocturnal emissions, masturbation, heterosexual petting, heterosexual and homosexual intercourse, and contacts with animals. Kinsey and his associates—Wardell Pomeroy, Clyde Martin, and Paul Gebhard—completed 18,000 interviews. The main results of these investigations were published in two landmark volumes, *Sexual Behavior in the Human Male* (1948) and *Sexual Behavior in the Human Female* (1953).

Although the Kinsey studies are still considered the benchmark data on marital sexuality, they have been criticized in several respects. Kinsey's critics charge that the population he studied—volunteers who offered a full account of their sexual experiences—was not representative. In particular, his sample has been criticized for including a disproportionate number of midwesterners and prison inmates. Some groups, such as blacks, farmers, and the poorly educated were seriously underrepresented in his data. Another criticism of his sample is that individuals who would volunteer information about their sex lives may have fewer inhibitions, and thus the entire sample may have contained a disproportionate number of sexual liberals. Nevertheless, if we take into account the character of the population used, the Kinsey studies do provide a useful, though now somewhat dated portrait of the sexual practices of white, middle-class college-educated people living in the Middle West and Northeast. And it is a tribute to the care with which Kinsey pursued that research that many of his main findings have been confirmed by subsequent research. Though some important changes have taken place in the generation since the Kinsey reports were published (more recent studies, for example, have not found the distinct differences among social classes that Kinsey describes) many of Kinsey's conclusions on such matters as reported frequency of marital intercourse are very similar to those reported in more recent studies based upon national samples (Westoff, 1974).

Just as Kinsey and his associates were pioneers in the use of interviews to investigate the sexual practices of a "normal" population, William Masters and Virginia Johnson were the first investigators to make systematic use of the direct observation of sexual acts. Their

(Box 10–2 continues on page 274)

(Box 10–2 continued from page 273)

main goal has been to understand the anatomical and physiological facts of human sexual response. For several decades, Masters and Johnson have studied the sexual behavior of males and females in a laboratory where precise observations can be made. They have observed and recorded more than 14,000 sexual acts. Although the 694 persons who volunteered as subjects for their first study (*Human Sexual Response,* 1966) included individuals of various races, ages, socioeconomic circumstances, and marital statuses, Masters and Johnson do not claim that theirs is a representative sample. Rather, they admit that many of their subjects have come from higher-than-average socioeconomic circumstances. Masters and Johnson have studied the responses of individuals in a variety of coital positions; the effects of self-stimulation; the effects of various contraceptive devices; as well as differences in sexual response between young and old people. Their studies have produced a detailed picture of how the body reacts to sexual stimulation, including a predictable sexual response cycle in which each stage is accompanied by physiological changes.

In recent years, as sex research has become more acceptable, there have been a variety of new studies. Because it is based upon a carefully drawn nationwide sample, one of the best of these is the National Fertility Study conducted by Charles Westoff (1974). The results of several other studies, such as Morton Hunt's *Sexual Behavior in the 1970's* (1974), which summarizes research commissioned by the Playboy foundation, and a study published in *Redbook* magazine (Levin and Levin, 1975) have to be examined with more caution. Hunt's study, which was conducted by an independent social science research firm, is based upon more than 2,000 completed questionnaires. Though the researchers tried to get a geographically representative sample by contacting individuals in twenty-four cities, questionnaires were completed by only about 20 percent of the individuals contacted by phone. Perhaps the most serious criticism of the study is that the respondents were people who agreed to participate in small, private group discussions—a group very likely to be more liberal and permissive than the population as a whole. Similarly, the major problem with the *Redbook* study (Levin and Levin, 1975) is that, despite the large number of respondents (about 100,000), it can hardly be assumed that people who fill out such reader surveys are a representative group.

One problem with these surveys of sexual practices is that while they generate data on such matters as frequency of intercourse or extramarital sex, they tell us very little about the qualitative and subjective aspects of sex. Two other studies *The Hite Report* (Hite, 1976) and *Beyond the Male Myth* (Pietropinto and Simenauer, 1977) offer some insight here, and give a better perspective on the psychological aspects of sex.

Among the new areas that sex researchers have been investigating are the sexual development of children, the biological basis of sexuality, and the psychology and physiology of impotence. And several new studies of homosexuality represent important advances in our understanding of this sexual minority. A recent report entitled *Homosexualities* (Bell and Weinberg, 1978) from the Institute for Sex Research attempts to do the same thing for homosexuality that the original Kinsey studies did for heterosexuality. It is an ambitious study, based upon some 1,500 interviews of homosexual men and women living in the San Francisco area in 1970, but many of the authors' comments, especially about the social consequences of a homosexual lifestyle, may not accurately describe the situation of homosexuals who live in other areas of the country where there are less liberal attitudes. With the publication of their long-awaited volume *Homosexuality in Perspective* (1979), Masters and Johnson present a detailed study of the sexual performance of 176 homosexuals, male and female, who are compared with heterosexuals who participated in earlier research.

adults, thus eliminating criminal penalties for such acts as oral copulation, which had been punishable by a maximum term of fifteen years, and sodomy, for which a California resident could formerly receive life imprisonment (*The New York Times,* May 14, 1975, p. 42). By 1977, there were eighteen states in which all of the prohibitions governing the private sexual behavior of consenting adults had been lifted.

Sociologist Nelson Foote, writing about the Kinsey studies in 1954, noted that they showed a great deal of sexual activity was going on, and that very little of it concerned reproduction. The most common motive, rather, was pleasure. Thus, Foote suggested, the most appropriate metaphor for sex is that of *play,* an activity engaged in for its own sake and one that generates rules allowing it to continue.

Foote's idea is certainly one whose time has come—in an avalanche of magazines and books that speak of sexual enjoyment to women readers as well as men with a candor that would have been scandalous only a few decades ago. Recent best sellers, such as David Reuben's 1969 book *Everything You Always Wanted to Know About Sex (. . . but were afraid to ask),* openly advocate "funsex." And one of the striking things about Alex Comfort's very popular *The Joy of Sex* (1972), a gourmet guide to sex, is the absence of disapproval of any potentially pleasurable experience.

Just how much attitudes toward sexual pleasure have changed is shown in the case of masturbation. A century ago, masturbation was widely regarded as a very serious kind of "self-abuse," and was condemned on medical as well as moral grounds. Arlene Skolnick describes the situation in this passage:

> The notion that masturbation not only is sinful but the leading cause of insanity, blindness, and epilepsy was put forth in the eighteenth century and reached its peak in the middle of the nineteenth. The preoccupation led to numerous devices for controlling masturbation, such as chastity belts and even surgical intervention. . . . Ironically, the very prevalence of masturbation made it possible for the proponents of masturbation as the cause of insanity to give the appearance of proving their point: they found that if they were to interrogate any mental patient, he would confess to being a masturbator. (1973, p. 175)

It was not until Kinsey's studies demonstrated that masturbation was almost universal among males that fears of "masturbation insanity" were entirely dispelled. Indeed, Kinsey's work served as a defense of masturbation. His evidence indicates that the act of masturbation is harmless for both males and females. There is no such thing, Kinsey asserted, as excessive masturbation (1953, p. 167).

Masters and Johnson go one step farther with masturbation, and in the process completely reverse nineteenth-century attitudes. Although they are mainly interested in sexual satisfaction in the marital relationship, intercourse seems at some places in their writings to take a back seat to the pleasures of masturbation. They report, for example, that female orgasms achieved through masturbation are more intense than those experienced in intercourse (1966, p. 34). Far from condemning it as medically harmful, Masters and Johnson advocate masturbation as a technique effective for some women in easing menstrual cramps and backache. In the treatment of some sexual disorders, therapists recommend self-stimulation before intercourse for men who do not have full erections, and postcoital masturbation for women who do not reach orgasm through intercourse.

It is highly significant that the Masters and Johnson research, and much of the public attention to sex over the past few years, focuses on orgasm, the peak of sexual pleasure. There could hardly be a clearer indication of the way attitudes have changed.

Sex as Work—Command Performance for Successful Sex

And yet when two sociologists, Lionel S. Lewis and Dennis Brissett, analyzed fifteen popular sex manuals, all of which were supposedly intended to help readers enjoy sexual play, they

Point of View

Box 10–3 / The Bedroom Olympiad

Not so very long ago, one might have answered the question of what role sex played in marital breakup by saying, quite simply, that if the marriage itself was satisfactory it generally followed that the sex within it would be satisfactory as well: physiology followed human feeling, and if love was there to begin with, making love posed no great problem. Not, one may be sure, that discreet couples didn't suffer difficulties, and often painful ones at that: frigidity, impotence, vastly unequal expectations, the brute lack of consideration for each other. But sex itself had not yet become, as it soon would, a highly compartmentalized activity, rather like high jumping; medals were not yet handed out for performance; no one as yet felt so clearly deprived, as they would later, if on the sexual side their lives fell somewhat short of *A Thousand and One Arabian Nights.* At a certain vague point, a good sex life stopped being a privilege and a delight and turned into a shrilly demanded right.

The good fight that such men as Bertrand Russell and Sigmund Freud fought in their time against ignorance, inhumane restraint, and hypocrisy in sexual life has been won, but can it be that the triumph has issued in not greater freedom but only in greater license, which is not at all the same thing?

Today's sexologists do not talk about human behavior but instead about the behavior of the human sexual apparatus. Such qualities as privacy, modesty, shame, fidelity fall outside the realm of their discussion, having long ago been replaced by such terms as foreplay, forepleasure, high-frequency impulses, ejaculation. Yet the sexologists have found a ready enough audience in America. Freud's campaign against undue abstinence in sex has come over the years to be translated into the tyrannical ideal that sexual activity is in itself a form of health; the more one has, the healthier one is.

It is all very easy to attack the sexologists, to demonstrate that where they are not sleazy they are shallow, yet in point of fact their influence has been extensive. Their presence hovers about bedrooms everywhere, their findings firmly lodged in the minds of lovers

found sex portrayed almost as a kind of work. Even the titles of the books, such as *Ideal Marriage: Its Physiology and Technique,* sounded more like something for a factory or laboratory than for a bedroom (1967). (See Box 10–3.)

The first lesson in these rather grim guides is that sex requires careful preparation. Many of the books recommend that couples begin by studying up on the subject, as they might for an important exam. One author presents a diagram of a woman's genitals and advises that it be "studied on the bridal night. . . . The husband should compare the diagram with his wife's genital region. . . ." (in Lewis and Brissett, 1967, p. 13) But preparation for sex is not all scholarship. The reader then graduates to the practical phase, which Lewis and Brissett refer to as "on-the-job training."

The second lesson taught by these guides is that sex, like any demanding job, requires competence. There are certain technical skills that must be mastered for a proper performance. One of the ironies of contemporary sexual life is that many people seem to have traded in a set of ethical "shoulds" and "should nots" for a set of technical rules that are just as inflexible.

as they go through their paces, their instructions recollected in the very rhythm of love-making.

In sex matters, imagination everywhere outdistances physical reality, with temperament as a consequence trained to permanent dissatisfaction. Through the courtesy of the sexologists, the brothel has been brought into the home, but to small avail. Everything is now permitted; nothing any longer good enough.

Clearly, as the old advertising tag had it, people seem to be getting more now and enjoying it less. Half a century ago, society, by imposing a strict code governing sexual behavior, would not let up on people; today, even though that code has long been dead, people will not let up on themselves. And so sex is asked to provide all that religion, work, and the family once provided—something greater than oneself, a means of relief from worldly concerns, a way of getting out of oneself and onto a higher plane of existence. Instead sex today does the very reverse: the relief it offers from the world is only as great as one's physical stamina, nothing is more sharply calculated to remind one of human limitations, and the completion of no other act so quickly brings one back to reality.

Perhaps nowhere is more asked of sex than in marriage, yet perhaps no other institution is less set up to deal with the modern sexual imagination. The ideal of the modern sexual imagination is variety and multiplicity. But in marriage—theoretically, at least—one person must serve where multitudes are forbidden. Sex looms larger today than ever before. Once people suffered sexual shortcomings in their partners, and while those shortcomings might be difficult, even painful to live with they were nonetheless generally deemed endurable. They are endurable no longer.

Once the old code of sexual repression was banished, married couples might have been able to affirm sex for what at its best it can be—a source of pleasure and delight and a means of potentially deepening and enriching their relationships. Once sex and the notion of sin were rightly riven, and guilt was removed from physical love, one might have looked to sex not as the main, but as another possibility for inward development. Alas, it was not to be. Instead of deepened and enriched relationships, instead of shedding guilt and developing inwardly, we have the bedroom olympics, with its accompanying tyranny of performance, unreal expectations, and misplaced salvationism.

Source: Excerpted from Joseph Epstein. *Divorced in America*. New York: Dutton, 1974.

A letter to the *Playboy* Advisor illustrates the point:

> Dear *Playboy*: I'll be damned if I can find out how long the average sex act lasts, not counting foreplay. Give me a break with some kind of norm, will you, so that I'll know how I'm doing?
> *L. L., Birmingham, Michigan* (*Playboy*, May 1969, p. 60)

What this reader seems to be asking for is a standard against which to judge his competence and normality. This is undoubtedly one of the chief reasons why people so avidly buy books about sexuality, even if, like some of the technical volumes published by Masters and Johnson, they turn out to be almost unreadable. People want to find out "how they're doing," which indicates the extent to which the work ethic, with its objective standards of competence, has invaded the bedroom.

If L. L. looked in the Kinsey volumes for standards of sexual competence, he must have been disappointed, for Kinsey points out that the range of sexual behavior from one individual to another is enormous. For example, Kinsey found one healthy male who had ejaculated just once over a thirty-year period, and another, equally healthy, who had ejaculated more than thirty times a week over the same period. Over a range this wide, averages are obviously not too meaningful (1948, p. 197).

A third lesson in the sex manuals that Lewis and Brissett analyzed is that sex should be done in a methodical, step-by-step way. A recurring theme in these books is that sex must proceed according to certain well-defined stages, none of which can be skipped, lest the entire operation be jeopardized. Couples are advised to control their immediate impulses so as to offer maximum satisfaction to the partner. There are even certain iron-clad rules, such as this one: "Foreplay should never last less than fifteen minutes even though a woman may be sufficiently aroused in five." Readers who take such suggestions seriously as the only correct way to enjoy sex are sure to end up with a less satisfactory sex life, not a better one. There is a certain irony in the fact that the writers of such manuals teach the lesson that "Not yet—later" applies even in sex, which is presumably one of the more spontaneous human activities.

Finally, the manuals assume that the goal of well-performed sex is orgasm, just as the object of a factory is to complete its product. By directing all effort toward the product, the manuals undoubtedly distract readers from the process, a pleasurable experience whether it leads to orgasm or not. "Getting there is half the fun" may be good advertising for an airline, but it is not the message in these work-oriented sex manuals.

In these manuals we see the triumph of performance over pleasure. Since sex is now widely accepted as a form of play, it follows that if it is not fun there must be something wrong with the way you are doing it. To correct the situation, you will have to work at it. Perhaps in a culture where many people still feel slightly guilty about sex, they can relieve their guilt by approaching it in a workmanlike way—and enhance their pleasure at the same time.

Sex manuals are not alone in turning play into labor. In a perceptive essay on the Masters and Johnson books, historian Paul Robinson comments on a long passage in which the authors describe in grueling physiological detail what happens as a prelude to orgasm. Robinson observes,

> This sounds more like an account of child labor in nineteenth-century Manchester than an experience of erotic excitement. Sex here has become tortuous and alienated, much of it, appropriately, carried out in the presence of, or aided by, machines. (1976, p. 178)

But in fairness to Masters and Johnson, who entitle one chapter of their recent book *The Pleasure Bond* (1976) "Why 'Working' at Sex Won't Work," it should be noted that in their role as sex therapists, they are keenly aware of the problems stemming from the "performance principle." A good deal of clinical evidence now shows that as a result of women's new assertiveness in claiming a right to equal sexual pleasure, some men are so threatened that they become impotent. Morton Hunt reports that

> women's liberation has altered the sexual relationships of countless married couples—often for the better, sometimes for the worse. . . . Many an angry woman gets even by deciding that her husband is a lousy lover and that she'll have no more of him except on her own terms; and many a man with traditional attitudes, alarmed or repelled by the new kind of woman, loses his drive or sexual self-assurance. Four out of five sexologists in a round-table discussion in the journal *Medical Aspects of Human Sexuality* held that impotence was definitely on the rise, and a team of three psychiatrists writing in *Archives of General Psychiatry* recently identified a syndrome they called "the new impotence"—the failure of the male to function, as a result of the new assertiveness of women. (1974, p. 186)

However, the latest sex manuals, those published since Lewis and Brisset made their survey, seem to allow some room for spontaneity, and picture sex as more playful than the older manuals did (Gordon and Shankweiler, 1971). And as we examine the role of sex in marriage, we shall see that recent studies have come to fairly optimistic conclusions about the quality of marital sexuality today.

THE SEXUAL BOND IN MARRIAGE

Despite all the TV commercials that sell every kind of product by associating it with sexual themes and yet never suggest sex between husband and wife, there is sex after marriage. In fact, one of the most important questions to ask about sex is what its significance in the marital relationship is.

A comparison of human sexual behavior with that of other species suggests our peculiar biological potential for a continuous bond. A unique fact about human biology is that, unlike other species, we have no period of conspicuous sexual excitability followed by a phase of indifference. Humans enjoy a relatively constant state of potential arousal in which sexual interest is influenced by emotional or psychological factors more than biological ones. This provides the basis for a continuous attachment between male and female, something that most other species do not have. In an important sense, human sexuality serves a social as well as a reproductive purpose.

This is not to say, of course, that throughout history intercourse has been a generally enjoyable experience for husband and wife, thus ensuring a lasting bond. The idea that spouses should share the "joys of sex" is a recent one, as the Church of England recognized in this statement, issued in 1958: "The new freedom of sexuality in our time . . . [provides] a gate to a new depth and joy in personal relationship between husband and wife" (in Krook, 1959, p. 336). Of course, our knowledge of the typical sexual satisfactions of marriage in other ages and cultures is scanty and unreliable, but it is not likely that marital sex has provided much mutual satisfaction for most couples. In fact, a survey of more than 190 societies concluded that in virtually all of them sex has been regarded as something a woman does for a man (Ford and Beach, 1951). It has had far more to do with the performance of conjugal duties than "the joy of sex," as the following account of marital sex in a traditional Japanese village illustrates:

> The sex act itself usually is a brief, businesslike affair with a minimum of foreplay. The husband, after waiting in the quilts at night for the rest of the household to settle into slumber, grasps his wife and satisfies himself as quietly and inconspicuously as possible, releasing his tensions and settling his duty to posterity at the same time. (Beardsley, Hall, and Ward, 1959, p. 57)

There are indications that not even in our own society does sex offer much mutual satisfaction for many couples. One of the most striking themes in interviews conducted by sociologists John Cuber and Peggy Harroff with several hundred upper-middle-class couples was the apathy many of them felt about sex. By middle age, a substantial number of couples "couldn't care less" about sex. One man described sex as "a damned nuisance," though he participated in it from time to time "with a minimum of fanfare." One woman, the wife of a prominent attorney, regarded sex as a duty, something she was expected to perform. Sex, she thought, is "a much overrated activity. . . . It's just not that important to either of us" (1968, pp. 172, 52).

Who Does What with Whom, How Quickly?

The Kinsey studies provide considerable evidence that for many couples a generation ago, intercourse was quite perfunctory. About three-quarters of the males surveyed in Kinsey's study (1948)—and probably, therefore, a clear majority of the American male population—were not able to delay orgasm for more than two minutes after the beginning of active copulation. For a "not inconsiderable number," climax was reached within a minute or less. Since many women cannot achieve an orgasm in less than about ten minutes of active copulation, and since most males normally reach only a single orgasm and do not continue intercourse afterward, these statistics suggest a lack of mutuality in intercourse and an indifference on the part of most males toward the female's satisfaction (1948, Chapter 3).

Though Kinsey was trained as a biologist, he showed that the kind of sexuality a male experiences is heavily influenced by social class membership. (However, he found that this factor is not so important for women.) Kinsey distinguished between what he called the upper-level group—college-educated, employed in the professions, usually living in suburban neighborhoods—and the lower-level group—people with no more than a high school education, working in semiskilled or manual labor, and living in less affluent neighborhoods. Typically, lower-level males experienced intercourse at earlier ages and were more active in premarital sex, patronizing prostitutes, and having homosexual experiences. Upper-level males, on the other hand, reported more masturbatory activities, petted more, and had more nocturnal emissions.

In marriage, too, the sexual experience of upper-level couples was different from that of lower-level couples. The upper-level couples reported more foreplay, more attention to female arousal, and in general a more mutually satisfying experience. As reported in *Sexual Behavior in the Human Female,* Kinsey found that upper-level women were more likely to reach climax in intercourse and to have orgasm more frequently. Among lower-level couples, lovemaking involved fewer preliminaries, less kissing, less fondling. Both nudity and oral sex were more often considered distasteful by such couples, and they experimented less with a variety of sexual positions (1953). In other words, the sexual practices of upper-level couples might be considered more sophisticated, more strongly guided by the belief that sex should be a mutually enjoyable experience.

In fact, there appear to be distinct similarities between the sexual attitudes and practices of lower-income couples in America and those in other countries. Sociologist Lee Rainwater has compared the meaning of sex for low-income groups in Mexico, Puerto Rico, England, and the United States, and found striking similarities with regard to certain basic assumptions (1964). Individuals belonging to the "culture of poverty" in all four countries agree, for example, that sex is a man's pleasure and a woman's duty. Women are assumed to be normally uninterested in sex; only "bad women" really enjoy it. Young women are sheltered from sexual knowledge. They are taught to regard marriage as desirable, but not because of the sexual experiences that go with it. Often, says Rainwater, husbands deliberately refrain from arousing their wives too much, for fear they might start to enjoy sex more than they should.

Rainwater believes that where the sex roles of spouses are highly segregated, there is little likelihood that the wife will enjoy marital sex, or that it will serve as a kind of intimate communication. In such marriages,

> husbands and wives tend to be fairly isolated from each other. They do not seem to depend on each other emotionally, though each performs important services for the other. . . . Mutually gratifying sexual relations are difficult because neither party is accustomed to relating intimately to the other. (1964, p. 463)

We might speculate that for centuries the meaning of marital sexuality for most couples more closely resembled the pattern that exists among today's low-income couples rather than that of upper-level couples, for whom sex more often offers a real means of intimate communication.

More than a generation has passed since the Kinsey studies were published, and it is interesting to examine the results of recent studies of marital sex to see what has changed during that period. In our discussion of marital sexuality today, we will take a closer look at recent studies of the frequency of marital intercourse. Overall, perhaps the most interesting conclusion from the more reliable studies that have been conducted in recent years (Bell and Bell, 1972; Levin and Levin, 1975; Westoff, 1974) is that rates of marital intercourse have *not* changed very much during the last thirty years, although as we shall see, there does appear to be more erotic variety today. Judging from the conclusions of at least one recent study that was based upon questionnaires completed by more than 4,000 men from a variety of educational and occupational backgrounds, it appears that there are fewer social class differences in sexual attitudes and behavior than there were when the original Kinsey studies were conducted (Pietropinto and Simenauer, 1977). If the social class background of spouses is no longer so closely associated with rates of marital intercourse as Kinsey suggested, their age still is. All of the recent sex surveys show the same pattern that was described in the Kinsey reports: as time passes, couples have intercourse less often. Among young couples, its average frequency is about three times a week; by the time couples are in their late twenties and early thirties, frequency has decreased to about one to two times per week; and by their fifties, frequency of intercourse declines to about once a week. One way of exploring why this decline occurs is to examine the differences between male and female sexuality.

Male and Female Sexuality

With today's general shift toward a companionship marriage comes the assumption that sex should be a mutually enjoyable experience. It is not uncommon now for wives to say they want more frequent sex in their marriage (Hunt, 1974, p. 217). The double standard for premarital sex, as we noted in Chapter 4, has begun to give way to a more liberal single standard. And in part, these changes have become possible because the old belief that women are sexually indifferent is being replaced by a belief in equal sexuality.

But are men and women really alike in their sexuality? Are male and female sexual patterns really similar enough to allow the kind of intense sexual bond in marriage that is often considered a realistic goal today?

Kinsey's studies conducted in the 1940s showed that before marriage, the average male experienced more than six times more orgasms—over 1,500 in all—than the average female. In marriage, some women were unable ever to achieve orgasm with their husbands, though the husbands almost never had this problem. Among the females Kinsey studied, 9 percent had never reached climax. And whereas men from all social class settings were similar in that they rarely went without sex for long, the sexual patterns of women appeared to be more irregular: women commonly alternated between periods of prolonged abstinence and periods of considerable sexual activity.

But Kinsey believed these differences could be explained by the different psychological influences that males and females experience. Had the sexual instructions given the two sexes been more similar, as indeed they have become since Kinsey conducted his studies, perhaps there would not have been quite so many differences between male and female sexual responsiveness.

Kinsey's data on sexual aging, however, do show one potentially serious difference between the sexes, one based on biological facts. In terms of total sexual outlet or capacity for frequent and repeated experiences, the male reaches his peak a few years after puberty. As Kinsey put it, "The high point of [male] sexual performance is, in actuality, somewhere around sixteen or seventeen years of age. It is not later" (1948, p. 219). Which is to say that by the time that most males marry, their sexual potential is past its peak. As the years go by, males gradually require somewhat more time to attain an erection and longer rest periods between sexual acts.

During adolescence, when the male is at his maximum capacity, the female is just beginning to develop her sexual responsiveness. She does not develop this responsiveness all of a sudden, as does the male. In fact, the average female does not reach her peak of sexual activity until about age twenty-eight, and after that she experiences a long plateau of sexual responsiveness. This does not taper off until late in middle age, and then only gradually. One writer sees the following implications in these two patterns:

> From a sexual standpoint men and women were like ships passing in the night. The male's years of greatest sexual capacity came at a time when women were relatively unresponsive, while the female's sustained years of maximum activity corresponded to the man's years of sexual decline. The mathematics of sex, it seemed, were unfavorable to marriage. (Robinson, 1976, p. 91)

But this view seems unduly pessimistic, for to be past one's peak is not to be out of commission. Kinsey's data also show that sexual activities continue for many men to a later age than was previously believed. Among the men Kinsey studied, only one-quarter had become impotent by age seventy (1948, p. 235). Masters and Johnson came to the same conclusion, and went on to state that in most cases impotence is caused by psychological factors such as the fear of not being able to perform sexually, and not by physiological ones. Thus, it is undoubtedly the different sexual scripts still taught to males and females, rather than biological differences, that best account for the declining rates of intercourse in marriage over the years. As Gagnon and Simon point out,

> the conditions under which we learn to be sexual in our society make it extremely difficult to maintain high levels of sexual performance with a single partner over long periods of time. (1973, p. 84)

The frequency of intercourse among lower-class couples apparently declines more rapidly than that of middle-class couples. But at all socioeconomic levels, the decline is due in part to the difficulty of relating sexually to a spouse who has taken on new roles such as parenthood, which he or she did not have during courtship. The reason middle-class couples maintain a more active sex life, Gagnon and Simon contend, is that they are better able to derive stimulation from such sources as romantic settings or erotic conversations, and to evoke sexual fantasies that stimulate a response to one's spouse (1973, p. 83).

While Kinsey's studies turned up many differences between male and female sexuality, Masters and Johnson are at pains to demonstrate some similarities. Like Kinsey, they aspire to scientific objectivity, but their emphasis on male–female similarities in sexual response and the way they argue their case betray a strong concern about the sexual compatibility of men and women in marriage (Robinson, 1976, p. 163). Their discoveries in female sexuality and insistence on the harmony of the male and female sexual response have had a very strong impact on contemporary thinking about marital sexuality.

Masters and Johnson announce in the introduction to *Human Sexual Response* that the similarities between male and female sexuality will be one of their themes: "Again and again attention will be drawn to direct parallels in human sexual response that exist to a degree never previously appreciated . . ." (1966, p. 8). Among these parallels are the heightened blood pressure, increased pulse, and muscular tension that accompany sexual excitement for both males and females, and a sex flush that may develop for either sex during arousal. Masters and Johnson also note that erection and vaginal lubrication appear to be parallel responses.

By examining and publicizing the multiorgasmic potential of women they have been very influential in destroying the old belief in natural female frigidity. And in this way, Masters and Johnson have indeed established a similarity between the sexes that was often denied in the past. They have even established that the timing of orgasmic contractions—at 0.8-second intervals—is precisely the same for both males and females. Although this similarity apparently has little practical significance in heightening sexual pleasure, one writer believes that for Masters and Johnson "it suggests that at the supreme sexual moment men and women are in perfect harmony. They march to the same drummer" (Robinson, 1976, p. 169).

But if Masters and Johnson seem at times to be straining to find similarities in male and female sexuality, they readily agree with Kinsey that sexual incompatibility in marriage is very common and a major factor in causing marital tensions. Although Kinsey's research was not directly concerned with the impact of sex on marital adjustment, he estimated that for at least 75 percent of the upper-middle-class couples in America who seek a divorce, sexual problems are a contributing factor. Masters and Johnson make a conservative estimate that in at least half of all American marriages there are some serious sexual problems (1970, p. 369).

In fact, Masters and Johnson are at least as well known for their success as sexual therapists as they are for their research. The rapid growth of clinics like theirs, where couples can go for treatment of sexual dysfunctions, is one of the most significant developments in marital counseling over the past decade (see Box 10–4). If the rocks on which many couples run aground are in bed, as Big Mama said in Tennessee Williams' play *Cat on a Hot Tin Roof,* such therapists offer new hope that they can be removed.

Yet the emphasis on shared sexual enjoyment in marriage, like other heightened expectations in today's marriages, may lead to greater marital instability. Influenced by the attention that Masters and Johnson have helped to focus on female orgasm, many young couples may conclude that there are unresolvable differences if sex is less than an earth-shaking experience for both of them in the early months of marriage. If sexual pleasure is often regarded today as a right to which both spouses are entitled, it is important to think of it too as a result of compatibility that typically takes a certain amount of time to acquire.

Both as researchers and pioneers in the direct treatment of sexual problems, William H. Masters and Virginia E. Johnson have substantially added to our knowledge of human sexuality.

Introducing the Marriage and Family Professionals

Box 10–4 / The Sex Therapists

Sexual problems used to be regarded mainly as symptoms of underlying psychological problems or interpersonal conflicts that could be treated only by a lengthy process of psychoanalysis. But since Masters and Johnson publicized the success of their direct treatment of sexual problems, sex therapy clinics have opened up all around the country. It is now recognized that, with the assistance of qualified therapists, many couples can resolve their sexual problems in a relatively short period of time.

What Is Sex Therapy?

Sex therapy differs from psychotherapy and marital counseling in that it focuses on sexual dysfunctions, and uses a direct learning approach rather than "talking therapies" to change sexual behavior. The most common dysfunctions are impotence or frigidity, premature or retarded ejaculation, and vaginismus (a condition in which the vaginal muscles close involuntarily, thus blocking penetration).

At the Masters and Johnson clinic, couples suffering from such sexual dysfunctions enter a two-week program. Masters and Johnson believe that sexual problems are never the fault of one person, but rather that they involve both partners, and must be treated as such. Thus, couples are always treated as a unit. In order to facilitate communication during therapy, a man and woman serve as cotherapists in the Masters and Johnson clinic.

The therapists first prepare a detailed sexual history for each partner. They try to persuade the couple that sex is a natural function, and that the greatest pleasure is to be gained simply by relaxing and letting it happen. The emphasis is on pleasure, not performance. The couple is instructed to practice certain sexual exercises in the privacy of the hotel room where they stay during the two-week session. Once elementary pleasuring techniques have been mastered, the couple gradually moves on to intercourse. In between sessions of sexual play, the couple meets with the therapists for frank discussions of their successes and failures: then the therapists suggest new exercises and ways of overcoming the problems that may remain.

Specific techniques are used for the treatment of each type of sexual dysfunction. If the problem is premature ejaculation, for example, the man is advised to lie on his back with the woman sitting in a comfortable position, with easy access to his genitals. She stimulates him to erection, but before he reaches orgasm, she grasps his penis below

Albert Ellis, a psychologist who often writes about marital sexuality, has had this to say about couples who have unrealistically high sexual expectations:

> Although there is nothing to be lost, and often much to be gained by a husband and wife trying to adjust themselves sexually so that they each achieve an orgasm during intercourse, and often achieve it simultaneously, there is a danger in their convincing themselves that mutual orgasm in intercourse is the only or even necessarily the best mode of sex satisfaction on all occasions. Orgasm is orgasm, however and whenever achieved, and may be thoroughly enjoyable on a nonsimultaneous basis. A husband may legitimately give his wife an orgasm before or after he has one himself—or without ever having one himself. Similarly, a wife may help her husband to

the glans and squeezes firmly between fingers and thumb. The man loses his urge to ejaculate, and partially loses his erection as well. This sequence is repeated until greater control over ejaculation has been gained. The couple then attempts intercourse, with the woman sitting astride the man. Again, if the man feels the need to ejaculate, he withdraws, and the woman uses the squeeze technique. Eventually, by this means, he develops the ability to control orgasm himself.

If the couple's sexual problem is that the woman is unable to experience orgasm, the emphasis is on her responses. During the first sessions, the couple assumes a position in which the woman sits with her back against her partner's chest, and her legs open. This allows the man easy access to her breasts and genitals, and also allows her to guide his hands, showing him the most effective ways of giving her pleasure. When the woman succeeds in responding orgasmically to these methods, the couple then tries intercourse in the same position used in the treatment of premature ejaculation.

Other sex clinics vary the treatment method somewhat: most do not insist upon the intensive two-week sequence used by Masters and Johnson; some use just one therapist rather than two. But all try to help couples to overcome sexual problems through active treatment.

How Effective Is It?

Most clinics report very impressive records of success with sex therapy. In *Human Sexual Inadequacy,* Masters and Johnson report an 80 percent success rate. Helen Singer Kaplan, author of *The New Sex Therapy* (1974), and director of the sex therapy program at the Payne Whitney Clinic of New York, reports about the same rate of success among couples who have no unusual psychological problems, and about a 50 percent success rate with those that do. Sex therapists are able to cure some problems, such as premature ejaculation, in virtually all cases.

How to Find a Qualified Sex Therapist

It is estimated that there are now about 5,000 clinics nationwide which offer sex therapy. But, as Masters and Johnson have stated, many are run by individuals who are either unqualified or inadequately trained, so the couple looking for sex therapy is well advised to examine carefully credentials and programs. Currently, no state has well-defined educational standards or licensing practices for sex therapists. The American Association of Sex Educators and Counselors has designed a certification program that insists upon academic training, written examinations, and supervised therapy experience. This organization publishes a useful volume, *A Guide to Certified Sex Therapists and Educators,* which is available from them at 5010 Wisconsin Avenue, N.W., Suite 304, Washington, D. C. 20016. The price is $3.00.

achieve a climax before, during, or entirely apart from her own climax(es). In many marriages, the achievement of simultaneous orgasm in intercourse will seldom or never occur; and still the spouses may have a truly satisfying and perfectly compatible sex life. (1962, p. 88)

If the sexual scripts taught to males and females today are not as different as they were several decades ago when Kinsey conducted his studies, the ideal of an intense sexual bond between husband and wife is still very difficult to achieve.

Marital Sexuality Today

The proliferation of clinics for the treatment of sexual problems, articles in mass circulation magazines about inorgasmic women and "the new impotence" among men, candid discussions about married couples who masturbate—all of these might be seen as signs that something is going wrong with marital sexuality. Do married couples today really experience more problems and fewer satisfactions in their sexual lives than people did a generation ago? Or does it just look that way because it is now more acceptable to talk candidly about sexual problems, and because our expectations of sexual pleasure in marriage are higher than they were?

Recent studies of marital sexuality suggest that rising expectations, rather than declining satisfactions, account for much of the current concern about sex in marriage. Morton Hunt puts it this way:

> The progress our society has made toward fuller and freer sexuality has revolutionized our expectations and made many of us so intolerant of our dissatisfactions that we forget the improvement that has taken place in our lives; like all partially liberated people, we are more discontented now than we were before our lot began to improve. Yet improvement is widespread and real. . . . (1974, p. 179)

Hunt's study, conducted under the auspices of the Playboy Foundation in 1972, provides comprehensive data allowing us to assess the changes that have taken place since the Kinsey studies. We should note, however, that the sampling procedures used by Hunt have been criticized (see Reiss, 1976, p. 177). Hunt began by making telephone inquiries in twenty-four cities around the country to locate a sample of the eighteen-and-over population willing to participate in the study. Not unexpectedly, considering the sensitivity of the topic, only one in five of the people contacted agreed to participate. Those who did agree were undoubtedly more sexually liberal than the adult population as a whole, and so probably overestimate the extent of change. Nonetheless, the study does provide data that allow us to see trends in marital sexuality, especially since they have proven similar to findings from the National Fertility Studies conducted in 1965 and 1970 (Westoff, 1974), and to responses from 100,000 female readers of *Redbook* magazine to a questionnaire about sexual attitudes and practices, designed by sociologist Robert R. Bell (Levin and Levin, 1975).

Summarizing the Playboy Foundation study, Hunt comments that "not only are today's married Americans having intercourse more frequently, but they seem to be doing so more imaginatively, voluptuously, and playfully than their counterparts of a generation ago" (1974, p. 195). Findings from the National Fertility Studies and the *Redbook* survey both seem to point to the same conclusion.

The level of erotic activity among married couples has increased substantially since Kinsey's studies in the 1940s. Whereas Kinsey found that four out of ten men in the age category twenty-six to thirty-five continued to masturbate after marriage, Hunt reports that seven out of ten now do so, and with greater frequency. Kinsey found that a third of the married women in the same age category masturbated, and that the median frequency for those women was about ten times a year. Hunt found that married women masturbate no more frequently than before, but twice as many of them do so (1974, p. 33). In the *Redbook* survey, about three-quarters of the married women of all age categories reported that they have masturbated at least occasionally since marriage (Levin and Levin, 1975, p. 56).

If Hunt's figures are to be trusted, they show that married couples of all ages are having coitus more frequently than their counterparts did in the 1940s (see Table 10–1). The National Fertility Studies, which were based on a more representative sample, show lower frequencies of intercourse for all age categories than do Hunt's data, but they still indicate that it takes place more often than it did in the 1940s. Significantly, when the data from the 1965 and 1970 National Fertility Studies are compared, they show that couples in all age categories were making love more frequently at the end of that five-year period (Westoff, 1974, p. 137).

And judging from reports on the percentage

of women who reach orgasm during intercourse, couples are not only having sex more often, they are enjoying it more. Hunt reports (1974) that about 75 percent of the young women in his sample were orgasmic, whereas only 57 percent in the Kinsey study experienced orgasm (1953, p. 339).

These studies provide data not only on how often, but also on *how* couples make love. The conclusion is that sex has become more varied, a more mutually enjoyable experience. Hunt's study indicates that couples today engage in more foreplay, and that the median duration of intercourse is longer (about ten minutes) than it was in the 1940s (about two minutes). Furthermore, oral sex is practiced by a higher percentage of couples today. And whereas Kinsey estimated that more than two-thirds of all married couples in the 1940s had never experimented with any position other than the one in which the woman lies on her back, with her husband above and facing her, both Hunt's data and the responses to the *Redbook* survey indicate that it is much more common today for couples to use other positions. The *Redbook* survey finds, for example, that a great majority of wives—78 percent—are active partners, "obviously rejecting the Victorian notion that a 'respectable' woman doesn't move" (Levin and Levin, 1975, p. 57).

Overall, it appears that the widely discussed sexual revolution has had at least as much of an impact among married couples as it has on premarital sex. (See Box 10–5.) Both the Hunt study and the *Redbook* survey indicate that there is much less conflict between the sexes about preferred frequency of sex than there used to be (Hunt, 1974, p. 217; Levin and Levin, 1975, p. 54).

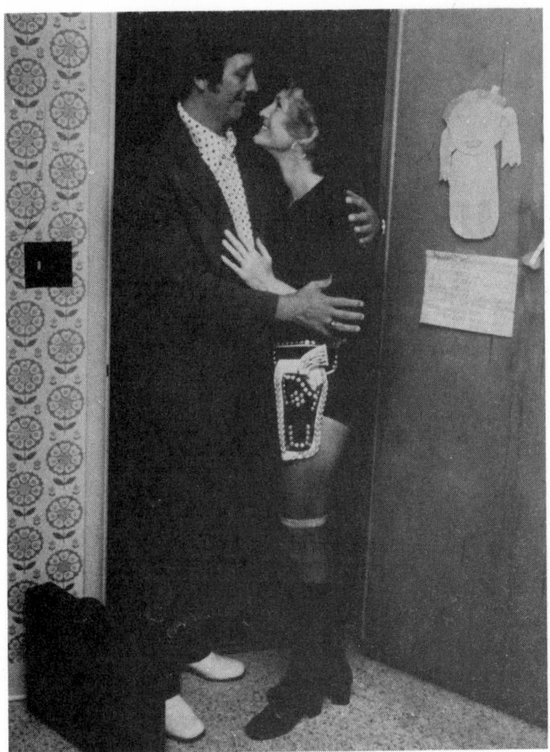

Sexual liberation within marriage means that many couples feel freer to explore their sexual fantasies.

Significantly, both studies reach quite optimistic conclusions about the state of the sexual union today:

Table 10–1 / Marital Coitus in the United States: Frequency per Week, 1938–1949 and 1972

1938–1949		*1972*	
Age	Median	Age	Median
16–25	2.45	18–24	3.25
26–35	1.95	25–34	2.55
36–45	1.40	35–44	2.00
46–55	0.85	45–54	1.00
56–60	0.50	55 and over	1.00

Source: Morton Hunt, *Sexual Behavior in the 1970's*. New York: Dell, 1974, p. 196.

Biological Aspects of Sex and Reproduction

Box 10–5 / Sexual Myths and Fallacies

Discussions about human sexuality are often more candid today than they were a generation ago, but many myths and fallacies persist. Here, in a series of excerpts from James McCary's book, *Human Sexuality*, is a list of common misconceptions.

1. *That each individual is allotted just so many sexual experiences, and that when they are used up, sexual activity is finished for that person.* This notion has troubled mankind for centuries, yet it is totally false. In fact, the degree of sexual activity that humans are capable of maintaining throughout the years seems to be correlated in quite an opposite manner: the earlier men or women mature physically, the longer their sexual reproductive ability continues; and the more sexually active a person is and the earlier the age at which he begins that activity, the longer it continues into old age.

2. *That sexual intercourse should be avoided during pregnancy.* There is no evidence to indicate that a pregnant woman with no unusual complications should not regularly engage in sexual intercourse or automanipulative activity to orgasm until late in the third trimester. Quite naturally, sensible precautions should be taken against excessive pressure on the abdomen, deep penile penetration, and infection.

3. *That there is a difference between vaginal and clitoral orgasms.* It has taken the recent Masters and Johnson research to convince many medical specialists and scientists

> The *Redbook* data stand as impressive evidence in support of the view that sex is alive and well and flourishing in most homes—unless, of course, one believes that 100,000 women have not told the truth. No matter how many years they have been married, seven out of every ten women report that the sexual aspect of marriage is "good" or "very good," and only two out of ten describe it as "fair." (Levin and Levin, 1975, p. 55)

The leveling of sex-role distinctions is an important contributing factor in the tendency toward more mutually enjoyable sex in marriage. We noted earlier in this chapter that where the sex roles of spouses are highly segregated, sex is less likely to offer mutual satisfaction, and data from the National Fertility Studies suggest the same conclusion. As demographer Charles F. Westoff says, three factors seem to be associated with higher-than-average marital intercourse: the wife's educational level, egalitarian attitudes, and commitment to a career. But obviously these are interrelated. A woman who has more education is also more likely to pursue a career and to have been exposed to egalitarian attitudes. Such women are more likely to believe in and practice a more sexually assertive role in marriage. In other words, they have sexual expectations that are more like their husbands' than do women with less education (Westoff, 1974, p. 137).

Thus, again it appears that many of the changing sexual practices in marriage can be explained as the result of new sexual scripts compatible with more egalitarian sex-role expectations. "One could argue," says Morton Hunt,

> that the principal effect of sexual liberation upon American life has been to increase the freedom

that women do *not* have two kinds of orgasms. From a purely physiological viewpoint, direct clitoral stimulation usually produces a somewhat stronger orgasmic response than does the indirect stimulation of the clitoris in vaginal penetration; but many women find the latter more satisfying because of various psychological factors.

4. *That menopause or hysterectomy terminates a woman's sex life.* Kinsey and other researchers have shown that a woman's sexual desire ordinarily continues undiminished until she is sixty years of age or older. Ordinarily no physical reasons exist for a woman's sex life to end because of menopause or hysterectomy.

5. *That a large penis is important to a woman's gratification, and that the man with a large penis is more sexually potent than the man with a small penis.* The size of the penis has practically no relationship to a man's ability to satisfy a woman sexually. The only exceptions would be when sexual pleasure is diminished because the penis is too large and causes the woman pain; or when the penis is so unusually small that penetration and pelvic contact cannot be maintained.

6. *That it is dangerous to have sexual intercourse during menstruation.* Menstrual blood is perfectly harmless in content to both man and woman; no damage occurs from penile penetration; and a woman's sex drive ordinarily does not diminish during the menstrual period.

Some other beliefs that are unfounded, and have been disproved, are:

7. *That an intact hymen is proof of virginity, and the absence of a hymen proves nonvirginity.*
8. *That masturbation is dangerous, and causes pimples or acne.*
9. *That men and women lose their sex drive after the age of fifty.*
10. *That sterilization diminishes the sex drive.*

Source: From *Human Sexuality*, by James Leslie McCary. Copyright © 1973 Litton Educational Publishing, Inc. Reprinted by permission of Van Nostrand Reinhold Company.

of husbands, and even more of wives to explore and enjoy a wide range of gratifying sexual practices within the marital relationship. Most discussions of sexual liberation concentrate upon its meaning for the unmarried, the unfaithful, and the unconventional, but by far the largest number of people whose sexual behavior has been influenced by it are the faithful (or relatively faithful) husbands and wives. (1974, p. 179)

FORSAKING ALL OTHERS—THE QUESTION OF SEXUAL FIDELITY

In many societies sex has been regarded as sacred or magical, and thus in need of control by rules and taboos. Every society regulates it in one way or another, but that does not always mean that husbands and wives are expected to confine their sexual activities to each other. In fact, the expectation that marriage should be both permanent and sexually exclusive is relatively rare. In a survey of sexual customs in 185 preliterate societies, anthropologist Clellan S. Ford and psychologist Frank A. Beach report that only about one-sixth of these societies formally restrict sexual activities to a single mate. The rest grant formal approval of certain types of extramarital liaisons, or at least tolerate them (1951).

In the United States, both religious organizations and legal authorities have tried to restrict sex to marriage. The Seventh Commandment, prohibiting adultery, reflects the restrictions that Judaism and Christianity place on sex. And although adultery is rarely prosecuted, it is still a crime in most states, punishable by up to five years imprisonment in states such as Maine, Vermont, Oklahoma, and South Dakota. Furthermore, adultery is an acceptable ground for divorce in many states; it is considered a breach of the marital agreement, something that no spouse is forced to tolerate.

Judging by recent polls, the ideal of fidelity in marriage is still considered important by most people. In 1978, the Gallup organization conducted a poll in which Americans of different backgrounds and ages were asked how they felt about a married person having sexual relations with someone other than their marriage partner. A large majority—81 percent—of those who answered the question said either that extramarital sex is "always wrong" or "almost always wrong." And although women consider sexual fidelity to be slightly more important than men do, both sexes generally disapprove of extramarital sex, with the strongest disapproval among older adults and those who had not attended college. Although survey findings such as these suggest that there has not been as much relaxation of the norm of sexual exclusivity as is often assumed, it is noteworthy that this poll indicates that 22 percent of the young adults in the eighteen to twenty-nine age category do reject the norm, stating that extramarital sex is either "wrong only sometimes" or "not wrong at all" (Gallup, 1978).

However, Kinsey's work and other more recent studies of sexual behavior have indicated that disapproval of extramarital sex does not mean that people refrain from it. On this subject actual behavior still differs conspicuously from most people's beliefs about how they *ought* to behave. Many of Kinsey's readers were shocked by his finding that by age forty about half of all men and one-fourth of all women had engaged in at least one extramarital affair. Kinsey's data also suggested that the affairs of married men are most likely to occur when they are younger, while women are more likely to stray when they are older. Kinsey found that most of the liaisons of both men and women were one-night stands, not extended affairs like the ones commonly depicted in popular fiction. And among those who did have extramarital liaisons, only a relatively small percentage—about 19 percent of the women—had been involved with five or more partners. After noting that nearly three-quarters of the men interviewed said they would like extramarital relations, Kinsey concluded that "the human male would be promiscuous . . . throughout the whole of his life if there were no social restrictions" (1948, p. 589).

How much has the incidence of extramarital sex changed since Kinsey's study a generation ago? Judging from the pattern described by Morton Hunt's study, surprisingly little. In the author's words,

> Our data in this area suggest that in the past generation there has been almost no measurable increase in the number of American husbands who ever have extramarital experience, and only a limited increase in the number of American wives who do so. The overall incidence for our sample of married men of all ages appears to be basically unchanged from that of a generation ago. Only among men under twenty-five do we find any significant increase, but even that increase is of moderate proportions. As for our sample of married women, there is no evidence of any overall increase in incidence compared to a generation ago. Among wives under twenty-five, however, there is a very large increase, but even this has only brought the incidence of extramarital behavior for these young women close to—but not yet on a par with—the incidence of extramarital behavior among under-twenty-five husbands. (1974, p. 254)

As Hunt acknowledges, this is a surprising conclusion in view of the recent widespread discussion of sexual latitude in marriage, swinging, and the contention that extramarital sex might improve a marriage. Hunt suggests that discussion of such topics today means only that the climate of opinion allows people to talk and write about such matters more openly. But even if there is no overall increase in the incidence of extramarital sex, as there definitely has been in premarital sex, there is one significant development: the large increase in extramarital sex for women under twenty-five. Today, about three-fourths as many young wives as husbands of this age venture outside of marriage for sex, suggesting that the double standard has broken down in extra- as in premarital sex (1974, p. 263).

In the survey that Hunt summarizes there was a series of questions about attitudes toward extramarital sex. The answers to these questions, like the responses in the Gallup survey we mentioned, were, in the author's words, "remarkably traditional." A large majority of young and old alike indicated they would not accept, even hypothetically, various forms of extramarital sex (1978, p. 256). As Hunt previously has observed:

> The most common attitude toward the extramarital affair is somewhat like the American attitude toward paying one's income tax: Many people cheat—some a little, some a lot; most who don't would like to but are afraid; neither the actual nor the would-be cheaters admit the truth or defend their views except to a few confidants; and practically all of them teach their children the accepted traditional code though they know they neither believe in it themselves nor expect that their children will do so when they grow up. (1969, p. 14)

Condemnation of any kind of extramarital sex has been so widespread that until recently almost everything written on the subject has been meant to express moral disapproval rather than to perform empirical analysis. Cuber once noted that even among social scientists, discussions of extramarital involvements had "a clear tendency to concentrate on negative aspects and to present them more vividly." Most discussions, he wrote, overlooked

> the enormous variations in adulterous experience with respect to its function in the lives of the participants, its relationship to marriage, and its impact on the mental health of the participants. . . . The effects on the marriage of the adulterous spouse have been presumed always to be destructive, and the effects on the mental health of all the participants have been assumed to be deleterious. (1969, p. 190)

Lately, however, researchers and clinicians have begun to point out that affairs are common in good marriages as well as bad ones, that they are not invariably destructive, and that in some cases they may actually help the marriage. Psychologist Albert Ellis (1969), for example, contends that there are healthy as well as disturbed reasons for having extramarital sex. Among the positive reasons he includes the desire to enjoy a variety of sexual partners, the desire for a richer life experience, the desire for adventure and escape from a humdrum existence, sexual curiosity, and the frustration brought on by sexual deprivation. Ellis does not declare that adultery under these conditions is morally right, merely that it is within the range of social and psychological normality and that it may lead to satisfaction for the parties involved. Among the disturbed reasons for infidelity he mentions hostility toward one's spouse, an inability to face the ordinary frustrations of daily life, the desire to find relief from sexual disturbances, a need for ego-bolstering, and the desire to escape from marital problems rather than facing them.

Perhaps the most significant feature of Ellis' discussion is that he regards extramarital sex exactly as he would any other behavior. Rather than being automatically ruled out by religious prohibitions, Ellis believes that extramarital sex should be judged as advisable or inadvisable according to both its motives and interpersonal consequences.

Even some theologians and religious leaders have suggested in recent years that, under certain conditions, extramarital sex might be acceptable. For example, a study group of Presbyterians produced a document for discussion that included this statement: "We recognize that there may be exceptional circumstances where extramarital sexual activity may not be contrary to the interests of a faithful concern for the well-being of the marriage partner." And Deane William Ferm, an ordained minister and chaplain at Mount Holyoke College, has written:

> We must give consideration to some couples who can either save their marriage or strengthen an

> already existing happy marriage through extramarital experiences. Are such extramarital relationships morally wrong? Once again, we should answer that question in terms of the total context and not in terms of the sex act itself. If extramarital sex harms the already existing human relationships, then it is morally wrong . . ." (in Francoeur, 1972, pp. 96, 99)

Thus, even in extramarital sex the ground for judging behavior is shifting. A case of adultery is no longer to be judged on moralistic or legalistic grounds but in terms of its contribution to intimate relationships.

Kinsey must have offended many readers with this statement in the *Male* volume: "There are some individuals," he wrote, "whose sexual adjustments in marriage have undoubtedly been helped by extramarital experience. . . . Extramarital intercourse has had the effect of convincing some males that the relationships with their wives were more satisfactory than they had realized" (1948, p. 593). And in the *Female* volume, he wrote that "Sometimes sexual adjustments with the spouse had improved as a result of the female's extramarital experience" (1953, p. 433). Furthermore, he found that in half of the cases where the husband knew or suspected that his wife was having an affair, most such incidents resulted either in no marital difficulty or only in minor ones. In this respect, Kinsey's data help us to avoid the stereotyped assumption that extramarital sex is invariably destructive.

Since the time of the Kinsey studies, several researchers have inquired into the connection between extramarital sex, dissatisfactions with sex in marriage, and more general feelings of marital satisfaction—and the results have been quite contradictory. In one study, where the investigators used personality tests to assess the characteristics of people involved in sex outside of marriage, the conclusion was that such people seem to be distinguished mainly by their disregard for conventional social restraints (Neubeck and Schletzer, 1962). In other studies, which differentiated between reported marital satisfaction of men and women, investigators came to different conclusions. In one study of this type, which used a large sample of subjects married for varying lengths of time, researchers noted that among men who have affairs, only those who engage in extramarital sex early in their marriages report less satisfaction, as compared with married men who have not had affairs. Among women there is a different pattern. In general, it appears that for them extramarital affairs are consistently associated with lower marital satisfaction, and those reports of low marital satisfaction are most marked among older women who are having affairs (Glass and Wright, 1977). Other studies have found this same pattern of lower self-reported marital satisfaction among women who have extramarital sex, but their authors are careful to point out that there are many people who engage in such affairs and also express considerable feelings of marital satisfaction (Bell, Turner, and Rosen, 1975).

Here is how Hunt summarizes the research on people who engage in extramarital affairs:

> (1) Many of the unfaithful—perhaps even a majority—are not seriously dissatisfied with their marriages nor their mates and a fair number are more or less happily married; (2) Only about a third—perhaps even fewer—appear to seek extramarital sex for neurotic motives; the rest do so for nonpathological reasons; and (3) Many of the unfaithful—perhaps even a majority—do not feel that they, their mates, nor their marriages have been harmed; in my own sample, a tenth said that their marriages had been helped or made more tolerable by their infidelity. (*Playboy*, August 1971, p. 168)

Swinging, Secret Affairs, and Intimate Friendships

There are various types of extramarital sex, each conforming to certain rules. The businessman who has a one-night fling on a trip to a distant city; the woman who has a long-term affair involving considerable emotional attachment, which she keeps secret from her husband; the young couple who occasionally enjoy sex with another couple, close friends—in each case extramarital sex has a different meaning. The first two are examples of nonconsensual adultery: the spouse does not consent and probably does not know. The third is an example of consensual adultery. Let us look briefly first at secret affairs, then at intimate friendships, and finally at the form of extramarital sex that receives the most attention: swinging.

The secret affair is still the most common form of extramarital activity. Hunt's data indicate that about half of the married men having affairs say their wives have no notion of what they are doing, and another three-tenths say their wives have only suspicions about it. The stress on concealing the matter from the spouse reflects the strength of the belief that marriage should be monogamous. "Our data indicate," writes Hunt,

> that there is still a very great emphasis on secrecy, based on the clear recognition that such extramarital acts will be perceived by the spouse as disloyalty, partial abandonment, and a repudiation of marital love. And this means that for the person engaged in extramarital acts there must be internal conflict, even if no perceived guilt. (1974, p. 270)

Perhaps we can partially explain the lure of the forbidden affair by noting that there is considerable evidence of heightened sexual attraction under conditions of high anxiety (Dutton and Aron, 1974). There is a frequently repeated tale about a coronary patient who asks his physician whether he should continue sexual activity. The doctor's reply is, "By all means—but only with your wife. I don't want you to get too excited." There may be more truth in that story than most people would want to admit. In one study of men with a history of heart failure who died after intercourse, it was determined that twenty-seven out of the thirty-four reported deaths of this type occurred after extramarital intercourse (in McCary, 1975, p. 268).

A very different form of extramarital sex, intimate friendship, is described by one researcher as an "otherwise traditional friendship in which sexual intimacy is considered appropriate behavior [and] which appears to be the natural outgrowth of practicing sexually open marriage over an extended period of time" (Ramey, 1976). Unlike secret affairs, intimate friendship involves the consent and approval of the spouse. In some marriages, sexual exclusivity is regarded as something not necessarily desirable. Intimate friendship is person-centered sex that may lead eventually to the establishment of a group marriage involving considerable complexity and commitment (see Chapter 13).

Swinging, in many ways, is just the opposite. Swingers adhere to an elaborate set of rules that limit personal involvement while allowing recreational sex. In the film *Bob and Carol and Ted and Alice,* Bob discovers Carol, his wife, with another man in their bedroom. Carol had known that Bob was having an affair and they had agreed that she was free to do the same, but now Bob is upset at the discovery that she has actually done it. Anxiously he asks, "Well, it's just sex, isn't it? I mean, you don't *love* him?" Bob is concerned about the possibility that his wife's sexual involvement might also become a committed relationship that would threaten their own—a common concern among swingers. Organizational swingers typically recognize this concern by adopting ways to meet, choosing places to meet, and recognizing ground rules for the encounter so that emotional involvements that might threaten the marriage are minimized. Swingers' publications such as *Select* magazine, for example, carry advertisements in which couples describe themselves and their sexual preferences and specify the distance they are willing to travel to meet potential partners.

When couples get together, there is usually an implied understanding that certain rules will be followed to minimize the risk of jealousy and other complications. According to the authors of one article, it is assumed "(1) that the marriage commands paramount loyalty; (2) that there is physical but not emotional interest in other partners; (3) that single persons are avoided; and (4) that there will be no concealment of sexual activities [between spouses]." Such rules amount to a strategy for no-strings-attached sex. They serve to make swinging "an adjunct to marriage rather than an alternative" (Denfeld and Gordon, 1970, pp. 85–100).

Judging by reports from several investigators of recreational sex, these rules are effective in preventing jealousy in most cases. In one study, only 34 percent of the females and 27 percent of the males who had participated in swinging reported feelings of jealousy (Smith and Smith, 1974). Against the potential drawbacks such as jealousy, there seem to be several benefits from swinging. Many couples report an increased sexual interest in their mates; others cite the social enjoyments of "replaying the mating game" as a couple. Women in particular report enjoyment of the positive reinforcement of being regarded as sexually desirable by men other than their husbands (Bartell, 1970). Hunt makes the interesting observation that the primary reward of swinging in group situations

> is that of doing forbidden, daring, ego-gratifying, voyeuristic and exhibitionistic things, all with the approval of the group. Significantly, one man admitted that as much as he enjoyed swinging parties (at which he performed heroically, performing with one woman after another), he almost never had an orgasm at them and could not make himself have one. After such an event, however, he and his wife would go home and have coitus, at which time he would reach orgasm easily and swiftly. (1974, p. 290)

And yet the individuals who practice swinging typically are not people who would otherwise engage in forbidden or deviant behavior. The profile of the typical swinger presented in various studies (Bartell, 1970; Gilmartin, 1974) is that of an otherwise conventional, even conservative and traditional middle-class couple, often in their late twenties or early thirties. For them, swinging or mate swapping is a way of finding sexual variety outside of marriage but in a less threatening way than secret affairs would be. Swinging might be compared to prostitution as a more or less institutionalized outlet for extramarital sex in an impersonal setting. But whereas prostitution has generally served men only, swinging allows sexual variety for both husband and wife.

How many American couples today actually engage in swinging? Hunt found that only 2 percent of his sample had participated in swinging as a couple, and as we noted before, his sample undoubtedly included a disproportionate number of sexual liberals. It is probably safe to assume that no more than 1 percent of the population is actively engaged in swinging. Despite the widespread fascination with swinging and the rewards it offers, Hunt believes the obstacles and problems it poses outweigh the advantages. Interviews, Hunt says,

> confirmed what the advocates and enthusiasts have claimed—namely, that marital swinging can provide physically intense experiences, that it can be immensely ego-gratifying, and that it is a temporary release from confinement and responsibility and a brief chance to live out one's wildest fantasies. In the end, however, for nearly all contemporary husbands and wives, its advantages are heavily outweighed by the manifold conflicts, emotional problems and practical dangers involved. This, at any rate, is the apparent meaning of the rarity and self-limiting nature of such behavior among married Americans in the early 1970s. (1974, pp. 273–274)

Conclusions

Judging from the attention devoted to sex today, it sometimes appears that we are trying to make up in just a few years for the silence that surrounded the topic for so long. It is highly significant that sex can be discussed with considerably more candor now than it was a generation ago, and yet—as we noted at several points in this chapter—what people say about sex has notoriously little relationship to what they actually do. One of the chief uses of systematic studies, such as those reviewed in this chapter, is to help us sort out frequently repeated beliefs from real changes in behavior.

To summarize what *has* changed in marital sexuality over the past generation:

(1) While extramarital affairs are apparently no more frequent than they were for the adults Kinsey studied, married couples today do enjoy slightly greater frequency of intercourse. Perhaps more significant is a shift toward a freer marital sexuality: spouses more commonly practice a variety of positions, women play a more active part and more frequently experience orgasm.

(2) There is a greater stress on the equal sexuality of men and women. As Kinsey noted, male and female sexuality are not entirely alike. But the recent emphasis on women's equal right to sexual pleasure, along with the Masters and Johnson research, which emphasizes women's multiorgasmic potential, substantially revises the traditional belief that sex is a man's pleasure and a woman's duty.

(3) Today, because of the availability of more effective contraceptives, conception can be more reliably controlled, thus minimizing the risk that sex might lead to pregnancy. This allows couples to define sex as play, something engaged in for its own sake. It also allows them to have less anxiety about its possible consequences.

(4) In several respects, sex has been secularized and demystified. Religious restraints have eroded, and there is a considerably greater tendency now than there was a generation ago to regard sex as no different from any other form of behavior. One of Kinsey's accomplishments was to demonstrate that it could be studied, just as we study other behavior. Similarly, the availability of sex therapy suggests that we are now beginning to regard sexual problems not as something unmentionable, but rather as behavior that might be changed, like any other.

Perhaps the most significant development in this area is rising expectations of sexual satisfaction. The point of most sex manuals, as well as mass market magazine articles and many discussions of sexuality, is that more pleasure, with greater intensity and variety, is possible. Indeed, one often gets the impression that sex is expected to compensate for a lack of intensity and a certain depersonalization in other aspects of life.

The quest for what one writer refers to as "an unending erotic sizzle" (Epstein, 1975, p. 305) brings new pressures to bear upon marriage. There is a certain tension created by the expectation that married couples should be monogamous, faithful to each other, yet at the same time be able to sustain an intense erotic life.

If permanence-and-permissiveness seems a practical way of satisfying two basic needs, for marital stability as well as for erotic satisfaction, it is also a peculiarly difficult arrangement to practice. "Thus far," writes Morton Hunt,

> all variations upon this theme have proven disruptive to the marriages of most of those who have practiced them, and too threatening to the majority. . . . Relatively few people, even today, manage to make permissive marriage work at all, let alone work better than exclusive marriage. For although marriage no longer has the structural support of religion, community, law or practical necessity, today there is something else that makes exclusivity, or the appearance of it, immensely important—namely, the loneliness and disconnectedness of modern life, which creates a deep need in modern man and woman to belong, and to have a binding emotional connection with someone else. And since for most people sex is so closely bound up with deep emotions, extramarital sex acts are severely threatening to the emotional identity and security that marriage seems to offer. (1974, p. 240)

One of the main questions about the future of sex in marriage is how the tensions between expectations of intense erotic satisfactions and exclusivity will be resolved. New expectations of sexual pleasure create a new intolerance of humdrum sexuality, or sex that offers pleasure to one spouse but not to the other. In the next few decades, many couples will undoubtedly experience new types of sexual dissatisfactions because of higher expectations, while others will enjoy heightened sexual pleasure in marriage.

REFERENCES

Gilbert Bartell. Group sex among the mid-Americans. *Journal of Sex Research,* May 1970, pp. 113–130.

Richard K. Beardsley, John W. Hall, and Robert E. Ward. *Village Japan*. Chicago: University of Chicago Press, 1959.

Alan P. Bell and Martin S. Weinberg. *Homosexualities.* New York: Simon and Schuster, 1978.

Robert R. Bell and Phyllis L. Bell. Sexual satisfaction among married women. *Medical Aspects of Human Sexuality* 6 (December 1972): 136–144.

Robert R. Bell, Stanley Turner, and Lawrence Rosen. A multivariate analysis of female extramarital coitus. *Journal of Marriage and the Family* 37 (May 1975): 375–384.

Jessie Bernard. In James R. Smith and Lynn G. Smith, eds. *Beyond monogamy*. Baltimore: Johns Hopkins Press, 1974.

Alex Comfort. *The nature of human nature*. New York: Avon, 1968.

———. *The joy of sex*. New York: Crown, 1972.

John F. Cuber. In Gerhard Neubeck, ed. *Extramarital relations*. Englewood Cliffs, N.J.: Prentice-Hall, 1969.

——— and Peggy B. Harroff. *Sex and the significant Americans*. New York: Penguin, 1968.

Duane Denfeld and Michael Gordon. The sociology of mate swapping. *Journal of Sex Research* 6 (1979): 85–100.

Donald G. Dutton and Arthur P. Aron. Some evidence for heightened sexual attraction under conditions of high anxiety. *Journal of Personality and Social Psychology* 30 (1974): 510–517.

Albert Ellis. Healthy and disturbed reasons for having extramarital relations. In Gerhard Neubeck, ed. *Extramarital relations*. Englewood Cliffs, N.J.: Prentice-Hall, 1969.

———. *The American sexual tragedy*. New York: Lyle Stuart, 1962.

Havelock Ellis. *Studies in the psychology of sex*. New York: Scribner's, 1936.

Joseph Epstein. *Divorced in America*. New York: Penguin, 1975.

Nelson Foote. Sex as play. *Social Problems* 1 (1954): 159–163.

Clellan S. Ford and Frank A. Beach. *Patterns of sexual behavior*. New York: Harper, 1951.

Robert Francoeur. *Eve's new rib*. New York: Delta, 1972.

John H. Gagnon and William Simon. *Sexual conduct*. Chicago: Aldine, 1973.

The Gallup Poll. Extramarital sex "not always wrong." Press Release, August 6, 1978.

Brian G. Gilmartin. Sexual deviance and social networks: A study of social, family, and marital interaction patterns among co-marital sex participants. In James R. Smith and Lynn G. Smith, eds. *Beyond monogamy*. Baltimore: Johns Hopkins Press, 1974.

Shirley P. Glass and Thomas L. Wright. The relationship of extramarital sex, length of marriage and sex differences on marital satisfaction and romanticism. *Journal of Marriage and the Family* 39 (1977): 691–703.

Michael Gordon and Penelope Shankweiler. Different equals less. *Journal of Marriage and the Family* 33 (1971): 459–465.

Shere Hite. *The Hite Report*. New York: Dell, 1976.

Morton Hunt. *The affair*. New York: World, 1969.

———. *Sexual behavior in the 1970's*. New York: Dell, 1974.

Alfred C. Kinsey, Wardell B. Pomeroy, and Clyde Martin. *Sexual behavior in the human male*. Philadelphia: Saunders, 1948.

———, Wardell Pomeroy, Clyde E. Martin, and Paul H. Gebhard. *Sexual behavior in the human female*. Philadelphia: Saunders, 1953.

Dorothea Krook. *Three traditions of moral thought*. Cambridge: Cambridge University Press, 1959.

Robert J. Levin and Amy Levin. Sexual pleasure: The surprising preferences of 100,000 women. *Redbook,* September 1975.

Lionel S. Lewis and Dennis Brissett. Sex as work: A study of avocational counseling. *Social Problems* 15 (1967): 8–17.

James L. McCary. *Freedom and growth in marriage*. Santa Barbara, Calif.: Hamilton, 1975.

William H. Masters and Virginia E. Johnson. *Human sexual response*. Boston: Little, Brown, 1966.

———. *Human sexual inadequacy*. Boston: Little, Brown, 1970.

———. *The pleasure bond*. New York: Bantam, 1976.

———. *Homosexuality in perspective*. Boston: Little, Brown, 1979.

John Money and Anke A. Ehrhardt. *Man and woman/boy and girl*. Baltimore: Johns Hopkins Press, 1974.

Gerhard Neubeck and Vera M. Schletzer. A study of extra-marital relationships. *Marriage and Family Living* 24 (1962): 279–281.

Anthony Pietropinto and Jacqueline Simenauer. *Beyond the male myth*. New York: New American Library, 1977.

Lee Rainwater. Marital sexuality in four cultures of poverty. *Journal of Marriage and the Family* 26 (1964): 457–466.

James Ramey. *Intimate friendships*. Englewood Cliffs, N.J.: Prentice-Hall, 1976.

Ira L. Reiss. *Family systems in America*. New York: Holt, Rinehart and Winston, 1976.

David Reuben. *Everything you always wanted to know about sex*. New York: McKay, 1969.

Paul Robinson. *The modernization of sex*. New York: Harper & Row, 1976.

John Scanzoni and Letha Scanzoni. *Men, women, and change*. New York: McGraw-Hill, 1976.

Arthur Schlesinger, Jr. An informal history of love, U.S.A. In Marcia E. Lasswell and Thomas E. Lasswell, eds. *Love, marriage, family—A developmental approach*. Glenview, Illinois: Scott-Foresman, 1973.

Arlene Skolnick. *The intimate environment*. Boston: Little, Brown, 1973.

Lynn G. Smith and James R. Smith. Co-marital sex: The incorporation of extramarital sex into the marriage relationship. In Smith and Smith, eds. *Beyond monogamy*. Baltimore: Johns Hopkins Press, 1974.

William N. Stephens. *The family in cross-cultural perspective*. New York: Holt, 1963.

Charles F. Westoff. Coital frequency and contraception. *Family Perspectives* 6 (1974): 136–141.

FOR FURTHER READING

The basic studies of marital sexuality are the ones mentioned in this chapter, beginning with the two Kinsey studies: Alfred C. Kinsey, Wardell B. Pomeroy, and Clyde E. Martin, *Sexual Behavior in the Human Male* (Philadelphia: Saunders, 1948) and Alfred C. Kinsey, Wardell B. Pomeroy, Clyde E. Martin, and Paul H. Gebhard, *Sexual Behavior in the Human Female* (Philadelphia: Saunders, 1953). Recent studies are Morton Hunt's *Sexual Behavior in the 1970's* (New York: Dell, 1974), and a useful analysis of how attitudes toward sexual behavior changed during the 1970s by Norval Glenn and Charles Weaver, "Attitudes Toward Premarital, Extramarital, and Homosexual Behavior in the United States in the 1970s," in the May 1979 issue of the *Journal of Sex Research*.

For a readable summary and commentary on the Masters and Johnson research, see *An Analysis of Human Sexual Response*, edited by Ruth and Edward Brecher (New York: Signet, 1966). Paul Robinson's *The Modernization of Sex* provides an intelligent and lively guided tour of the major studies of sex, beginning with those of Havelock Ellis (New York: Harper & Row, 1976).

By consulting several different types of studies about female sexuality, readers can get a reasonably well-balanced perspective on the topic. See Robert R. Bell and Phyllis L. Bell, "Sexual Satisfaction among Married Women," *Medical Aspects of Human Sexuality*, December 1972, pp. 136–144; *The Redbook Report on Female Sexuality*, by Carol Tavris and Susan Sadd (New York: Delacorte, 1977); and *The Hite Report* by Shere Hite (New York: Dell, 1976). Chapter 8 in Lillian Rubin's *Worlds of Pain* (New York: Basic Books, 1976) provides an interesting perspective on how working-class women are responding to new, more liberated attitudes toward marital sex.

Dennis Brissett and Lionel S. Lewis have taken a look at how the manuals on marital sex published over the past decade differ from the earlier books on the same topic (discussed in their 1967 article "Sex as Work"). See "The Big Toe, Armpits, and Natural Perfume: Notes on the Production of Sexual Ecstasy," which appeared in the January/February 1979 issue of *Transaction* magazine. Philip Slater has written an insightful essay on the implications of regarding sex as work in his volume *Footholds* (New York: Dutton, 1977). For a discussion of how the Roman Catholic church has reevaluated its attitudes toward love and sex, see "Christianity, Marriage and Sex," by Francis X. Murphy, which appeared in the June 16, 1978 issue of *Commonweal*.

For a useful collection of articles on the sociology of sex, see James M. Henslin, ed., *Studies in the Sociology of Sex* (New York: Appleton Century Crofts, 1971), and for a review of the cross-cultural evidence, see William H. Davenport's "Sex in Cross-Cultural Perspective," in *Human Sexuality in Four Perspectives*, edited by Frank A. Beach (Baltimore: Johns Hopkins Press, 1977).

Much has been written since the early 1970s on sexual alternatives. Two good anthologies are edited by Roger W. Libby and Robert N. Whitehurst, *Renovating Marriage: Toward New Sexual Life-Styles* (Danville, Calif.: Consensus Publishers, 1973); and James R. Smith and Lynn G. Smith, eds., *Beyond Monogamy: Recent Studies of Sexual Alternatives in Marriage* (Baltimore: Johns Hopkins Press, 1974). For a recent report on swinging, its appeal and its drawbacks, see *The Gilmartin Report* by Brian Gilmartin (Secaucus, N.J.: Citadel Press, 1979).

If you're convinced that students of sex take the matter altogether too seriously, you might want to consult a delightful spoof that promises no reliable new information, just some entertaining answers to such important questions as "What Should Children Tell Their Parents About Sex?" The reference is to James Thurber and E. B. White, *Is Sex Necessary: Or, Why You Feel the Way You Do* (New York: Harper, 1957).

"Ginny & Lee, II" Shirley Gorlick

11 Marriage Throughout the Life Cycle—Will You Still Need Me/Will You Still Feed Me

The end of the fairy tale, "and they lived happily ever after," is the beginning of marriage. But countless writers, most of them men, have been at pains to correct the impression that married life is uninterruptedly happy. "Marriage is like life in this," wrote Robert Louis Stevenson, "that it is a field of battle, and not a bed of roses." Marriage, it has been said, is like a pair of scissors: two people joined together so that they cannot be separated, but moving in opposite directions. Perhaps the most frequent theme in such pronouncements is that love, over the years, gives way to disenchantment. As essayist André de Missan writes, "You study one another for three weeks, you love each other for three months, you fight for three years, and you tolerate the situation for thirty."

If it is only in fairy tales that a happy-ever-after ending can be taken for granted, how do real marriages change as time goes by? No matter how well matched two people are, it would be surprising to find that their initial attraction remains constant. Situations change, and so do individual needs, interests, and values. One psychologist who studied couples married for twenty years showed just how substantial those changes are: on the average, his subjects had changed 52 percent of their values, 55 percent of their vocational interests, 69 percent of their self-rated personality characteristics, and 92 percent of their answers to attitude questions since their marriage (Kelly, 1955, p. 654). In other words, very few people wake up on their twentieth wedding anniversary to find that they are the same as when they married.

But even if our personal traits remained the same, the changing demands of the adult life cycle would cause substantial alterations in the partnership. Occupational demands, the burdens of child rearing, the new freedoms of the postparental years all have their effect on the marital relationship.

In this chapter, we will examine studies of marital satisfaction over time. Because both marital "satisfaction" and "adjustment" are subjective matters that are not so easily observed or measured as what people actually do, we will look first at some of the problems that confront researchers in this area. Then, in order to understand why satisfaction changes over time, we will explore four different phases: (1) the newlywed marriage; (2) the parental marriage; (3) the middle-aged marriage; and (4) the retirement marriage.

Until about a decade ago, social scientists paid relatively little attention to adulthood. Psychologists focused their attention on infancy and childhood and showed little concern for mapping the stages of adult development. And although some students of the family used the entire life cycle as a frame of reference as early as the turn of the century, most of the interest in this area focused on the events of the early adult years—on such matters as mate selection, courtship, and the mutual adjustments of young married couples. There was some study of the impact of certain events that occur in the later years—such as women's adjustment to the "empty nest" phase, or the impact of retirement—but in general, knowledge of adult life, and how marriage and family change over time remained fairly sketchy.

Recently, there has been a good deal of scholarly as well as popular interest in exploring the life cycle in its entirety and in better understanding the stages of adult development. "There is a growing desire in our society," writes psychologist Daniel Levinson, "to see adulthood as something more than a long, featureless stretch of years with childhood at one end and senility at the other" (1978, x). Levinson is the author of one major study that developed a time-table according to which adults continue to change over the years. This study received considerable public attention because it provided much of the research upon which Gail Sheehy's very popular book, *Passages*, was based (1976). Among students of marriage and family life there has been renewed interest in studying the temporal aspects of marriage, such as the sequence and timing of the various roles that most people take over the course of a lifetime (Elder, 1977). Another recent development in the social sciences has been the rapid growth of a field called gerontology, which is devoted to the study of aging and the later stages of the life cycle. As a result of these developments in the social sciences, we are beginning to get a better understanding of what happens over the years, both to individuals and to their relationships.

MEASURING MARITAL SATISFACTION

In 1974, the Roper Organization conducted a poll asking thousands of people how they felt about love and marriage. When asked "What happens to love in marriage?" a majority agreed that after a while couples stop being in love and a different kind of affection replaces the initial attraction. Only 4 percent believed that "after a couple is married, sooner or later they stop being in love, and once this ends the marriage is pretty dull." It appears, in other words, that most Americans do not believe in a continuing romance in marriage, but neither do they think marriage inevitably declines into a situation that can be tolerated, but not enjoyed.

However, two other questions in that survey reveal a basic dilemma about marriage. When asked "Should people expect romance to last for years after they are married?" about two-thirds said yes. But when asked "Does romance last in most marriages?" a majority of both men and women answered no. Apparently, many Americans today are aware that the high expectations they bring to marriage are not entirely realistic, and that romance is quite difficult to sustain.

Of the questions about marriage that we would like to answer, few have such practical implications as these: What happens to marital satisfaction over time? What are the ingredients of successful marriages? If we could identify the elements of a successful marriage, we might be able to avoid less-than-successful ones. Students of marriage and family life have by no means ignored these questions. They have tried

Most of the studies discussed in this chapter show the impact that childbearing and child rearing have on marital satisfaction.

to chart the trajectory of marital satisfaction and predict successful marriages, but the harder they looked for "marital success," the more diffiult they found it was to define and measure. The success of a business enterprise or baseball team can be measured by a single, widely agreed upon goal such as profits or games won, but marriages have many different goals, not all of them consistent with each other. The personal values that couples bring to marriage take on as many different forms as the houses these couples live in.

What you mean by the expressions "marital success," "adjustment," and "happiness" is probably quite different from what those words mean to others, even those who are like you in many other ways. Marital satisfaction is a quality, not a quantity, and there are many difficulties in applying an objective yardstick to so subjective an experience. In fact, some sociologists insist that there is no objective reality corresponding to the expression "a successful marriage." Sociologist Robert Ryder argues,

> There is no descriptively defined entity that can reasonably be called a successful marriage, because there is no general agreement as to what marriages should be. Yet study after study has contrasted "good" marriages with "bad" marriages as if there were such an entity. A successful marriage is clearly one of which we approve. The concept is a value judgment dressed up to look like a matter of objective descriptive fact. (in Skolnick, 1973, p. 208)

If ever the social sciences are guilty of trying to "define the indefinable, and to measure the unmeasurable," as essayist Joseph Wood Krutch once charged, it is surely here, in studies of marital happiness. Before we pass final judgment on these studies, however, let us examine some of them, asking what they really tell us about the changes that take place in marriage as the years go by.

Of Time and Disenchantment

One of the earliest and most ambitious studies of satisfaction through the course of marriage was conducted by sociologists Ernest Burgess and Paul Wallin (1953). This longitudinal study (see Box 11–1) was begun in 1936, when Burgess and Wallin administered questionnaires designed to predict marital success to 1,000 engaged couples in the Chicago area. Three to five years later the couples who were still together were studied again, and then again after they had been married eighteen to twenty years (Pineo, 1961). The study demonstrates a pattern of disenchantment not very different from the conception of marriage expressed at the beginning of this chapter by André de Missan. Over the years most marriages declined in companionship, demonstration of affection (including both kissing and intercourse), common interests, beliefs, and values. Belief in the permanence of the marriage declined as well.

Sociologists Robert Blood and Donald Wolfe conducted another ambitious study attempting to assess marital satisfaction in the Detroit area in the 1950s. They interviewed more than 1,000 wives of different ages, racial backgrounds, and social statuses in urban, surburban, and rural settings at different points in the course of marriage. Their study examined how marital satisfaction is affected by such factors as social status, the specific background of the husband and wife, the degree of companionship, and the presence of children. They concluded,

> In the first two years of marriage, 52 percent of the wives are very satisfied with their marriages, and none notably dissatisfied. Twenty years later, only 6 percent are still very satisfied, while 21 percent are conspicuously dissatisfied. These figures suggest that a majority of wives become significantly less satisfied in later marriage than they were at the beginning. (1960, p. 264)

Blood and Wolfe found black wives, who are far more likely to experience the stresses of economic hardship, expressing considerably more dissatisfaction than white wives (1960, p. 264).

Blood later performed the same study in the Tokyo metropolitan area and found that in Japan, too, wives' dissatisfaction with marriage increases as the years go by (Blood, 1967). The researchers characterize this gradual ebbing of marital satisfaction as "the corrosion of time." Their summary of what happens to marriage with the passing of time corroborates most other studies of this subject.

> The first few years of marriage are a honeymoon period which continues the romance of courtship.

Research Perspectives on Marriage and Family

Box 11–1 / Cross-Sectional and Longitudinal Studies—Measuring Change Over Time

To assess how social attitudes or behavior changes over time is very difficult because changes are too slow to be easily observed. Social scientists use two research tools to overcome this problem. One is the *cross-sectional* study, which simultaneously examines several groups of people at different stages. For example, if you were interested in determining how attitudes toward cohabitation change over the four years of a college career, you might administer questionnaires to freshmen, sophomores, juniors, and seniors at the same time to see what differences, if any, exist in their attitudes. A second tool for studying change over time is the *longitudinal* study, which follows the same people over a number of years. If you used this method to study changing attitudes toward cohabitation, you would administer a questionnaire to a group of students as freshmen and then in each subsequent year ask the same group of students to fill out a new questionnaire.

Both methods are superior to the procedure of simply asking people to think back to what their attitudes were several years before and then to describe how they have changed. Memory is fallible; subsequent experiences distort our recollections of what we believed or how we acted. This method is especially inaccurate for assessing changes that took place over a period of many years.

But cross-sectional and longitudinal studies also have their disadvantages. Take, for example, Boyd Rollins and Harold Feldman's study of marital satisfaction (1970), which, like most other studies on this subject, is a cross-sectional study. The researchers set out to determine how marriage adjustment and satisfaction fluctuate over the course of marriage by questioning 1,598 husbands and wives in eight groups corresponding to the eight stages in the course of family life. Husbands and wives at each stage were asked about such matters as companionship and level of satisfaction with the partnership. Comparing the answers of those at various stages, the researchers noticed that a high percentage of couples at the early stages, as well as the latest, reported very satisfactory marriages. The group reporting the least satisfaction was the one whose children were being launched from the family. In other words, the results described a U-shaped curve of marital satisfaction over time.

The major drawback of this study—and of all cross-sectional studies—is that it does not really measure changes in marital satisfaction over time. Couples at each stage of the course of marital life were studied at the same point in time; the researchers had to infer a relation between the marital stage and level

(Box 11–1 continues on page 304)

With the birth of the first baby, satisfaction with the standard of living and companionship declines. In subsequent years, love and understanding sag, too. If children do not come, their absence is an alternative source of dissatisfaction.

These trends do not involve all couples, but they do affect a very large proportion. . . . Some of this decline involves the calming of enthusiasm into satisfaction as a result of getting used to the partner, no matter how fine he may be. Newlyweds *ought* to be enthusiastic because they are tasting new satisfactions for the first time. However, much of the decline in satisfaction reflects observable decreases in the number of things hus-

(Box 11–1 continued from page 303)

of reported satisfaction. There is no guarantee, in other words, that a couple at the earliest stage of marriage would actually report a decline in satisfaction over time. The young couples studied by Rollins and Feldman might bring to marriage expectations and inclinations that are very different from those of the older group.

Another problem with cross-sectional studies of marital satisfaction is cohort attrition: couples in the older age categories are those who have stayed together. Part of the upswing in reported satisfaction among older couples may be due to the fact that the least satisfied couples have divorced, leaving as married those who are relatively more satisfied.

The major advantage of the longitudinal study is that it shows how satisfaction changes over time. Thus, researchers can check the accuracy of predictions about such factors as role expectations and husband–wife similarity in causing marital satisfaction. Burgess and Wallin's study provides an example of the longitudinal design. It began in 1936 with a group of 1,000 engaged couples. Three to five years after their marriage, marital satisfaction scores were obtained from the 666 couples out of the original 1,000 who had actually married and stayed together. The tests divided marital satisfaction into seven dimensions: marital adjustment, love, permanence, consensus, absence of complaints, happiness, and sexual adjustment. When satisfaction scores were obtained from the 400 couples still married after eighteen to twenty years of marriage, it was found that husbands tended to report statistically significant declines in four of the seven dimensions (marital adjustment, love, permanence, and consensus) while wives reported declines in five dimensions (the four mentioned most often by men plus absence of complaints) (Pineo, 1961). The study's overall conclusion is that marital satisfaction declines over time.

Longitudinal studies require much more time than do cross-sectional studies, and they are more costly to conduct. One of their major difficulties is keeping track of a large number of people over several years. Because the group is widely scattered after just a few years, it is almost impossible to collect data at frequent intervals. As a consequence, the Burgess and Wallin study says nothing about year-to-year fluctuations in marital satisfaction. The most serious drawback of longitudinal studies is attrition. Burgess and Wallin started out in the 1930s with a sample of 1,000 couples and ended up in the 1950s with only 400. Our understanding of the process of gradual disenchantment in marriage is incomplete because we know nothing about the other 600 couples.

Each of these techniques, then, has its flaws. The cross-sectional study ignores generational differences. The longitudinal study is expensive, slow, and complicated by the fact of attrition. In this area, as in others, social researchers choose the most appropriate tool from among several alternatives. In the assessment of change over time, both cross-sectional and longitudinal studies provide more reliable data than retrospective accounts.

bands and wives do with and for each other. Hence, "corrosion" is not too harsh a term for what happens to the average marriage in the course of time. Too many individuals allow their marriages to go to seed for any milder term to be appropriate. As individuals, middle-aged husbands and wives may find satisfaction elsewhere—in friends, the husband in his work, the wife in her children—they seldom find as much in each other. (1960, p. 264)

This passage contains almost as many of Blood and Wolfe's assumptions about what marriage *should* be as it does findings from their research. In this respect, as well as the overall pattern described, it is a representative study of marital satisfaction.

Blood and Wolfe's conclusions are similar to those reached by John Cuber and Peggy Harroff (1968) in a very different type of study—one using extensive interviews rather than structured questionnaires. Cuber and Harroff limited their study to occupationally successful upper-middle-class couples between the ages of thirty-five and fifty-five. They conclude that many of these marriages can be characterized as either utilitarian ("established or maintained for purposes other than to express an intimate, highly important *personal* relationship between a man and a woman") or devitalized (apathetic); relatively few were still what might be called vital or total relationships. The characteristic feature of the devitalized marriage is, according to Cuber and Harroff,

> the clear discrepancy between middle-aged reality and the earlier years. These people usually characterized themselves as having been "deeply in love" during the early years, as having spent a great deal of time together, having enjoyed sex, and most importantly, having had a close relationship with one another. The present picture, with some variation from case to case, is in clear contrast—little time is spent together, sexual relationships are far less satisfying qualitatively and quantitatively, and interests and activities are not shared, at least not in the deeper and meaningful way they once were. Most of their time together now is "duty time"—entertaining together, planning and sharing activities with children, and participating in various kinds of community responsibilities. (1968, p. 47)

Of course, such couples do have some common interests—the children, shared property, the husband's career—but this is a very different matter from the intrinsic sharing they experienced as newlyweds.

Two more recent studies describe a generally similar pattern of declining satisfaction, but they both agree that marital satisfaction increases again in the later years of marital life. Rollins and Feldman found that marital satisfaction graphed over time yields a U-shaped curve (Figure 11–1). Satisfaction was highest for newlyweds, then declined steadily until the children left home, and then turned upward again.

Social psychologist Angus Campbell studied a random nationwide sample of more than 2,000 married people and came to the same conclusions as Rollins and Feldman did. Newly married couples without children were the happiest group surveyed. With the birth of children, satisfaction dropped, but later, when the children left home, the couples reported their happiness returning to its previous level (1975, p. 40).

Not surprisingly, considering the variety of populations studied and measures of marital satisfaction employed, there are several points that researchers do not agree on. One study, for example (Burr, 1970), found no evidence of gradual decline, but rather a number of highs and lows on specific dimensions of marital satisfaction over the years.

In general, however, the research on marital satisfaction over the years suggests that the cynics are closer to the truth than the happy-ever-after romantics. Most studies indicate a pattern of deepening dissatisfaction with marriage until the children are launched and the parents have the house to themselves again.

In his old age, novelist Thomas Mann—who had advocated marriage as "a creative sexual union . . . transmuted into an enduring partnership of life and fortune which outlives it"—made this entry in his diary:

> Marriage—a problem. This too has become a problem, as everything else has, with time. Truly, one may, even without malice, easily gather the impression that today 90 percent of all marriages are unhappy—admitting the assumption that percentage calculations are permitted and possible with such relative and fleeting concepts as happiness and unhappiness. (in Epstein, 1975, p. 41)

Figure 11–1. Rollins and Feldman found, as other investigators have, that reported satisfaction declines in the middle years of marriage, but returns to its previous high level during the postparental period.

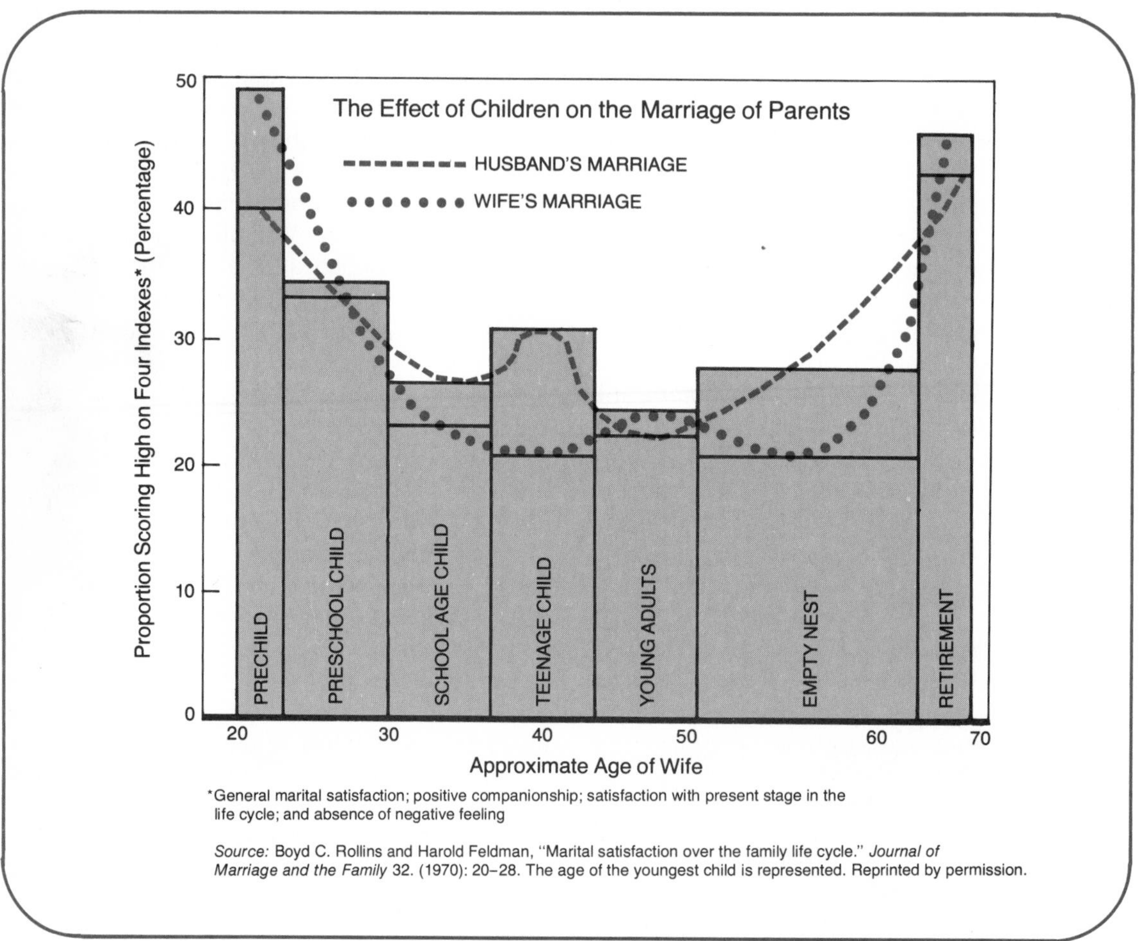

Mann's observations of marital satisfaction were, of course, informal, but in reaching the same conclusion as systematic sociological studies he may have discovered the same truth—or fallen victim to the same errors. What are the potential sources of error in trying to measure marital happiness?

The Problem of Interpretation

Any assessment of success in marriage depends on self-reports. That is, the subjects themselves judge how satisfactory their marriages are. But how accurate are their judgments? How honest are their answers to personal questions asked by strangers? One researcher, Vernon Edmonds, suspected that many people would be reluctant to describe themselves and their marriages in an unfavorable light. To test this hypothesis, he asked 100 married couples at Florida State University to respond "true" or "false" to a series of statements such as: "My marriage is a perfect success," "If my mate has any faults, I am not aware of them," and "Every new thing I have learned about my mate has pleased me." Though these statements were so idealized as to be unbelievable, many respondents said they were true. Edmonds concluded that when people are asked to report about their own marriages, they often tell more about what they think *ought* to be than about what really is going on in their married lives (1967). Although, as we have seen, some people do candidly admit a lack of satisfaction, if Edmonds is right, studies based upon self-reports undoubtedly underreport marital dissatisfaction.

Another criticism of marital adjustment studies is that the conclusions reached by their authors are heavily influenced by the specific meanings they attach to the key words "adjustment," "satisfaction," and "happiness." Since there is no general consensus on exactly what these words mean, researchers try to give them a fixed definition—but not necessarily the same definition as those given by other researchers. In Burgess and Wallin's research, for example, a well-adjusted marriage is defined as

> a union in which the husband and wife are in agreement on the chief issues of marriage, such as handling finances and dealing with in-laws; in which they have come to an adjustment on interests, objectives and values; in which they are in harmony on demonstrations of affection and sharing confidences; and in which they have few or no complaints about their marriage. (1953, p. 470).

Is this your idea of a well-adjusted marriage? Perhaps your definition would not value harmony in the marriage over individual satisfaction, as Burgess' does. Notice, too, that a couple in which one of the spouses is pathologically dependent might do very well on Burgess' adjustment scorecard.

Instead of using the word "adjustment," other studies tend to use such words as "satisfaction," thus reflecting the current assumption that a good marriage should foster individual development. In sociologist Wesley Burr's research, for example, satisfaction is defined in terms of individual accomplishment rather than mutual accommodation, "a subjective condition in which the individual experiences a certain degree of attainment of a goal or desire" (1970, p. 30).

Again, considering the variety of measures of satisfaction used in these studies, it is hardly surprising to note that there is no consensus about the percentage of marriages that might be termed happy or unhappy at any stage. But as Angus Campbell remarks, if we compare the reported happiness of the entire married population with that of the unmarried, we get a very different perspective from that suggested by these findings of gradually declining satisfaction. "All of the married groups," Campbell writes, "—men and women, over thirty and under, with children and without—reported higher feelings of satisfaction and general good feelings about their lives than all of the unmarried groups—the single, divorced, or widowed." And then he adds an important reminder: "Remember, though, that I am talking about group averages—there are plenty of miserable married people and satisfied singles. But the link between marriage and satisfaction is striking and consistent, whichever the cause or effect: marriage may make people happy, or perhaps happy people are more likely to marry" (1975, p. 40).

Campbell points out that the most important factor determining a person's feelings of satisfaction or dissatisfaction, for both males and females, is the stage of life that the individual is passing through. Now, therefore, we turn to the stages of the family life cycle, and their effects on marital satisfaction.

STAGES IN THE FAMILY LIFE CYCLE

The course of family life with its four major stages might be regarded as a schedule for the performance of certain tasks and the accomplishment of certain goals, just as the stages of infant development can be defined in terms of specific tasks to do. One of the tasks of early marriage, for example, is the establishment of the couple's own, independent home. Later on, parental roles must be accommodated within the marital relationship (Duvall, 1971).

Each couple is unique in certain ways, of course. Not all couples are the same age when they marry; some choose not to have children; in others, family size or the spacing of children creates unusual patterns. Nevertheless, typically there is a fairly predictable progression of expansions and contractions in the size and complexity of the family and a progression of role responsibilities thrust upon adults of a certain age and later taken away. Furthermore, no family lives in a vacuum; every marriage is strongly affected by the occupational system and by such other social institutions as the educational system. Male and female role requirements typically change as the individuals grow older, and these changes also affect the marital relationship.

We must note, too, that the stages in the course of family life vary in length not only from family to family but from generation to generation. Increased longevity and preferences for fewer children have combined to increase the number of years that most couples spend in the stage of retirement marriage, with consequences we shall soon explore.

There is no consensus among social scientists about the exact number of stages in the course of marriage. Inevitably, the division is somewhat arbitrary. Here we will discuss four basic stages; the *newlywed* marriage, a relatively short period ending with the birth of the first child; the *parental* marriage, which lasts until the youngest child leaves home; the *middle-aged* marriage, sometimes called the empty-nest period; and the *retirement* marriage, which begins at retirement and ends with the death of either spouse.

Most of the literature on how marriage changes with time presumes that the couple will have children and is largely designed to help people understand how children and the demands of parental roles affect marriage. Most couples, of course, do have children, and it is undeniable that children have a strong influence on the marital relationship. Thus there is little in the literature on how the marriages of childless couples change over time.

The Newlywed Marriage

Our comments about the newlywed marriage will be short and sweet. Both words describe this stage accurately. There are, of course, many personal adjustments that people have to make when they marry. Spouses not only have to take on the husband and wife roles, but they also have to work out discrepancies between each other's assumptions about what those roles involve. And they have to arrive at workable strategies for resolving differences. There are other tasks of the newlywed period as well, such as forming a new set of ties with the family and friends of one's spouse. The fact that divorce is more likely to happen in the earliest years of marriage than later on indicates that some couples discover their incompatibility very quickly. But for most couples the satisfactions of this early phase of marriage are considerable.

"The best of all possible worlds for most Americans," writes Angus Campbell, "is to be newly married and not have children. If single people in their twenties feel that something is lacking in their lives, married couples of that age are the happiest of all groups" (1975, p. 39).

This aptly summarizes one of the most consistent findings in marital satisfaction studies. Early marriage is in many ways a continuation of courtship. Even if the newly married couple learns that they do not agree with each other in as many ways as they thought, they still enjoy many satisfactions together, particularly in shared activities and companionship. They prize individual responsivity and have few role responsibilities that conflict with person-oriented interaction. Most young wives, moreover, have jobs, making the couple's combined income considerably higher than it will be when she drops out of the labor force for a period of at least a few years, as most married women do, to give birth and take care of their young children.

The Parental Marriage

For most couples, the newlywed phase is relatively brief. More than one-third of all white women who married for the first time in the late 1960s—and a considerably higher fraction of black women—had their first child within the first year of marriage. More than half became mothers within eighteen months after their wedding (Presser, 1975).

At this point, primary role responsibilities change abruptly, and so does reported marital satisfaction. "Almost as soon as a couple has kids," writes Campbell,

> their happy bubble bursts. For both men and women, reports of happiness and satisfaction drop to average, not to rise again significantly until their children are grown and about to leave the nest (age eighteen). Couples with young children also report feeling more stress and pressure than any other group. The mothers, most of whom are between the ages of twenty-five and thirty-four, carry the burden of child rearing, and the pressures are most acute for them. They are the most likely group to describe themselves as feeling tied down, to express doubts about their marriages, and to wish occasionally to be free of the responsibilites of parenthood. The husbands feel less satisfied with children, too; but they don't show the great swing that their wives do, partly because they were less euphoric about marriage to begin with. (1975, p. 41)

On this point there is some research allowing us to compare the satisfactions of marriage in families that have young children with childless families (the word "child-free" might be more descriptive of these couples). After conducting a study of almost 7,000 adults in Alameda County, California, sociologist Karen Renne reports that "contrary to popular belief, childless marriages are more satisfactory than others; parents, especially those currently raising children, were definitely less apt to be satisfied with their marriages. But the number of children had no consistent effect on the rate of dissatisfaction" (1970, p. 66). The Rollins and Feldman study helps us to understand why the presence of young children contributes to marital dissatisfaction. Couples with young children reported a dramatic drop in companionship activities; child-free couples did not (1970).

Though most couples experience considerable rewards from parenthood—which we will examine more closely in the next chapter—the relationship between husband and wife changes in certain ways with the birth of children. In the newlywed marriage, as we saw, interactions between spouses are person-centered, stressing the individual traits of the spouse; parents, on the other hand, soon begin responding to each other more in terms of role obligations. It is significant that many parents call each other Mom and Dad.

Becoming a mother, as Campbell noted, often causes women to feel tied down. In the next chapter we will look into the efforts being made today to redefine parenthood so that its responsibilities do not fall so heavily on the shoulders of women. One of the effects of more readily available day-care facilities, for example, might be fewer feelings of dissatisfaction on the part of young mothers.

Becoming a father can be a disturbing experience, too. Men often report feeling neglected by their wives, who must suddenly devote so much of their time to mothering. In effect, there may be a competition between the husband and the child for the woman's attention. Helena Lopata's study of role priorities among young women suggests that the child is often the winner in that competition. When Lopata asked more than 600 housewives to list what they thought were women's most important roles, 80 percent mentioned motherhood and only 62 percent mentioned the role of wife. When the same women were asked how they viewed their husbands, the provider role was listed more often than any other (87 percent), followed by the father role (65 percent). Only 46 percent listed the husband role. Even in an era of companionship marriage, the father and provider roles apparently take priority during the child-rearing years (Lopata, 1965, p. 24).

A recent in-depth study of the effects that a newborn has on its parents and their marriage calls attention both to the emotional impact of the experience, and also to its effect in redefining their roles. Two husband-wife teams conducted an intensive study of fourteen couples from the midpoint in the woman's pregnancy to a point about six months after childbirth (Cowan and Coie, 1978). Like several of the studies to which we have already referred, this one found that all of the parents felt some discontent about the loss of shared leisure time caused by the new demands of parenthood. Although all of the couples said they felt an emotional "high" and a sense of fulfillment following the birth, the investigators also found that most of the couples experienced significant changes in self-esteem during this period—changes that on the whole were more negative than positive.

Both spouses redefined their roles, often in ways they had not planned. For most of the fathers, this was a period of considerable turmoil associated with work or career: several were laid off, and others seriously considered switching careers or felt a heightened concern about the adequacy of their income. And soon after childbirth, all of the couples—regardless of the way they had formerly divided up household chores, and regardless of the employment of the wives—shifted to a more traditional division of household labor. This was true of both decision-making roles as well as the responsibility for such child care tasks as nightly feedings. At least in this early phase of child rearing, when spouses are making the transition to parenthood, and when infants make particularly heavy demands on the time and attention of their parents, the husbands and wives commonly experience very mixed feelings. They discover that they had underestimated the demands and difficulties of parenthood and the problems involved in balancing domestic and work commitments (Cowan and Coie, 1978).

But perhaps we have exaggerated the negative aspects of parenthood to account for declining marital satisfaction during these years. "The arrival of a child," as Campbell recognizes, "is a happy event, but one that puts unanticipated strains on the marriage—both economic and psychological ones" (1975, p. 41).

The Middle-Aged Marriage

As we noted in Chapter 5, the typical family life cycle for today's adults is different from what it was for their parents and grandparents. Today most people live longer and have fewer children—and as a result are preoccupied with the duties of child care for a smaller part of their adult lives. A typical American woman born in the 1950s gave birth to her last child at age twenty-nine. A century before, a typical woman would have been about thirty-two when she did so. The most dramatic change in the timing of our lives results from increased life expectancy. A typical woman born in the 1950s can expect to live with her spouse until her mid-sixties, whereas a woman born in the 1880s could expect to have her marriage terminated by the death of the spouse about eight years earlier. As a result of these two trends—a more compressed childbearing period and longer life expectancy—the couple who marry today can anticipate spending more than forty years together. They will spend about half of their married lives alone together, with no children in the house. Because this postparental phase is unprecedentedly long, it is particularly important to look at the characteristics of the middle-aged marriage.

"So here we are, Lucille. Down to basics. You and me."

Various terms have been used to characterize the third stage of marriage, which begins when the children are old enough to leave their parents' home. It has been called the postparental period, the launching stage, and the empty-nest phase. All of these expressions call attention to the transitions that are required of middle-aged couples.

Looking at the dissatisfactions of the parental marriage, Campbell says:

> There is hope for the disgruntled or disappointed parent, however. Wait seventeen years or so until you are alone with your spouse again. Your satisfaction with life and your all-around good mood will return to where it was before you had kids. Indeed, parents of older children were among the happiest groups in the study, and this was true for both sexes. Couples settled back in the "empty nest" reported feelings of companionship and mutual understanding even higher than they felt as newlyweds. Raising a family seems to be one of those tasks, like losing weight or waxing the car, that is less fun to be doing than to have done. (1975, p. 41)

But there is not much agreement among various studies on the relative satisfactions of the middle-aged marriage. Rollins and Feldman found that the husband's reported satisfaction with marriage increases dramatically during the empty-nest period, but the wife's experience is somewhat different. Her reported marital satisfaction goes down slightly at the beginning of the period and begins to rise only just before the retirement years (1970). Looking at the overall picture of marital satisfaction in middle-aged marriages portrayed in these studies, Campbell's remarks seem too cheerful.

It is an oversimplification to say there is an overall rise or fall in reported satisfaction in the middle-aged marriage. A variety of changes take place during these years: some cause new problems, others allow new freedoms and a renewed sense of intimacy and companionship. The family is reduced to the original dyad, and the couple can look forward to a much longer period of being alone together than they enjoyed as newlyweds. Sociologist Irwin Deutscher found that

> this phase of the family cycle is seen by the majority of middle-aged spouses as a time of new freedoms: freedom from the economic responsibilities of children; freedom to be mobile (geographically); freedom from housework and other chores. And, finally, freedom to be oneself for the first time since the children came along. (1967, p. 516)

There is reason to conclude that the postparental phase is a somewhat different experience for couples in different socioeconomic circumstances. Among working-class couples who have fewer financial resources than their middle-class counterparts, one of the major changes in the postparental years is that they are relieved of the financial burdens of child rearing. As a consequence of greater discretionary income, there is a more discernible improvement in their lifestyle at this point.

In a study of role shifts in the postparental marriage, sociologist Marvin Sussman found that, particularly at higher socioeconomic levels, couples started spending more time and doing more things together (1960). In other words, the middle-aged marriage does often allow for a renewal of the kind of companionship that most newly married couples have.

But there are, of course, crucial differences. The exhilarating feeling of discovering each other, common in newlywed marriages, obviously cannot be recaptured. There is at this point "a kind of vulnerability to newly sensed alternatives that characterizes the family relationship that has settled down to a sort of deadly routine, with only task orientations and interlocking roles to hold it together" (Turner, 1970, p. 94). For some couples, the kind of companionship they enjoyed when first married is no longer possible because husband and wife have since gone through different experiences and their interests have diverged.

At middle age, moreover, one has already become much of what one will ever be; the sense of limitless possibilities that an individual feels in youth is gone. Instead, one has a very tangible reminder from the physical changes of middle age that time is beginning to run out. By the time most men reach their late forties or early fifties, they have reached the peak of their career advancement. Some men in middle age, having met cultural expectations and invested themselves heavily in their work, look over their shoulder at what they have accomplished and wonder if it was worth the effort. This reaction is expressed by Bob Slocum, the narrator of Joseph Heller's novel *Something Happened.* "Is this all there is for me to do?" Slocum asks himself. "Is this really the most I can get from the few years left in this one life of mine?" In an interview, author Heller echoes Slocum's doubts:

> From age forty on, something starts to happen. The dissatisfaction with work may be a dissatisfaction with one's life: the realization that it has pretty much passed. While you may have achieved a lot, what you've achieved isn't as valuable as you thought it would be. (in *Forbes,* June 15, 1975, p. 58)

Recent studies of adult development suggest that the midlife turmoil that Heller expresses is a rather common experience. Indeed, one of the major contributions of these studies to an understanding of adult life is that they remind us of the normality of a midlife crisis (Levinson, 1978; Vaillant, 1977). Perhaps this explains the enormous popularity of Gail Sheehy's book, *Passages* (1976), which summarizes, and in certain respects misrepresents, the findings of these studies. *Passages* provides for a general audience a much-needed map of adult development. Today, many people look to the social sciences for something that seems to have been lost, the perception of life as a sequence of well-defined stages. Thus *Passages* provides, as *Pilgrim's Progress* did for so many eighteenth-century readers, a schema for growth, a guidebook for a journey of self-discovery. It allows readers to locate and define themselves, as "late baby superachievers," as victims of "Catch-30," or beneficiaries of the "mellowing 50s."

Judging from Daniel Levinson's intensive, long-term study of forty adult males, it appears that midlife crises are not only normal, they even come at fairly predictable points in the life sequence. Levinson found that for about 80 percent of his subjects, the midlife transition—which begins at about age forty and lasts for about five years—is a time of considerable personal turmoil, when men typically question the pattern of their lives, engage in a profound personal reappraisal, and try to make certain modifications in their lives. It is not that middle age is without its satisfactions. As Levinson points out, it is at this point that the tyranny of social demands for success and achievement begins to subside, and many men begin to yearn for a more balanced life. If there is no longer the same preoccupation with proving one's success that tends to concern younger men, this period is normally accompanied by the realization of the disparity between one's dreams and one's accomplishment. It is a time when many relationships undergo considerable change, including the man's relationship to his children, who are now late teenagers. How, exactly, is marriage affected by these midlife changes? Levinson's research suggests that it is at this point that couples become fully aware of differences in the rate and direction of their development, begin to reappraise their marriages, and decide whether they should make new choices or recommit themselves on new terms to older choices (1978).

The experience of middle-aged women is quite different from that of men. A man in his late forties or early fifties has typically achieved some occupational security, if not success, and can anticipate the satisfactions of another ten or more years of work. In contrast, most women, after having committed themselves primarily to the mother's role, find themselves with an empty nest. Often with little preparation or cultural support, they have to enter a "second act" to sustain a sense of usefulness—and there is no script defined by tradition telling them what to do.

The more demanding role transition that middle-aged women are expected to make may help to explain why, as psychologist Marjorie Lowenthal and her associates point out in their book *Four Stages of Life:* "Middle-aged women mention the most difficulties in getting along with their husbands. . . . On nearly all counts, middle-aged women confronting the postparental period were more clearly in a critical period than were their male counterparts" (1975, pp. 26, 242).

There has been considerable discussion of the problems experienced by women in the "empty-nest" phase—including depression and a sense of uselessness. But the evidence on the extent of such traumatic responses is inconsistent. Although, as we have noted, the Rollins and Feldman (1970) study found that reported satisfaction of women goes down at the beginning of this period and does not rise again until several years later, the results from a variety of small-scale surveys—as summarized by Glenn (1975)—suggest that, on the whole, marital satisfaction does not decline for women in the postparental phase; and the departure of children from the home does not typically cause any long-lasting psychological problems for middle-aged mothers. The results from a recent intensive study of 160 women whose children had just left home point to the same conclusion. The investigator, Lillian Rubin (1979), found that many mothers responded to the departure of their children with a sense of relief, and they typically managed the transition to new jobs and responsibilities without major problems. We might assume that as more women work in the labor force for much of their adult lives, the transition to the postparental phase will become somewhat easier than it was for their mothers, who were more likely to be full-time homemakers.

The Retirement Marriage

It has been said that old age is the minority group to which most of us will belong at some point. This was by no means true in the past. At the turn of the century, parents only occasionally outlived the departure of the last child from the home. Life expectancy for persons born in 1900 was only about forty-seven years, and persons sixty-five or older made up only 4 percent of the United States population then. Today, life expectancy for women is about seventy-six, for men about sixty-eight. The elderly number over 20 million and comprise about 10 percent of the population. This means that many married couples today live long enough to share a fourth stage of marriage, the retirement stage.

At retirement, most men reorient their interests and activities after years of making a heavy investment in their occupational role. At the same time, especially among couples who earlier in life had a fairly clear-cut division of role responsibilities—she being responsible for household tasks and he for bringing in an income—retirement often means a substantial redefinition of household routines and responsibilities. For many couples it also means that husband and wife spend more hours together each day than they ever did before, even more than they did in the early years of marriage.

The abruptness of mandatory retirement, which causes problems for some Americans in their early retirement years, is not unavoidable. In the Israeli kibbutzim, retirement is more gradual. To compensate the elderly for the loss of their occupational role, the kibbutz provides alternative activities: some work in light industries or crafts; others serve on governing committees; still others are retrained to resume the nonmanual occupations they gave up when they joined the kibbutz. "Gradual retirement," one writer notes,

> spares the workers the shock of an abrupt and total loss of their major social function and enables them to adjust to retirement stage by stage. Moreover it enables the community to utilize the productive capacities of all members fully and spares aging members the long period of involuntary idleness. (Talmon, 1961, p. 287.)

There is some evidence that in the United States, professional or managerial couples are more likely to look forward to retirement, and to enjoy it when it happens, than are people who worked at lower occupational levels (Kerckhoff, 1964). An obvious reason is that professional or managerial workers earn higher salaries, receive more generous pensions, and end up in a better financial position after retirement. For many other couples, retirement brings a radically reduced standard of living.

Other problems of the retirement years result from a legacy of stereotypes about what it means to grow old. One of the most serious misconceptions about old age—and sadly, one that many older people share—is that sexual interests are abandoned as the years go by. It is often assumed that older men can no longer perform sexually. Jokes about sex among "golden agers" often reveal our squeamishness about a sensitive topic. (Comedian Bob Hope was once asked if there is sex after sixty-five. He replied, "You bet, and awfully good, too—especially the one in the Fall.") Older couples sometimes take these attitudes to heart and feel guilty about their sexual urges. One gerontologist recalls the complaint of an eighty-four-year-old man that the sexual activity his seventy-nine-year-old wife enjoyed was "not natural for such an old man and woman" (Lobsenz, 1974, p. 8).

Research has shown, however, that satisfying lovemaking among older couples can be and often is more than the seasonal occurrence Bob Hope jokes about. The Kinsey research reported that 80 percent of men over sixty said in interviews that they were still capable of intercourse, and that women do not experience a sexual decline until very late in life (1948). More recently, the Masters and Johnson research has

In recent years there has been a good deal of scholarly as well as popular interest in understanding what happens over the years, both to individuals and their marriages.

provided the information we need to discard many stereotypes about declining sexuality among the elderly. Masters and Johnson observe that sexual response, like other physical responses, slows down in older couples. Older men require more time to develop an erection, which is sometimes incorrectly interpreted as evidence of impotence. However, these researchers point out that impotence is more often a consequence of fears of declining abilities than a result of aging. "There are only two basic needs for regularity of sexual expression in the seventy- to eighty-year-old woman," they write. "These necessities are a reasonably good state of health and an interested and interesting partner" (in Puner, 1974, p. 44).

As we saw in discussing the studies conducted by Campbell, and Rollins and Feldman, elderly couples seem to regain what many of them gave up in their middle years—companionship. In fact, if the elderly couples in the Rollins and Feldman study were not exaggerating their marital satisfaction, we could aptly call this last stage a second honeymoon (1970).

DISCUSSION: THE SATISFACTIONS OF MARRIAGE

We began this chapter by raising the question "What happens to marriage over time?" We have examined two different types of studies in order to answer that question. First, we examined several of the studies that have attempted to assess marital adjustment, satisfaction, or happiness. Then we looked at the various stages of the family life cycle, and drew upon descriptive accounts to understand the characteristic stresses and rewards of each of those stages.

What, then, in general, *does* happen to marriage over time? To a considerable extent, the answer depends on which studies you consult and how you interpret them. On the one hand is a series of studies conducted over a thirty-year period, each of which asked couples to rate their own marriages as very happy, pretty happy, or not too happy. If these studies are at least a generally accurate portrait of marital happiness, they provide impressive and consistent evidence that most marriages are quite satisfactory. Five studies conducted in various states produced generally similar happiness ratings. The least optimistic was an Illinois study in which 63 percent of the couples reported they were very happy and 22 percent were not too happy. The most optimistic was a California study in which 85 percent of the respondents said they were very happy and only 5 percent reported being not too happy (Orden and Bradburn, 1968).

On the other hand, you might consult the studies summarized earlier in this chapter and conclude with sociologist Peter Pineo that "loss of satisfaction is . . . generally an inescapable consequence of the passage of time in a marriage" (1961, p. 11). Again with Pineo, however, you might choose to emphasize that as the years go by, personal satisfaction comes to depend less and less upon one's spouse. Though couples who have been married for years may derive less satisfaction from their spouses, it is not because of a lower estimate of the spouse but because there are alternative sources of satisfaction outside the marriage (1961).

But if studies of all types cannot agree on how many marriages stay satisfactory, or for how long, they do show that some marriages remain much more satisfactory than others. Why? Sociologist Jan Dizard (1968) finds one clue in his analysis of the Burgess and Wallin study discussed earlier in this chapter. Dizard comes to the rather surprising conclusion that the couple most likely to experience declining marital satisfaction over the years is the one in which the husband has become very successful, and has—at the same time—involved himself in a variety of community organizations.

In several other studies, too, including Cuber and Harroff's book on unusually successful adults, we find that men who have many outside commitments, satisfactions, and role responsibilities are likely to have what Cuber and Harroff call utilitarian rather than vital marriages—practical arrangements that offer a considerable amount of security and stability, but not much vitality. Cuber and Harroff observe that this type of marriage is tailor-made for the man whose primary commitment is to his career (1968, p. 116). In other words, the occupational role takes priority over the marital relationship.

Another clue may lie in the studies we have examined which indicate that a reason for declining satisfaction in marriage is that the mother role takes priority over the wife and companion role. During the parental marriage, *role incompatibility*—"the degree to which the demands of one role are incompatible with the demands of other roles a person is occupying"—may help to explain declining marital satisfaction (Burr, 1973, p. 129). Such incompatibility is minimal at first:

> Newlyweds, both men and women, gave almost exclusive attention to personality characteristics and emotional responsivity, and made minimal references to roles and statuses, norms which they were still in the process of clarifying. They were eager to convey the unique features of the partners they had just chosen, and dwelt on themes of mutual understanding, caring, shared interests, and enjoyment of each other's company. (Lowenthal, Thurnher, and Chiriboga, 1975, p. 25)

But when the authors of this study describe the characteristics of middle-aged parents, role expectations take precedence over unique personal traits:

> While the older groups also touched upon personality attributes (such as the wife's gregariousness, compassion, or attractive appearance) their descriptions were set within the framework of normative role expectations. More than those of others, the middle-aged men's descriptions of spouses were centered on their performance as wives and mothers. . . . In comparison, men and women in the preretirement stage expressed what appears to be a renewed interest in the personalities of their spouses, and their descriptions were more expressive. Though these oldest men also paid tribute to the roles of housewife and mother, they were more likely to mention marital companionship and the wife's personal talents and qualities. Similarly, the women, while not omitting the husband's role of worker and provider,

Introducing the Marriage and Family Professionals

Box 11–2 / Marriage Enrichment Programs

Every Monday and Thursday evening for a period of three weeks, six married couples meet for several hours in a university auditorium in Birmingham, Alabama. With the assistance of a husband-and-wife team trained in marriage counseling, they learn how to express feelings, to communicate more openly, and to experiment with new roles. Then, when each couple returns home, they complete a homework assignment by bathing together and giving each other a foot massage.

These couples are participating in the Pairing Enrichment Program (PEP), designed by Robert P. Travis and Patricia Y. Travis for married couples who wish to enhance their marriage. PEP is just one of a growing number of marriage enrichment programs across the country that are attempting to teach married couples the interpersonal skills that appear to enhance marital satisfaction. According to Herbert A. Otto, a pioneer in the marriage enrichment movement, these programs "are for couples who have what they perceive to be a fairly well functioning marriage and who wish to make their marriage even more mutually satisfying. The programs are *not* designed for people whose marriage is at a point of crisis, or who are seeking counseling help for marital problems" (1975, p. 137). In other words, they are preventive rather than remedial. And they are a relatively recent phenomenon—before the 1960s, they were virtually unknown.

Otto conducted a survey of such enrichment programs in this country. "Sixty-five percent of those reporting," writes Otto, "stated that their programs were approved by a church or church-related organization. Seven percent of the remainder were approved by other organizations and the rest conducted by professionals in private practice" (p. 138). Most of these programs employ a variety of techniques to facilitate marital interaction, including group discussions, sensitivity training, and certain exercises in nonverbal communication. Otto also found that topics such as sexual relationships, roles, and conflict resolution are frequently discussed. It is estimated that almost 200,000 couples have participated in such programs over the past few years (Otto, 1975).

The most popular program so far has been the Roman Catholic Marriage Encounter, attended by more than 40,000 couples, not all of them Catholics. The Marriage Encounter is a weekend program conducted by a team of one to three couples and a priest, and attended by anywhere from six to fifteen couples. These programs place particular emphasis upon helping couples differentiate between role relationships (mother–father, husband–wife) and interpersonal ones; and in dispelling misconceptions about masculinity by encouraging men to express their feelings more freely.

Marriage enrichment programs such as these focus on the interpersonal competence required in a companionship marriage where there are high expectations for both emotional and sexual satisfaction. If marital satisfaction generally seems to decline over the years, such programs may help some couples to sustain more vital relationships.

Sources: Herbert A. Otto. Marriage and family enrichment programs in North America—Report and analysis. *The Family Coordinator,* April 1975, pp. 137–142; Robert P. Travis and Patricia Y. Travis. The pairing enrichment program: Actualizing the marriage. *The Family Coordinator,* April 1975, pp. 129–136. Copyright © 1975 by National Council on Family Relations. Reprinted by permission.

> gave greater consideration to emotional ties and to the individuality of the spouse. (Lowenthal et al., 1975, p. 25)

One of the main reasons for declining satisfaction in the middle-aged marriage, then, is that spouses interact more in terms of roles than in terms of unique personalities. In the unusual marriages that Cuber and Harroff call vital or total relationships, spouses manage to maintain companionship, continuing to emphasize each other's personal traits and needs despite the demands of occupational and parental roles. In many of the marital enrichment programs that have been initiated across the country, too, one of the objectives is to help spouses maintain personal sensitivity and responsiveness (see Box 11–2).

As we have noted often throughout this book, many of the problems in marriage today result from the high expectations that people bring to it. In societies where spouses do not expect to be companions, role incompatibility is far less likely to cause problems. Perhaps as people approach marriage with somewhat more realistic expectations and more awareness of the stresses caused by parental and occupational roles, they will also be better prepared for the continual adjustments required in modern marriage.

Conclusions

"What happens to marriage over the years?" is a difficult question to answer because, among other things, the investigator must try to measure the elusive quality known as marital adjustment, success, or happiness. Different studies define and measure this factor in somewhat different ways, so comparison of their results is inexact. Cross-sectional and longitudinal designs, the two research tools for studying change over time, both have certain drawbacks. And with either design, all such studies are based on self-reports, which probably tell more about the respondents' conventionality than about the reality of their marriages.

Nevertheless, the studies agree generally that marital satisfaction soon begins to decline after the unscripted spontaneity of the newlywed period. As the young parents take on more role obligations, companionship declines along with common interests and demonstrations of affection. But eventually marital satisfaction increases again in the later years of marriage.

Dividing the course of family life into four stages, we saw that in the first stage, the newlywed marriage, marital satisfaction is high. Spouses typically enjoy each other's companionship and engage in many shared activities. With the birth of children, however, role obligations become paramount, and many couples report less marital satisfaction. Middle-aged marriage begins as the children leave home. The spouses find new freedoms and have to make many adjustments; the wife in particular has to prepare for her "second act." Then finally in the retirement years, as occupational roles are discarded, too, marital satisfaction increases again. Many couples become as happy together as they were when first married.

But why does marital satisfaction decline in the middle years of marriage? A leading cause is role incompatibility. The demands of parental and occupational roles cause spouses to neglect emotional needs, to pay less attention to each other's personal traits than they did as newlyweds.

REFERENCES

Robert O. Blood. *Love match and arranged marriage.* New York: Free Press, 1967.

——— and Donald M. Wolfe. *Husbands and wives.* New York: Free Press, 1960.

Ernest W. Burgess and Paul Wallin. *Engagement and marriage.* Philadelphia: Lippincott, 1953.

Wesley R. Burr. Satisfaction with various aspects of marriage over the life cycle: A random middle-class sample. *Journal of Marriage and the Family,* February 1970, pp. 29–37.

———. *Theory construction and the sociology of the family.* New York: Wiley, 1973.

Angus Campbell. The American way of mating: Marriage si, children, only maybe. *Psychology Today,* May 1975, pp. 39–42.

Philip Cowan, Carolyn Cowan, Lynne Coie, and John Coie. The impact of children upon their parents. In Lucille Newman and Warren Miller, eds. *The first child and family formation.* Chapel Hill: University of North Carolina Press, 1978.

John F. Cuber and Peggy Harroff. *Sex and the significant Americans.* Baltimore: Penguin, 1968.

Irwin Deutscher. Socialization for postparental life. In Arnold Rose, ed. *Human behavior and social process.* Boston: Houghton Mifflin, 1967.

Jan Dizard. *Social change in the family.* Chicago: Community and Family Study Center, University of Chicago, 1968.

Evelyn M. Duvall. *Family development.* Philadelphia: Lippincott, 1971.

Vernon Edmonds. Marriage conventionalization: Definition and measurement. *Journal of Marriage and the Family* 29 (1967): 681–688.

Glen Elder. Family history and the life course. *Journal of Family History* 2 (1977): 276–304.

Joseph Epstein. *Divorced in America.* Baltimore: Penguin, 1975.

Norval D. Glenn. Psychological well-being in the postparental stage. *Journal of Marriage and the Family* 37 (1975): 105–110.

E. Lowell Kelly. Consistency of the adult personality. *American Psychologist* 10 (1955): 654–681.

Alan C. Kerckhoff. Husband–wife expectations and reactions to retirement. *Journal of Gerontology* 19 (1964): 510–516.

Alfred Kinsey, Wardell Pomeroy, and Clyde E. Martin. *Sexual behavior in the human male.* Philadelphia: Saunders, 1948.

Gerald R. Leslie. *The family in social context.* New York: Oxford University Press, 1973.

Daniel J. Levinson. *The seasons of a man's life.* New York: Knopf, 1978.

Norman Lobsenz. Sex and the senior citizen. *The New York Times Magazine,* January 20, 1974, pp. 8 et passim.

Helena Lopata. The secondary features of a primary relationship. *Human Organization,* Summer 1965, pp. 116–123.

Marjorie Fiske Lowenthal, Majda Thurnher, and David Chiriboga. *Four stages of life.* San Francisco: Jossey-Bass, 1975.

Susan R. Orden and Norman M. Bradburn. Dimensions of marriage happiness. *American Journal of Sociology* 73 (1968): 715–731.

Peter C. Pineo. Disenchantment in the later years of marriage. *Marriage and Family Living* 23 (1961): 3–11.

Harriet Presser. Age differences between spouses. *The American Behavioral Scientist,* November/December 1975, pp. 190–205.

Morton Puner. Will you still love me? *Human Behavior,* June 1974, pp. 42–48.

Karen Renne. Correlates of dissatisfaction in marriage. *Journal of Marriage and the Family* 32 (1970): 54–67.

Boyd C. Rollins and Harold Feldman. Marital satisfaction over the family life cycle. *Journal of Marriage and the Family* 32 (1970): 20–28.

The Roper Organization. *The Virginia Slims American women's opinion poll.* New York: The Roper Organization, 1974.

Lillian Rubin. *Women of a certain age.* New York: Harper & Row, 1979.

Gail Sheehy. *Passages.* New York: Dutton, 1976.

Arlene Skolnick. *The intimate environment.* Boston: Little, Brown, 1973.

Marvin Sussman. Intergenerational family relationships and social role changes in middle age. *Journal of Gerontology* 15 (1960): 71–75.

Yonina Talmon. Aging in Israel, a planned society. *American Journal of Sociology* 67 (1961): 284–295.

Ralph Turner. *Family interaction.* New York: Wiley, 1970.

George E. Vaillant. *Adaptation to life.* Boston: Little, Brown, 1977.

FOR FURTHER READING

For different perspectives on the satisfactions of marriage, and problems in assessing them, see an article by Boyd C. Rollins and Kenneth L. Cannon, "Marital Satisfaction Over the Family Life Cycle: A Reevaluation" (*Journal of Marriage and the Family,* May 1974), which discusses why role strain helps to explain the U-shaped curve of marital satisfaction; Graham B. Spanier, Robert A. Lewis, and Charles L. Cole are the authors of an article entitled "Marital Adjustment Over the Family Life Cycle: The Issue of Curvilinearity" (*Journal of Marriage and the Family,* May 1975), which presents data on a new research project, and discusses some of the problems in interpreting cross-sectional studies of satisfaction; Joseph Harry's "Evolving Sources of Happiness for Men Over the Life Cycle: A Structural Analysis" (*Journal of Marriage and the Family,* May 1976) analyzes the principal sources of satisfaction for men at different points in the life cycle.

For a comprehensive study of the pressures and preoccupations of people at various stages of the life cycle, see *Four Stages of Life* by Marjorie Fiske Lowenthal, Majda Thurnher, and David Chiriboga (San Francisco: Jossey-Bass, 1975). Joan Aldous has written a useful book from the developmental perspective entitled *Family Careers* (New York: Wiley, 1978). Among the new books on adult development, Daniel J. Levinson's *The Seasons of a Man's Life* (New York: Knopf, 1978) is an outstanding combination of disciplined inquiry and felicitous prose.

Glen Elder has made several outstanding contributions to an understanding of how families change over the life course. You might consult his article "Family History and the Life Course," which appeared in the *Journal of Family History,* vol. 2, 1977, for an overview, and his book *Children of the Great Depression* (Chicago: University of Chicago Press, 1974), which is based upon a rich source of longitudinal data provided by the Oakland Growth Study. This is a particularly valuable analysis of how personal and family histories are affected by massive historical forces.

For a more personal perspective on the process of mutual adjustment of spouses in the early years of marriage, and for some insights about how working-class marriages differ from the middle-class marriages that sociologists most often study, see Chapters 5 and 6 in Lillian Rubin's *Worlds of Pain* (New York: Basic Books, 1976). Rubin has also written a new book, *Women of a Certain Age* (New York: Harper & Row, 1979), which provides a useful perspective on middle-aged women.

For further reading on the later stages of the family life cycle, see Gary R. Lee's "Marriage and Morale in Later Life" in *Journal of Marriage and the Family,* vol. 40, February 1978; and Norval D. Glenn's "Psychological Well-Being in the Postparental Stage" in *Journal of Marriage and the Family,* vol. 37, February 1975.

V

Extensions of Intimacy— Children, Relatives, and Community Ties

"Robinson Family, 1977" Alice Neel

12 Parents and Children—To Beget or Not to Beget?

This year 3 million American couples will experience an event with profound consequences for them and for the entire society: they will have a child.

Of all of the personal decisions discussed in this text, none has more lasting significance or poses more burdens. As we saw in the previous chapter, the birth of a child has a dramatic effect on marital satisfaction. First, pregnancy and childbirth disrupt the couple's sexual relationship, and then the infant makes heavy demands on its parents' time and attention. The birth of a child also represents a substantial financial commitment. Parents spend more on each of their children than they do on any purchase they make. To complicate the matter, having a child is one of the few irreversible decisions that most people make in a lifetime.

Considering the consequences of childbirth, it is startling and depressing that in many cases today we still cannot accurately call it a decision. Nature has connected the intensely pleasurable experience of sex with the responsibilities of childbearing and rearing, and although contraceptives are widely available, many couples still do not take the precautions required to separate the two. As a result, many pregnancies are unintended. Worse yet, a high percentage of babies born today are unwanted.

But if children create such a burden for their parents, why does anyone want them? Why do so many couples each year shoulder that burden quite willingly? Whether or not there is any such thing as a maternal instinct, every society, ours included, offers various incentives for having children—wages a kind of propaganda campaign for parenthood. One of the main reasons why groups such as the National Alliance for Optional Parenthood (NAOP) have formed is to provide a different perspective, one that urges couples to make a conscious decision about childbirth in light of personal preferences and abilities as well as the potential costs.

As *Look* magazine writer Betty Rollin said,

> It is not a question of whether children are sweet and marvelous to have and rear. The question is,

> even if that's so, whether or not one wants to pay the price for it. . . . If God were still speaking to us in a voice we could hear, He would probably say, "Be fruitful, *don't* multiply." (1970, p. 15)

Judging by the smaller average family size today, the smaller family size preferences expressed by young women, and the increasing number of couples who choose not to have children at all, that is exactly what many people are doing.

Until recently, one could hardly speak of marriage without implying parenthood. The institution of marriage was designed primarily to provide a durable and socially acceptable vehicle for parenthood. Bearing and rearing children was considered an inescapable duty, one that naturally involved certain sacrifices and pains. "Standing by the crib of one's own baby with that world-old pang of compassion and protectiveness toward this little creature," essayist Christopher Morley wrote,

> the heart flies back in gratitude to those who felt the same way toward oneself. Then for the first time one understands the homely succession of sacrifices and pains by which life is transmitted and fostered down the stumbling generations of men.

But for many people today personal freedom and growth have begun to take precedence over the ancient obligation to bear children.

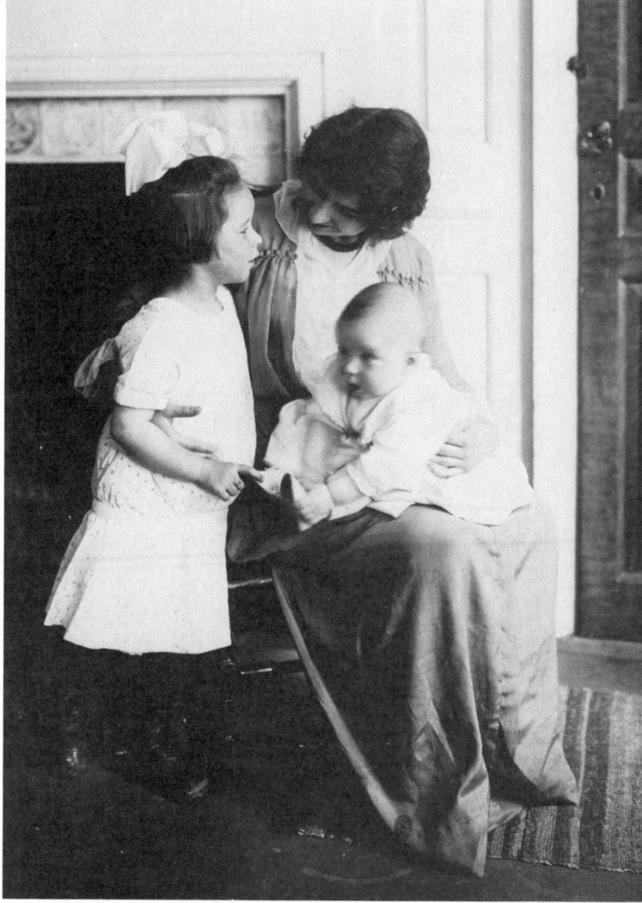

Early twentieth-century sentimentalized view of motherhood.

And if you decide to have children, you are faced with further choices about how to raise them. "The trick nature played on humans," Arlene Skolnick says, "was to give them the most burdensome infants of all the primates while removing the detailed genetic instructions that guide maternal behavior among other species" (1973, p. 278). For us, child rearing is a cultural process; we must *learn* how to raise our children, and there is no consensus in our society on how it should be done. Should parents be strict or permissive? What is the best way to help a child achieve her potential? How much fondling and attention does an infant really need? Is it bad for a child if his mother returns to her job? Even the advice given in child care books written by pediatricians and psychologists is inconsistent. "It is evident," columnist Max Lerner once observed, "that in no other culture has there been so pervasive a cultural anxiety about the training of children" (1957, p. 562).

Obviously, however, the first question of all is: Do you really want to have children?

PARENTHOOD AS DUTY OR CHOICE

Considering how often it is assumed that there is a "maternal instinct," it is remarkable that so many incentives exist to encourage us to do "what comes naturally." There are strong social pressures to bear children. Failure to do so requires an explanation. Having children is often considered an inevitability, not an option, as expressed in such refrains as "When you grow up and have your own children. . . ." Later, parents drop hints to their married children about their desire to become grandparents and thus add to the social pressures to bear children.

Pronatalist Pressures—Be Fruitful and Multiply

In a great variety of ways, from subtle, often unspoken assumptions to outright cash grants to parents, most societies encourage people to have children. One of the most common themes in Western art for centuries was the happy Madonna cradling a contented infant. Today advertisements convey the same message: baby food ads, for example, sell motherhood at the same time that they sell certain brand names. These pronatalist pressures might be regarded as inducements to convince couples to do what is necessary in order to satisfy the most basic requirement of any society—to reproduce itself.

In the Soviet Union, where slumping birth rates and a labor shortage have prompted official concern, pronatalist programs have been instituted by the regime. Parents who have three or more children receive substantial cash grants. Women who bear five children are eligible for the Medal of Motherhood, and those who have ten get the Mother Heroine award (Geiger, 1968, p. 191).

In the United States, most of the inducements to have children are less obvious, but very strong nonetheless. In one study of pronatalism in women's magazine fiction, the researcher found that a majority of stories picture motherhood as a profoundly fulfilling occupation and portray the lives of women without children as frustrated and empty (Franzwa, 1974). Pronatalist themes predominate on television, too. Pregnancy and motherhood receive even more time in the daytime soap operas than the commercials, and women are often portrayed as seeking fulfillment by having children. They often become pregnant out of a desire to appear more attractive to their husbands. "The message to viewers is clear," as one writer concludes: "Whoever conceives, wins" (Peck, 1974, p. 79).

Although the federal government makes no direct cash grants to parents, it does encourage having children by allowing special tax exemptions for parents. A more subtle but perhaps more effective inducement is the popular belief in the joys of parenthood. As sociologist E. E. LeMasters has pointed out, there is a long list of popular beliefs that encourage parents to have children. It starts with such items as "rearing children is fun," "children are sweet and cute," "children will turn out well if they have good parents," and "children appreciate all the advantages their parents give them." It continues with such frequently repeated beliefs as "two parents are always better than one," "love is enough to sustain a good parental performance," "all married couples should have children," "children improve a marriage," and "child rearing is easier today because of modern medicine, modern appliances, child psychology, and so on"(1957, pp. 353–4). Even though most parents would say that these folk beliefs tell only half the story at best, they remain an important inducement to having children.

It is often assumed that the lives of men as well as women are incomplete if they do not have children. Here is an excerpt from an article that appeared in *Bride's* magazine: "A man without children," writes the male author,

> is not complete. . . . Children establish my place in the long chain of generations. . . . Children are my continuity. Through children, I fling my seed into the future. Reproduction is the act of life, is life itself. In reproducing, I affirm my place in the system of life, inhabiting the earth. The man without children has lost his place in history. (Peck, 1974, p. 136)

Faced with the loss of their place in history, few men could ignore the implications of that passage. Do not think about all the potential costs of parenthood. You have a *duty* to sire children.

In the past, of course, these pressures served a very practical purpose, for even in Western Europe until the eighteenth century, the "population problem" was to replenish the population in each generation. Disease and recurrent food shortages kept the population from increasing very rapidly. High fertility rates were matched by high mortality rates; a very large percentage of infants and children died before reaching maturity. Under those circumstances, the commandment to be fruitful and multiply was an eminently practical instruction.

From the point of view of the parents as well as society as a whole, having children could be very beneficial. Under some circumstances it still is today, for the parents at least, as a poor laborer with eight children in a village north of New Delhi explained to a journalist. "It's good to have a big family," the man said. "They don't cost much, and when they get old enough to work they bring in money. And when I am old, they will take care of me." Thus, the birth control programs promoted by the Indian government have had only a limited success because among the Indian poor, children are one's only Blue Cross policy and Social Security program. In India, as in many societies of the past, people have large families because they are poor and children are their only wealth. It is very common in such societies to regard pregnancy as a matter over which the individual has little control. "Children are the gods' gifts," the Indian laborer said. "Who are we to say they should not be born?" (Borders, 1976, p. 18).

The rewards and costs of parenthood for most Americans today are very different from those of an Indian villager. In the past few years several organizations have been formed to expose the pronatalist pressures that still exist in our society and to encourage people to think of parenthood as an option, not a duty—an alternative, not an absolutely foregone conclusion.

Parenthood by Choice

Had you been in New York's Central Park on the evening of August 1, 1974, you might have witnessed a celebration that illustrated and dramatized today's changing attitudes toward fertility. The event was an infertility rite, and it featured a dance performed by three white-gowned women celebrating the freedoms of nonmotherhood. Dan Wakefield, a novelist, and Stephanie Mills, a feminist writer, were crowned with laurel wreaths and named Nonparents of the year. Among those speaking at the ceremonies was Alvin Toffler, author of *Future Shock*. "Once, the encouragement to breed was a necessity to perpetuate the species," he said, but today pronatalism has become "an obsolete cultural hangover."

Among the organizers of that ceremony were several of the founders of the National Alliance for Optional Parenthood. One of them explains the group's purpose this way: "We're not going around saying people shouldn't have children. But we say people shouldn't automatically assume they *should* have children. Parenthood is a matter to be thought over quite carefully—both for the parents' and the children's sake." But haven't people always had the freedom not to have children? Spokespeople for the NAOP don't think so.

> It's true in a technical sense, of course, that because of the contraceptive devices available today, people can decide not to have children. But, in a deeper sense, one can only really make a free choice in an unprejudiced social context. And we don't have that today. (Katz, 1972, p. 18)

Members of NAOP criticize what they call the motherhood myth, a glorified picture of a child-centered life for women who never really consider the alternatives or think about whether they are well suited to motherhood. NAOP charges that the duty to procreate has been kept alive by "babysell," the efforts of business enterprises to encourage motherhood in order to expand the market for family-related consumer goods (Katz, 1972).

Figure 12–1 United States Population Growth with Two- or Three-Child Families. It may not seem as if the decision to have "just one more" child has important social consequences. But, as this graph demonstrates, there is a marked difference between the population growth of a nation in which families have, on the average, two children as opposed to three. If American families continue to have an average of three children, the national population would, by the year 2013, be double what it was in 1968. Even if the current preference for two-child families continues, it is estimated that there will be another one hundred million Americans by 2013.

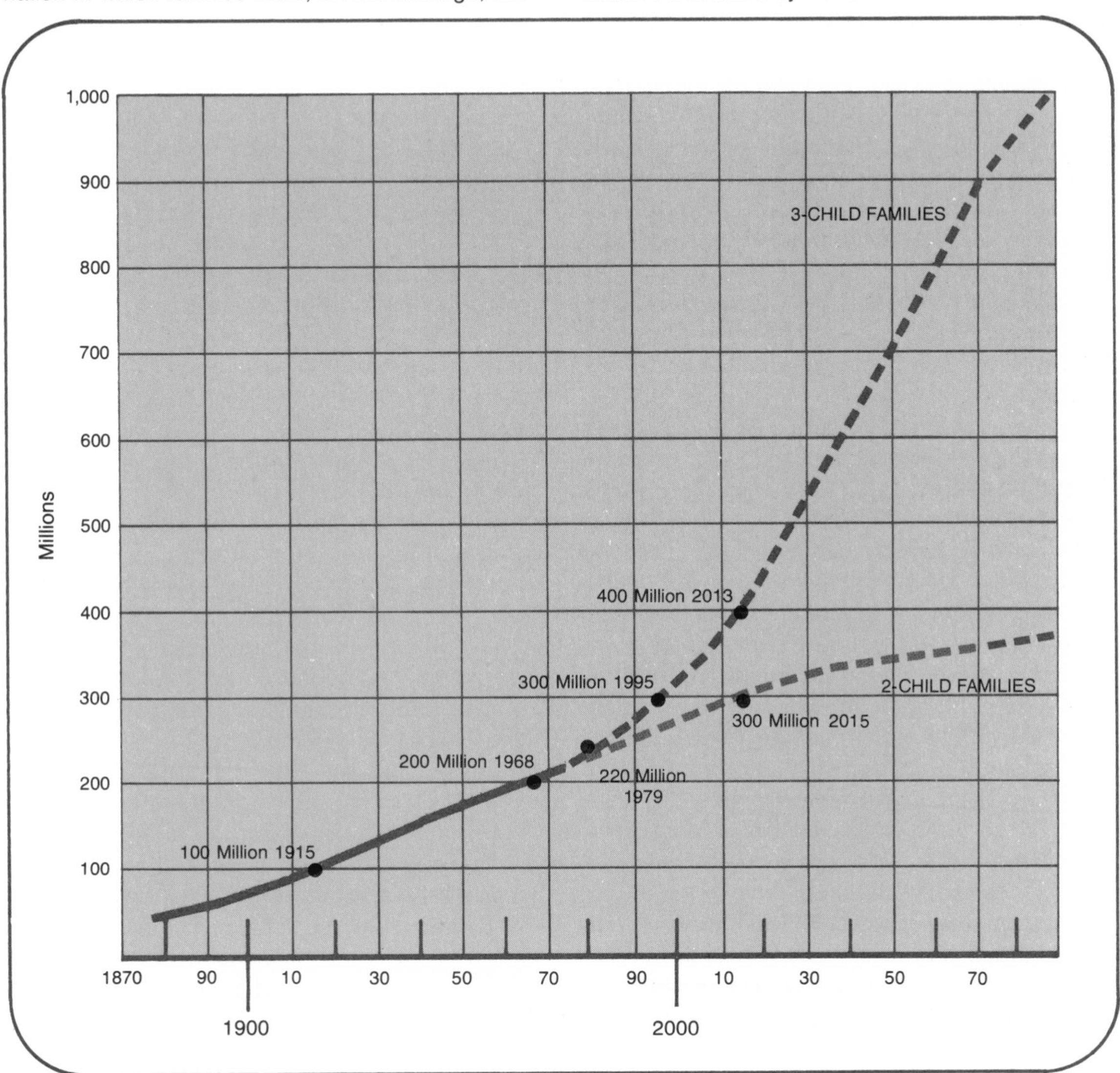

Source: Population and the American Future. The Report of the Commission on Population Growth and the American Future (Washington, D.C.: Government Printing Office, 1972).

Organizations such as NAOP and activities like the infertility rite in Central Park both illustrate how rapidly attitudes toward parenthood and family size in the United States are changing today; survey studies of family size preferences and declining birth rates also demonstrate how widespread the new attitudes have become (see Figure 12–1). In one poll of American college students, 56 percent of the males and 49 percent of the females said they wanted only two children. Only about 33 percent of the males in this study and a slightly higher percentage of females revealed a preference for three children (Blake, 1974). Although only about 5 percent of the young adults surveyed in another poll plan to have marriages without children, there is wide acceptance among them of both intentionally childless marriages and a delay of childbirth for several years. Four out of five under age thirty agreed that it was "perfectly all right" for a married couple to have no children at all (Institute of Life Insurance, 1974, p. 5).

Data from the June 1978 Census Bureau report on *Fertility of American Women* show that the preference for relatively small families is widely shared among young women and not confined to the college-educated or to any one racial group. The number of births expected over their entire lifetime by women between the ages of eighteen and thirty-four is 2,113 per 1,000 women, which is almost exactly the same as the fertility level (2,115) required for natural replacement of the population. The birth expectations of women between eighteen and twenty-four are particularly important, because this group will account for a large percentage of all the births over the next few years. Among women in this category, lifetime birth expectations are slightly below the replacement level, at 2,033 per 1,000 women. Considering that the fertility rate among black women has been considerably higher than that of white women, it is significant that the 1978 Population Survey found that black women under twenty-five had the *lowest* birth expectations of any of the racial groups (U.S. Bureau of the Census, 1978).

The birth rate since the 1960s indicates that couples are not just planning to have smaller families, they are actually doing so. In 1972, the Census Bureau revised its projections of what the United States population would be by the year 2000 because the fertility rate—the number of births per 1,000 women in the childbearing years—was dropping well below the high levels of the 1950s. In 1972, despite the relatively large number of women who could potentially give birth, the actual number of babies born was smaller than it had been in twenty-seven years. This tendency toward lower fertility rates was christened the "birth dearth" or the "baby bust," in contrast to the "baby boom" that followed World War II. In 1974, the fertility rate started to climb slightly, but—influenced perhaps by the economic recession—it dropped again in 1975 to 66.7 per 1,000 women of childbearing age, the lowest ever recorded. When the fertility rate began a modest rise in 1977—to 68.4—people began to speculate that the "baby boomlet" might indicate a reversal of the recent trend toward low fertility. But in the following year, 1978, the fertility rate dropped to a new record low, 66.4 births per 1,000 women of childbearing age (*Vital Statistics Report,* 1978; see Figure 12–2).

Since 1972, when births in the United States fell below the replacement level for the first time, some people have referred to this phenomenon as zero population growth. But even though the fertility rate may remain relatively low compared with what it was in the 1950s, the population of the United States is likely to keep growing because the total number of women in the prime childbearing years will be larger than it was in the past. It is estimated, for example, that by 1980 the total number of women in their prime childbearing years—a group that includes about 20 million people—will be about twice as large as that group was in 1960. As a result, even with fertility rates at or slightly below the 2.1 replacement level rate, it will take several decades for the population to stabilize.

What are the main factors that have contributed to this trend toward lower fertility rates? One important factor is the educational attainment of women, for in recent years there has been a consistent connection between the number of years of formal education that a woman completes and her fertility. The effect of more education is especially striking among black women. In recent years, black women with less

Figure 12–2 The Baby Boom and the Birth Dearth. As this graph shows, since the 1950s, there has been a sharp drop in the fertility rate.

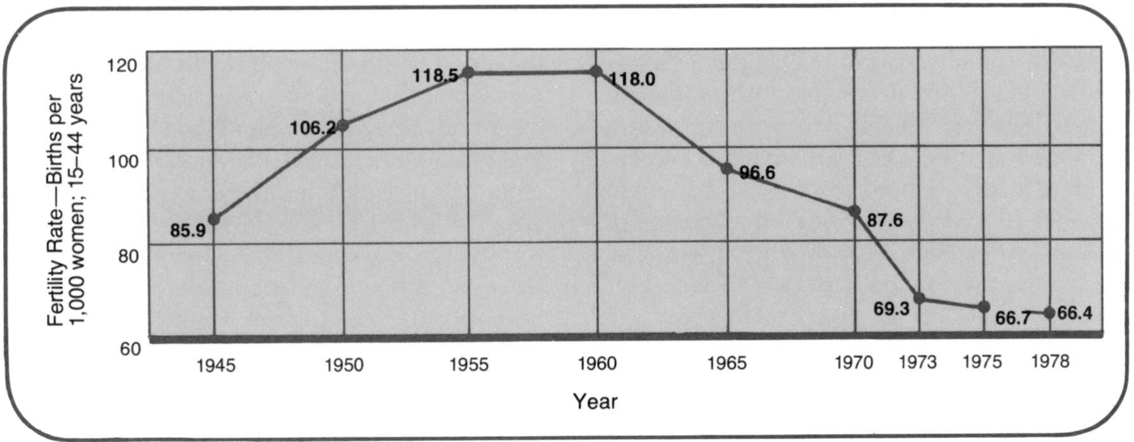

Source: Statistical Abstract of the United States 1976 (Washington, D.C.: Government Printing Office, 1976); and *Vital Statistics Report,* "Births, Marriages, Divorces and Deaths for 1978" (Washington, D.C.: Department of Health, Education, and Welfare, March 15, 1979).

than a high school diploma have had, on the average, about four children. Those who graduate from high school have about three children—which is similar to the fertility of their white counterparts. But among black women who complete four years of college, average family size is less than two children, well below the replacement level, and considerably lower than the average family size of their white counterparts (Population Reference Bureau, 1975).

It also appears that the lower fertility rates of recent years are a result of the growing expectation among women that they will spend many of their adult years in the labor force. Among young women in their late teens, plans to enter the labor force do not have much effect on their fertility expectations. But as women grow older, they become more aware of the extent to which bearing and rearing children will interrupt their jobs or careers. Consequently, as women grow older, their employment plans have a more marked effect on fertility expectations (Stolzenberg and Waite, 1977).

There are two final factors that help to explain the low fertility rates of the past few years. Today, just as in previous decades (such as during the Depression of the 1930s, when the fertility rate fell) economic stresses affect family size preferences. In 1978, as in 1975, the threat of economic recession undoubtedly contributed to low fertility. We will discuss another important contributing factor, the availability of more effective contraceptives, after examining the extent of voluntary childlessness.

For the society as a whole, the trend toward smaller families means more resources per person, fewer demands on educational facilities, and a shift toward a slightly older population. For individual families, it means—among other things—a shorter childbearing period and more years for women to spend in other pursuits.

Voluntary Childlessness

As we have noted, there has been an unprecedented decline in childbearing in the United States since the 1960s. Because voluntary childlessness is widely discussed today, and because there is more social support for couples who choose to have no children, it would be reasonable to conclude that childbearing has declined in part because a substantial minority has chosen the child-free option. If we examine recent statistics on childlessness among ever-married women in their twenties, it appears that this is what has happened. Among ever-married women between the ages of twenty and twenty-four, for example, the percentage who were childless had increased from 24 to 42 percent between 1960 and 1976. During that same period, the percentage of ever-married women in their late twenties who had not had a child increased from 13 to 22 percent (U.S. Bureau of the Census, 1977). Even if a small percentage of these women remained childless because they were unable to bear children, these statistics seem to show a marked increase in voluntary childlessness.

However, we get a different perspective on this phenomenon by taking into account the trend toward delayed childbearing and by noting that the incidence of childlessness among women in their early thirties is no higher than it was a few decades ago. Indeed, among women thirty-five and over the incidence of childlessness has actually *declined* since 1960; only 7 percent of ever-married women between thirty-five and thirty-nine were childless, compared with about 11 percent among women of the same age in 1960. To put this in historical perspective, it is interesting to note that in the mid-seventies the percentage of child-free couples in the United States was less than one-quarter what it had been in the 1920s (Glick, 1977). Even if the women who married during the sixties are different from their predecessors, and bear out the Census Bureau's prediction that about 10 percent will remain childless, we can still conclude that the overwhelming majority of American couples can be expected to have at least one child, and most will have several. The main reason for the decline in childbearing has been, and very likely will continue to be, that the number of large families has declined, not that many couples decide to forego childbearing altogether, or decide to have only one child.

What are the characteristics of that small minority of couples who choose not to have children? In her research on voluntarily childless couples, sociologist Jean Veevers (1973) conducted in-depth interviews with more than fifty women to understand what they perceived as the disadvantages of parenthood. She remarks that child-free couples, like those who do have children, often find it difficult to articulate why they made that choice. In some cases it is the result of a conscious decision reached after weighing the alternatives in the first few years of marriage; more often it results from the successive postponement of childbearing. Veevers found that these couples, usually well-educated, making relatively high incomes, living in or near metropolitan areas, and not strongly religious, resist the social pressures to have children because they are happy with a child-free lifestyle. Other studies underline the importance for such couples of seeking approval for childlessness from friends and relatives; in other words, although child-free couples are part of a small, even deviant minority, they are influenced by and seek out reference groups that support their decisions (Houseknecht, 1977).

The Costs and Rewards of Parenthood

One of the costs of parenthood that may influence some child-free couples is the pattern of declining marital satisfaction after the birth of children, as we saw in the previous chapter. Another cost is the restriction that motherhood puts on women to pursue their own interests and careers. There is no way to determine how much this factor has contributed to the smaller family size of recent years, but it has been noted that the women who express the greatest interest in pursuing a career of their own also express a desire for relatively few children.

Some of the costs of parenthood can be expressed in dollars and cents. In agricultural societies children are an economic asset, but in the United States children are very costly.

The costs, then, are high, but what about the rewards? Many of the old rewards, as we have already seen, have lost their allure. Children can no longer be counted upon to provide a pension in one's old age. It is rare today for parents to have children just so that they can perform family religious rituals, although this may still be a factor in some Jewish families, where a son is needed to say the *kaddish* for his dead father. And historian Edward Shorter is undoubtedly right when he says that people today care far less than our ancestors did for the "posterity business." As family name and lineage become less important, we are less likely to have children in order to extend the chain of generations stretching down through time (Shorter, 1975, p. 8). Nevertheless, nineteen out of twenty couples today have at least one child, and they are not merely yielding to pronatalist pressure. For many people, to provide nurture and to be needed are rewards in themselves, and children do offer many personal satisfactions, difficult as they are to list and analyze (see Box 12–1).

When sociologist Lee Rainwater asked more than 400 husbands and wives at various income levels why they wanted children, he found a common belief that parents are selfish if they have fewer children than they can afford. Many people think that "one should not have more children than one can support, but one should have as many children as one can afford" (1965, p. 181). In view of this belief, it seems paradoxical that lower-class parents, on the average, have larger families than other parents, but Rainwater explains that children offer rewards to these parents that they cannot get in any other way. Lower-class women often do not have the option of a satisfying job or career, so for them motherhood is destiny. There is really no alternative, nothing that promises to make her life complete the way motherhood does. It provides a worthwhile and socially recognized role (1960). At the same time, fatherhood provides special satisfactions for the lower-class male, for if he often cannot take as much pride in his work as does a middle-class male, he can take pride in his family. Family life also offers an arena for exercising a kind of power that he does not have at his job. Two other investigators have put it this way:

> Whereas successful achievers have their status as adult men supported by their superior occupational roles and authority, the unsuccessful find a substitute in the authority they exercise in their role as fathers over a number of children. (Blau and Duncan, 1967, p. 428)

There are several reasons, then, why lower-class parents might choose to have more children than do their middle-class counterparts. In the past few pages, we have been examining the costs and rewards of having children, assuming that these are factors that parents consider as they plan their families. There is, however, convincing evidence that at all social levels many children are unplanned, and some are unwanted.

Pregnancy, Planned and Unplanned

For centuries, humans have been trying to find an effective contraceptive—something that would allow sex and reproduction to be disconnected. Long before overpopulation became a social concern, there were many individuals who for personal reasons wanted to prevent pregnancy. Both the Bible and the Talmud mention the use of *coitus interruptus* (male withdrawal before ejaculation) as one means of controlling fertility. Most of the techniques used were highly unreliable or totally ineffective. The Egyptians, for example, used a vaginal suppository made out of crocodile dung and honey. This was apparently more effective than many of the other contraceptive methods that have been prescribed over the centuries, including magic potions, jumping up and down after intercourse, and induced sneezing (McCary, 1973, p. 87).

In this respect, young people today have grown up in a situation that is historically unique. Sheldon Segal, one of the directors of the Population Council, refers to the recent era as the "population years." Unlike their parents, today's young people

Point of View

Box 12–1 / Choosing Motherhood

Certainly women have been oversold and wrongly sold on motherhood. Little girls have been taught roles that narrowly focus on the pleasures of child care, promoting excess domesticity and shrinking of brains—but that is by now an old story. The evils of a male-chauvinist society have not been cured or eliminated, but certainly they have been exposed. But the reaction against motherhood—the scorn poured on the nurturing role, particularly if performed by the mother—nevertheless is falling into its own error of excess.

Having a child by birth or adoption profoundly changes and forever alters the woman. In our excessively child-oriented society, we have only begun to examine what the care and relationship to children actually mean for the parent. This is not an easily categorized experience. It results in one of the most intricate weavings of the human mind, where terror, joy, hate, anger, love, guilt, memory, pride, and fear form patterns, each unique, that finally can be recognized and called a "mother and child relationship." As we forge this relationship we are creating parts of ourselves, extending ourselves, not so we live through our children (though the temptation is there and the error is there) but so that we become enriched with the knowledge and experience, both intellectual and gut, of ourselves in this most special of human encounters. The experience of the mother–child pair as it goes through its metamorphosis, no less dramatic than many others in nature, leaves on the parent weathering marks, disfiguring and beautifying.

All of this sounds rather abstract, but I mean something very concrete. For example, if you are a mother, you must have experienced the fear that you might die at a time when a three-year-old is still having nightmares, and wakes up to come into your room. What if you weren't there? What if the child reached out and called for you half asleep and you were dead? The particular terror of that thought, while painful, also expresses the fact that you are absolutely needed and connected to the center of someone else's emotional life.

There are new feelings in motherhood of tenderness, closeness, and a new sense of awe at some special sense of the miracle of the mind—the first words, the first steps, the first game, the first smile, the first sign of intelligence under a still-bald head. These wonders have been turned into confectionary garbage by some women's magazines but are still experienced privately and deeply by new mothers over and over again.

This is just a small part of the emotional experiences of a woman in the early years of her baby's life. The routines, the boring, deadening menial work that surrounds child care also surrounds this storm of feelings that shapes the changing interior landscape of the young mother.

I remember the moment, now some twelve years ago, when I suddenly knew my child was being taken care of. I was bathing my daughter—who was trying to put the soap in her mouth—and I felt this sudden kinship with all the other women who had done the same

have heard since childhood of the population explosion, planned parenthood, and family planning. They have grown up and into an era of highly effective contraception, voluntary sterilization, and legal abortion. They are the first generation to include many post-pill babies born to mothers who used oral contraception and are themselves prodigious consumers of contraceptives on a steady basis. In 1970, nine out of ten married American women under thirty used some thing—this feeding, cleaning, disposing of urine and feces, smiling, hugging, and touching. And with this sense of a common bond, I entered a new phase in my life. I had grown to value my wonderful individuality a little less and my common humanity more.

How often the idealistic, possibly grandiose dreams of one's adolescence seem to appear again, like sturdy weeds, as one views one's child. He or she will be a concert pianist, will be a billionaire or an Einstein or da Vinci. He or she will travel where I never went and be more beautiful, get better grades, excel where I failed, be emotionally perfect, healthy in every way. One imagines that the scars of one's own childhood will be removed by the success of the new generation. But in fact all of us who have survived the adolescence of our children have learned to view them sometimes as enemies, sometimes as strangers; finally, hopefully, realistically, as separate people with feelings as personal, unique, and marked as our own.

Before the Women's Movement, child raising was just another part of the female experience that was covered with distortions, left to male supervision and expertise, and considered unimportant. The details of the struggle were hushed up. While I was pregnant, I found no less than twenty-four books on the subject of giving birth and the physical experience and biology of the event. I found nothing to explain or help me with my emotional reactions to the needs of the baby in the postnatal period. I was totally unprepared by anything in my college education for the onslaught of real life in the form of a crying baby who needed comforting.

We know that being human is only partially the pleasures of mind, esthetics, travel, music, etc. It is also in the touching of bodies, the primitive smells, the catching of the force of sex, as it surges in the physical self. Maternity may not be an instinct such as aggression or sex, but it is intimately connected, twined onto the process of life. The other side of dying is the creation of life, and one can hardly say this is merely a learned social role.

The social distortion has been in the assumption that beyond the first nine months of gestation and the several months of nursing, maternity need be the preserve of the natural mother. The time of one's life that is required in taking care of small children is so limited that women who have made child care their sole function may be left emptied and used up at an early age, rattling like ghosts through their uninhabited houses, nursing memories of times when they served a more useful function.

But if one thinks of the maternal instinct as the urge to nurture, tend, feed, measure, care for, teach, lead, clean, watch, empathize with, identify with, fill up one's empty rooms with (and who doesn't have empty space inside), then the maternal instinct can easily be shared with men. In sharing, one can avoid such obvious traps of motherhood as possessiveness, slavery to one's child, loss of self to another, or diminution of identity.

In no sense do I feel that a woman is less of a success or less of a woman if she does not feel maternal or does not have an interest in spending time with children. But neither do I feel this nonmaternal freedom is a wonderful ideal that all women should strive for.

Source: Anne Roiphe. "Can You Have Everything and Still Want Babies?" *Vogue*, December 1975, pp. 153, 201, 202.

form of contraception, and half of them were using the pill. (1976, p. 40)

The two major developments to which Segal refers—new, low-risk contraceptive methods and legal abortion—mean that we have entered an era in which the phrase "family planning" accurately applies in many cases. The 1970 National Fertility Study found that since the 1950s there has been a significant decline in

"Wrong Reasons"

60-Second Television Message

ANNCR(VO): A lot of people have children for the wrong reasons.

GRANDMOTHER: You've been married a year now. When are we going to see some grandchildren?

YOUNG MAN: You want to have a baby, Evelyn? All right, we'll have a baby! Maybe that'll patch things up!

YOUNG WIFE: We only want two children. But if one of them isn't a boy— we'll keep trying.

WOMAN: Why knock myself out working when I can have a baby.

MAN: Heh-heh, hey Harry. What are you and Marge waiting for— huh?

YOUNG GIRL: Sure I want another baby. What else is a woman for?

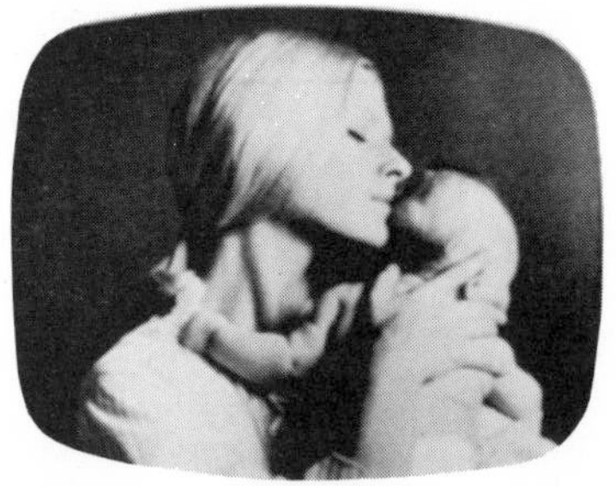

ANNCR(VO): As we said, there are a lot of wrong reasons to have a child— but only one right reason: because you really want one. And that takes planning.

ANNCR(VO): For more information, write Planned Parenthood, Box 840, New York, 10019.

Television ad for Planned Parenthood.

the number of unwanted births. This decline can be attributed to the more consistent use of more reliable contraceptive techniques. During the mid-1970s, there was a slight decline in the percentage of women using oral contraceptives ("the Pill"), but it was still by far the most commonly employed contraceptive. Particularly among white couples aged thirty and over, there has been a dramatic increase in surgical sterilization (National Center for Health Statistics, 1979). There is also some evidence that many couples today are more highly motivated to prevent unwanted births; and thus use even the older techniques with greater effectiveness (Ryder, 1973; Westoff, 1972). The effect of liberalized abortion laws on the birth rate has not been so dramatic in the United States as it was in Japan and several European nations, which legalized abortion in the 1950s. America's changing attitudes toward abortion have been reflected in two recent Supreme Court decisions. The first, *Roe* v. *Wade,* held in 1973 that abortion during the first twenty-four weeks of pregnancy was a private matter between a woman and her physician, thus making unconstitutional any state laws that prohibited abortion except to save the mother's life. A 1976 decision declared that no woman should have to seek parental consent to get an abortion, thus supporting a woman's right not to bear an unwanted child.

Abortion is still a highly controversial question, however. Despite the Supreme Court decisions, many people bitterly oppose it, some arguing that it is a form of murder. Judging from polls taken over the past few years, it appears that the Supreme Court decisions did not reflect the opinion of the majority. A majority of Americans believes that life begins before birth; that women should *not* have the right to obtain an abortion without their husband's consent; and that abortion should not be publicly financed (Blake, 1977). Advocates of legal abortion, on the other hand, point out that many women will get abortions whether they are legal or not; the procedure should always be performed under proper medical supervision to minimize the health risks. In countries such as Japan and Czechoslovakia, where abortion is legal, death caused by it is an exceedingly rare phenomenon. Moreover, insistence on the birth of an unwanted child is a far more serious matter than the destruction of a fetus, the advocates of legal abortion say, pointing out that unwanted children often become "battered children" and, if they survive, eventually become inadequate parents themselves.

While people continue to argue about whether legal abortion is right or wrong, we can get an idea of the likely effects of more liberal abortion laws by looking at what happened in New York, the first state to allow abortion on request. Christopher Tietze of the Population Council examined the birth rates in New York City before and after the legalization of abortion and found that although the number of legal abortions increased from about 5,000 in the year before legalization to about 75,000 in the year following, the birth rate in the city did not drop correspondingly. In other words, most of the 75,000 abortions probably would have been carried out anyway, legal or illegal. Tietze estimates that the legalization of abortion meant that only about 20 to 30 percent more were actually performed (1973).

Most population experts agree that it is the more consistent use of more reliable contraceptives, and not the legalization of abortion, that accounts for most of the declining fertility of the past few years.

But even in an era of more effective contraception, unwanted pregnancy is still very common. Investigators have estimated that one-fifth of all births between 1960 and 1965 were unwanted (Bumpass and Westoff, 1970). The 1970 National Fertility Study found that of all births to married women from 1966 to 1970, 15 percent were unwanted, and another 44 percent, though wanted eventually, came at the wrong time in their parents' plans (Westoff, 1972).

Unplanned pregnancy takes place among all groups in the population, but it is most common among the very young, the poor, and the uneducated. The reason, Segal believes, is that imperfect contraception methods are used—and often used carelessly or intermittently (1976). Many people are still uninformed about the facts of human reproduction and the reliability of various contraceptive techniques (see Box 12–2).

Nevertheless, the significance of what has been called the contraceptive revolution should not be underestimated. It has had profound effects not only on average family size but on premarital sexual behavior, and it has undoubtedly been an important contributing factor to the increasing popularity of the single life. It has also had a direct effect on the status of women. The achievement of a condition in which most children are both wanted and planned would be a transition to a society in which most individuals exert some control over the paramount factors shaping their lives.

THE DIFFICULTIES OF PARENTHOOD TODAY

"Is there any other occupation in the world," asks Catherine Storr,

> on which almost everyone is prepared to embark without training, without experience, and without any more specialized knowledge than is provided by having been, so to speak, on the receiving end a good many years before? An occupation, too, which will affect the health and happiness if not the actual survival of one or more people? . . . I am referring, of course, to the job of being a parent, which most of us undertake so light-heartedly, and which, for most of us again, turns out to be so different from anything we had expected. Our surprise takes innumerable and varied forms, some pleasant, some disagreeable . . . (1972, p. 98)

Whether or not most people undertake parenthood light-heartedly, as Storr suggests, it is indisputably true that few are either trained or prepared for the experience. Until a few years ago, much of what was written about parenthood dwelled on the fulfillment and satisfactions it offers, and did little to give couples realistic expectations about it or the ways it might affect their marriage—a situation that has prompted E. E. LeMasters to remark that in America it is not marriage but parenthood which is the real "romantic complex" (1957, p. 461).

The changes brought on by parenthood begin with pregnancy, which for many women is accompanied by discomfort ranging from waves of nausea or feelings of severe fatigue to unusual irritability, leg cramps, and abdominal pains. The baby's appearance at birth very often comes as something of a shock to its parents. Newborn babies do not look like those healthy, plump little things in the baby food ads until they are about six months old. But as LeMasters found out, that is only the first of many surprises for some parents. "We knew where babies came from," said one of the young fathers interviewed, "but we didn't know what they were like."

Rather than the immediate fulfillment that so many accounts of child rearing promise, the birth of a child provoked a crisis for many of the couples studied by LeMasters. Young mothers reported

> loss of sleep (especially during the early months); chronic tiredness or exhaustion; extensive confinement to the home and resulting curtailment of their social contacts; giving up the satisfactions and the income of outside employment; additional washing and ironing; guilt at not being a "better" mother; the long hours and seven days (and nights) a week necessary in caring for an infant; decline in housekeeping standards; and worry over their appearance (due to factors such as increased weight after pregnancy). (1957, p. 354)

Fathers may experience some of these effects, too, depending on how much they share child care duties, but they are also troubled by other problems, including

> decline in sexual response of wife; economic pressure resulting from the wife's retirement plus additional expenditures necessary for the child;

Biological Aspects of Sex and Reproduction

Box 12–2 / Human Reproductive Anatomy

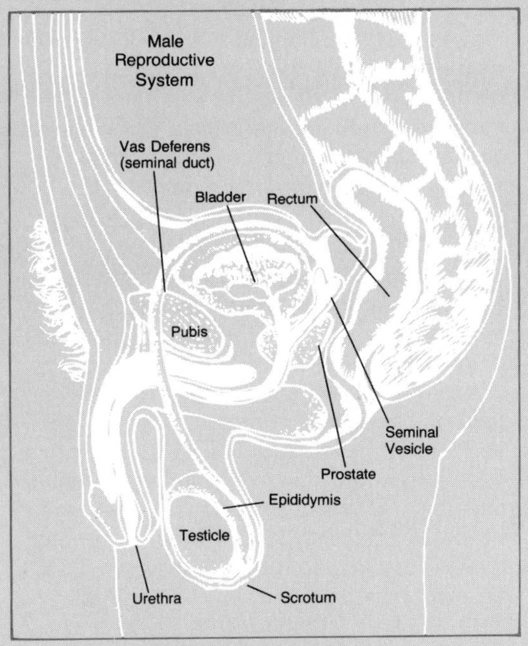

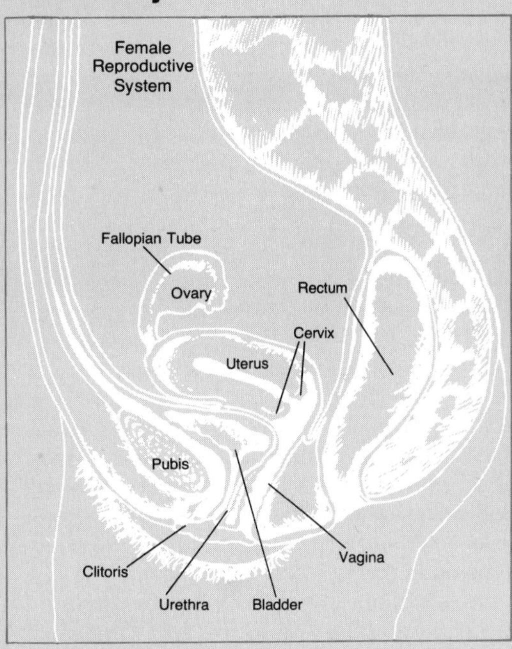

(Left) the male reproductive system. (Right) the female reproductive system.

"Vive la différence!" say the French. Indeed, there *is* something to celebrate in the distinctions between men and women. While those differences may seem self-evident, it is worthwhile to describe them precisely because a knowledge of the sex organs and their functions is indispensable to an understanding of one's own sexual responses, as well as those of one's partner.

Male Sexual Anatomy

The *penis* consists of a tube composed of three distinct spongy bodies wrapped in a fleshy sheath. When sexual stimulation occurs, these bodies fill with blood until they are distended, which is the cause of the erection. The surface of the penis is richly supplied with nerve endings which make it highly sensitive to touch. The most sensitive area is the rounded head of the penis, called the *glans,* particularly the ridge on top called the *corona,* and the thin strip of skin on the bottom known as the *frenulum.* Running through the center of the penis is a thin tube called the *urethra,* which serves as a passageway for both urine and semen.

Suspended inside a bag of loose flesh called the *scrotum* are two egg-shaped organs, the *testes.* They manufacture the male sex cells *(spermatozoa)*, and also furnish the male hormone, *testosterone.* Inside the testes are hundreds of yards of tiny hollow tubes called *seminiferous tubules,* where the sperm are manufactured. The sperm then travel through a series of ducts until they reach a C-

(Box 12–2 continues on page 338)

(Box 12–2 continued from page 337)

shaped chamber on top of the testis called the *epididymis.* It is here that the sperm grow to maturity. Once mature, they continue on their journey through a tube called the *vas deferens,* through a structure known as the *seminal vesicle,* and finally to the *prostate gland.* Here the sperm mix with *semen,* a milky, alkaline fluid. During the male orgasm, the prostate gland and seminal vesicles contract rhythmically, causing ejaculation of sperm and semen through the urethra.

Female Sexual Anatomy

The external sex organs in the female are known collectively as the *vulva.* They include the *mons,* the *labia minora,* the *labia majora,* and the *clitoris.* The mons is a fleshy mound over the pubic bone. The *labia majora* are folds of fatty flesh at the entrance to the vulval cleft. They too contain abundant nerve endings, as do the *labia minora,* a second pair of folds below them. Most sensitive of all, however, is the *clitoris,* a small, cylindrical body located at the top of the vulval cleft. The clitoris is analogous to the penis in several respects. Like the male organ, it is composed of spongy tissue and becomes erect during sexual arousal.

The *vagina* is a muscular tube that leads from the vulval cleft to the entrance of the *uterus,* or *womb.* Normally, there is no space between its walls, but in response to sexual stimulation, it becomes both wider and longer. It is extremely elastic, adjusting during intercourse to the size of the penis.

The *uterus* is a hollow, muscular organ about the size of a pear. Like the vagina, it is highly elastic, expanding to many times its normal size during pregnancy. Leading from the uterus are the two *fallopian tubes* which end in a fringed funnel shape near each of the *ovaries.* The ovaries are the female reproductive glands corresponding to the male *testes.* Like the testes, they perform a dual role. They produce the female sex cells, or *ova*, and also manufacture the two female sex hormones, *estrogen* and *progesterone.*

The Reproductive Process

The reproductive process begins during intercourse when the male ejaculates sperm into the vagina of the female. Propelling themselves with undulations of their long, whiplike tails, the sperm swim through the neck of the womb (the *cervix*), into the uterus, and then to the fallopian tube. If an ovum has been released by the ovary and is present in the tube, it will most likely be fertilized by one of the sperm. The fertilized ovum divides, then divides again, eventually becoming a little ball of cells. Meanwhile, it floats slowly down the tube into the uterus, finally anchoring itself in the blood-rich lining of the uterus, which has been prepared to receive it.

At this point, the ovum consists of two parts: an inner-cell mass that will develop into the *fetus,* and an outer layer of streamer-like cells that absorbs nourishment from the mother's blood and will develop into the *placenta.* Initially, the ovum is no larger than the dot above this "i." After five weeks, it has

> interference with their social life; worry about a second pregnancy in the near future; and general disenchantment with the parental role. (LeMasters, 1957, p. 354)

Other researchers suggest that although becoming a parent does cause certain stresses, LeMasters' use of the word "crisis" in this context overstates those stresses and understates the gratifications of parenthood (Russell, 1974).

Judging from much of what has been written and said over the past few years about family life, one might conclude that the word "crisis" accurately describes the entire institution of parenthood today. It is now commonly assumed that the needs of children are not being ade-

grown to about one-twelfth of an inch long and has the beginning of a backbone. A week later, the *embryo* has a head, a heart, buds from which arms and legs will form, and depressions in the head where eyes will appear. It is about one-quarter inch long. After seven weeks it has doubled in length and developed recognizable fingers, toes, and eyes. A week later there are ears and the beginning of a face. The formation of the face is completed about the twelfth week along with the partial formation of the arms, legs, hands, and feet. After eleven weeks, differences begin to appear in the external genital organs, making it possible to determine the sex of the fetus, which is now about three inches long and weighs one ounce. At four months, the mother can normally feel the fetus moving within her, and its heartbeat can be detected with a stethoscope. After five months, the fetus has grown to a length of about one foot, weighs about one pound, and has hair on its head. After nine months, it is normally about twenty inches long, weighs about seven pounds, and is ready to be born.

While the fetus is growing, certain important changes take place in the mother's body, too. The fetus is attached by the *umbilical cord* to the placenta. In the placenta, a continuous and complex interchange takes place between the mother and the fetus. Nourishment and oxygen are carried through the placenta and absorbed by the fetus. Meanwhile the waste products of the fetus filter into the placenta and are removed by the mother's bloodstream. Virtually any substance that the mother ingests is quickly passed to the fetus, be it nicotine, alcohol, or drugs of any kind. By the same token, the mother's immunity to certain diseases is also passed to the fetus. This immunity is retained by the infant for a few months after birth. During pregnancy, the mother's body is also preparing to give birth to the baby and feed it after it is born. The glands in the breasts swell, filling with a clear substance called *colostrum,* which will be the baby's food during the first few days of life. The pelvic girdle widens in preparation for the passage of the infant down the birth canal.

Abortion of the fetus may be either spontaneous or induced. Spontaneous abortions may be caused by some dysfunction of the ovum, the placenta, or the umbilical cord. Displacement of the fetus, endocrine imbalances, electric shock, or radiation may also bring on a spontaneous abortion. Contrary to popular belief, however, falls are rarely the cause of an abortion because the fetus is too well protected to be affected by any but the most violent shocks. The most common method of induced abortion is *dilation and curettage* (D & C), which can be performed only in the early months of pregnancy. The physician dilates the cervix, then inserts an instrument to scrape the lining of the womb. Another method is to remove the developing fetus with a vacuum device. During the early months of pregnancy, abortion induced by such methods under proper medical supervision is a fairly simple and safe procedure, but if performed later it is difficult and more dangerous.

quately met by their parents, the school system, the federal government, or society in general. According to one recent survey, half of all single parents, about two-fifths of all mothers who work full time, and about a third of all parents today worry about the job they are doing in raising their children (Yankelovich, 1977). It is the view of one prominent student of child development, Urie Bronfenbrenner, that despite well-intentioned parents, child rearing has undergone some marked changes in recent years, with alarming effects on children.

> In today's world parents find themselves at the mercy of a society which imposes pressures and priorities that allow neither time nor place for

> meaningful activities and relations between children and adults, which downgrades the role of parents and the functions of parenthood, and which prevents the parent from doing things he wants to do as a guide, friend, and companion to his children. . . . In our modern way of life, children are deprived not only of parents but of people in general. A host of factors conspires to isolate children from the rest of society. . . . *We are experiencing a breakdown in the process of making human beings human.* (1976, p. 161)

If it is accurate, this diagnosis needs to be taken quite seriously. But statements like this one—particularly because it was delivered at a White House Conference and intended to provoke action from policymakers who commonly deal with problems only when they think they have become crises—need to be carefully scrutinized. America has long been regarded as a child-centered society, and that concern has often impelled people who are seeking to initiate certain reforms to declare a "crisis" in child-care. Thus, we need to inquire about what, exactly, has changed in our child-rearing practices, and with what consequences.

If a certain anxiety about the adequacy of child-rearing practices is typically American, the intensity of that feeling today seems to stem largely from the accelerating changes that have been discussed in previous chapters of this book. For the first time in American history, the mother of a typical school-age child works in the labor force, which gives rise to the concern that Bronfenbrenner voices about whether children are being neglected. That concern about neglect is only heightened by the rising divorce rate; today, roughly one in three marriages ends in divorce, and today's parents are less likely to stay together "for the sake of the children" than people used to be. Furthermore, there is concern about the evidence of child abuse, which suggests that some of the interactions that do occur between parents and children are not at all in the children's best interests. And, as discussed in Chapter 1, there is evidence from recent surveys that the 1970s produced a "new breed" of parents, more self-oriented, less inclined to sacrifice for their children, skeptical of traditional values such as the institution of marriage, religion, material success, and hesitant about passing on their own values to their children. In short, there appear to be a substantial number of parents who feel that they do not have any secure guidelines for how to raise children, who are quite uncertain about the right way to be parents.

There are other indications of concern about the quality of child care in American society today. Although child-rearing manuals have been common for years, bookstores now carry advice books on nearly every aspect of child rearing, from toilet training to raising a child's IQ. There is no way of knowing whether such books allay more anxieties than they create. As one writer remarks, "Among certain strata of the American middle class, children are studied and read up on as intensely as is the subject of sex, though the added homework hasn't seemed to improve the quality of either" (Epstein, 1975, p. 177). That such books are so popular, though, does seem to be symptomatic of deep concern among parents. Perhaps in recognition of this concern, Dr. Benjamin Spock, the granddaddy of child-rearing manuals, entitled his latest book, *Raising Children in a Difficult Time* (1974).

Child Rearing by the Book—Goals and Techniques

Dr. Spock's first book, *Baby and Child Care,* came out in 1945. Like other child-care manuals, which had been available for more than a century, Dr. Spock's entry was a how-to book about the art and science of parenting. It gave information and advice about hundreds of practical matters from toilet training to left-handedness, from the medical problems of infants to their nutritional needs. It reached the bookstores just in time for the postwar baby boom, and for some reason it captured this huge market. Since its publication it has sold almost 30 million copies, achieving the status of a standard reference work in middle-class homes. It is

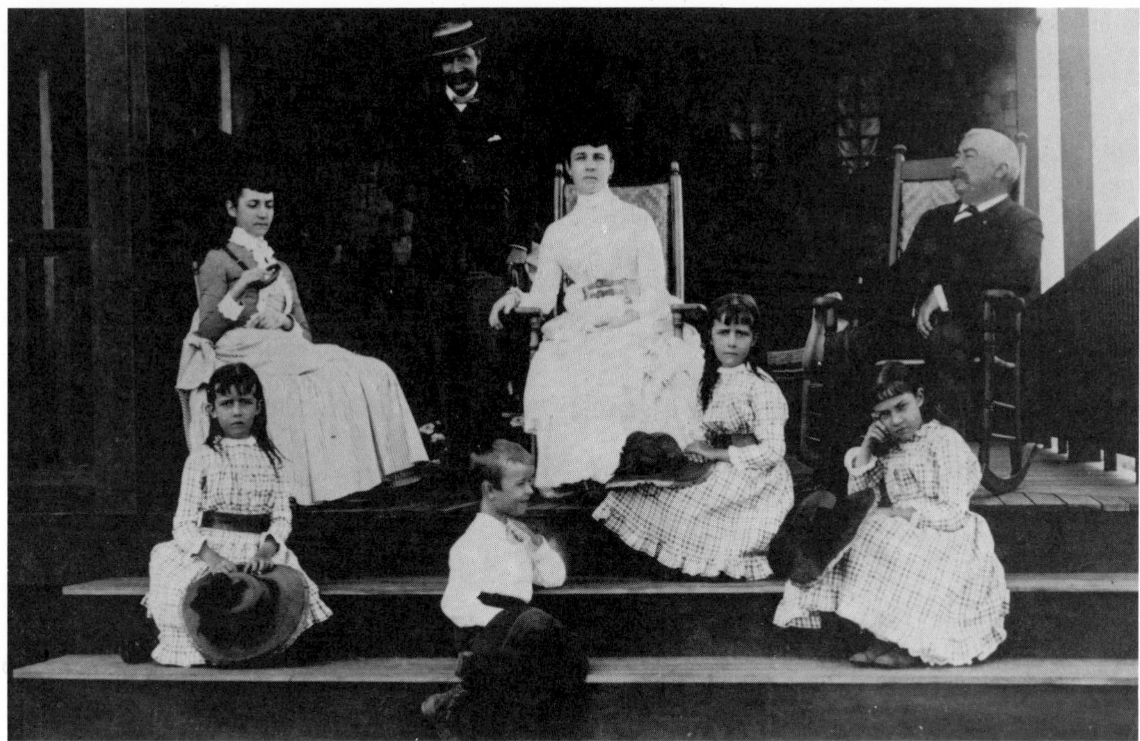

In the past, when there was more of a consensus about what good parents should be, parenthood was less difficult than now.

no exaggeration to say that *Baby and Child Care* has had a considerable influence, either direct or indirect, on most of the postwar generation. This book—including the revisions in each of the successive editions—can be used as a prism through which we can examine what is most distinctive about parenting in America.

One of the interesting things about the success of this and other child-rearing manuals available today is that it was written by an "expert," a man who presumably knows better than we (or our mothers) do about how to bring up children. For centuries, women learned how to be mothers from *their* mothers, who knew the traditional answers, passed down from one generation to the next, to the questions that mothers were likely to ask. But today, says psychologist Jerome Kagan, parents are anxious because there is "a lack of consensus on values." "Parenting," Kagan explains, "means implementing a series of decisions about the socialization of your child—what do you do when he cries, when he's aggressive, when he lies or when he doesn't do well in school." Fifty years ago, parenting was easier because there was more agreement about what parents should do. But now "there is no consensus as to what a child should be like when he is an adult—or about how you get him there" (*Newsweek*, 1975, p. 48). Thus, Spock and the other child-rearing advisers have taken over from grandmother the task of giving advice—but in the process, it seems, mothers have become more anxious about whether they are doing the right thing.

If there is no consensus among mothers, neither is there much consistency among experts. An analysis of the advice given in successive editions of the pamphlet *Infant Care,* published by the federal government and based on expert consultation, finds remarkably little consistency on the needs of children, the goals of childhood socialization, or recommended parental behavior (Wolfenstein, 1953).

Any advice on how to bring up children is based on one's assumptions about the child's essential nature. If, for example, we assume, as the Puritans did, that the child is unruly and depraved at birth, then too much parental tenderness or indulgence is a serious mistake. The child's natural desires cannot be encouraged; considerable parental discipline is appropriate. If, on the other hand, it is assumed that the child is innocent at birth, parents are obliged to shelter and protect it. The underlying assumption in *Baby and Child Care* is closer to the second of these views. Spock assumes the baby to be innocent, sturdy, and responsive to the right environment (Winch, 1968).

Looking back over the various expert instructions on child rearing, we can also see a substantial shift in the adult personality that socialization practices were supposed to produce. At the turn of the century, an adult with good moral character was the objective. The ideals of honesty, orderliness, and industry were supreme. Today, most child-rearing manuals take an uninhibited, spontaneous adult as their goal.

The shifting currents of advice are revealed most clearly when parents refer to the books to find out how strict they should be, and how they should deal with such matters as toilet training and masturbation. In the 1920s and 1930s, they were told to enforce rigid feeding schedules and early toilet training and to restrain themselves from rushing to the baby's side when it cried. John Watson, an early behavioral psychologist, advised parents that immediate gratification is not in the child's interest and warned against excessive displays of affection, too.

By the 1940s, however, parents were encouraged to be more indulgent. Spock advised mothers to feed infants when they were hungry. Rigid toilet training schedules were no longer in fashion. The baby's needs achieved a new priority. Thumb sucking and masturbation, which earlier had been considered pernicious habits to be broken, were now regarded as wholesome expressions of the child's need for exploration and experience.

Today it is widely assumed that parents should gratify an infant's needs for food, sucking, and reassurance, and should allow children to satisfy their curiosity by exploring without the restrictions of playpens or leashes. Parents are advised to avoid punishments or lectures, and to employ instead clever diversions that avoid conflicts.

Whereas psychologists such as Watson were advising parents in the early part of this century to avoid reinforcing the wrong types of behavior, many of today's advice books are based on a very different insight. The mind of an infant works differently from that of an older child or an adult. As one writer remarks, the practical consequences of this insight are enormous:

> Today's experts point out, for example, that a six-week-old infant has no sense of time, and therefore can't possibly learn patience, or respect for regularity, from being fed on a set schedule, as babies once invariably were. Hunger, they say, teaches despair, not patience, so feed a child as soon as she cries. (McGrath, 1976, p. 26)

Perhaps the most basic question about the child-rearing manuals written by experts like Spock is whether they are really scientific—that is, based on information that is more reliable than the traditional lore of grandmothers. Is there much solid evidence that parents should perform certain actions and avoid others? There is some social science research that helps to specify the probable outcomes of certain parental actions. For example, research supports common sense in suggesting that inconsistency is bad for children and that parental consistency will lead to more stable behavior patterns in children. Studies also help to specify the probable consequences of different styles of child rearing. It appears in general that parents who take a punitive approach to discipline and characteristically resort to physical punishment rather than verbal reproof are more likely to produce children who are overtly aggressive (Becker, 1964). There is evidence that harsh parental discipline leads to a more defensive interpersonal style and also inhibits the development of intellectual competence (Blau, 1972). Children who act on the basis of internalized standards of judgment (rather than fear of detection or punishment) report little use of force or direct commands by their parents; rather, they are moved by the use of rational appeals and explanations of the consequences of their behavior (Becker, 1964). Overall, studies of how children develop to become responsible and self-reliant, uninhibited but not overly aggressive, suggest that parents should combine warmth and encouragement with firm but not harsh control and discipline.

But these are general guidelines, not specific instructions about what parents should or should not do. Like other students of child development, Jerome Kagan has pointed out that research does not suggest any specific list of parental actions. After the child's basic needs have been met, he says,

College-educated adults, more so than other parents, are convinced that what they do as parents will make a great deal of difference in how their children turn out.

> Children do not require any specific actions from adults in order to develop optimally. There is no good evidence that children must have a certain amount or schedule of cuddling, kissing, spanking, holding, or deprivation of privileges in order to become gratified and productive adults. The child does have some psychological needs, but there is no fixed list of parental behaviors that can be counted on to fill those requirements. (1976, p. 88)

Arlene Skolnick makes the same point when she observes that

> Researchers as well as parents have been frustrated in the search for clear or simple cause-and-effect relationships between things parents do or don't do, and the way children turn out. There are no cookbook recipes for producing a particular kind of child. (1973, p. 302)

The changing currents of advice reflected in such manuals as the various editions of the government pamphlet *Infant Care* tell us more about changing conceptions of the child's nature and the desired adult personality type than they do about how certain types of child care influence development.

If researchers have had a hard time pinning down the effects of specific parental actions, perhaps parents will be relieved to find out that there is more than one right way to raise children.

Recipe for Perfection

One of the themes in Spock's manual helps to explain the peculiar susceptibility of American parents to feelings of guilt and inadequacy. As Philip Slater points out, Spock endorses the idea that each child has a certain "potential" that can be realized only with the right kind of parental guidance (1970, p. 62). The parent is thus made responsible not just for the child's physical welfare, but also for its personality as well. If the child grows up with any personality flaws, the parents (and the mother in particular) are held responsible. Slater says that

> most middle-class, Spock-oriented mothers believe, deep in their hearts, that if they did their job well enough all of their children would be creative, intelligent, kind, generous, happy, brave, spontaneous, and good—each, of course, in his or her own special way. (1970, p. 64)

We do not have to look very far back in history or very far afield in the variety of cultural practices to see how peculiar this attitude is. Until recent times the attitudes of parents toward their children were quite pragmatic. Of course there were bonds of affection between parents and children in times past, but parents then were not so personally invested in their children's psychological development as they are now. The emphasis on the quality of parenting is largely a modern invention.

The belief that each child has a unique potential that the parents must help to realize is alien to most cultures other than our own. In the highlands of Guatemala, for example, Indian mothers believe that the disposition of a child depends on the day it was born. Thus, the mother has little personal responsibility for how the child turns out. She is convinced, Kagan says, "that there is little she can do to change these fixed developmental directions, and her fatalism leads her to stand aside so that her child can grow as nature intended" (1976, p. 87).

When Americans were asked in a 1974 poll, "How much effect can parents have in determining how children will turn out?" there was an interesting pattern to the answers. There was not a very substantial difference between the answers of men and women, or between people who have children and people who do not. But 59 percent of the whites surveyed, and only 39 percent of the blacks, believed that parents have a great deal of influence over how their children turn out. Furthermore, 66 percent of people with a college education but only 48 percent of those with a grade school education believed in strong parental influence (The Roper Organization, 1974, p. 77).

Perhaps college-educated people know enough about psychology to be convinced of the importance of the early childhood years and thus of the potential importance of parents in shaping the experience of their infants. Or it may be a social class difference: parents who are better educated and have higher incomes may invest more energy and attention in shaping the development of their children. In any case, Spock certainly reflected and contributed to this middle-class belief that what parents do makes a great deal of difference in how their children turn out.

The Permissive Parent?

In many discussions of the influence of Spock's *Baby and Child Care,* nothing receives so much attention as his alleged permissiveness. Because of his advocacy of relaxed feeding, weaning, and toilet training practices, Spock was blamed for a great variety of things, including the violence of student protests in the 1960s. The Reverend Norman Vincent Peale, for example, said that permissive child rearing led young people to expect "instant gratification" and that the result of such training was a generation that thought it could get what it yelled for.

Actually, Spock's relatively indulgent attitudes toward such matters as weaning and toilet training were nothing new. He advocated no more permissiveness than did several other writers of child-rearing manuals. Perhaps many parents were looking for a scapegoat for their own guilt feelings about allowing children too much freedom. In a 1974 survey, 84 percent of the women said that in most homes today, discipline is not strict enough, while only 2 percent thought discipline to be too strict. Men's responses were almost identical (The Roper Organization, 1974, p. 74).

As various studies have shown, the question of obedience has very different meanings to parents at different social class levels. By looking at the different child-rearing patterns practiced today, we can explore some of the problems caused by the newer, nonauthoritatrian style of parental control which is common among middle-class parents.

Imagine the following situation. You are the parent of a four-year-old girl, and she is supposed to be taking a nap. When you check on her you find that she has gotten out of bed and discovered a paint set that was stored in a closet. At this point she has succeeded mainly in covering herself with paint, but she is intent on her creation, a nondescript finger painting that adorns the wall.

As with most of the situations that parents confront every day, there are several ways you might respond. Furious at the mess and angry at the child's disobedience, you might slap her for "painting all over the wall" and pronounce a rule: "Don't every play with those paints again!" If the child should ask why, you could answer: "Because I said so!" Another response would be to approve the child's absorption in such "creative" play, irritated though you might be at the mess. In this case you would probably encourage your daughter by example to clean up, scold her for not being in bed, and explain why an afternoon nap is so important.

As several studies have shown (Bronfenbrenner, 1961; Kohn, 1959; Newson and Newson, 1968), the style of parenting that is characteristic of the middle class today is different from that of blue-collar families. There is no right way of responding to a situation like the one we just described, but there are ways characteristic of each social setting, and they reveal different assumptions about the good child and the roles parents should take.

The first response exemplifies the so-called traditional or authoritarian pattern, which was more common in the past and today is more characteristic of blue-collar parents. The second response exemplifies the so-called modern or "democratic" style of child rearing commonly advocated in the baby books and usually put into practice by the middle-class parents who read these books. It is difficult to describe these two patterns without implying that the second one is preferable, but we can show that it has disadvantages as well as advantages.

For parents who follow the traditional pattern, a good child is one who has learned obedience, neatness, and cleanliness. A study of 400 Washington, D.C., families showed that obedience in particular is highly valued in working-class families (Kohn, 1959). The aim of this style of upbringing is to control the child's impulses, not to explore or express them. Traditional parents view themselves as unquestioned authority figures who have a right to give orders and lay down unexplained rules. It is assumed in such families that the children should adjust to their parents' needs and preferences, not vice versa. Setting limits and making rules is assumed to be an important part of the parents' role. And when the children break these rules, physical punishment, not verbal reproof, is considered appropriate. As one working-class wife said,

> I don't believe in all those books which tell you, "Don't smack your kids." If you're going to *talk* the child out of it, you're going to spend half your day standing there *talking* to them. I think it does them good to have a smack if they've done something wrong. I think it lasts longer than simply talking to them. (Newson and Newson, 1968, p. 74)

Parents who follow the "democratic" pattern, on the other hand, make different assumptions about what constitutes the good child and the proper parental role. Such parents prize curiosity, happiness, consideration, and self-control in the child more than obedience (Kohn, 1959). The child's impulses are often accepted and encouraged; in a number of respects, in fact, these families are far more child-centered than are those of the other type. One writer comments that middle-class parents "are more willing to play with a child on *his* level (the you-be-the-engine-I'll-be-the-caboose sort of game) because it develops his imagination and verbal facility" (Fishman, 1968, p. 97). When four-year-old children invent fictitious friends and imaginary animals, middle-class parents are more likely to approve of them as signs of a fertile imagination. The parental role, according to this model, is that of counselor, not disciplinarian. As many child-rearing manuals advise, parents explain rules to children, and children are encouraged to understand this reasoning and apply it for themselves. This verbal style of discipline and direction is quite democratic, and often frustrating for parents who discover that the cool voice of reason does not often persuade an unruly four-year-old. This style of parenting is more egalitarian than the traditional style; the middle-class parent, more concerned about the child's development than its obedience, often acts like its friend. If, as at least one study indicates (Newson and Newson, 1968), such parents do have fun with their children, they are also the ones most troubled by "permissiveness."

Two researchers (Wright and Wright, 1976) replicated Kohn's 1959 study, and they found that there is still a definite relationship between social class and parental values. Middle-class parents still place more of an emphasis on developing internalized standards for behavior than their working-class counterparts. But this later study suggests that it is the parents' educational level, and not their occupation, that best explains the distinctive child-rearing values of each group, because education is important in determining how much autonomy and self-direction a person is allowed at work.

Each of these two styles of child rearing has its advantages and its disadvantages. Disciplining children in the "democratic" style may cause more anxiety in children than do the physical punishments of the traditional style. In many respects, the "democratic" style makes more demands on parents. If, for example, the infant is allowed to feed on demand, the mother's activities are often interrupted by her child's needs. As one writer points out, the "permissive" parent must have tremendous patience and energy.

> To permit children to wander, experiment, and test requires constant vigilance to protect their physical safety. To provide children with intellectual stimulation and sensory variety requires intensive involvement in the quality of their activities. But if parents are to provide the quantities of time, energy, and patience required to achieve these goals they must limit their own recreation and pursuits. (Flacks, 1974, p. 352)

Thus parenthood comes as a heavy strain for many people.

Why have child-rearing patterns changed so dramatically? One possible explanation is that in an era of rapid social change parents can no longer say "do as I have done." They have to prepare their children for a future that is substantially different from the present. It is partly because there is no consensus about what type of personality will be best suited to tomorrow's realities that the parents' role is so complicated today.

Is a Full-Time Mother Necessary?

If Spock's "permissiveness" was mainly an endorsement of a widely accepted trend in child rearing, *Baby and Child Care* did depart from other child-rearing manuals in the answers it gave to two basic questions about parenting: (1) How much care or attention do children need? and (2) Does it make any difference who supplies that attention? Spock's answers to these questions contributed to the domesticity and emphasis on full-time motherhood that characterized the 1950s. In the first edition of *Baby and Child Care* and in every revision until the most recent one, Spock equated proper child care with mothering, and described mothering as a full-time job. Only in the most recent revision does he suggest that, at least in some families, both the child's and the mother's needs might be better served by some other arrangement than full-time mothering. One has the feeling that the child-rearing expert is now following public opinion, not leading it. The present shift away from full-time mothering is well worth examining because it represents a fundamental change in our ideas about what is proper parenting.

The first edition of *Baby and Child Care* was written during a period when researchers were devoting much attention to the problems that arose from inadequate mothering, a subject first opened by studies of institutionalized children (Ribble, 1943; Spitz, 1945). It was discovered that children brought up in settings such as orphanages, and thus deprived of normal mothering, suffered withdrawal, a dazed inactivity, and various medical symptoms.

This research, plus their own clinical studies of the childhood experiences of noninstitutionalized children who developed various psychological disorders, led psychologists to draw some implications of inadequate mothering for normal families. One of the most influential writers on what came to be regarded as maternal deprivation was the British psychoanalyst John Bowlby. In a book entitled *Child Care and the Growth of Love,* Bowlby tried to summarize the evidence on the effect of parental care upon the child's development (1953).

"What is believed to be essential for mental health," Bowlby wrote, "is that an infant and young child should experience a warm, intimate, and continuous relationship with his mother (or permanent mother-substitute—one person who steadily 'mothers' him) in which both find satisfaction and enjoyment." Without such continuous attention, even the effects of what Bowlby referred to as "partial deprivation" can be serious ones, such as "nervous disorders and instability of character." When Bowlby asserted "the absolute need of infants and toddlers for the continuous care of their mothers," many of the mothers who read this book must have wondered if they could ever stray from the child's side. For them, Bowlby offered this advice: "We must recognize that leaving any child of under three years of age is a major operation only to be undertaken for good and sufficient reasons, and, when undertaken, to be planned with great care . . ." (1953, pp. 13, 18).

Thus, for people who were influenced by the idea of maternal deprivation in the 1950s, there were very practical implications for mothers. Based on what appeared to be well-founded advice from clinicians and researchers with impressive credentials, many people concluded that continuous, full-time mothering was required to guarantee the proper development of the child. Like Spock, Bowlby equated proper child care with mothering, and he advocated full-time motherhood.

Other writers, such as the widely respected American psychiatrist Theodore Lidz, brought the argument full circle. Not only do children need full-time mothering, but women need to bear children. Lidz wrote that woman's

> biological purpose seems to require completion through conceiving, bearing, and nurturing children. . . . Her generative organs seem meaningless unless her womb has been filled, her breasts suckled. . . . The woman's creativity as a mother becomes a central matter that provides meaning and balance to her life. (1968, p. 443)

This statement affirmed the existence of a maternal instinct, and the practical implications of such a thing are enormous. If there is a maternal instinct, one need not ask who should take care of children. As Bowlby and Lidz suggested—and Spock assumed—mothers are uniquely qualified for the task. If mothering is not learned but instinctive, then all women must have an interest in and aptitude for child rearing. And if infants and young children need their mothers' undivided attention and care, then a mother should not work outside the home, even part time; and day-care centers, no matter how well equipped and staffed, may be harmful to children. A letter that appeared in *The Times* of London reflected this belief:

> It is with horror and a sinking heart that I read of the Government's intention to expand nursery education. It is an established fact that children are

> closely attached to their mother . . . from before birth to about five or six. . . . For a child to develop fully and with its potential undamaged, it is essential that it should move through this period of intense attachment to its mother. Not even toys, brightly painted rooms or the companionship of other similarly deprived children can compensate for the withdrawal of this relationship. . . . (in Oakley, 1974, p. 204)

Over the past decade, however, both the idea of maternal deprivation and the belief in a maternal instinct have been widely criticized. There do appear to be certain ways in which both mothers and infants are biologically predisposed to a mutual attraction. There are certain unlearned maternal responses that are conducive to a close mother–child bond. For example, the crying of an infant triggers the secretion of the hormone oxytocin, which in turn causes nipple erection and prepares a woman for nursing (Rossi, 1977). But to acknowledge the relevance of such biological facts to an understanding of the mother–child bond is only to say that biology shapes what is learned, which is a very different thing from assuming that "blind" instinct leads women to conceive, bear, and nurture children. Most of what we mean by mothering is learned, not instinctive. Some women are good at it, and others are not—which is true of any acquired skill. The belief that infants and young children need the continuous attention of their mothers has been attacked, and so has the idea that women need to be mothers. Psychiatrist Richard Rabkin, for example, has said: "Women don't need to be mothers any more than they need spaghetti. But if you're in a world where everyone is eating spaghetti, thinking they need it and want it, you will think so too" (in Rollin, 1970, p. 69).

The idea of maternal deprivation has been criticized on several grounds. It has been argued, for example, that the institutionalized children who provided the basis for the idea do not represent a normal separation of mother and child, and other inadequacies in the care provided by orphanages explain the children's problems (Casler, 1961). As one writer noted,

> There seems to have occurred a dangerously unscientific extrapolation of assumptions from studies of institutionalized infants to the much more common situation in which infants leave their homes for part of the day, are cared for by other responsible adults, and are returned again to their homes. As a result, women are taught to believe that infants require their undivided attention during the first two or three years of life, at least. (Wortis, 1971, p. 740)

The emphasis that Bowlby and Spock placed on full-time mothering seems quite strange, moreover, when we compare it with child care in other societies, particularly traditional societies. There, child care is generally regarded as a part-time activity, one that women pursue while carrying out other tasks such as food gathering or crafts. In very few societies can women afford to devote most of their time to child care.

It would be alarming, if true, that infants and young children need the continuous attention of their mothers, for fewer and fewer of them are getting it in the United States. Between 1950 and 1976, the percentage of married women in the labor force increased quite rapidly, but the most striking increase in labor force participation was among mothers with children younger than six. In 1950, only about 12 percent of the mothers (in families with the husband present) with such young children worked outside the home; by 1976 that figure had increased to more than 37 percent (see Figure 12–3). Today, the mothers of more than 6 million preschool children have outside jobs.

Fortunately, recent studies of the children of mothers with jobs are much more optimistic than Bowlby was. Several studies of school-age children with working mothers have found no negative consequences. A summary of these studies concludes that when working mothers derive satisfaction from their employment and do not feel guilty about its effects, they are likely to perform the mother's role at least as well as nonworking women. It also appears that daughters of women who work have less traditional sex-role expectations and a higher evaluation of female competence (Hoffman, 1974, pp.

Over the past several decades there has been a striking increase in labor force participation among mothers with young children.

152, 136). Fewer studies have been made of the infants of working mothers, but there is substantial evidence that babies benefit from a generally predictable environment, and they form special attachments to their regular caretaker, whoever it is. No evidence shows, however, that the caretaker has to be the mother, and there is little support for Bowlby's suggestion that any separation between mother and child may be hazardous for the child (Hoffman, 1974).

Researchers in almost any field conclude their papers by saying that additional studies are necessary, but the infants of working mothers really do need more research attention, particularly in view of their rapidly increasing numbers. Although the belief that infants and young children need the continuous attention of a full-time mother has been generally dismissed, many questions remained unanswered about the effect of maternal employment on infants.

Is Full-Time Mothering Good for Women?

While it is still being debated whether children need a full-time mother, it has become more common in the past few years to ask whether full-time mothering is good for women. One of the chief reasons for concern about the welfare of both mothers and children is that parenting takes place in a relatively private, isolated household. American parents have more exclusive responsibility for their children than do parents in other cultures. Relatives and neighbors are not readily available to take over when a mother's patience wears thin. In the absence of other adults, the fury of a distraught mother sometimes goes unchecked:

> In our culture, babies are a private enterprise—everyone is in the baby business as soon as he gets married. He produces his own babies; they are his; only he has a say-so in their management. . . . Pinched off alone in one's house, shielded from critical eyes, one can be as irrational as one pleases with one's children as long as severe damage does not attract the attention of the police. (Henry, in Skolnick, 1973, p. 296)

It sounds reasonable that the more time and effort a parent invests in child rearing, the better the results. In practice, however, things do not always seem to work that way. For example, a study of child-rearing practices in six cultures comes to the conclusion that mothers are more

Figure 12–3 Mothers in the Labor Force, in Families with Husband Present (by Presence and Age of Own Children 1950–1976).

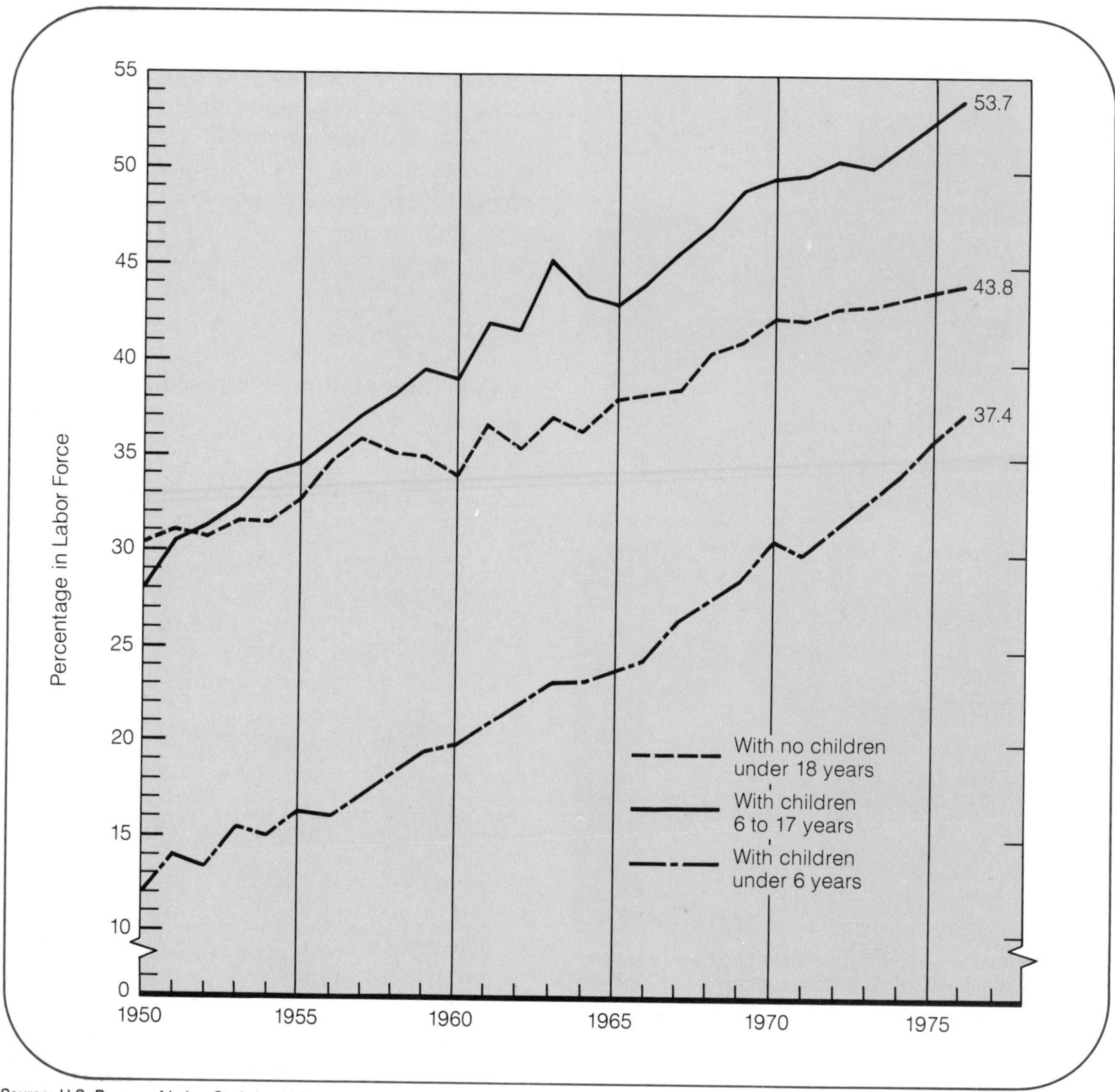

Source: U.S. Bureau of Labor Statistics. *U.S. Working Women: A Databook.* Washington, D.C.: Government Printing Office, 1977, p. 22.

stable and meet their children's needs better when parental substitutes are available. The emotional health of both mother and child is best, it appears, where others are ready to help with the tasks of parenthood (Lambert, 1971; Whiting, 1963).

The exclusive mother–child attachment made possible in middle-class communities by relatively isolated, self-sufficient households, and encouraged by the belief expressed by Spock and others that motherhood should be a continuous, full-time job, creates considerable tensions. According to the motherhood myth, women are supposed to feel nothing but love and warmth for their children, whereas in reality, the frequent demands of young children, their stubborn refusal to follow instructions, and such common behavior as throwing away food that they have just asked for all wear down a mother's patience. If a child cries constantly despite being comforted, the mother may understandably feel rejected and angry, and without any other adults to turn to, her anger and rejection may build up to the point of enraged reaction. When the child becomes the target of its parent's rage child abuse may result.

It is shocking to realize that small children are far more likely to be injured by their parents than by anyone else. It is not at all uncommon for physicians to be asked to treat small children suffering from unexplained fractures, severe bruises, or abrasions. The extent of the problem of child abuse is difficult to estimate accurately. As we noted in Chapter 9, the author of one recent study extrapolated from the data provided by interviews with more than 1,000 families and estimated that of the 46 million children between the ages of three and seventeen who live with both parents, roughly 2 million are beaten up by their parents in any given year, and at least 1 million are threatened by a parent wielding a gun or a knife (Gelles, Straus, and Steinmetz, 1978).

Child abuse poses a difficult dilemma for everyone concerned—parents, children, physicians, and social service agencies. Parents have a legal right to discipline their children, and it is not easy to determine the point at which reasonable discipline becomes unreasonable and harmful abuse. Studies of abused children and their parents have identified no traits that would allow us to separate "normal" parents from potential child abusers (Gil, 1970). "Is there any mother or father," asks one writer,

> who has not been provoked almost to the breaking point by the crying, wheedling, whining child? How many parents have not had moments of concern and self-recrimination after having, in anger, hit their own child much harder than they expected they would? How many such incidents make a "child abuser" out of a normal parent? (Zalba, 1971, p. 460)

In other words, many parents are potential child abusers because of the normal frustrations of being a parent. In exasperation, a parent hits a child who will not behave for the same reasons that a motorist kicks a car that will not start; he or she simply does not know what else to do. "It's not a matter of villains or bad parents," Arlene Skolnick points out, "but rather an ecological one: great demands being placed on limited parental resources of time, energy, and money" (1973, p. 292).

Some of the suggested remedies for child abuse seek to provide the kind of assistance that is readily available in cultures where the mother can turn for help to neighbors or relatives. For example, "crisis nurseries" have been provided in Colorado. Parents can use these facilities, with no questions asked. They are safe places where children can be left for a few hours or a few days, until the parent is ready to resume responsibility for the child (Kempe, 1976, p. 180).

Over the past thirty years, since the publication of the first edition of Spock's *Baby and Child Care,* assumptions about the mother's role have changed substantially. (See Box 12–3.) As we have seen, it is not just that the idea of "maternal deprivation" has been widely attacked, and replaced with a concern for the welfare of the mother, and the things that can go wrong when a mother and child are isolated from other adults. The belief in a "maternal instinct" has been generally discarded, too. Femininity is no longer equated with motherhood so often as it was a generation ago. Recognizing that the mother's role is learned, and that some women do not want the role, we are entering an era of optional motherhood. If the fear of "maternal deprivation" was one reason why facilities such as day care centers were not widely available in the 1950s, many programs that have been proposed or enacted in the past few years seek to relieve women of the responsibil-

Guidelines for Decision Making

Box 12–3 / How Late Can You Wait to Have a Baby?

As a consequence of the recent tendency to defer marriage and childbearing, it is not uncommon today for couples to decide to have their first child as late as their mid-thirties. The timing of first birth is partly a matter of personal preference, of course, but it is also a question of biological capability. Although it is commonly assumed that age thirty-five is the biological boundary for women to bear their first child, there is no reason to conclude that the risks of childbearing increase dramatically in any given year. However, the woman who waits much past the normal age of first marriage to bear children does take a greater risk, both to her own health and the baby's, and that risk gradually increases with age.

One age-related factor in both males and females is fertility, the capacity to bear children. Fertility depends upon the proper coordination of both partners' reproductive systems. In order for conception to occur, the woman has to be able to release healthy eggs; her fallopian tubes must allow the passage of the fertilized egg into the uterus; and the lining of the uterus must be prepared for the implantation of the embryo. The man has to be able to produce healthy sperm capable of propelling themselves up the uterus to the fallopian tubes where they meet the ovum, and those sperm must be compatible with the chemical balance of the woman's reproductive system. Anything that restricts the production of sperm and eggs or impedes their interaction lowers the chances of conception.

The fecundity of men and women declines after age thirty. Although male fecundity declines more slowly than that of females (some men father children as late as their seventies or eighties) aging does have an effect on their reproductive ability. With increasing age men produce fewer sperm and less active ones. The fecundity of women is typically highest in their mid-twenties, then it declines gradually during their thirties and more rapidly in their forties. The main reason why the fecundity of women decreases with age is that ovulation—which does not necessarily accompany each menstrual cycle—takes place less frequently. Women who have experienced irregular menstruation, repeated abortions, or prolonged use of the Pill (which suppresses the functioning of the ovaries) may have special difficulties in conceiving during their thirties and forties.

The most common fear about late pregnancy is that it may produce retarded or deformed children. Although recent developments in obstetrics have reduced the risk of late childbearing, the chance of producing a child with congenital abnormalities does increase with the age of the parents. A genetic defect known as Down's syndrome (sometimes referred to as mongolism) is one of the

ities of twenty-four-hour mothering. We will look more closely at some of those programs after a discussion of what Spock largely ignored—fatherhood.

Fatherhood

If, as Margaret Mead said, a family is "a woman with a child, and a man to look after her," the man's role is not to take care of the child himself but to provide economic support so that the woman can do it. Spock reflected this assumption in all the editions of *Baby and Child Care* until the most recent one. In the earlier editions, father was mentioned in just two brief sections.

In this respect, as in the others we have examined, the evolution of the various revisions most widespread abnormalities associated with aging parents. Mongolism is the single most common cause of mental retardation and is often the cause of severe heart defects. Among mothers in their twenties, the chances of producing a child with Down's syndrome are very low—about 1 in 1,500. Those odds change to about 1 in 800 for women in their early thirties, to about 1 in 280 for women in their late thirties, and then to about 1 in 100 for women in their early forties. In the case of other abnormalities, such as Klinefelter's syndrome—a condition in which male children are born with two X chromosomes and abnormally small testes that make them incapable of producing sperm—the age of the father seems to be an important factor. And there are other abnormalities associated with advancing parental age, such as the fact that women who give birth for the first time in their early thirties have about twice as many stillbirths—about 112 per 1,000 deliveries—compared with women who are in their early twenties. It is also important to note that the risk to the mother increases as she gets older. Delivery is more often complicated, and the risk of maternal heart failure and cervical cancer increases with age.

Childbirth at a relatively late age is safer for women today than it was a generation ago because parents can now avail themselves of a relatively new diagnostic technique, amniocentesis, which allows the early diagnosis of Down's syndrome and other congenital disorders. This involves the insertion of a thin needle into the womb to remove fluid and cells for analysis, which can be performed fourteen to sixteen weeks after conception. If such examination indicates the presence of Down's syndrome, or other genetic disorders, the mother can seek an abortion. Amniocentesis also allows doctors to determine the sex of the unborn child, which allows the selective abortion of male fetuses if the parents are carriers of any of several dozen disorders that are passed on only to sons. However, parents who intend to use amniocentesis should be aware of its limitations. It cannot yet be used to detect the presence of all birth defects. It is a relatively expensive procedure, and the results of the test are not available until several weeks after the test is taken. And although medical researchers at the University of California concluded on the basis of a study of 3,000 women that the procedure is safe, highly reliable, and extremely accurate, many doctors are still concerned about the possibility that amniocentesis may damage the fetus.

For women in their mid-thirties who are wondering if it is too late to give birth to a first child, the following advice might be offered. In general, it appears that the risks of childbirth to healthy women of this age have been exaggerated. Although the risk of producing a congenitally malformed child does increase with age, those risks are still fairly low for a woman in her mid-thirties who is married to a man no more than about ten years older than she is. For the prospective mother of this age who has "passed" her amniocentesis test, and who uses the facilities of a well-equipped medical center to minimize possible birth complications, there is little reason for concern about the special risks of late childbearing.

of this book over the past thirty years provides a perspective on how ideas about parenting have changed. In the 1976 revision, the father's role is much more important than before. Particularly when the wife has an outside job, Spock now recommends that both partners contribute equally to the tasks of parenthood.

A mother's involvement with her child is, of course, initially determined by biological factors, whereas fatherhood is a cultural invention to a greater extent than motherhood. As Margaret Mead has written,

> As far as we know, there is no biological instinct that makes a man into a good father. It is necessary to persuade him to want to be a father, and

Traditionally, in our society, the father's role was to provide status and economic support for his children. Recently, however, there has been considerable emphasis on fathering itself.

> each society uses different means of doing so. Sometimes he is persuaded to be a father because he needs an heir to inherit his land. The French Canadians used to persuade him to be a father by not giving bachelors hunting or fishing licenses. Sometimes he was persuaded to be a father through a system of ancestor worship, in which a man lacking children to worship him after death had no proper existence in the next world. There have been all varieties of inducements, and they all tend to break down. . . . (1953, p. 3)

One indication that these inducements still tend to break down is the Parent Locater Service that is operated by the federal government. This service uses Social Security numbers to help states track down fathers who have defaulted on their child support payments. About 85 percent of the 3.4 million families that receive Aid to Families of Dependent Children (AFDC) payments have absent fathers. This service is expected to collect an estimated $1 billion a year in child support from fathers who are currently avoiding those payments (*The New York Times,* April 7, 1976, p. 15).

In the eyes of the law, as we saw in Chapter 6, a mother is obligated to provide child care services and a father is obligated to provide support, though biologically a father is necessary only for conception. However, parenthood is a social as well as a biological fact, and it is the father's status in the community that generally determines the child's social standing. Bronislaw Malinowski, an influential social anthropologist, described the principle of legitimacy as a rule which states that "no child should be brought into the world without a man—and one man at that—assuming the role of sociological father, that is, guardian and protector, the male link between the child and the rest of the community" (1930, p. 137). William Goode added that the really important thing is not so much the child's protection as its status placement (1960, p. 27). This has been particularly important in patrilineal societies where one's social status and wealth (in the form of property) are largely inherited, and thus the social status of a child with no acknowledged father is ambiguous. To be born a bastard is to bear a highly undesirable, stigmatized status.

In our own society, where the occupational status of one's father rather than his place in the kinship system is what determines the circumstances in which one is raised and one's chances for achievement, illegitimacy in itself is not such a handicap, though the stigma has been disappearing only in recent years. When actress Ingrid Bergman gave birth in the 1950s to what was then popularly called a love child, her career went into a decline from which it never completely recovered, whereas a generation later, when actress Catherine Deneuve gave birth to a child and publicly announced her intention to bring it up by herself, her career suffered no comparable decline. Nevertheless, illegitimate birth has been far slower to gain public acceptance than premarital sex.

Of course, many other women besides movie stars are perfectly capable today of providing for children they may bear and rear on their own. One reason for the continuing concern about illegitimacy, however, is that many of the children born to unwed mothers do become dependent on state support. In recent years, about one out of three AFDC children has been illegitimate, and the annual cost of supporting these children and their mothers is about $2 billion (Cutright, 1972).

The number of single-parent families in the United States is rapidly growing, and more than 85 percent of them are headed by women. The phenomenal increase in the number of single-parent families over the past decade describes one of the most important trends in American family life. In 1978, single-parent households headed by a woman comprised 11 percent of all American households, and the number of such households had increased by about half over the previous decade (U.S. Bureau of the Census, 1978). However, illegitimacy is only one of the reasons for the rapid increase in single-parent families. More of them are caused by the death of a spouse, and more still by divorce.

We can put this trend toward single-parent families in better perspective by looking at how the living arrangements of children under eighteen have changed in recent decades. In recent years, about 80 percent of all American children under eighteen have lived in households with two parents (though not necessarily both their natural parents). This figure varies widely among different racial groups: for example, only about 50 percent of all black children live in two-parent families. The Census Bureau estimates that, among children born in recent years, about 45 percent are likely to live for a while in one-parent families. The 1970 Census showed that only about 66 percent of all children under eighteen were then living in families with both of their natural parents present, and the 1980 Census will show a substantially lower percentage than that because of the rising divorce rate (Carter and Glick, 1976). As we have noted, it is the impact of divorce on family life, and a rising number of single-parent families, that have caused much of the current anxiety about child rearing in America today. Most people assume that it is in the children's best interest to grow up in households with both natural parents, and thus it is assumed that the rise of the single-parent family is an undesirable trend.

What is not often noted is that in the decades

since 1940 the proportion of children living with at least one of their parents—rather than with foster parents, relatives, or in child care institutions—has risen. In 1940, the percentage of children living with at least one of their natural parents in a separate household was about 90 percent; in the 1970s, it increased to about 95 percent. There are several reasons for this, but the most important one is that widowed or divorced women are much more likely to maintain their own households, to keep the family together, and not to send their children to orphanages or to live with relatives (Bane, 1976, p. 13). Most commentators on family life express considerable concern about the trend toward single-parent families; very few acknowledge that while fewer of today's children live with both of their natural parents, more of them live with at least one.

But of course this does not mean that we should overlook the potential problems of single-parent families or ignore the possible consequences. In particular, since nine out of ten children living with a divorced parent live with their mother, we need to inquire about the impact of this pattern.

Does the absence of a father impair the socialization of children? Is it particularly difficult for boys to have no father in the home providing a masculine role model? These questions have been studied, but the results are inconclusive (Herzog and Sudia, 1968). There is no convincing evidence that the absence of a father, in and of itself, is critical in affecting the behavior or adjustment of the children.

However, single-parent families often have two problems that are beyond dispute. The first problem is that the children are deprived of the attention of the remaining parent because she is overburdened by having to carry both the child-rearing and the wage-earning responsibilities. The second problem is poverty. A 1976 U.S. Department of Labor report showed that in the previous year about 40 percent of all female-headed households had incomes of less that $5,000, compared with only about one in ten families headed by a man. And whereas only 28 percent of female-headed households had incomes in excess of $10,000, about 70 percent of male-headed households were in that category (U.S. Department of Labor, 1976).

In a study of the problems of female-headed households, two economists observe:

> The inadequate incomes of most female-headed families stem from the loss of a male earner, the mother's continuing responsibility for the care of young children, and the inability of most women to earn enough to support a family. However, the loss of a male earner within the household need not mean the loss of all of the father's income. Alimony and child-support payments as well as more informal gifts of money and other items help to maintain women and children living on their own. But indications are that the flow of those private transfers is somewhat smaller than is commonly believed. They are certainly inadequate to the task of keeping many women and children out of poverty. (Ross and Sawhill, 1975, p. 175)

Many people believe that the rapid increase of female-headed households is a good reason to establish a large, federally assisted day-care program. Convenient day-care facilities might not only relieve some of the stress suffered by the solo parent, but might also enable mothers to work at full-time jobs and earn higher salaries.

The Father in Intact Families

A glance at the relatively small number of studies of fathers and children in intact families indicates that researchers have generally shared Dr. Spock's opinion: except for his indirect importance as wage earner, the father is considered less important to his children than is the mother. What research there is on this topic suggests that fathers and mothers contribute to the development of their children in somewhat different ways. Not surprisingly, systematic observation of the interactions of parents with infants at three weeks and three months of age suggests that even when mothers have outside jobs fathers have relatively few regular responsibilities for child care. Nearly half the fathers in one study indicated that they had never changed the baby's diapers. The father's main role appears to be that of playmate, and the play between fathers and their infants is typically less verbal and more tactile than is play between mothers and young children. As contrasted to mothers, who characteristically stimulate their children verbally, fathers more often engage in physical activities such as rough-and-tumble play (Parke and Sawin, 1977).

Fathers also appear to be more concerned than mothers that their children develop distinctly masculine or feminine gender roles. In their child-rearing practices, fathers more often treat their young boys and girls very differently. Perhaps as a consequence of the greater stress on autonomy and independence in males, various studies suggest that parents have more influence over their daughters than they have over their sons (Lynn, 1976, p. 192).

In recent years, there have been some discernible changes in the father's role. With the decline of the traditional family, the father is no longer the undisputed authority who commands the respect and obedience of his children. In times of family crisis, outside professionals such as social workers or family therapists now share part of the father's power as final arbiter of disputes. And fathers are not called in to administer punishment as often as they once were. Rather, the new image of the father is that of an active, sharing helper.

In the decades to come, it will be interesting to see how the father's role changes in response to a redefined mother's role. There is a commonly expressed feeling today that, just as women have invested too much of themselves in the mother's role, men have invested themselves too heavily in their work roles. As one man, a psychiatrist and family therapist, writes:

> Today's father is overworked at work, played out and unable to give himself to full-time fathering when he gets home. His wife is also fed up with full-time mothering. Both seem to want part-time work and part-time parenting. Perhaps we should redefine fatherhood entirely. It should not be the full-time job of one parent but the part-time function of both parents in accord with their ability and knowledge. (Beels, 1974, p. 10)

While women have been moving into the traditionally male world of full-time work and careers, men have begun to move into what has traditionally been the woman's world of child rearing. Both trends signal a redefinition of what it means to be male or female.

THE FUTURE OF PARENTHOOD—SOME ALTERNATIVES

Since the quality of parenting is a matter of such widespread concern in the United States today, many different proposals and programs have been suggested to improve it. Some people, for example, feel that child rearing is so difficult, and at the same time so important to society, that it should be granted only to a select few. "Raising children, after all," writes Alvin Toffler,

> requires skills that are by no means universal. We don't let just anyone perform brain surgery or, for that matter, sell stocks and bonds. Even the lowest-ranking civil servant is required to pass tests proving competence. Yet we allow virtually anyone, almost without regard for mental or moral qualification, to try his or her hand at raising young human beings, so long as these human beings are biological offspring. Despite the increasing complexity of the task, parenthood remains the greatest single preserve of the amateur. (Toffler, 1970, p. 243)

Most of us would agree that parents need certain skills and knowledge to be able to meet a child's needs, but how are we to tell the competent parents from the incompetent? Who would be empowered to make that decision? How would we prevent the unqualified from having children? Roger McIntire has a plan that addresses all these problems. A special contraceptive drug would be administered to all women of childbearing age, making them permanently incapable of conceiving. Fertility could be restored only through the use of an antidote, and the antidote would be strictly regulated by the government. In order to qualify for child rearing, a couple would have to prove their competence for the task, much as all motorists are now required to pass a driving test. If licensing parents seems a serious invasion of individual rights, why is it that no one minds the stringent screening procedures that adoption agencies use when placing children? Why, McIntire asks, does "our society care more about the selection of a child's second set of parents than it does about his original parents?" (1973, p. 38).

Parent licensing would involve the government quite deeply in parenting—compared, at the least, to the provision of day-care facilities, and that by itself has been enough to provoke constant debate.

For the past decade, there has been a heated debate over day-care facilities, whether the federal government should extend its support for them, and what the consequences of a more comprehensive day-care system would be. Recent surveys of the child care facilities for children aged three to six years old whose mothers are in the labor force show conclusively that only a small minority—about 4 percent—are currently enrolled in a day-care center. Among the young children who are without daytime parental care, a much higher percentage are taken care of by relatives or friends (*Current Population Survey*, 1975).

The proponents of an expanded day-care system argue that expanded federal subsidies for such centers would not only ease the burden of working women who now have trouble obtaining adequate child care, but that they would also enhance children's development, and provide new jobs for women. Critics believe that any such system might undermine both parental authority and parental involvement with children, and that it would be a costly system whose consequence may be to impair the development of children. Many of the critics of an expanded day-care system have argued that the same money would be better spent if it were used to provide the support and services women need to stay at home and care for their children rather than working at full- or part-time jobs.

There is evidence from research studies on at least one crucial question in this debate, the effect of day care on the development of children. One study followed the development of a group of infants who entered a day-care center at between three and five months of age and left at twenty-nine months. Those children were then compared with a similar group who had been raised at home. After two and one-half years of formal assessments of development as well as informal observation, the investigators could find no differences between the children in day care and those raised at home. The attachments between day-care infants and their mothers did not weaken, and there was no observable difference between the two groups in separation anxiety. As the investigators conclude, "Day care, when responsibly and conscientiously implemented, does not seem to have hidden psychological dangers." If this conclusion was what the proponents of an expanded day-care system were hoping for, another finding—that there were no differences in social and cognitive development between the children who attended day care centers and those raised at home by their mothers—suggests that some of the expectations about day care are unrealistic (Kagan, Kearsley, and Zelazo, 1978, p. 261).

"Day care" is not just one proposal. Instead, the phrase covers an assortment of backup facilities that might be provided for the part-time care of children. One form it might take is already being tested on a limited basis in certain offices and factories. Child-care centers are provided right in the work place, which not only acquaints children with their parents' working world, but may have advantages for the employer as well by cutting down on the absentee and turnover rates and thus saving money (Farrell, 1975, p. 132).

For the past decade, there has been heated debate over day-care facilities, whether the federal government should extend its support for them, and what the consequences of a more comprehensive day-care system would be.

Another way businesses can help parents spend more time with their children is to allow greater flexibility in work hours, which might enable husband and wife to alternate child care duties while each contributes toward family income (Farrell, 1975, p. 135).

Day-care centers could also form a part of complete child-care communities—apartment complexes designed especially for parents, with child-care centers where children could be left while the parents are working. Such complexes might even include communal dining facilities for parents and children, so as to relieve parents of some of their domestic duties (Platt, 1969).

Some critics of our current child-rearing practices suggest a more radical approach: separating biological parenthood from social parenthood. One or both functions might be well-paid specialties, full-time professions for which applicants would have to qualify much as they do for any other profession. In a short time,

> a system of completely professional breeders and child rearers could be developed. Childbearing could be a profession and could be conducted with the best of modern technology—fertility drugs for multiple births, sperm banks, embryo transplants, and uterine implants to expand the gene pool, and so on. Professional breeders could be paid top salaries, like today's athletes, for the fifteen to twenty years of their prime childbearing time. Those who are impregnated could live in well-run dormitories, with excellent physical care, food, and entertainment. . . . (Lorber, 1975, p. 468)

This idea is a long way from current beliefs and practices, but perhaps it is not so far-fetched as it seems. Over the past thirty years, we have made the transition from a society in which parenthood was virtually obligatory to one in which it is a right, an option—not an inevitability. Looking ahead to a society in which having children is a privilege rather than a right, we can expect the institution of parenthood to take on forms that depart from current practices even more than the current ones differ from those of the past.

In the immediate future, however, the key question is who will take on the job of having children in an era when the burdens of parenthood seem prohibitively heavy. Perhaps if parenthood can be made compatible with other creative activities, optional parenthood need not pose a very serious problem. "Many will still decide," writes Bernice Lott,

> for all sorts of personally valid reasons, that parenthood is not for them, but others, remembering their own joyful childhoods, will be eager to participate in such an experience again, as parent now instead of child. (1973, p. 582)

Conclusions

Despite the many pronatalist pressures that still exert considerable force in our society, having children is no longer obligatory for every married couple. *Not* having them is now a realistic option.

Just as there are many bad reasons to get married in the first place, there are many bad reasons to have children. Here are just a few: "Our parents want grandchildren." "It'll improve our marriage." "It's a sure way to prove you're an adult." "We don't want to be different." "A child is my only claim to immortality." Instead of falling back on formulas like these, couples should ask what the real costs and rewards of parenthood are.

The costs include the possibility of lowered marital satisfaction, the usual crises and stresses of pregnancy and childbirth, the limitations that child rearing places upon the mother's freedom to pursue interests outside the home, and of course the economic burden of parenthood.

The rewards include the considerable satisfactions of nurturing a child, shaping its development, and sharing its growth. Being a parent gives many adults a sense of fulfilling an important and socially recognized role, and children often provide for their parents the satisfactions of closeness and connectedness that this special bond offers.

But parenthood seems particularly difficult today. The belief that the mother is responsible not just for the child's physical welfare but for molding its personality as well contributes to this difficulty, and so does the relative isolation of the mother and child in single-family households where no other adults share the responsibilities of parenthood. There is also considerable confusion today about how children should be brought up. Manuals written by child rearing "experts" can provide some help, but research on specific practices does not provide any clear guidelines. That research points to certain child-rearing practices that can harm children, but it does not produce any clear-cut advice about what specific socialization practices are in the child's best interest.

We do know that the early years of infancy—particularly the first three years of a child's life—are very important to its development. The full-time attention of its mother is not essential. But consistent care from parents and part-time parent-substitutes who are loving and who share the parents' general approach to child rearing is important. It is in the first three years of the child's life that the parents must plan carefully to give the child the attention it needs. After that, there is a wider range of alternatives, for both parents and children, including a variety of day-care facilities.

Today, relatively few households include grandparents or other relatives who can assist in child rearing, and yet a large percentage of mothers, many with preschool children, work outside the home. The number of fatherless families, moreover, is increasing. All of these factors make parenting more stressful, and all have been cited as reasons for expanding and improving day-care facilities.

REFERENCES

Mary Jo Bane. *Here to stay.* New York: Basic Books, 1976.

Wesley C. Becker. Consequences of different kinds of parental discipline. In M. L. Hoffman and L. W. Hoffman, eds. *Review of child development research,* vol. 1. New York: Russell Sage, 1964.

C. Christian Beels. Whatever happened to father? *The New York Times Magazine,* August 25, 1974, pp. 10 et passim.

Judith Blake. Coercive pronatalism and American population policy. In Ellen Peck and Judith Senderowitz, eds. *Pronatalism: The myth of mom and apple pie.* New York: Crowell, 1974.

———. The Supreme Court's abortion decisions and public opinion in the United States. *Population and Development Review,* March 1977, pp. 45–62.

Zena Smith Blau. Maternal aspirations, socialization, and achievement of boys and girls in the white, working class. *Journal of Youth and Adolescence* 11 (1972): 35–57.

Peter Blau and Otis Dudley Duncan. *The American occupational structure.* New York: Wiley, 1967.

William Borders. Indian sees benefits in his eight children. *The New York Times,* May 30, 1976, sect. 1, p. 18.

John Bowlby. *Child care and the growth of love.* Baltimore: Penguin, 1953.

Urie Bronfenbrenner. The changing American child—A speculative analysis. *The Journal of Social Issues* 17 (1961): 6–18.

———. The roots of alienation. In Nathan B. Talbot, ed. *Raising children in modern America.* Boston: Little, Brown, 1976.

Larry L. Bumpass and Charles F. Westoff. *The later years of childbearing.* Princeton, N.J.: Princeton University Press, 1970.

Hugh Carter and Paul C. Glick. *Marriage and divorce: A social and economic study.* Cambridge, Mass.: Harvard University Press, 1976.

Lawrence Casler. Maternal deprivation: A critical review of the literature. *Social Research and Child Development* 26 (1961): 1–64.

Phillips Cutright. Historical and contemporary trends in illegitimacy. *Archives of Sexual Behavior* 2 (1972): 97–117.

Joseph Epstein. *Divorced in America.* Baltimore: Penguin, 1975.

Warren Farrell. *The liberated man.* New York: Bantam, 1975.

Katharine Davis Fishman. In praise of the middle-class mother. *The New York Times Magazine,* November 3, 1968, pp. 97–100.

Richard Flacks. "Growing up confused." In Arlene Skolnick and Jerome Skolnick, eds. *Intimacy, family and society.* Boston: Little, Brown, 1974.

Helen H. Franzwa. Pronatalism in women's magazine fiction. In Ellen Peck and Judith Senderowitz, eds. *Pronatalism: The myth of mom and apple pie.* New York: Crowell, 1974.

Kent Geiger. *The family in Soviet Russia.* Cambridge, Mass.: Harvard University Press, 1968.

Richard J. Gelles, Murray A. Straus, and Suzanne K. Steinmetz. *Violence in the American family.* Garden City, N.Y.: Doubleday Anchor, 1978.

David G. Gil. *Violence against children.* Cambridge, Mass.: Harvard University Press, 1970.

Paul C. Glick. Marrying, divorcing and living together in the U.S. today. *Population Bulletin* 32, No. 5 (1977).

William F. Goode. Illegitimacy in the Caribbean social structure. *American Sociological Review* 25 (1960): 21–30.

Elizabeth Herzog and Cecelia E. Sudia. Fatherless homes: A review of research. *Children* 15 (1968): 177–182.

Lois Wladis Hoffman. Effects on child. In Lois Wladis Hoffman and F. Ivan Nye, eds. *Working mothers.* San Francisco: Jossey-Bass, 1974.

Sharon K. Houseknecht. Reference group support for voluntary childlessness: Evidence for conformity. *Journal of Marriage and Family* 39 (May 1977): 285–292.

Institute of Life Insurance. *Youth—1974.* New York: Institute of Life Insurance, 1974.

Jerome Kagan. The psychological requirements for human development. In Nathan B. Talbot, ed. *Raising children in modern America*. Boston: Little, Brown, 1976.

Jerome Kagan, Richard B. Kearsley, and Philip R. Zelazo. *Infancy: Its place in human development*. Cambridge, Mass.: Harvard University Press, 1978.

Barbara J. Katz. Cooling Motherhood. *National Observer,* December 20, 1972.

C. Henry Kempe. Child abuse and neglect. In Nathan B. Talbot, ed. *Raising children in modern America*. Boston: Little, Brown, 1976.

Melvin L. Kohn. Social class and parental values. *The American Journal of Sociology* 64 (1959): 337–351.

W. W. Lambert. Cross-cultural backgrounds to personality development and the socialization of aggression: Findings from the six-culture study. In W. W. Lambert and Rita Weisbrod, eds. *Comparative perspectives on social psychology*. Boston: Little, Brown, 1971.

E. E. Lemasters. Parenthood as crisis. *Marriage and Family Living* 19 (1957): 352–355.

Max Lerner. *America as a civilization*. New York: Simon and Schuster, 1957.

Theodore Lidz. *The person: His development through the life cycle*. New York: Basic Books, 1968.

Judith Lorber. Beyond equality of the sexes: The question of the children. *The Family Coordinator* 24 (1975): 465–472.

Bernice E. Lott. Who wants the children? *American Psychologist* 28 (1973): 573–582.

David B. Lynn. Fathers and sex-role development. *Family Coordinator* 25 (October 1976): 403–409.

James Leslie McCary. *Human sexuality: A brief edition*. New York: D. Van Nostrand, 1973.

Nancy McGrath. By the book. *The New York Times Magazine,* June 27, 1976, p. 26.

Roger W. McIntire. Parenthood training or mandatory birth control: Take your choice. *Psychology Today,* October 1973, pp. 34–39, et passim.

Bronislaw Malinowski. Parenthood: The basis of social structure. In V. F. Calverton and S. D. Schmalhausen, eds. *The new generation*. New York: Macauley, 1930.

Margaret Mead. The impact of cultural changes on the family. In *The family in the urban community*. Detroit: The Merrill-Palmer School, 1953.

National Center for Health Statistics. *Vital Statistics Report,* vol. 27, no. 12, March 15, 1979.

John Newson and Elizabeth Newson. *Four years old in an urban community*. Chicago: Aldine, 1968.

Newsweek. The parent gap. September 22, 1975, pp. 48–50, et passim.

Ann Oakley. *Woman's work*. New York: Pantheon, 1974.

Ross D. Parke and Douglas B. Swain. Fathering: It's a major role. *Psychology Today* (November 1977): 28–32.

Ellen Peck. Television's romance with reproduction. In Ellen Peck and Judith Senderowitz, eds. *Pronatalism: The myth of mom and apple pie*. New York: Crowell, 1974.

John R. Platt. Child care communities. *The Urban Review* 3 (1969): 17–18.

Population Reference Bureau. Family size and the black American. *Population Bulletin,* 30, no. 4. Washington, D.C., 1975.

Lee Rainwater. *And the poor get children*. Chicago: Quadrangle, 1960.

———. *Family design: Marital sexuality, family size and contraception*. Chicago: Aldine, 1965.

Margaretha Ribble. *The rights of infants*. New York: Columbia University Press, 1943.

Betty Rollin. Motherhood: Who needs it? *Look,* September 22, 1970, pp. 15–17.

The Roper Organization. *The Virginia Slims American women's opinion poll*. New York: The Roper Organization, 1974.

Heather L. Ross and Isabel Sawhill. *Time of transition*. Washington, D.C.: The Urban Institute, 1975.

Alice S. Rossi. A biosocial perspective on parenting. *Daedalus* (Spring 1977): 1–31.

Candyce Smith Russell. Transition to parenthood: Problems and gratifications. *Journal of Marriage and the Family* (1974): 294–301.

Norman Ryder. Contraceptive failure in the United States. *Family Planning Perspectives* 5 (1973): 133–142.

Sheldon J. Segal. Limiting reproductive potential. In Nathan B. Talbot, ed. *Raising children in modern America*. Boston: Little, Brown, 1976.

Edward Shorter. *The making of the modern family*. New York: Basic Books, 1975.

Arlene Skolnick. *The intimate environment*. Boston: Little, Brown, 1973.

Philip Slater. *The pursuit of loneliness*. Boston: Beacon Press, 1970.

René A. Spitz. Hospitalism: An inquiry into the genesis of psychiatric conditions in early childhood. Part I. *Psychoanalytic Studies of the Child* 1 (1945): 53–74.

Benjamin Spock. *Baby and child care* (originally published under the title *The common sense book of baby and child care*). New York: Duell, Sloan and Pearce, 1945.

———. *Raising children in a difficult time*. New York: Norton, 1974.

Ross M. Stolzenberg and Linda J. Waite. Age, fertility expectations and plans for employment. *American*

Sociological Review 42 (October 1977): 769—783.

Catherine Storr. Freud and the concept of parental guilt. In Jonathan Miller, ed. *Freud: The man, his world, his influence.* Boston: Little, Brown, 1972.

Christopher Tietze. Two years' experience with a liberal abortion law, its impact on fertility trends in New York City. *Family Planning Perspectives* 5 (1973): 36–41.

Alvin Toffler. *Future shock.* New York: Random House, 1970.

U.S. Bureau of the Census. *Population characteristics.* Washington, D.C.: Government Printing Office, August 1978.

———. *Fertility of American Women.* Current Population Survey, series P-20, no. 330. Washington, D.C.: Government Printing Office, June 1978.

Jean E. Veevers. Voluntarily childless wives: An exploratory study. *Sociology and Social Research* 57 (1973): 356–365.

Charles F. Westoff. The modernization of U.S. contraceptive practices. *Family Planning Perspectives* 4 (1972): 9–12.

——— and R. H. Potvin. *College women and fertility values.* Princeton, N.J.: Princeton University Press, 1967.

Beatrice Whiting. *Six cultures: Studies of child rearing.* New York: Wiley, 1963.

Robert F. Winch. Rearing by the book. In Marvin Sussman, ed. *Sourcebook in marriage and the family.* Boston: Houghton Mifflin, 1968.

Martha Wolfenstein. Trends in infant care. *American Journal of Orthopsychiatry* 23 (1953): 120–130.

Rochelle Paul Wortis. The acceptance of the concept of maternal role by behavioral scientists: Its effect on women. *The American Journal or Orthopsychiatry* 41 (1971): 733–746.

James D. Wright and Sonia R. Wright. Social class and parental values for children. *American Sociological Review* 41 (June 1976): 527–548.

Yankelovich, Skelly, and White, Inc. *The General Mills American Family Report 1976–77.* Minneapolis, Minn.: General Mills, Inc., 1977.

Serapio R. Zalba. Battered children. *TransAction,* July/August 1971, pp. 58–61.

FOR FURTHER STUDY

For a comprehensive discussion of the long-term decline in fertility not only in the United States, but also in other industrial nations, see "Marriage and Fertility in the Developed Countries," by Charles F. Westoff, in *Scientific American* (December 1978). Another recent publication, co-authored by Westoff (with Norman B. Ryder) is *The Contraceptive Revolution* (Princeton, N.J.: Princeton University Press, 1977), which discusses the effects of new techniques for birth control. In addition to new contraceptive techniques, one of the main reasons for the decline in population growth is a change in the economic value of children, discussed in a Population Reference Bureau publication, *The Value and Cost of Children* (Population Bulletin, vol. 32, no. 1, Washington, D.C., 1977).

For different perspectives on the influence of Dr. Spock and other child-rearing experts, see Michael Zuckerman's "Dr. Spock: The Confidence Man," in *The Family in History,* edited by Charles E. Rosenberg (University of Pennsylvania Press, 1975); an article by Christopher Jencks, "Is It All Dr. Spock's Fault?" which appeared in the *New York Times Magazine,* March 3, 1968; and Chapter 2, "Social Expectations of Parenting—The Impact of Experts" in *Fathers, Mothers, and Society,* by Rhona and Robert Rapoport (New York: Basic Books, 1977). The Rapoports' book also includes a useful discussion of the variety of modern parental situations.

Jessie Bernard's *The Future of Motherhood* (New York: Penguin, 1974) is a good discussion of the forces that influence the mother's role. Over the past few years, more attention has been paid to fathering. The reader might want to consult a special issue of *The Family Coordinator* (October 1976), which was devoted entirely to this topic. Two other discussions of fatherhood that are well grounded in research are David B. Lynn's *The Father—His Role in Child Development* (Belmont, Calif.: Wadsworth, 1974), and an anthology edited by Michael Lamb, *The Role of the Father in Child Development* (New York: Wiley, 1976).

For two contrasting perspectives on the child care debate, see Selma Fraiberg's *Every Child's Birthright: In Defense of Mothering* (New York: Basic Books, 1978), and *Infancy: Its Place in Human Development* by Jerome Kagan, Richard Kearsley, and Philip Zelazo (Cambridge, Mass.: Harvard University Press, 1978). The latter shows that good day care is not necessarily detrimental to infant development. This volume also provides an interesting perspective on the widely accepted but unproven belief that infant experience is crucial in shaping the character and intellect of adults.

Much has been written in recent years about the need for a comprehensive family policy. For different perspectives, see Mary Jo Bane's *Here to Stay* (New York: Basic Books, 1976); Gilbert Y. Steiner, *The Children's Cause* (Washington, D.C.: The Brookings Institution, 1976); and *All Our Children,* a volume prepared by Kenneth Keniston and the Carnegie Council on Children (New York: Harcourt, Brace, 1977).

"The Barbecue" Rosalind Shaffer

13 Kinship and Community—It's Nice to Know They're There When You Need Them

Perhaps the most revealing documents about the type of society we live in are the ones we carry around in our wallets. Social Security cards, credit cards, hospitalization and health care cards, plastic ID cards—all are peculiar to modern society and reveal one of its basic features, for as recently as fifty years ago they were unnecessary. Social Security was not in effect, nor was group medical insurance or any of the other large programs that one turns to in case of unemployment, medical emergency, or disability. Then it was the family, not some impersonal bureaucracy operating with nine-digit ID numbers and computerized correspondence, that was supposed to provide assistance.

One of the most telling facts about the family today is that it is no longer called upon to perform certain functions. Most of us, for example, will never be expected to take care of a cousin who is temporarily unemployed. The care of family members who are retarded, chronically ill, or old and infirm is increasingly given over to outside institutions.

Credit cards tell the same story. Formerly, one's face, name, and family reputation were all the identification one needed, but in today's large-scale society, ID cards bearing your photograph and signature are often necessary because the members of a particular group—a company, a club, or college—do not necessarily recognize one another.

For several generations, one of the chief preoccupations of sociologists was to describe this shift from traditional to modern society. "Time was," as Peter Laslett writes in *The World We Have Lost,* "when the whole of life went forward in a circle of loved, familiar faces, known and fondled objects, all to human size. That time has gone forever. It makes us very different from our ancestors" (1965, p. 6). It was commonly argued that industrialization caused the breakup of the extended family, which consisted of grandparents and collateral relatives—aunts, uncles, cousins. Judging from the size of most modern households, many sociologists concluded that it had dwindled into the smaller, portable, isolated nuclear family composed of a husband and wife and their children.

It was also assumed by many sociologists that the bonds of kinship had eroded; family members no longer depended on each other as they had in the past. The modern family was considered by many to be little more than a launching pad for the children, who would soon be in their own orbit at some distance from their parents and kinfolk, both geographically and emotionally.

But is this really what happened? Clearly, something important has changed. We no longer live in a society where the bonds of kinship are commonly considered more important than the marital union, and it is tempting to conclude that the ties of kinship have eroded almost completely for many American families. And yet studies conducted since the 1950s have repeatedly demonstrated that kinship ties are still important.

If most American families have not really abandoned their kinfolk, however, there is another respect in which many families today are somewhat isolated. Compared with family life in the past, it is common for today's families to be relatively isolated from their neighbors and the surrounding community. The household has become a more self-contained and self-sufficient unit, and family life has become a more private affair. Many people have complained about the feeling of isolation that such private households promote. "I feel like I'm in a vacuum," said one woman who lives with her husband and son in suburban Atlanta. "I've got everything I always wanted—a swimming pool and a private patio—but it's so damn private that it's driving me crazy" (*Newsweek*, September 22, 1975, p. 50).

There are many indications that people are interested in exploring new forms of connectedness and breaking down the fences that have been erected around the nuclear family. In many cities, there are "hotlines" or "dial-a-shoulder" services for potential suicides, alcoholics, even for people who want to lose weight. There are youth centers bearing names like Project Trust and Sanctuary where troubled youngsters can go and find help.

More significantly, new forms of marriage and family life are being tested in thousands of group marriages and family clusters that have redefined the household and rewritten some of the rules about intimate relationships. These quiet social experiments have received far less media attention than the hippie communes of the late 1960s and early 1970s, but they may have a greater impact as agents of social change. They are attempts to create a new type of extended family unit based on shared interests and mutual commitment rather than the fact of kinship.

These experiments illustrate some of the most radical alternatives to traditional forms of marriage and the family. Even if they do not provide a blueprint that a majority of families would want to follow, they may help us to understand some of the problems associated with our marriage and family arrangements.

THE BONDS OF KINSHIP

Until just a few generations ago, a person's family name was his fate. Like skin color or fingerprints, it could hardly be changed. Much of what anyone might ask about you could be answered by saying "I am the son or daughter of X, the cousin of Y." Especially in small towns where a few dozen families had lived together for generations, it was assumed that your family name said much about who you are. Here, for example, is Harper Lee's description of the life of a small town in the South during the Depression, from her novel *To Kill a Mockingbird*:

> The people who had lived side by side for years and years were utterly predictable to one another: they took for granted attitudes, character shadings, even gestures, as having been repeated in each generation and refined over time. Thus the dicta "No Crawford minds his own business," "Every third Merriweather is morbid," "The truth is not in the Delafields," "All the Bufords walk like that," were simple guides to daily living: Never

> take a check from a Delafield without a discreet call to the bank; Miss Maudie Atkinson's shoulder stoops because she was a Buford; if Mrs. Grace Merriweather sips gin it's nothing unusual—her mother did the same. (1962, p. 134)

In such towns, your family name was your credit card—unless, of course, you happened to be a Delafield.

Kinship was an important factor even in large cities in the past. Edith Wharton's novels, for example, describe "good society" in New York at the turn of the century as an almost tribal community consisting of five or six great families, each related to the others through marriage.

In many societies other than our own, kinship provides the very basis of the social fabric. Describing the Navajo tribe, Dorothea Leighton and Clyde Kluckhohn write that

> the importance of his relatives to the Navajo can scarcely be exaggerated. The worst that one might say of another person is "He acts as if he doesn't have any relatives. . . ." Conversely, the ideal of behavior often suggested by headmen is "Act as if everyone were related to you." (1948, p. 54)

In contrast to our own language, which provides few kinship terms—and not very precise ones at that—most preliterate societies are characterized by a complex kinship vocabulary. In such societies, the kinship system indicates a precise code of responsibilities, rights, and obligations. People function not as autonomous individuals but as members of certain kinship groups. Virtually all relationships are defined by the type and degree of kinship that exist between two people.

Because we place such a high value on individual freedom and personal autonomy, societies that are organized around the principle of kinship seem confining to us. American literature in the early decades of this century was sprinkled with figures like Carol Kennicott in Sinclair Lewis's novel *Mainstreet,* who wanted so much to escape from the ascribed status and constant surveillance of small-town life. For most people in American society today, the ties and obligations that Carol Kennicott resented have been cast off. Most of our population now resides in metropolitan areas, not small towns. Family name and kinship ties are no longer as important as they were.

Is the Nuclear Family Isolated?

Like most people, scholars sometimes mistake frequently repeated beliefs for established fact. Such was the case for several generations of sociologists who tried to understand the nature of modern family life. Twentieth-century sociologists inherited from the founders of the discipline a series of contrasting terms—for example, the contrast between societies based on status or contract. Perhaps the most influential statement on the breakdown of traditional community was written in 1887 by Ferdinand Tönnies, a German sociologist who contrasted *Gemeinschaft,* the integral community characterized by a fusion of feeling, thought, commitment, and tradition, with *Gesellschaft,* the rationally ordered society in which most associations are more impersonal.

These early theorists all stressed the differences between folk and urban society. They believed that much of the history of the family could be understood as the decline of the large, extended family unit and the rise of the nuclear family. Theorists pointed out that the modern family had been stripped of many of its old functions, and explained that the strong bonds of the extended family were not consistent with the needs of modern society.

What, exactly, had caused the extended family to break down? Several influential theorists answered the question by pointing to the process of industrialization. Here, for example, is Raymond Firth's explanation of why industrialization ushered in the nuclear family:

> Industrial employment alters the occupational structure, lessens the time spent together by family and kin members, attracts able-bodied men away from their natal homes, loosens the bonds of ob-

> ligation and control in respect to their elders, gives them a personal cash income which is easily convertible to their own purposes. Able to induce their wives to follow them to their place of employment or to obtain wives away from their home and the conventional local ties, they can form family units of an independent character, and take the responsibility for the support of their own wives and children. (1964, p. 74)

And, it was argued, this small nuclear family is ideally suited to the requirements of industrial society. In such a society mobility is necessary, and the nuclear family is a portable unit that also provides a refuge from the competitive pressures of industrial society. It is well suited to a society in which individual achievement is more important than the accident of birth into a particular family and kin group.

The idea that the distinguishing feature of the modern family is its isolation from the bonds of kinship seemed so plausible that it was accepted as self-evident truth. It was an attractive hypothesis that gained the status of accepted fact without having been subjected to the test of inquiry.

The hypothesis of the isolated nuclear family seemed especially plausible in American culture, which had been characterized since the colonial period by rapid mobility (Parsons, 1943). From the very beginning, Americans seemed to have developed more isolated social units than did people in Europe. In European agricultural communities, as historian Oscar Handlin observes, "the peasants still lived in villages and walked out each day to labour in the fields." But in the American colonies, except for New England, the isolated family farm or plantation quickly became the dominant pattern. And even in New England, where the Puritans tried to control migration and establish settled towns, the control exerted by the Puritan leaders lasted no longer than about thirty years (Handlin, 1966, p. 45).

Americans were—and still are—more rootless and mobile than other people. Nineteenth-century English novels usually end as two people get married, and that ending symbolizes not only the triumph of romantic love, but also the fact that the couple has found a place in the established social structure. By contrast, American novels of the same period are more likely to end with the hero riding off into the sunset, as does Huckleberry Finn: "I got to light out for the Territory ahead of the rest, because Aunt Sally she's going to adopt me and civilize me and I can't stand it. I been there before."

In nineteenth-century America there was a saying, "If you can see your neighbor's chimney, it's time to move on." One of the most persistent themes in our folk songs, like the lyrics of "Get Along, Little Dogie," is the idea of freedom and loneliness, the necessity of leaving family and friends, and moving on:

> *You ain't got no father, you ain't got no mother,*
> *You left them behind when first you did roam,*
> *You ain't got no sister, you ain't got no brother,*
> *You're just like a cowboy, a long way from home.*

For Americans, the self-made man became a cultural ideal. The phrase itself suggests how far we have moved from those societies of the past in which one's name was one's fate. "*Self-made,*" not the product of parents, ancestors, or kin; but self-created, sprung—like the hero of Scott Fitzgerald's *The Great Gatsby*—"from his Platonic conception of himself."

Kinship in Contemporary Society

It is no doubt true that kinship is less important for us today than it has been in the past, and that the mobility characteristic of American society since the colonial period has created social patterns unlike those in Western Europe. But research conducted since the 1950s suggests that the theorists who drew a sharp contrast between folk and urban society, and thus concluded that kinship is no longer important in modern society, did not present a very accurate picture of the present or the past.

In the first place, these theorists incorrectly assumed that the typical household of the past consisted of an extended family. That may have been true of the wealthier households in eighteenth- and nineteenth-century Europe, but in North America and Britain and among poorer families especially, the typical household of the past contained the same members we find in most families today—a husband, his wife, and their children. "Prior to the modern era in the Western world," writes William Goode,

> several generations of one family did not live under the same roof, and did not carry on all their productive activities there. If only because of the brute facts of mortality and the necessity of living on small plots of land, this was true for both urban and rural strata. (1963, p. 371)

The assumption that industrialization and urbanization caused the breakdown of the extended family has also been challenged over the past few decades as historians have assembled evidence showing that the nuclear family structure was common *before* industrialization, and indeed that its existence was an important prerequisite for industrial development (Lasch, 1975, p. 35). One study of the residential patterns in nineteenth-century England found that compared with families in rural areas, those in the new factory towns were *more* likely to have aging relatives living with them. In factory towns, a widowed grandmother might provide real assistance to a married daughter and son-in-law by looking after their children while both husband and wife were at work in the mills (Anderson, 1971).

In addition, several dozen studies conducted in Great Britain and the United States since the 1950s provide more of the kind of information we need to understand the meaning of kinship today. This research suggests that we should substantially modify the hypothesis of the isolated nuclear family. It was so frequently assumed that the bonds of kinship had eroded that, at first, researchers remarked about the unexpected pattern they discovered. "We were surprised," remarked Michael Young and Peter Wilmott in a summary of a study conducted in the mid-1950s, "to discover that the wider family, far from having disappeared, was still very much alive in the middle of London" (1957, p. xvi). When the same pattern was repeatedly demonstrated by researchers such as Marvin Sussman (see Box 13–1) and Bert Adams (1975), students of contemporary kinship systems turned their attention to the specific types of assistance that kinfolk offer each other.

In our society today, the norm is that a married couple should be financially independent, needing no assistance from their parents or kinfolk. Young couples frequently view continuous assistance from their parents as a threat to their independence. Nonetheless, a majority of young married couples struggling to maintain their lifestyle do take substantial assistance from parents. One study showed that 56 percent of the young couples who were asked disapproved of receiving such help, but did not reject it (Sussman, 1965, p. 397).

Rather than providing continuous financial help, parents more frequently offer assistance in the form of no- or low-interest loans or money for inexpensive vacations or household equipment. Like gifts given on ceremonial occasions such as anniversaries or birthdays, assistance of this sort is less threatening to the young couple trying to maintain their independence than regular subsidies would be.

Parents and other kin are also called upon for assistance in times of emergency. When people are in trouble or need help, they turn to relatives more readily than to friends. The bonds of kinship are still considered by most people to involve certain "inalienable rights" as well as obligations. When struck by major disasters such as fires or floods, victims seek help from their relatives even before they turn to outside agencies (Sussman and Burchinal, 1962, p. 144). The more impersonal forms of assistance—hospitalization plans and government relief for disaster victims—are important, but relatives are still called upon in times of need. Blue Cross will not take care of the children when a woman is hospitalized (for whatever reason), but her mother frequently will.

Research Perspectives on Marriage and Family

Box 13–1 / Measuring Mutual Assistance Patterns Among Kinfolk

Among the functions of empirical studies are the testing of theoretical beliefs and the detection of patterns that otherwise escape notice. A 1959 study conducted by Marvin Sussman on the hypothesis of the isolated nuclear family shows how empirical studies can be used to correct and guide sociological theory. Sussman's study, like others conducted in the 1950s and 1960s, was an attempt to answer several basic questions about the importance of kinship in urban society: Do relatives often live close to one another, and interact frequently? Do they offer any substantial assistance to one another? If so, what types of assistance are most likely to be offered? Sussman set out to determine empirically how important the bonds of kinship are in urban, industrial society.

He began by drawing samples from two census areas in Cleveland, one in a lower-middle-class district, the other in a working-class area. His sample consisted of a total of eighty families. He then designed a series of questions about visiting patterns among relatives, assistance of various types—financial aid, housekeeping or child care, advice, gift-giving, and family ceremonies such as birthdays or anniversaries.

Responses to these questions demonstrated a very clear pattern of kin interdependency. Almost all of the families had offered some form of kin assistance within the one-month period preceding the interview. Contrary to the assumption that in industrial society the conjugal family moves wherever the chief wage earner can get the best job, this study found that 70 percent of the working-class respondents and 45 percent of the middle-class families have relatives living in the neighborhood.

Even families that lived at some distance from their relatives offered assistance of various sorts with some regularity. The percentage of families involved in various types of assistance, the types of help offered, and which family members most often received it are shown in the accompanying table.

Despite hospitalization and disability insur-

Families commonly exchange more routine types of assistance, too. Day-to-day activities such as shopping, child care, helping with household tasks, and giving advice are among the types of assistance that kinfolk extend to one another. As one study of help patterns among middle-class families indicates, parents more frequently offer services to their young, married daughters; male children are more likely to receive financial aid. Usually parents offer the type of assistance that will allow their son or daughter to fulfill conventional sex-role expectations in marriage (Sussman, 1953).

Parents whose children have formed their own households clearly indicate that they want to remain a significant part of their children's lives. Judging from the assistance that is offered and accepted by their children, they do indeed remain significant. Parents are also emphatically against receiving support from their children. And although survey studies show that married children are willing, in theory, to support their elderly parents, not many actually do (Sussman, 1963).

Such studies demonstrate that family means considerably more than just a "launching pad"

HOW FAMILY MEMBERS HELP EACH OTHER

	Direction of Service Networks				
Major Forms of Help and Service	*Between Respondent's Family and Related Kin*	*From Respondents to Parents*	*From Respondents to Siblings*	*From Parents to Respondents*	*From Siblings to Respondents*
Any form of help	93.3	56.3	46.6	79.6	44.8
Help during illness	76.0	47.0	42.0	46.4	39.0
Financial aid	53.0	14.6	10.3	46.8	6.4
Care of children	46.8	4.0	29.5	20.5	10.8
Advice (personal and business)	31.0	2.0	3.0	26.5	4.5
Valuable gifts	22.0	3.4	2.3	17.6	3.4

Note: Totals do not add up to 100 percent because many families received more than one form of help or service.
Source: Marvin B. Sussman. "The Isolated Nuclear Family: Fact or Fiction?" *Social Problems* 6 (Spring 1959): 336.

ance, family members are frequently called upon to help during illness. And although a widely accepted norm is that couples should be financially independent of their parents and other kinfolk, financial assistance was reported as one of the most common ways in which relatives help each other. By comparing the second and fourth columns in this table, it is evident that assistance patterns between married couples and their parents do not follow the principle of reciprocity. Parents give their children more assistance of every type than vice versa.

Because of this study and others like it which measured mutual assistance patterns among kinfolk in various metropolitan areas across the country, the existence of a kin network in contemporary society has been conclusively demonstrated. Kinship today does mean something different from what it meant in simpler societies, but it remains important (Sussman, 1959).

for children. The ties of kinship—particularly those between parents and children, and brothers and sisters who once shared the same household—remain important in today's society. In an age of transient friendships, kin relations are often defined as people that one can depend on. In comparison with friendships, primary kin relationships are more likely to endure over time and distance.

Although there is an element of obligation in kin relationship, we cannot assume that these bonds are expedient or superficial. Various studies show that between kin a real bond of affection, shared interests, and companionship exists as well. A study conducted in San Francisco, for example, found that about 90 percent of the respondents named a kinsman as one of their closest friends (Bell and Boat, 1957). Especially among urban, blue-collar families, get-togethers involving the extended family are a very important part of leisure-time activities (Dotson, 1951). The frequency with which kinfolk visit each other says something about the nature of the bond, too. According to a national survey conducted in 1974, more than a third of the respondents said that they get together with

Research show not only how common mutual assistance patterns among kinfolk are, but also that many people consider kinfolk to be their closest friends.

relatives at least once a week, and about three-fifths do so at least several times a month (National Opinion Research Center, 1974).

Women more often maintain close relationships with their parents than men do. As the proverb says, "A son's a son till he takes a wife; a daughter's a daughter for all her life." Ours is a society in which family name is transmitted through the male line. But judging by continued bonds between parents and their offspring, we more closely resemble a matrilineal pattern, in which the female line is more important. Kinship studies confirm not only that women take a more active part than their husbands do in maintaining kin relationships, but that the mother–daughter bond is closer than either the father–daughter bond or that between parents and their sons. Perhaps this is one consequence of the emphasis in childhood socialization on male independence, but Peter Wilmott and Michael Young offer an additional explanation for the closeness of the mother–daughter bond. They point out that the major role expectation for women is still that they be wives and mothers, thus giving successive generations of females certain interests and experiences in common (1960, p. 84). Young women who have just taken on the housewife and mother roles often feel a common bond with their mothers, and say things like "Now I know what my parents went through in raising me" (Adams, 1975, p. 368). Because men only rarely choose occupations that are like their fathers', there is no similar basis for a close father–son bond.

That the housewife and mother roles expected of the young wife resemble the roles her husband's mother has been performing for years also helps to explain that common family complaint, in-law problems. True, the stereotypical mother-in-law of countless jokes is the *wife's* mother: "If I had it to do over again," sighs the American husband, "I'd marry a Japanese girl. They're pretty, graceful, obedient—and your mother-in-law's in Yokohama" (Adams, 1975, p. 312). Surprisingly, though, the in-law named most frequently as the source of trouble is the husband's mother, not the wife's (Duvall, 1954, p. 187).

The most common complaints about mothers-in-law fit the stereotypes. They do tend to interfere, to criticize, to be possessive and overprotective. There may be a grain of truth in all the mother-in-law jokes and in novels such as Philip Roth's *Portnoy's Complaint,* which depict the mother who refuses to acknowledge that her children might be able to get along without her. Could Mama Portnoy *ever* be convinced that another woman would take good care of her son Alex?

The universality of mother-in-law jokes suggests that the special attachment between mother and child is difficult to sever. Because in our culture most families have relatively few children, and thus an intense mother–child bond, it is understandable that mothers have a difficult time allowing their children to be independent. The situation is further complicated, as sociologist Gerald Leslie points out, because

> the wife is thrown into direct competition with the husband's mother, and will be judged in terms of her ability to keep house, cook, and otherwise cater to her husband's needs. Moreover, she competes with a woman with twenty or more years' experience on the job. (1976, p. 318)

It is no wonder that more women than men complain about their mothers-in-law.

Moving On—How Mobility Affects Kinship Ties

Most families today are not isolated from their kinfolk. Patterns of mutual assistance, frequent visits, and mother-in-law problems all illustrate the continuing importance of kinship bonds. But how has geographical mobility, such a distinctive feature of American society, affected those bonds?

In Saul Bellow's 1970 novel, *Mr. Sammler's Planet,* a character is asked whether he would like to inherit an uncle's house to acquire roots. "Roots?" the man replies, "roots are not modern. That's a peasant concept." Certainly it has been alien to many Americans since colonial times; today, half the American population changes its place of residence every five years. The average American moves about fourteen times in a lifetime. Even if many of those moves are from one residence to another within the same city, long-distance moves have become a much more common fact of life over the past few decades. A United Van Lines official reports that its average client family in 1960 moved about 400 miles. Ten years later, in 1970, that figure had increased to 500 miles (Melville, 1972).

One woman, the wife of a corporate executive, reports that she and her husband moved nine times in fourteen years, living in cities as widely separated as Phoenix, Los Angeles, Philadelphia, and New York. She comments that she feels like a displaced person. "It's like a rerun of 'The Lone Ranger,' " she says. "We're constantly riding out of one town or another, and there are our new-found acquaintances waving good-bye and wondering who we are." (Melville, 1972) This is an extreme example, but the problems this woman encountered are typical of many college-educated couples working in professional or technical occupations, or in managerial positions where geographical mobility is commonly required for career advancement. A report from the Census Bureau shows how clear a connection there is between higher educational achievement and greater geographical mobility. Between 1975 and 1978, only 23 percent of persons with eight years of schooling or less had moved to a different house in the United States, while 33 percent of those with one to four years of high school, and fully 42 percent of those with some college had moved (U.S. Bureau of the Census, 1979). Some real estate firms now specialize in locating "equivalent towns" in metropolitan areas across the country for such mobile couples. But even if the new town to which the couple moves looks and feels like the last one they lived in, the problem that such highly mobile couples face is that the only long-term intimate relationships they maintain on an active basis are with each other.

There is some evidence that such rapid mobility, while encouraged by large corporations which shift top-level employees from one corporate site to another, is also being resisted by some families. Moving is commonly regarded today as a traumatic event, particularly for the wife, and now that women make up a larger percentage of the work force, the loss of the wife's job has become a more common reason to stay put. It is significant that when Atlas Van Lines, a company that specializes in long-distance moves, conducted a survey of 300 corporate customers in 1974, over half of the firms reported some refusal by employees to relocate, an increase of more than 20 percent over the 1973 figure. In the year before that, 1972, so few corporate employees had refused to relocate that the moving firm had decided that no systematic survey was necessary (Vecsey, 1975).

Despite these signs of resistance, however, geographical mobility is still very common, especially among upper-middle-class families. One reason the hypothesis of the isolated nuclear family was so convincing was that it seemed obvious that such rapid mobility would weaken kinship ties by separating family members.

Several studies conducted over the past two decades help us to understand the effect of mobility on kinship bonds. It has been found, for example, that mobility has one meaning for lower-class or blue-collar families and another for middle- and upper-middle-class families. The mobility pattern of lower-class and blue-collar families is illustrated by Lewellyn Hendrix's study of families that moved from a small town in Arkansas. Hendrix found that over half of the people who left moved to cities where kinfolk were already living. Typically, those who had first settled in the new location helped their kinfolk to follow by offering the newcomers assistance in finding jobs and a place to live (Hendrix, 1975).

This study, like others, demonstrates a pattern of chain migration for many lower-class and blue-collar families. Most industrial cities contain clusters of families that have migrated from the same town or region in the South. This pattern of migration might be compared with that of nomadic peoples in other societies, who move as a group and establish new settlements that retain many of the characteristics of the older one.

Upper-middle-class couples, on the other hand, move for somewhat different reasons. Having more specialized occupational skills, they are more likely to move for occupational

For families in which the chief wage earner is like the man portrayed in this ad "getting somewhere," moving from one place to another may be an occupational requirement. As Lloyd Warner and James Abegglen comment in their book *Big Business Leaders in America* (Harper, 1955, p. 62), ". . . these are men on the move. They left their homes, and all that this implies. The physical departure is only a small part of the total process of leaving that a mobile man must undergo. He must leave behind people as well as places. . . . Most important of all, and this is the great problem of the man on the move, he must, to some degree, leave his father, mother, brothers and sisters, along with other human relationships of his past."

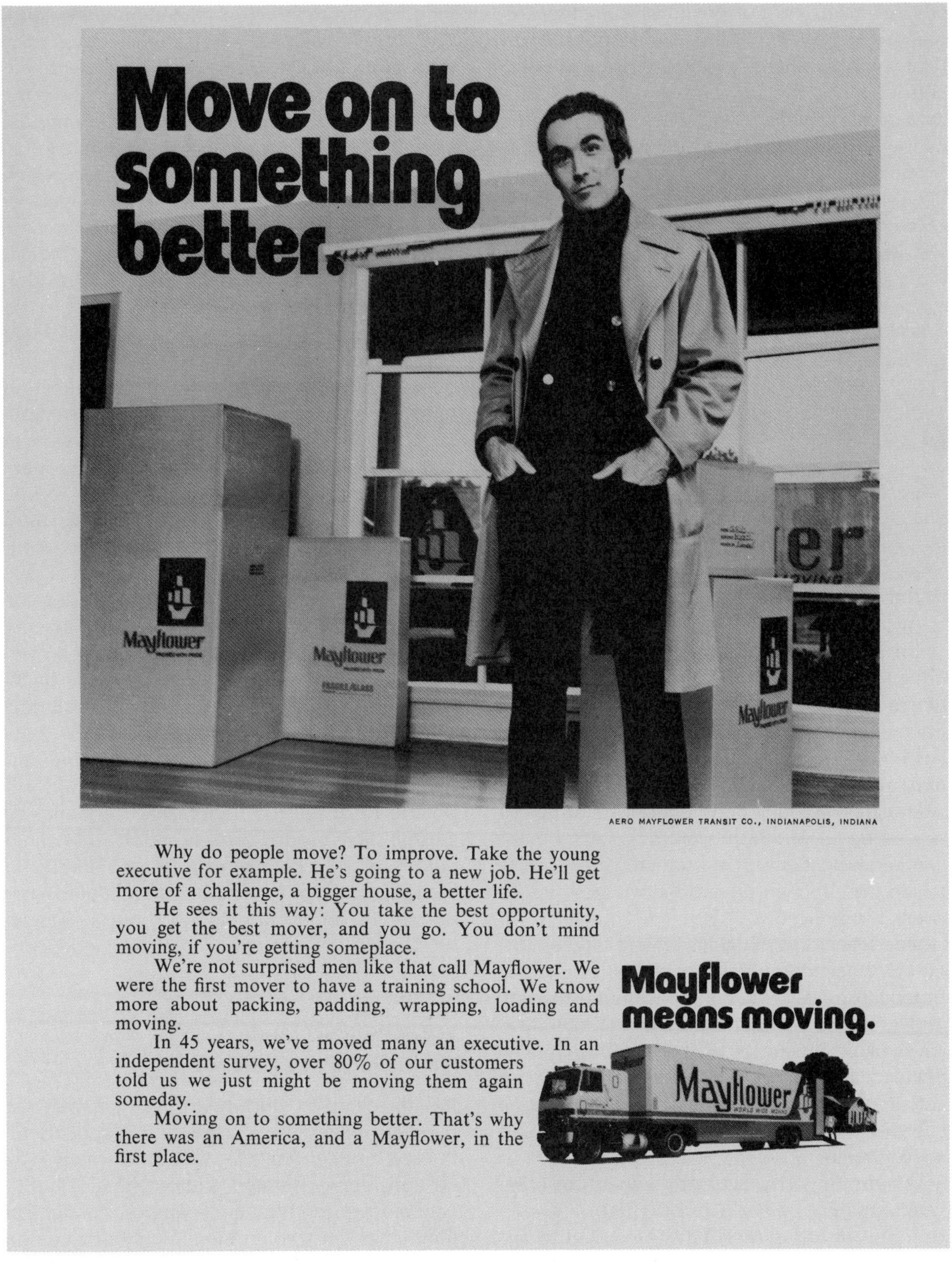

Move on to something better.

AERO MAYFLOWER TRANSIT CO., INDIANAPOLIS, INDIANA

Why do people move? To improve. Take the young executive for example. He's going to a new job. He'll get more of a challenge, a bigger house, a better life.

He sees it this way: You take the best opportunity, you get the best mover, and you go. You don't mind moving, if you're getting someplace.

We're not surprised men like that call Mayflower. We were the first mover to have a training school. We know more about packing, padding, wrapping, loading and moving.

In 45 years, we've moved many an executive. In an independent survey, over 80% of our customers told us we just might be moving them again someday.

Moving on to something better. That's why there was an America, and a Mayflower, in the first place.

Mayflower means moving.

advancement and not just to find another job. Nor are they likely to move to a location where relatives have already settled. For middle-class couples more than lower-class or blue-collar families moving from one place to another often causes certain feelings of isolation.

Sociologist Robert Weiss compares the loneliness of wives who have just moved to a new community to the loneliness of divorced and widowed women. For the wives,

> the relationship with the husband could to an extent ameliorate the loneliness of social isolation, but it could not entirely dissipate it. Husbands could not really discuss with interest the dilemmas of child care nor the burdens of housework, and though they sometimes tried, they simply could not function properly as a friend. Moreover, what the women needed was not so much a single friend as access to a social network, to a community of friends who might together exchange information about matters of common interest, establish values, and create events and activities (1975, p. 17).

For mobile upper-middle-class couples, the ties of kinship are typically less intense than they are for blue-collar or lower-class families. But many middle-class couples still consider the ties of kinship to be important. Air transportation and long-distance phone calls enable kinfolk to keep in touch despite the wide distances separating them. Both emotional attachment and certain patterns of assistance can be maintained even though the amount of face-to-face contact is reduced.

One researcher, Eugene Litwak, argues that the most accurate phrase for the kinship ties in American society today is "modified extended-family" structure. More typical than the isolated family, Litwak believes, is the pattern of related nuclear families depending on each other for certain forms of assistance. Unlike the extended families of the past, the contemporary pattern does not depend on physical proximity and has no single authority figure to whom the other family members defer (Litwak, 1960).

In one of his studies, Litwak wanted to test the idea of a modified extended family by finding out whether the couples who move away from kinfolk have fewer feelings of identification with them than couples who stay in the vicinity. To measure their family orientation, Litwak asked the people in this study to respond to such statements as "I want a location which would make it easy for relatives to get together." He found that couples living at some geographical distance from their relatives are as likely to have an extended family identification as those who live nearby (1960).

But responses to such questions tell us more about family norms than they do about actual behavior. That extended family identification remains strong even when people are geographically distant reveals feelings of obligation to stay in touch with relatives. The more important point is that—as we would expect—family members who are physically separated from one another have much less face-to-face contact (Litwak, 1960).

Some researchers who have assessed the meaning of kinship in contemporary society seem so eager to deny the hypothesis of an isolated nuclear family that they lean over backward to prove how important extended family ties still are. It is no doubt useful to know how frequently family members call upon one another for certain forms of assistance, and important to dispel the notion that the bonds of kinship have eroded entirely. But it still cannot be denied that compared to most societies in the past, kinship bonds are not particularly important for many families in today's society. Most nuclear families are relatively independent.

THE MODERN FAMILY AS REFUGE AND RETREAT

If with regard to kinship we must characterize most families as only relatively independent, there is another sense in which they might well be considered isolated without much qualification. Over the past few centuries, the nuclear family has become an increasingly private unit that promises a retreat from the outside world. While some ties to the extended family remain, connections with the local neighborhood and community have eroded. The modern family is thus very different from what it was in the past. "What really distinguishes the nuclear family," writes historian Edward Shorter,

> is a special sense of solidarity that separates the domestic unit from the surrounding community. Its members feel that they have much more in common with each other than they do with anyone else on the outside—that they enjoy a privileged emotional climate that they must protect from outside intrusion, through privacy and isolation. (1975, p. 205)

To understand what is so unique about this conception of family life, we need to turn from sociological studies to the historical record. The French social historian Philippe Ariès has shown how drastically the meaning of the family has changed over the past four centuries, and in so doing has shed much light on some basic features of contemporary social life.

Studying the images of society that have been preserved in paintings and engravings since the sixteenth century, Ariès discovered something that was too commonplace to merit the attention of writers in those times, for the conventions of everyday life changed so slowly that they hardly seemed worth commenting on. Yet over a few centuries both the meaning of the family and the texture of community life underwent a basic transformation. In the sixteenth century, art was rarely devoted to family scenes. As in the memorable peasant wedding painted by Pieter Bruegel, art depicted the crowd, "not the massive, anonymous crowd of our overpopulated cities," Ariès observes, "but the assembly of neighbors, women and children, numerous but not unknown to one another" (1962, p. 405). In the sixteenth century, most of one's life was lived in public, and there was neither time nor place for solitude or privacy.

Even the seventeenth-century family was distinguished from the modern family by the "enormous mass of sociability which it retained" (Ariès, 1962, p. 403). Homes, particularly of wealthier families, were public places. There was a constant flow of people at all hours—clients, clerks, apprentices, servants, social callers. In the morning, a nobleman might have a dozen people waiting to see him, and he might receive them in the same room he slept in, wearing his dressing gown. Ariès points out that until the eighteenth century, no barrier of privacy was drawn around the house, and even within the house there was no privacy. People ate, slept, danced, worked, and received visitors in the same general-purpose rooms. They lived much of their "private lives" in public, or at least within view of a sizable number of neighbors and acquaintances. Child rearing, family squabbles, even sexual activities took place without the wall of privacy that surrounds most modern households.

But by the eighteenth century, something began to happen that made family life much more like what it is today. Ariès refers to it as the triumph of the family over other types of relationships.

> The family began to hold society at a distance, to push it back beyond a steadily extending zone of private life. . . . The old code of manners was an art of living in public and together. The new code of manners emphasized the need to respect the privacy of others. (1962, p. 398)

A new concern arose for the individual, for privacy, children, and domestic matters.

> Starting in the eighteenth century, people began defending themselves against a society whose constant intercourse had hitherto been a source of education, reputation, and wealth. . . . Everywhere the family reinforced private life at the expense of neighborly relationships, friendships and traditional contacts. The history of modern manners can be reduced in part to this long effort to break away from others, to escape from a society whose pressure had become unbearable. (Ariès, 1962, p. 398)

Ariès comments that he was tempted to conclude that "sociability and the concept of the

family were incompatible, and could develop only at each other's expense (1962, p. 407). Gradually, family life became a much more private affair, until today we expect many of the needs that used to be satisfied in the wider arena of the community to be met within the nuclear family.

Other writers have observed that the family began to be idealized as an island of harmony and a retreat from the outside world just when the most rapid urbanization was taking place, about the middle of the nineteenth century (Jeffrey, 1972). If the rise of the modern city and its bustling heterogeneity were threatening to many people, family life could provide a refuge. The simple virtues of domestic life began to be celebrated in the inscription that can still be found on many walls: "Be it ever so humble, there's no place like home."

Historian John Demos vividly describes the division between the world in which we live our private lives and the impersonal world outside. In modern society, he writes,

> the family stands quite apart from most other aspects of life. We have come to assume that whenever a man leaves his home "to go out into the world" he crosses a very critical boundary. Different rules, different values, different feelings apply on either side, and any failure to appreciate this brings, inevitably, the most painful kind of personal distress. The contrast has, of course, a pejorative character. The family becomes a kind of shrine for upholding and exemplifying all of the softer virtues—love, generosity, tenderness, altruism, harmony, repose. The world at large presents a much more sinister aspect. Impersonal, chaotic, unpredictable, often characterized by strife and sometimes by outright malignity, it requires of a man that he be constantly "on guard." It goads and challenges him at every point, and occasionally provokes response of a truly creative sort; but it also exhausts him. So it is that he . . . retreat periodically within the family circle. (1970, p. 186).

The Private Family

When social anthropologist Elizabeth Bott (1957) conducted an intensive study of urban working-class families in England in the 1950s, she noticed something that helps to explain the intensity of family life in American middle-class suburbs today. Among many of the families she studied, husbands and wives did not expect to be friends; masculine and feminine roles were highly segregated. After inquiring about many aspects of these marriages, Bott concluded that the definition of conjugal roles is generally influenced to a considerable extent by the social environment surrounding the family. Where there is a close-knit network of relatives, friends, neighbors, and co-workers, many of whom know each other and interact frequently, conjugal roles are more likely to be segregated.

But why does the social environment of the family have such a striking effect on the definition of male and female roles within a marriage? Bott suggests two reasons for it: (1) wives with a close circle of friends and relatives can depend on them rather than their husbands for assistance; and (2) close-knit groups tend to agree on certain norms and put pressure on individuals to conform. Thus, where there is a close-knit family network, both males and females are under pressure to conform to traditionally masculine or feminine roles.

A very interesting pattern of role redefinition followed when families moved away from these close-knit groups. Bott found that the typical couple soon developed a marriage with certain middle-class characteristics, including more companionship between spouses and less role segregation. As couples moved away from close friends and relatives, they were forced to "seek in each other some of the emotional satisfactions and help with familial tasks that couples in close-knit networks can get from outsiders" (1957, p. 60).

Bott's research provides an important insight into the changes that have taken place in the family and how they are affected by the kinship network and the community in which the couple lives. As walls of privacy are erected around the nuclear family, spouses come to depend on each other for many of the social and emotional satisfactions that used to be provided by a number of friends, relatives, and neighbors.

Around the turn of the century, most middle-class houses were built with front porches. What took place on those porches was fairly public behavior. The neighbors, who spent a good deal of time on *their* front porches, could see and hear much of what went on. But over the next few decades, new architectural conventions reflected changing social ideals. The relatively public front porch gave way to the more private enclosed patio, sun room, or family room. In most suburban middle-class communities today, the front lawn, which is carefully mowed and manicured, is mainly for ceremonial display. Not much of family life is visible from the street. Outdoor activities take place in the *backyard,* which is far more private than the front porch was in the grandparents' generation.

And, as certain walls of privacy have been erected around the nuclear family, private spaces have been created within the household as well. Unlike the all-purpose rooms of sixteenth- and seventeenth-century households, most of the rooms in suburban middle-class homes are designed for particular uses. Indeed, "family rooms" would not be necessary if the other rooms were not special-purpose rooms. One of the main objectives of the architects who design such homes is to ensure privacy. Two leading architects, Serge Chermayeff and Christopher Alexander, have described privacy as "that marvelous compound of withdrawal, self-reliance, solitude, quiet, contemplation, and concentration." They offer the following criteria for the design of an ideal house:

1. Is there an entry "lock" to give the house as a whole an adequate buffer zone against intrusion?
2. Is the children's domain directly accessible from outside so as not to interfere with the adults' privacy and family domains?

3. Is there a buffer zone between the children's private domain and the parents' private domain?
4. Is there a lock to the parents' private domain?
5. Can a "living room" be isolated . . . from the rest of the house?
6. Are the outdoor spaces private? (1963, pp. 37, 219)

Such design criteria for the houses in which modern families live both reflect and encourage the belief that maximum privacy, not only between the family and the surrounding community but within the house as well, is something that is highly desirable.

Richard Farson believes that the family may become increasingly important because it is the only place where the expression of intense emotions is appropriate. The family may become, he says,

> a rehabilitative agent, a buffer against a very complex and demanding world in which family members constitute our only advocate, the only people who are for us. So we shall depend upon them increasingly. Furthermore, in one sense, the family may be one of the few places in the world of the future—one of the last places—in which we can find privacy. As such, it will be a safe place for expressing our aggressive and hostile impulses. So family life will be highly emotional, intimate, infantile, aggressive, hostile, and irrational. . . . We can expect a great deal more emotionality and intimacy, a broader range of emotional expression. This will come about simply because people everywhere are increasingly demanding it; they no longer want to live composed, serene, calm, bland lives. They want more of both ends of the continuum—emotionality and serenity—and the family will become the matrix for such experience. (1969, p. 60)

The privatization of the family has made the relationships within it emotionally more intense. Children depend almost entirely on the good will of a full-time mother and a part-time father. Often there are no other adults around to serve as a safety valve. Between spouses as well as between parents and children, so much is at stake that family members often avoid conflict because its consequences would be too threatening (Sennett, 1970).

After centuries of increasing privacy for the family, the apparent reaction starting in just the last few years could be considered, as Philippe Ariès remarked, a kind of "prison revolt" (Ariès, 1975). The recent experiments with new family forms, though they include a wide variety of alternatives from cooperatives to group marriages, might all be seen as attempts to open up family life, to reverse the tendency toward a small, emotionally exclusive family. Significantly, the young people who have shown the most interest in exploring such alternatives come from middle-class homes that epitomize the nuclear family characteristics we have been examining.

REINVENTING AN INTIMATE NETWORK—SOME ALTERNATIVES

One of the most significant themes that emerged from the protest movement of the 1960s was the re-creation of community. First at Berkeley, and then on many campuses across the country, students protested against increasingly impersonal, bureaucratic regulations. In campus demonstrations, students carried signs reading "Do Not Fold, Spindle, or Mutilate" and demanded a "campus community." By the late 1960s, thousands of communes began to appear, many of them tucked away in the hills of California, Vermont, and Oregon or perched on arid mesas in New Mexico, and all consisting of people convinced that the only way they could change society was to form small, self-sufficient communities in which radically different lifestyles might be practiced.

Then the political and economic climate changed, and so did the interests and preoccupations of college students. By the mid-

In the nuclear family, much of a child's emotional satisfaction centers on the time he has with a father who is away from home much of the day. Later, when he is grown, this communication may have to be kept up long-distance.

"We're 2,000 miles apart now, but still just as close."

Before I could tell time, I knew when my dad would be home from work. I'd be waiting at the window, watching for him to turn the corner.

When I was old enough, I'd run to the bus stop to wait for him. And we'd race each other to the porch, then sit on the steps and talk about everything from football to cowboys.

That part of the day was ours. Now, we're 2,000 miles apart, but I still get a kick out of sharing my day with him.

Long Distance is the next best thing to being there.

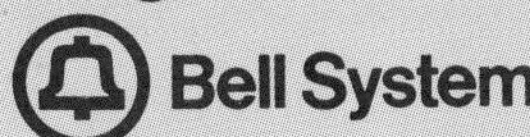

1970s, most of the themes of the protest movement seemed dated. But the idea of creating new types of communities and breaking down some of the boundaries around the nuclear family survived. True, the media no longer carry colorful stories about rural communes in which young people have radically redefined sex, marriage, and child rearing; indeed, one of the lessons of the late 1960s was that lifestyle experiments such as communes or group marriages are fragile, easily shattered by publicity or curious strangers. Publicity-shy but far from extinct, such experiments are still being conducted today.

The people most interested in exploring alternative forms of community life are, of course, often college students, for they find themselves "between acts" in several respects, and not securely situated in any durable group. However, two other categories of the population have also shown a lively interest. Advertisements for retirement communities featuring shared leisure facilities and activities are aimed at one of these categories, the elderly, who may have disengaged from some of their former roles and social contacts. The people belonging to the second category are also somewhat isolated, though for different reasons. In a comprehensive study of group marriage, investigators found that it is "young couples in their late twenties who have been married for six to eight years and have two or three children who are the most likely to attempt a multilateral marriage" (Constantine and Constantine, 1973). For these couples, the burdens of child care in a small family where few of these responsibilities can be handed off to other adults often create a feeling of isolation from the wider community.

The alternative forms of marriage and family life that exist today take a great variety of forms. There are some rural households containing several couples and their children who are trying to combine farming with new forms of extended family units, ones based on common interests rather than kinship. There are urban group marriages in which the adults pursue conventional jobs or careers while experimenting with unconventional lifestyles. There are part-time communities dedicated to personal growth, in which couples let down some of the walls normally surrounding the nuclear family for a few days or weeks each year. In some experiments several couples share the same household; others assume that boundaries can be dissolved without living under the same roof. Some groups share property or child care responsibilities, but maintain conventional beliefs about emotional or sexual exclusivity. Some erase the sexual boundaries but maintain the others.

There are many different kinds of barriers around the nuclear family today. Most people assume, for example, that it should be economically self-sufficient, that child care is the exclusive responsibility of the parents, and that many of the spouses' emotional needs and all of their sexual needs will be satisfied within its boundaries. There are many ways of opening up the family unit by erasing some of these boundaries. A group of parents who form a babysitting cooperative, for example, in which each parent takes care of the others' children for one morning a week, breaks down one kind of self-sufficiency normally associated with the nuclear family. In the rest of this section we will examine the whole spectrum of alternatives, from cooperatives that modify only one or another of those boundaries to group marriages that redefine almost all of them.

Cooperatives and Family Clusters

Cooperatives provide an alternative for couples who want to modify family boundaries in some respects without substantially redefining the family unit. Essentially, cooperatives imply nothing more than the willingness of several couples to pool their resources to provide certain goods or services that they all need. A child care cooperative can be set up with only a few families participating; other types of cooperatives, such as food coops, may involve a wider circle of families and substantial amounts of money.

If you add an element of emotional commitment to the sharing that coops encourage, the arrangement can be what psychologist Frederick Stoller (1970) calls an intimate network and therapist Herbert Otto (1971) calls a family cluster. For many American families, a cluster develops spontaneously; it has no name, no formal rules. A compromise between the need for privacy and the need for connectedness, it does not require a shared household. Stoller describes it as

> a circle of three or four families who meet together regularly and frequently, share in reciprocal fashion any of their intimate secrets, offer one another a variety of services, and do not hesitate to influence one another in terms of values and attitudes. (1970, p. 151)

Such groups break down several of the boundaries which normally surround the nuclear family. Three of the most important things that normally take place only *within* the family unit—child rearing, providing for material needs, and fighting, as well as other forms of "impolite" communication among intimates—are redefined as appropriate to share within the family cluster.

A group consisting of three or four couples and their children might share many experiences with more commitment to each other, and a greater willingness to dissolve certain conventional boundaries, than friends ordinarily have. A family cluster offers a wider circle of intimates to provide a variety of viewpoints and services and can share certain possessions as well—vacation homes, cars, and other things normally used only by the members of one family.

When many people hear about the family cluster concept, their first reaction is to remark that they know of several such arrangements, sometimes involving single, widowed, or divorced persons in addition to married couples and their children. Whether or not they were planned in advance, they allow some of the barriers of privacy that normally surround the nuclear family to be dissolved.

Intimate Friendship

As Stoller defines a family cluster, it excludes one of the most private and personal activities—sex. That sexual activity is not defined as appropriate behavior except among spouses might well serve to maintain other conventional boundaries. One of the main reasons why relatively few adults in our culture have emotionally intense friendships with members of the opposite sex is that the emotion might turn into sexual interest, and that of course is prohibited by the norm of marital fidelity. It is noteworthy that in a report on group marriage, researchers stipulate that their "definition of multilateral [group] marriage does not require that partners be sexually involved with anyone. A committed multilateral relationship without sex is possible; we just have never found one" (Constantine and Constantine, 1973, p. 163). Thus, if family clusters are arrangements encouraging emotional but not sexual closeness among the adults, their emotional closeness may be limited by the fear that active sexual interest will follow. Much of the current interest in extramarital relationships might be understood as an attempt to penetrate the barriers drawn around the nuclear family.

If a sexual dimension is added to the bonds of interdependence characteristic of the family cluster, the result is the intimate friendship defined by researcher James Ramey as an "otherwise traditional friendship in which sexual intimacy is considered appropriate behavior" (1975, p. 516). As Cuber and Harroff found in their study, *Sex and the Significant Americans,* this may be a more widely practiced pattern than most people acknowledge. The researchers say such couples "simply do not accept the monogamous commitment with respect to their personal lives, although they still feel committed to and fulfilled in marriage and parenthood" (1965, p. 35).

There is an important difference between intimate friendship and either of the two more commonly discussed types of extramarital relationships, secret love affairs and swinging.

Married people who engage in secret affairs cut off a whole area of their lives—one that may have great significance to them—from their spouses; and that secrecy may create a barrier between them, weakening their communications with each other. Couples who engage in intimate friendships, on the other hand, agree that there is no reason to hide them from each other. Ramey found that it is common in such a friendship for a person's spouse to become friends with his or her lover (1975, p. 522).

Intimate friendship is also different from swinging in that swingers typically do not seek emotional intimacy with their sexual partners. In fact, the settings in which swinging often takes place, as well as the transient nature of those contacts, seem to minimize the possibility of intimacy. In contrast, people who engage in intimate friendships view sex as one aspect of a committed, enduring relationship—as normal behavior between friends in situations where they decide it is appropriate. "The key factor in defining intimate friendship patterns," Ramey observes, "appears to be the *potential* for sexual intimacy, not *actual* sexual intimacy" (1975, p. 178). Because sex is allowed, emotional closeness can develop between friends who need not keep their distance to avoid forbidden extramarital relationships.

Of course, intimate friendships of this nature may be neither desirable nor practical for most couples today, because such relationships require a redefinition of one of the most sensitive aspects of marriage—the sexual bond between spouses.

Group Marriage

Group marriage represents an even more radical redefinition of the marital relationship. It presumes not just the interdependency of family clusters and the sexual openness of intimate friendships but a common household and a long-term commitment. Even when they consist of only three persons, group marriages are quite complex because they include additional bonds. Because of that complexity and the necessity to maintain each interpersonal bond, most group marriages consist of no more than six or seven people. In this respect, group marriages are quite different from what most people think of when the term "commune" is mentioned. As most communes involve a larger number of people, they might be regarded as communities rather than families. In most communes, moreover, the commitment to the entire group is less intense than the commitment to one's partner, whereas in group marriages it is assumed that there is a primary attachment to at least two others. (See Box 13–2.)

Considering how radical the idea of group marriage is, and how many of the conventional boundaries drawn around the family disappear in such settings, it is interesting to ask how common they actually are. Larry and Joan Constantine, who have conducted the only extensive study done on this subject, were able to locate only slightly more than 100 group marriages (1973, p. 63), but there is far more interest in the idea than this number suggests. Of the 20,000 readers of *Psychology Today* who responded to a poll conducted a few years ago, a quarter indicated that they were either in favor of or personally interested in group marriage (Athenasiou, 1970).

Who are the people who have chosen to form group marriages? As mentioned previously, married couples in their late twenties with several young children are most likely to attempt such experiments. Judging by their scores on tests for achievement, self-actualization, and capacity for intimacy, they are well adjusted (Constantine and Constantine, 1973, p. 93). "As a group," the Constantines report,

> participants are seeking growth, a better family for their children, a community, and sexual and intellectual variety; most of them are *not* rebelling, seeking escape, acting on religious principles, or improving what they consider to be unsatisfactory marriages. (1973, p. 109)

It is significant, considering the structural char-

Point of View

Box 13–2 / A Commune in Disguise in the Suburbs

When the word "commune" is mentioned, most people imagine a rural farmhouse in Vermont or New Mexico, populated by a handful of bearded or braless dropouts. Communes of that description received much attention in the late 1960s and early 1970s, but as agents of social change they may be less significant than communes like one in a New York suburb, which refers to itself as the Elm Lane Eight. This group illustrates a quiet experiment in opening up the nuclear family and creating a wider community.

> We are an experimental, nontraditional family—a commune. We are not part of the drug scene, political activism, religious fanaticism, or any other cause. We came together more than three years ago simply to seek the rewards of the communal lifestyle, and we have found them many times over.
>
> We don't know whether our experiment has been duplicated elsewhere. Our history convinces us, however, that the idea of communal living in the suburbs could become a reality for others quite easily.
>
> We attribute our freedom from problems with the community to a policy of low profile. We dress conventionally and pay moderate attention to the lawn. While hiding nothing on the occasion of various local registrations, school censuses, and the like, we have volunteered a full explanation to none. As it happens, no one has asked whether we are in violation of the zoning code, which, it could be argued, we are.
>
> Our presence has brought certain concrete benefits to the property, the neighborhood, and the community at large: (1) We have rescued an elegant dowager of a house from deterioration or worse. (2) The rescue was good news for the neighborhood. Prior to our arrival, adjacent owners had a deserted property in view, a target for vandals, a temptation for curious children, and a threat to the block's correct conception of itself as highly desirable. (3) The community benefits when the tax roles carry ratables at their full potential. When we install a swimming pool next spring we will add further to our community value in the form of more tax revenue.
>
> Perhaps we embody a solution for those directly affected by the housing shortage, a match between the many young families, retired persons, and singles who cannot find adequate housing on the one hand, and the large stock of big, underused homes on the other.
>
> We would never use so provocative a term as "commune" if confronted locally. There are academic terms to describe intentional communities such as we are, but they ring of structure. We are a family, and that's that.
>
> By occupation, we are equal parts business, professional, and the artistic. There is a practicing Catholic, an ex-Jesuit (not one and the same), and the rest celebrate Jewish holidays culturally.

(Box 13–2 continues on page 386)

acteristics of the families most of them had lived in before, that the most common reason given for forming these experiments was that they wanted more companionship (1973, p. 260).

How do intimate relationships change when the household expands to include more adults? What happens to the relationship between a man and wife who formerly lived in a separate household? How do their relationships with their children change? How, in brief, is a collective living situation different from conventional family life?

(Box 13-2 continued from page 385)

There are three couples who were married before the group's formation, and three dependent children among them. The two singles met when they joined the group, and have become a couple. Ages range from twenty-three to forty-seven. There does not appear to be any common element in everyone's background that would account for organizing a large family. All come from middle-sized, typical families. Our parents and old friends are occasional visitors, most expressing mild approval and managing to keep their skepticism to themselves.

Although each marriage was healthy, there was a restlessness to do better what we were already doing well: caring, enjoying involvement, sorrowing, rejoicing, and simply sharing the daily routine of life with a wider circle of enriching friends. Our ideal is to live and feel as a single family, in which there are naturally special intimacies but in which each person responds to every other with the commitment of a spouse or sibling.

The secondary benefits, some intentional and some unforeseen, are many. The cooperation of the group's staggered work schedules partly freed our infant's mother to resume her career. And since all the adults have some outside occupation, the combined income has made hired help feasible.

We met over a period of time, mostly through ads in a weekly newspaper. One summer we rented a beach house together. At summer's end, we knew we had found the people and the pattern we wished to make permanent.

It took us nine months to locate a property the right size, at our price, within commuting distance to our jobs. There is a contract dealing with the eight partners' ownership, as well as insurance policies payable to the partnership and an Elm Lane Eight savings account. But there are no other written rules. We have a weekly formal meeting, at which menus for the coming week are listed, cooks volunteer for the evening of their choice, and other chores are dispensed on a sharing basis.

This meeting concludes with open time to raise personal problems and feelings about one another or the group as a whole. In addition, anyone may and does call a meeting on the spot in times of stress or conflict.

We think of ourselves as skilled in resolving conflicts. All major decisions are unanimous, not arrived at by taking a vote, but by listening to everyone's view in turn. If there is no unanimity on a matter of substance, we talk some more next time, until there is a self-evident compromise.

What we hope to gain from this report is a recognition that for some, alternatives to the present American family system are workable. Specifically in suburbia, we hope that people who write ordinances, and neighbors protective of property values, will view housing uses on a performance basis. Experiments like ours are often precluded by zoning laws.

Being pragmatic, we have no inclination to apply for variances, or change them by tampering with the definition of "family." But it is an abuse of common sense to judge that a number of unrelated persons sharing a home are invariably drug-crazed orgiasts, or at best noisier and sloppier than a crowd of brothers and sisters.

Let's allow people to expand their lifestyle options and at the same time enhance older housing that is underused.

Source: The New York Times, December 7, 1975, R-8.

In a very interesting exploration of these questions, three sociologists, Rosabeth Kanter, Dennis Jaffe, and D. Kelly Weisberg, studied thirty-five experimental households. They noticed first that new alliances develop, and the power structure between partners is altered. The presence of other adults as an audience has several effects: couples commonly experience a loss of control over their partners; certain types of "childish" behaviors are less likely to take

In communal living, one of the chief goals seems to be the creation of a family-like intimacy.

place because others observe and comment on what is happening; and spouses can gain more power by forming coalitions with others in the household (1975, p. 433).

Just as the presence of others changes relationships among adults, it also affects the parent–child relationship. There are both advantages and disadvantages associated with child rearing in collective families. "Parents experience diminishing abilities to make and enforce rules and increased self-consciousness about child rearing, as well as important help in many of the tasks of parenting" (Kanter et al., 1975, p. 434). Children have a larger number of adults to turn to and deal with, and they experience a wider variety of exchanges among adults, conflict as well as cooperation.

One of the most significant effects of group marriages and communes is that people begin functioning within the group as individuals rather than members of a pair. Moreover, having other people to turn to for intimacy may decrease the emotional intensity of the pair bond. Here is how one man described the changes in his marriage when he and his wife entered a relationship involving several other adults:

> We began more and more doing things on a completely individual basis, following our interests whether or not they included the other. . . . The biggest change is this recognition of our individual lives outside of our relationship. (Kanter et al., 1975, p. 439)

This change is desirable in some ways and undesirable in others.

> Almost every couple interviewed remarked that living collectively resulted in their learning that if and when their mate cannot meet a particular need, there are others who can. They find that many of the conflicts they had as a nuclear couple are less intense, because the other no longer represents a unique and irreplaceable resource. This both takes pressure off their relationship, and decreases its intensity—a potential gain and a potential cost. (Kanter et al., 1975, p. 437)

One of the most common reasons given for forming group marriages is the desire for personal growth. In what way can a group marriage encourage growth better than a conventional family? Perhaps the answer stems from the fact that we reveal different aspects of ourselves to different people. Thus, a setting that consists of several other adults might encourage people to explore various facets of themselves.

One aspect of group marriage that many people are understandably curious about is sex. This appears to be one of the chief differences between many communal settings and group marriages. According to Kanter and her associates,

> Nearly all of our communes show a preference for couple members not developing sexual relationships with their housemates. After a while, most groups develop an "incest taboo" which seems to be a source of stability, and sexual experimentation for couples occurs largely outside the commune. . . . It seems that the family-like intimacy that is the goal of communes does not include shared sexual relationships probably because the jealousy and comparisons which occur tend to disrupt the weaker of the relationships even more dramatically than other forms of sharing, leading to one of the participants leaving the commune. (1975, p. 442)

All of the group marriages examined by the Constantines, on the other hand, did involve sexual relationships beyond the original couples. But group marriages did not necessarily mean group sex. In most groups this occurred only rarely, if at all. In some, especially the larger groups, there was a regular rotation according to which bed partners, if not sexual partners, were agreed on beforehand. One of the interesting conclusions of the Constantines' report is that, based on information from a variety of sources, "sex is rarely a real problem" (1973, p. 169). As in most marriages, sexual problems sometimes arise, and are a symptom of interpersonal problems. But for most of the respondents in the study, sexual satisfactions increased after moving into group marriages (1973, p. 169).

But if sex does not pose serious problems for most group marriages, maintaining a long-term commitment does. Among the sixteen groups studied intensively, eleven dissolved before the study was completed. The median length of time those groups stayed together was only sixteen months (Constantine and Constantine, 1972).

Why are group marriages apparently so unstable? The Constantines noted that "many participants, especially those in short-lived experiments in alternate marital forms, become involved through fascination with the form more than through relationships with specific people" (1972, p. 461). In the same way that choosing the right partner is important in conventional relationships, it is important in group marriages. But it is complicated in group marriages because, with more positions to fill, there are more problems in finding suitable mates.

Some of the problems reported in group marriages are exactly the same as in ordinary marriages. The two difficulties most frequently mentioned are communication and friction between personalities. Indeed, the most common reason for groups to split up is simply personal incompatibility (1973, p. 204).

One final factor should be acknowledged. The Constantines comment that it is not uncommon for people to express a need to be primary in group marriage situations. "Many people have told us that they felt a need to be first in somebody's heart, to be in one relationship in which they are the most important person to the other." If, as the Constantines suggest, "pair bonding is an innate human propensity," then we might well turn our attention elsewhere, and assume that anything resembling a group marriage is a structural impossibility. It might be argued that pair bonding as well as the "need to be primary" is an attitude taught to all of us in this culture from a very early age, but until children are socialized differently, these needs will remain a substantial obstacle to the formation of group marriages (1973, p. 169).

Group marriage is an intriguing response to the problems created by the high walls of privacy around the nuclear family, but it can hardly be regarded as a practical alternative for many people today or tomorrow. Alternatives such as family clusters and even intimate friendship are more likely to be adopted in the near future. They may provide that sense of greater connectedness that many people seem to be yearning for.

Conclusions

In this chapter we first examined studies that demonstrate the continuing importance of kin ties in our society, particularly those between older parents and children who have formed their own households. Despite the availability of assistance programs such as unemployment compensation and health care benefits, kinfolk are still an important source of help in times of emergency—and provide routine assistance the rest of the time. These studies provide the evidence needed to test the hypothesis of the isolated nuclear family. If "isolation" implies that the bonds of kinship are no longer important in today's society, the hypothesis is refuted. Even in urban industrial society, extended family ties remain important in many respects.

The family has not changed so much as the hypothesis of the isolated nuclear family suggests, but it has been transformed in several ways, and that transformation has been profoundly significant in shaping contemporary family life and creating new expectations for the marital relationship.

Edward Shorter gives this description of the transformation:

> In the sixteenth and seventeenth centuries, the family was held firmly in the matrix of a larger social order. One set of ties bound it to the surrounding kin, the network of aunts and uncles, cousins and nieces who dotted the old regime's social landscape. Another set fastened it to the wider community, and gaping holes in the shield of privacy permitted others to enter the household freely, and, if necessary, preserve order. A final set of ties held this elementary family to generations past and future. Awareness of ancestral traditions and ways of doing business would be present in people's minds as they went about their daily business. Because they knew that the purpose of life was preparing coming generations to do as past generations had done, they would have clear rules for shaping relations within the family. . . . In its journey into the modern world, the family has broken all those ties. It has separated from the surrounding community, guarded now by high walls of privacy. It has cast off its connections with distant kin, and has changed fundamentally even its relationship to close relatives. And it has parted from the lineage, that chain of generations stretching across time: whereas once people had been able to answer the question, "Who am I?" by pointing to those who had gone before and would come after, in the twentieth century, they would have other replies. (1975, p. 3)

The American middle-class family has become a tightly self-contained unit, surrounded by walls of privacy. Much of the experimentation with new family forms, such as family clusters and group marriage, might be interpreted as an attempt to reach through these walls of privacy, to create new forms of interdependence and connectedness. Whether or not these alternatives provide a practical solution that might be attractive to many people, they help us to understand some of the problems caused by today's privatized family unit.

REFERENCES

Bert N. Adams. *The family*. Chicago: Rand-McNally, 1975.

M. Anderson. Household structure and the industrial revolution: Mid-nineteenth-century Preston in comparative perspective. In P. R. Laslett, ed. *The comparative history of family and household*. Cambridge: University Press, 1971.

Philippe Ariès. *Centuries of childhood*. New York: Knopf, 1962.

———. The family, prison of love—A conversation with Philippe Ariès. *Psychology Today,* August 1975.

Robert Athenasiou. Sex. *Psychology Today,* July 1970.

Wendell Bell and Marion D. Boat. Urban neighborhoods and informal social relations. *American Journal of Sociology* 62 (1957): 391–398.

Elizabeth Bott. *Family and social network*. London: Tavistock, 1957.

Serge Chermayeff and Christopher Alexander. *Community and privacy: Toward a new architecture of humanism*. New York: Anchor, 1963.

Larry L. Constantine and Joan M. Constantine. Dissolution of marriage in a nonconventional context. *The Family Coordinator,* October 1972, pp. 36–42.

———. *Group marriage*. New York: Macmillan, 1973.

John F. Cuber and Peggy Harroff. *Sex and the significant Americans*. Baltimore: Penguin, 1965.

John Demos. *A little commonwealth*. New York: Oxford University Press, 1970.

Floyd Dotson. Pattern of voluntary associations among working class people. *American Sociological Review* 16 (1951): 687–693.

Evelyn M. Duvall. *In-laws: Pro and con*. New York: Association Press, 1954.

Richard E. Farson. *The future of the family*. New York: Family Service Association, 1969.

Raymond Firth. Family and kinship in industrial society. Sociological Review Monograph no. 8. *The Development of Industrial Societies,* October 1964.

William J. Goode. *World revolution and family patterns*. New York: Free Press, 1963.

Scott Greer. *The emerging city: Myth and reality*. New York: Free Press, 1962.

Oscar Handlin. *The American people: The history of a society*. London: Penguin, 1966.

Lewellyn Hendrix. Kinship ties: Movers and stayers in the Ozarks. In Nona Glazer-Malbin, ed. *Old family/new family*. New York: Van Nostrand, 1975.

Kirk Jeffrey. The family as utopian retreat from the city: The nineteenth-century contribution. In Sallie TeSelle, ed. *The family, communes, and utopian societies*. New York: Harper & Row, 1972.

Rosabeth Moss Kanter, Dennis Jaffe, and D. Kelly Weisberg. Coupling, parenting, and the presence of others: Intimate relationships in communal households. *The Family Coordinator,* October 1975, pp. 433–452.

Christopher Lasch. The family and history. *The New York Review of Books,* November 13, 1975.

Peter Laslett. *The world we have lost: England before the industrial age*. New York: Scribner's, 1965.

Gerald R. Leslie. *The family in social context*. New York: Oxford University Press, 1976.

Harper Lee. *To kill a mockingbird*. New York: Popular Library, 1962.

Dorothea Leighton and Clyde Kluckhohn. *Children of the people*. Cambridge, Mass.: Harvard University Press, 1948.

Eugene Litwak. Geographic mobility and extended family cohesion. *American Sociological Review* 25 (1960): 385–394.

National Opinion Research Center. *General social survey, 1974*. Question 57, unpublished data. Chicago: University of Chicago.

Herbert A. Otto. *The family cluster: A multi-base alternative*. Beverly Hills: Holistic Press, 1971.

The parent gap. *Newsweek,* September 22, 1975, pp. 48–56.

Talcott Parsons. The kinship system of the contemporary United States. *American Anthropologist* 45 (1943): 22–38.

James Ramey. Intimate groups and networks. *Family Coordinator* 24 (1975): 515–530.

Richard Sennett. *The uses of disorder*. New York: Knopf, 1970.

Edward Shorter. *The making of the modern family*. New York: Basic Books, 1975.

Frederick Stoller. The intimate network of families as a new structure. In Herbert Otto, ed. *The family in search of a future*. New York: Appleton Century Crofts, 1970.

Marvin Sussman. The help pattern in the middle-class family. *American Sociological Review* 15 (1953): 22–28.

———. The isolated nuclear family: Fact or fiction? *Social Problems* 6 (1959): 333–340.

———. Relationships of adult children with their parents in the United States. In Ethel Shanas and Gordon F. Streib, eds. *Social structure and the family: Generational relations*. Englewood Cliffs, N.J.: Prentice-Hall, 1965.

——— and Lee Burchinal. Kin family network: Unheralded structure in current conceptualizations of family functioning. *Marriage and Family Living,* August 1962, pp. 231–240.

U.S. Bureau of the Census. *Geographical mobility: March 1975–March 1978,* series P-20, no. 331. Washington, D.C.: Government Printing Office, 1979.

George Vecsey. More executives refusing to relocate. *The New York Times,* November 7, 1975, p. 1.

W. Lloyd Warner and James Abegglen. *Big business leaders in America.* New York: Harper, 1955.

Robert S. Weiss. *Marital separation.* New York: Basic Books, 1975.

Peter Wilmott and Michael Young. *Family and class in a London suburb.* London: Routledge & Kegan Paul, 1960.

Michael Young and Peter Wilmott. *Family and kinship in East London.* Glencoe, Ill.: Free Press, 1957.

FOR FURTHER STUDY

For a comprehensive discussion of the overall pattern traced in this chapter, William Goode's book *World Revolution and Family Patterns* (New York: Free Press, 1963) is indispensable. Chapter 6, "The Rise of the Nuclear Family," in Edward Shorter's book *The Making of the Modern Family* places the modern family in historical perspective (New York: Basic Books, 1975). Barbara Laslett provides an intelligent discussion of the privatized family in "The Family as a Public and Private Institution: An Historical Perspective," which appeared in the *Journal of Marriage and the Family,* August 1973.

David Handlin's book *The American Home: Architecture & Society, 1815–1915* (Boston: Little-Brown, 1979) provides an analysis of how changes in domestic architecture reflect changing social ideas and conceptions of family life.

Howard M. Bahr and F. Ivan Nye have some interesting things to say about contemporary perceptions of the kinship bond in "The Kinship Role in a Contemporary Community," which appeared in *The Journal of Comparative Family Studies,* Spring 1974. For a careful analysis of family and kinship organization in a black ghetto community, see Carol B. Stack's *All Our Kin: Strategies for Survival in a Black Community* (New York: Harper & Row, 1974). And for a more comprehensive discussion of the meaning of kinship in American society, see David M. Schneider and Raymond T. Smith, *Class Differences in American Kinship* (Ann Arbor: University of Michigan Press, 1978).

Jane Howard's book, *Families* (New York: Simon and Schuster, 1978), is a popular account that deals with many of the themes of this chapter, the characteristics of the human ties to friends and relatives that we all depend upon. "We must devise new ways, or revive old ones, to equip ourselves with kinfolk," she writes. She then goes on to describe the characteristics of intentional extended families.

To avoid what Mary Jo Bane refers to as "the general agitation about the decline of the family and the demise of community," read Chapter 4, "The Expanded Family: Kith and Kin," in her book *Here to Stay* (New York: Basic Books, 1978). It provides a well-documented discussion on what has—and has not—changed.

Of the many books written about alternate forms of family arrangements and community life, two of the best are Rosabeth Moss Kanter's *Commitment and Community* (Cambridge, Mass.: Harvard University Press, 1972) and Benjamin Zablocki's account of the Bruderhof community, *The Joyful Community* (Baltimore: Penguin, 1971). One of the best-informed observers of alternate family arrangements is James Ramey, who is director of the Center for the Study of Innovative Life Styles. In a recent book, *Intimate Friendships* (Englewood Cliffs, N.J.: Prentice-Hall, 1976), he analyzes the relationships between people both in and outside marriage.

VI
Terminating Intimate Relationships

"Billboard, Emporia, Kansas, November 1940" John Vachon

14

The Fragile Family–Crisis and Divorce

Few social statistics attract so much attention and generate so much concern as the divorce rate. Every year since the mid-1960s newspapers have run headlines like "Divorces Break Record" whenever the Census Bureau announces the annual divorce count. And indeed, there has been a substantial increase in the number of divorces every year. Over the past decade the number of divorces granted each year in the United States has more than doubled.

While many view these statistics with alarm, satirist Jules Feiffer ridicules the hip marriage ceremony that is stripped not only of pretense but also of any hope of a long-term commitment. The very casual Reverend Dupas, about to join the young couple in matrimony, says:

> First, let me state frankly to you, Alfred, and to you, Patricia, that of the two hundred marriages I have performed, all but seven have failed. So the odds are not good. . . . If it works, fine! If it fails, fine! Look elsewhere for satisfaction. Perhaps to more marriages. (Feiffer, 1968, p. 64)

This is only satire, to be sure, but it is also a pointed comment on one of the most basic alterations in the meaning of marriage today. In the traditional Christian ceremony, the newlyweds and their witnesses are sternly informed that a lifelong commitment has just been made: "Whom therefore God hath joined together, let no man put asunder." In the Jewish ceremony a glass is crushed, illustrating for everyone present that it would be as difficult to reassemble the fragments of that glass as to break the marital bond. But for about a third of all couples who marry today, the union will *not* last till death do them part.

In this chapter we will explore the legal and the personal processes of separation and divorce, and the reasons for our rising divorce rate. By comparing divorce and remarriage statistics we will question the assumption that marriage is breaking down—and see that in several respects it makes more sense to say that marriage is breaking *up*. The rising divorce statistics can be interpreted as evidence that many people today are unwilling to stay in emotionally unsatisfying relationships, and that the new, more liberal divorce laws encourage more couples to seek new relationships.

But even in an era of no-fault divorce laws, it is a rare divorce that does not bring serious emotional pain and personal trauma in its wake. As one sociologist comments,

> Few events in the life cycle require more extensive changes in activities, responsibilities, and living habits (or cause greater alterations in attitudes, reranking of values, and alterations of outlook on life) than does a change from one marital status to another. (Bogue, 1949, p. 212)

How do most people weather this transition? Not very well. Most separations take place only after a long, bruising process of mutual alienation that leaves both people with lowered self-esteem. Then the legal process of divorce often requires them to face each other as adversaries, exacerbating their already bitter feelings. Sympathetic social support is offered the newly widowed, but divorced people commonly find themselves in the position that one woman described by saying: "I had this feeling that I had failed, that I had disappointed society. You just feel so rejected. You don't belong to anyone, and nobody wants you" (*Newsweek,* 1973, p. 55).

Over one million couples will be divorced in the United States this year.

For most people, divorce is indeed a crisis. About a quarter of the men and roughly two-fifths of the women who undergo a divorce seek some form of professional help for their personal problems (Gurin, Veroff, and Feld, 1960). And surveys consistently show that the divorced and the widowed have the highest rates of unhappiness and dissatisfaction with their lives.

Recently we have seen a flurry of new books on how to initiate and survive a divorce. In addition, seminars on divorce adjustment, and organizations like Parents Without Partners, which offer counsel and companionship to divorced persons, indicate a new willingness to deal with the problems of divorce. People have always received advice on how to choose partners and how to form intimate attachments, but we are only now recognizing the need to learn how to break off partnerships when they are no longer satisfactory. In this chapter we will examine the process of severing intimate attachments. Throughout most of this discussion, our main concern will be sociological, not psychological. We will dwell mainly on the social and economic factors that help to explain changing divorce rates among various groups in American society. We will begin by looking at the stresses that cause family crises and at the traits of families which, in these crises, most often lead to divorce.

CRISIS AND RESPONSE

Students taking an experimental class in a Portland, Oregon, high school engage in an experiment designed to acquaint them with the realities of married life. The students pair off and go through a mock wedding ceremony. Then, as married couples, they settle down to coping with the problems of marital life: planning the family budget, resolving personal differences, and so on. In order to gain an understanding of what married life is really like, each couple takes a spin on a "wheel of misfortune" which provides them with instant disasters. A fire destroys their house, the chief wage earner is laid off, or the wife unexpectedly gets pregnant. Such stress-producing events may happen to any couple, but are rarely anticipated. Through this exercise students see how unexpected disasters can result in the dissolution of a marriage (*U.S. News & World Report,* October 27, 1975, p. 36).

It is natural and desirable to be optimistic about the future of a marriage, to hope for the best and avoid morbid thoughts about what might go wrong. Very few couples anticipate when they marry that their marriage might end in divorce, or even be threatened by a major crisis. Nevertheless, at some point almost every couple confronts a potentially crippling crisis. The family is a fragile alliance; its equilibrium can be upset by many different stresses or crises. Compared to other groups, the family is not particularly well suited to cope with stress-producing events. As one prominent family researcher, Reuben Hill, remarks,

> The average family is badly handicapped organizationally. Its age composition is heavily weighted with dependents, and it cannot freely reject its weak members and recruit more competent team mates. . . . This group is not ideally manned to withstand stress, yet society has assigned to it the heaviest of responsibilities: the socialization and orientation of the young, and the meeting of the major emotional needs of all citizens, young and old. (1958, p. 140)

When one member of the family is incapacitated or absent, or when some stressful event takes place, disequilibrium is likely to result. Family equilibrium can be restored, of course, depending on the seriousness of the stress-producing event and the ability of the family to adjust to it. But when equilibrium is totally destroyed, family members can no longer perform their accustomed roles, the family ceases to function as a unit of interdependent people, and dissolution follows.

Some families, of course, undergo extremely stressful experiences and yet stay together. This outcome is most likely when the stress-producing event comes from outside the family. As Hill observes, "war bombings, political persecutions, religious persecutions, floods, tornadoes, hurricanes, and other 'acts of God' " can even improve family solidarity (1958, p. 142). It is noteworthy that in fictional family dramas like the television series *The Waltons,* the problems that the family must overcome invariably arise from outside, not from within.

Stresses that originate from within the family, like those portrayed in the televised documentary series *An American Family,* are another matter. They fall into several different categories. One type involves the removal of a family member, whether temporarily or permanently. The death of a child, the hospitalization or imprisonment of one of the parents, the absence of a runaway child, and the absence of a wage earner who has gone to take a job in another city are all common examples. A second type of stress involves the addition of an extra member to the family unit. Events in this category include unwanted childbirth, the birth of a physically handicapped child, and the adoption of an aged grandparent. A third type does not diminish or enlarge the family but demoralizes all concerned, as for example when the main source of income is lost, a parent slips into alcoholism, or one of the children is arrested and labeled a delinquent. Such stresses often break down family solidarity because they interrupt expected role performances (Hill, 1958).

Another crisis-provoking event, the death of a spouse, is in a class by itself. Death cannot be coped with in the same sense that other stressful situations can; it must be adjusted to. Over the past century the rate of marital dissolution has not changed much, but the proportion of that rate which can be attributed to death of a spouse has. The annual rate of marital dissolution in the United States has remained constant at about 30 per 1,000 marriages. At the beginning of the century about 29 of the 30 dissolutions were due to death. By 1970 divorce accounted for almost half of the 30. Despite the rising divorce rate, death is still the main reason for marital dissolution (Jacobson, 1959; Ross and Sawhill, 1975, p. 195).

No two families react to stress in the same way. Some families, though, have emotional and economic assets that help them cope with stress and avoid dissolution. As we might expect, families that are neither emotionally stable nor economically secure have few resources on which to fall back. Thus it is not the wealthy who have the highest rate of divorce but rather those with relatively low income.

Besides having relatively few resources that would allow them to maintain stable marriages, lower-class families not uncommonly have to face several stresses all at the same time. "This is a category of unskilled, irregular workers," writes sociologist S. M. Miller,

> broken and large families, and a residual bin of the aged, physically handicapped, and mentally disturbed. . . . A number of forces can lead families into chronic dependence. "Lower-class" life is crisis-life, constantly trying to make do with string where rope is needed. Anything can break the string. . . . Low-paid and irregularly employed individuals do not develop an image of the world as predictable and as something with which they are able to cope. (1970, p. 40)

As sociologist William Goode explains the divorce proneness of the lower classes,

> The internal strains of marriage are greater among the lower classes; marital satisfaction scores are lower; romantic attachment between spouses is less common; the husband is less willing to share household tasks when the wife is working, and so on. (1962, p. 509)

Thus, the higher divorce rates among such individuals are understandable, given the alternatives open to them, for they have less to lose by dissolving a marriage and starting over again.

If low income is one predictor of relatively high divorce rates, it would be reasonable to assume that if the government were to provide income supplements to low-income families one result would be greater family stability. In fact, this was the assumption behind President Carter's proposal that welfare support for two-parent families might be a way to encourage families to stay together. But evidence from a study that has been conducted at the University of Wisconsin's Institute for Research on Poverty suggests that even well-intentioned efforts to "end poverty" might backfire. In this experiment, certain families were chosen to receive support payments equivalent to those in a "negative income tax" system, in which there would be a guaranteed minimum income, with payments gradually lowered as family members earned enough to offset the loss of benefits. When the researchers compared family stability among those who received the augmented benefits with a matched sample of families who received no unusual benefits, they found that the families receiving such special support payments had separation, divorce, and desertion rates 70 percent *higher* than the others. Apparently, sharply altered income caused stresses in many of these families because it precipitated certain changes, and those changes—like others induced by stresses such as unemployment or health problems—contributed to marital instability.

If lower-class families are the most vulnerable, crisis threatens families at other social class levels too. What, then, are the other factors that are responsible for family deterioration? Several sociologists have pointed out how important certain shared values—such as feelings of common interest, affection, and interdependence, or the subordination of personal ambitions to family goals—are in responding to crises. In their absence, families at all social class levels are less able to cope with stress (Hill, 1958).

Another factor that marks the crisis-prone family is its habit of defining unfavorable events as crises. A given event—for example, loss of employment—happening to one family might be interpreted by them as a catastrophe, while another might shrug it off as a temporary inconvenience. As Hill puts it, "Crisis proneness in families also proves related to outlook—to whether or not the event is defined as challenging or crisis provoking" (1958, p. 145).

Many families that cannot overcome their difficulties typically go through a regular process of deterioration consisting of six sequential phases. The process begins with (1) the initial stress-provoking event—the loss of a job, alcoholism, the birth of a handicapped child. Family members soon (2) attach certain meanings to the event: an individual feels ashamed at not having a job or unworthy because of his alcoholism, which has further effects on family dynamics and role performances. These reactions persist and worsen until finally, (3) someone tries to remedy the situation. The other spouse goes to work or social service organizations are consulted for assistance. But this may only exacerbate the situation by producing (4) negative side effects, such as feelings of inadequacy at the inability to perform expected roles. In order to prevent further hurt, one or both spouses (5) withdraw emotionally, which leads to (6) a decrease in emotional satisfaction from the relationship. Further withdrawal of interdependency and the elimination of shared activities, such as sex, soon follow.

Marriage counselors (see Box 14–1) or social service agencies can be helpful in stopping this process of deterioration and reversing its direction. But for more than a million American couples this year, it will lead to divorce as the only way out of an intolerable situation.

THE LEGAL FACTS OF DIVORCE

As we noted in Chapter 6, marriage is a contract, a legal agreement in which two people promise to fulfill certain responsibilities to each other, but unlike other contracts, which can be dissolved whenever the parties agree to do so, marriage is not so easy to dissolve. Like the armed forces, marriage is easy to get into and hard to get out of.

The state is a third party to any marriage. A couple wishing to terminate their marriage is required by law to obtain the state's permission by going through a legal process.

Our present divorce laws reflect religious beliefs. Divorce has never been permitted in the Roman Catholic tradition, and for centuries a marriage could be dissolved only by an annulment granted by high ecclesiastical authority on strictly limited grounds. After the Protestant Reformation, divorce laws in some countries were eased somewhat, but still the principle remained that divorce could be granted only to a party who had demonstrably been injured by the spouse. To some extent, today's laws are still based upon this principle. "So too, for the state as it had been for the church," observes one writer, Joseph Epstein, "was the idea of guilt at the center of divorce—divorce, in other words, was viewed as retribution for serious marital misconduct" (1975, p. 108).

The traditional divorce procedure required that one party publicly accuse the other of certain specific offenses that are legally recognized as grounds for divorce. By making the husband and wife legal adversaries, the divorce process is often responsible for turning all the ill will of an unsuccessful marriage into a public spectacle. As the prominent trial lawyer Louis Nizer says in his book *My Life in Court,* "Litigations between husbands and wives exceed in bitterness and hatred those of any other relationship." Other cases may involve extreme emotions, he writes, "but none of them, even in their most aggravated form, can equal the sheer, unadulterated venom of the matrimonial contest" (1972, p. 153).

Introducing the Marriage and Family Professionals

Box 14–1 / Marriage Counselors—When You Need Help

Under what circumstances might a trained marriage counselor help?

No couple needs the help of a trained counselor to resolve routine differences. Not even bitter arguments necessarily call for professional help. But when a couple reaches the point where recurrent tensions or frustrations seem impossible to relieve, when the air is heavy with recrimination and no real communication is taking place, then a counselor may be able to help.

Why can't a mutual friend do as well? Friends can and do provide valuable help in many situations, but sometimes they unwittingly allow themselves to be used by one spouse as a weapon or ally against the other. Marriage counselors are trained to act as objective referees, who can open the channels of communication and point out the difference between the symptoms of a problem and its source.

How do you find a suitable marriage counselor?

Choosing a competent counselor whose approach and techniques are suitable to your needs and preferences is considerably harder than finding a dentist or an accountant. Essentially, marriage counseling is not a specific profession but a service offered by different types of professionals—doctors, ministers, social workers, and psychologists. Over the past decade, a considerable variety of counseling strategies has appeared. Many of them, such as gestalt therapy, transactional analysis, and behavior modification, use specific techniques for understanding and changing behavior.

In order to decide which approach is most compatible, you are well advised to shop around, to be skeptical, and to compare various forms of therapy. Since you are looking for marriage counseling and not individual therapy, find a counselor who treats couples, or groups of couples. Be as specific as possible about your objectives. What is it that you want help in changing? For certain types of problems it is helpful to get the entire family involved (see Box 9–1, p. 245). If the difficulties are sexual, consult a sex therapist specifically trained to deal with those problems (see Box 10–4, p. 284).

What kinds of qualifications should you look for?

Some states, like California, license marriage counselors. Most others do not. There are several ways to check on the training and competence of counselors. One is to write or call the American Association of Marriage and Family Counselors, 225 Yale Avenue, Claremont, California 91711, telephone (714) 621-4749, for a list of accredited counselors in your area. This association requires that its members have at least a master's degree in

Personal Complaints and Legal Grounds

Why do marriages fall apart? From the point of view of the spouses involved, the question is often difficult, even impossible to answer. The causes of marital breakup can be discussed by referring to certain themes—sexual or financial difficulties, different attitudes or expectations—

one of the behavioral sciences (psychology, sociology, education, etc.), and at least two years of clinical experience under approved supervision.

Another group that will refer you to trained and experienced counselors is the American Group Psychotherapy Association, 1865 Broadway, New York, New York 10023, telephone (212) 245-7732. Members of the AGPA must have at least 1,800 hours of supervised therapy, involving individual, group, and family therapy.

Among the various professionals who offer marriage counseling, such as clergymen, social workers, psychologists, and psychiatrists, it is psychiatrists who generally have the highest status and demand the highest fees—usually at least $50 for a fifty-minute session. But a psychiatrist may not be the best choice for marriage counseling, because psychiatrists normally do not receive specific training in dealing with spouses who are in therapy together. So if you seek the help of a psychiatrist, it is important to find out whether he or she will see both you and your spouse at the same time.

To avoid misunderstandings, as well as counselors who are unqualified, you should have no qualms about asking what qualifications a trained therapist has. Then discuss your goals, the counselor's philosophy and therapeutic techniques, and professional fees. You may also want to do what many transactional therapists insist upon: draw up a contract in which you and your therapist define your responsibilities in the agreement.

What do marriage counselors do?

Depending on their orientation and the type of training they received, counselors use various techniques to help couples resolve their problems. Some focus mainly on communication problems, or an understanding of hostility or guilt. At times, counselors serve mainly as referees. Or they may point out how each spouse might work toward a solution to a specific problem. Most counselors will, on occasion, offer direct advice, guidance, or assistance.

How effective is marriage counseling?

This is a difficult question to answer, because it depends so much on your personal goals and expectations. For example, do you want the counselor to salvage your marriage above all, or to promote the individual growth of the spouses even if it requires divorce? Most counselors today consider it more important to save individuals than to save marriages. This attitude is summed up in a statement issued as part of a proposed code of ethics by the American Association of Marriage Counselors:

> While the marriage counselor will feel satisfaction in the strengthening of a marriage, he should not feel obliged to urge that the married partners continue to live together at all costs. There are situations in which all resources fail, in which continued living together may be severely damaging to one or both persons. In such event it is the duty of the counselor to assess the facts as he sees them. However, the actual decision concerning separation or divorce is a responsibility that must be assumed by the client, and this should be made clear to him. If separation or divorce is decided upon, it is the continuing responsibility of the counselor to give further support and counsel during a period of readjustment, if that appears to be wanted and needed, as it often is. (in Udry, 1974, p. 420)

yet it may be impossible to identify specific events or issues which, in and of themselves, destroyed the marriage. Every divorce has a very complex, drawn-out story behind it, and that story invariably has two different versions.

But since divorce is a legal matter, the reasons for marital dissolution must be fit into a legal framework. The law specifies the conditions under which a divorce may be granted and it judges each marriage according to those specifications. The tangled stories behind each breakup must be considerably simplified before they reach the courtroom.

The result is a curious incongruity between the personal experience and the law's interpretation. "What is involved," writes Joseph Epstein,

> are two quite different orders of truth—the truth that the law asserts, and the truth that experience teaches. The law's truth holds that one party to a marriage must be guilty of grave misconduct before it will allow the marriage to be dissolved. The truth of experience holds that in a relationship as intricate as marriage guilt can rarely be so decisively allocated—can usually, indeed, be found to lie with both parties—nor need acts of misconduct be of so blatant a nature as grounds prescribe to destroy a marriage. . . . Although the truth of experience is more widely held—even among lawyers and judges—in the courtroom it is the law's truth that prevails. "Please," says the plaintiff's attorney to the defendant, who vainly attempts to explain his actions, "just answer the question yes or no." (1975, p. 117)

Grounds for divorce differ from one state to another. There are three favorite legal grounds, however, which account for about three-quarters of all divorces: desertion, nonsupport, and cruelty. These legal grounds are not meant to be understood as the actual causes of marital dissolution but only as convenient categories into which lawyers translate the complaints of their clients. The reason these three grounds are so popular is that they are less embarrassing and painful to discuss in public than other grounds might be. For example, all states allow adultery as a possible ground for divorce, and research such as the Kinsey studies shows that a very substantial percentage of the population does, in fact, practice extramarital sex. Yet adultery is not a popular ground for divorce because to accuse one's spouse of having chosen another sex partner is both embarrassing, and also a very awkward charge to prove. Thus, most couples apply for divorce on less specific grounds, such as mental cruelty, which can mean almost anything.

About 85 percent of all divorces are uncontested. That is, the defendant makes no attempt to answer the charges of the complainant. Most divorce cases, therefore, are actually brought to court by mutual agreement, though our legal system (except in states with no-fault laws) makes no provision for dissolving marriages on this basis. Technically, such collaboration is called collusion and is against the law, but the courts regularly wink at it because most people who want a divorce would not otherwise be able to get one. Couples whose reasons for divorcing do not fit the accepted categories must sometimes go to great lengths to manufacture acceptable grounds.

The No-Fault Concept

After thirteen years of marriage, a husband and wife, Matthew and Anne Surrey, decided they would both prefer to live alone. They began legal proceedings and sent cards to their friends announcing that they were having an amicable divorce. After the divorce was granted (reluctantly, since the judge was unfavorably impressed by the couple's evident friendliness toward each other), the Surreys had a party to celebrate the end of their marriage. Friends watched while they cut a wedding cake, the knife blade symbolically inserted *between* the figures of the bride and groom. The celebration ended with an improvised religious ceremony in which the officiant said

> Almighty and loving God, who has ordered that seasons shall change and that human lives shall proceed by change, we ask thy blessing upon thy children who now, in their commitment to thee, have severed their commitment to each other. Send them forth in the bond of peace. (Shideler, 1971, p. 554)

Few divorcing couples are able to part as am-

Introducing the Marriage and Family Professionals

Box 14–2 / What You Should Know About Divorce Law and Lawyers

"A woman who proceeds to get a divorce without legal help," writes Barbara Hirsch, "is engaging in an activity that is nearly as dangerous as self-taught brain surgery." Ms. Hirsch, who is a Chicago attorney and the author of a recent book, *Divorce: What a Woman Needs to Know* (1973), might be regarded as a biased observer. But few people who are familiar with the divorce process would disagree with her. And her advice applies to men as well as women.

The law does not require that spouses who want to end their marriages hire an attorney, and legal fees commonly run anywhere from $400 to $800 for an uncontested divorce. Why, then, is legal assistance generally advisable, even in states with no-fault laws that simplify the divorce procedure? In divorce cases, feelings of bitterness and resentment are the rule rather than the exception. Hair-trigger emotions combined with a sketchy legal knowledge can be a lethal combination for the person trying to manage divorce proceedings without legal assistance.

A divorce lawyer's job is to protect the client's interests and make sure that the action satisfies the requirements of the law. In most states the first task is to translate the actual situation into terms that the law recognizes. For the complainant's attorney, this means choosing a specific ground for divorce, assembling the evidence for that complaint, and acting as an advocate for the client when the case comes to court.

Essentially, there are four matters to be decided in divorce cases: (1) whether the divorce will be granted; (2) how property will be divided; (3) who will receive custody of the children; and (4) whether alimony or child support payments will be required. In each of these matters, a lawyer informs and advises

(Box 14–2 continues on page 404)

icably as the Surreys did. Although the majority of divorces are mutually desired, a good deal of bitterness usually emerges during the course of divorce proceedings. Most critics blame this ill will on the adversary nature of divorce laws. Others condemn our divorce laws as holdovers from a time when continuing an unhappy marriage was seen as a form of punishment for spouses who were both to blame for conjugal misery. "Where neither spouse was innocent of wrongdoing," said a 1799 English court ruling, "both should live together and find sources of mutual forgiveness in the humiliation of mutual guilt" (Gough, 1970, p. 18).

Sometimes the divorce process can erupt into real horror. In order to gain evidence of adultery, a complainant may hire a detective to follow the spouse. If the laws of the state are stringent, a hotel room maid may even be necessary to complete a scene recorded by camera and popping flashbulbs. Children, too, may be victimized by the process. As one judge remarked, "they are treated as negotiable debris from the marriage, not much different from the hi-fi set or the family car" (Wylie, 1970, p. 99). In some states, a person can secure a court order forcing a spouse to vacate the home merely by swearing to a judge that the spouse was guilty of "cruel treatment." Many married couples find that the divorce laws give them potent weapons for venting their immediate anger and resentment, but which they may later regret using. (For further discussion of divorce law and lawyers, see Box 14–2 above.)

(Box 14–2 continued from page 403)

the client, negotiates with the spouse's lawyer, and argues for certain rights or concessions.

In many instances the divorce case does not end even when the decree is final. Obligations change, and so do the financial situations of each of the former spouses. The husband, for example, may fall behind in his child support payments, or the wife may remarry. Whenever one of these things happens, the divorce may again require the attorney's attention.

How do you go about finding a good lawyer? For many people seeking a divorce, this is the first time they need the assistance of an attorney, and they know very little about how lawyers and their clients work together. Particularly because of the personal nature of such cases, it is essential to find an attorney you trust, one who has the time to give adequate information and advice, and one who respects your own preferences about how the matter should be settled.

Lawyers specialize in certain types of cases. Those who mostly handle divorces call their specialty matrimonial law. The best advice in finding a suitable attorney is to ask friends, perhaps ones who have already gone through a divorce, or to ask lawyers who do not take matrimonial work themselves. They are likely to know who the competent and reliable attorneys are. Another source of information is the city and state bar associations, or the office of the American Academy of Matrimonial Lawyers, a national organization.

In the first meeting with an attorney, it is important to reach agreement on your mutual expectations about the relationship. The attorney should be clear about how much time he or she will make available to the client, what the professional fees are, and how long the proceedings are likely to take. It is standard practice for husbands to pay a retainer in advance. If the wife has no separate income from which to pay a retainer, the attorney has to win a settlement for payment. The reason why an advance is normally required is that the lawyer might otherwise never be paid; the couple can always reconcile their differences, even after a considerable amount of legal work has been done.

Because of the legal complexities of divorce, anyone contemplating it is well advised to read more about it. One useful source is a twenty-four page booklet entitled "About Divorce," which explains many aspects of the process in question-and-answer form and is available from Lawyers and Judges Publishing Co., 817 East Broadway, PO Box 6081, Tucson, Arizona 85733. Also, Norman Sheresky and Marya Mannes have co-authored the informative book *Uncoupling: The Art of Coming Apart* (New York: Viking, 1972). Robert Weiss' *Marital Separation* (New York: Basic Books, 1975) includes a chapter on legal matters.

It has been evident for some time that drastic reform in our divorce laws is urgently needed, and in recent years most states have initiated a reform based on a new concept of marital dissolution. This concept is known as no-fault divorce.

In 1970 California passed the Family Law Act, a revolutionary piece of legislation that does away with the term "divorce" altogether, replacing it with "dissolution of marriage." In order to dissolve a marriage, one spouse is no longer required to bring charges against the other. All that is necessary is that irreconcilable differences exist and that both parties feel it impossible for their marriage to survive. Even the traditional mode of naming divorce cases, "*Applegate* versus *Applegate,*" has been changed. California now employs this form: "In re the marriage of Applegate and Applegate." Today, all but three states—Illinois, Pennsylvania, and

South Dakota—have some form of no-fault procedure, and the Pennsylvania legislature is considering one.

Under the old divorce laws, the division of property and the awarding of alimony payments were determined according to the concept of fault. In other words, property and support were given to the innocent party as a reward and extracted from the guilty party as punishment. The no-fault concept changes this pattern. Under California's Family Law Act, property is divided equally between the spouses, although they may agree to divide it unequally if they wish. In the matter of alimony, the court is required to take into account the duration of the marriage, the needs of each party, and the ability of the supported spouse to earn his or her own living (Gough, 1970).

Unfortunately, the Family Law Act has not been so successful in dealing with the problem of child custody. Divorcing spouses may still contest each other's right to care for the children, and since custody must be decided on the basis of which parent can best serve the child's interests, custody disputes may still turn into bitter personal battles. Some critics have proposed that the situation might be improved if the child had his or her own legal representative. "A lawyer appointed for the child," as Michael Wheeler, a law professor who has studied no-fault divorce, points out, "could investigate the case by speaking with members of the family, as well as teachers and friends, and then advocate to the court what course would be best for the child" (1974, p. 85).

Whether this proposal is feasible or not, there is clearly a need to protect the rights of children in divorce. "The danger," as Wheeler says, "is that after a divorce reform bill is enacted, there may be a sense that the job is done, when actually one of the most important issues is still unresolved" (1974, p. 97).

Trends in Divorce Statistics

Critics of no-fault laws often argue that if divorce becomes too easy, a great many more couples will get one. This argument assumes that the expense, difficulty, and unpleasantness of the traditional procedure are major deterrents to divorce. Such critics insist that easy divorce laws will lead to a society in which marriage is contracted and dissolved on a casual basis, leading to all the social problems that result from family instability.

How plausible is this alarming scenario? Perhaps a look at recent divorce statistics will shed some light on the matter. Some states have changed their divorce laws so recently that the effect of these changes cannot be assessed, but it is still interesting to examine recent divorce statistics to see how long-term trends are being modified.

The problem with analyzing divorce rates is that these statistics, even more so than most social statistics, can be used to support very different conclusions. Using certain statistics, one can demonstrate a dramatic increase in divorce; pointing only to the number of marriages that remain intact over many years, one can just as convincingly argue that most marriages are quite stable today. Like birthday party magicians, people who use divorce statistics often conceal as much as they reveal. In order to really understand the current divorce rate we must look at tendencies in remarriage as well as divorce, noticing both the steady, long-term increase in the divorce rate and the fact that a majority of marriages still remain intact (see Box 14–3).

Figure 14–1 shows the rates of divorce, marriage, and remarriage in the years between 1921 and 1977. The peaks and valleys show how such events as the Great Depression and World War II influenced marital decisions. As demographers Paul Glick and Arthur Norton (1973) point out, marriage, divorce, and remarriage were all at a low point during the Depression years in the 1930s. Many people delayed marriage and divorce as well during those years because both cost money. In the period immediately after World War II, the opposite trend took place. The jump in the divorce rate at that time is generally attributed to the breakup of

Research Perspectives on Marriage and Family

Box 14–3 / Using Statistics to Understand Divorce

Statistics from government agencies such as the Justice Department, the Census Bureau, and the National Office of Vital Statistics are indispensable in gauging the direction and extent of certain social trends.

However, certain questions should be kept in mind when using statistics for research purposes: (1) How accurate and comprehensive are the data? Do they come from a reliable source, and do they represent a complete enumeration of the phenomenon they describe? (2) Are the data combined in categories or rates that accurately express their meaning? (3) What inferences can properly be made from the data presented?

Most people are aware that statistics can be used in misleading ways. It is quite appropriate, for example, to be skeptical about whether advertisers' claims expressed as statistics are indeed factual. Behind the apparently persuasive statement, "Four out of five doctors recommend. . . ." may lurk a doctoring of the facts. Sometimes statistics are misrepresented by well-intentioned people who are not trying to sell us anything, but only to persuade us to act in our own self-interest. For example, before every holiday weekend, the media tell us how many people are expected to die on the nation's highways. Invariably, those statistics indicate that more people will be killed on the roads during this Memorial Day weekend (or whatever holiday it is) than ever before. Presumably, the media announce these projected fatalities to persuade us to drive carefully.

When most people hear these statistics they conclude that the nation's highways are more dangerous than ever before, or that its drivers are worse than they used to be. But the figures are misleading because they are uncorrected for volume. What we would really like to know is whether, per mile traveled, a driver is more likely to be involved in a serious accident over a holiday weekend than at any other time. Data collected by the National Safety Council indicate that people actually drive more safely over holiday weekends than at other times. The reason there are so many fatalities is that the total volume of traffic is so much higher than usual. If you make allowance for the fact that the average driver travels much farther today than he did several decades ago, you find that drivers are considerably safer than they used to be. Correcting for volume, traffic fatalities in the 1960s were less than one-third of what they had been three decades before (Biderman, 1966, pp. 28–29).

Divorce statistics, too, are sometimes presented so as to deceive us. In the first place, it is seldom pointed out that divorce statistics are incomplete. Recognizing the inadequacy of divorce statistics, in 1958 the Office of Vital Statistics established a new procedure for gathering the data, but it still does not generate comprehensive statistics. Only about half of the fifty states report complete information to the federal government on the number and characteristics of divorces granted.

Even in states that record complete data,

spur-of-the-moment wartime marriages. Then during the 1950s there was a period of relative stability. The divorce and remarriage rates were at a plateau, while the rate of first marriage declined somewhat (Glick and Norton, 1973).

Disregarding temporary fluctuations, the pattern up until the mid-1960s can be described as follows. For more than half a century, since there is no adequate information on desertion. Because divorce involves substantial legal fees, it is a luxury that many poor people cannot afford. (As the black comedian Godfrey Cambridge once said, "I have just gone through a white, middle-class divorce. I mean, man, lawyers and a judge were involved.") Thus when legal services for the poor improve, as they did briefly because of the antipoverty programs of the mid-1960s, many desertions are made official, and in some places a rising divorce rate might better be understood as a consequence of improved legal services than of growing dissatisfactions with marriage.

Divorce statistics are particularly difficult to interpret because their rates are calculated in several ways. What impression the statistics give depends on which technique is used to compute the rate. One of the most commonly used rates, the current-marriage-to-current-divorce ratio, is also one of the most misleading and one that most lends itself to the impression that the incidence of marital breakdown is alarmingly high. This technique seems quite simple, and superficially at least, seems to provide an accurate measure of divorce. It is computed by comparing the number of marriage licenses granted in a certain month with the number of divorce decrees. If, for example, 400 marriage licenses were granted and 200 divorce decrees issued during a certain month, we might conclude that 50 percent of all marriages end in divorce.

For all its appealing simplicity, however, this rate is highly deceptive. It compares two very different populations, the mostly young people who marry in a given year and people who married before, any time from one to thirty years ago. Furthermore, if a substantial number of people decide to defer marriage the marriage rate will go down, causing the divorce rate to increase even if the number of divorces stays the same. Finally, this measure provides no way to estimate the likelihood that a first marriage will end in divorce. Among those 200 divorces granted, some were issued to people who have been married at least twice before. Such individuals are counted in the divorce statistics every time they go through the process, thus causing the divorce rate to be inflated.

There are other, less misleading ways to calculate the divorce rate. The crude rate, for example, is defined as the number of divorces per 1,000 population. The problem with this measure is that the "1,000 population" includes many people, such as children or adults who have decided never to marry, who are not "at risk" to divorce. A better measure is the refined divorce rate, which is the number of divorces per 1,000 married women.

The best way to determine how many marriages eventually end in divorce would be to take a national sample of individuals marrying in a given year and then to follow them through life until their marriages are dissolved either by death or by divorce. But this has never been done because it would be very expensive and time consuming. As demographers Hugh Carter and Paul C. Glick have pointed out, however, we do have data on marriages begun some years ago, and these data show that as of 1960, "For ever-married persons 65 years of age and over, 79 percent of the men and 84 percent of the women had been married only once" (1970, p. 83).

We can conclude, then, that the divorce rate *is* increasing, but not as rapidly as some statistics would suggest. On the subject of divorce, even more than most others in social research, it is important to be aware of what statistics reveal and what they conceal.

the latter part of the nineteenth century, the divorce rate climbed slowly but steadily. In 1900, the divorce rate per 1,000 population was 0.7; in 1920, it was 1.6; in 1940, 2.0; in 1960, 2.2. But in the mid-1960s, *before* no-fault laws were passed, the divorce rate started to accelerate more dramatically, from 2.5 in 1966 to 2.9 in 1968; then to 3.5 in 1970, 4.0 in 1972, and 4.6

Figure 14–1 Rates of Marriage, Divorce, and Remarriage in the United States: 1921–1977. The graph shows, among other things, how large-scale external events affected the rates of marriage, divorce, and remarriage in this country.

Source: Reprinted courtesy of the Population Reference Bureau, Inc., Washington, D.C. From Paul C. Glick and Arthur J. Norton, "Marrying, Divorcing and Living Together in the U.S. Today," Population Bulletin, Vol. 32, No. 5, 1977, p. 5.

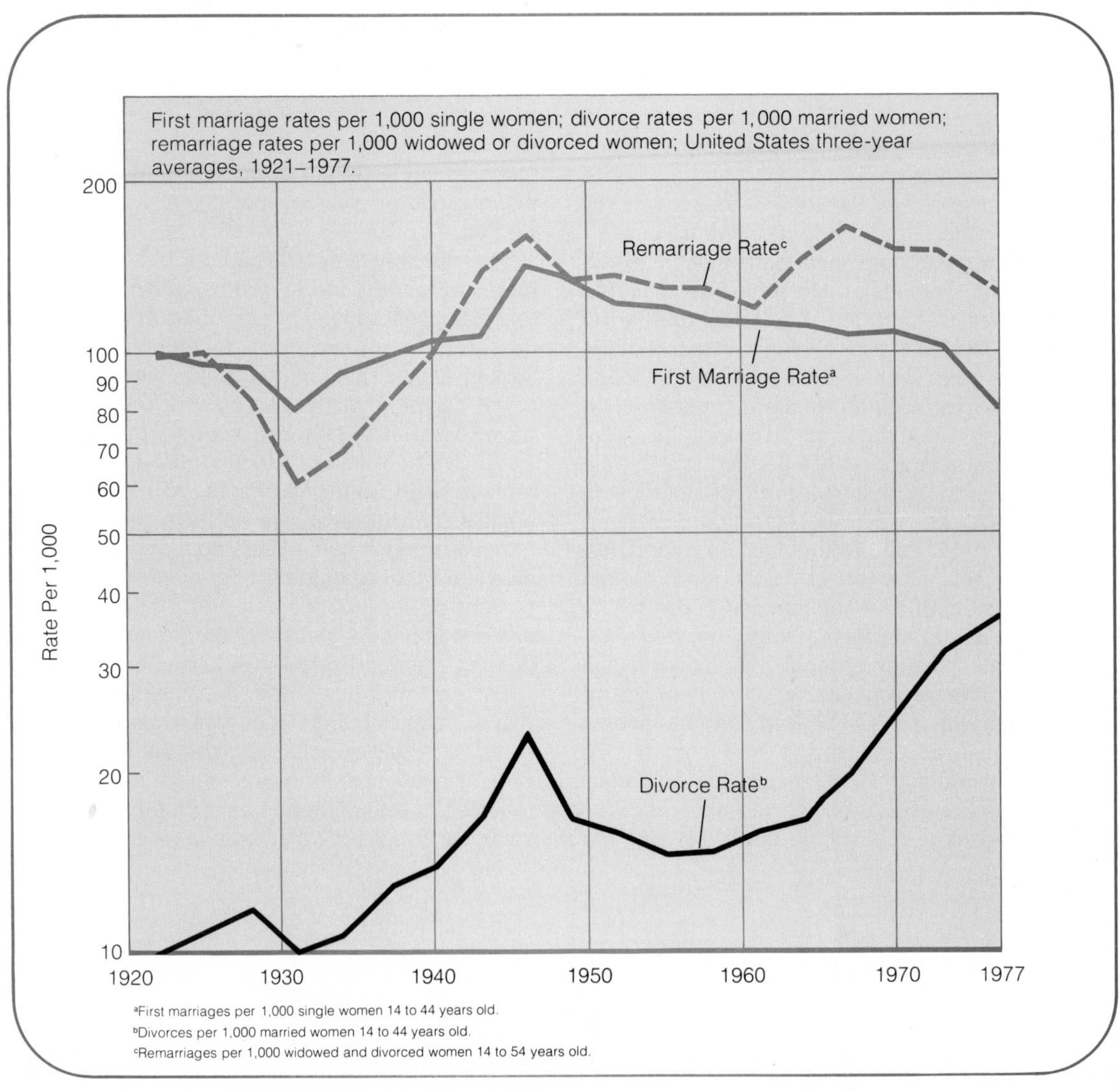

in 1974 (*Statistical Abstract,* 1974, p. 38).

Since 1975, the divorce rate has almost stabilized. In 1976, it reached 5.0; by 1977 the rate was virtually unchanged, at 5.1 per 1,000 population (National Center for Health Statistics, 1979).

It is interesting to note that this pattern of rapid acceleration in the divorce rate during the mid-1960s appeared not only in the United States, but in every nation in Western Europe as well, except France and Portugal (Shorter, 1975, p. 277). This suggests that the relative instability of modern marriage is a factor that we can adequately explain only by looking at very broad currents of social change.

How, then, has no-fault legislation affected the divorce rate? In the first seven years after California's no-fault legislation went into effect, the divorce rate there increased by 54 percent between 1970 and 1977; but during that same period, the national rate increased even more, by 56 percent. Observing the number of divorces per month over a six-year period in Nebraska, both before and after no-fault laws were enacted in 1972, investigators concluded that the new legislation had had no discernible effect on the overall divorce rate. (Mazur-Hart and Berman, 1977). A more comprehensive study of the impact of liberalized divorce laws in twenty-five states came to the same conclu-

Divorce greeting cards, such as this, are now sold in shops alongside more familiar staples—birthday and anniversary cards.

sion. Comparing divorce rates in the reform states with those in "fault" states, the authors of this comprehensive study found that the new laws had had little effect on the incidence of divorce. "Whatever the effects of no-fault reforms on the lives of individual couples, they do not seem to have contributed to the nation's rising divorce rates" (Wright and Stetson, 1978).

Divorce and Remarriage One of the most significant facts revealed in Figure 14–1 is that for more than thirty years, the remarriage rate has closely followed the divorce rate. A relatively high divorce rate, then, does not mean that people are giving up on marriage, but that for a substantial minority, marriage is no longer viewed as a necessarily permanent arrangement. That most people divorce in order to remarry is demonstrated by an interesting fact: when divorced and widowed women are compared age for age, remarriage is more than twice as likely for the divorced woman (Hetzel and Cappetta, 1971, p. 28).

The inclination of most people to remarry after divorce helps to explain why the age of the spouses is such a good predictor of marital breakup. In each successive year of marriage after the first two, a couple is increasingly likely to stay together. Even though the average duration of marriages that end in divorce is now slightly more than six years, the breakup is most likely in the first few years because both spouses usually want to remarry before increasing age makes it more difficult. Older couples who are just as dissatisfied with their marriages may choose alternatives other than divorce because their chances of remarrying are not so good.

In recent years, however, by far the most rapid percentage increase in divorce has been among people married fifteen to twenty years (Bernard, 1975, p. 584). The remarks of a father of three children, filing for divorce after sixteen years of marriage, illustrate new attitudes toward middle-aged divorce. "We've grown apart over the years," the man explained,

> and . . . have nothing in common any more other than the children. There are at least twenty years of enjoyable life still ahead of me. I was worried about the children until we discussed it with them. So many of their schoolmates have had divorced parents or parents who had remarried that they are accustomed to the idea. It's part of life. My wife is still a good-looking woman, younger than I, and probably will remarry. I'm not thinking of it now, but I'll probably remarry someday. (in Otto, 1970, p. 38)

The Statistics of Stability Looking mainly at divorce rates can give a mistaken impression about marital stability. Most marriages do not end in divorce, even in an era of greater life expectancy. Glick and Norton have compared three groups of women born roughly a generation apart in terms of their likelihood to divorce at some point in their lifetime. Among women in the first group, born about 1900, only 12 percent of their first marriages are expected to end in divorce. For women born about 1920, the rate increases to about 19 percent. Among women born about 1940, 25 to 29 percent will eventually be involved in a divorce. In other words, slightly less than one in three women who are in their thirties today are likely to experience a divorce at some point. And 5 to 10 percent of these divorcées will go through the process again and get a second divorce (1973, p. 311).

The same figures show unquestionably that most marriages remain intact. Among women who are in their thirties now, two-thirds will never experience a divorce. And if we set aside groups that have unusually high divorce rates—blacks, the poor, the uneducated—the chances that a marriage will *not* end in divorce are even better.

Why Is the Divorce Rate Increasing?

The fact that most marriages still remain intact does not, however, permit us to ignore the rising divorce rate. Why do so many more marriages end in divorce today? Is it a symptom of social disorganization, a measure of a growing prob-

"If you can give me some idea of how long you expect to be together, I can suggest a price range."

lem? Or should we regard it as one result of a more readily available solution?

Statistics tell us only how many couples are legally divorced, not how many marriages fail, or why. It is paradoxical but probably true that good marriages fail more often than bad ones. Good marriages are more likely to raise the expectations of the spouses to a point where disappointment can be fatal. Divorces, one writer believes, are like revolutions:

> Neither is likely to break out when conditions are at their worst, but they are when the situation has begun to get better. Once reforms have started, people gain strength and, more importantly, a vision of what their lives might be like. (Farson, 1971, p. 111)

For every marriage that breaks up so the spouses can seek greener pastures, there are undoubtedly several marriages in which the partners remain unhappily yoked together. In their interviews with more than 400 men and women, John Cuber and Peggy Harroff found it common for couples to remain in relationships the researchers classified as devitalized. Such couples are described as "apathetic, lifeless, numb. . . . Their relationship has become a void. The original zest is gone" (1968, p. 49).

A marriage counselor in Highland Park, Illinois, reports on one such couple. The man openly admitted that he was "a nobody . . . a complete flop." His wife agreed, and took every opportunity to remind him of it. Yet their marriage survived because of the powerful need each had developed for the other. "Says Joe, with an air of explaining the obvious: 'Oh, I *couldn't* leave Lucille. I love her very much. I decided one night to leave and did. But I couldn't sleep for thinking about her, wondering what she was doing and if she was all right.' " And his wife Lucille is equally incapable of imagining life without him: "What would I do if I left him? I would be absolutely lost. I have thought of it often enough, but when I try to imagine what it would be like without him, I know I just couldn't . . ." (Hunt, 1959, p. 376).

Marriages like this one remain intact out of habit more than anything else. The quality of the relationship, as both Joe and Lucille readily admit, is painfully bad, but more painful still is the prospect of facing life alone. Such marriages endure because neither spouse has the strength or the vision to see what their lives might be like without the other.

A rising divorce rate may mean not that our marital aptitude is lower than it used to be, but rather that we bring different expectations to marriage than our grandparents did. In a sense, then, the divorce rate has risen not because people care less about marriage nowadays, but because they care more. As Peter Berger and Hansfried Kellner put it,

> Typically, individuals in our society do not divorce because marriage has become unimportant to them, but because it has become so important that they have no tolerance for the less than completely successful marital arrangement they have contracted with the particular individual in question. (1964, p. 23)

With the increasing emphasis in our culture on personal fulfillment, divorce has become a way of asserting the importance of the self, of publicly proclaiming that one's own development takes priority over other concerns. Meanwhile, the barriers that formerly prevented most people from performing this act—religious prohibitions, legal regulations, economic restraints, and widely shared attitudes that condemned divorce—have come tumbling down. "The most striking change in this area," writes William Goode, "is the lessened social stigma attached to divorce. At the turn of the century, almost everyone who divorced was viewed as having lost respectability to some extent, and from many circles the divorcée was excluded" (1963, p. 81). Today divorce is far more respectable, even for candidates running for office, for whom divorce used to be a serious liability.

Jobs for Women Another factor contributing to the rising divorce rate is the employment of women. Part of the reason the divorce rate was so much lower several decades ago is that the great majority of women were financially dependent on their husbands. As more women want jobs and the opportunities become available to them, the economic barrier to divorce begins to crumble.

A recent study has shown that as the wife's earnings increase, so does the likelihood that her marriage will end in divorce (Ross and Sawhill, 1975, p. 57). One interpretation of this finding might be that because the job takes so much of her time and energy, the working wife performs her marital roles less adequately and thus strains her marriage. Or it may be that wives seek employment in preparation for divorce. There are no data supporting or denying either of these interpretations, but it is evident that women who can afford to leave an unsatisfactory marriage and can manage on their own do so more often than those who cannot.

The rising divorce rate, finally, gains impetus from the snowball effect: as more people get divorced, less of a stigma attaches to it. If your child has several friends whose parents have divorced, you will probably be less inclined to stay in an unsatisfactory marriage for the child's sake. More middle-aged couples divorcing become more potential new mates for *other* middle-aged couples who are considering a divorce.

The rising divorce rate does not indicate a general pattern of social disorganization. What it does mean is that a sizable minority of people have decided that if forced to choose, they will take a new partnership, with all its uncertainties, rather than one that is permanent but unsatisfactory.

WITHDRAWAL AND DETACHMENT—THE PERSONAL PROCESS OF TERMINATING A PARTNERSHIP

Just as there is a great deal more to marriage than the wedding ceremony that starts it, there is more to divorce than the courtroom procedure that makes it legal. What is it like, personally, to sever the marital bond?

We can think of the deterioration of a marriage as the process of falling in love in reverse. For most people, falling in love is an intoxicating experience because the most flattering mirrors are held up to oneself; the lovers dwell on each other's strengths and virtues, and their self-esteem soars. They feel trusted and accepted, so it is safe to reveal who they really are. And when love leads to marriage, the radiant bride and the proud groom surrounded by family and friends symbolize the fact that in the eyes of the community they are doing the "right thing."

Now run this process in reverse, and you begin to understand what happens when a marriage deteriorates. First, little acts of thoughtlessness and minor betrayals become highly significant symptoms. Rather than the euphoric feeling of high self-esteem that accompanied the beginning of the relationship, each feels the sting of systematic, destructive criticism. Before, they had focused on each other's strengths and virtues; now the spotlight turns to frailties and shortcomings. Instead of enthusiastic plans for a shared future, there are bitter recriminations over unmet promises. Where before there was increasing trust, now the partner's loyalty can no longer be taken for granted. At some point sexual accessibility may be withdrawn, and with it go companionship and emotional support. Just as lovers cherish certain momentos of special times together, when they stray apart they find many sad reminders of love's labor lost. Finally, the bitterness of the divorce is the mirror image of the wedding's joy. And afterwards, two households must be maintained on the same income that formerly supported one.

In several respects, divorce can be even more emotionally upsetting than the death of a spouse. Devastating though death is for the survivor, it at least is final, whereas divorce may be agonizing precisely because it lacks finality. Even after the legal termination of the marriage, feelings of attachment often remain. There is always the possibility, however remote, that things can be patched up, that the lost satisfaction can be recaptured. The ambiguity of this situation can be extremely painful. As one woman said, referring to the husband from whom she had been divorced: "He, who was the cause of my despair, was the only available human being, the only person I felt close to" (Weiss, 1975, p. 36).

Whether one loses a spouse because of death or divorce, the result is a hollow place where the spouse used to be, and "the natural reaction to the loss of a loved object or person (and sometimes a hated one as well) is grief" (Bohannan, 1971, p. 42). But it is often more difficult to cope with the grief brought on by divorce than that caused by death, because our society offers little in the way of formal consolation to the divorced person. Society allows, even encourages, the widow or widower to express grief. Emotional breakdown, reduced efficiency, even drunkenness are all to some extent condoned, and expressions of sympathy, though sometimes a formality, serve at least to tell the bereaved that he or she is not alone in grief. Divorce is different. Our society provides no recognized way to mourn it. As one writer has observed, "The grief has to be worked out alone and without benefit of traditional rites, because few people recognize it for what it is" (Bohannan, 1971, p. 43).

Only in the past few years have facilities such as the Transition Institute in Berkeley, California been formed to help people deal with the emotional problems associated with the transition to the divorced status. For most of the newly divorced—in recent years about 2 million people have been in that category—no such facilities are readily available, and it may be difficult for them to turn to family for support. The originator of Seminars for the Separated, sociologist Robert Weiss, has described the difficulties that divorced people often have in breaking the news to their parents. Parental approval is very important to most people, whatever their age. The rejection and disapproval that people expect in response to an announcement of divorce can shame them into postponing it almost indefinitely (Weiss, 1975, p. 130).

The reaction of friends is likely to be more sympathetic, at least superficially. When the marriage splits up, relations with "couple friends"—people formerly seen mainly on a couple-to-couple basis—may become strained. Married couples sometimes feel that the divorce of friends is indirectly a challenge to their own marriage.

In many cases, friends feel pressured to take the side of one or the other of the former spouses. Not wishing to play favorites, they may prefer to disengage themselves from both. Such desertion is particularly galling to people who are in the midst of emotional turmoil and in need of support. Many divorcées complain about ex-friends. "Friends?" one woman exclaimed.

> They drop you like a hot potato. The exceptions are those real ones you made before marriage, those who are unmarried, and your husband's men friends who want to make a pass at you. (Bohannan, 1971, p. 59)

What Happens to the Children?

Some of the most startling statistics about divorce today describe the children affected by it. In earlier generations parents generally subscribed to the belief that for the sake of the children it was better to stay together even though unhappy. Today, more and more people feel otherwise. This is just one more constraint to divorce that has loosened over the past few decades. More than 60 percent of the couples who are granted divorces have children at home. In each of the past few years, the parents of more than a million children under age eighteen have divorced, so that by now only about 70 percent of American children younger than eighteen are living with both of their natural parents in families undisturbed by divorce. The children of divorce are no longer a tiny minority (Glick, 1975).

Apparently one of the reasons why parents more willingly seek divorces today is that they believe an unhappy marriage may cause more psychological damage to their children than a divorce would. Is this belief true? Unlike many other questions that have practical consequences in marriage and family life, researchers have devoted a good deal of time and attention to this matter, but their research studies and clinical observations have not yet yielded any easy generalizations.

One of the most thorough studies of the effects of divorce, William Goode's *Women in Divorce* (1956), summarizes interviews with more than 400 women. Most of the mothers were concerned about the possibility that divorce would be harmful for their children, but felt they had to go through with it anyway. After it was over, most of them, particularly those who had remarried, felt that their children's lives were better. A majority said the divorce had little effect on the difficulty of handling their children. Clearly, these mothers were attempting, as most of us do, to justify a difficult decision they had made. It is interesting that so many of them felt satisfied with the consequences of divorce (and in many cases, remarriage) for their children, but they can hardly be considered objective observers.

More reliable observations on the effects of divorce have emerged from a study in progress in California since 1970. The investigators, Judith Wallerstein and Joan Kelly (1974), asked parents who were filing for divorce to bring their children between two and one-half and eighteen years to a counseling center designed to help them cope with the divorce. Sixty couples accepted the invitation. A family therapist interviewed parents and children several times during a six-week counseling period, and then again a year later.

Reports from this study agree in general with what parents have said about the effects of divorce. Initially, children are upset when their parents decide to separate; it is a painful experience for older adolescents as well as for younger children. Extreme anger, certain types of regression to earlier forms of behavior, and physical symptoms such as asthma are not uncommon responses. Younger children especially seem to blame themselves for their parents' separation. Older adolescents more often feel angry at the disruptions caused by the divorce, or ashamed at the disgrace. For the first few months most children wish the separation could be repaired. They want the father or mother to rejoin the household.

But within a year most children of all ages return to a normal pattern of development and appear to be undamaged by the divorce. Less than one-fourth of the children studied became increasingly distressed as time went on. Their difficulties showed up as reduced self-esteem, problems in relating to others, and continued feelings of sadness or anger (Wallerstein and Kelly, 1974).

This and other studies suggest certain things parents can do to help their children deal with divorce (see Box 14–4). They also suggest that for most children divorce is not as devastating as some people have feared. There are still many unanswered questions about the specific circumstances under which children may be harmed by the experience, but in general it appears that after the first shock has been absorbed, most children are able to cope with it. Children are tougher, more resilient, and more realistic than many parents give them credit for. It seems clear that in the long run it is usually easier for children to survive a divorce than to cope with the constant strife and irritation of unhappily married parents.

STARTING OVER

For that growing number of people who emerge from the process of divorce each year, regaining a sense of independence and autonomy is no easy matter. It requires a redefinition of self, changed living habits, and a partial change of friends and social patterns. As many recently divorced people discover, the freedoms of the single life, so appealing to a person in the toils of an unsatisfactory marriage, can turn out to be terrifying when the person actually regains them.

Starting over means using the pronoun "I" again, after years of saying "we." Whatever tasks were delegated to one's spouse during marriage—washing the dishes, choosing a wine, fixing the wiring, making social arrangements—become one's own responsibility again. "All too often," writes Paul Bohannan, "mar-

Guidelines for Decision Making

Box 14–4 / Helping Children Adjust to Divorce

Based on his experience as a sociologist and founder of the popular Seminars for the Separated, Robert Weiss offers the following advice to parents who are seeking a divorce. In his book Marital Separation *(New York: Basic Books, 1975), Weiss admits that it is often difficult to translate the findings of researchers or clinicians into practical advice. However, these ten suggestions, excerpted from his book, might be helpful for many parents wondering how to assist their children through a difficult transition. It should be noted that although Weiss assumes the mother will be the children's caretaker in case of divorce, in a small but growing minority of divorces the father has been granted custody.*

1. *Children, even very young children, should be kept informed, without overwhelming them with information they cannot assimilate.* Children should be told enough to explain the father's departure. Failing to do so imposes on the children not only the experience of disruption, but also the burden of working out for themselves why it happened. Parents who are less than honest with their children encourage them to develop confused or distorted understandings of threats they cannot avoid recognizing. In general, explanations of the separation should as far as possible display respect for the worth of all involved: mother, father, and child.

2. *Children are likely to react to the separation with upset and to need appropriate solicitude.* Very young children are apt to become sad at the loss of a loved figure and fearful that they may lose all the figures on whom they depend. Somewhat older children may be sad, angry, or bitter because of what appears to be a parental action taken without concern for their well-being. No matter what age the child is, the parent should try to be understanding and appropriately solicitous.

3. *Children who fail to resume normal development within a year of the separation may need special attention.* If the child's sadness, anger, bitterness or other early reactions to the separation have not faded by the end of the first year after the separation, or if the child is not again functioning normally, something may be going wrong. At this point, modifications in the parents' relationship with the child might be considered. A consultation with a professional child therapist might also be helpful.

4. *A competent and self-confident parent as head of the household is the child's most important source of security.* Children whose mothers function adequately are less likely to be upset by parental separation. They learn that their mothers are people on whom they can rely. They also learn from their mothers how to deal effectively with problems. Fathers who do not have custody should recognize that they contribute to their children's well-being by being supportive of the mother. The single parent should try to use whatever resources are available to help her function effectively: babysitting exchanges with friends or neighbors, paid help or the contributions of older children . . . in the home, as well as any help that the other spouse is able to furnish.

riage is used as a shield against becoming whole or autonomous individuals'' (1971, p. 61). Many of the problems normally associated with late adolescence or one's early twenties—establishing autonomy, developing self-esteem and self-confidence—come up all over again after a divorce. Facing life by oneself again is filled with ambiguities. After the routines of

5. *Preadolescent children need a parent's full attention at least part of the time.* It is easy for the newly separated mother to become preoccupied with the tasks of reorganizing her life. Yet it is essential for the children's well-being that she set aside time, preferably every day, when she can give the children her full attention. Otherwise the children may feel that they have in large measure lost their mother as well as their father.

6. *Ordinarily, children gain if the noncustody parent remains in the picture.* Clinical experience suggests strongly that the father can continue to play a valuable role in his children's lives even though he is no longer a member of the household. If the mother remarries, the relationship of the father and the children might have to be reconsidered. Attention would have to be given to coordinating that relationship with obligations to the new household. We do not know enough at this point to say that one custody arrangement or visitation pattern is superior to another. But it does appear that a consistent pattern on which the children can rely is desirable.

7. *It is important for the children to retain as many regions of safety in their lives as possible.* Children lose a guarantor of their safety when their father leaves their home. They should be permitted to retain as many other supports for feelings of safety as possible. For a time, if possible, they should be protected from anxiety-arousing situations. This means keeping the children within the same house and the same school, and encouraging them to see the same friends.

8. *Insofar as there is change, children are likely to profit from parental support in establishing a satisfactory living situation for themselves.* Parents should try to assist their children's efforts to come to terms with their new situation. If the children have moved away from their former neighborhood, the parents might try to help their children establish new friendships and might talk with their children about problems they may be having in the new school.

9. *Children should be permitted to mature at their own pace, and neither be encouraged to become prematurely mature nor held back in their development through overprotection.* It is bad for the child to become responsible for the emotional well-being of one or both parents. Becoming a parent's companion, confidant, or advisor can divert them from the interests and social activities that are more appropriate for their age. It may become an obstacle to their emotional development. Some parents go to the other extreme. They try to protect their children from every sort of anxiety, frustration, or risk. This can be as dangerous to the child's development as continuous requests for their advice and support.

10. *Parents can help their children by establishing satisfactory life situations for themselves.* The self-sacrificing parent, like the overprotective one, can cause children to feel extraordinarily deserving, or guilty, or both. The children easily come to mean too much for the self-sacrificing parent, both positively and negatively. It is natural for parents whose lives are otherwise empty to attempt to fill them by forming inappropriate relationships with their children. But this can be burdensome for the children and ultimately is likely to be unsatisfactory for the parent.

Source: Robert Weiss. *Marital Separation.* New York: Basic Books, 1975.

married life, one often feels adrift, directionless. But there are moments of triumph and exhilaration as well.

As one newly separated woman writes:

There is no one whose rules I have to live up to now. This aimless freedom is heady and terrifying and I guess I have to find rules inside myself. Who cares what I do? I have to account to no one ex-

> cept myself. But I find it impossible to locate my self, my rules, so I guess I'll experiment. I am not the person I was brought up to be. (Braudy, 1975, p. 180)

Starting over also commonly requires forming new friendships, since, as Goode noted (1956, p. 243), a divorced person often loses contact with some friends. Conflicts arising from the divorce may make some old friendships awkward and inconvenient.

Unfortunately, those are not the only circumstances in which friends are lost. Overwhelmed by feelings of failure or rejection, many divorced persons conclude that their friends are no longer interested in seeing them. Most often, those feelings are false, and a simple phone call is enough to prove that the divorce has not made one a social outcast. One divorced woman, whose way of starting over was to invite her old friends to a party, describes the pleasant surprise of discovering that they had not rejected her. "It was a real effort to pick up the telephone after all those months," she says. "I kept thinking that no one would want to come, now that I was divorced. But all my friends—my old married friends—accepted! They all sounded so glad to hear from me" (Krantzler, 1973, p. 130).

Nor are all connections between the former spouses completely severed in most cases. Even when they have no children, the bonds they have established in marriage are not easily dissolved, no matter what the grievances were that led to their divorce. If most human relationships can be explained by the exchange principle (you maintain a relationship as long as its advantages outweigh its disadvantages), the continued attachment between ex-spouses is undoubtedly an exception. "Attachment," Robert Weiss observes, "is not willed into being after calculation of its advantages." In many cases, it has very little to do with love, esteem, or compatibility. Divorced persons may feel anger and contempt for one another, yet still find it impossible to break off the relationship completely (Weiss, 1975, p. 44).

In some cases, divorced couples find it possible to achieve a reconciliation after the turmoil of the initial separation. The relationship may assume the "we're just good friends" quality so often claimed by separated Hollywood stars. As one woman says of her ex-husband,

> It's rather pleasant to be able to see him and have a drink together, and not fight with him. We were married for sixteen years, and you just don't tune out that many years of your life. (Weiss, 1975, p. 125)

A common problem among the recently divorced is reentering the pool of eligibles after a long absence. The rituals of dating and courtship seem strangely inappropriate to middle-aged people looking for new partners. There is a common feeling that the entire process—waiting for phone calls, the sexual tension, the awkwardness associated with new people in unfamiliar situations—should have been left behind in adolescence. Some divorced women complain that their new status causes dates to think of them as easy sexual conquests: "There is no dignity, no honor, in divorce. The divorced woman is pictured as a sleazy character. Men think a divorced woman is horny, or else that she's hard and cold" (Weiss, 1975, p. 77).

Despite these objections, however, dating is an important part of a return to a normal, active life. "Dating for the divorcée," says Goode, "is in part an index of her willingness to start a new life. It is at the same time an introduction and a stimulus to that new life" (1956, p. 258). For the recently divorced person, dating is generally valuable in helping to restore a sense of autonomy, self-worth, and sexual attractiveness. As one young divorcée wrote after several months of dating,

> I have a growing knowledge that the loss of any lover, friend, job, or money won't tear me apart. If I do fall apart only a small percentage of me will disintegrate, and then I know I will put myself back together. I feel tougher. (Braudy, 1975, p. 242)

One way of starting a social life after a divorce is to find individuals who are in a similar situation.

As we noted in Chapter 5, ours is still very much a marriage-oriented society. The young person who divorces after a few years of marriage can mix with those who never married and find a variety of facilities that make the single life more congenial. People who are older may find living alone rather difficult, as the pressures to remarry come from all sides. There are personal needs for companionship, sex, and regaining self-esteem, which for most people are most easily satisfied in marriage. There are economic incentives to remarry, particularly for the divorcée who has no adequate income of her own. And there are the social needs, for a more acceptable status in the eyes of the community, for help in the tasks of child rearing. One of the most significant statements about the institution of marriage in our society, and perhaps one of the most telling comments about the problems of the single state for those who have divorced, is the fact that so many of those who can marry again do so.

Remarriage

A few years ago, a cartoon in *The New Yorker* showed a pair of stylishly dressed newlyweds leaving the office of the justice of the peace. The beaming bride turns to the groom and exclaims, "Darling, our first marriage!"

This may not be what most newlyweds are thinking when they marry, but it does reflect what actually happens to a growing minority. Since the mid-1960s there has been an impressive increase in serial monogamy—the practice of having at least two spouses during a lifetime, one after the other. And it has been increasing at all socioeconomic levels.

As we noted before, until recently the remarriage rate has been climbing almost as fast as the divorce rate. We might interpret this, in Samuel Johnson's cynical words, as "the triumph of hope over experience." Or we might view it as evidence that people believe they cannot do without marriage because they expect it to meet so many of their needs.

The statistics on remarriage are an impressive

Throughout the 1960s the remarriage rate, like the divorce rate, increased sharply. Then, in the mid-1970s, as the divorce rate flattened out, the remarriage rate began to move rapidly downward.

reminder not only of the appeal of marriage but also of the problems associated with the divorced status. These statistics clearly demonstrate that a very high percentage of those who divorce, and especially the young, can be expected to remarry. Age for age, persons who have divorced are more likely to remarry than are the widowed, more even than persons who have yet to marry for the first time. It is estimated that about 94 percent of women who divorce at age thirty will eventually remarry, and the remarriage rates are even higher for men. As Jessie Bernard comments, referring to the numerous "ball and chain" jokes,

> The actions of men with respect to marriage speak far louder than words. They speak, in fact, with a deafening roar. Once men have known marriage, they can hardly live without it. . . . Indeed, it might not be far-fetched to conclude that the verbal assaults on marriage indulged in by men are a kind of compensatory reaction to their dependence on it. (1972, p. 18)

These statistics also demonstrate that many people remarry very soon after they divorce. Just as the divorce rate rose during the 1960s, so did the speed of remarriage. In 1969, for example, 50 percent of divorced men remarried within twelve months; 50 percent of the women did so within fourteen months. Taking both sexes together, 75 percent of the divorced remarried within about three years. In the 1950s, by contrast, the average number of years before remarriage was about four (U.S. Department of Health, Education, and Welfare, 1973).

It may be that a substantial number of people do not seek a divorce until they have found someone they want as a new partner. Another point to keep in mind when reading these statistics is that couples are commonly separated for a year or more before the divorce is granted. Thus, people do not rush into another marriage quite so quickly as these figures would seem to indicate.

Are Second Marriages Better? Compared with first marriages, how successful are remarriages? Judging by the responses of the more than 400 women interviewed in William Goode's study, we would have to say that remarriage is quite successful. A very large majority—92 percent—said their second marriage was happier than their first. Most said their first marriage had made the second one easier (1956, p. 336).

This is perhaps the most interesting feature of remarriage: for most people it is *not* the same experience the second time around. To be sure, there are a few who marry again and again, and in their case we might assume that certain personality traits cause them to repeat the same mistakes. But interviews with twice-married people often reveal a different story. The first marriage, which they regret, was undertaken for the wrong reasons and perhaps at the wrong time. In retrospect they see it as an apprenticeship for a more successful second marriage. Here, for example, is what one man said about his first marriage:

> My first marriage was an almost completely automatic act, the thing I was supposed to do after graduation from college, something expected of me at that point in my life. Nobody made me even remotely aware of the preparation or skills I would need in relating to women, or sex, or child rearing. I had to face most of those important things just winging it, by trial and error. (Westoff, 1975, p. 11).

After interviewing dozens of people in their second marriage, a writer comments:

> In retrospect, many of the couples saw their first marriage as a kind of training school, like the college they had left with academic degrees but little knowledge of themselves. Divorce was their diploma. All agreed that the second marriage was the real thing at last. They had entered it with much clearer ideas about the things that really mattered to them, whether those things were love, friendship, understanding, sex, or money. (Westoff, 1975, p. 11)

Again, however, we ought to be skeptical about statements that might be regarded as justifications of one's choices. For most people, admitting that their second marriage had worked out no better than their first would be an acknowledgment of failure, perhaps of an inability to sustain any intimate relationship. And, indeed, if we judge the success of second marriages by their rate of divorce, we get a different picture from that painted by self-report. As one sociologist, Thomas Monahan, found when he compared the divorce rates of once-married people with those who married twice or more, remarriages are not very stable. In fact, where either or both partners have been married once before, the divorce rate is twice as high as it is in first marriages. And when either spouse has been married more than once before, the rate doubles again (1958).

Many explanations have been offered for the relative instability of subsequent marriages. It is no doubt true that people who are incapable of a satisfactory marriage with *any* partner contribute to these statistics, but sociological factors are also involved. For one thing, the large group of people who marry only once includes some who for religious or other reasons are almost "divorce proof." Then, too, people who have gone through the divorce process once may be less reluctant to do it again if the second marriage does not work out. And, finally, there are many situational factors that may create a strain for couples who remarry. Where one partner brings children from a previous marriage, for example, visiting privileges for the ex-spouse may create tensions. It is also important to remember that the most divorce-prone people are the poor, the disadvantaged, the uneducated—people with problems that are not solved by remarriage.

Owing to all these factors, then, remarriage is not as successful as first marriage—if marital success is measured by divorce rate. If we judge success by scores on various marital adjustment tests, however, the verdict is in doubt. As Jessie Bernard concluded after summarizing a number of studies of marital success, no clear-cut pattern of lower success among the remarried can be discerned (1956). This conclusion need not contradict the divorce statistics if we note that the once-divorced category includes a considerable number of people who are impatient with anything less than very satisfactory partnerships. Compared with the once-married, they are more likely to choose divorce (and remarriage) rather than live in a lukewarm relationship. If we set aside people with personality problems and those who for situational reasons are not likely to be satisfied in any relationship, the remaining remarriages are no less successful than first marriages.

Perhaps as the divorced status becomes more common and more acceptable, fewer people will remarry for the wrong reasons. If that happens, then the success of remarriage, no matter how it is measured, may be somewhat higher than it is today.

THE SOCIAL IMPACT OF MARITAL INSTABILITY

Edward Gibbon, the historian, once remarked about Corsica—an island renowned for the bandits it harbored—that it is easier to deplore than to describe. The same thing might be said of divorce. In most discussions where the divorce rate is mentioned, it is deplored as a sign of the times, an indication that the social fabric is unraveling. Only rarely is that rising divorce rate understood as a consequence of new expectations. As we have noted, divorce is very often accompanied by personal crisis and trauma. That bloodless statistic telling us that more than a million divorces will be granted in the United States over the next twelve months must cover an enormous amount of personal suffering. Few people stop to think, however, that a great deal of personal suffering must also be *relieved* by those divorces, as they allow people to escape unsatisfying partnerships. We can hardly use the divorce rate as a measure of social disorganization when such a large percentage of the divorced remarry within a short period of time.

It is common to deplore the high divorce rate as a sign that many couples are either incapable of, or unconcerned about, keeping the marital commitment. Yet two of the factors that contribute to the high divorce rate have nothing to do with personal failures or a decreasing "marital aptitude." One of these factors is the standard against which we compare today's divorce rates. Social commentators often compare today's rates with those of the 1950s, without noticing that United States divorce rates in that decade were quite low as compared with other urban industrial nations. As compared with those unusually low rates, today's look disturbingly high. Another factor in today's high divorce rate is increased longevity. When life expectancy was shorter, most marriages were terminated by death. Divorce terminates a larger proportion of marriages today in part because people are living longer than they did before.

A relatively high divorce rate is a problem mainly if we assume that all marriages should remain intact until the death of a spouse. Most societies have some provision for the dissolution of marriages in which the contract between husband and wife is not being fulfilled. We might view the new, more liberal grounds for divorce as a reflection of newer assumptions about the satisfactions that marriage is supposed to offer. In the past, as we have seen, companionship was not an important or widely shared expectation in marriage, and so it made sense that the only allowable grounds for divorce were those that clearly specified a breach of contract, such as adultery, desertion, drunkenness, or neglect of support.

New laws that allow divorce because of irretrievable breakdown or incompatibility reflect the increasingly widespread quest for personal fulfillment and companionship in marriage. (See Box 14–5.) In one 1974 survey (Institute of Life Insurance, p. 59), young people across the country were asked which of four broad goals was most important to them—a happy family life, a fulfilling career, the opportunity to develop as an individual, or making a lot of money. The most common choice was the opportunity to develop as an individual, which was chosen slightly more often than a happy family life. Significantly, these values among young people came in marked contrast to the answers given by adults in a survey conducted the previous year. A happy family life was most important to 80 percent of the adults; the opportunity to develop as an individual was picked by only 12 percent. In a society that places more and more emphasis on personal fulfillment, a rising divorce rate is almost inevitable.

Jessie Bernard believes there is a contradiction between emotional intensity and permanence, between marriages designed to maximize personal growth and those designed to promote stability. She writes,

> There is an intrinsic and inescapable conflict in marriage. Human beings want incompatible things. They want to eat their cake and have it too. They want excitement and adventure. They also want safety and security. These are difficult to combine in one relationship. . . . In the future, the emphasis among both men and women may well be on freedom rather than on security, at least to a far greater extent than today. Conceivably to a too great extent. (1972, p. 81)

In his popular book *Future Shock,* Alvin Toffler looks ahead to the next few decades and anticipates that

> couples will enter into matrimony knowing from the first that the relationship is likely to be short-lived. . . . Serial marriage, a pattern of successive temporary marriages, is cut to order for the Age of Transience in which all of man's relationships, all his ties with the environment, shrink in duration. (in Rollin, 1971, p. 62)

Perhaps Toffler will turn out to be right. Other writers have seriously proposed that the state should recognize limited-term, renewable marriage contracts. With the blessing of the state, couples would agree to a commitment for a specified period of time, and if the relationship was still satisfactory for both spouses at the end of the period, it might be renewed. If not, it

Point of View

Box 14–5 / Divorce in an Age of Disposable Relationships

During this year, I will be among about 2 million Americans who will be divorced.

I don't want to be. I am horrified by the prospect. I think it is the most devastating thing that could happen to my family. But it is going to take place.

My wife wants it.

We would seem to have everything to live together for. We have four wonderful sons who need us both; they range in age from six to sixteen. We have a large, comfortable house in Connecticut.

I thought we were a perfectly happy family until my wife told me, without any advance warning, that she didn't love me any more and wanted a divorce. Not a matter of infidelity or alcoholism or beating or arguments or desertion, but that I didn't mean anything to her any more and she wanted out.

My wife and I really were married in a different world. We are both forty-four. We were married twenty years ago. Those were the times when you looked for "togetherness." You found someone who was the "other half," who had qualities that complemented yours and filled you out, and you put them together and marched in lockstep through marital happiness. And we did. I enjoyed fully my role as husband and father; my wife appeared to be enjoying hers as wife and mother; she does not feel the same today in hindsight.

After my wife told me she wanted a divorce, we went to marital counseling for about a year. We learned many things about destructive patterns which we were not aware of before: things like dominance and dependence and imposing of wills and acquiescence and blocked and thwarted growth. We learned probably as much, too, about the way outlooks have changed concerning roles, marriages, and divorce.

And I guess that is where my problem really lies. The world, or at least the part of it concerned with psychological counseling, has changed in ways I am unwilling to accept. Not that I want to cling to negative destructive pat-

would be terminated without legal obstacles and, ideally, without the shattered hopes that make most of today's divorces so devastating. Limited-term contracts would undoubtedly be attractive to some people, and might, as their advocates believe, keep people from sliding into the unresponsiveness that is likely to happen in a relationship that is taken for granted.

Perhaps. Or it might turn out that an emotional commitment intended to last a lifetime will be even more attractive in an age of transience. William Goode comments,

> Marriage *feels* permanent, and that's the important thing. It's buying instead of renting. It's "even-if-you're-acting-like-an-S.O.B.-we'll-stick-it-through." It's going home at night to somebody you don't have to keep winning. It's having decided. (in Rollin, 1971, p. 64)

In a transient society like ours the appeal of a permanent commitment—one that promises to last longer than a new car or a good pair of gloves—is enormous. It seems unlikely that most people will abandon the hope of a permanent relationship, even if many do not achieve it.

Conclusions

In this chapter we examined the stresses that cause families to break down, the legal facts of terns, or "the old way." But we are now in a time which says that you get in touch with yourself, find out what your needs are, and then fill them. That is paramount.

My wife accepts this completely. She needs freedom, independence, out from under what she felt was a smothering relationship. Her whole outlook on life has changed. I don't fit into it any longer. So, divorce.

I don't feel this way, but I am left with a crumbled view of a marital world which doesn't have much popularity anymore. I feel that relationships aren't disposable; that you don't just throw them away after more than two decades.

Nobody is saying I can't hold these views. They are just saying that they are a little old-fashioned, a little quaint, a little square, and a little unreal in our present-day world.

I ask myself: at some point, doesn't a counterrevolution have to take place? Don't the excesses in favor of the liberation of the individual have to be met by a consideration of the needs of families, of the other party? Doesn't a psychology which hands license to a wife to do what she wants in these times fueled by the themes of women's lib have to be called to some accounting of responsibility? Doesn't someone have to come forward and say: "My God, wait a minute, what are we doing to ourselves?"

I think of what it is to be a child today—one of my own children—and what a dreadful experience that must be. Who speaks for them? While the adults are fulfilling themselves, finding their identities, liberating themselves from restrictive life situations, who is taking into account the welfare and well-being of the children? What happened to notions like commitment, responsibility, and an even more discredited concept, suffering?

Am I just feeling sorry for myself? Am I just full of self-pity? I don't think so. I don't think that I am unique. I am one man, hurt, groping. I do not have answers to the most important questions of my life. But I think that for the good of us all, as a people and as a society, we had better start coming up with better ones than we have now.

Source: Albert Martin, I Am One Man, Hurt, *The New York Times,* June 25, 1973, p. 33.

divorce, and the personal process of terminating a marriage and starting over again afterwards.

Unanticipated crises such as serious illness, alcoholism, or unemployment can put an intolerable strain on a marriage and cause it eventually to break down. It is because lower-class families more often lack the resources to cope with these crises that they have the highest rates of marital dissolution.

We explored the legal process of divorce and noted some of the consequences of having to petition the state to dissolve a marriage. Especially where divorce laws require spouses to face each other as adversaries, the process often adds to the bitterness of separation. Legislation permitting no-fault divorce responds to these problems and to the increasingly widespread belief that companionship and personal fulfillment are paramount in marriage. A breakdown of companionship can rarely be said to be the fault of one partner or the other.

We examined divorce statistics which show that, except for fluctuations during wars and depressions, there has been a long, steady rise in the percentage of marriages that end in divorce. Since the mid-1960s, that rise has accelerated. We explored the reasons for the higher divorce rate, including new expectations in marriage, lowered barriers to divorce, and greater economic independence for women.

We then turned to the personal aspects of divorce, the process of withdrawal and detachment. For many people it is a time of considerable turmoil and personal crisis, even when both spouses want to end the relationship. This can be understood by viewing the process of detachment as falling in love in reverse: self-esteem plummets, trust declines, and instead of the social approval given newlyweds, one feels the social stigma still attached to the divorced status.

There are many signs of recent interest in helping people who divorce. Books on how to survive divorce, divorce announcement cards, match-up services for divorced people who are looking for new partners, and organizations such as Parents Without Partners all recognize the fact that divorce is an increasingly common experience in our society.

We are curious about marital crises and divorce for a very practical reason. We would like to be able to cope effectively with crises before they lead to divorce. As in studies of physical disease, we would like to be able to recognize the symptoms of trouble and know what to do about them. But aside from the information that there are various types of marriage counselors trained to help couples cope with marital crises, there is very little general advice to be offered.

In severing a marriage, as in so many other subjects we have discussed, people have more personal options today than they had before. With fewer obstacles to the termination of an unsatisfying relationship, more people have to consider the potential costs and benefits and then decide for themselves between saving a marriage and seeking a divorce. One way of summarizing this chapter is to review those costs and benefits.

One of the main costs of divorce for many people is personal suffering. Severing a relationship can be a traumatic experience. The fact that many people seeking a divorce need some form of professional help with personal problems is an indication of their pain. Another cost is the social stigma attached to the divorced status. We noted this stigma in the comments of many of the recently divorced about the reactions of both family and friends.

Despite cheerful books about "creative divorce," divorced people face problems that are different from those of their married or single friends. As Angus Campbell, the author of a study of personal satisfaction and happiness, notes:

> Divorce hits women hardest. Most of them have to work (71 percent) and care for children (84 percent) without moral, economic, or psychological support from a husband or partner. They earn less than single women their age, certainly less than divorced men. . . . And they lack the opportunities that divorced men have to date and remarry. For all these reasons, divorced women feel the greatest pressure and stress of any group, report the greatest dissatisfaction with their lives, and describe the emotional quality of their lives in gloomy terms. (1975, p. 41)

On the other side of the ledger is the high percentage of divorced people who remarry. It is also encouraging that divorce apparently does not leave permanent emotional scars on most of the children who are affected by it. Couples who have tried unsuccessfully to resolve their difficulties and finally admit that divorce is the only way out may take further comfort in the increasing number of others who are in the same situation, since a higher divorce rate provides a larger number of potential mates. Perhaps the best reassurance for the person seeking a divorce is the testimony of so many people who have remarried that it is better the second time around.

REFERENCES

Peter Berger and Hansfried Kellner. Marriage and the construction of reality. *Diogenes* 46 (1964): 1–24.

Jessie Bernard. *Remarriage: A study of marriage.* New York: Holt, Rinehart and Winston, 1956.

———. *The future of marriage.* New York: Bantam, 1972.

———. Notes on changing life styles, 1970–1974. *Journal of Marriage and the Family* 37 (1975): 582–593.

Albert Biderman. Social indicators and goals. In Raymond Bauer, ed. *Social indicators*. Cambridge, Mass.: MIT Press, 1966.

Donald Bogue. *The population of the United States*. Glencoe, Ill.: The Free Press, 1949.

Paul Bohannan. *Divorce and after*. New York: Anchor Books, 1971.

Susan Braudy. *Between marriage and divorce*. New York: Morrow, 1975.

Angus Campbell. The American way of mating. *Psychology Today*, May 1975, pp. 37–43.

Hugh Carter and Paul C. Glick. *Marriage and divorce*. Cambridge, Mass.: Harvard University Press, 1970.

John F. Cuber and Peggy B. Harroff. *Sex and the significant Americans*. Baltimore: Penguin, 1968.

Joseph Epstein. *Divorced in America*. Baltimore: Penguin, 1975.

Richard Farson. Why good marriages fail. *McCall's*, October 1971, pp. 110–111, 165–166.

Jules Feiffer. *Little murders*. New York: Random House, 1968.

Paul Glick. A demographer looks at American families. *Journal of Marriage and the Family* 37 (1975): 15–26.

——— and Arthur J. Norton. Perspectives on the recent upturn in divorce and remarriage. *Demography* 10 (1973): 301–314.

William J. Goode. *Women in divorce*. New York: Macmillan, 1956.

———. Marital satisfaction and instability: A cross-cultural class analysis of divorce rates. *International Social Science Journal* 14 (1962): 507–526.

———. *World revolution and family patterns*. New York: Free Press, 1963.

Aidan R. Gough. Divorce without squalor. *The Nation*, January 12, 1970, pp. 17–20.

Gerald Gurin, Joseph Veroff, and Sheila Feld. *America looks at its mental health*. New York: Basic Books, 1960.

Alice M. Hetzel and Marlene Cappetta. *Marriages: Trends and characteristics*. Vital and Health Statistics, series 21. Washington, D.C.: National Center for Health Statistics, 1971.

Reuben Hill. Generic features of families under stress. *Social Casework* 39 (1958): 139–158.

Barbara Hirsch. *Divorce: What a woman needs to know*. Chicago, Ill.: Regnery, 1973.

Morton Hunt. *The natural history of love*. New York: Knopf, 1959.

Institute of Life Insurance. *Youth*. New York: Institute of Life Insurance, 1974.

Paul H. Jacobson. *American marriage and divorce*. New York: Holt, Rinehart and Winston, 1959.

Mel Krantzler. *Creative divorce*. New York: Evans, 1973.

Stanley F. Mazur-Hart and John J. Berman. Changing from fault to no-fault: An interrupted time series analysis. *Journal of Applied Social Psychology* 7 (1977): 300–312.

S. M. Miller. The American lower classes. In Paul H. Glasser and Lois N. Glasser, eds. *Families in crisis*. New York: Harper & Row, 1970.

Thomas Monahan. The changing nature and instability of remarriages. *Eugenics Quarterly* 5 (1958): 73–85.

National Center for Health Statistics. Divorce, child custody and child support, series P-23, no. 84. Washington, D.C.: Government Printing Office, 1979.

Louis Nizer. *My life in court*. Benwood, W. Va.: Pyramid Publications, 1972.

Herbert A. Otto. Has monogamy failed? *Saturday Review*, April 25, 1970, pp. 23 et passim.

Betty Rollin. The American way of marriage: Remarriage. *Look*, September 1971, pp. 62–64.

Heather L. Ross and Isabel V. Sawhill. *Time of transition*. Washington, D.C.: The Urban Institute, 1975.

Mary McDermott Shideler. An amicable divorce. *The Christian Century*, May 5, 1971, pp. 553–555.

Edward Shorter. *The making of the modern family*. New York: Basic Books, 1975.

Statistical Abstract. Washington, D.C.: Government Printing Office, 1974.

Richard J. Udry. *The social context of marriage*. Philadelphia: Lippincott, 1974.

U.S. Department of Health, Education, and Welfare. *Marital status and living arrangements, March 1973*. Current Population Reports, series P-20, no. 255. Washington, D.C.: Government Printing Office, 1973.

Judith S. Wallerstein and Joan B. Kelly. The effects of parental divorce: The adolescent experience. In E. James Anthony and Cyrille Koupernik. *The Child and his family: Children at psychiatric risk*, vol. 3. New York: Wiley, 1974.

Robert S. Weiss. *Marital separation*. New York: Basic Books, 1975.

Leslie Aldridge Westoff. Two-time winners. *The New York Times Magazine*, August 10, 1975, pp. 10–11, 13, 15.

Michael Wheeler. *No-fault divorce*. Boston: Beacon, 1974.

Gerald C. Wright and Dorothy M. Stetson. The impact of no-fault divorce law reform on divorce in American states. *Journal of Marriage and the Family*, 40 (August 1978): 575–580.

FOR FURTHER STUDY

For an up-to-date review of the literature on coping with the death of one's spouse, see Starr Roxanne Hiltz's "Widowhood: A Roleless Role," which appeared in the November/December 1978 issue of the *Marriage and Family Review.*

Hugh Carter and Paul C. Glick's *Marriage and Divorce: A Social and Economic Study* (Cambridge, Mass.: Harvard University Press, 1976) is a basic and well-documented source on the topics discussed in this chapter. For an analysis of more recent developments, see the National Center for Health Statistics report "Divorce and Divorce Rates," published in March 1978 (series 21, no. 29).

Robert Weiss' *Marital Separation* discusses the problems of ending an intimate partnership and making the transition to the single life again (New York: Basic Books, 1975). Two unusually well-informed journalists, Morton and Bernice Hunt, have collaborated to write *The Divorce Experience* (New York: McGraw-Hill, 1977) in which they provide a portrait of separated and divorced Americans.

Michael Wheeler, an attorney who has studied no-fault divorce, presents a well-written discussion in his book *No-Fault Divorce* (Boston: Beacon Press, 1974). For an assessment of the effects of no-fault legislation, see Gerald C. Wright and Dorothy M. Stetson's "The Impact of No-Fault Divorce Law Reform on Divorce in American States," in the August 1978 issue of the *Journal of Marriage and the Family.*

For a more personal perspective on what separation and divorce mean, the reader might want to see Joseph Epstein's *Divorced in America* (Baltimore: Penguin, 1975) or Susan Braudy's *Between Marriage and Divorce* (New York: Morrow, 1975).

VII
Looking Ahead

"The Garden" Sylvia Sleigh

15

Trends and Forecasts—The Future Isn't What It Used to Be

Writing a textbook is very much like assembling a jigsaw puzzle. You start with a pile of thousands of tiny pieces—research reports, descriptive accounts, census data, facts of varying significance and reliability. As you fit these pieces together, certain patterns begin to emerge. It is frustrating to see that certain pieces are missing, that the research studies required to understand a part of the pattern have not been conducted. But of course this is a puzzle that can never be complete. Every year new pieces come in, and all of them have to be put into place so that new trends can be seen developing out of older patterns. In this final chapter, we will look at some of these broader patterns.

Many of the changes and much of the turbulence in marriage and family life today result from four factors that have come up time and again in this book. They are:

1. Gender roles—particularly those of women—are being rapidly redefined.
2. Parenthood has taken on new meanings, and is now less obligatory.
3. The life cycle has been substantially redefined, with new stages added.
4. Many people now approach marriage with new priorities and expectations. Individual fulfillment and personal growth are given a higher priority than they were a generation ago.

A clearer understanding of these factors may allow us to make some tentative forecasts about things to come. But first we should understand that, like the weatherman who makes his forecast by leaning out the window, looking at what's happening, and saying that there will be more of the same, social scientists have very limited powers of prediction. Recognizing and understanding long-range trends can be a guide to the future, but it is just as possible for the social scientist as for the weatherman to be surprised by the unexpected.

Like everyone else, social scientists sometimes make the mistake of throwing up their hands in dismay at changes that seem to foreshadow the disintegration of marriage and family. The generation of sociologists who studied urban society and found it wanting as compared with small-town life illustrates the constant temptation to judge emerging institutions by the standards of the past. Here, for example, is the prediction of one prominent scholar, Pitirim Sorokin, in 1941:

> Divorces and separations will increase until any profound difference between socially sanctioned marriages and illicit sex relationship disappears. . . . The main functions of the family will further decrease until it becomes a mere incidental cohabitation of male and female, while the home will become a mere overnight parking place mainly for sex relationship. (1941, p. 776)

Sorokin was partly right, of course. The popularity of cohabitation provides evidence of his first assertion, and the functions of the family have indeed changed. But few people today would agree that marriage and family could fairly be described as "a mere incidental cohabitation." It was Sorokin's overriding concern for permanence and stability that led to his gloomy prediction; he missed the mark because he did not pay enough attention to new expectations, to the new values of companionship and individual growth, which may be better satisfied by the new forms of marriage and family.

In this chapter, then, we will explore some of the structural changes that marriage and family are likely to undergo in the decades to come, noticing changes in ideals and expectations at the same time. These educated guesses will provide a basis for a discussion of some of the practical suggestions and public policy solutions that have been proposed in response to new marriage and family forms.

FOUR TRENDS

In almost every chapter of this book, we have noticed how rapid—and in many respects, how fundamental—recent changes in marriage and family arrangements have been. These changes illustrate the point that family sociologists have stressed so often: these are highly adaptable institutions that are forced to change as the social environment around them does. It is easy to assume that "the family" is timeless and unchanging, and terribly misleading to do so.

One of the most powerful engines of social change, and one that prompted many of the innovations we have been examining in this book, is technology. Here, for example, are five kinds of changes in marriage and family life caused by technology:

1. The invention of the telephone and the automobile has transformed the courtship process, making it increasingly difficult for parents to monitor their children.
2. The timing of our lives has been changed by medical technologies and nutritional improvements, thus allowing new stages in the life cycle.
3. New building technologies, as well as a rising standard of living, have enabled the construction of houses that provide more privacy. New walls of privacy have changed the meaning of community and encouraged a new type of individualism within the family unit.
4. Industrialization, facilitated by technology, has profoundly affected family life. As the work place shifted to factories, child rearing became more exclusively a woman's specialty, and wage earning a man's.
5. If the technologies that had the greatest impact on marriage and family arrangements in the eighteenth and nineteenth centuries were those that facilitated industrialization, the ones likely to cause the most dramatic changes in the decades to come are the medical and biotechnologies. For example, techniques for detecting birth defects long before a child is born enable women to postpone childbearing more safely than they could before. Another example is that doctors now know how to identify the sex of a fetus soon after conception. If the parents wanted their child to be male, they might decide to abort if the fetus is female. If, in general, parents preferred children to be male, substantially more males than females might be born. Left unregulated, this practice

What's Happening Today

Box 15–1 / The Brave New World of Biotechnology

In his novel *Brave New World,* Aldous Huxley imagined a society of the future in which sex and procreation are entirely separate, where children are mass-produced in state-run "hatcheries" and "conditioning centers." Fortunately, this is still a dim prospect. But to many people, the birth of the world's first "test tube" baby appeared to be a significant step in that direction. In one of the most widely publicized cases in medical history, two English doctors, Dr. Patrick Steptoe and Dr. Robert Edwards, accomplished something that had not been done before: working with a couple who could not bear children because the wife, Mrs. Lesley Brown, had blocked fallopian tubes, they removed a ripe egg from her ovary, fertilized it in a petri dish with sperm from her husband, allowed the ovum to incubate, and then planted the developing embryo in Mrs. Brown's uterus. That experiment led, in July 1978, to the first human birth from an egg that was fertilized in a laboratory.

Rarely has a scientific breakthrough been greeted with such mixed feelings. On the one hand, the potential benefits of this procedure for couples who want children but cannot conceive them are considerable. Using this procedure, doctors can now help women whose fallopian tubes are defective to bear children. Drs. Steptoe and Edwards also anticipate that the same procedure can be used to overcome sterility due to inadequate sperm production. Judging from a poll conducted for *Parent's* magazine by Louis Harris and Associates soon after the Brown's child was born, there is considerable interest in the method, called *in vitro* fertilization. More than 25 percent of the married women polled said they had had trouble in getting pregnant, and 58 percent of the women of childbearing age said they would consider using the method.

On the other hand, many people viewed the birth of the "test tube" baby as a mixed blessing, an ominous step toward the manipulation of basic life processes, and one that raises a whole new set of ethical, legal, and social questions. Some people object to the procedure on religious grounds, insisting that any meddling with the birth process is a violation of the natural order. Others are more concerned about legal and ethical dilemmas: Should such embryo implants be allowed only for married couples? Should parents who use *in vitro* fertilization be offered some of the options that this procedure allows, such as choice of gender? Using this technique, a woman with a healthy uterus but no ovaries might borrow an egg from a donor, just as semen for artificial insemination can be obtained from a donor. But, in such cases, how should the donor be chosen? Which qualities should be sought for the purposes of better breeding, which defects screened out?

Consider the possibilities that arise if this process is carried one step further: A woman who has had her uterus removed (which is not uncommon) but has intact ovaries might

(Box 15–1 continues on page 434)

could lead to a staggering problem for the labor force and the marriage system (Nimkoff, 1962; Etzioni, 1968; Keller and Lindenberg, 1972; Largey, 1973). (See Box 15–1.)

We are assuming, of course, that the trends listed above will continue in the future. It is true that some basic factors—preferences in family size, for example—change dramatically from one decade to the next, but the four we are about to discuss seem well enough established to help us foresee what is likely to happen in marriage and family over the next few decades.

(Box 15–1 continued from page 433)

ask a doctor to have a baby conceived from her eggs and her husband's sperm to retain their genetic features. And then she might arrange for the fertilized egg to be carried in another woman's uterus. What, exactly, would be the legal status of the child? Who would be its real mother? And what would be the consequences if a woman who is fully capable of bearing a child decided—for reasons of vanity or convenience—to pay another woman to do the job of carrying her child nine months? Would this be unreasonable exploitation, or a new option created by the separation of sex and procreation? How would this innovation—which would mean that mothers would contribute no more to the birth of a child than fathers—affect the bond between mother and child and the division of labor between the sexes?

It has been suggested that in the future natural parenthood may become an anachronism. Upon reaching sexual maturity, both males and females might, as a matter of course, deposit sex cells at a special bank. Then they would be sterilized by means of tubal ligation for women and vasectomy for men, in order to enjoy sex without the risk of unwanted conception. Should a couple marry and desire children, they would simply request that the woman's eggs be inseminated with the man's sperm. Then the fetus would develop in an artificial womb that would reduce the incidence of birth defects by maintaining an absolutely safe and consistent environment. Unlike a human mother, the artificial womb would not smoke cigarettes, take harmful drugs, catch German measles, or fall down stairs. The growth of the fetus could be carefully monitored, and it could be immunized against disease before it entered the world. From the point of view of the parents, there would be various advantages: not only would unwanted pregnancies be eliminated, but women would no longer have to endure the discomfort of bearing children, nor the uncertainty of an imperfect fetal environment. This procedure would have the added advantage of allowing the couple to have children whenever they please, regardless of their age. When he wrote *Brave New World* in 1932, Huxley imagined that such artificial wombs might be developed several hundred years in the future; considering recent developments in embryology, it appears that something resembling Huxley's "hatcheries" might be developed in the near future, if anyone wanted to do so.

Throughout history, new technologies—such as the plow, the printing press, the automobile and the television—have drastically altered the external environment and caused dramatic changes in the social structure. The effect of the biotechnologies, which have been developing at such a rapid rate over the past generation, is to alter our internal environment. New technologies of contraception and reproduction, techniques for determining the sex of the fetus and for performing transsexual operations, and breakthroughs that promise a greatly extended life span, all cause us to rethink some of the most basic questions about human nature. Because the new biotechnologies pose some fundamental questions about marriage as well as parenthood, and about the meaning of male and female, their influence on marriage and family life in the coming years will be profound.

Redefining Women's Roles—and Men's

We explored the movement toward greater equality of the sexes in Chapter 8. Now let us consider how a continuation of this trend might affect marriage and the family in the future.

The women's movement is just one recent aspect—although a highly visible and influential one—of a long-term trend toward equality of the sexes. As we noted before, the percentage

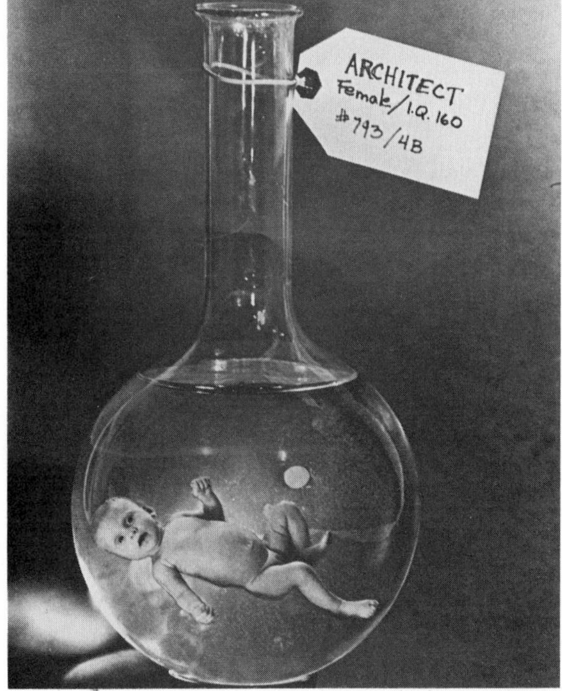

New developments in biotechnology prompt us to rethink some of the most basic questions about human nature.

of women in the labor force started its steady increase long before the women's movement gathered momentum in the 1960s. Participation by married women in the labor force has important consequences. As more women spend much of their adult lives in the labor force, the two sexes no longer live in distinctly different worlds during the work day.

For at least the next generation, the jobs that most women hold will not be equal in status or pay to those of most men. But this inequality will probably not deter many women from entering the labor force. There are several reasons to assume that the percentage of married women who work will continue to increase. First, the jobs that will be most readily available over at least the next decade are in areas traditionally defined as women's work. Then, too, more women will have completed a college degree, making them more likely to enter the labor force. An additional factor is that, as two economists have remarked,

> there will be strong economic pressures on the remaining single-earner families who will find themselves increasingly at a competitive disadvantage in terms of standard of living. It is difficult enough to keep up with the Joneses under normal circumstances, but when both of them are working, it becomes virtually impossible. (Ross and Sawhill, 1975, p. 171)

Women are more nearly men's equals than they were a generation ago not only in education and occupational opportunity, but also in sexual attitudes and behaviors. Readily available contraceptives, more liberal abortion laws, and day-care facilities for children are all steps in the gradual emancipation of women from a lifetime filled with childbearing and rearing. As average family size declines and more couples choose not to have children, it becomes increasingly possible for women to pursue careers as men's equals.

The tensions associated with this shift toward sexual equality can be expected to continue. Many husbands will still want their wives to be interesting companions, and at least part-time wage earners, but will refuse to redefine their own roles and share the tasks of housekeeping and child rearing. So far, most of the change has come in women's attitudes and behaviors, not men's. One of the most basic questions about the future of marriage and family is whether men's roles, too, will be substantially redefined.

Several consequences of greater sex role equality are already evident. One is that women wage earners, being more capable of supporting themselves, are apparently less reluctant than other women to dissolve an unsatisfactory marriage. Thus we might expect the divorce rate to continue at a high level. We might also anticipate some improvement in many wives' lives, as the problems now plaguing the full-time housewife and mother may become less common. And as women invest more of themselves in occupational roles, they may no longer report more marital dissatisfaction than their husbands do.

The shift toward sexual equality causes fundamental changes in many areas of marriage and family life, including expectations of companionship between spouses, communication and conflict patterns, expectations about sexual satisfaction, and decisions about family size and child-rearing responsibilities.

One of the most basic questions about the future of marriage and family is whether men's roles will change as much as women's roles.

Redefining Parenthood

The redefinition of parenthood will also have a wide range of consequences for marriage and the family. As we noted in Chapter 12, the "population problem" for many societies has been to produce enough children to insure the perpetuation of the group; parenthood therefore was an obligation. In such societies, sexual equality existed neither as an ideal nor a practical alternative because women spent most of their adult years bearing and caring for children. In our society, by contrast, childbearing has become a matter of individual choice. It has recently become clear to many people that it is not in our society's interest to encourage everyone to have children. And the increase in the number of voluntarily childless marriages indicates that some couples are deciding that it is also not in their individual interest to have any children.

The family is a social invention whose main purpose traditionally has been to provide a durable vehicle for childbearing and rearing. Both church and state have provided instructions and incentives to make sure that these functions will be performed. Although the policy objectives of the federal government with regard to parenthood have never been clearly spelled out, in most respects they have been pronatalist. Tax deductions for children, for example, and certain forms of public assistance for families, help to offset the costs of child rearing.

With few exceptions, however, legislators in the United States have been wary of intruding more directly into family life. Most governmental policies and programs, such as day-care facilities for children, provide optional services that parents can take advantage of as they please. Whereas the regime in the Soviet Union expresses a very direct interest in and control over the child-rearing process, the United States has no policy that the family should fulfill the larger goals of the society in any specific way.

In contrast to the 1950s, when it was often assumed that the family was an island unto itself, a realm unaffected by public policy, in recent years there has been widespread discussion of the need for a comprehensive and coherent family policy. As we noted in Chapter 1, a Senate subcommittee examined the influence that government policies have on American families and came to the conclusion that new legislative proposals should be accompanied by "family impact statements." If nothing else, such statements might focus more attention on the many ways in which governmental programs and policies in such areas as housing, transportation, taxation, and income maintenance affect family life.

Federal housing policy, for example, which has been formulated with other objectives in mind, has had a far-reaching impact on family life. In the post-World War II period, various programs encouraged the suburbanization of middle-class America. To alleviate an acute housing shortage that had developed by the end of the war, the federal government guaranteed mortgages for suburban homes, but not inner-city housing, and offered certain tax advantages for home ownership; in addition, it encouraged the flight of middle-class families to the suburbs by constructing highway systems that made it easier for commuters to get to their jobs in the cities. In such ways, the government subsidized what many people regarded as a very favorable environment for family life in the suburbs, while at the same time contributing to the deterioration of inner-city areas. As a result of the relatively abundant housing that was available by the 1960s, the average size of households dropped because family members such as young unmarried people and the elderly could find adequate housing for themselves. The housing situation may also have contributed indirectly to the rising divorce rate, because by the mid-1960s it was easier for husbands and wives to find separate residences than it had been before. The government also indirectly encouraged the trend toward age-segregated communities: it is significant that over the past generation many new communities have been designed for specific age groups, as either "retirement communities" or "singles complexes." Although there has been relatively little systematic attention paid to the effects of such age-segregated communities, the spatial separation of family members and relatives has undoubtedly had an impact on the types of assistance they offer to each other and on the bonds among family members (Downs, 1977).

Family life has long been affected by public policy. In the early decades of this century, for example, social reformers who lobbied for compulsory education laws, the creation of new child welfare services, and changes in the juvenile court system, did so in part because they felt the family was deteriorating, and that the new institutions might stand *in loco parentis,* in the place of parents. But in recent years, some of the most influential proposals about new directions in family policy have been based upon a different set of assumptions. When the Carnegie Council on Children completed a five-year study in 1977, it proposed the adoption of a family policy "as comprehensive as the nation's defense policy." But rather than urging the creation of new outside institutions to provide for the needs of children, as so many of the social reformers of the past have done, the Council suggested that the government should help to provide parents with more resources—including jobs, money, time, and influence (Keniston, 1977).

Whether a more coherent family policy will be adopted remains to be seen. But in any case, child care is very likely to become a prominent concern in public policy in the United States, as it already is in many other industrialized nations.

Redefining the Life Cycle

As we noted in our discussion of the single life, the timing of our lives is quite different from that of our grandparents. Formal education lasts longer, the childbearing period is considerably shorter than it was when families were larger, and life expectancy is much longer. The new stages that have been added to the life cycle, a single stage in early adulthood and a considerably expanded retirement stage later on, reflect the fact that for more of our adult years we are free from the responsibilities of child rearing and full-time employment.

One reason why the life cycle is being redefined is that there is no longer an inescapable connection between one's age and certain role responsibilities. The concept of continuing education illustrates this. Formal schooling, once limited to the young, is now being pursued by more and more adults who drop out of the labor force, either to study a subject of personal interest or to train for a new occupation. In the next few years, retraining may be particularly

Just as it is becoming more common to have multiple careers, it is also becoming more common to move from one type of marital arrangement to another at various points in the life cycle.

popular among recent college graduates who, because of a tight labor market, have been forced to take unsatisfying jobs.

Just as formal education is no longer restricted to the young, retirement is no longer restricted to the elderly. There is more support now than there was a few years ago for sabbaticals, temporary periods of retirement for younger workers. It is also more common today for adults to switch jobs or careers. One survey done by the American Management Association found that of 2,821 management-level employees polled, nearly half had either changed or considered changing their occupation during the past five years (American Council of Life Insurance, 1974). Evidently adults have more options than they did before, more potential transition points enabling them to move from one status to another.

People also make more moves from one type of marital arrangement to another. In the past, people spent most of their lives as a member of just two families, first the one they were born into (called the family of orientation), then the one they established at marriage (called the family of procreation). Today it is becoming increasingly common to move not only from one marriage to another but even from one *type* of marital arrangement to another at various points in the life cycle.

Three features of the redefined life cycle with far-reaching implications for marriage and family are: (1) the postponement of first marrage; (2) a longer postparental or "empty-nest" period after the children move out of their parents' home; and (3) an increasing number of potentially stressful transition points for adults as they move from one status or lifestyle to another.

As we noted in Chapter 5, a growing number of people in their twenties are deciding to defer marriage, but for most of them, remaining single is a transitional stage, not a permanent status. Increased life expectancy and preferences for a smaller family have made it possible to defer marriage and childbearing. In several respects, the single status might be regarded as a way of postponing some of the obligations traditionally associated with adulthood. Rather than the rush toward adulthood characteristic of the 1950s, when the average age of first marriage was at an all-time low, young people today have several reasons for postponing marriage. A certain wariness about the idealized happy-ever-after marriage is one of these reasons, and the growing desire of women for independent identities and careers of their own is another. This accelerating trend toward later marriages will probably continue.

Other changes in the life cycle have resulted in a considerably longer postparental or "empty-nest" period for most people. The typical woman who marries at the median age of slightly over twenty-one will have completed her childbearing by age twenty-six. All her children will be in school when she is in her early thirties, and by the time she is in her mid-forties, they will be out of the house. Then she will be left with far more years than her grandmother enjoyed to spend as she pleases. As more married women with children become aware of these facts, they will be more likely to prepare for these extra years by entering continuing education or retraining programs, or by not interrupting their education or employment for long, or at all, even while their children are young.

The growing phenomenon of middle-aged divorce suggests that many couples are separating at about the time their children leave the household. Perhaps they want to find more compatible partners with whom to spend the extended postparental period. In fact, increased life expectancy is a major reason for higher divorce rates. In 1910, marriage "till death do us part" lasted (on the average) for twenty-eight years. By 1970, it lasted more than forty years. A typical married couple today, in other words, spends over twelve more years together than did the average couple around 1910.

The redefined life cycle has also brought a greater number of occupational and marital transitions in the average person's lifetime. Since such transitions are potentially stressful, more professional assistance or some sort of "transition clinics" might be provided to help people absorb the shock and cope with the personal problems associated with them.

New Ideals and Priorities—Marital Instability and Individual Fulfillment

The final "master trend" has an even wider range of implications than the other three. It is one of the most common reasons given for switching careers in middle age and for moving in and out of various marital arrangements. We are referring to the long-term, recently accelerating tendency to value personal growth, happiness, and fulfillment over all else. Today, that alluring and elusive goal called self-realization often takes precedence over the ancient obligations to conform to community standards, to perform socially defined roles, and to stay in one marital relationship whose stability is a matter of considerable importance to many people.

A fundamental reason for changing marriage and family arrangements is that many people now bring new expectations for growth and personal fulfillment to institutions that were designed for very different purposes. As we noted in Chapter 6, the O'Neills' popular book *Open Marriage* explores a relatively new ideal, the growth-oriented marriage, which stresses "*un*-dependent living, individual freedom, flexible roles, mutual trust, and expansion through openness" (1974, p. 62). Judging from surveys, in which thousands of men and women were asked to describe what is most important to them in a good marriage, the O'Neills' book (1972) describes the values held by millions of Americans today (The Roper Organization 1974, p. 43).

Personal growth, happiness, and self-realization are unquestionably important and worthwhile goals. What we need to understand, however, is how the institutions of marriage and family change in an era when these personal aspirations have a virtually unchallenged priority. Throughout this book, whether discussing the single life, the marriage contract, contemporary sexual standards, or attitudes toward childbearing and divorce, we have observed the consequences of this shift toward a society in which there are fewer obligations and greater freedom.

One observation on this trend might help us to anticipate the shape of things to come. Over the past few years, much attention has been devoted to the task of "demythologizing" the unrealistic ideals and expectations that lie behind what the O'Neills refer to as the traditional closed-contract marriage. They note, for example, how unrealistic it is to expect that any one partner will be able to fulfill all of the other's needs. But the new ideal of growth and fulfillment which they articulate—and which many people share—may turn out to be just as unrealistic. As we have seen, marriage in the past was largely an economic arrangement in which each spouse performed certain role responsibilities for the other. Gradually, the personal relationship began to take precedence. More and more emphasis was placed on companionship, mutual affection, and then individual growth. With each step, the satisfactory marriage has become a more elusive and subjective matter.

In a searching examination of his own separation and divorce, Joseph Epstein asks again the question that bedeviled Sigmund Freud half a century ago: "What does woman want?" In trying to answer the question, he sheds some light on the modern problem of personal fulfillment—through work as well as marriage—for men and women.

In the past, Epstein writes,

> Self-fulfillment came through living honorably in one's community, and exploring the terrains of new forms of experience was left to artists and social bohemians. When the sense of community vanished . . . fullfillment was desperately searched for in new forms of experience—sex, drugs, psychoanalysis, revolutionary politics, wherever it seemed likely to be available. . . . With the disappearance of community, something else disappeared as well: The phenomenon of necessity

> in life. By necessity is meant that body of obligations that were once owed to an entity greater than oneself and whose discharge was imperative. The old obligations could be burdensome, and indeed sometimes crushing, but they did provide an anchor of sorts, and so one was not cut loose to search out a new life except by one's own volition. (1974, p. 95)

But today, Epstein believes, a wide range of personal alternatives creates a good deal of confusion, especially for women now looking beyond domestic roles for personal fulfillment. For women in the past, he writes,

> Fulfillment came, or at least was expected to come, in marriage and family and through running and raising families. No longer. The nearly universal search for fulfillment on the part of American women outside their marriages is beyond question the most radical development to confront the institution of marriage in this century. . . . It is now commonly understood, at least among the ever-increasing membership of the American middle class, that a wife is permitted to remain at home until the last of the children is off to school; then she, too, must be off, off beating the bushes to find fulfillment, something that will give meaning to her life. But what will it take to fill her up? . . . In order for work to be fulfilling, according to the gospel of fulfillment, it must be exciting, creative, intellectually stimulating, and bring about more good than harm for society. How many such jobs are there in America, or for that matter in any country? This is precisely the tyranny behind the notion of fulfillment—that it sets the goal of human happiness impossibly high. (1974, pp. 76, 79)

The same thing might be said about the new ideal of the growth-oriented marriage. As described by such writers as Herbert Otto, this is "an exciting union which has as its main purpose the involvement of both partners in the adventure of actualizing each other's potential" (1970, p. 11). But what of the obligations, the constraints, and the sacrifices that are part of *any* enduring commitment? At its worst, this new ideal may cause new dissatisfactions and greater instability by encouraging people to expect too much from marriage.

The future of marriage depends to a considerable extent on the answers to these two questions: What shape will marriage take if it is understood mainly as a vehicle for personal growth? What is the future of commitment and stability in a society where the yardstick of personal fulfillment is used to measure the adequacy of marriage and family arrangements? These are questions we cannot answer yet.

OPTIONS AND ALTERNATIVES IN THE LIFESTYLE SUPERMARKET

It was only a few years ago that Margaret Mead had this to say about marriage in American society:

> Ours is a terribly overmarried society, because we can't think of any other way for anybody to live, except in matrimony, as couples. It's very, very difficult to lead a life unless you're married. So everyone gets married, and unmarried, and remarried. But they're all married to someone most of the time. We have, in a sense, overdepended upon marriage in this country. We've vastly overdone it. (1971, p. 52)

But even as she was writing these words, and certainly in the years since then, society has increasingly recognized and begun to tolerate a wider variety of sexual and marital arrangements. It is no longer true that "we can't think of any other way to live except in matrimony." It is still true, of course—and will undoubtedly continue to be—that most adults live in two-person primary relationships, either as married couples or committed cohabitors. However, the interest in individually tailored contracts reflects a trend in modifying the meaning of marriage.

Among these other ways to live are two increasingly popular alternatives. Later age at marriage and a larger number of one-person households indicate the growing popularity of the single life as one alternative to matrimony, and experiments with plural marriage and new forms of community exemplify another.

Single-Person Households, Single-Parent Families

The first alternative is to live by yourself in order to be free to develop any or all of a variety of intimate relationships, while not making any exclusive commitment. Because of greater sexual freedom outside of marriage, as well as the increasing acceptance of single persons, this is becoming—as we have seen—a more popular choice than ever before.

The deferring of marriage among many young adults in their twenties, and a relatively high divorce rate are two of the reasons for the dramatic rise in the number of single-person households, and it would be very surprising if either of these trends did not continue in the near future.

More and more people in their twenties are willingly staying single for a few years. But for most young never-marrieds (as well as for the middle-aged divorced population) being single is a transitional status. The same is true of most single-parent families, whose numbers increased by about one-third between 1965 and 1975, mainly because of the higher divorce rate.

Thus it seems we can definitely anticipate that more adults will be spending a greater number of years in single-person households or as heads of single-parent families.

New Forms of Community, Connectedness, and Cooperation

Several new kinds of households are being tried as a way of coping with the problems of the single life or the single-parent family. Some single mothers, for example, are forming small collectives to share the burdens of child rearing without a spouse. When two divorced women with five children jointly purchased a three-bedroom house in California, one of them explained, "It certainly doesn't fit my mother's concept of 'family,' but I'm really living now. I felt vulnerable as a single parent, financially and in functional things" (*Newsweek,* March 12, 1973, p. 55). And although both women admit they have had differences over how much authority each has to discipline the other's children, they agree that their present arrangement is better than the separate households they had before. "We have an understanding that we are all in this together," said one of them, "and that we must have a group effort in order to survive" (p. 55).

Another kind of new household has been proposed to answer the problems of another segment of our society: elderly widows. According to writer Victor Kassel, polygynous marriage might be an acceptable alternative for persons over sixty. In view of the considerable surplus in this age category of females over males, a marriage of one man with two or more women could offer some important advantages. First, it obviously would provide companionship for more elderly widows than does our present marriage system. Then, too, the pooled income of at least three people would enable all of them to live more comfortably and to take care of each other's needs. It would also allow the expression of sexual needs that are so often repressed in widowhood because there are no available partners (1970).

Is it probable that many older adults would choose polygyny after sixty? Would this arrangement be practical in an era of more nearly equal sex roles? True, it *is* a radical redefinition of marriage. However, the idea that marital arrangements can be redesigned to meet people's needs is much more widely accepted than it was a few years ago. The elderly have many needs that under present arrangements are either frustrated or denied entirely. Furthermore, because there is a considerably larger gap between the life expectancy of males and females than there was even a few decades ago, the problems of elderly widows will become increasingly prominent. In 1940, the difference in life expectancy of males and females was only 4.3 years; by 1976, with life expectancy

That some retired couples, such as the one shown here, return to the classrooms to continue their education reflects the fact that for more of our adult years, we are free from the responsibilities of child rearing and full-time employment.

for males at 69.0 years and for females at 76.7, the difference was 7.7 years (Siegal, 1979). Thus we might anticipate considerable experimentation among the elderly with new types of relationships and new forms of community.

Among young adults, there will undoubtedly continue to be considerable interest in communal arrangements. (One real estate developer in California who wants to attract young singles currently offers a "communium"—a cross between a commune and a condominium—which allows more shared spaces in kitchen, dining, service, and living areas than most conventional developments.) It is important to remember that communes are alternative forms of community life, not alternatives to marriage. Especially for young people who do not want to pair off into exclusive couple relationships, communes provide a social network that is more stable than a series of short-term intimate relationships. We might even speculate that people will increasingly make long-term commitments involving economic interdependence and personal dedication to the commune, but not involving sexual relationships, which have proved to be an extremely divisive element in many communes.

For the Majority, More of the Same—But with a Difference

For most people, however, the need for intimacy will continue to be met by a much more familiar arrangement, the one-to-one commitment, whether it takes the form of marriage or cohabitation. Again, the popularity of the O'Neills' book *Open Marriage* is revealing. For all the modifications they suggest, their premise is quite traditional.

> The one-to-one relationship, whether it is realized through monogamy or within other forms of marriage, fulfills man's profoundly human needs—those developmental and psychological needs for intimacy, trust, affection, affiliation, and the validation of experience. It need not be permanent, exclusive, or dependent, but the relationship of two people to each other allows a closeness and psychological intimacy that no other kind of relationship offers. (1972, p. 24)

Jessie Bernard, who can hardly be considered a staunch defender of traditional marriage patterns, reaches the same conclusion:

> The future of marriage is as assured as any social form can be, for men and women will continue to want intimacy, they will continue to want to celebrate their mutuality, to experience the mystic unity which once led the church to consider marriage a sacrament. . . . There is hardly any probability such commitments will disappear or that all relationships between men and women will become merely casual or transient. The commitment may not take the form we know today, although that too has a future. (1972, pp. 269–270)

Judging from recent surveys, a fairly traditional conception of marriage is still the overwhelming preference of most adults. Although sex-role expectations have indeed changed, and there is growing feeling among women that the marital vows should be rewritten, deleting the wife's promise to obey her husband, nine out of ten people still choose marriage as the most desirable lifestyle, and sexual fidelity is still important to most adults of both sexes (The Roper Organization, 1974).

The Custom-Designed Marital Contract—A Choice of Commitments

For the great majority of adults over the next few decades, the most significant of the new alternatives is the wider latitude for personal choice in drawing up the marriage contract. This is the main idea behind "open marriage": to allow more room for personal development and separate interests, while at the same time maintaining a long-term commitment.

As suggested in Chapter 6, what we will undoubtedly see is the social recognition of various types and degrees of commitment. They will be judged not by their conformity to traditional norms, but by their adequacy in providing for the needs of both spouses. For example, there will undoubtedly be a greater number of "weekend marriages," especially among dual-career couples who take jobs in different cities and live together only a few days a week (see Box 15–2). Limited-term contracts may also become more common, especially among couples who anticipate changing needs and preferences at various stages in the life cycle. Options such as these, which substantially redefine the marital commitment, will undoubtedly be viewed by some as appalling misuses of individual freedom, and by others as appealing alternatives well suited to personal needs.

In the future, rather than being asked to "Check one: Single _____ , Married _____ " we might be offered a dozen or more alternatives specifying the nature and extent of the commitment that the two spouses have agreed on.

PERSONAL PREFERENCES AND PUBLIC POLICY

Many people today believe that lifestyle preferences should not be regulated by the state, and so far we have discussed them as if they were solely a matter of individual preference. In reality, however, laws are often used to discourage or prohibit some of the alternatives we have been discussing. As we noted in Chapter 6, for example, couples are not free to define the marital contract as they please. In the eyes of the law, the wife is responsible for the per-

What's Happening Today

Box 15–2 / Redefining the Marital Commitment—Weekend Marriages

A small but growing number of people who, though married, live apart for at least several days a week in order to pursue jobs in different cities, illustrates the greater freedom that couples have today to choose the type of commitment they want. This report, on the experience of several couples who have chosen long-distance marriages, illustrates both their appeal and their drawbacks.

Because they say that they have a relationship characterized by love, understanding, and respect for each other's individuality, Yves and Harriet Michel have separated after two children and ten years of marriage. As incongruous as it seems, such qualities were important in the couple's decision to part. For, unlike the traditional marital separation, theirs is not the beginning of the end of marriage. Mrs. Michel has left her husband, her sons, and a comfortable home on the West Side of Manhattan to pursue a career in Washington, more than 200 miles away.

The Michels are members of a growing group of American couples who choose to live apart, usually to pursue independent careers, but to maintain a marriage. The decision to separate often is made at the beginning of the peak of a person's career, when he or she is trying to pursue the best opportunities or rewards. The practice, sometimes called "commuter," "weekend," or "long-distance" marriage, is becoming more common as women attain higher status in the labor market and are offered positions that they often consider too attractive to refuse. It underscores the changing pattern of American family life, and the greater acceptability of divergent lifestyles.

Like many partners in long-distance marriages, Jan Hodgson, who now works in Kansas City, 150 miles from Jefferson City, Mo., where her husband is employed as director of the Missouri Department of Social Services, said the decision to live apart was a difficult one. "There's a lot more sacrifice involved than you'd ever imagine," she said. "It's not a relationship. It's a weekend romance. It's not a marriage." But despite the drawbacks, the separation was necessary to career fulfillment for both her and her husband, she said. "I'm the kind of person—my husband is too—who needs to be challenged, stimulated, and interested in my daily work. Even though I was happy being with him, I was unhappy in my work, and that worried him."

(Box 15–2 continues on page 446)

formance of certain tasks such as housekeeping and child care; the husband is responsible for providing support. In certain cases, personal contracts that reverse these assumptions have not been honored by the courts. This does not, of course, prevent couples from defining role responsibilities within marriage according to personal preferences. But when cases involving marriage and family arrangements end up in the courts, judges often rule in favor of a traditionally defined unit.

The tendency to preserve and protect the traditional family unit is expressed most clearly in cases involving individuals who have chosen such alternatives as cohabitation, homosexual marriages, or communes, none of which is legally recognized. Most people who choose these alternatives do so in the privacy of their

(Box 15–2 continued from page 445)

The degree of planning for such a separation varies widely, with some couples defining values, rights, and responsibilities and others simply relying on the strength of their relationship to weather dangers. The presence of children, which is a rarity among these couples, usually complicates matters. Couples with children do much more planning before they separate. But despite such careful planning, these relationships are sometimes subject to stress, anxiety, loneliness, and guilt. Some couples say they continually have to justify their arrangements to family and friends. Sometimes the couples themselves are uncomfortable about living apart and, in an attempt to rationalize it, stress that it is only temporary.

Nancy Schirm could not adjust. She gave up a job at a television station in Phoenix, where her family lives, for one in hospital public relations in Newport Beach, California. She went to Phoenix a few times a month to visit her husband, David, who manages a furniture store, and her five-year-old daughter, Tiffany. She loved her new job, worked ten to twelve hours a day and was successful. But after a year, she gave it up. The concentrated weekends, cramming seven days into two, were not enough. "I was slowly, but surely, being cut out of the family group and being replaced by a number of people," she said. "When I was home on weekends, Tiffany would no longer say 'Mommy, would you fix my hair,' but 'Daddy's going to fix my hair' . . ."

Terry Samuelson, thirty-two, a lawyer in Houston, was divorced in July from George Stransky, thirty-three, an obstetrician in Anchorage. When they decided to live apart, they discussed—as many couples do—whether they would date other people. "My husband was willing to allow me to have new sexual experiences," Miss Samuelson said. "He was liberated or wide open or thought it was sort of neat to see what would happen. . . . I wasn't so willing to have him fool around with other women." It took a while, but Miss Samuelson began seeing other men. At first, she said, she felt married. But slowly that changed. "I think we were apart too long," she said. "Too many little things, good and bad, happened where we couldn't applaud the other or support them. All of a sudden, we were two people who didn't even know each other, trying to be together. But I still believe marriage can work out and be a lifelong thing, it you're careful."

The Michels of New York and Washington plan to be careful. They are steeling themselves for expected and unexpected problems. They say they are neither frightened nor intimidated by the challenge.

Source: Excerpted from an article by Sheila Rule, *The New York Times,* October 31, 1977, p. 33. Reprinted with permission.

own homes. They are undeterred by the fact that the laws do not recognize them as valid marriage and family units. But without the sanction of the law, cohabitors or people living in homosexual marriages or communes are denied the privileges extended to married couples. For example, they often cannot qualify for group medical insurance or claim Social Security survivor's benefits or benefits from Workmen's Compensation. Also, people who choose alternative family styles may face serious problems with inheritances and with custody of children (if, for example, parents separate, or one of them dies). To mention one other example, the law recognizes the right of legally married spouses to refuse to testify against each other in criminal cases, whereas the courts can force cohabiting couples to do so (Weisberg, 1975).

The legal problems faced by people who choose to form communes are illustrated by a

1974 Supreme Court decision. The legal weapon most frequently used against communes is the restrictive zoning ordinance, which excludes multiadult households from areas specifically zoned for single-family dwellings. Although it is discriminatory to deny housing on the basis of race, religion, or nationality, such zoning ordinances can be used to exclude communal groups that consist of several unrelated adults. In 1972, in the village of Belle Terre, New York, six university students rented a house. Village residents maintained that this action violated a local ordinance stipulating that no more than two unrelated adults may share the same house. When the students were informed of the violation, they brought suit to have the ordinance declared unconstitutional. Two years later, in 1974, the Supreme Court ruled that such zoning ordinances are constitutional, a legitimate exercise of the rights of local citizens. As one writer notes, "Although this decision may constitute a step forward in terms of legal recognition of unmarried couples—'two unrelated persons living together'—it appears to be a serious legal setback for the communal family" (Weisberg, 1975, p. 556). But five years after that court ruling, the New Jersey Supreme Court—indicating that it found Federal opinion in the Belle Terre decision "to be both unpersuasive and inconsistent"—overturned the "unrelated persons" law. The majority opinion was that regulations based on legal or biological relationships "do not reflect the real world," and are in violation of Constitutional guarantees of due process and personal right to privacy (*New York Times,* July 31, 1979, p. 1).

A new interest in family law has been prompted by the awareness of the wide range of marriage and family arrangements actually in existence, whereas the laws recognize and serve to protect only one model: the legally constituted heterosexual marriage. Courts have seen a "compelling interest" for the state to uphold this kind of family, arguing that no other structure can adequately perform its functions. Consequently, the courts have often looked on alternative family units as unstable and undesirable, and thus not in the public interest. For example, in the opinion set down by a New Jersey district court judge, who denied welfare services to illegitimate children:

> Marriage is a permanent or at least semipermanent institution. The State has reinforced it with a great deal of protection in its statutory and case laws. Its whole domestic relations law is designed to protect marriage and family. . . . The State has determined that it only wants to subsidize what it considers to be legitimate families, ones where the likelihood is greater for the instillment of proper social norms. It is certainly both a proper and a compelling State interest to refuse to subsidize a living unit which may lead to the state of anomie and which violates its laws against fornication and adultery (in Weisberg, 1975, p. 554).

The standing law on marriage and the family might well be regarded as an example of what sociologist William Ogburn called cultural lag. There are many discrepancies between the assumptions and practices upheld by the law and the beliefs people actually hold and practice today. Recent public opinion surveys show considerable willingness to allow a wide range of marriage and family alternatives for people with different preferences and needs. Thus, we might anticipate that over the next few decades the wide diversity of arrangements that already exist will find increasing support in public policy. In the meantime, however, people who choose cohabitation or communal living should know something about the legal implications—and possible complications—of their choice.

Easing the Transitions, Searching for Solutions

As we make the transition to a society in which a considerable variety of marriage and family forms is acknowledged and encouraged, more than laws have to be changed. It has been proposed, for example, that the work week be restructured to allow more flexible employment, particularly for the benefit of single-parent and dual-career families. Another proposal is to change the physical environment by redesigning housing and communities to ease some of the problems caused in part by currently prevalent designs. Yet another proposal is to provide new counseling services to meet new needs.

"Flex-Time" Jobs College graduates, in interviews with prospective employers, might well ask not just about salary and fringe benefits, but also about whether the employer offers "flex-time." It is estimated that about one out of every eight American corporations has already adopted this plan, which allows employees to begin and end their workday at a time of their choice—within certain limits, of course (*The New York Times,* November 9, 1977, p. 32). If you got a job with the Scott Paper Company in Philadelphia, for example, you might arrive for work any time between 8 and 10 A.M., have lunch between noon and 2 P.M., and leave between 4 and 6 P.M., provided that you put in the required number of hours per day. This may not sound like much of a change from the traditional 9-to-5 job, but it does allow employees more freedom to arrange their daily activities as they choose. It might, for example, allow parents to share the tasks of child rearing more equally, or it might provide more leisure time together for the entire family.

Other companies are making more radical modifications of the work week. The Honeywell Corporation now offers a school shift that allows women to tailor their work week to the schedules of their school-age children. The Lipton Company has gone even further, allowing a three-day work week with staggered hours. These variations on the conventional 9-to-5, 35-hour-a-week work routine allow more flexibility in the performance of marital roles and family responsibilities.

A report from Catalyst, a nonprofit organization that helps to expand career opportunities for college-educated women, describes three other plans for restructuring jobs. The first plan, called pairing, allows two women to share one full-time job. Both women have equal responsibility, but each works only half time. The second plan is for a split-location job that permits an employee to work both at home and at the office as the nature of the work dictates, thus allowing more freedom to share household and child-rearing responsibilities. The third plan, called the split-level job, could apply to jobs that require two different levels of training or skills. Instead of one person doing both kinds of tasks full time, the job might be filled by two employees, each working half time at different skill and pay levels (Catalyst, 1973).

Such newly structured jobs could provide a solution for mothers who have been forced to choose between not working at all, taking a low-prestige, low-paying, part-time job, or a full-time, fixed-hour job that makes it difficult to perform family roles. Flexible-hour employment is one way business establishments can respond to the needs of working mothers and dual-career couples who want to share household and child care responsibilities.

Housing and Community Design Housing developments reflect their designers' assumptions about the social needs of the people who will live in them. Architects help to shape behavior every time they make a major design decision. Environments can bring people together or keep them apart, make living easy or stressful. There has been a gradual recognition over the past few years among architects that, in collaboration with social scientists, they might produce buildings that are better suited to their inhabitants' needs.

Most of the housing units available today are either small apartments designed for single-person households—the young, not-yet-married person or the elderly widow or widower—or single-family dwellings designed for the nuclear family with children. There is very little housing designed to meet the needs of people living in any other arrangement. To overcome this shortage, sociologists Betty Cogswell and Marvin Sussman suggest the construction of

> model towns or housing estates which include physical structures to match the characteristics of various family forms. Living accommodations would reflect their needs, desires, and aspirations. The environment would include single apartment-type units; units for extended families with connecting doors which could be opened or closed; one-family homes; dormitories for young people; efficiency units for individuals or small families; and larger units for commune-type families. (1972, p. 511)

Not even the nuclear family is always well served by present designs. Jessie Bernard calls attention to the problems created for young mothers in suburban communities:

> While many young women are looking for ways to live more cooperatively, there is little provision for such a lifestyle in suburbia. Both privacy and community recreation are highlighted, but architectural designs that facilitate cooperation are notable by their absence. Young women themselves cannot jump this hurdle. As Buckminster Fuller reminds us, we have to provide the environment if we wish to change the behavior of people. Not until the architects have designed the setting that makes it possible for families to cooperate while at the same time retaining their coveted privacy will young women find ways to practice the lifestyle so many of them now crave. (1975, p. 235)

New Counseling Services A high divorce rate, a large number of single-parent families, rapidly changing sex-role expectations, more frequent transitions from one type of living arrangement to another—any of these situations can cause stress severe enough to require the help of a well-trained counselor. The counselor's task in such a case, however, is quite different from simply promoting marital adjustment. One therapist, Sidney Jourard, has discussed the counselor's role in a society that offers so many intimate alternatives. "As a psychotherapist," he writes,

> I have often been called upon to do "marriage counseling." And I have been struck by the incredible lack of artistry and creativity in marriage partners. Either person may be imaginative in making money or decorating a house, but when it comes to altering the design of their relationship, it is as if both imaginations had burnt out. For years, spouses go to sleep night after night, with their relationship patterned one way, a way that perhaps satisfies neither—too close, too distant, boring or suffocating. . . . It is both possible and difficult to reinvent a relationship. In America, the most affluent nation that has ever existed, reasons for enforcing conformity are diminishing. Indeed, not to capitalize on our release from economic necessity, not to "play" creatively with such forms as marriage, family life, schooling, and leisure pursuits is a kind of madness, a dread of and escape from freedom and the terror it engenders. Forms of family life that were relevant in rural frontier days or in earlier urban life, that produced a mighty industrial nation and immense wealth, are obsolete today. There exists, in fact, a great diversity of man-woman, parent-child relationships. . . . Both the myriad ways of living married that are secretly being explored by consenting adults in this society, and the designs that have existed since time immemorial in other cultures, represent a storehouse of tested possibilities available to those who would experiment with marriage. Anything that has been tried in any time and place represents a mode for exploration by men and women who dare to try some new design when the conventional pattern has died for them. Not to legitimize such experimentation and exploration is to make life unlivable for an increasing proportion of the population. (1970, pp. 44–45)

Then, turning specifically to the role that a new sort of counselor might perform, Jourard says,

> We could even envision a new profession, that of "marriage inventor" who would develop and catalogue new ways for men and women to cohabit and raise children, so that no one would be at a loss for new forms to try when the old forms have died. It is curious to me that college courses and textbooks on marriage all turn out to be propaganda for the prevailing cliché of the middle-class marriage. . . . There is an implication here for

therapists who engage in marriage and divorce counseling. Is the therapist committed to the social *status quo,* or to a more pluralistic society? If to the latter, his role is akin to that of a guru, or existential guide. He will encourage people who find themselves in marital impasses to explore new ways; he will be able to help his client invent a new way of being married to someone, rather than persuade him to perpetuate the conventional marriage form with his present partner in despair, or with a new partner in unfounded hope. (p. 46)

Clearly, Jourard's vision of a marriage inventor radically redefines the marriage counselor's role. In a society where marriage is increasingly regarded as a vehicle for personal growth, such marriage inventors might well perform an essential service.

Conclusions

It is unlikely that any of the new alternatives we have examined in this book will replace the traditional forms as the prevalent modes in marriage and family life. But the mere presence of these alternatives is highly significant, for new freedoms create new choices. "No one should be led to ignore the increasing hazards that marriage will encounter," writes Jessie Bernard.

> Options make great demands. . . . Offer people marital options and they are exposed to conflict. No matter which option they choose, they wonder if they should have made a different choice. Some will run from one to another, in the hope that some other kind of relationship will be better. That possibility is a genuine hazard. (1973, p. 303)

At the close of his book *World Revolution and Family Patterns* (1963), William Goode steps back from his detailed description of recent changes in family life and asks how we might evaluate the consequences.

> Some see them as the advent of a new and fruitful era, a period in which men and women will find a richer personal life, in which they will have a greater range of choices in their own emotional fulfillment. Others will view all these processes with suspicion, skepticism, or dismay. (p. 379)

Some of the options create problems because they are new forms of behavior, untested; we are unprepared for them, says Goode.

> Under the old system, everyone at least knew what his obligations were, and learned to carry them out over many years. Now, increasingly, each person must work out an individual system of role relationships—some of them perhaps even more burdensome than the older ones would have been, but in any event somewhat difficult to adjust to, simply because there has been little prior socialization and experience that might fit them to assume those burdens easily and willingly. (p. 380)

Are these new arrangements likely to allow greater happiness or personal adjustment? Probably not, says Goode. But ultimately, as he admits, it is an unanswerable question.

> I do not believe we shall ever know how to balance the ecstasy and agony of the family systems now coming into being against that of older systems. I suspect that, on the average, the older family patterns did yield greater contentment to the people who lived out their lives under them, but any careful reading of the folklore and literature of those cultures reveals countless instances of extreme pain, and happiness as well. (p. 380)

"And yet," Goode writes in conclusion,

> I welcome the great changes now taking place. I see in them the hope of greater freedom . . . the unleashing of personal potentials, the right to love, to equality within the family, to the establishment of a new marriage where the old has failed. I see the world revolution in family patterns as a part of a still more important revolution that is sweeping the world in our time, the aspiration on the part of billions of people to have the right for the first time to *choose* for themselves. (p. 380)

And so we end where we began, with the problem of choosing in an age of alternatives.

The ancient Chinese had a curse that expresses with delicious irony the situation we all face today: "May you be born in interesting times." This is one thing we can say with certainty about the decades to come. They will indeed be "interesting times."

REFERENCES

American Council of Life Insurance. *The life cycle.* Trend Analysis Program, Report no. 8. New York, 1974, pp. 14–15.

Jessie Bernard. *The future of marriage.* New York: Bantam, 1972.

———. *The future of motherhood.* Baltimore: Penguin, 1975.

The broken family—Divorce U.S. style. *Newsweek,* March 12, 1973, pp. 47–57.

Catalyst. *Flexible work schedules.* New York: Catalyst, 1973.

Betty E. Cogswell and Marvin B. Sussman. Changing family and marriage forms: Complications for human service systems. *The Family Coordinator* 21(1972): 505–516.

Anthony Downs. The impact of housing policies on family life in the United States since World War II. *Daedalus,* Spring 1977, pp. 163–180.

Joseph Epstein. *Divorced in America.* Baltimore: Penguin, 1974.

Amitai Etzioni. Sex control, science, and society. *Science,* September 13, 1968, p. 1107.

William J. Goode. *World revolution and family patterns.* New York: Free Press, 1963.

Sidney M. Jourard. Reinventing marriage: The perspective of a psychologist. In Herbert A. Otto, ed. *The family in search of a future.* New York: Appleton Century Crofts, 1970.

Victor Kassel. Polygamy after sixty. In Herbert A. Otto, ed. *The family in search of a future.* New York; Appleton Century Crofts, 1970.

Suzanne Keller and Siegwart Lindenberg. When parents can choose—Which sex will it be? *The Futurist,* October 1972.

Kenneth Keniston and the Carnegie Council on Children. *All Our Children.* New York: Harcourt, Brace, Jovanovich, 1977.

Gale Largey. Sex control and society. *Social Problems* 20(1973): 310–318

Margaret Mead. Future family. *Transaction,* September 1971, pp. 50–53.

Meyer F. Nimkoff. Biological discoveries and the future of the family. *Social Forces* 41(1962): 121–127.

Nena O'Neill and George O'Neill. *Open marriage.* New York: Evans, 1972.

———. Open marriage: The conceptual framework. In James R. Smith and Lynn G. Smith, eds. *Beyond monogamy.* Baltimore: Johns Hopkins University Press, 1974.

Herbert Otto. The new marriage: Marriage as a framework for developing personal potential. In Herbert Otto, ed. *The family in search of a future.* New York: Appleton Century Crofts, 1970.

The Roper Organization. *The Virginia Slims American women's opinion poll.* New York: The Roper Organization, 1974.

Heather L. Ross and V. Sawhill. *Time of transition.* Washington, D.C.: The Urban Institute, 1975.

Jacob S. Siegel. Prospective trends in the size and structure of the elderly population. *Current Population Reports,* series P-23, no. 78. Washington, D.C.: U.S. Department of Commerce, Bureau of the Census, 1979.

Pitirim Sorokin. *Social and cultural dynamics,* vol. 4. New York: Harper, 1941.

D. Kelly Weisberg. Alternative family structures and the law. *The Family Coordinator,* October 1975, pp. 549–559.

"Dollar Bills, 1962" Andy Warhol

APPENDIX Managing the Financial Partnership—Dollars and Sense

If love provides much of life's poetry, money provides most of its prose. In marriage, which is a business partnership, money is the most common source of problems. When two investigators questioned more than 900 wives in the Detroit area about disagreements with their husbands, they found that money, not children, in-laws, or sex, was at the top of the "trouble" list (Blood and Wolfe, 1960, p. 241).

But why is money so frequently a source of trouble? Morton Hunt, who has been writing about marriage for years, suggests that money is not so much the *cause* as it is a *symbol* of other problems. "There are unmistakable similarities in the roles both sex and money play in marriage," Hunt notes (1970, p. 38). Like sex, money can be used to symbolize a great variety of feelings. Husbands withhold it to express anger. Wives go on spending binges when they feel neglected. Gifts are a way of expressing affection. Spouses who feel trapped in marriage sometimes save up a secret nest egg as an expression of their need for independence.

There are two other respects in which money and sex might be compared: both are surrounded by secrecy and taboos, and just as Victorian ladies were supposed to have no interest in sex, or knowledge of it, women are often ignorant about personal finance. In the past, most women assumed their husbands would take care of such matters for them. Today, ignorance about money management is a luxury no one can really afford.

Even women who never go through a divorce can anticipate spending ten to fifteen years of their adult lives without a husband to depend on. A few of those years might be spent as a young, not-yet-married single, but most of them will be spent as an elderly widow. The average American wife is younger than her husband and can expect to outlive him by seven years. Thus, long-range plans for financial security in marriage will ultimately affect the wife more than the husband—which is one reason why women no less than men should be well informed about financial management.

"There is nothing so degrading as the constant anxiety about one's means of livelihood," wrote novelist Somerset Maugham. "Money is like a sixth sense without which you cannot make complete use of the other five." What should you know about marital finances in order to acquire that sixth sense? After a brief discussion about the meaning of money, this appendix turns to the practical matter of designing a family budget. Every dollar spent is a decision made. A carefully constructed budget is one way to make sure that your spending decisions express not just your immediate preferences but also your long-term goals.

Then we will examine what will probably be your largest single expense—taxes. While everyone is legally obligated to pay taxes, many people are unaware that they are actually overpaying taxes because they are ignorant of certain allowable deductions.

Another area in financial management we will explore is the use of credit. Depending on how and when you use it, and what credit sources you draw upon, it can be either a flexible tool in financial management or a dangerous and expensive trap.

In the final sections of this appendix, we will look at two elements in any long-range financial plan, insurance programs that serve as financial "shock absorbers" and saving and investment plans that allow families to work toward long-term financial security.

This discussion is unique in that it is based on the information and advice of financial analysts rather than social science researchers, but like the other chapters in this book it describes alternative ways of acting.

THE MEANING OF MONEY

Money is never simply a matter of dollars and cents. It is obviously a means of acquiring essentials—food, shelter, clothing, transportation—as well as the things and experiences that make life more enjoyable. But it is far more than that, too.

Ours is a society in which the traditional symbols of one's status in the community—family name, for example—are no longer as important as they were. In a highly mobile society, money provides portable status. If, as we are so often reminded, you cannot buy happiness with it, money can purchase such visible symbols of success as a home in an attractive neighborhood or an expensive car. Money does bring power and esteem. In this society, one's earning power is often used as a yardstick of one's personal worth. It is almost inevitable that, for many people, having money is synonymous with self-respect.

The amount of money people earn and the way they spend it are also seen as measures of competence and intelligence. This view is reflected in such common refrains as "If you're so smart, why aren't you rich?"

Money becomes an even more complicated matter in marriage. It is a crucial element in maintaining sex-role expectations, for in most marriages the husband's primary responsibility is to earn the family income and the wife's is to spend much of it. In many marriages the man still sees his role as the manager of family funds: since he makes the money, he feels he has the right to say how it will be allocated. Because there is no widely accepted standard that determines the percentage of family income that the wife can spend as she pleases, conflicts often arise over the power of the purse strings. But in many marriages, money is not the real issue in such conflicts. Rather, the issue is male dominance.

Quarrels about money are often an expression of something else, too—a conflict in goals and lifestyles. For example, a wife might disagree with her husband because she feels they are not saving enough money. Her main goal is to buy a house, to settle down and gain a sense of permanence. But her husband has a different set of values: he prefers to spend money as quickly as he earns it, to take expensive vacations and buy designer clothes.

Each spouse brings to marriage a highly individual sense of what money means. A woman who felt that her parents scrimped on her wardrobe as a child might become extravagant with clothes as an adult. Similarly, a man whose mother bought fancy cuts of meat and gourmet foods might not understand the intentions of a wife who thinks she is being thrifty and creative with her repertoire of a hundred ways to fix hamburger.

Of course, the lifestyle aspirations of young married couples do not necessarily correspond to their earning power. It is important to determine not just short-term preferences but long-term goals. For some people, merely to sustain the lifestyle of their parents is sufficient. But even this seemingly realistic goal may pose considerable problems, for many young people today grew up in a period of economic boom; their parents benefited from a rapidly rising standard of living. However, in recent years the national economy has been characterized by recession, inflation, and a generally tight labor market.

If money is often a symbol of other things, it can also be a weapon used to express marital hostilities and differences. In fact, most couples find it easier to quarrel about money management than to talk about the emotional dissatisfactions that lie behind certain spending decisions. A wife who feels neglected, for example, might seek attention by deliberately, if unconsciously, misusing family funds. A husband who feels dominated by his wife might fight back by indulging in expensive hobbies or gambling.

Money, then, symbolizes acceptance, power, lifestyle preferences, even self-esteem. Thus, if money is the most common source of marital disagreement, it is not necessarily a result of ignorance about money management—though sound advice and information can help in managing the financial partnership of marriage. In the next few pages we will examine one such source of information—the family budget.

THE FAMILY BUDGET—PREFERENCES AND PRIORITIES

When two people get married and become financially interdependent, their spending patterns are radically altered. Before, the woman might have been quite impressed by the man's willingness to spend money on their entertainment, but once married and apprised of the family income, she may consider the same expenditures terribly wasteful.

While dating, a couple spends most of the time they have together enjoying some entertainment or recreation, instead of preparing for financial interdependence or the practical concerns of running a household together. In fact, the man, trying to convince the woman that he is worthy of her love, may not think it will help his cause to be completely honest with her about his financial situation.

Then, to make matters worse, the newly married couple is under considerable pressure to overspend. Advertisers play on their anxieties and lure them into expensive purchases with the promise of easy credit, which often turns out to be terribly expensive. Especially for young people who have just married and do not want to deny each other anything, it can be difficult to resist making purchases.

Short-Term Needs, Long-Term Goals

Before they marry, many single people indulge themselves. Long-term financial planning does not seem necessary. Money is viewed mainly as a source of pleasure and enjoyment in the present—something to use for clothes, cars, entertainment, vacations.

Marriage means redefining goals and priorities, particularly for young couples with children. Concerned now with long-term objectives, they make savings, investment plans, and insurance important items in their budget.

The transition from short-term pleasures to long-term goals is typically a difficult one for a young couple. Sometimes the very expenditures they most enjoyed before marriage now have to be deferred to meet their long-term objectives, such as the purchase of a house.

All of the important decisions about the financial partnership depend on carefully defined goals. How important is it to have an expensive house or a vacation retreat? Will both spouses

A family with two incomes needs to protect both.

It used to be that most families had one breadwinner. The husband. The father. And most people thought that only he needed life insurance protection.

No more. Today, almost everybody recognizes that the death of the wife and mother is cause for more than grief. If she is a working wife, the loss of her income can prove a crippling jolt to a family heavily dependent on it. And whether she works inside the home or out, someone must care for the children—and that may be a major, continuing expense.

The fact is, almost every man and woman should have life insurance. Talk to your New York Life Agent about your family's needs—soon.

New York Life. For all of your life. NEW YORK LIFE

New York Life Insurance Company, 51 Madison Avenue, New York, New York 10010. Life, Group and Health Insurance, Annuities, Pension Plans.

work, or will one retire at least temporarily to pursue interests or hobbies that do not generate income? Do both agree whether or not to have children, and about how to allocate responsibility for meeting such expenses as the children's education? Just as every expenditure is a decision, every major decision implies a commitment to pay for it. For couples in every income bracket, the most basic financial fact is this: there is never enough money to meet every need or preference. Therefore, pursuing any goal means deferring certain others.

Thus, financial planning begins when the couple defines their necessities and their luxuries, what they *have* to have and what they *want* to have. It is often true that what one spouse regards as a luxury the other defines as a necessity. This is one reason why spouses have to be involved in family financial planning. If the family budget is not to become a constant source of irritation and arguments, the needs and desires of every member of the family must be recognized. Even for those on the most modest budget, there are many different ways to spend family money. Like a fingerprint, each family's budget is a highly individual thing, different in many ways from the budget of any other family.

Another reason for designing a budget is to identify the spending leaks that exist for most couples. Leaks are the unintended spending decisions that account for a substantial percentage of the family expenditures. Eating dinner out several times a week, for example, can become an expensive habit. By adding up the unanticipated expenses that do not really offer long-term satisfactions, couples often see how they might more efficiently meet important long-term goals (see Box 1).

Items in the Family Budget

A budget is a basic tool in money management. It helps couples to see how family income is actually spent, so they can work realistically toward their goals. It is helpful in deciding what expenses might be reduced in order to save money for more important things. For couples who have trouble living within their means, a well-designed budget can help to avert financial disaster. If properly designed, a budget allocates enough money for the necessities of food, clothing, and shelter. It anticipates certain crises such as medical problems, allows the family to enjoy vacations together, and sets some money aside for the future.

Since no two families, even those at the same income level, allocate money in the same proportions, budgeting cannot consist of applying a predetermined percentage for each category of a family's expenditures. Budgeting begins with the dull but important job of record keeping. Using a checklist like the one in Box 1, family members keep track of their actual expenditures for about two months. Careful records of how money is spent generally demonstrate at least two things: first, what the actual spending priorities are, and second, what everyone spends is, in fact, more than he or she is aware of. The cost of an evening for two at the movies includes not just the $5.00 you spend on tickets, but more than twice that much when you include the cost of transportation, the snack you buy at the theater, the coffee or drinks afterward, the babysitting fees. Keeping careful records of actual expenses for a month or two will probably help to construct a more realistic budget and to identify the spending leaks.

The second step in budgeting is to list anticipated income on a monthly basis. For the purposes of budgeting, you are interested only in spendable income, so deduct taxes and contributions toward Social Security and insurance plans. Include salary, interest from savings, tax refunds, and other income you are sure to have. If you do this for a whole year in advance, remember to anticipate those months when you will have extra income from seasonal bonuses, or when investments or savings certificates mature. You are inviting problems if your budget is based on future income that is uncertain.

One significant change in the financial partnership that marriage implies is that so many of today's couples consist of two wage earners.

Involvement Exercises

Box 1 / Designing a Family Budget—A Checklist

A budget is a basic tool in financial management. It helps you to keep track of the monthly cash flow, to spot leaks in your expenditures, and to see whether your expenses are realistic for your income.

MONTHLY INCOME For purposes of budgeting, list only *spendable* income. Remember to deduct taxes, Social Security payments, and insurance premiums.

Source	*Amount*
______________________________	______________________________
______________________________	______________________________
______________________________	______________________________
______________________________	______________________________

MONTHLY TOTAL $____________

FIXED EXPENSES Use receipts and canceled checks, wherever possible, to recall the amount spent for each of these items.

Housing Monthly rental or mortgage payment. ____________

Utilities

Gas ____________

Electric ____________

Telephone ____________

Food This figure should include all food consumed by the family, that prepared at home, as well as food eaten out. Remember to include snacks and coffee breaks, taxes, and tips. ____________

Household operations This category includes small items that may be hard to anticipate, even though they are regular expenditures. For example: soap, laundry and cleaning supplies, stamps and stationery. ____________

Personal care Barber and beauty care services, cosmetics, toilet articles, and medicine cabinet supplies. ____________

Transportation Include costs of public transportation as well as automobile maintenance, depreciation, registration, repairs, insurance, as well as gas, oil, and lubrication. ______

Insurance If insurance premiums must be paid every few months, include the average monthly cost. ______

Medical care Remember to include fees for professional services, drugstore supplies, and such items as eyeglasses. ______

Debt repayment Include monthly repayments for loans, installment purchases, etc. ______

Education Tuition, textbooks, supplies. ______

Additional fixed expenses The budget of every family includes certain items that are individual, unlike the expenses of other families. First indicate what those expenses are, and then list the average monthly expense.

______ ______

______ ______

MONTHLY TOTAL FOR FIXED EXPENSES $ ______

SPENDABLE INCOME MINUS FIXED EXPENSES = AMOUNT AVAILABLE FOR DISCRETIONARY EXPENSES $ ______

DISCRETIONARY EXPENSES These variable expenses are harder to estimate than the fixed ones. Make sure you allow enough in each category to avoid feeling tyrannized by your budget.

Personal allowance Pocket money. ______

Recreation and entertainment Be sure to include entertaining at home as well as the expenses of going out. Include family outings as well as money for vacations. ______

Clothing Remember to add in the costs of laundry and dry cleaning. ______

Replacement of family possessions Family possessions such as furniture, appliances, and linens deteriorate and must be repaired or replaced. Figure out an approximate figure for the depreciation of those household possessions. ______

Periodic expenses Certain expenditures, such as holiday shopping, need to be anticipated. ______

Odds and ends These miscellaneous expenditures—pets, smoking, newspapers, magazines, charity contributions, and union dues—add up and should be accounted for. ______

Savings ______

Investments ______

MONTHLY TOTAL FOR DISCRETIONARY EXPENSES $ ______

The next step is to list your fixed expenses, the ones you are already committed to, such as rent or mortgage payments, utilities, and transportation costs. These fixed expenses are the result of past choices.

It is a common mistake to make so many purchases on "time" that future earnings are almost entirely committed to meeting the monthly payments. When buying on credit one too often ignores the total cost of the item and counts only the monthly payment. Especially with "big ticket" items such as household appliances, credit purchases not only reduce a family's financial flexibility until the payments are completed, but cost a lot in interest charges too.

The last step in constructing a budget is to assign the remaining income to discretionary, or variable, expenses—clothing, recreation, personal allowances, and such odds and ends as cigarettes and newspapers. It may seem natural to save only what is left over at the end of the month, but by then any money that has not been set aside for a special purpose will have been spent. Therefore, a realistic savings plan requires setting aside a fixed amount at the beginning of the month. Most people find that savings plans work best if they are followed systematically, and if the money is set aside to meet specific long-term goals.

Once a budget is constructed, you should ask these questions about it: Is too much money committed in advance? Do both spouses have a personal allowance large enough to keep them from feeling straitjacketed by the budget? Any budget should allow for some impulse buying. Although it is useful to follow the budget as a guide for family spending, no budget should be inflexible. It is not a rigid plan but a road map designed to lead to certain long-term goals.

In most families, the budget has to be revised periodically, not just in response to changing income but to new needs as well. Typically, the family budget has to change drastically with the birth of the first child. It changes again in ten or fifteen years, as the father's earnings increase and the mother returns to full- or part-time work.

A difficult point for a young couple to remember is that not everything can be done at once. It is foolish to try within the first few years to attain the lifestyle that may have taken one's parents twenty years to attain. Many couples are not able to set aside money for long-term security until they have been married ten years or more, partly because inflation causes prices to rise at least as rapidly as income, especially in the early years of one's career. (See Box 2.)

Designing a budget should help to distinguish short-term capabilities from long-term goals. It should also provide a road map for moving toward those goals.

The "Big Ticket" Items—Children, Housing, Cars

We can see how hard it is to put a realistic price tag on certain long-term goals when we consider the cost of having a child. The decision to have a child is different from any other financial decision: unlike a couple's purchases, children are neither rentable nor returnable. The fact that birth rates are relatively low among affluent, well-educated, urban couples suggest that they, at least, think of children in terms of their cost. And indeed, when all the hidden costs of bearing and rearing a child are added up, most children turn out to be more expensive than the houses they are brought up in. No young couple can afford to minimize such costs as they plan for their future.

How much do children cost today? The expenses begin with medical care during pregnancy and include hospital facilities for the delivery. Then the newborn needs medicine, a layette, a crib, baby clothes, and diapers. For most children there will be an additional room in the house and visits to a pediatrician. Over the next few years, in addition to the obvious costs—clothing, food, medical care—a family with young children will also have to pay for babysitters, toys and birthday parties, and perhaps nursery school. Throughout childhood and adolescence there will be the expenses for en-

What's Happening Today

Box 2 / Coping With Double-Digit Inflation

For years, the rate of inflation in the American economy—which averaged about 2.8 percent a year during the 1960s—was a matter of concern mainly to economists. But when the consumer price index began to climb at an annual rate of 6 percent in the early 1970s, almost 8 percent in 1978, and more than 10 percent during the first six months of 1979, inflation became a household word and a source of daily concern for millions of Americans who found that even with rising salaries they could not keep up with soaring costs.

Inflation means that the buying power of the dollar dwindles. The rate of inflation over the past twenty years means, according to figures compiled by the Conference Board, an independent research organization, that someone who earned $25,000 in 1960 would have to earn more than $60,000 in 1980 to support the same lifestyle. Even though there have been substantial increases in the income of most American workers in recent years, those increases have in many cases been wiped out by inflation. In general, unionized blue-collar workers—such as steelworkers, autoworkers, and truck drivers—have received pay increments that have allowed them to stay ahead of inflation. Like businessmen and professionals who can raise their prices to cover rising costs, they have not been the victims of inflation. But many others have been. It is estimated, for example, that a typical middle-level corporate lawyer experienced an actual decline of more than 8 percent of his income between 1967 and 1978 because of the combined effects of taxes and inflation. During that same period, university professors experienced a drop of more than 17 percent in their real income.

Prices have increased rapidly in almost every category of consumer spending. Between 1967 and 1977, the cost of a pack of cigarettes increased by 68 percent in a typical American city, while the cost of a car increased by 86 percent; the cost of a pair of blue jeans increased by more than 200 percent, and the cost of a three-bedroom house

(Box 2 continues on page 462)

tertainment, hobbies and sports, family pets, and perhaps summer camp. Later on, of course, the expenses may include such items as a car (along with the costs of maintaining and insuring it) and a college education.

One of the major costs of child rearing is the lost income of the wife who leaves her job to bring up the children. If the woman was earning $8,000 a year and then earns no income for ten years, $80,000 has been lost. Leaving lost income out of the total, however, it now costs about three years of the father's income to rear each child. Obviously, having children requires long-range financial planning.

Buying a Car So does buying a car. To assess the cost accurately, it should be amortized—that is, spread out over every year of its useful life. Gas, oil, lubrication, tires, repairs, and insurance should also be taken into account. Depreciation is an important cost factor, too, for one of the differences between a house and a car is that the market value of a house often increases over time, whereas the value of a car depreciates. A new car does not necessarily represent the best value because its selling price typically depreciates by about one-third the first year. The depreciation is about 18 percent of the original price the second year and 10 per-

(Box 2 continued from page 461)

rose by 69 percent. One way of making ends meet in a period of rapid inflation is to cut back on nonessential items; but since the most rapid increases in prices have been in necessities such as food, shelter, and transportation, there is not much that many families can do to insulate themselves against soaring prices. Some people, such as recipients of Social Security or retired civil servants, are protected by escalator clauses which specify that their benefits have to rise at the same rate as inflation. But, particularly for the millions of Americans who retired on their savings, rapid inflation has meant that the dollars they saved do not purchase very much in today's marketplace. If inflation were to continue at a 10 percent annual rate, every $1,000 in retirement savings at this year's prices would be worth only $150 in twenty years.

What are the implications of rapid inflation for personal financial planning? One word of advice would be to save in the form of real assets—such as real estate or other durable goods that have a secure value such as diamonds, fine art, or jewelry—rather than in the form of financial assets. Many people who decided ten years ago to put their savings in apparently secure places like savings accounts or government bonds have found that they actually lost money, because the interest on their investments has been less than the rate of inflation. Judging by the fact that American consumers are accumulating debt at a faster rate than ever before in American history, it appears that many people believe in an inflationary psychology. They have begun borrowing heavily to support their buying habits on the belief that things will only be more expensive later on. There is some logic to this, because inflation favors debtors at the expense of creditors. If you borrow $1,000 today, and pay it back in a year, the inflation that will have taken place between now and then means that you will be paying back money that has less purchasing power than it would have in a noninflationary period.

The high inflation rates of the past few years have caused many Americans not only to forgo certain purchases, but also to wonder whether they can maintain the standard of living to which they have been accustomed.

cent the third. If a car depreciates in value most rapidly in its first two years and begins to need costly repairs in its fifth year, the best advice might be to buy a recent-year used car and drive it for several years before trading it in.

In purchasing and maintaining a car, as in any other major investment, good information and sound advice are indispensable. Automotive magazines, the *Consumer Reports'* annual *Auto Buying Guide,* and the *Bluebook* estimate of a car's trade-in value are all useful references. And a reliable mechanic who can make a well-informed judgment about the condition of a used car is a valuable consultant before you make the purchase.

Buying a House The choice of housing is even more complex than that of transportation. For most couples, the purchase of a house is the family's largest single investment. Living in an apartment could be a convenient alternative, involving fewer responsibilites and less maintenance. How should you decide what type of housing best suits your needs?

Before deciding to buy a house, couples might sit down and figure out their long-range housing costs. The cost of renting over a period of years can easily be calculated by adding up the annual rental, plus an increase of several percent each year. The cost of home ownership is more difficult to determine, for maintenance

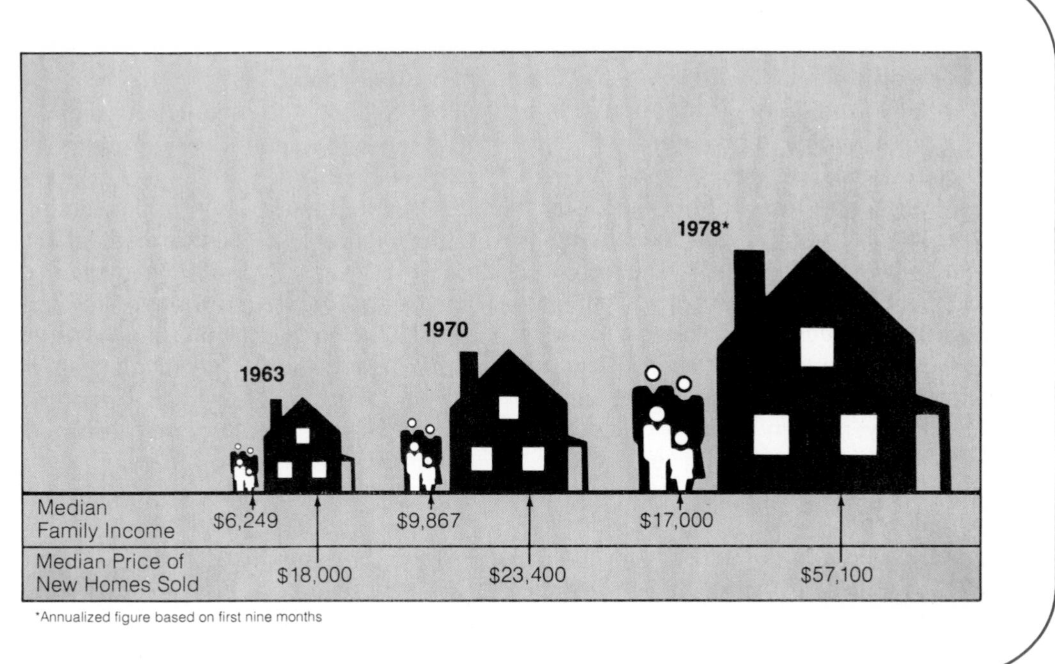

Data from the National Association of Realtors

Despite the tight credit situation in recent years, demand for housing has remained high. For many families, home ownership is a hedge against inflation, for the rate at which real estate has been appreciating has been faster than the increase in the rate of inflation. As this chart shows, although median family income in the United States has risen 2.7 times over the fifteen-year period between 1963 and 1978, the price of a new home more than tripled during that period.

and repair, insurance, and taxes must be added to the mortgage payments.

The traditional rule of thumb on how much a family can afford for housing is that it should cost no more than one-quarter of the spendable monthly income. When buying a house, families have been advised to pay no more than two or three times their yearly income. However, inflation and rising interest rates have made this rule useless. The only measures of how much a family can spend on a house today are the amount of cash they have saved or can borrow for a down payment and the amount they can afford for the monthly mortgage payment.

A mortgage amounts to a long-term purchase on the installment plan. Examine a mortgage and you may be dismayed to find that the interest over the entire payment period is at least as much as the principal. This may seem unreasonable, but actually it may not be as disadvantageous as renting a house. First, property taxes, house insurance, and interest charges on the mortgage are all allowable tax deductions. Those who choose to rent are allowed no equivalent deductions. And second, real estate often increases in value, enabling investors to recover their equity if they wish. Despite the interest charges on a mortgage, therefore, many couples find that it is cheaper in the long run to buy a house than to rent one.

As with any other purchase, it pays to shop around before signing a mortgage agreement. The availability of mortgages depends on the general economic situation and on the availability of money from lending institutions. In a generally poor economy, mortgages are hard to get and interest rates are high. Interest rates on mortgages vary considerably from one source to another. Banks, savings and loan associations, and some builders offer mortgages, and there are private mortgage companies that usually charge higher rates but are willing to make loans to some who would not qualify at other lending institutions. The lending institution usually asks the buyer to pay 25 to 30 percent of the purchase price in cash, and the rest is financed over a period of twenty to thirty years. Monthly payments, which often include real estate taxes, cover a portion of the principal as well as the interest, so that at the end of the mortgage, the entire loan is paid off.

TAXES

As is commonly said, nothing is certain but death and taxes. Taxes are the biggest single expense for most families, though of course they have no choice about paying them. Federal income taxes make the main difference between take-home pay and gross income, and most states and some localities have also levied additional taxes. The total bill for most families—taxes on income, property, and purchases, plus "hidden" or indirect taxes—is staggering; it is no wonder that people so frequently complain about their taxes. The surprising thing is that millions of people every year pay *more* taxes than they are legally required to.

Most of this overpayment is a result of overlooking allowable deductions—all too easy to do if you report your personal income tax on the short form, which allows only a specific percentage (15 percent of gross income, but no more than $2,000) as a deduction. The advantages of this form are obvious: it is simple, uncomplicated, and quick; and for people with few deductions or a low income, it is generally adequate. But for families with more income or more allowable deductions, it can be a very expensive timesaver.

Many allowable deductions seem so minor that you might tend to ignore them in the rush to meet the deadline for filing. For example, you can deduct travel to and from a doctor's office or hospital as part of the medical deduction. You are allowed to deduct medical expenses for a dependent even though she is not a tax exemption for you. Some people do not know that a dependent may be an adult son or daughter who works, or even a married child or an elderly relative. The Internal Revenue Service defines a dependent as anyone who receives more than half of his or her support from someone else.

There is a long list of allowable deductions that many people are unaware of, including interest payments on loans and credit purchases, the costs of moving when it is required for a new job, and the fees paid to an employment agency. Tax laws change from year to year. It is important to be well informed about the newest allowable deductions before filling out the annual tax forms. The best source of information for most people is the government publication *Your Federal Income Tax,* which is available from the Superintendent of Documents, Washington, D.C. 20402.

Once they list all allowable deductions, most people can compute their own taxes and not overpay, but when the family's financial situation is particularly complex, it may be advisable to consult a private accountant or tax service. Accountants, like attorneys, are required to prove their competence by taking state-administered tests, whereas individuals who work in tax service firms are not.

Accountants often make these two suggestions to their clients who want to avoid overpayment of taxes: (1) keep careful records of bills and purchases; and (2) think ahead to the tax consequences of certain financial decisions you make. Your records should include paid bills and canceled checks, an account of money spent for the support of dependents not living with you, and expenditures that relate to business, such as the business use of your home or car. It is especially important to keep permanent records of all expenses related to owning a house, because if you buy a house and then sell it a few years later at a profit, the profits are taxable. Many expenses—capital improvements on the house, closing costs, brokerage fees—are recognized by the IRS as factors in reducing the tax on profits.

It is possible to avoid some taxes by being alert to the tax consequences of certain financial decisions you make. For example, by deferring income from stock options into a later tax year when total income may be less, you may be able to save money.

CREDIT—A TOOL OR A TRAP?

"These are three faithful friends," wrote Benjamin Franklin, "an old wife, an old dog, and ready money." As those words suggest, "ready money"—which in today's society means available credit—can be not only a "faithful friend," but also a useful tool in managing the family finances.

Credit is the mainstay of the business world. Without it, few companies could grow. Businesses borrow money in order to increase their productivity and earning power; properly managed, money is used to make more money.

There are some instances in which individuals might use money as businesses do. A low-cost student loan, for example, might reasonably be considered a type of borrowing that will pay for itself by increasing future earning power. But generally, credit has one use for a business (a producer of commodities) and another for an individual or family (a consumer). For the consumer, credit is a means of deferring payment or breaking down the cost of a purchase into manageable installments. Those "small monthly payments" have a remarkable way of looking inconsequential at the time a purchase is made, but they appear much larger when added to the payments for several other installment purchases. For a business, credit can be used to increase income. For a family, credit amounts to a mortgage on future income, without in any way increasing it.

Most people find credit easy to get. When you first apply you will be judged by your job, your income, your other assets, the way you have managed a checking account, and your record in paying routine bills. Credit records are compiled by more than 2,000 local credit bureaus throughout the country. The information stored in their files serves as a credit history for more than 100 million Americans. The files are confidential: only stores, banks, and other businesses that extend credit, as well as the individual concerned, have a legal right to examine them.

A credit rating is based on several indications of your ability to make payments. Before extending credit, a lending institution will ask:

1. How capable are you of repaying a debt? The answer is based on your estimated monthly income minus your fixed expenses, including other debts.
2. What is your capital worth? What assets—savings, life insurance, stocks, or real estate—do you own? The creditor wants to know whether your assets will cover the loan if you cannot repay it.
3. What is your past credit experience? Have you paid bills consistently and promptly? You may also be asked how long you have lived at the same address, or at least in the same community. Obviously, a person who moves often from one place to another is a relatively bad credit risk because she may be hard to trace if she defaults on a loan.

Maintaining a good credit rating is important, if for no other reason than to have it available for emergencies. Some people believe they will be regarded as a good credit risk if they pay cash for all their purchases and maintain a good employment record. But this is not necessarily true. Potential creditors are interested in proof that you have already repaid borrowed money.

Thus it may be a good idea to apply for a bank credit card—which will establish your credit rating—even if you never use it.

Anyone who is turned down on a credit application is entitled by law to know why. Credit bureaus sometimes make mistakes. Stores or banks sometimes deny credit, illegally, on the basis of sex or race. The legal right to review one's own credit rating means that anyone can protect that rating against mistakes or discriminatory practices.

Credit comes in many forms—charge cards, checking plus accounts, installment plans, holiday credit—and most people use it for major purchases. Whatever the form, it costs money. The interest charges are usually buried in payments and often go unnoticed, but they can be quite high. Buying credit from the most convenient source is like shopping at the most convenient store—without looking at the prices. Ironically, many people who carefully compare prices on commodities and save money by getting the best bargain, lose perhaps as much by using an expensive type of credit. There are, in fact, three types of credit—credit cards, installment buying, and loans. Each bears a different price tag.

Credit Cards

Credit cards can be a great convenience. They allow impulse purchases on items too expensive to buy with cash. They serve as security when renting cars. Some cards offer the added convenience of borrowing cash quickly and easily. But it is precisely the convenience of credit cards that leads to their misuse. For people who have trouble living within their means, credit cards are a passport to disaster because they make spending so much easier. Banks encourage their use because they are highly profitable. People begin using cards as a convenience and assume they will avoid late-payment charges, but many soon get in the habit of making minimum payments toward a fairly large balance—while the bank profits from the interest charges.

More and more people pay for their purchases with credit cards without realizing that certain kinds of cards are more expensive to maintain than others.

There are three different types of credit cards. The first is the travel and entertainment card offered by such companies as American Express, Carte Blanche, and Diners Club, which charge a membership fee of about $25 a year, but no interest, if you pay on time. Most people need no more than one card of this type, for it enables you to cash checks, obtain travelers checks, and pay for restaurants, hotel bills, airline tickets, and other purchases. If you are in the habit of paying on time, the membership fee is a low price to pay for the convenience it offers.

The second type of credit card is the most familiar—the bank card, like Master Charge or Visa. This card costs nothing to obtain, but it can be more expensive to use than the travel and entertainment card for several reasons. The period of time allowed to pay bills is generally less—usually within twenty-five days of the billing date—than that allowed with travel and entertainment cards, which means you are more likely to run up interest charges. If you use the borrowing privilege that most bank cards offer, the interest starts immediately and the rates are high. This is a convenient but expensive form of credit and should be used only when necessary.

The third type of card is the single-use card. Oil companies, hotel chains, and car rental firms, among other companies, offer these cards as an incentive to use their products and services. Most of them cost nothing to obtain, and no interest is charged if you pay on time—generally within about thirty days of the billing date.

Installment Buying

"Buy now, owe nothing for sixty days, then pay a small monthly charge." Such offers persuade people to buy things they would not be able to afford if they had to pay cash, especially "big ticket" items such as appliances or furniture. Without realizing it, many people end up paying a great deal for this convenience. Installment purchases often involve high interest rates. For the consumer, it turns out to be more expensive to buy credit from the dealer selling the item than from almost any other source. In general, consumers are well advised to borrow money elsewhere, preferably from the low-interest credit sources discussed below, and then pay cash for such purchases.

The important thing to remember about installment buying, as with any other type of credit, is to read the contract carefully and understand the interest charges clearly. You may be required to sign a contract giving the retailer the right to repossess if you fail to make payments on time. Some stores require an "add on" clause in installment contracts, providing that if you have bought several things from the same store, all of them may be repossessed even if you have already paid more than the price of any one.

Loans

It takes a well-informed consumer to shop wisely for a loan. You have a wide range of lending institutions to choose from and a sometimes confusing vocabulary of credit terms and discount methods to learn. As you might expect, the cost of credit varies widely from one lending institution to another.

There are several types of lending institutions that are best to avoid because of the high interest rates they charge. Small loan companies, for example, are both costly and unreliable. Using the cash-advance privilege that most bank credit cards offer you is, as we noted above, quite convenient and very expensive. It is also unwise to use the "instant credit" option that some checking accounts allow.

One of the best and cheapest ways to borrow money is to "borrow it from yourself." For example, a life insurance loan permits you to borrow against the cash value of your life insurance policy.

If you have a good credit rating, you may qualify for a personal bank loan. After dealing with one bank long enough to have an established account, you may be able to borrow as much as $1,000 on a personal note, payable monthly on a declining-interest basis. Or the bank may prefer to offer you a collateral loan, for which you put up stocks or bonds whose value is fairly stable. The interest rates charged by different banks for the same type of loan vary, so make sure to shop at several banks before signing an agreement.

Credit unions are another good source of

money. These organizations consist of members belonging to a particular profession or employed by a particular company and offer their members high interest on savings. Credit unions also loan money to their members, usually at a more favorable interest rate than banks can offer because the banks have higher overhead expenses.

There are several ways of computing interest on a loan. If you qualify for it, you should choose a loan with interest calculated on the declining balance, which means simply that interest is charged only on the unpaid balance.

Women and Credit

Traditionally it has been assumed that the husband has the primary responsibility for family support, and thus the power to manage family income and property. Women have been kept financially dependent on their husbands by all kinds of social and legal restrictions—including the assumption by creditors that when women marry, they give up their own credit status—even if they go on working in secure, well-paid jobs. Credit card companies have refused to issue cards in the name of a married woman without her husband's signature. Some women who qualified for store charge accounts as singles found that when they tried to change the name of their account because of marriage, they had to reapply for credit, which included giving information about their husbands' credit history. Even highly paid professional women found that banks refused to count their salary fully in determining the couple's eligibility for a loan. Creditors assumed that women might drop out of the labor force, and so their income was not very reliable.

These discriminatory practices on the basis of sex and marital status placed a special burden on women, particularly on the recently divorced middle-aged woman. First, if she was a full-time housewife and mother, she had no means of earning a substantial income. Then, to complicate her problems, creditors commonly discounted alimony and child support as reliable sources of income. Because most women gave up their own credit ratings when they married, the recently divorced woman emerged from marriage with no credit history of her own. And if her former husband had a bad credit history, it was possible to use it against her, but if he was a good credit risk, she did not necessarily benefit. For years, divorced women, even those receiving substantial alimony payments, were not considered creditworthy unless they had property or a substantial income of their own. Thus, in a society where credit plays an important part in financial management, divorced women were at a severe disadvantage.

The Equal Credit Opportunity Act, passed by Congress in 1975, was designed to eliminate financial discrimination on the basis of sex or marital status. Among other provisions, it prohibits creditors from viewing married people as more creditworthy than those who are single or divorced. Also, creditors can no longer terminate a woman's credit account because she marries, nor can they require a woman to reapply in her husband's name. Although creditors can still request information about continued ability to pay, they cannot ask a couple about their birth control methods, or whether they plan to have children. Furthermore, creditors are no longer allowed to discount any part of personal income because of sex or marital status. This means, for example, that if alimony and child support payments are reliable, they cannot be disregarded as income sources.

Several provisions of this act improve the position of the divorced woman. For example, a woman's charge account cannot any longer be closed down when she divorces, so long as she is able and willing to pay her bills. Furthermore, the information reported to credit agencies on joint accounts must now be reported in both spouses' names, so that divorced women will have their own credit histories.

Although this legislation does much to equalize the financial position of men and women, it does not make credit an automatic right. Creditworthiness is still based on such criteria as reliable income, payment record, and personal assets—for example, savings or real estate ownership. Besides, one cannot assume the new law will deliver all it promises, for it is still untested. Thus, a woman should maintain her own credit identity by keeping some charge accounts in her maiden name after she marries. It may also prove useful to open a savings or checking account in her own name, or to apply for credit cards to prove her creditworthiness.

Of course, no one enters marriage with the thought that it will end in divorce or premature death, but it is best to be prepared for such an eventuality. A sound credit rating can be very useful in getting through a difficult transition.

ANTICIPATING CRISES—THE FINANCIAL "SHOCK ABSORBERS"

A crisis can strike any family. After working and saving for years in order to afford a house and furnishings, for example, a family may have everything wiped out by fire. Sickness and accidents bring medical expenses that add financial woes to physical ones. Unexpected death leaves in its wake not only heartache but a tangle of financial problems. Thus, one of the main goals of any family's long-range financial plans should be to provide "shock absorbers" against such crisis.

A first step in designing a family protection package is to conduct an inventory of the benefits you are already entitled to, such as Social Security payments and hospitalization, disability, and retirement benefits provided by most employers.

The Social Security program provides insurance protection for a family whose breadwinner dies, as well as disability benefits for the seriously ill, injured, or disabled. It also provides, of course, pension benefits and medical care at retirement as well as death benefits. The amount of benefits depends on the person's average earnings that were subject to Social Security taxes. To find out what benefits you are entitled to, contact your local Social Security office. You will probably find that they are quite minimal. Most people supplement them with other programs and policies. Remember, you will not collect anything unless you apply for it.

In addition, most businesses supplement this protection by offering medical insurance, life insurance, and a pension plan for their employees. When looking for a job, few young people pay much attention to these fringe benefits, but they vary widely from one firm to another, so they should be examined closely. In choosing among several job offers, you might do better to take a job at a slightly lower salary if the firm offers a superior benefits package. What the company pays in benefits will not seem as tangible as salary or bonuses, but it can add up to a substantial amount. Check to see what kind of medical insurance is provided, how much life insurance is included, and what type of pension plan employees are enrolled in. In some companies, employees have to contribute to the pension plan; in others, the employer pays the full amount. Another feature to look for is an employee investment plan, sometimes referred to as profit-sharing programs.

Once you have completed this inventory of benefits to which you are already entitled, you can figure out what additional coverage you need to anticipate possible crises. An adequate protection plan for most families consists of at least five types of insurance: disability, hospitalization, property, automobile, and, finally, life insurance. (See Box 3.)

Protecting Yourself Against Death, Disability, and Disaster

Of all the types of insurance, property insurance is the easiest to understand. Loss of property due to such causes as fire or theft is covered by this insurance. An inventory of personal belongings, along with copies of the bills for them, is invaluable in settling property loss claims. Such records should be kept in a safety deposit box in a bank and updated regularly. Remem-

Guidelines for Decision Making

Box 3 / Ten Ways to Waste Money

There are as many ways to waste money as there are to spend it. Any couple that makes more than a few of these mistakes has some major leaks in the family finances.

Mistake 1. You thought a family budget wasn't necessary. Putting together a budget like the one outlined in Box 1 might not seem worthwhile. After all, you know where your money goes, don't you? Most couples who keep track of their expenses for a few months are surprised at the results. A budget is a most useful tool in making sure that your real expenses express your priorities.

Mistake 2. You don't keep careful records of family finances. It may seem a bother to keep records and stay in the habit of filing receipts and bills, check stubs, and evidence of other purchases and transactions. However, these records will repay the time and effort when you sit down to figure your taxes or when you need to settle an insurance claim.

Mistake 3. When you buy you think mainly about the item's price tag, not its usable life. When buying clothes, cars, appliances, and just about anything else, an essential factor in figuring out whether you *really* got a bargain is how long the item will last.

Mistake 4. You shop carefully for prices but you don't pay much attention to the cost of credit. Especially on "big ticket" items, the interest charges you pay amount to a substantial percentage of the total cost. Be aware of the fact that some kinds of credit, including the cash-advance privilege attached to bank credit cards and most installment credit plans at stores, carry a high price tag.

Mistake 5. You keep all your money in joint accounts, and most of your family property is jointly owned. Joint accounts and joint own-

ber, too, that the value of a house may increase over time; your policy should reflect its market value.

Many young, unmarried people see no reason to be concerned about property or life insurance. But even the single person with little property and no dependents has to be concerned about hospitalization and disability coverage. If you are unable to support yourself because of sickness or injury, disability insurance provides benefits. In some cases disability is included in comprehensive health insurance policies. The important questions to ask about a disability insurance policy are:

1. How much will you receive, and for how long, if you are disabled?
2. How does the policy define sickness and accident disability?
3. If you are only partially disabled, does the policy provide benefits?
4. Must you be hospitalized or confined at home in order to receive payments?

Compared with other types of coverage, the purchase of life insurance seems very complicated. But if you approach it as you would any other purchase, two essential facts become clear: first, the purpose of life insurance is to provide a continuing source of income for dependents if the breadwinner dies; and second, one should shop around for the lowest premium, or cost, of the insurance one needs.

Why does it often seem so complicated? Most people don't buy insurance, it is sold to them.

ership may seem the fairest way to arrange family finances, but if a spouse dies the joint account is frozen and the family may be denied access to it until the court appoints an executor—weeks, even months, later. Joint ownership of all family property is also a bad idea for tax purposes. You might need the help of a financial adviser to determine the best way to divide assets.

Mistake 6. Insurance policies are in the husband's name. In general, it's a better idea for the wife to own the policies, so that fewer of the proceeds will be taxed. But the wife must be able to prove that she paid the premiums.

Mistake 7. You file taxes jointly, and you always use the short form. The short form is more convenient, but the reason millions of people overpay their taxes is that they do not fully list their allowable deductions. Although filing jointly is generally advisable, there are certain cases where couples can save money by filing separate returns. A large raise or huge medical bills might mean that you would benefit from separate returns.

Mistake 8. You put off drawing up a will because "it's not necessary to do that yet." The unexpected does sometimes happen. Putting together a will is a relatively simple matter, and it is the only way you can be sure that family assets will be distributed as you want them to be.

Mistake 9. Family finances are the man's responsibility, and women need not be bothered with them. No woman can afford the luxury of ignorance about family finances. The experience of millions of bewildered widows and divorcées who always depended on men to take care of financial matters suggests that the woman who is ignorant in this area may well pay a price for it.

Mistake 10. You do all your own financial planning, without consulting expert advice. Some matters of family finance—unusually complicated taxes, estate planning—involve such intricacies that most people need expert advice on them. Reliable, well-informed experts such as accountants, lawyers, and bankers are well worth the fees they charge.

They sign up without first determining what they really need or whether they could get it elsewhere at a lower price. Thus no buyer resistance prevents insurance companies from turning simple plans into complex programs to make them seem more attractive. The insurance business is highly competitive, and salespeople promote policies that bring them the highest commission, whether or not they are the best policies for the insured, in either coverage or cost.

Basically, there are two kinds of life insurance, term and ordinary. Term insurance is the simplest and the least expensive. For a certain period of time—the *term* of the policy—the insurance company receives a specified premium (often payable in monthly installments) and promises to pay the face value of the policy if the insured dies. The term is generally five years, after which the policy has to be renewed with a somewhat higher premium to account for the greater probability of death as the insured gets older. Term insurance has no savings or lending provisions and gives no refund if the policy is canceled or expires, but it is the best buy because it is considerably cheaper than other kinds of insurance and does exactly what it is designed to do. The commission for term insurance is lower than for other kinds of policies, so salespeople always try to sell something else.

The second type of life insurance—ordinary life, sometimes called straight or whole life—requires premium payments as long as the insured is alive, and unless the cause of death is one of the policy's exemptions, pays the beneficiary a predetermined amount of money when the insured dies. The premium remains unchanged throughout the life of the insured because it is an average of the lifetime premium. At the beginning, therefore, it is higher than needed to pay for the same protection. The excess is invested by the company and returns more than enough money to cover the higher cost of protection in later years. At the same time, this reserve is available to the policyholder as cash value that can be borrowed. If the policy is dropped at any point, the reserve is returned to the policyholder.

Analysis of the cost difference between term and ordinary life shows why it is cheaper to buy term insurance. If you were to deposit an amount equivalent to the difference between what these two types of coverage cost in a savings account, the interest would be greater than the accumulation of the reserve.

Enterprising insurance companies have put together many different insurance packages. One of the favorite phrases is "cradle-to-grave" coverage. Almost without exception, however, these plans are designed to benefit the insurance company, not the insured.

In order to buy what you need and nothing more, remember what life insurance should do: provide an income for dependents if the wage earner dies. How much insurance do you need? The answer depends of a number of factors. Like other aspects of financial planning, life insurance has to be tailored to family income and budget, but must also take account of such factors as whether the mother would get a job if her husband died and how much of the family's expense she could meet. If no such alternative income can be expected, add up family expenses for every year until the youngest child completes college, and then add what the wife will need to support herself for the rest of her life. Typically, couples who are in their mid-thirties need at least $100,000 worth of life insurance to protect the family.

Keep these points in mind when you buy insurance:

1. The cost of similar coverage varies from one insurance company to another, so compare prices before you buy.
2. The basic purpose of life insurance is to provide protection for dependents if the breadwinner dies. Policies that include a savings program or a lending privilege may sound more attractive, but they invariably cost more than simple term insurance.
3. There are several ways of buying cheaper coverage than that offered by insurance companies. Group plans at your place of employment and GI term insurance are two examples. In some states, savings banks offer low-cost insurance policies.
4. It is cheaper to pay premiums annually than monthly. Some companies even offer a small discount for prepayment of premiums.
5. Take advantage of the low-cost insurance options on personal loans, mortgages, and auto loans. These policies cover the unpaid portion of the loan in case of death. Without such coverage, a widow could well be liable for the remainder of the loan.
6. Who should buy the policy? This is an important question, for if the insured buys the policy on his or her own life, the proceeds are income-tax free—but not exempt from estate tax. It is best, therefore, for the wife to buy an insurance policy on her husband's life, and vice versa. In that case the proceeds are free from both estate and income taxes.
7. Should a husband take out insurance on his wife? If she has an income that constitutes an important part of the total family income, the answer is obvious. Even if she does not contribute to the family income, however, insurance can help to provide all the services normally performed by a housewife that will have to be purchased after her death.

Estate Planning

Many couples who have carefully arranged insurance coverage for their family fail to take another important step in managing family finances—designing a will. Some think it unnecessary because they assume the surviving spouse will automatically get everything the other owned. Others, especially in the early years of marriage, do not believe they have enough assets to make it worthwhile. (They might change their minds if they added up the value of their personal possessions, their house, car, furnishings, profit-sharing rights, and so on.) And finally, no one likes to contemplate the possibility of premature death.

But here is an example of what can happen if a spouse dies without a will. Imagine a case in which a thirty-four-year-old man with a wife and two young children is killed in a freak accident. By law, his bank accounts are frozen and his wife must go through an involved series of legal proceedings to be appointed administrator of his estate as well as legal guardian for the children. She may be forced to submit accountings of family expenses to the court until the children reach age twenty-one. In this case, the husband's failure to write out a will caused his wife substantial inconvenience and legal fees, and the court may not have distributed his estate as he would have wished.

Even young couples need a carefully prepared will in order to avoid such problems. The will is your only assurance that family money and property will be distributed according to your preferences. It is necessary to ensure that most family resources will pass directly to the surviving spouse and children, and to avoid stiff court expenses and estate taxes.

A will, to be valid, must adhere to law, and so it should be drawn up with the assistance of an attorney. The process involves, first, listing all your beneficiaries, including family, friends, and charitable organizations, and then listing all the assets to be distributed. The will names an executor of the estate, who can be the surviving spouse or a business associate, and appoints a guardian for the children. In drawing up a will, you should consult with your attorney about the advisabiltiy of arranging family assets so as to avoid excessive estate taxes. Finally, any will should be reviewed regularly. Relationships change, and the nature and value of the estate change. Periodic review will help to ensure that property and money will be distributed as you want them to be.

Considering that so many women outlive their husbands by at least several years, one of the most common mistakes in managing family finances is for the wife to remain ignorant about family assets, liabilities, and the provisions of the will. Widowhood is difficult enough without the added burden of ignorance about financial matters.

SAVINGS AND INVESTMENTS—WORKING TOWARD FINANCIAL SECURITY

Attitudes toward regular savings today are quite different from what they were a generation or two ago. Even though most people still think some money should be saved, there is a greater emphasis today on immediate enjoyment, even if it means going into debt temporarily. It used to be customary for financial advisors to recommend that couples build up a "savings cushion" equivalent to at least six months' income. This was supposed to provide enough cash to cover emergencies, most illnesses, the loss of a job, or unexpected major bills. Today, because government programs and employee benefit plans cover some of these emergencies, few families feel it necessary to keep that much money in savings, but savings amounting to at least a few months' income can still prove to be very helpful.

The total assets of many families grow even without specific saving or investment plans. For example, the market value of most houses increases, and pension or profit-sharing plans accumulate "hidden" assets. The disadvantage with such assets is that they are not liquid: they cannot easily be converted into cash. That is one of the main reasons to maintain a savings "nest egg."

The simple advice that a family should save regularly is easy to give and hard to follow. However, here are some savings strategies that have been used successfully:

1. If you write yourself a check and deposit it in a savings account at the *beginning* of the

month when bills are paid, you are much more likely to save regularly than if you save only what is left over at the end of the month. Some employers offer payroll deduction plans for this purpose.

2. You might find that the payments you have been making on long-term purchases such as a car or a major appliance can be continued after the item is paid off. Simply make the same payments to yourself and deposit them in a savings account.
3. If you kick a habit such as smoking, set aside the money you might have spent for cigarettes and save it.
4. If you have difficulty saving anything from your ordinary income, you might plan to save money from such unusual sources as tax refunds, expense account reimbursements, and even raises.

What kind of bank should you use for your savings account? There are three types of banks: savings banks, savings and loan associations, and commercial banks. The first two types of banks generally offer the highest interest rates.

Families today are usually advised to keep no more in savings than they need to have available as ready cash, because in an era of rapid inflation, the purchasing power of money decreases substantially in each year. Money left in a low-interest savings account over a number of years may not accumulate enough interest to cover the cost of inflation.

There are a number of ways to earn higher interest rates on long-term savings. For example, you can qualify for a high-interest savings account by promising to leave a certain amount in the account for one to two years or more. A certificate of deposit amounts to the same thing, a relatively long-term deposit on which you receive high interest. Bonds issued by government agencies are another way to get high interest on small sums of money, but you must hold the bond until it matures to qualify for the full return.

If you already have ample insurance, an adequate family protection plan, and several months' income in savings, you might want to consider investing money to make greater profits. For the family with surplus funds, sound investment can mean addtional income.

But it must be done intelligently. In recent years, the securities industry—the people who buy and sell stocks and bonds—has promoted the idea of investing for the common person. As a result, one in every seven Americans has some investment in the stock market. Many of these investors, however, find themselves speculating on things they know nothing about. A considerable amount of knowledge is needed to invest wisely in the stock market—not to mention real estate, art, gold, and commodities such as wheat and corn. When the economy was booming, everyone was an expert because everyone was making money. But when the market turned around, a great many people learned the hard way that there is no such thing as a sure investment. Stocks can go down as well as up. Therefore, no investment should be made in which the investor cannot afford to lose as much as he or she might gain.

It takes no great skill to buy a stock that rises in a strong economy. Knowing how to invest in an uncertain economy, however, is a job for a professional. The private investor should rely on professional brokers with strong credentials and a record of reasonable success. For the inexperienced investor, the best bet is still a mutual fund in which the choice of stocks or bonds purchased is determined by professional analysts.

As in other areas of financial management that require special skills and knowledge, any individual is well advised to seek professional advice before risking the loss of family income in uncertain investments.

REFERENCES

Robert O. Blood, Jr., and Donald M. Wolfe, *Husbands and wives.* New York: Free Press, 1960.

Morton Hunt. Money and sex: Two marital problems or one? *Redbook,* January 1970.

FOR FURTHER STUDY

There are many practical guides to family finance that include more detailed information than that offered in this appendix. Make sure that the book you consult reflects the current situation with regard to such matters as allowable tax deductions, credit laws, and investment opportunities. One such book is Sylvia Porter's *New Money Book for the 1980's* (New York: Doubleday, 1979). Several periodicals feature useful information on the topics discussed here. One of the best is *Consumer Reports,* which also publishes buying guides on such purchases as life insurance.

For further information on the problems that women encounter when applying for credit, see Martha Garrison's article "Credit-Ability for Women," in the July 1976 issue of *The Family Coordinator.*

One of the best discussions on the meaning of money and the impact of changing standards of living is Lee Rainwater's *What Money Buys: Inequality and the Social Meanings of Income* (New York: Basic Books, 1974).

Name Index

Subject Index

Permissions Acknowledgments

CHAPTER 1

John F. Cuber and Peggy B. Harroff, from *Sex and the Significant Americans*. Copyright © 1968 by Hawthorn Books, Inc. Reprinted by permission of the publisher. All rights reserved.

Howard Kirschenbaum and Sidney B. Simon, from "Values and the Future Movement in Education," in Alvin Toffler, ed., *Learning for Tomorrow*. Copyright © 1973 by Random House, Inc. Reprinted by permission of the publisher.

Hyman Rodman, from "The Textbook World of Family Sociology," from *Social Problems*. Copyright © 1965 by The Society for the Study of Social Problems. Reprinted by permission.

Arlene Skolnick, from *The Intimate Environment*. Copyright © 1973 by Little, Brown and Company. Reprinted by permission of the publisher.

CHAPTER 2

Robert Blood, from *Love Match and Arranged Marriage*. Copyright © 1967 by The Free Press. Reprinted by permission of Macmillan Publishing Company, Inc.

Inge Bell Powell, from "The Double Standard." Published by permission of Transaction, Inc. from *Transaction*, Vol. 8, #1–2. Copyright © 1970 by Transaction, Inc.

Ernest Van den Haag, from "Love or Marriage," from *Harpers*. Copyright © 1962 by Harpers Magazine. Reprinted by permission of the publisher.

Elaine Walster, Jane Allyn Piliavin, and G. William Walster, from "The Hard-To-Get Woman." Reprinted from *Psychology Today*. Copyright © 1973 by Ziff-David Publishing Company.

CHAPTER 3

George R. Bach and Ronald M. Deutsch, from *Intimacy*, Peter Wyden, 1970. Reprinted by permission of the authors.

Peter L. Berger, from *Invitation to Sociology*. Copyright © 1963 by Peter L. Berger. Reprinted by permission of Doubleday & Company, Inc.

Eleanor Macklin, from "Unmarried Heterosexual Cohabitation," in Jacqueline Wiseman, *The Social Psychology of Sex*, Harper & Row, 1975. Reprinted by permission of the author.

William McWhirter, from " 'The Arrangement' at College," from *Life*. Copyright © 1968 by Time Inc. Reprinted by permission.

Excerpt from *Marriage, Divorce and Family Newsletter*, September 1, 1975, p. 4. Copyright © 1975 by The Marriage and Divorce Press, Inc. Reprinted by permission.

Bernard I. Murstein, from "Theory of Marital Choice and Its Applicability to Marriage Adjustment," in B. I. Murstein, ed., *Theories of Attraction and Love*, p. 116. Copyright © 1971 by Springer Publishing Company. Reprinted by permission of the publisher.

Ira L. Reiss, from "Toward a Sociology of the Heterosexual Love Relationship," from *Journal of Marriage and the Family*. Copyright © 1960 by the National Council on Family Relations. Reprinted by permission.

James Skipper and Gilbert Nass, from "Dating Behavior: A Framework for Analysis and an Illustration," from *Journal of Marriage and the Family*. Copyright © 1966 by the National Council on Family Relations. Reprinted by permission.

George Thorman, from "Cohabitation: A Report on the Married-Unmarried Life Style," from *The Futurist*, a Journal of Forecasts, Trends and Ideas About the Future. Reprinted by permission of World Future Society. An Association for the Study of Alternative Futures, 4916 St. Elmo Avenue, Washington, D.C. 20014.

William Waller as quoted by D. Bromley and F. Britten, "The Sex Lives of College Students," in William O'Neill, ed., *The American Sexual Dilemma*. Copyright © 1972 by Holt, Rinehart and Winston. This material originally appeared in D. Bromley, *Youth and Sex*. Copyright © 1938 by Harper & Row, Publishers, Inc. Reprinted by permission.

CHAPTER 4

Robert Bell, from "Parent-Child Conflict in Sexual Values," *Journal of Social Issues*, Vol. 22, No. 2 (1966). Reprinted by permission of author and publisher.

Robert Bell and Jay Chaskes, from "Premarital Sexual Experience Among Coeds—1958 and 1968," from *Journal of Marriage and the Family*. Copyright © 1970 by the National Council on Family Relations. Reprinted by permission.

Winston Ehrmann, from "Marital and Nonmarital Sexual Behavior," in Harold T. Christensen, ed., *Handbook of Marriage and the Family*. Copyright © 1964 by Rand McNally Publishing Company. Reprinted by permission of the publisher.

Morton Hunt, from *Sexual Behavior in the 1970's*. Reprinted with permission of Playboy Press. Copyright © 1974 by Morton Hunt.

David Kirk, et al., from *Biology Today*, second edition, pp. 742–743. Copyright © 1975 by Random House, Inc. Reprinted by permission.

Robert J. Levin and Amy Levin, from "Sexual Pleasure: The Surprising Preferences of 100,000 Women," from *Redbook Magazine*, September 1975. Copyright © 1975 by The Redbook Publishing Company. Reprinted by permission of the publisher.

Constance Lindemann, from *Birth Control and Unmarried Young Women*, pp. 15, 20, 25, 28, 29. Copyright © 1974 by C. Lindemann. Reprinted by permission of author and Springer Publishing Company.

Excerpts from an interview with Betty Ford in *The New York Times Magazine*, August 11, 1975. Copyright © 1975 by The New York Times Company. Reprinted by permission.

Anne Roiphe, from "Teen-Age Affairs," from *The New York Times Magazine*. Copyright © 1975 by The New York Times Company. Reprinted by permission.

J. Richard Udry, from *The Social Context of Marriage*. Copyright © 1974 by J. B. Lippincott Company. Reprinted by permission of the publisher.

Charles Winick, from "Sex and Advertising," in Robert J. Glessing and William P. White, eds., *Mass Media: The Invisible Environment*. Copyright © 1975 by Charles Winick. Reprinted by permission of the author.

CHAPTER 5

Natalie Allon and Diane Fishel, from "Urban Courting Patterns: Singles' Bars," a paper presented at the annual meeting of the American Sociological Association, New York, August 1973. Reprinted by permission of the American Sociological Association.

Ingrid Bengis, from "Being Alone," in *Couples*, New York Magazine, 1973. Reprinted by permission.

Jessie Bernard, from *The Future of Marriage*. Copyright © 1971 by Jessie Bernard. Originally published by World Publishing Company, used with permission of Thomas Y. Crowell Company, Inc.

Caroline Bird, from "Women Should Stay Single," in Harold H. Hart, ed., *Marriage: For and Against*. Copyright © 1972 by Hart Publishing Company, Inc. Reprinted by permission of the publisher.

Susan Jacoby, from "49 Million Singles Can't Be All Right," from *The New York Times Magazine*. Copyright © 1974 by The New York Times Company. Reprinted by permission.

Manfred Kuhn as quoted in Howard Becker and Reuben Hills, eds., *Family, Marriage and Parenthood*. Copyright © 1955 by Heath. Reprinted by permission of the editors.

Excerpts from "Games Singles Play," from *Newsweek*. Copyright 1973 by Newsweek, Inc. All rights reserved. Reprinted by permission.

Cynthia Prouly, from "Sex as Athletics in the Singles Complex," *Saturday Review/Society*, May 1973, pp. 61–66. Reprinted by permission of Saturday Review.

Peter Stein, from "Singlehood: An Alternative to Marriage," from *The Family Coordinator*. Copyright © 1975 by the National Council on Family Relations. Reprinted by permission.

CHAPTER 6

Excerpts from *Booklet for Women Who Wish to Determine Their Own Names After Marriage*. Copyright © 1974 by the Center for a Woman's Own Name, 261 Kimberley, Barrington, Illinois 60010. Reprinted by permission.

Susan Edmiston, from "How to Write Your Own Marriage Contract," *Ms.* magazine, Spring 1972. Reprinted by permission.

Karl Fleishmann, from "Marriage by Contract: Defining the Terms of Relationship," from *Family Law Quarterly*, 1974. Reprinted by permission of the Editor-in-Chief, Sanford N. Katz.

James Ramey, et al., from "The Impact of Legal Regulations on Alternative Life Styles," a paper delivered at the annual meeting of the American Sociological Association. Reprinted by permission of the American Sociological Association.

Marcia Seligson, from *The Eternal Bliss Machine*. Copyright © 1973 by Marcia Seligson. Adapted by permission of William Morrow and Company, Inc.

Norman Sheresky and Mary Mannes, from "A Radical Guide to Wedlock," *Saturday Review*, July 29, 1972. Reprinted by permission of Saturday Review.

Edward Shorter, from *The Making of the Modern Family*. Copyright © 1975 by Basic Books, Inc., Publishers, New York.

Philip Slater, from "Some Social Consequences of Temporary Systems," in W. G. Bennis and P. E. Slater, eds., *The Temporary Society*. Copyright © 1968 by Harper & Row. Reprinted by permission.

CHAPTER 7

Excerpt from an advertisement placed in *Advertising Age* by the Cadwell Compton Agency. Reprinted by permission of the Cadwell Compton Agency.

Louis Harris, from *ABC News—Harris Survey*, Vol. 1, No. 29, Chicago Tribune-New York News Syndicate, March 8, 1979. Reprinted by permission.

Excerpt from the 1970 Virginia Slims American Women's Opinion Poll. Reprinted by permission of Louis Harris and Associates and Virginia Slims/Philip Morris.

CHAPTER 8

Helen Andelin, from *Fascinating Womanhood*, Bantam, 1974. Reprinted by permission.

Robert Blood, from "Long Range Causes and Consequences of the Employment of Married Woman," from *Journal of Marriage and the Family*. Copyright © 1965 by the National Council on Family Relations. Reprinted by permission.

Graph entitled "Percentage of Professional Degrees Awarded to Women, 1967–1977," *The Chronicle of Higher Education*, November 13, 1979, p. 13. Reprinted with permission. Copyright 1979 by The Chronicle of Higher Education, Inc.

Germaine Greer, from *The Female Eunuch*. Copyright © 1970, 1971 by McGraw-Hill Book Company. Reprinted by permission of the publisher.

Susan Jacoby, from "What Do I Do For the Next Twenty Years?" from *The New York Times Magazine*. Copyright © 1973 by The New York Times Company. Reprinted by permission.

Mirra Komarovsky, from "Cultural Contradictions and Sex Roles: The Masculine Case," from *American Journal of Sociology*, 78 (1973):873–884. Copyright © 1973 by The University of Chicago Press. Reprinted by permission of The University of Chicago Press and the author.

Helen Z. Lopata, from *Occupation: Housewife*. Copyright © 1971 by Oxford University Press. Reprinted by permission of the publisher.

Marabel Morgan, from *The Total Woman*. Copyright © 1973 by Marabel Morgan. Used by permission of Fleming H. Revell Company.

Philip Slater, from "What Hath Spock Wrought?" from *The Washington Post*. Copyright © 1970 by The Washington Post. Reprinted by permission.

CHAPTER 9

George Bach and Ronald Deutsch, from *Pairing*, copyright George Bach and Ronald Deutsch, © 1970. Published by Peter Wyden and reprinted by permission of The David McKay Company, Inc.

Colin Cherry, from *On Human Communication: A Review, A Survey, and A Criticism*, 2nd ed. Copyright © 1966 by MIT Press, Cambridge, Mass. Reprinted by permission of the publisher.

Antonio Ferreira, from "Family Myth and Homeostasis," from *Archives of General Psychiatry*, 9 (1963):457–464. Copyright © 1963 by the American Medical Association. Reprinted by permission of the author and the AMA.

William J. Lederer and Don D. Jackson, M.D., from *The Mirages of Marriage*. Copyright © 1968 by W. W. Norton & Company, Inc., New York, N.Y. Reprinted by permission of the publisher.

McCroskey, Larson, and Knapp, from *An Introduction to Interpersonal Communication*, © 1971, pp. 161–170. Reprinted by permission of Prentice-Hall, Inc., Englewood Cliffs, New Jersey.

Keith Melville, from "On Our Way to Where," from *The Sciences*, November 1972. Copyright © 1972 by The New York Academy of Sciences. Reprinted by permission.

Lillian Breslow Rubin, from *Worlds of Pain: Life in the Working Class Family*. Copyright © 1976 by Lillian Breslow Rubin, Basic Books, Inc., Publishers, New York. Reprinted by permission.

CHAPTER 10

Alex Comfort, from *Sex in Society*. Copyright © 1963 by the Citadel Press, Inc. Reprinted by permission of the publisher.

John Cuber, from "Adultery: Reality Versus Stereotype," in G. Neubeck, ed., *Extramarital Relations*, Prentice-Hall, 1969. Reprinted by permission of the author.

Joseph Epstein, from *Divorced in America*. Copyright © 1974 by Joseph Epstein. Reprinted by permission of E. P. Dutton & Company, Inc.

J. L. McCary, from *Human Sexuality*, 3rd Edition. Copyright © 1978 by Litton Educational Publishing, Inc. Reprinted by permission of D. Van Nostrand Company.

Excerpts from "The Vatican Position," *The New York Times Magazine*, January 16, 1976. Copyright © 1976 by The New York Times Company. Reprinted by permission.

CHAPTER 11

Angus Campbell, from "The American Way of Mating: Marriage Si, Children Only Maybe," from *Psychology Today*. Copyright ©

1975 by Ziff-Davis Publishing Company. Reprinted by permission of Psychology Today Magazine.

Irwin Deutscher, from "Socialization for Postparental Life," in Arnold Rose, ed., *Human Behavior and Social Processes*. Copyright © 1962 by Houghton Mifflin Company. Reprinted by permission.

Excerpts from "The Cruelest Task-Master of All," *Forbes*, June 15, 1975, p. 58. Reprinted by permission.

Herbert A. Otto, from "Marriage and Family Enrichment Programs in North America—Report and Analysis," *The Family Coordinator*, April 1975, pp. 137–142. Copyright © 1975 by the National Council on Family Relations. Reprinted by permission.

Graph from Boyd C. Rollins and Harold Feldman, "Marital Satisfaction over the Family Life Cycle," *Journal of Marriage and the Family* 32:20–28. Reprinted by permission.

Yonina Talmon, from "Aging in Israel, A Planned Society," from the *American Journal of Sociology*, 67 (1961):284–295. Copyright © 1961 by The University of Chicago Press. Reprinted by permission of The University of Chicago Press.

CHAPTER 12

C. Christian Beels, from "Whatever Happened to Father?" from *The New York Times Magazine*. Copyright © 1974 by The New York Times Company. Reprinted by permission.

Richard Flacks, from *Youth and Social Change*. Copyright © 1971 by Rand McNally Publishing Company. Reprinted by permission of the publisher.

Jerome Kagan, from "The Psychological Requirements for Human Development," in Nathan Talbot, ed., *Raising Children in Modern America*. Copyright © 1976 by Little, Brown and Company. Reprinted by permission of the publisher.

Barbara Katz, from "Cooling Motherhood." Reprinted with permission from *The National Observer*, copyright Dow Jones & Company, Inc. 1972.

Judith Lorber, from "Beyond Equality of the Sexes: The Question of the Children," from *The Family Coordinator*. Copyright © 1975 by the National Council on Family Relations. Reprinted by permission.

F. N. McGrath, from "By the Book," *The New York Times Magazine*, June 27, 1976. Copyright © 1976 by The New York Times Company. Reprinted by permission.

Margaret Mead, from "The Impact of Cultural Change on the Family," from *The Family in the Urban Community*, published by the Merrill-Palmer School, 1953. Reprinted by permission of the author.

Ellen Peck, from "Television's Romance with Reproduction," in Ellen Peck and Judith Senderowitz, eds., *Pronatalism: The Myth of Mom and Apple Pie*. Copyright © 1974 by Apollo Editions, Inc. Reprinted by permission of Thomas Y. Crowell, Inc.

Betty Rollin, from "Motherhood: Who Needs It?" from *Look*. Copyright © 1970 by Cowles Communications, Inc. Reprinted by permission.

Sheldon J. Segal, from "Limiting Reproductive Potential," in Nathan Talbot, ed., *Raising Children in Modern America*. Copyright © 1976 by Little, Brown and Company. Reprinted by permission of the publisher.

Catherine Storr, from "Freud and the Concept of Parental Guilt," in Jonathan Miller, ed., *The World of Freud: The Man, His World, His Influence*. Copyright © 1972 by Little, Brown and Company. Reprinted by permission.

CHAPTER 13

Raymond Firth, from "Family and Kinship in Industrial Society," from *Sociological Review*. Copyright © 1964 by *Sociological Review*. Reprinted by permission of the publisher.

William J. Goode, from *World Revolution and Family Patterns*. Copyright © 1963 by Macmillan Publishing Company, Inc. Reprinted by permission.

Rosabeth Kanter, Dennis Jaffe, and D. Kelly Weisberg, from "Coupling, Parenting, and the Presence of Others," from *The Family Coordinator*. Copyright © 1975 by the National Council on Family Relations. Reprinted by permission.

Excerpts from *The New York Times Magazine*, December 7, 1975, R–8. Copyright © 1975 by The New York Times Company. Reprinted by permission.

Marvin B. Sussman, from "The Isolated Nuclear Family: Fact or Fiction?" from *Social Problems*. Copyright © 1959 by the Society for the Study of Social Problems. Reprinted by permission.

Robert S. Weiss, from *Marital Separation*. Copyright © 1975 by Basic Books, Inc., Publishers, New York. Reprinted by permission of the publisher.

CHAPTER 14

Peter Berger and Hansfried Kellner, from "Marriage and the Construction of Reality," *Diogenes*, 46, 1964. Reprinted by permission of the publisher.

Paul Glick and Arthur J. Norton, graph from "Perspectives on the Recent Upturn in Divorce and Remarriage," *Demography*, Vol. 10, pp. 301–314. Reprinted by permission of the publisher.

Reuben Hill, from "Social Stress on the Family," from *Social Casework*. Copyright © 1958 by the Family Service Association of America. Reprinted by permission.

Barbara Hirsch, from *Divorce: What a Woman Needs to Know*. Published by the Henry Regnary Company, Chicago. Copyright © 1973 by Barbara Hirsch. Reprinted by permission.

Albert Martin, from "I Am One Man, Hurt," *The New York Times Magazine*, June 25, 1973. Copyright © 1973 by The New York Times Company. Reprinted by permission.

Herbert A. Otto, from "Has Monogamy Failed?" *Saturday Review*, April 25, 1970. Reprinted by permission of the publisher.

Leslie Aldridge Westoff, from "Two-Time Winners," from *The New York Times Magazine*. Copyright © 1975 by The New York Times Company. Reprinted by permission.

CHAPTER 15

Betty Cogswell and Marvin Sussman, from "Changing Family and Marriage Forms: Complications for Human Service Systems," from *The Family Coordinator*. Copyright © 1972 by the National Council on Family Relations. Reprinted by permission.

Sydney M. Jourard, from "Re-Inventing Marriage: The Perspective of a Psychologist," in Herbert A. Otto, ed., *The Family in Search of a Future*, Appleton-Century-Crofts, 1970. Reprinted by permission of the publisher.

Margaret Mead, from "Future Family." Published by permission of Transaction, Inc. from *Transaction*, Vol. 8 #11, Copyright © 1971 by Transaction, Inc.

Sheila Rule, "What's Happening Today?" *The New York Times*, October 31, 1977. Copyright © 1977 by The New York Times Company. Reprinted by permission.

Picture Credits

Title Page—Michael Weisbrot & Family

Chapter One Understanding Marriage and Family Today
9–Peter Simon/Stock, Boston; 18–Raimondo Borea/Photo Researchers, Inc.; 22–Courtesy, CBS TV Network; 31–Elliott Erwitt/Magnum.

Chapter Two Mate Selection—The Choice Is Yours
44–Courtesy, Video-Mate; 45–Courtesy, Gingiss; 54–(left) Hank Lebo/Jeroboam; (right) Jill Freedman; 59–Museum of Modern Art/Film Stills Archive.

Chapter Three Getting to Know You—Dating, Getting Together, Living Together
76–Courtesy, Al Capp; 81–Susan Meiselas/Magnum; 88–Bob Adelman/Magnum.

Chapter Four Premarital Sex in the 1970s—Is There a Revolution?
102–© Dan Jury/Rapho/Photo Researchers, Inc.; 118–(both photos) The Bettmann Archive; 121–Mitchell Payne/Jeroboam; 125–Museum of Modern Art/Film Stills Archive.

Chapter Five Choosing the Single Life—In the Land of the Married
140–Victoria Rouse; 149–Museum of Modern Art/Film Stills Archive; 155–Shelly Rusten.

Chapter Six The Marriage Contract—Do You Promise to Love, Honor, and Obey?
169–The Bettmann Archive; 173–From the collection of Skirball Museum, Hebrew Union College, Los Angeles. Photo by Erich Hockley; 175–Donna Gray; 182–Dennis Stock/Magnum.

Chapter Seven Male and Female—Biological and Sociological Perspectives
200–Timothy Eagon/Woodfin Camp & Assoc.; 206–(both photos) Courtesy, Modern Woodman of America; 203–Courtesy, Faberge; 200–Jean Boughton/The Picture Cube.

Chapter Eight His Marriage and Hers—Redefining Sex Roles and Relationships
217–Abigail Heyman/Magnum; 223–Hank Lebo/Jeroboam; 226–Drawing by Weber, © The New Yorker Magazine; 231–Leif Skoogfors/Woodfin Camp & Assoc.

Chapter Nine Communication and Conflict—Talking Without Speaking, Listening Without Hearing
252–Drawing by George Price © The New Yorker Magazine; 253–Thomas Hopker/Woodfin Camp & Assoc.; 257–Museum of Modern Art/Film Stills Archive; 259–Courtesy, The Advertising Council.

Chapter Ten Marital Sexuality—As Work and Play
268–Joel Gordon; 283–Dirck Halstead/Liaison; 287–Jill Freedman.

Chapter Eleven Marriage Throughout the Life Cycle—Will You Still Need Me/Will You Still Feed Me
301–(All three photos) Michael Weisbrot; 311–Drawing by Whitney Darrow © 1975 The New Yorker Magazine; 315–Marion Bernstein/EPA, Inc.

Chapter Twelve Parents and Children—To Beget or Not to Beget?
324–The Bettman Archive; 334–Courtesy, Planned Parenthood; 341–The Granger Collection; 343–Charles Gatewood; 349–Susan Wilson; 354–Anna Kaufman Moon/Stock, Boston; 359–Suzanne Szasz.

Chapter Thirteen Kinship and Community—It's Nice to Know They're There When You Need Them
373–Karen Preuss/Jeroboam; 375–Courtesy, Mayflower Transit Company; 378–Drawing by Osborne © The New Yorker Magazine; 381–Courtesy, American Telephone & Telegraph Co., Long Lines Dept.; 387–Tim Carlson/Stock, Boston.

Chapter Fourteen The Fragile Family—Crisis and Divorce
396–Courtesy, Richard Goldberg; 409–© Greeting Cards, Inc., Art by Vivian Taylor; 410–Drawing by Whitney Darrow © 1975 The New Yorker Magazine; 419–Courtesy, Parents Without Partners, Inc.; 420–Phil Preston/© The Boston Globe.

Chapter Fifteen Trends and Forecasts—The Future Isn't What It Used to Be
435–Montage by Joan Menschenfreund, Baby photo by Mariette Allen; 436–Bruce Roberts/Rapho/Photo Researchers, Inc.; 438–Poster art by Milton Glaser, photo courtesy, SVA; 443–Timothy Eagan/Woodfin Camp & Assoc.

Appendix Managing the Financial Partnership—Dollars and Sense
456–Courtesy, New York Life Insurance; 466–Jeff Perkell.

About the Author

SUZANNE KELLER (the consulting editor) is currently Professor of Sociology at Princeton University, where she has served as Chairperson of the Department of Sociology. She was born in Vienna, Austria, and came to the United States as a child. After college she spent several years in Europe, mainly in Paris and Munich, where she worked as a survey analyst and translator. She received a Ph.D. in sociology from Columbia in 1953. In 1957, she became an Assistant Professor at Brandeis University, where she taught courses in social theory, stratification, and the sociology of religion. A Fulbright Lectureship in 1963 at the Athens Center of Ekistics marked the beginning of her interest in architecture and community planning. At the completion of her Fulbright in 1965, Professor Keller joined the Center, where she remained until 1967. That year she came to Princeton University as a Visiting Professor, and in 1968 she was the first woman to be appointed to a tenured Professorship there. She has also been Vice-President of the American Sociological Association.

Today, Professor Keller is pursuing her interests in teaching, writing, research, public lectures, and world-wide travel. A Federal Grant is currently permitting Professor Keller and an interdisciplinary team to investigate methods for the assessment of a planned environment. She is also active in the women's movement. The author of numerous articles and two books, she has just completed a module on sex roles for General Learning Corporation.

KEITH MELVILLE (the author) did his undergraduate studies at Colgate University, and completed the Ph.D. in sociology at Columbia University. He has been a professor at the City University of New York since 1972 and is also a Research Associate at the Center for Policy Research. He is the author of three books and several dozen articles that have appeared in both popular magazines and professional journals. As an interpreter of the social sciences for a general audience, Professor Melville was a consulting editor and wrote more than a dozen articles for *The Sciences*, a magazine published by the New York Academy of Sciences.

The focus of much of his work over the past ten years has been applied social research. His doctoral dissertation is a study of the uses of the social sciences in formulating educational programs and policy. Since working at the Center for Urban Education in the late 1960s, where he was part of a research team that studied the TV viewing habits of lower-income families for the Children's Television Workshop, two of his main interests have been educational innovation and mass media studies. He has taught several courses on the social impact of the electronic media at the Center for Understanding Media, and he developed a film series on science and society, which was distributed by the National Endowment for the Humanities. His interest in developing new types of learning materials that encourage training in noncognitive skills led to the preparation of the workbook—*Exploring Marriage and Family Today*—that serves as a companion volume to this text.